Everyman's

DICTIONARY OF
QUOTATIONS AND PROVERBS

A volume in
EVERYMAN'S REFERENCE LIBRARY

Other volumes in preparation

Everyman's

DICTIONARY OF
QUOTATIONS
AND
PROVERBS

Compiled by

D. C. BROWNING
M.A. (Glasgow), B.A., B.Litt. (Oxon.)

LONDON: J. M. DENT & SONS LTD
NEW YORK: E. P. DUTTON & CO. INC

SBN: 460 03011 6

CONTENTS

INTRODUCTION

CONTAINING just over 10,000 quotations and proverbs, this dictionary is to all intents and purposes an entirely new compilation. That, of course, is not to deny its debt to other dictionaries, including its predecessor in Everyman's Library. But fashions change in quotation as in everything else, and by modern standards the dictionaries of a past generation seem ill-proportioned. For example, the previous *Everyman's Dictionary of Quotations* allotted over 200 entries to Byron, and over 70 to Young (of *Night Thoughts* fame), while Browning had only seven, and Kipling only ten.

It has been the editor's aim to readjust the balance by giving less space to old-fashioned authors and more to those now popular. The net has also been cast wider, for extracts are given from nearly a thousand authors—about double the number that appeared in this volume's predecessor. The newcomers are by no means all modern, for they include—to take a few names at random—Aubrey, Jane Austen, Bismarck, Beau Brummell, Catullus, Clough, De Quincey, Evelyn, Kenneth Grahame, Hogg, Lang, Lear, Luther, Maeterlinck, Marryat, Nelson, Patmore, Sallust, Spooner, Traherne, Queen Victoria, Artemus Ward, Xenophon, and Zola.

VARIETY OF CONTENTS.

The quotations are of the most varied kind. There are famous sayings, from Lord Acton's ' Power tends to corrupt, and absolute power corrupts absolutely ' to Zamoyski's ' The king reigns, but does not govern '; the greatest lines and passages of the best-known poems are quoted, from *Paradise Lost* (which provides 121 extracts) to *Mary had a little Lamb*, and including such old forgotten favourites as *Somebody's Darling* and ' I have no pain, dear mother, now '; solitary tags like ' The villain still pursued her ' or ' It's a long time between drinks ' are given a local habitation and a name ; and for the more frivolous there is a small but select collection of limericks in the Anonymous section.

Among the newcomers, perhaps the most interesting are the extracts from Mr. Churchill's war speeches, where the most famous of his phrases are given with context and date—' I have nothing to offer but blood, toil, tears, and sweat '; ' Never in the field of human conflict was so much owed by so many to so few '; ' Give us the tools and we will finish the job '; ' Some chicken; some neck.' Readers who have a weakness for detective fiction may find the Holmesiana worthy of study— ' You see, but you do not observe '; ' The curious incident of the dog '; ' You know my methods '; ' " Elementary," said he.'

Two Innovations.

In the setting-out of the quotations there are two innovations which it is hoped will add to the usefulness of the volume. The first is the indication of the calling and nationality of each author. In most dictionaries of quotations the only clue to an author's identity is the date, and even well-informed readers may be at a loss with some of the less-known British or American names. Where no nationality is mentioned in the references here, the author is English.

The second innovation is the giving of day and month, as well as year, of each author's birth and death. This, it is hoped, will be helpful to journalists and others who want the exact date for centenary celebrations and similar purposes. All dates have been checked and rechecked, and if they are found at variance with those of any other work of reference, it should be remembered that dates are sometimes in dispute.

Order and Arrangement.

The arrangement of the authors is alphabetical, as before, a single list being used and foreign authors put in their place among English ones. The name under which each is listed is the one most commonly used. For instance, quotations from *Alice in Wonderland* are given under ' Lewis Carroll,' to which there is a cross-reference from the author's real name, C. L. Dodgson. Similarly, Latin authors are given under their familiar anglicised names, with the Latin form in brackets, e.g. ' Horace (Quintus Horatius Flaccus).' Quotations of doubtful authorship are placed at the end and grouped according to literary forms.

Within each author, the arrangement of the quotations is as far as possible chronological, and this rule has been extended even to Shakespeare, following the order of composition given by the latest authorities. In the case of the Bible the usual order of the books has been followed. An Index is provided to the plays of Shakespeare on page 269, and to the books of the Bible on page 411.

Allotment of Space.

In allotting space among the different authors, the editor has tried to hold a just balance and to avoid favouritism of any kind.

It is instructive to see how the numbers work out, though it must always be borne in mind that the ' quotability ' of an author is not a reliable index of his greatness, and that it is not necessarily the finest passages that have become the most familiar. Shakespeare, of course, has the lion's share, with nearly 1,300 entries ; indeed, the play of *Hamlet* alone, with 180 entries, supplies more quotations than any other single author except Milton, who has just over 250, though the Bible exceeds this with 567.

Pope comes third of the authors, with over 150 entries, and Tennyson fourth, a little behind him. Then there is a big gap till we come to Browning and Wordsworth, both about 90. Johnson, Byron, and Kipling have just over 80, and Burns just under. Dickens has 70 and Walter Scott 60, with Dryden in between. Coleridge, Cowper, Gilbert, and Goldsmith are all in the fifties. Shelley, Keats, and Lewis Carroll have a little over 40 each, Gray and Stevenson a little under. Among foreign writers Horace and Virgil easily top the list with 25 each.

PROVERBS.

Like the quotations, the proverbs are an entirely fresh selection, in which quality rather than quantity has been aimed at. It would have been quite easy to have increased the number ten times over, but the list would have lost instead of gaining in usefulness. There has been ample space for including all that are well-known or of special interest, and the opportunity has been taken of indicating the earliest appearance of each and also explaining obscure points. It is often the pithiest proverbs whose meaning is not at once apparent. For example, ' Back may trust, but belly won't,' ' Let alone makes many a loon,' ' No money, no Swiss,' all call for explanatory comment.

Annotation is particularly necessary in the case of Scottish proverbs. For instance, the familiar ' Jouk and let the jaw gae by ' was given in the previous volume as ' Joke and let the jaw gae o'er,' apparently under the impression that the ' jaw ' was a ' telling-off ' instead of a pailful of slops. Foreign proverbs have, of course, been provided with a translation.

INDEX.

It is hoped that the value of the index has been increased by incorporating the proverbs with the quotations. This enables the proverbs to be much more fully and clearly indexed ; and if the reader wishes to keep the two sets of references distinct, he has only to remember that all numbers up to 6387 are quotations, while the higher numbers are proverbs. There is an obvious advantage in having a separate number for each entry, since it is irritating to be referred only to a page, which may have anything up to a score of entries.

Every effort has been made to choose the right key-words, that is, those that form the salient point in each quotation, and are the most memorable part of it. Generally speaking, nouns have been preferred to verbs or adjectives for reference words, but when the noun is quite colourless, like 'man' or 'thing' there did not seem much point in indexing all its occurrences. Foreign and Old English words are inserted alphabetically with the rest, Greek letters being identified with their nearest English equivalents. On an average there are three index references per quotation, but, of course, the number varies with the size of the quotation; Hamlet's 'To be or not to be' speech requires 48.

USES OF THE DICTIONARY.

It will be observed that the index takes up a very large proportion (about one-third) of the total space. This is necessary if the reader is to depend upon it for two of his main objectives —selecting suitable quotations for special occasions and obeying the time-honoured admonition, 'Always verify your references.' A further use of the dictionary is that it forms a series of samples giving an idea of what each author is like. It is difficult to run over, for example, the list of extracts from Dickens or Johnson without wanting to read the books they are taken from; and there is no one so widely read but that he may make pleasant discoveries among authors that are new to him.

1950   D. C. B.

For the sixth edition the whole volume has been carefully gone over and one or two errors and misprints corrected. A few dates of early authors have been newly inserted or adjusted in conformity with the latest researches, and dates have also been filled in of those moderns who have died since the work was first published.

1965   D. C. B.

QUOTATIONS

QUOTATIONS

*(Arranged alphabetically under authors ; for the full
subject-reference index, see page 527.)*

ABRANTES, DUC D', *see* Junot, Andoche

ACCIUS, LUCIUS, Roman dramatist, 170–86 ? B.C.
  1. Oderint dum metuant.—Let them hate as long as they fear.
                                                          Atreus.

ACTON, JOHN EMERICH EDWARD DALBERG ACTON, 1st BARON,
  historian, 10 Jan. 1834—19 June, 1902
  2. Power tends to corrupt, and absolute power corrupts absolutely.
Great men are almost always bad men.
                              Historical Essays and Studies, appendix.

ADAMS, CHARLES FOLLEN, U.S. poet, 21 April, 1842—8 March, 1918
  3.   I haf von funny leedle poy
               Vot gomes schust to mine knee :
               Der queerest schap, der createst rogue
               As efer you dit see.   *Yawcob Strauss.*

ADAMS, FRANKLIN PIERCE, U.S. journalist, 15 Nov. 1881—
  4.   Go, lovely Rose that lives its little hour !
               Go, little booke ! and let who will be clever !
               Roll on ! From yonder ivy-mantled tower
               The moon and I could keep this up for ever.
                    Lines on and from " Bartlett's Familiar Quotations."

ADAMS, JOHN QUINCY, U.S. President, 11 July, 1767—23 Feb. 1848
  5. Think of your forefathers ! Think of your posterity !
               Speech at Plymouth, Massachusetts, 22 Dec. 1802.

ADAMS, SARAH FLOWER, poetess, 22 Feb. 1805—14 Aug. 1848
  6.   Nearer, my God, to Thee,
               Nearer to Thee !
               E'en though it be a cross
               That raiseth me.   *Nearer, my God, to Thee.*

ADDISON, JOSEPH, author, 1 May, 1672—17 June, 1719
  7. And, pleased the Almighty's orders to perform,
  Rides in the whirlwind and directs the storm.
                                            The Campaign, 291.

  8. The spacious firmament on high,
  With all the blue ethereal sky,
  And spangled heavens, a shining frame,
  Their great Original proclaim.   *Ode.*

*A²

3

9. Soon as the evening shades prevail,
The moon takes up the wondrous tale,
And nightly to the listening earth
Repeats the story of her birth. *Ibid*

10. Poetic fields encompass me around,
And still I seem to tread on classic ground.

A Letter from Italy.

11. 'Tis not in mortals to command success,
But we'll do more, Sempronius ; we'll deserve it. *Cato*, I. ii.

12. Blesses his stars and thinks it luxury. *Ibid, iv.*

13. The woman that deliberates is lost. *Ibid., IV. i.*

14. It must be so—Plato, thou reason'st well !—
Else whence this pleasing hope, this fond desire,
This longing after immortality ?
Or whence this secret dread and inward horror
Of falling into naught ? Why shrinks the soul
Back on herself and startles at destruction ?
'Tis the Divinity that stirs within us,
'Tis Heaven itself that points out an hereafter,
And intimates Eternity to man.
Eternity !——thou pleasing-dreadful thought ! *Ibid, v. i.*

15. The soul, secured in her existence, smiles
At the drawn dagger and defies its point.
The stars shall fade away, the sun himself
Grow dim with age, and nature sink in years ;
But thou shalt flourish in immortal youth,
Unhurt amidst the war of elements,
The wrecks of matter, and the crush of worlds. *Ibid.*

16. Sir Roger told them, with the air of a man who would not give his judgment rashly, that much might be said on both sides.

The Spectator, 122.

17. I have often thought, says Sir Roger, it happens very well that Christmas should fall out in the middle of winter. *Ibid, 269.*

18. A woman seldom asks advice before she has bought her wedding clothes. *Ibid, 475.*

19. I have but ninepence in ready money, but I can draw for a thousand pounds. [Contrasting his powers in conversation and in writing.] Boswell, *Life of Johnson*, an. 1773.

20. See in what peace a Christian can die. *Dying words.*

ADELER, MAX (CHARLES HEBER CLARK), U.S. author, 11 July, 1847—
10 Aug. 1915

21. Oh no more he'll shoot his sister with his little wooden gun ;
And no more he'll twist the pussy's tail and make her yowl
for fun.
The pussy's tail now stands out straight ; the gun is laid
aside ;
The monkey doesn't jump around since little Willie died.
In Memoriam.

22. We have lost our little Hanner in a very painful manner.
Little Hanner.

ADY, THOMAS, author, 17th century

23. Matthew, Mark, Luke, and John,
The bed be blest that I lie on.
Four angels to my bed,
Four angels round my head,
One to watch, and one to pray,
And two to bear my soul away.
A Candle in the Dark.

Æ (GEORGE WILLIAM RUSSELL), Irish poet, 10 April, 1867—17 July,
1935

24. The blue dusk ran between the streets : my love was winged
within my mind,
It left to-day and yesterday and thrice a thousand years
behind.
To-day was past and dead for me, for from to-day my feet
had run
Through thrice a thousand years to walk the ways of ancient
Babylon. *Babylon.*

AESCHYLUS, Greek dramatist, 525–456 B.C.

25. Οὐ γὰρ δοκεῖν ἄριστος, ἀλλ' εἶναι θέλει.
—He wishes not to seem, but to be, the best.
Seven against Thebes, 588.

26. Ποντίων τε κυμάτων
'Ανήριθμον γέλασμα.
—And sea waves' unnumbered laughter. *Prometheus Bound,* 89.

27. Τὸ δ' εὖ νικάτω.
—But let the good prevail. *Agamemnon,* 121.

À KEMPIS, THOMAS, *see* Kempis, Thomas à

AKENSIDE, MARK, doctor and poet, 9 Nov. 1721—23 June, 1770

28. Such and so various are the tastes of men.
The Pleasures of the Imagination, III. 567.

AKERS, ELIZABETH CHASE, U.S. authoress, 9 Oct. 1832—7 Aug. 1911

29. Backward, turn backward, O Time, in your flight,
Make me a child again just for to-night !
Rock me to Sleep.

ALDRICH, HENRY, Dean of Christ Church, Oxford, 1647—14 Dec.
1710

30. If all be true that I do think,
There are five reasons we should drink :
Good wine—a friend—or being dry—
Or lest we should be by and by—
Or any other reason why. *Reasons for Drinking.*

ALDRICH, JAMES, U.S. poet, 1810—Oct. 1856

31.   Her suffering ended with the day,
           Yet lived she at its close,
        And breathed the long, long night away
           In statue-like repose.

        But when the sun in all his state
           Illumed the eastern skies,
        She passed through Glory's morning gate
           And walked in Paradise.   *A Death Bed.*

ALEXANDER, CECIL FRANCES, poetess, 1818—12 Oct. 1895

32.   All things bright and beautiful,
           All creatures great and small,
        All things wise and wonderful,
           The Lord God made them all.
           All Things Bright and Beautiful.

33.   Do no sinful action,
           Speak no angry word ;
        Ye belong to Jesus,
           Children of the Lord.   *Do no Sinful Action.*

34.   There is a green hill far away,
           Without a city wall,
         Where the dear Lord was crucified,
           Who died to save us all.
           There is a Green Hill.

35.   By Nebo's lonely mountain,
           On this side Jordan's wave,
         In a vale in the land of Moab,
           There lies a lonely grave.   *The Burial of Moses.*

ALEXANDER, SIR WILLIAM, EARL OF STIRLING, Scottish poet and
    statesman, 1567 ?—12 Sept. 1640

36.   The weaker sex, to piety more prone. *Doomsday. Hour* v. 55.

37.   Those golden palaces, those gorgeous halls,
           With furniture superfluously fair;
        Those stately courts, those sky-encount'ring walls
           Evanish all like vapours in the air.
           The Tragedy of Darius, IV. iii.

ALFORD, HENRY, Dean of Canterbury, 10 Oct. 1810—12 Jan. 1871

38.   Ten thousand times ten thousand,
           In sparkling raiment bright,
         The armies of the ransomed saints
           Throng up the steeps of light.
           Ten Thousand Times Ten Thousand.

ALLAINVAL, LÉONOR JEAN CHRISTINE SOULAS D', abbé, French author,
    1700 ?—2 May, 1753

39.   L'embarras des richesses.—The embarrassment of riches.
           Title of play.

ALLEN, ELIZABETH AKERS, *see* Akers, Elizabeth Chase

ALLINGHAM, WILLIAM, Irish poet, 19 March, 1824—18 Nov. 1889

40.   Up the airy mountain,
Down the rushy glen,
We daren't go a-hunting
For fear of little men. *The Fairies.*

41.   Four ducks on a pond,
A grass-bank beyond,
A blue sky of spring,
White clouds on the wing:
What a little thing
To remember for years—
To remember with tears! *A Memory.*

ANSTEY, CHRISTOPHER, poet, 31 Oct. 1724—3 Aug. 1805

42.   If ever I ate a good supper at night,
I dream'd of the devil, and wak'd in a fright.
The New Bath Guide, iv. *A Consultation of the Physicians.*

APPLETON, THOMAS GOLD, U.S. author, 31 March, 1812—17 April, 1884

43.   Good Americans, when they die, go to Paris.
O. W. Holmes, *Autocrat of the Breakfast Table*, vi.

ARCHIMEDES, Greek scientist, 287 ?–212 ? B.C.

44.   Εὕρηκα.—I have found it. [Eureka !] *On making a discovery.*

45.   Δός μοι ποῦ στῶ, καὶ κινῶ τὴν γῆν.—Give me somewhere to stand, and I will move the earth. *In reference to the lever.*

ARIOSTO, LUDOVICO, Italian poet, 8 Sept. 1474—6 July, 1533

46. Natura il fece, e poi ruppe la stampa. —Nature made him, and then broke the mould. *Orlando Furioso*, x. 84.

ARISTOPHANES, Greek dramatist, 448 ?–380 ? B.C.

47.   Νεφελοκοκκυγία.—Cloudcuckooborough. [The city built by the birds.] *The Birds*, 821.

ARISTOTLE, Greek philosopher and scientist, 384–322 B.C.

48.   "Ανθρωπος φύσει πολιτικὸν ξῷον.—Man is by nature a civic animal. *Politics*, I. ii.

49.   Προαιρεῖσθαι τε δεῖ ἀδύνατα εἰκότα μᾶλλον ἢ δυνατὰ ἀπίθανα.—Plausible impossibilities should be preferred to unconvincing possibilities.
Poetics, xxiv.

ARMSTRONG, NEIL, U.S. astronaut, 5 Aug. 1930—

50.   That's one small step for a man, one giant leap for mankind.
On setting foot on the moon, 3.56 a.m. B.S.T., 21 July, 1969.

ARNOLD, SIR EDWIN, poet, 10 June 1832—24 March, 1904

50a.   Shall any gazer see with mortal eyes,
Or any searcher know by mortal mind?
Veil after veil will lift—but there must be
Veil upon veil behind. *The Light of Asia*, VIII.

ARNOLD, GEORGE, U.S. poet, 24 June, 1834—9 Nov. 1865

51. The living need charity more than the dead.
The Jolly Old Pedagogue.

ARNOLD, MATTHEW, poet and critic, 24 Dec. 1822—15 April, 1888

52.　　　　　　　　　　　　　　　　　　　Be his
My special thanks, whose even-balanc'd soul,
From first youth tested up to extreme old age,
Business could not make dull, nor passion wild :
Who saw life steadily, and saw it whole :
The mellow glory of the Attic stage ;
Singer of sweet Colonus, and its child.　[Sophocles.]
To a Friend.

53.　　　Others abide our question.　Thou art free.
We ask and ask : Thou smilest and art still,
Out-topping knowledge.　　　　　　*Shakespeare.*

54.　　　And thou, who didst the stars and sunbeams know,
Self-school'd, self-scann'd, self-honour'd, self-secure,
Didst walk on earth unguess'd at.　Better so !
All pains the immortal spirit must endure,
　All weakness that impairs, all griefs that bow,
Find their sole voice in that victorious brow.　　　*Ibid.*

55.　　　Now the great winds shoreward blow ;
Now the salt tides seaward flow ;
Now the wild white horses play,
Champ and chafe and toss in the spray.
The Forsaken Merman, 4.

56.　　　Children dear, was it yesterday
(Call yet once) that she went away ?　　　*Ibid., 48.*

57.　　　'Tis Apollo comes leading
His choir, the Nine.
The leader is fairest,
But all are divine.　　　　*Empedocles on Etna, II.*

58.　　　Too fast we live, too much are tried,
Too harass'd, to attain
Wordsworth's sweet calm, or Goethe's wide
And luminous view to gain.　　　　*Obermann, 77.*

59.　　　We cannot kindle when we will
The fire that in the heart resides,
The spirit bloweth and is still,
In mystery our soul abides :
　But tasks in hours of insight will'd
　Can be through hours of gloom fulfill'd.　　　*Morality.*

60. Truth sits upon the lips of dying men.
Sohrab and Rustum, 656.

61. But the majestic River floated on,
Out of the mist and hum of that low land,
Into the frosty starlight, and there mov'd,
Rejoicing, through the hush'd Chorasmian waste,
Under the solitary moon : he flow'd
Right for the Polar Star, past Orgunjè,
Brimming, and bright, and large : then sands begin
To hem his watery march, and dam his streams,

And split his currents ; that for many a league
The shorn and parcell'd Oxus strains along
Through beds of sand and matted rushy isles—
Oxus, forgetting the bright speed he had
In his high mountain cradle in Pamere,
A foil'd circuitous wanderer—till at last
The long'd-for dash of waves is heard, and wide
His luminous home of waters opens, bright
And tranquil, from whose floor the new-bath'd stars
Emerge, and shine upon the Aral Sea.   *Ibid.*, 875.

62.   Strew on her roses, roses,
                    And never a spray of yew.
                 In quiet she reposes :
                    Ah ! would that I did too.   *Requiescat.*

63.   To-night it doth inherit
                    The vasty Hall of Death.   Ibid.

64. Crossing the stripling Thames at Bablock-hithe.
                                        The Scholar Gipsy, 74.

65.   Still nursing the unconquerable hope,
                    Still clutching the inviolable shade.   *Ibid.*, 211.

66.   And that sweet city with her dreaming spires.   *Thyrsis*, 20.

67. So have I heard the cuckoo's parting cry,
       From the wet field, through the vext garden-trees,
       Come with the volleying rain and tossing breeze.
                                        Ibid. 57.

68.   The foot less prompt to meet the morning dew,
       The heart less bounding at emotion new,
       And hope, once crush'd, less quick to spring again.
                                        Ibid. 138.

69.   Hath man no second life ?—Pitch this one high !
       Sits there no judge in heaven, our sins to see ?—
       More strictly, then, the inward judge obey !
       Was Christ a man like us ?—Ah ! let us try
       If we then, too, can be such men as he !
                                        Anti-desperation.

70.   Whispering from her towers the last enchantments of the Middle
Age . . . Home of lost causes, and forsaken beliefs, and unpopular
names, and impossible loyalties ! [Oxford.]
                 Essays in Criticism, 1st series, preface.

71.   I am bound by my own definition of criticism : a disinterested
endeavour to learn and propagate the best that is known and thought
in the world.
                 Ibid., *Functions of Criticism at the Present Time.*

72.   Poetry is simply the most beautiful, impressive and widely
effective mode of saying things, and hence its importance.
                                        Ibid., *Heinrich Heine.*

73.   In poetry, no less than in life, he is ' a beautiful and ineffectual
angel, beating in the void his luminous wings in vain.'
[Quoting from his own essay on Byron.] Ibid., 2nd series. *Shelley.*

74.   The pursuit of perfection, then, is the pursuit of sweetness and
light.   *Culture and Anarchy.*

75. The word which our Bibles translate by ' gentleness ' means more properly ' reasonableness with sweetness,' ' sweet reasonableness.'
St. Paul and Protestantism, preface.

76. Culture, the acquainting ourselves with the best that has been known and said in the world, and thus with the history of the human spirit. *Literature and Dogma*, preface.

ARNOLD, SAMUEL JAMES, dramatist, 1774–1852.

77. For England, home, and beauty.
The Death of Nelson.

ARNOLD, THOMAS, Headmaster of Rugby, 13 June, 1795—12 June, 1842

78. What we must look for here is, first, religious and moral principles; secondly, gentlemanly conduct; thirdly, intellectual ability. *Address to his scholars.*

ASQUITH, HERBERT HENRY, EARL OF OXFORD AND ASQUITH, Prime Minister, 12 Sept. 1852—15 Feb. 1928.

79. Wait and see. *Various Speeches*, 1910.

AUBREY, JOHN, antiquary, born 12 March, 1626, buried 7 June, 1697.

80. *Anno* 1670, not far from Cirencester, was an apparition : being demanded, whether a good spirit, or a bad ? returned no answer, but disappeared with a curious perfume and most melodious twang. Mr. W. Lilly believes it was a fairy. *Miscellanies. Apparitions.*

81. He was a handsome, well-shaped man : very good company, and of a very ready and pleasant smooth wit.
Brief Lives. William Shakespeare.

AUCHINLECK, ALEXANDER BOSWELL, LORD, Scottish Judge, 1706—31 Aug. 1782

82. He gart kings ken that they had a *lith* in their neck. [Of Cromwell. Lith = joint.]
Boswell, *Journal of a Tour to the Hebrides*, 6 Nov. 1773, note.

AUGIER, GUILLAUME VICTOR ÉMILE, French dramatist, 17 Sept. 1820—25 Oct. 1889

83. La nostalgie de la boue.—Home-sickness for the gutter.
Le mariage d'Olympe—The Marriage of Olympe, i. i.

AUGUSTINE (AURELIUS AUGUSTINUS), SAINT, Bishop of Hippo, 13 Nov. 354—28 Aug. 430 A.D.

84. Da mihi castitatem et continentiam, sed noli modo.—Give me chastity and continence, but not now. *Confessions*, VIII. vii.

85. Securus judicat orbis terrarum.—The verdict of the world is final. *Contra Epistolam Parmeniani*, iii. 24.

AUGUSTUS (GAIUS JULIUS CAESAR OCTAVIANUS, *formerly* GAIUS OCTAVIUS), Roman Emperor, 23 Sept. 63 B.C.—19 Aug. A.D. 14.

86. Quintili Vare, legiones redde.—Quintilius Varus, give me back my legions.
When three legions were annihilated by the Germans, A.D. 9.

87. Ad kalendas Graecas.—On the Greek calends.   [I.e. never.]
Suetonius, *Divus Augustus*, lxxxvii.

AURELIUS, MARCUS (MARCUS AURELIUS ANTONINUS), Roman Emperor,
April, 121—17 March, 180.

88.   Ἐκεῖνος μέν φησιν · 'πόλι φίλη Κέκροπος', σὺ δὲ οὐκ ἐρεῖς· 'ὢ πόλι φίλη Διός';
—The poet says ' Dear city of Cecrops ' ; and wilt not thou say ' O
dear city of God ' ?   *Meditations*, IV. xxiii.

AUSTEN, JANE, novelist, 16 Dec. 1775—18 July, 1817

89. But are they all horrid, are you sure they are all horrid ?
[Catherine Morland, of a list of novels.]   *Northanger Abbey*, vi.

90. It is a truth universally acknowledged, that a single man in
possession of a good fortune must be in want of a wife.
Pride and Prejudice, i.

91. How can you contrive to write so even ?   [Miss Bingley]
Ibid., x.

92. It is happy for you that you possess the talent of flattering with
delicacy. May I ask whether these pleasing attentions proceed from
the impulse of the moment, or are the result of previous study ?
[Mr. Bennet.]   Ibid., xiv.

93. Nobody is on my side, nobody takes part with me ; I am
cruelly used, nobody feels for my poor nerves. [Mrs. Bennet.]
Ibid., xx.

94. You ought certainly to forgive them as a Christian, but never
to admit them in your sight, or allow their names to be mentioned
in your hearing. [Mr. Collins.]   Ibid., lvii.

95. A basin of nice smooth gruel, thin, but not too thin.   *Emma*, xii.

96. All the privilege I claim for my own sex . . . is that of loving
longest, when existence or when hope is gone. [Anne Elliot.]
Persuasion, xxiii.

97. What dreadful hot weather we have ! It keeps me in a continual state of inelegance.   *Letters*, 18 Sept. 1796.

98. Miss Blachford is agreeable enough.   I do not want people
to be very agreeable, as it saves me the trouble of liking them a great
deal.   Ibid., 24 Dec. 1798.

99. The little bit (two inches wide) of ivory on which I work with
so fine a brush as produces little effect after much labour.
Ibid., 16 Dec., 1816.

AUSTIN, ALFRED, Poet Laureate, 30 May, 1835—2 June, 1913

100. An earl by right, by courtesy a man.   *The Season*.

AYTOUN, WILLIAM EDMONSTOUNE, Scottish poet, 21 June, 1813—
4 Aug. 1865

101.   News of battle !—news of battle !
Hark ! 'tis ringing down the street :
And the archways and the pavement
Bear the clang of hurrying feet.
Edinburgh after Flodden, 1.

102.　　　　　Come hither, Evan Cameron !
　　　　　　　Come, stand beside my knee.
　　　　　　　　　　　　The Execution of Montrose, 1.

103.　　　　　Do not lift him from the bracken,
　　　　　　　　Leave him lying where he fell—
　　　　　　　Better bier ye cannot fashion :
　　　　　　　　None beseems him half so well.
　　　　　　　　　　　　The Widow of Glencoe, 1.

104.　　　　　Take away that star and garter—
　　　　　　　　Hide them from my aching sight !
　　　　　　　Neither king nor prince shall tempt me
　　　　　　　　From my lonely room this night.
　　　　　　　　　*Charles Edward at Versailles on the Anniversary
　　　　　　　　　　of Culloden,* 1.

105.　　　　　Fhairshon swore a feud
　　　　　　　　Against the clan McTavish ;
　　　　　　　Marched into their land
　　　　　　　　To murder and to rafish.
　　　　　　　　　　　The Massacre of the Macpherson, 1.

BACON, FRANCIS, VISCOUNT ST. ALBANS, Lord Chancellor, 22 Jan. 1561
　　　—9 April, 1626

106.　Come home to men's business and bosoms.
　　　　　　　　　　　　　　　Essays, dedication.

107.　What is truth ? said jesting Pilate, and would not stay for
an answer.　　　　　　　　　　　　Ibid., i. *Of Truth.*

108.　Men fear death as children fear to go in the dark ; and as
that natural fear in children is increased with tales, so is the other.
　　　　　　　　　　　　　　　Ibid., ii. *Of Death.*

109.　It is as natural to die as to be born ; and to a little infant
perhaps the one is as painful as the other.　　　　　Ibid.

110.　Revenge is a kind of wild justice.　　Ibid., iv., *Of Revenge.*

111.　He that hath wife and children hath given hostages to fortune ;
for they are impediments to great enterprises, either of virtue or
mischief.　　　　　Ibid., viii., *Of Marriage and Single Life.*

112.　The remedy is worse than the disease.
　　　　　　　　　　Ibid., xv., *Of Seditions and Troubles.*

113.　A little philosophy inclineth man's mind to atheism, but
depth in philosophy bringeth men's minds about to religion.
　　　　　　　　　　　　Ibid., xvi., *Of Atheism.*

114.　God Almighty first planted a garden ; and, indeed, it is the
purest of human pleasures.　　　　　Ibid., xlvi., *Of Gardens.*

115.　Studies serve for delight, for ornament, and for ability.
　　　　　　　　　　　　Ibid., l., *Of Studies.*

116.　Some books are to be tasted, others to be swallowed, and
some few to be chewed and digested.　　　　　Ibid.

117.　Reading maketh a full man, conference a ready man, and
writing an exact man.　　　　　Ibid.

118.　Histories make men wise; poets, witty ; the mathematics,
subtile ; natural philosophy, deep ; moral, grave ; logic and rhetoric,
able to contend.　　　　　Ibid.

119. If a man will begin with certainties, he shall end in doubts ; but if he will be content to begin with doubts, he shall end in certainties.
Advancement of Learning, i. v. 8.

120. I have taken all knowledge to be my province.
Letter to Lord Burleigh, 1592.

121. Nam et ipsa scientia potestas est.—For knowledge itself is power.
Meditationes Sacrae. De Haeresibus.—
Religious Meditations. Of Heresies.

122. The world's a bubble ; and the life of man
Less than a span. *The World.*

123. Who then to frail mortality shall trust,
But limns the water, or but writes in dust. Ibid.

BAILEY, PHILIP JAMES, poet, 22 April, 1816—6 Sept. 1902

124. We live in deeds, not years ; in thoughts, not breaths ;
In feelings, not in figures on a dial.
We should count time by heart-throbs.   He most lives
Who thinks most—feels the noblest—acts the best.
Festus, v.

BAILLIE, LADY GRISELL *or* GRIZEL, Scottish poetess, 25 Dec. 1665—
6 Dec. 1746

125. And werena my heart licht I wad dee.
Werena my Heart Licht.

BAILLIE, JOANNA, Scottish dramatist, 11 Sept. 1762—23 Feb. 1851
126. The wild-fire dances on the fen
The red star sheds its ray ;
Uprouse ye then, my merrie men !
It is our op'ning day. *Orra,* iii. i.

BAIRNSFATHER, BRUCE, artist, July, 1888—29 Sept. 1959.

127. Well, if you knows of a better 'ole, go to it.
Caption of war cartoon, 1915.

BALFOUR, ARTHUR JAMES BALFOUR, 1st EARL OF, 25 July, 1848—
19 March, 1930

128. The energies of our system will decay, the glory of the sun will be dimmed, and the earth, tideless and inert, will no longer tolerate the race which has for a moment disturbed its solitude.   Man will go down into the pit, and all his thoughts will perish.
The Foundations of Belief, i. i.

129. A frigid and calculated lie.
Speech, Constitutional Club, 26 Oct. 1909.

BALL, JOHN, priest, died 15 July, 1381
130. When Adam dolve and Eve span,
Who was then the gentleman ? *Attributed.*

BALZAC, HONORÉ DE, French novelist, 20 May, 1799—17 Aug. 1850
131. Elles doivent avoir les défauts de leur qualités.—They are bound to have the defects of their qualities.
Le Lys dans la vallée.—The Lily in the Valley, 369.

BAMPFYLDE, JOHN CODRINGTON, poet, 27 Aug. 1754—1796 ?

132.   Rugged the breast that beauty cannot tame.
Sonnet in Praise of Delia.

BANKS, GEORGE LINNAEUS, author, 2 March, 1821—3 May, 1881

133.   For the cause that lacks assistance,
         For the wrong that needs resistance,
         For the future in the distance,
           And the good that I can do.   *What I Live for.*

BANVILLE, THÉODORE FAULLAIN DE, French poet, 14 March, 1823—15 March, 1891

134.   Nous n'irons plus aux bois, les lauriers sont coupés.
   —We'll go no more to the woods, the laurel trees are cut.
      [*Taken from a folk song.*]   *Les Stalactites,* iii.

BARBAULD, ANNA LETITIA, authoress, 20 June, 1743—9 March, 1825

135.   Life ! we've been long together
    Through pleasant and through cloudy weather ;
      'Tis hard to part when friends are dear ;
      Perhaps 'twill cost a sigh, a tear ;
      Then steal away, give little warning,
        Choose thine own time ;
    Say not ' Good night,' but in some brighter clime
    Bid me ' Good morning.'
Life.

BARBOUR, JOHN, Scottish poet, 1316 ?—13 March, 1395

136.   A ! fredome is a nobill thing !
      Fredome mayss man to haiff liking !
      Fredome all solace to man giffis :
      He levys at ese that frely levys.   *The Bruce,* I. 225.

BARÈRE DE VIEUZAC, BERTRAND, French revolutionary, 10 Sept. 1755—13 Jan. 1841

137. L'arbre de la liberté ne croît qu'arrosé par le sang des tyrans.—
The tree of Liberty only grows when watered by the blood of tyrants.
Speech, National Convention, 1792.

BARHAM, RICHARD HARRIS, clergyman, 6 Dec. 1788—17 June, 1845

138. You intoxified brute !—you insensible block !—
  Look at the clock !—Do !—Look at the clock !
The Ingoldsby Legends. Patty Morgan, i.

139. And, talking of epitaphs—much I admire his,
 ' Circumspice, si monumentum requiris ' ;
 Which an erudite verger translated to me,
 ' If you ask for his monument, Sir-come-spy-see ! '
Ibid., *The Cynotaph.*

140.   The Jackdaw sat on the Cardinal's chair !
    Bishop, and abbot, and prior were there ;
      Many a monk, and many a friar,
      Many a knight, and many a squire.
Ibid., *The Jackdaw of Rheims.*

141.　　　Never was heard such a terrible curse !
　　　　　　　But what gave rise
　　　　　　　To no little surprise,
　　　　　Nobody seemed one penny the worse !　　　　　　*Ibid.*

142. Heedless of grammar, they all cried, ' That's him ! '　　　*Ibid.*

143. She drank prussic acid without any water,
　　　And died like a Duke-and-a-Duchess's daughter.
　　　　　　　　　　　　　　　　　　Ibid., The Tragedy.

144. She help'd him to lean, and she help'd him to fat,
　　　And it look'd like hare—but it might have been cat.
　　　　　　　　　　　　　　　　　Ibid., The Bagman's Dog.

145. The sacristan, he says no word that indicates a doubt,
　　　But he puts his thumb unto his nose, and spreads his fingers
　　　　　out !　　　　　　　　　　　　　　*Ibid., Nell Cook.*

146. 'Twas in Margate last July, I walk'd upon the pier,
　　　I saw a little vulgar boy—I said, ' What make you here ? '
　　　　　　　　　　　　　　　Ibid., Misadventures at Margate.

147. What Horace says is,
　　　Eheu fugaces
　　　Anni labuntur, Postume, Postume !
　　　Years glide away, and are lost to me, lost to me !
　　　　　　　　　　　　　　Ibid., Epigram : Eheu Fugaces.

BARING, MAURICE, author, 27 April, 1874—15 Dec. 1945.

148.　　　Because of you we will be glad and gay,
　　　　　　　Remembering you, we will be brave and strong;
　　　　　And hail the advent of each dangerous day,
　　　　　　　And meet the great adventure with a song.
　　　　　　　　　　　　　　　Julian Grenfell (1888-1915).

BARING-GOULD, SABINE, clergyman and author, 28 Jan. 1834—2 Jan.
　　　1924

149.　　　　　　　Onward, Christian soldiers,
　　　　　　　　　Marching as to war,
　　　　　　　　With the Cross of Jesus
　　　　　　　　Going on before.
　　　　　　　　　　　　Onward Christian Soldiers.

150.　　　　　　　Hell's foundations quiver
　　　　　　　　　At the shout of praise.　　　　　*Ibid.*

151.　　　　　　　Now the day is over,
　　　　　　　　　Night is drawing nigh,
　　　　　　　　Shadows of the evening
　　　　　　　　Steal across the sky.
　　　　　　　　　　　　Now the Day is over.

BARNARD, LADY ANNE, Scottish poetess, 8 Dec. 1750—6 May, 1825

152. When the sheep are in the fauld, when the kye's a' at hame,
　　　And a' the weary warld to rest are gane.
　　　　　　　　　　　　　　　　　Auld Robin Gray.

153. My father urged me sair—my mother didna speak,
　　　But she looket in my face till my heart was like to break ;
　　　They gied him my hand—my heart was in the sea—
　　　And so Robin Gray was gudeman to me.　　　*Ibid.*

BARNERS *or* BERNES *or* BARNES, JULIANA, authoress, born 1388 ?

154. Of the offspring of the gentilman Jafeth come Habraham, Moyses, Aron, and the profettys ; also the Kyng of the right lyne of Mary, of whom that gentilman Jhesus was borne.

Blasyng of Armys.

BARNFIELD, RICHARD, poet, baptised 13 June, 1574, buried 6 March, 1627

155. As it fell upon a day
In the merry month of May. *An Ode.*

156. King Pandion, he is dead,
All thy friends are lapp'd in lead. Ibid.

BARNUM, PHINEAS TAYLOR, U.S. showman, 5 July, 1810—7 April, 1891

157. You can fool some of the people all the time, and all of the people some of the time ; but you can't fool all of the people all the time. *Attributed.*

BARRETT, EATON STANNARD, Irish author, 1786—20 March, 1820

158. Not she with trait'rous kiss her Saviour stung,
Not she denied Him with unholy tongue ;
She, while apostles shrank, could danger brave,
Last at His cross, and earliest at His grave.

Woman, I. 143.

BARRIE, SIR JAMES MATTHEW, Scottish author, 9 May, 1860—20 June, 1937

159. I do loathe explanations. *My Lady Nicotine,* xvi.

160. If it's heaven for climate, it's hell for company.
The Little Minister, iii.

161. It's a weary warld, and nobody bides in't. Ibid., iv.

162. You canna expect to be baith grand and comfortable. Ibid., x.

163. Let no one who loves be called altogether unhappy. Even love unreturned has its rainbow. Ibid., xxiv.

164. When the first baby laughed for the first time, the laugh broke into a thousand pieces and they all went skipping about, and that was the beginning of the fairies. *Peter Pan,* I.

165. To die will be an awfully big adventure. Ibid., III.

166. It's a sort of bloom on a woman. If you have it, you don't need to have anything else ; and if you don't have it, it doesn't much matter what else you have. [Of charm.]
What every Woman knows, I.

167. A young Scotsman of your ability let loose upon the world with £300, what could he not do ? It's almost appalling to think of ; especially if he went among the English. Ibid.

168. You've forgotten the grandest moral attribute of a Scotsman, Maggie, that he'll do nothing which might damage his career.
Ibid., II.

BARTHÉLEMY, AUGUSTE MARSEILLE, French poet, 1796—23 Aug. 1867

169. L'homme absurde est celui qui ne change jamais.—The absurd man is the one who never changes.

Ma justification—My Justification.

BASHFORD, SIR HENRY HOWARTH, doctor, 1880—15 Aug. 1961

170.
As I came down the Highgate Hill
I met the sun's bravado,
And saw below me, fold on fold,
Grey to pearl and pearl to gold,
London like a land of old,
The land of Eldorado. *Romance.*

BASSE *or* BAS, WILLIAM, poet, died 1653 ?

171. Renowned Spenser, lie a thought more nigh
To learned Chaucer, and rare Beaumont lie
A little nearer Spenser, to make room
For Shakespeare in your threefold, fourfold tomb.

On Shakespeare.

BATES, KATHERINE LEE, U.S. poetess, 29 Aug. 1859—28 March, 1929

172.
America ! America !
God shed His grace on thee
And crown thy good with brotherhood
From sea to shining sea !

America the Beautiful.

BAXTER, RICHARD, clergyman, 12 Nov. 1615—8 Dec. 1691

173. I preached as never sure to preach again,
And as a dying man to dying men.
Love breathing Thanks and Praise, II.

BAYLY, THOMAS HAYNES, author, 13 Oct. 1797—22 April, 1839

174.
I'd be a butterfly ; living a rover,
Dying when fair things are fading away.
I'd be a Butterfly.

175.
Oh ! no ! we never mention her,
Her name is never heard ;
My lips are now forbid to speak
That once familiar word.
Oh ! no ! we never mention her.

176.
We met—'twas in a crowd. *Song.*

177.
Why don't the men propose, mamma,
Why don't the men propose ?
Why don't the Men propose ?

178.
She wore a wreath of roses,
The night that first we met.
She wore a Wreath of Roses.

179.
O pilot ! 'tis a fearful night,
There's danger on the deep. *The Pilot.*

180.
Absence makes the heart grow fonder.
Isle of Beauty.

181.   Gaily the Troubadour
               Touched his guitar.   *Welcome me Home.*

182.   I'm saddest when I sing.   *Song.*

183.   The mistletoe hung in the castle hall,
      The holly branch shone on the old oak wall.
                                   The Mistletoe Bough.

BEATTIE, JAMES, Scottish poet, 25 Oct. 1735—18 Aug. 1803

184.   Mine be the breezy hill that skirts the down,
      Where a green grassy turf is all I crave,
      With here and there a violet bestrewn,
      Fast by a brook or fountain's murmuring wave ;
      And many an evening sun shine sweetly on my grave !
                                The Minstrel, II. 17.

185.   At the close of the day, when the hamlet is still,
      And mortals the sweets of forgetfulness prove,
      When naught but the torrent is heard on the hill,
      And naught but the nightingale's song in the grove.
                                    The Hermit.

186.   He thought as a sage, though he felt as a man.   Ibid.

BEAUMONT, FRANCIS, dramatist, 1584—6 March, 1616

187.   What things have we seen
    Done at the Mermaid ! heard words that have been
    So nimble and so full of subtile flame
    As if that every one from whence they came
    Had meant to put his whole wit in a jest,
    And had resolved to live a fool the rest
    Of his dull life.   *Letter to Ben Jonson.*

188.   Mortality, behold and fear !
          What a change of flesh is here !
             On the Tombs in Westminster Abbey.

189.   Here are sands, ignoble things,
          Dropt from the ruin'd sides of kings.   Ibid.

BEDDOES, THOMAS LOVELL, poet, 20 July, 1803—26 Jan. 1849

190.   If there were dreams to sell,
                 What would you buy ?
             Some cost a passing-bell,
                 Some a light sigh.   *Dream-Pedlary.*

BEERS, ETHEL LYNN, U.S. poetess, 13 Jan. 1827—11 Oct. 1879

191. All quiet along the Potomac to-night,
      No sound save the rush of the river,
    While soft falls the dew on the face of the dead—
      The picket's off duty forever.   *The Picket Guard.*

BEITH, JOHN HAY, *see* Hay, Ian

BELL, HENRY GLASSFORD, Scottish author, 8 Nov. 1803—7 Jan. 1874

192. I looked far back into other years, and lo ! in bright array
   I saw, as in a dream, the forms of ages passed away.
   It was a stately convent, with its old and lofty walls,
   And gardens with their broad, green walks, where soft the
   footstep falls. *Mary Queen of Scots.*

193. The scene was changed. It was the court—the gay court of
   Bourbon ;
   And 'neath a thousand silver lamps a thousand courtiers throng.
   Ibid.

BELLOC, JOSEPH HILAIRE PIERRE, author, 27 July, 1870—16 July, 1953

194. Child, do not throw this book about ;
   Refrain from the unholy pleasure
   Of cutting all the pictures out !
   Preserve it as your chiefest treasure.
   The Bad Child's Book of Beasts, dedication.

195. When I am living in the Midlands,
   That are sodden and unkind,
   I light my lamp in the evening :
   My work is left behind ;
   And the great hills of the South Country
   Come back into my mind. *The South Country.*

196. I will hold my house in the high wood,
   Within a walk of the sea,
   And the men that were boys when I was a boy
   Shall sit and drink with me. Ibid.

197. Balliol made me, Balliol fed me,
   Whatever I had she gave me again;
   And the best of Balliol loved and led me,
   God be with you, Balliol men.
   To the Balliol Men still in Africa.

198. There's nothing worth the wear of winning
   But laughter and the love of friends.
   Dedicatory Ode.

199. Remote and ineffectual Don
   That dared attack my Chesterton. *Lines to a Don.*

200. He does not die that can bequeath
   Some influence to the land he knows,
   Or dares, persistent, interwreath
   Love permanent with the wild hedgerows ;
   He does not die, but still remains
   Substantiate with his darling plains. *Duncton Hill.*

201. His sins were scarlet, but his books were read.
   Epigrams. On his Books.

202. The chief defect of Henry King
   Was chewing little bits of string.
   Cautionary Tales for Children. Henry King.

BENNETT, ENOCH ARNOLD, novelist, 27 May, 1867—27 March, 1931

203. There was no influenza in my young days. We called a cold
a cold. *The Card,* viii.

204.   There was a young man of Montrose,
              Who had pockets in none of his clothes.
                When asked by his lass
                Where he carried his brass,
              He said, ' Darling, I pay through the nose.'   *Limerick.*

BENSON, ARTHUR CHRISTOPHER, Master of Magdalene College, Cam-
      bridge, 24 April, 1862—17 June, 1925
205.   By feathers green, across Casbeen
                The pilgrims track the Phoenix flown,
                By gems he strew'd in waste and wood,
                And jewell'd plumes at random thrown.
                                                The Phoenix.

206.   Land of Hope and Glory, Mother of the Free,
         How shall we extol thee, who are born of thee ?
         Wider still and wider shall thy bounds be set ;
         God, who made thee mighty, make thee mightier yet.
                                        Land of Hope and Glory.

BENTHAM, JEREMY, jurist, 15 Feb. 1748—6 June, 1832
   207. All punishment is mischief ; all punishment in itself is evil.
                                Principles of Morals and Legislation, xiii.

BENTLEY, EDMUND CLERIHEW, author, 10 July, 1875—30 March, 1956
208.   Geography is about maps,
                But biography is about chaps.
                                        Biography for Beginners.

209.   What I like about Clive
                Is that he's no longer alive.   Ibid., *Clive.*
210.   George the Third
                Ought never to have occurred.
                                        Ibid., *George III.*
211.   They say, ' Shall these things perish utterly,
         These that were England through the glorious years—
           Faith and green fields and honour and the sea ?'
         I simply wag my great, long, furry ears.
                                Ballade of Plain Common Sense

BENTLEY, RICHARD, classical scholar, 27 Jan. 1662—14 July, 1742
   212. It is a maxim with me that no man was ever written out of
reputation but by himself.   Monk's *Life of Bentley*, 90.

   213. A very pretty poem, Mr. Pope, but it's not Homer. [Of Pope's
translation of the Iliad.]   *Attributed.*

BERKELEY, GEORGE, BISHOP OF CLOYNE, Irish philosopher, 12 March,
      1685—14 Jan., 1753
214.   Westward the course of empire takes its way ;
           The four first acts already past,
         A fifth shall close the drama with the day :
           Time's noblest offspring is the last.
                        *On the Prospect of Planting Arts and Learning
                        in America.*

BERNES, *see* Barners, Juliana

BETHMANN HOLLWEG, THEOBALD VON, German Chancellor, 29 Nov. 1856—1 Jan. 1921

215. Just for a scrap of paper, Great Britain is going to make war on a kindred nation who desires nothing better than to be friends with her. *To the British Ambassador*, 4 Aug. 1914.

BICKERSTAFFE, ISAAC, Irish dramatist, 1735 ?—1812 ?

216.   There was a jolly miller once,
                  Lived on the river Dee ;
             He worked and sung from morn till night
                  No lark more blithe than he.
             And this the burthen of his song
                  For ever used to be—
             I care for nobody, no, not I,
                  If no one cares for me.   *Love in a Village*, I. iii.

BICKERSTETH, EDWARD HENRY, BISHOP OF EXETER, 25 Jan. 1825—16 May, 1906

217. Peace, perfect peace ? in this dark world of sin !
         The blood of Jesus whispers peace within.
                                             Peace, Perfect Peace.

BIERCE, AMBROSE, U.S. author, 24 June, 1842—1914 ?

218. Woman would be more charming if one could fall into her arms without falling into her hands. *Epigrams.*

BINYON, ROBERT LAURENCE, poet, 10 Aug. 1869—10 March, 1943

219. With proud thanksgiving, a mother for her children,
         England mourns for her dead across the sea.
                                             For the Fallen.

220. They shall grow not old, as we that are left grow old :
         Age shall not weary them, nor the years condemn.
         At the going down of the sun and in the morning
         We will remember them.   Ibid.

BIRKENHEAD, FREDERICK EDWIN SMITH, 1ST EARL OF, Lord Chancellor, 12 July, 1872—30 Sept. 1930

221. The world continues to offer glittering prizes to those who have stout hearts and sharp swords.
         Rectorial Address, Glasgow University, 7 Nov. 1923.

BIRRELL, AUGUSTINE, M.P. and author, 19 Jan. 1850—21 Nov. 1933

222. That great dust-heap called ' history.'
                                 Obiter Dicta, 1st series. *Carlyle.*

223. Libraries are not made ; they grow.
                                 Ibid., 2nd series. *Book-Buying.*

BISMARCK, OTTO EDUARD LEOPOLD, PRINCE VON, German Chancellor, 1 April, 1815—28 July, 1898

224. Blut und Eisen.—Blood and iron.
                 Speech, Prussian House of Deputies, 28 Jan. 1886.

BLACKSTONE, SIR WILLIAM, jurist, 10 July, 1723—14 Feb. 1780

225. The royal navy of England hath ever been its greatest defence
and ornament; it is its ancient and natural strength—the floating
bulwark of the island.   *Commentaries*, I. xiii.

226. Time whereof the memory of man runneth not to the contrary.
Ibid., xviii.

227. That the king can do no wrong, is a necessary and fundamental
principle of the English constitution.   Ibid., III. xvii.

BLAIR, ROBERT, Scottish minister, 1699—4 Feb. 1746

228.   The schoolboy, with his satchel in his hand,
           Whistling aloud to bear his courage up.
                                              The Grave, 58.

229.   Its visits
           Like those of angels, short and far between.   Ibid., 588.

BLAKE, JAMES, U.S. song-writer, 1862–1935

230. East Side, West Side, all around the town,
      The tots sang ' Ring-a-rosie,' ' London Bridge is falling down ';
      Boys and girls together, me and Mamie Rorke,
      Tripped the light fantastic on the sidewalks of New York.
                                  The Sidewalks of New York.

BLAKE, WILLIAM, poet and artist, 28 Nov. 1757—12 Aug. 1827

231.   How have you left the ancient love
           That bards of old enjoy'd in you !
           The languid strings do scarcely move !
           The sound is forc'd, the notes are few !
                                              To the Muses.

232.   Piping down the valleys wild,
           Piping songs of pleasant glee,
           On a cloud I saw a child.
                                  Songs of Innocence, introduction.

233.   My mother bore me in the southern wild,
           And I am black, but O my soul is white.
                              Ibid., *The Little Black Boy.*

234. When the voices of children are heard on the green,
      And laughing is heard on the hill.
                                  Ibid., *Nurse's Song.*

235.   Tiger ! Tiger ! burning bright
               In the forests of the night,
               What immortal hand or eye
               Could frame thy fearful symmetry ?
                          Songs of Experience. The Tiger.

236.   Never seek to tell thy love,
               Love that never told can be ;
               For the gentle wind does move
               Silently, invisibly.   *Love's Secret.*

237.   Mock on, mock on, Voltaire, Rousseau ;
               Mock on, mock on, 'tis all in vain !
           You throw the sand against the wind,
               And the wind blows it back again.
                              Mock on, mock on, Voltaire.

238.   To see a World in a grain of sand,
            And Heaven in a wild flower,
            Hold Infinity in the palm of your hand,
            And Eternity in an hour.   *Auguries of Innocence.*

239.   A robin redbreast in a cage
            Puts all Heaven in a rage.   Ibid.

240.   He who bends to himself a Joy
            Doth the winged life destroy ;
            But he who kisses the Joy as it flies
            Lives in Eternity's sunrise.   *Gnomic Verses*, xvii. 1.

241.   A petty sneaking knave I knew—
            O ! Mr. Cr[omek], how do ye do ?
                                        On Friends and Foes, xxi.

242.   I will not cease from mental fight,
            Nor shall my sword sleep in my hand,
            Till we have built Jerusalem
            In England's green and pleasant land.
                                        Milton, preface.

243.   A fool sees not the same tree that a wise man sees.
                    Marriage of Heaven and Hell. Proverbs of Hell.

244.   Damn braces.   Bless relaxes.   Ibid.

BLAMIRE, SUSANNA (THE ' MUSE OF CUMBERLAND '), poetess, 12 Jan.
        1747—5 April, 1794

245.   And ye sall walk in silk attire,
                        And siller hae to spare.   *The Siller Crown.*

BLANCHET, PIERRE, French dramatist, 1459 ?–1519

246.   Revenons à nos moutons.—Let us get back to our sheep
[=to our subject].   *Patelin*, 1191

BLAND, MRS. HUBERT, *see* Nesbit, Edith

BLISS, PHILIP, U.S. evangelist, 9 July, 1838—29 Dec. 1876

247.   Hold the fort, for I am coming.
                            Ho, my Comrades, see the Signal.

BLOOMFIELD, ROBERT, poet, 3 Dec. 1766—19 Aug. 1823

248.   Strange to the world, he wore a bashful look,
                The fields his study, Nature was his book.
                            The Farmer's Boy. Spring, 31.

BLUNT, WILFRID SCAWEN, poet, 17 Aug. 1840—10 Sept. 1922

249.   He who has once been happy is for aye
                Out of destruction's reach.   *Esther*, l.

250.   I like the hunting of the hare
                Better than that of the fox.   *The Old Squire.*

BOBART, JACOB, botanist, 2 Aug. 1641—28 Dec. 1719

251.   Think that day lost whose [low] descending sun
            Views from thy hand no noble action done.
                            Virtus sua Gloria.

BOETHIUS *or* BOETIUS, ANICIUS MANLIUS SEVERINUS, Roman
    philosopher, 480 ?–524 ?

252. In omni adversitate fortunae infelicissimum est genus infor-
tunii fuisse felicem.—In every adversity of fortune the most unhappy
kind of misfortune is to have been happy.
    Consolatio Philosophiae—Consolation of Philosophy, II. iv.

BOLINGBROKE, HENRY ST. JOHN, VISCOUNT, statesman, 1 Oct. 1678—
    12 Dec. 1751

253. Nations, like men, have their infancy.
    On the Study and Use of History, letter iv.

254. The dignity of history. Ibid., letter v.

255. All our wants, beyond those which a very moderate income
will supply, are purely imaginary. *Letter to Swift*, 17 March, 1719.

BONAR, HORATIUS, Scottish minister, 19 Dec. 1808—31 July, 1889
256. A few more years shall roll,
        A few more seasons come,
        And we shall be with those that rest
        Asleep within the tomb. *Hymn.*

BONE, JAMES, Scottish journalist, 1872–
257. The City of Dreadful Height.
    Description of New York.

BOOTH, BARTON, actor, 1681—10 May, 1733
258. True as the needle to the pole,
        Or as the dial to the sun.
    Song.

BORROW, GEORGE HENRY, author, 5 July, 1803—26 July, 1881
259. There's night and day, brother, both sweet things; sun,
moon, and stars, brother, all sweet things; there's likewise a wind
on the heath. Life is very sweet, brother; who would wish to die?
    Lavengro, XXV.

BOSQUET, PIERRE FRANÇOIS JOSEPH, French Marshal, 8 Nov. 1810—
    5 Feb. 1861

260. C'est magnifique, mais ce n'est pas la guerre.—It is magnificent,
but it is not war.
    On the charge of the Light Brigade at Balaclava, 25 Oct. 1854.

BOSSIDY, JOHN COLLINS, U.S. doctor, 17 June, 1860—1928
261. And this is good old Boston,
        The home of the bean and the cod,
        Where the Lowells talk only to Cabots
        And the Cabots talk only to God.
    On the Aristocracy of Harvard

BOSWELL, ALEXANDER, *see* Auchinleck, Lord

BOSWELL, JAMES, Scottish biographer, 29 Oct. 1740—19 May, 1795

262. Yes, Sir ; you tossed and gored several persons. [When Johnson said ' We had a good talk.'] *Life of Johnson*, an. 1769.

263. He [Dr. Johnson] has no formal preparation, no flourishing with his sword ; he is through your body in an instant.

Ibid., an. 1775.

BOTTOMLEY, GORDON, author, 20 Feb. 1874—25 Aug. 1948

264. When you destroy a blade of grass
      You poison England at her roots.
                    To Ironfounders and others.

265. Your worship is your furnaces,
      Which, like old idols, lost obscenes,
      Have molten bowels ; your vision is
      Machines for making more machines.

Ibid.

BOULTON, SIR HAROLD EDWIN, 2ND BARONET, poet, 7 Aug. 1859—1 June, 1935

266. Speed, bonny boat, like a bird on the wing ;
        ' Onward ! ' the sailors cry ;
      Carry the lad that's born to be king
      Over the sea to Skye. *Skye Boat Song.*

267. When Adam and Eve were dispossessed
      Of the garden hard by Heaven,
      They planted another one down in the west,
        'Twas Devon, glorious Devon ! *Glorious Devon.*

BOURDILLON, FRANCIS WILLIAM, author, 22 March, 1852—13 Jan. 1921

268. The night has a thousand eyes,
        And the day but one ;
      Yet the light of the bright world dies
        With the dying sun. *Light.*

BOWEN OF COLWOOD, CHARLES SYNGE CHRISTOPHER BOWEN, BARON, judge, 1 Jan. 1835—10 April, 1894

269. The rain it raineth on the just
      And also on the unjust fella :
      But chiefly on the just, because
      The unjust steals the just's umbrella.
                    Sichel, Sands of Time.

BOWEN, EDWARD ERNEST, schoolmaster, 30 March, 1836—8 April, 1901.

270. Forty years on, growing older and older,
        Shorter in wind, as in memory long,
      Feeble of foot, and rheumatic of shoulder,
        What will it help you that once you were strong ?
                Forty Years On. Harrow School Song.

BRADFORD, JOHN, Protestant martyr, 1510?—1 July, 1555

271. But for the grace of God there goes John Bradford.
On seeing some criminals taken to execution.

BRADLEY, FRANCIS HERBERT, philosopher, 30 Jan. 1846—18 Sept. 1924

272. Metaphysics is the finding of bad reasons for what we believe upon instinct.   *Appearance and Reality*, preface.

BRAMSTON, JAMES, poet, 1694?—16 March, 1744

273.   What's not destroy'd by Time's devouring hand ?
Where's Troy, and where's the Maypole in the Strand ?
Art of Politics, 71.

BRATHWAITE, RICHARD, poet, 1588?—4 May, 1673

274.   Hanging of his cat on Monday
For killing of a mouse on Sunday.
Barnabee's Journal, I.

BRERETON, JANE, poetess, 1685—7 Aug. 1740

275.   The picture, plac'd the busts between,
Adds to the thought much strength ;
Wisdom and Wit are little seen,
But Folly's at full length.
*On Mr. Nash's Picture at Full Length between the
Busts of Sir Isaac Newton and Mr. Pope.*
[Also attributed to Lord Chesterfield.]

BRETON, NICHOLAS, poet, 1545 ?—1626 ?

276.   Much ado there was, God wot ;
He would love, and she would not.
Phillida and Coridon.

277.   I wish my deadly foe no worse
Than want of friends, and empty purse.
A Farewell to Town.

278.   A mad world, my masters.   *Title of dialogue.*

BRIDGES, ROBERT SEYMOUR, Poet Laureate, 23 Oct. 1844—21 April, 1930

279.   I heard a linnet courting
His lady in the spring.
I heard a Linnet courting.

280.   Whither, O splendid ship, thy white sails crowding,
Leaning across the bosom of the urgent West,
That fearest nor sea rising, nor sky clouding,
Whither away, fair rover, and what thy quest ?
A Passer-by.

281. Perfect little body, without fault or stain on thee,
With promise of strength and manhood full and fair !
On a Dead Child.

282.   Spring goeth all in white,
                           Crowned with milk-white may :
                       In fleecy flocks of light
                           O'er heaven the white clouds stray.
                                     Spring goeth all in White.

283.   So sweet love seemed that April morn,
              When first we kissed beside the thorn,
              So strangely sweet, it was not strange
              We thought that love could never change.
                                     So Sweet Love seemed.

284.   I never shall love the snow again
                       Since Maurice died.
                           I never shall love the Snow again.

285.   My delight and thy delight
              Walking, like two angels white,
              In the gardens of the night.
                                     My Delight and thy Delight.

BRIGHT, JOHN, statesman, 16 Nov. 1811—27 March, 1889

286. The Angel of Death has been abroad throughout the land ;
you may almost hear the beating of his wings.
                       Speech, House of Commons, 23 Feb. 1855.

287. I am for " Peace, retrenchment, and reform," the watchword
of the great Liberal party thirty years ago.
                       Ibid., *Birmingham,* 28 April, 1859.

288. England is the mother of Parliaments.   Ibid., 18 Jan. 1865.

289. The right honourable gentleman . . . has retired into what
may be called his political Cave of Adullam.
                       Ibid., *House of Commons,* 13 March, 1866.

BROMLEY, ISAAC HILL, U.S. journalist, 6 March, 1833—11 Aug. 1898

290. John A. Logan is the Head Centre, the Hub, the King Pin,
the Main Spring, Mogul and Mugwump of the final plot by which
partisanship was installed in the Commission.
                       Editorial, New York Tribune, 16 Feb. 1877.

BRONTË, EMILY JANE, authoress, 30 July, 1818—19 Dec. 1848

291.   Riches I hold in light esteem
                           And love I laugh to scorn ;
                       And lust of fame was but a dream,
                           That vanished with the morn.   *The Old Stoic.*

292.   No coward soul is mine,
              No trembler in the world's storm-troubled sphere :
              I see Heaven's glories shine,
              And faith shines equal, arming me from fear.
                                                 Last Lines.

293.   Though earth and man were gone,
                       And suns and universes ceased to be,
                       And Thou wert left alone,
                       Every existence would exist in Thee.   Ibid.

BROOKE, RUPERT CHAWNER, poet, 3 Aug. 1887—23 April, 1915

294.   Breathless, we flung us on the windy hill,
        Laughed in the sun, and kissed the lovely grass.
           The Hill.

295.   Unkempt about those hedges blows
         An English unofficial rose.
           The Old Vicarage, Grantchester.

296.   Curates, long dust, will come and go
         On lissom, clerical, printless toe ;
         And oft between the boughs is seen
         The sly shade of a Rural Dean.   *Ibid.*

297.   For England's the one land, I know,
         Where men with Splendid Hearts may go.   *Ibid.*

298.   And in that Heaven of all their wish,
         There shall be no more land, say fish.   *Heaven.*

299.   Live hair that is
    Shining and free ; blue-massing clouds ; the keen
    Unpassioned beauty of a great machine ;
    The benison of hot water ; furs to touch ;
    The good smell of old clothes.   *The Great Lover.*

300.   Blow out, you bugles, over the rich Dead.   *The Dead.*

301.   If I should die, think only this of me :
         That there's some corner of a foreign field
         That is for ever England.   *The Soldier.*

BROOKS, NOAH, U.S. author, 24 Oct. 1830—16 Aug. 1903

302.   Punch, brothers, punch with care,
         Punch in the presence of the passenjare.
       Inspired by a notice to conductors of New York horse-cars.
[This has been claimed for Mark Twain, probably because he used
it without acknowledgment, and for Isaac Hill Bromley.]

BROOKS, PHILLIPS, Bishop of Massachusetts, 13 Dec. 1835—23 Jan.
     1893

303.   O little town of Bethlehem,
         How still we see thee lie ;
        Above thy deep and dreamless sleep
         The silent stars go by.
           O Little Town of Bethlehem.

BROUGH, ROBERT BARNABAS, author, 10 April, 1828—26 June, 1860

304.   My Lord Tomnoddy is thirty-four ;
         The Earl can last but a few years more.
         My Lord in the Peers will take his place :
         Her Majesty's councils his words will grace.
         Office he'll hold and patronage sway ;
         Fortunes and lives he will vote away ;
         And what are his qualifications ?—ONE !
         He's the Earl of Fitzdotterel's eldest son.
           My Lord Tomnoddy.

BROUGHAM AND VAUX, HENRY PETER BROUGHAM, BARON, Lord
  Chancellor, 19 Sept. 1778—7 May, 1868

305. The schoolmaster is abroad, and I trust to him, armed with
his primer, against the soldier in full military array.
  Speech, House of Commons, 29 Jan. 1828.

306. In my mind, he was guilty of no error, he was chargeable
with no exaggeration, he was betrayed by his fancy into no metaphor,
who once said, that all we see about us, Kings, Lords, and Commons,
the whole machinery of the State, all the apparatus of the system,
and its varied workings, end in simply bringing twelve good men
into a box.   *Speech on the Present State of the Law*, 7 Feb. 1828.

307. The great Unwashed.   *Attributed*

BROWN, JOHN, clergyman and author, 5 Nov. 1715—23 Sept. 1766

308.   Truth's sacred fort th' exploded laugh shall win ;
       And coxcombs vanquish Berkeley by a grin.
         An Essay on Satire, occasioned by the Death of Mr. Pope,
           II. 223.

BROWN, THOMAS, author, 1663—16 June, 1704

309.   I do not love thee, Doctor Fell,
               The reason why I cannot tell ;
               But this alone I know full well,
               I do not love thee, Doctor Fell.
         Translation of Martial, *Epigrams*, I. xxxii.   [No. 2581.
             infra.]
           [A slightly different version is given in Brown's
           Works.]

BROWN, THOMAS EDWARD, Manx poet, 5 May, 1830—30 Oct. 1897

310.   O blackbird, what a boy you are !
               How you do go it.   *The Blackbird.*

311. A garden is a lovesome thing, God wot.   *My Garden.*

BROWNE, CHARLES FARRAR, *see* Ward, Artemus

BROWNE, SIR THOMAS, doctor and author, 19 Oct. 1605—19 Oct. 1682

312. At my devotion I love to use the civility of my knee, my
hat, and hand.   *Religio Medici*, part I. 3.

313. I love to lose myself in a mystery, to pursue my Reason to
an *O altitudo !*   Ibid., 9.

314. We carry within us the wonders we seek without us. There
is all Africa and her prodigies in us.   Ibid., 15.

315. All things are artificial, for nature is the art of God.
                                                        Ibid., 16.

316. It is the common wonder of all men, how among so many
millions of faces there should be none alike.   Ibid., part II. 2.

317. What song the Syrens sang, or what name Achilles assumed when he hid himself among women, though puzzling questions, are not beyond all conjecture.   *Hydriotaphia*, v.

318. But the inequity of oblivion blindly scattereth her poppy, and deals with the memory of men without distinction to merit of perpetuity.   Ibid.

319. Man is a noble animal, splendid in ashes and pompous in the grave.   Ibid.

320.   Sleep is a death, O make me try
                By sleeping, what it is to die,
                And as gently lay my head
                On my grave, as now my bed.
                    Religio Medici, part II. 12.

BROWNE, WILLIAM, poet, 1590?—1645?

321.   Underneath this sable hearse
                Lies the subject of all verse,
                Sidney's sister, Pembroke's mother,
                Death ! ere thou hast slain another
                Learn'd and fair and good as she,
                Time shall throw a dart at thee.
                    Epitaph on the Countess of Pembroke.
[This was formerly attributed to Ben Jonson.]

BROWNE, SIR WILLIAM, doctor, 1692—10 March, 1774

322.   The King to Oxford sent a troop of horse,
                For Tories own no argument but force :
                With equal care to Cambridge books he sent,
                For Whigs allow no force but argument.
                    Epigram in reply to Trapp's. [No. 5358 *infra.*]

BROWNING, ELIZABETH BARRETT, poetess, 6 March, 1806—30 June, 1861

323. Or from Browning some 'Pomegranate,' which, if cut deep down the middle,
    Shows a heart within blood-tinctured, of a veined humanity.
                    Lady Geraldine's Courtship, 41.

324.   Do you hear the children weeping, O my brothers,
            Ere the sorrow comes with years ?
                    The Cry of the Children, 1.

325.   But the child's sob in the silence curses deeper
            Than the strong man in his wrath.   Ibid., 13.

326.   And kings crept out again to feel the sun.
                    Crowned and Buried, 11.

327.   In the pleasant orchard closes,
                ' God bless all our gains,' say we ;
                But ' May God bless all our losses '
                Better suits with our degree.   *The Lost Bower*, 1.

328.   Our Euripides, the human,
           With his droppings of warm tears.

Wine of Cyprus, 12.

329.   ' Yes,' I answered you last night ;
          ' No,' this morning, sir, I say.
       Colours seen by candle-light
          Will not look the same by day.   *The Lady's ' Yes.'*

330.   Unless you can muse in a crowd all day
          On the absent face that fixed you ;
       Unless you can love, as the angels may,
          With the breadth of heaven betwixt you ;
       Unless you can dream that his faith is fast,
          Through behoving and unbehoving ;
       Unless you can die when the dream is past—
          Oh, never call it loving !   *A Woman's Shortcomings.*

331. ' Guess now who holds thee ? '—' Death,' I said. But, there,
    The silver answer rang, . . . ' Not Death, but Love.'
                        Sonnets from the Portuguese, i.

332.   How do I love thee ? Let me count the ways.
       I love thee to the depth and breadth and height
       My soul can reach, when feeling out of sight
       For the ends of Being and ideal Grace.
       I love thee to the level of every day's
       Most quiet need, by sun and candle-light.
       I love thee freely, as men strive for Right ;
       I love thee purely, as they turn from Praise.
       I love thee with the passion put to use
       In my old griefs, and with my childhood's faith.
       I love thee with a love I seemed to lose
       With my lost saints,—I love thee with the breath,
       Smiles, tears, of all my life !—and, if God choose,
       I shall but love thee better after death.   Ibid. xliii.

333.   Since when was genius found respectable ?

Aurora Leigh, vi.

334.   What was he doing, the great god Pan,
          Down in the reeds by the river ?
       Spreading ruin and scattering ban,
       Splashing and paddling with hoofs of a goat,
       And breaking the golden lilies afloat
          With the dragon-fly on the river.

A Musical Instrument.

BROWNING, ROBERT, poet, 7 May, 1812—12 Dec. 1889

335. Sun-treader, life and light be thine for ever. [Shelley.]

Pauline, 148.

336.   Over the sea our galleys went,
       With cleaving prows in order brave.   *Paracelsus,* iv.

337.   Who will, may hear Sordello's story told.

Sordello, i. 1.

338.   And still more labyrinthine buds the rose.   Ibid. 476.

ᴁ

339.   Any nose
May ravage with impunity a rose.   Ibid. VI. 877.

340.   O'er night's brim, day boils at last.
                        Pippa Passes, introduction.

341.   Say not ' a small event ! '   Why ' small ' ?
Costs it more pain that this, ye call
A ' great event,' should come to pass,
Than that ?   Untwine me from the mass
Of deeds which make up life, one deed
Power shall fall short in or exceed !   Ibid.

342.   The year's at the spring
       And day's at the morn ;
       Morning's at seven ;
       The hill-side's dew-pearled ;
       The lark's on the wing ;
       The snail's on the thorn :
       God's in his heaven—
       All's right with the world !   Ibid. I. *Morning.*

343.   Some unsuspected isle in far-off seas.   Ibid. II. *Noon.*

344.   You'll love me yet !—and I can tarry
       Your love's protracted growing :
June reared that bunch of flowers you carry,
       From seeds of April's sowing.   Ibid. III. *Evening.*

345.   All service ranks the same with God—
With God, whose puppets, best and worst,
Are we : there is no last nor first.   Ibid. IV. *Night.*

346.   Marching along, fifty-score strong,
Great-hearted gentlemen, singing this song.
                Cavalier Tunes.   Marching Along.

347.   Boot, saddle, to horse, and away !
                        Ibid. *Boot and Saddle.*

348.   Just for a handful of silver he left us,
       Just for a riband to stick in his coat.
                        The Lost Leader.

349.   We shall march prospering,—not thro' his presence ;
Songs may inspirit us,—not from his lyre ;
Deeds will be done,—while he boasts his quiescence,
   Still bidding crouch whom the rest bade aspire.   Ibid.

350.   Never glad confident morning again.   Ibid.

351.   I sprang to the stirrup, and Joris, and he ;
I galloped, Dirck galloped, we galloped all three.
       ' *How they brought the Good News from Ghent to Aix,*' I.

352.   Where I find her not, beauties vanish ;
       Whither I follow her, beauties flee ;
Is there no method to tell her in Spanish
   June's twice June since she breathed it with me ?
                Garden Fancies.   The Flower's Name, 6.

353.   Gr-r-r—there go, my heart's abhorrence !
       Water your damned flower-pots, do !
                Soliloquy of the Spanish Cloister, I.

354. There's a great text in Galatians,
         Once you trip on it, entails
         Twenty-nine distinct damnations,
            One sure, if another fails.   *Ibid.* 7.

355. 'St, there's Vespers ! *Plena gratiâ*
         Ave, Virgo !   Gr–r–r—you swine !   *Ibid.* 9.

356. There are flashes struck from midnights,
         There are fire-flames noondays kindle,
         Whereby piled-up honours perish,
            Whereby swollen ambitions dwindle,
         While just this or that poor impulse,
            Which for once had play unstifled,
         Seems the sole work of a lifetime
            That away the rest have trifled.   *Christina,* 4.

357. Round the cape of a sudden came the sea,
         And the sun looked over the mountain's rim :
         And straight was a path of gold for him,
         And the need of a world of men for me.
                                    Parting at Morning.

358. Nay but you, who do not love her,
         Is she not pure gold, my mistress ?   *Song.*

359. Beautiful Evelyn Hope is dead.   *Evelyn Hope,* 1.

360. Something to see, by Bacchus, something to hear, at least !
                  Up at a Villa—Down in the City, 2.

361. Your ghost will walk, you lover of trees,
               (If our loves remain)
               In an English lane,
         By a cornfield-side a-flutter with poppies.
                                    ' *De Gustibus*——'

362. A castle, precipice-encurled,
         In a gash of the wind-grieved Apennine.   *Ibid.*

363.   Open my heart and you will see
            Graved inside of it, ' Italy.'   *Ibid.*

364. Oh, to be in England
         Now that April's there.   *Home Thoughts, from Abroad.*

365. That's the wise thrush ; he sings each song twice over,
         Lest you should think he never could recapture
         The first fine careless rapture !   *Ibid.*

366. Nobly, nobly Cape St. Vincent to the North-west died away ;
      Sunset ran, one glorious blood-red, reeking into Cadiz Bay.
                                    Home-Thoughts, from the Sea.

367. 'Tis not what man Does which exalts him, but what man
         Would do !   *Saul,* 18.

368. Oh, the little more, and how much it is !
         And the little less, and what worlds away !
                                    By the Fire-Side, 39.

369.   Only I discern—
            Infinite passion, and the pain
            Of finite hearts that yearn.
                                    Two in the Campagna, 12.

370.   This is a spray the Bird clung to,
           Making it blossom with pleasure.

                                  Misconceptions.

371.   Lose who may—I still can say,
           Those who win heaven, blest are they !

                           One Way of Love.

372. It is but to keep the nerves at a strain,
      To dry one's eyes and laugh at a fall,
  And, baffled, get up and begin again.   *Life in a Love.*

373. Better sin the whole sin, sure that God observes ;
  Then go live his life out ! Life will try his nerves,
  When the sky, which noticed all, makes no disclosure,
  And the earth keeps up her terrible composure.   *Before*, 4.

374.   Ah, did you once see Shelley plain,
           And did he stop and speak to you
           And did you speak to him again ?
           How strange it seems and new !   *Memorabilia.*

375.   Hobbs hints blue,—straight he turtle eats :
           Nobbs prints blue,—claret crowns his cup :
        Nokes outdares Stokes in azure feats,—
           Both gorge. Who fished the murex up ?
        What porridge had John Keats ?   *Popularity*, 13.

376. There's a woman like a dewdrop, she's so purer than the
        purest.   *A Blot in the 'Scutcheon*, i. iii.

377.   It was roses, roses, all the way.

                                     The Patriot.

378.   The air broke into a mist with bells.   *Ibid.*

379. That's my last Duchess painted on the wall,
  Looking as if she were alive.   *My Last Duchess.*

380. ' For I '—so I spoke—' am a poet :
  Human nature,—behoves that I know it ! '   *The Glove.*

381. There may be heaven ; there must be hell ;
  Meantime, there is our earth here—well !

                                Time's Revenges.

382. 'Tis an awkward thing to play with souls,
      And matter enough to save one's own.

                            A Light Woman, 12.

383. Who knows but the world may end to-night ?

                      The Last Ride Together, 2.

384. Sing, riding's a joy ! For me, I ride.   *Ibid.*, 7.

385. And you, great sculptor—so, you gave
  A score of years to Art, her slave,
  And that's your Venus, whence we turn
  To yonder girl that fords the burn !   *Ibid.*, 8.

386. So munch on, crunch on, take your nuncheon,
  Breakfast, supper, dinner, luncheon !

                    The Pied Piper of Hamelin, 7.

387.   A thousand guilders ! Come, take fifty !   *Ibid.*, 9.

388. He said, ' What's time ? Leave Now for dogs and apes !
      Man has Forever.'   *A Grammarian's Funeral.*

389.   That low man seeks a little thing to do,
                Sees it and does it :
            This high man, with a great thing to pursue,
                Dies ere he knows it.
            That low man goes on adding one to one,
                His hundred's soon hit ;
            This high man, aiming at a million,
                Misses an unit.   *Ibid.*

390.   He settled *Hoti's* business—let it be !—
                Properly based *Oun*—
            Gave us the doctrine of the enclitic *De*,
                Dead from the waist down.   *Ibid.*

391.   Here's the top-peak ; the multitude below
                Live, for they can, there :
            This man decided not to Live but Know—
                Bury this man there ?   *Ibid.*

392. And the sin I impute to each frustrate ghost
          Is—the unlit lamp and the ungirt loin.
                            The Statue and the Bust.

393.   You should not take a fellow eight years old
                And make him swear to never kiss the girls.
                            Fra Lippo Lippi, 224.

394.   Ah, but a man's reach should exceed his grasp,
            Or what's a heaven for ?   *Andrea del Sarto,* 97.

395.   And have I not Saint Praxed's ear to pray
            Horses for ye, and brown Greek manuscripts,
            And mistresses with great smooth marbly limbs ?
            The Bishop orders his Tomb at Saint Praxed's Church, 73.

396.   Aha, ELUCESCEBAT quoth our friend ?
            No Tully, said I, Ulpian at the best !   *Ibid.,* 99.

397.   Just when we are safest, there's a sunset-touch,
            A fancy from a flower-bell, someone's death,
            A chorus-ending from Euripides,—
            And that's enough for fifty hopes and fears
            As old and new at once as nature's self.
                            Bishop Blougram's Apology, 182.

398.   No, when the fight begins within himself,
            A man's worth something.   *Ibid.,* 693.

399. God be thanked, the meanest of his creatures
      Boasts two soul-sides, one to face the world with,
      One to show a woman when he loves her.
                            One Word more, 17.

400. Oh, good gigantic smile o' the brown old earth.
                James Lee's Wife, vii. *Among the Rocks.*

401. On earth the broken arcs ; in heaven, a perfect round.
                            Abt Vogler, 9.

402.   Grow old along with me !
                The best is yet to be.   *Rabbi Ben Ezra,* 1.

403.   Then, welcome each rebuff
        That turns earth's smoothness rough,
    Each sting that bids nor sit nor stand but go !
    Be our joys three-parts pain !
    Strive, and hold cheap the strain ;
    Learn, nor account the pang ; dare, never grudge the throe.
                                                Ibid., 6.

404.   Setebos, Setebos, and Setebos !
        'Thinketh, He dwelleth i' the cold o' the moon.
                                    Caliban upon Setebos, 24.

405.   What is he buzzing in my ears ?
            ' Now that I come to die,
        Do I view the world as a vale of tears ? '
            Ah, reverend sir, not I !   *Confessions*, 1.

406.   How sad and bad and mad it was—
            But then, how it was sweet !   *Ibid.*, 9.

407.   Fear death ?—to feel the fog in my throat,
        The mist in my face.   *Prospice.*

408.   I was ever a fighter, so—one fight more,
        The best and the last !   *Ibid.*

409.   No ! let me taste the whole of it, fare like my peers
        The heroes of old,
    Bear the brunt, in a minute pay glad life's arrears
        Of pain, darkness and cold.   *Ibid.*

410.   Each life unfulfilled, you see ;
        It hangs still, patchy and scrappy :
        We have not sighed deep, laughed free,
            Starved, feasted, despaired,—been happy.
                                        Youth and Art, 16.

411.   It's wiser being good than bad ;
        It's safer being meek than fierce :
        It's fitter being sane than mad.   *Apparent Failure*, 7

412.   O lyric Love, half angel and half bird
        And all a wonder and a wild desire.
                                    The Ring and the Book, 1. 1391.

413.   What I call God
        And fools call Nature.
                            Ibid., x. *The Pope*, 1073.

414.   Why comes temptation but for man to meet
        And master and make crouch beneath his foot,
        And so be pedestalled in triumph ?   *Ibid.*, 1185.

415.   Abate,—Cardinal,—Christ,—Maria,—God, . . .
        Pompilia, will you let them murder me ?
                                    Ibid., xi. *Guido*, 2426.

416.   ' With this same key
        Shakespeare unlocked his heart,' once more !
        Did Shakespeare ? If so, the less Shakespeare he !
                                            House, 10

417.   I want to know a butcher paints,
           A baker rhymes for his pursuit,
       Candlestick-maker much acquaints
           His soul with song, or, haply mute,
           Blows out his brains upon the flute !   *Shop*, 21.

418.   Good, to forgive ;
                   Best, to forget !
                   Living, we fret ;
                   Dying, we live.   *La Saisiaz*, introduction.

419.   Such a starved bank of moss
               Till that May-morn,
           Blue ran the flash across :
               Violets were born !
                       The Two Poets of Croisic, introduction.

420.   Sky—what a scowl of cloud
               Till, near and far,
           Ray on ray split the shroud
               Splendid, a star !   Ibid.

421.   Never the time and the place
               And the loved one all together !
                       Never the Time and the Place.

422.   Truth, that's brighter than gem,
       Trust, that's purer than pearl,—
       Brightest truth, purest trust in the universe—all were for me
           In the kiss of one girl.   *Asolando. Summum Bonum*.

423.   One who never turned his back but marched breast forward,
           Never doubted clouds would break,
       Never dreamed, though right were worsted, wrong would
           triumph,
       Held we fall to rise, are baffled to fight better,
           Sleep to wake.   Ibid., epilogue.

424.   No, at noonday in the bustle of man's worktime
               Greet the unseen with a cheer !   Ibid.

BRUCE, MICHAEL, Scottish poet, 27 March, 1746—5 July, 1767

425.   Sweet bird ! thy bow'r is ever green,
               Thy sky is ever clear ;
           Thou hast no sorrow in thy song,
               No winter in thy year.   *Ode to the Cuckoo*.

BRUMMELL, GEORGE BRYAN (' BEAU BRUMMELL '), dandy, 7 June,
       1778—30 March, 1840

   426.   Who's your fat friend ?   *Of the Prince of Wales*.

BRYAN, WILLIAM JENNINGS, U.S. statesman, 19 March, 1860—26 July,
       1925.

   427.   The humblest citizen of all the land, when clad in the armour
ot a righteous cause, is stronger than all the hosts of Error.
       Speech, National Democratic Convention, Chicago, 10 July, 1896.

428. We will answer their demand for a gold standard by saying to them : You shall not press down upon the brow of labour this crown of thorn. You shall not crucify mankind upon a cross of gold.

Ibid.

BRYANT, WILLIAM CULLEN, U.S. poet and journalist, 3 Nov. 1794— 12 June, 1878

429.   So live, that when thy summons comes to join
         The innumerable caravan which moves
         To that mysterious realm, where each shall take
         His chamber in the silent halls of death,
         Thou go not, like the quarry-slave at night,
         Scourged to his dungeon, but, sustained and soothed
         By an unfaltering trust, approach thy grave,
         Like one that wraps the drapery of his couch
         About him, and lies down to pleasant dreams.

Thanatopsis, 73.

430.   The visions of my youth are past—
              Too bright, too beautiful to last.   *The Rivulet.*

BRYDGES, SIR SAMUEL EGERTON, genealogist, 30 Nov. 1762—8 Sept. 1837

431.   The glory dies not, and the grief is past.
                     Sonnet on the Death of Sir Walter Scott.

BUCHANAN, ROBERT WILLIAMS, Scottish author, 18 Aug. 1841— 10 June, 1901

432.   She just wore
              Enough for modesty—no more.
                     White Rose and Red, part i. v. 60.

433. The Fleshly School of Poetry.
                     Article in Contemporary Review, Oct. 1871.

BUCKINGHAM, GEORGE VILLIERS, 2ND DUKE OF, 30 Jan. 1628—16 April, 1687

434. What the devil does the plot signify, except to bring in fine things ?   *The Rehearsal,* iii. i.

BUCKINGHAM AND NORMANBY, JOHN SHEFFIELD, 1ST DUKE OF, 7 April, 1648—24 Feb. 1721

435.   Read Homer once, and you can read no more,
              For all books else appear so mean, so poor,
              Verse will seem prose ; but still persist to read,
              And Homer will be all the books you need.
                     Essay on Poetry, 322.

BUCKSTONE, JOHN BALDWIN, actor and dramatist, 14 Sept. 1802—
31 Oct. 1879

436. On such an occasion as this,
All time and nonsense scorning,
Nothing shall come amiss,
And we won't go home till morning.

Billy Taylor. I. ii.

BUFFON, GEORGES LOUIS LECLERC, COMTE DE, French scientist,
7 Sept. 1707—16 April, 1788.

437. Le style est l'homme même.—The style is the man himself.

Discours sur le style—Discourse on Style

438. La génie n'est autre chose qu'une grande aptitude à la patience
—Genius is nothing else but a great aptitude for patience. *Attributed*

BUNN, ALFRED, theatre manager, 1796 ?—20 Dec. 1860

439. I dreamt that I dwelt in marble halls,
With vassals and serfs at my side.

The Bohemian Girl, II.

440. The heart bow'd down by weight of woe
To weakest hopes will cling. Ibid.

441. When other lips and other hearts
Their tales of love shall tell. Ibid., III.

BUNNER, HENRY CUYLER, U.S. author, 3 Aug. 1855—11 May, 1896

442. Love must kiss that mortal's eyes
Who hopes to see fair Arcady.
No gold can buy you entrance there ;
But beggared Love may go all bare—
No wisdom won with weariness ;
But Love goes in with Folly's dress—
No fame that wit could ever win ;
But only Love may lead Love in
To Arcady, to Arcady. *The Way to Arcady.*

BUNYAN, JOHN, author, baptised 30 Nov. 1628, died 31 Aug. 1688

443. The name of the slough was Despond.

Pilgrim's Progress, part I

444. Set down my name, Sir. Ibid

445. Then Apollyon straddled quite over the whole breadth of the
way. Ibid

446. It beareth the name of Vanity Fair, because the town where
'tis kept is lighter than vanity. Ibid.

447. So soon as the man overtook me, he was but a word and a
blow. Ibid.

448. A castle called Doubting Castle, the owner whereof was Giant
Despair. Ibid.

449. So he passed over, and all the trumpets sounded for him on
the other side. Ibid., part II.

*B

450.   Some said ' John, print it ' ; others said, ' Not so.'
         Some said, ' It might do good ' ; other said, ' No.'
                                   Ibid., Apology for his Book.

451.   He that is down need fear no fall,
                       He that is low, no pride.
             Ibid., Shepherd boy's song in the Valley of Humiliation.

BURCHARD, SAMUEL DICKINSON, U.S. clergyman, 6 Sept. 1812—
     25 Sept. 1891

    452. We are Republicans, and don't propose to leave our party
and identify ourselves with the party whose antecedents have been
Rum, Romanism, and Rebellion.
             Speaking for a deputation of clergymen, New York, 29 Oct. 1884.

BURDETTE, ROBERT JONES, U.S. clergyman, 30 July, 1844—19 Nov.
     1914.

453.   Yet though I'm full of music
                       As choirs of singing birds,
                     ' I cannot sing the old songs '—
                       I do not know the words.   *Songs without Words.*

BURGESS, FRANK GELETT, U.S. humorist, 30 Jan. 1866—18 Sept. 1951

454.   I never saw a Purple Cow
                       I never hope to see one ;
                     But I can tell you, anyhow,
                       I'd rather see than be one.   *The Purple Cow.*

455.   Ah, yes, I wrote the ' Purple Cow '—
                       I'm sorry, now, I wrote it !
                     But I can tell you, anyhow,
                       I'll kill you if you quote it !   *Cinq Ans Après.*

BURGON, JOHN WILLIAM, clergyman, 21 Aug. 1813—4 Aug. 1888

456.   Match me such marvel save in Eastern clime,
            A rose-red city half as old as Time.   *Petra,* 132.

BURGOYNE, JOHN, General and dramatist, 24 Feb. 1722—4 June, 1792

    457. You have only, when before your glass, to keep pronouncing
to yourself nimini-pimini—the lips cannot fail of taking their plie.
                                   The Heiress, III. ii.

BURKE, EDMUND, Irish statesman, 12 Jan. 1729—9 July, 1797

    458. I am convinced that we have a degree of delight, and that no
small one, in the real misfortunes and pains of others.
             On the Sublime and Beautiful, part I. 14.

    459. There is, however, a limit at which forbearance ceases to be a
virtue.
             Observations on a Publication, ' The Present State of the Nation.'

460. When bad men combine, the good must associate ; else they will fall, one by one, an unpitied sacrifice in a contemptible struggle.
Thoughts on the Cause of the Present Discontents.

461. The cant of *Not men, but measures.* Ibid.

462. A wise and salutary neglect.
Speech on Conciliation with America.

463. The worthy gentleman who has been snatched from us at the moment of the election, and in the middle of the contest, whilst his desires were as warm, and his hopes as eager as ours, has feelingly told us what shadows we are, and what shadows we pursue.
Speech at Bristol on Declining the Poll, 1780.

464. It is now sixteen or seventeen years since I saw the Queen of France, then the Dauphiness, at Versailles ; and surely never lighted on this orb, which she hardly seemed to touch, a more delightful vision. I saw her just above the horizon, decorating and cheering the elevated sphere she just began to move in,—glittering like the morning star, full of life, and splendour, and joy. . . . Little did I dream that I should have lived to see such disasters fallen upon her in a nation of gallant men, in a nation of men of honour and of cavaliers. I thought ten thousand swords must have leaped from their scabbards to avenge even a look that threatened her with insult. But the age of chivalry is gone. That of sophisters, economists, and calculators, has succeeded ; and the glory of Europe is extinguished for ever.
Reflections on the Revolution in France.

465. That chastity of honour which felt a stain like a wound. Ibid.

466. Vice itself lost half its evil, by losing all its grossness. Ibid.

467. Kings will be tyrants from policy, when subjects are rebels from principle. Ibid.

468. Learning will be cast into the mire and trodden down under the hoofs of a swinish multitude. Ibid.

469. The men of England, the men, I mean, of light and leading in England. Ibid.

470. And having looked to government for bread, on the very first scarcity they will turn and bite the hand that fed them.
Thoughts and Details on Scarcity.

471. He was not merely a chip of the old block, but the old block itself. *Of Pitt's first speech,* 26 Feb. 1781.

472. It is not a good imitation of Johnson ; it has all his pomp, without his force ; it has all the nodosities of the oak without its strength ; it has all the contortions of the Sybil without the inspiration. [On Croft's life of Dr. Young.] Boswell, *Life of Johnson,* an. 1781.

BURNEY, FRANCES *or* FANNY (MME. D'ARBLAY), novelist, 13 June, 1752—6 Jan. 1840.

473. ' True, very true, ma'am,' said he [Mr. Meadowes], yawning, ' one really lives nowhere ; one does but vegetate, and wish it all at an end.' *Cecilia,* VII. v.

BURNS, ROBERT, Scottish poet, 25 Jan. 1759—21 July, 1796

474.   Tho' this was fair, and that was braw,
                  And yon the toast of a' the town,
              I sigh'd, and said among them a',
                  ' Ye are na Mary Morison.'   *Mary Morison.*

475.   Auld Nature swears, the lovely dears
                  Her noblest work she classes, O ;
              Her prentice han' she tried on man,
                  And then she made the lasses, O !
                                          Green grow the Rashes.

476.   Nature's law
              That man was made to mourn.
                                          Man was made to mourn.

477.   Man's inhumanity to man
                  Makes countless thousands mourn !   Ibid.

478.   The heart aye's the part aye
                  That makes us right or wrang.
                                  Epistle to Davie, a Brother Poet.

479.   O Thou, who in the heavens does dwell,
              Who, as it pleases best Thysel',
              Sends ane to heaven, and ten to hell,
                      A' for Thy glory,
              And no for ony gude or ill
                      They've done afore Thee !
                                          Holy Willie's Prayer.

480.   I was na fou, but just had plenty.
                                  Death and Doctor Hornbook.

481.   Some wee short hour ayont the twal'.   Ibid.

482.   There's some are fou o' love divine,
                  There's some are fou o' brandy.   *The Holy Fair, 27.*

483.   Wee sleekit, cowrin, tim'rous beastie,
                  O, what a panic's in thy breastie !   *To a Mouse.*

484.   The best-laid schemes o' mice and men
                      Gang aft a-gley.   Ibid.

485.   The mother, wi' her needle and her shears,
                  Gars auld claes look amaist as weel's the new.
                                  The Cotter's Saturday Night, 5.

486.   The halesome parritch, chief of Scotia's food.   Ibid., 11.

487.   He wales a portion with judicious care,
              And ' Let us worship God ! ' he says with solemn air.
                                                          Ibid., 12.

488.   From scenes like these old Scotia's grandeur springs,
                  That make her lov'd at home, rever'd abroad :
              Princes and lords are but the breath of kings,
                  'An honest man's the noblest work of God.'   Ibid., 19.

489.   O thou ! whatever title suit thee—
                  Auld Hornie, Satan, Nick, or Clootie.
                                          Address to the Deil.

490.
But fare-you-weel, auld Nickie-ben !
O wad ye tak a thought an' men' !
Ye aiblins might—I dinna ken—
    Still hae a stake :
I'm wae to think upo' yon den,
    Ev'n for your sake !   Ibid.

491.
His lockèd, letter'd, braw brass collar,
Show'd him the gentleman and scholar.
                              The Twa Dogs, 13.

492.
Freedom and whisky gang thegither !
    The Author's Earnest Cry and Prayer, postscript, 7.

493.
Then gently scan your brother man,
    Still gentler sister woman ;
Though they may gang a kennin wrang,
    To step aside is human.
                    Address to the unco Guid.

494.
What's done we partly may compute,
    But know not what's resisted.   Ibid.

495.
O wad some Power the giftie gie us
To see oursels as ithers see us !
It wad frae mony a blunder free us,
    And foolish notion.   *To a Louse.*

496.
Wee, modest, crimson-tippèd flow'r.
                              To a Mountain Daisy.

497.
I waive the quantum o' the sin,
    The hazard of concealing ;
But och ! it hardens a' within,
    And petrifies the feeling.
                    Epistle to a Young Friend.

498.
To catch dame Fortune's golden smile,
    Assiduous wait upon her ;
And gather gear by ev'ry wile
    That's justified by honour ;
Not for to hide it in a hedge,
    Nor for a train attendant ;
But for the glorious privilege
    Of being independent.   Ibid

499.
But facts are chiels that winna ding,
    An' downa be disputed.   *A Dream*

500.
The poor inhabitants below
Was quick to learn and wise to know,
And keenly felt the friendly glow,
    And softer flame ;
But thoughtless follies laid him low,
    And stain'd his name.
                              A Bard's Epitaph.

501.
Your poor, narrow foot-path of a street,
Where twa wheel-barrows tremble when they meet.
                              The Brigs of Ayr

502.
Great chieftain o' the pudding-race.
                              Address to a Haggis.

503.
Here lie Willie Michie's banes,
O Satan, when ye tak him,
Gie him the schulin o' your weans,
For clever deils he'll mak them !
Epitaph for a Schoolmaster.

504.
Whoe'er he be that sojourns here,
I pity much his case,
Unless he come to wait upon
The Lord their God,—His Grace.

505.
There's naething here but Highland pride,
And Highland scab and hunger :
If Providence has sent me here,
'Twas surely in an anger. *The Bard at Inveraray.*

506.
Up in the morning's no for me,
Up in the morning early. *Up in the Morning.*

507.
Of a' the airts the wind can blaw,
I dearly like the west,
For there the bonnie lassie lives,
The lassie I lo'e best. *Of a' the Airts.*

508.
Aye waukin', O !
Waukin' still and wearie :
Sleep I can get nane
For thinking on my dearie.
Simmer's a Pleasant Time.

509.
Should auld acquaintance be forgot,
And never brought to mind ?
Should auld acquaintance be forgot,
And auld lang syne ! *Auld Lang Syne.*

510.
We'll tak a cup o' kindness yet,
For auld lang syne. *Ibid.*

511.
We twa hae run about the braes,
And pu'd the gowans fine ;
But we've wander'd mony a weary fit,
Sin' auld lang syne. *Ibid.*

512.
And there's a hand, my trusty fere,
And gie's a hand o' thine !
And we'll tak a right gude-willie waught,
For auld lang syne. *Ibid.*

513.
Go, fetch to me a pint o' wine,
And fill it in a silver tassie ;
That I may drink before I go.
A service to my bonnie lassie. *My Bonnie Mary.*

514.
John Anderson my jo, John,
When we were first acquent,
Your locks were like the raven,
Your bonnie brow was brent ;
But now your brow is beld, John,
Your locks are like the snow ;
But blessings on your frosty pow,
John Anderson, my jo. *John Anderson my Jo.*

515. My love she's but a lassie yet. *Title.*

516. Whistle o'er the lave o't. *Title.*

517. Hear, Land o' Cakes, and brither Scots,
Frae Maidenkirk to Johnny Groat's ;—
If there's a hole in a' your coats,
    I rede you tent it :
A chiel's amang you takin' notes,
    And, faith, he'll prent it !
      *On the late Captain Grose's Peregrinations
      thro' Scotland.*

518. My heart's in the Highlands, my heart is not here,
My heart's in the Highlands, a-chasing the deer ;
A-chasing the wild deer, and following the roe,
My heart's in the Highlands wherever I go.
[Traditional.]   *My Heart's in the Highlands.*

519. To make a happy fireside clime
    To weans and wife,
That's the true pathos and sublime
    Of human life.   *Epistle to Dr. Blacklock.*

520. Where sits our sulky sullen dame,
Gathering her brows like gathering storm,
Nursing her wrath to keep it warm.
      Tam o' Shanter. 10.

521. Auld Ayr, wham ne'er a town surpasses
For honest men and bonnie lasses.   Ibid., 15.

522. Ah, gentle dames ! it gars me greet
To think how mony counsels sweet,
How mony lengthen'd, sage advices
The husband frae the wife despises !   Ibid., 33.

523. His ancient, trusty, drouthy crony :
Tam lo'ed him like a very brither ;
They had been fou for weeks thegither.   Ibid., 43.

524. Kings may be blest, but Tam was glorious,
O'er a' the ills o' life victorious.   Ibid., 57.

525. But pleasures are like poppies spread,
You seize the flow'r, its bloom is shed ;
Or like the snow falls in the river,
A moment white—then melts for ever ;
Or like the Borealis race,
That flit ere you can point their place ;
Or like the rainbow's lovely form
Evanishing amid the storm.   Ibid., 59.

526. Ah, Tam ! ah, Tam ! thou'll get thy fairin !
In hell they'll roast thee like a herrin !   Ibid., 201.

527. Ye banks and braes o' bonnie Doon,
    How can ye bloom sae fresh and fair ?
How can ye chant, ye little birds,
    And I sae weary fu' o' care ?   *The Banks o' Doon.*

528. What can a young lassie do wi' an auld man ?   *Title.*

529.   Critics !—appall'd I venture on the name,
        Those cut-throat bandits in the paths of fame.
                        Second Epistle to Robert Graham of Fintry.

530.   Ae fond kiss and then we sever.   *Ae Fond Kiss.*

531.   But to see her was to love her,
            Love but her, and love for ever.   *Ibid.*

532.   Had we never lov'd sae kindly,
            Had we never lov'd sae blindly,
            Never met—or never parted,
            We had ne'er been broken-hearted.   *Ibid.*

533.   The deil's awa wi' the Exciseman.   *Title.*

534.   O saw ye bonnie Lesley
                    As she gaed o'er the Border ?
                She's gane, like Alexander,
                    To spread her conquests farther.
                To see her is to love her,
                    And love but her for ever ;
                For Nature made her what she is,
                    And never made anither !   *Bonnie Lesley.*

535.   Here awa, there awa, wandering Willie.
                                        Wandering Willie.

536.   Whistle, and I'll come to ye, my lad.   *Title.*

537.   Scots, wha hae wi' Wallace bled,
            Scots, wham Bruce has aften led,
            Welcome to your gory bed,
                    Or to victory.   *Bannockburn.*

538.   Now's the day, and now's the hour ;
            See the front o' battle lour ;
            See approach proud Edward's power—
                    Chains and slavery !   *Ibid.*

539.   Liberty's in every blow !—
                    Let us do or die !   *Ibid.*

540.   O my luve's like a red, red rose,
                That's newly sprung in June :
            O my luve's like the melody
                That's sweetly play'd in tune.   *A Red, Red Rose.*

541.   And I will luve thee still, my dear,
                Till a' the seas gang dry.   *Ibid.*

542.   He turn'd him right and round about
                Upon the Irish shore ;
            And gae his bridle-reins a shake,
                With adieu for evermore, my dear ;
                With adieu for evermore.
[Found in a ballad.]   *It was a' for our Rightfu' King.*

543.   Contented wi' little, and cantie wi' mair.
                                        Contented wi' Little.

544.   When I think on the happy days
                I spent wi' you, my dearie ;
            And now what lands between us lie,
                How can I be but eerie ?

545.   How slow ye move, ye heavy hours,
                As ye were wae and weary !
            It wasna sae ye glinted by,
                When I was wi' my dearie.
                                How Long and Dreary is the Night.

546.   The rank is but the guinea's stamp ;
                The man's the gowd for a' that.
                                A Man's a Man for a' That.

547.   A king can mak a belted knight,
                A marquis, duke, and a' that ;
            But an honest man's aboon his might,
                Guid faith, he mauna fa' that.   *Ibid.*

548   For a' that, and a' that,
                It's coming yet for a' that,
            That man to man, the warld o'er,
                Shall brothers be for a' that.   *Ibid.*

549.   O wert thou in the cauld blast.   *Title.*

550.   Gin a body meet a body
                Coming through the rye ;
            Gin a body kiss a body,
                Need a body cry ?   *Coming through the Rye.*
    [Old song rewritten.]

551.   Some hae meat, and canna eat,
                And some wad eat that want it ;
            But we hae meat, and we can eat,
                And sae the Lord be thankit.   *The Selkirk Grace.*
    [Authorship doubtful.]

BURTON, ROBERT, clergyman and author, 8 Feb. 1577—25 Jan. 1640

    552. Naught so sweet as melancholy.
                    Anatomy of Melancholy. The Author's Abstract.

    553. They lard their lean books with the fat of others' works.
                            Ibid., *Democritus to the Reader.*

    554. We can say nothing but what hath been said. . . .   Our poets
steal from Homer. . . . . He that comes last is commonly best.
                                                            Ibid.

    555. One was never married, and that's his hell ; another is, and
that's his plague.   Ibid., part I. II. iv. 7.

    556. Tobacco, divine, rare, superexcellent tobacco, which goes far
beyond all their panaceas, potable gold, and philosopher's stones, a
sovereign remedy to all diseases.   Ibid., part II. IV. ii. I.

    557. But, as it is commonly abused by most men, which take it as
tinkers do ale, 'tis a plague, a mischief, a violent purger of goods, lands,
health, hellish, devilish, and damned tobacco, the ruin and overthrow
of body and soul.   Ibid.

BUTLER, JOSEPH, BISHOP OF DURHAM, 18 May, 1692—16 June, 1752.

    558. Things and actions are what they are, and the consequences
of them will be what they will be : why then should we desire to be
deceived ?   *Fifteen Sermons*, vii. 16.

BUTLER, NICHOLAS MURRAY, President of Columbia University, 2 April, 1862—7 Dec., 1947.

559.   An expert is one who knows more and more about less and less.
Commencement Address.

BUTLER, SAMUEL, poet, baptised 8 Feb. 1612, died 25 Sept. 1680.

560.   And pulpit, drum ecclesiastic,
           Was beat with fist instead of a stick.   *Hudibras*, I. i. 11.

561.   Beside, 'tis known he could speak Greek
           As naturally as pigs squeak ;
           That Latin was no more difficile
           Than to a blackbird 'tis to whistle.   Ibid., 51.

562.   He was in logic a great critic,
           Profoundly skill'd in analytic.
           He could distinguish and divide
           A hair 'twixt south and south-west side.
           On either which he would dispute,
           Confute, change hands, and still confute.   Ibid., 65.

563.   For rhetoric, he could not ope
           His mouth, but out there flew a trope.   Ibid., 81.

564.   For he by geometric scale
           Could take the size of pots of ale.   Ibid., 121.

565.   And wisely tell what hour o' th' day
           The clock does strike, by algebra.   Ibid., 125.

566.   For every why he had a wherefore.   Ibid., 132.

567.   He knew what's what, and that's as high
           As metaphysic wit can fly.   Ibid., 149.

568.   Such as take lodgings in a head
           That's to be let unfurnished.   Ibid., 161.

569.   'Twas Presbyterian true blue.   Ibid., 191.

570.   Such as do build their faith upon
           The holy text of pike and gun.   Ibid., 195.

571.   And prove their doctrine orthodox
           By apostolic blows and knocks.   Ibid., 199.

572.   Compound for sins they are inclin'd to
           By damning those they have no mind to.   Ibid., 215.

573.   The trenchant blade, Toledo trusty,
           For want of fighting was grown rusty,
           And eat into itself, for lack
           Of some body to hew and hack.   Ibid., 359.

574.   For rhyme the rudder is of verses,
           With which, like ships, they steer their courses,
                                                           Ibid., 463.

575.   With many a stiff thwack, many a bang,
           Hard crab-tree and old iron rang,   Ibid., ii. 831.

576.   Ay me ! what perils do environ
           The man that meddles with cold iron.   Ibid., iii. 1.

577.   If he that in the field is slain
         Be in the bed of honour lain,
         He that is beaten may be said
         To lie in honour's truckle-bed.   Ibid., 1047.

578.   But those that write in rhyme still make
         The one verse for the other's sake ;
         For one for sense, and one for rhyme,
         I think's sufficient at one time.   Ibid., II. i. 27.

579.   Not by your individual whiskers,
         But by your dialect and discourse.   Ibid., 155.

580.   Some have been beaten till they know
         What wood a cudgel's of by th' blow ;
         Some kicked until they can feel whether
         A shoe be Spanish or neat's leather.   Ibid., 221.

581.   The sun had long since in the lap
         Of Thetis taken out his nap,
         And, like a lobster boiled, the morn
         From black to red began to turn.   Ibid., ii. 29.

582.   Have always been at daggers-drawing,
         And one another clapper-clawing.   Ibid., 79.

583.   What makes all doctrines plain and clear ?
         About two hundred pounds a year.
         And that which was proved true before,
         Prove false again ?   Two hundred more.
                                                      Ibid., III. i. 1277.
584.   He that complies against his will
         Is of his own opinion still.   Ibid., iii. 547.

BUTLER, SAMUEL, author, 4 Dec. 1835—18 June, 1902.

   585. Life is one long process of getting tired.
                    Note Books.   Lord, What is Man ?   Life.

   586. Life is the art of drawing sufficient conclusions from insufficient
premises.   Ibid.

   587. The phrase ' unconscious humour ' is the one contribution I
have made to the current literature of the day.
                    Ibid., *The Position of a Homo unius Libri.*

   588. I keep my books at the British Museum and at Mudie's.
                    The Humour of Homer.   Ramblings in Cheapside.

589.   Stowed away in a Montreal lumber room
         The Discobulus standeth and turneth his face to the wall ;
         Dusty, cobweb-covered, maimed and set at naught,
         Beauty crieth in an attic and no man regardeth.
                    O God !   O Montreal !   *A Psalm of Montreal.*

BUTLER, WILLIAM, doctor, 1535—29 Jan. 1618

   590. Doubtless God could have made a better berry, but doubtless
God never did.   [Of the strawberry.]   Walton, *Compleat Angler*, I. v.

BYROM, JOHN, poet, 29 Feb. 1692—26 Sept. 1763

591.   God bless the King !—I mean the Faith's Defender ;
                God bless (no harm in blessing) the Pretender !
                But who Pretender is, or who is King,—
                God bless us all !—that's quite another thing.
                                    To an Officer of the Army.

592.   Some say, compar'd to Bononcini,
                That Mynheer Handel's but a ninny ;
                Other aver that he to Handel
                Is scarcely fit to hold a candle.
                Strange all this difference should be
                'Twixt Tweedledum and Tweedledee.
                     On the Feuds between Handel and Bononcini.

593.   Christians awake ! Salute the happy morn,
                Whereon the Saviour of the world was born !
                         Hymn for Christmas Day.

BYRON, GEORGE GORDON NOEL BYRON, 6TH LORD, 22 Jan. 1788—
     19 April, 1824

594.   When we two parted
                    In silence and tears,
             Half broken-hearted
                    To sever for years.   *When we two parted.*

595.   If I should meet thee
                    After long years,
              How should I greet thee ?—
                    With silence and tears.   Ibid.

596.   Fools are my theme, let satire be my song.
                    English Bards and Scotch Reviewers, 6.

597.   'Tis pleasant, sure, to see one's name in print ;
        A book's a book, although there's nothing in 't. Ibid., 51.

598.   With just enough of learning to misquote.   Ibid., 66.

599.   As soon
        Seek roses in December—ice in June ;
        Hope constancy in wind, or corn in chaff ;
        Believe a woman or an epitaph,
        Or any other thing that's false, before
        You trust in critics who themselves are sore.   Ibid., 75.

600.   Better to err with Pope, than shine with Pye.   Ibid. 102.

601.   Oh, Amos Cottle ! Phoebus ! what a name !   Ibid., 399.

602.   So the struck eagle, stretch'd upon the plain,
        No more through rolling clouds to soar again,
        View'd his own feather on the fatal dart,
        And wing'd the shaft that quiver'd in his heart ;
        Keen were his pangs, but keener far to feel
        He nursed the pinion which impell'd the steel. Ibid., 841.

603.   Maid of Athens, ere we part,
             Give, oh give me back my heart !   *Maid of Athens.*

604.   Maidens, like moths, are ever caught by glare.
                           Childe Harold's Pilgrimage, 1. 9.

605.   Adieu, adieu ! my native shore
          Fades o'er the waters blue.   Ibid., 13.

606.   My native land—good night !   Ibid.

607.   Once more upon the waters ! yet once more !
    And the waves bound beneath me as a steed
    That knows his rider.   Ibid., iii. 2.

608.   Stop !—for thy tread is on an Empire's dust !
    An earthquake's spoil is sepulchred below !   Ibid., 17.

609.   There was a sound of revelry by night,
    And Belgium's capital had gather'd then
    Her beauty and her chivalry, and bright
    The lamps shone o'er fair women and brave men ;
    A thousand hearts beat happily ; and when
    Music arose with its voluptuous swell,
    Soft eyes look'd love to eyes which spake again,
    And all went merry as a marriage bell ;
    But hush ! hark ! a deep sound strikes like a rising
            knell !   Ibid., 21.

610.   Did ye not hear it ?—No ; 'twas but the wind,
    Or the car rattling o'er the stony street ;
    On with the dance ! let joy be unconfined ;
    No sleep till morn, when Youth and Pleasure meet
    To chase the glowing Hours with flying feet.   Ibid., 22.

611. Arm ! Arm ! it is—it is—the cannon's opening roar !   Ibid.

612. He rush'd into the field, and. foremost fighting, fell.

                                        Ibid., 23.

613.   And there was mounting in hot haste.   Ibid., 25.

614.   Rider and horse,—friend, foe,—in one red burial blent.
                                        Ibid., 27.

615.   The castled crag of Drachenfels
          Frowns o'er the wide and winding Rhine.   Ibid., 55.

616.   By the blue rushing of the arrowy Rhone.
                                      Ibid., 71.

617.   Sapping a solemn creed with solemn sneer.
                                    Ibid., 107.

618.   I have not loved the world, nor the world me ;
    I have not flatter'd its rank breath, nor bow'd
    To its idolatries a patient knee.   Ibid., 113.

619.   I stood in Venice, on the Bridge of Sighs ;
      A palace and a prison on each hand.   Ibid., iv 1.

620. Where Venice sate in state, throned on her hundred isles.
                                        Ibid.

621.   Then farewell, Horace ; whom I hated so,
        Not for thy faults, but mine.   Ibid., 77.

622.   Yet, Freedom ! yet thy banner, torn, but flying,
    Streams like the thunder-storm *against* the wind.

                                        Ibid., 98.

623.   He reck'd not of the life he lost nor prize,
          But where his rude hut by the Danube lay,
          There were his young barbarians all at play,
          There was their Dacian mother—he, their sire,
          Butcher'd to make a Roman holiday.   *Ibid.*, 141.

624.   While stands the Coliseum, Rome shall stand ;
          When falls the Coliseum, Rome shall fall ;
          And when Rome falls—the World.   *Ibid.*, 145.
              [Saying of the ancient pilgrims, quoted from Bede
                  by Gibbon, *Decline and Fall of the Roman
                  Empire*, lxxi.]

625.   There is a pleasure in the pathless woods,
          There is a rapture on the lonely shore,
          There is society, where none intrudes,
          By the deep sea, and music in its roar :
          I love not Man the less, but Nature more,
          From these our interviews, in which I steal
          From all I may be, or have been before,
          To mingle with the Universe, and feel
          What I can ne'er express, yet cannot all conceal.

                                                  Ibid., 178.

626.   Roll on, thou deep and dark blue Ocean—roll !
          Ten thousand fleets sweep over thee in vain ;
          Man marks the earth with ruin—his control
          Stops with the shore.   *Ibid.*, 179.

627.   He sinks into thy depths with bubbling groan,
          Without a grave, unknell'd, uncoffin'd, and unknown.
                                                  Ibid.

628.   Time writes no wrinkle on thine azure brow :
          Such as creation's dawn beheld, thou rollest now.
                                                  Ibid., 182.

629.   Muse of the many-twinkling feet !   *The Waltz.*

630.   Know ye the land where the cypress and myrtle
              Are emblems of deeds that are done in their clime ?
          Where the rage of the vulture, the love of the turtle,
              Now melt into sorrow, now madden to crime.
                                          The Bride of Abydos, i. 1.

631.   The blind old man of Scio's rocky isle.   *Ibid.*, ii. 2·

632.   Hark ! to the hurried question of Despair :
          ' Where is my child ? '—an echo answers, ' Where ? '

                                                  Ibid., 27·

633.   O'er the glad waters of the dark blue sea,
          Our thoughts as boundless, and our souls as free,
          Far as the breeze can bear, the billows foam,
          Survey our empire, and behold our home !
                                          The Corsair, i. 1.

634.   She walks in beauty, like the night
                  Of cloudless climes and starry skies ;
              And all that's best of dark and bright
                  Meet in her aspect and her eyes :
              Thus mellow'd to that tender light
                  Which heaven to gaudy day denies.
                                          She walks in Beauty.

635. Oh ! snatch'd away in beauty's bloom,
  On thee shall press no ponderous tomb.
      Oh ! snatch'd away in Beauty's Bloom.

636. The Assyrian came down like the wolf on the fold,
  And his cohorts were gleaming in purple and gold ;
  And the sheen of their spears was like stars on the sea,
  When the blue wave rolls nightly on deep Galilee.
      The Destruction of Sennacherib.

637.   There be none of Beauty's daughters
    With a magic like thee ;
   And like music on the waters
    Is thy sweet voice to me. *Stanzas for Music.*

638. Then the few whose spirits float above the wreck of happiness
  Are driven o'er the shoals of guilt or ocean of excess :
  The magnet of their course is gone, or only points in vain
  The shore to which their shiver'd sail shall never stretch
   again.   *Stanzas for Music.*

639. Eternal Spirit of the chainless Mind.
        Sonnet on Chillon.

640. My hair is grey, but not with years.
      The Prisoner of Chillon. 1.

641. Fare thee well ! and if for ever,
  Still for ever, fare thee well. *Fare thee well.*

642. And both were young, and one was beautiful.
       The Dream, 2.

643. A change came o'er the spirit of my dream. Ibid., 3.

644. So we'll go no more a-roving
   So late into the night.
     So we'll go no more a-roving.

645. My boat is on the shore,
   And my bark is on the sea
      To Thomas Moore.

646. Here's a sigh to those who love me,
   And a smile to those who hate ;
   And, whatever sky's above me,
   Here's a heart for every fate.   Ibid.

647. The nursery still lisps out in all they utter—
  Besides, they always smell of bread and butter.
       Beppo, 39.

648. In virtues nothing earthly could surpass her,
  Save thine ' incomparable oil ', Macassar !
      Don Juan, i. 17.

649. But—Oh ! ye lords of ladies intellectual,
  Inform us truly, have they not hen-peck'd you all ?
      Ibid., 22.

650. A little while she strove, and much repented,
  And whispering ' I will ne'er consent '—consented.
      Ibid., 117

651. 'Tis sweet to hear the watch-dog's honest bark
      Bay deep-mouth'd welcome as we draw near home ;
      'Tis sweet to know there is an eye will mark
      Our coming, and look brighter when we come.

      Ibid., 123.

652. Sweet is revenge—especially to women. *Ibid., 124.*

653. Man's love is of man's life a thing apart,
      'Tis woman's whole existence. *Ibid., 194.*

654. A solitary shriek, the bubbling cry
      Of some strong swimmer in his agony. *Ibid., ii. 53.*

655. The best of life is but intoxication. *Ibid., 179.*

656. Alas ! the love of women ! it is known
      To be a lovely and a fearful thing. *Ibid., 199.*

657. In her first passion woman loves her lover,
      In all the others all she loves is love. *Ibid., iii. 3.*

658. He was the mildest manner'd man
      That ever scuttled ship or cut a throat. *Ibid., 41.*

659. The isles of Greece, the isles of Greece !
      Where burning Sappho loved and sung. *Ibid., 86.*

660. The mountains look on Marathon—
      And Marathon looks on the sea ;
      And musing there an hour alone,
      I dream'd that Greece might still be free. *Ibid.*

661. Place me on Sunium's marbled steep,
      Where nothing, save the waves and I,
      May hear our mutual murmurs sweep ;
      There, swan-like, let me sing and die. *Ibid.*

662. And if I laugh at any mortal thing,
      'Tis that I may not weep. *Ibid., iv. 4.*

663. The tocsin of the soul—the dinner-bell. *Ibid., 49.*

664. When Bishop Berkeley said ' there was no matter,'
      And proved it—'twas no matter what he said.

      Ibid., xi. 1.

665. But Tom's no more—and so no more of Tom.

      Ibid., 20.

666. 'Tis strange the mind, that very fiery particle,
      Should let itself be snuff'd out by an article. *Ibid., 60.*
      [Of Keats's death.]

667. The English winter—ending in July,
      To recommence in August. *Ibid., xiii. 42.*

668. Society is now one polish'd horde,
      Form'd of two mighty tribes, the *Bores* and *Bored*.

      Ibid., 95.

669. The world is a bundle of hay,
      Mankind are the asses who pull ;
      Each tugs in a different way,
      And the greatest of all is John Bull. *Epigram.*

670.   Who kill'd John Keats ?
                         ' I,' says the Quarterly,
                         So savage and Tartarly ;
                       ' 'Twas one of my feats.'   *John Keats.*

671.   Oh, talk not to me of a name great in story ;
            The days of our youth are the days of our glory ;
            And the myrtle and ivy of sweet two-and-twenty
            Are worth all your laurels, though never so plenty.
                 Stanzas written on the Road between Florence and Pisa.

672.   My days are in the yellow leaf ;
                   The flowers and fruits of love are gone ;
                 The worm, the canker, and the grief
                         Are mine alone.
                       On this Day I complete my thirty-sixth Year.

673.   Seek out—less often sought than found—
                A soldier's grave, for thee the best ;
            Then look around, and choose thy ground,
                    And take thy rest.   *Ibid.*

   674. I awoke one morning and found myself famous.
              Entry in memoranda, on the success of ' Childe Harold.'

BYRON, HENRY JAMES, dramatist, Jan. 1834—11 April, 1884

   675. Life's too short for chess.   *Our Boys*, I.

CAESAR, GAIUS JULIUS, Roman statesman, 12 July 102 B.C.—15 March,
       44 B.C.

   676. Gallia est omnis divisa in partes tres.—All Gaul is divided
into three parts.   *De Bello Gallico—On the Gallic War*, I. i.

   677. Iacta alea est.—The die is cast.
                            On crossing the Rubicon, 49 B.C.

   678. Veni, vidi, vici.—I came, I saw, I conquered.
                 Letter after victory at Zela in Asia Minor, 47 B.C.

   679. Et tu, Brute ?—You too, Brutus ? *As he was being assassinated.*

CAINE, SIR THOMAS HENRY HALL, novelist, 14 May, 1853—31 Aug.,
       1931

   680. I reject the monstrous theory that while a man may redeem
the past a woman never can.   *The Eternal City*, VI. xviii.

CALHOUN, JOHN CALDWELL, U.S. statesman, 18 March, 1782—31 March,
       1850

   681. The very essence of a free government consists in considering
offices as public trusts, bestowed for the good of the country, and not
for the benefit of an individual or a party.   *Speech*, 13 Feb. 1835.

CALIGULA, GAIUS CAESAR, Roman Emperor, A.D. 12—41

   682. Utinam populus Romanus unam cervicem haberet !—Would
that the Roman people had but one neck !   Suetonius, *Caligula*, xxx

CALLIMACHUS, Greek poet and librarian, 310 ?—240 ? B.C.
683. Μέγα βιβλίον, μέγα κακόν—Great book, great evil. *Attributed.*

CALVERLEY (*formerly* BLAYDS), CHARLES STUART, poet, 22 Dec. 1831—
17 Feb. 1884

684. I love to gaze upon a child ;
  A young bud bursting into blossom ;
Artless, as Eve yet unbeguiled,
  And agile as a young opossum :
And such was he. A calm-brow'd lad,
  Yet mad, at moments, as a hatter.
  Gemini and Virgo.

685. Thou who, when fears attack,
  Bidst them avaunt, and Black
Care, at the horseman's back
  Perching, unseatest ;
Sweet, when the morn is grey ;
Sweet when they've cleared away
Lunch ; and at close of day
  Possibly sweetest. *Ode to Tobacco.*

686. Grinder, who serenely grindest
  At my door the Hundredth Psalm.
  Lines on hearing the Organ.

687. The sports, to which with boyish glee
  I sprang erewhile, attract no more ;
Although I am but sixty-three
  Or four. *Changed.*

688. O my own, my beautiful, my blue-eyed !
  To be young once more, and bite my thumb
At the world and all its cares with you, I'd
  Give no inconsiderable sum. *First Love.*

689. I deal in every ware in turn,
  I've rings for buddin' Sally
That sparkle like those eyes of her'n ;
  I've liquor for the valet. *Wanderers.*
[Parody of Tennyson's *The Brook.*]

690. The auld wife sat at her ivied door,
  (*Butter and eggs and a pound of cheese*)
A thing she had frequently done before ;
  And her spectacles lay on her apron'd knees.
  Ballad.

691. In moss-prankt dells which the sunbeams flatter.
  Lovers, and a Reflection.

CAMBRONNE, PIERRE JACQUES ÉTIENNE, COMTE, French General,
26 Dec. 1770—8 Jan. 1842

692. La garde meurt, mais elle ne se rend pas.—The Guard dies,
but does not surrender. *At Waterloo*, 18 June, 1815.
[His real answer, according to French authorities, was ' shorter and
not less forcible.']

CAMDEN, WILLIAM, antiquary, 2 May, 1551—9 Nov. 1623

693.   Betwixt the stirrup and the ground
            Mercy I asked, mercy I found.
                    Epitaph for a Man killed by falling from his Horse.

CAMPBELL, IGNATIUS ROY DUNNACHIE, South African poet, 2 Oct.
        1902—22 April, 1957

694.   They use the snaffle and the curb all right,
            But where's the bloody horse ?
                            On some South African Novelists.

CAMPBELL, JANE MONTGOMERY, translator, 1817—15 Nov. 1878

695.   We plough the fields, and scatter
            The good seed on the land,
            But it is fed and watered
            By God's almighty hand.   *We plough the Fields.*

696.   He paints the wayside flower,
            He lights the evening star.   Ibid.

CAMPBELL, JOSEPH, Irish poet, 1879—13 July, 1944

697.   As a white candle
                In a holy place,
                So is the beauty
                Of an aged face.   *The Old Woman.*

CAMPBELL, THOMAS, Scottish poet, 27 July, 1777—15 June, 1844

698.   'Tis distance lends enchantment to the view.
                        The Pleasures of Hope, I. 7.

699.   Hope, for a season, bade the world farewell,
        And Freedom shrieked—as Kosciusko fell !   Ibid., 381.

700.   What though my winged hours of bliss have been,
        Like angel-visits, few and far between.   Ibid., II. 377.

701.   Lochiel, Lochiel ! beware of the day
            When the Lowlands shall meet thee in battle array !
                        Lochiel's Warning, 1.

702.   'Tis the sunset of life gives me mystical lore,
        And coming events cast their shadows before.   Ibid., 55.

703.   A chieftain to the Highlands bound
              Cries ' Boatman, do not tarry !
            And I'll give thee a silver pound
              To row us o'er the ferry.'   *Lord Ullin's Daughter.*

704.   Ye Mariners of England
            That guard our native seas,
            Whose flag has braved, a thousand years,
            The battle and the breeze—
            Your glorious standard launch again
            To match another foe !
            And sweep through the deep,
            While the stormy winds do blow—
            While the battle rages loud and long,
            And the stormy winds do blow.
                        Ye Mariners of England.

705.
> Britannia needs no bulwarks,
> No towers along the steep ;
> Her march is o'er the mountain waves,
> Her home is on the deep.   *Ibid.*

706.
> The meteor flag of England
> Shall yet terrific burn,
> Till danger's troubled night depart
> And the star of peace return.   *Ibid.*

707.
> There was silence deep as death,
> And the boldest held his breath
> For a time.   *Battle of the Baltic.*

708.
> On Linden, when the sun was low,
> All bloodless lay the untrodden snow,
> And dark as winter was the flow
> Of Iser, rolling rapidly.   *Hohenlinden.*

709.
> Wave, Munich ! all thy banners wave,
> And charge with all thy chivalry !   *Ibid.*

710.
> Our bugles sang truce—for the night-cloud had lowered,
> And the sentinel stars set their watch in the sky ;
> And thousands had sunk on the ground overpowered,
> The weary to sleep, and the wounded to die.
> *The Soldier's Dream.*

711.
> There came to the beach a poor exile of Erin.
> *Exile of Erin.*

712.
> O leave this barren spot to me !
> Spare, woodman, spare the beechen tree.
> *The Beech-Tree's Petition.*

713.
> To live in hearts we leave behind
> Is not to die.   *Hallowed Ground,* 35.

714.
> Star that bringest home the bee,
> And sett'st the weary labourer free !
> *Song to the Evening Star.*

CAMPION, THOMAS, poet, 12 Feb. 1567—1 March, 1620

715.
> Follow thy fair sun, unhappy shadow.
> *Follow thy Fair Sun.*

716.
> Follow your Saint, follow with accents sweet ;
> Haste you, sad notes, fall at her flying feet.
> *Follow your Saint.*

717.
> Good thoughts his only friends ;
> His wealth a well-spent age ;
> The earth his sober inn,
> And quiet pilgrimage.   *The man Upright of Life.*

718.
> When thou must home to shades of under ground,
> And there arriv'd, a new admired guest,
> The beauteous spirits do ingirt thee round,
> White Iope, blithe Helen, and the rest.
> *When thou must Home.*

719.   Never love unless you can
           Bear with all the faults of man :
           Men will sometimes jealous be,
           Though but little cause they see ;
           And hang the head, as discontent,
           And speak what straight they will repent.   *Never Love.*

720.   There is a garden in her face
            Where roses and white lilies blow.
                    There is a Garden in her Face.

CANNING, GEORGE, Prime Minister and wit, 11 April, 1770—8 Aug. 1827

721.   Needy Knife-grinder ! whither are you going ?
        Rough is the road, your wheel is out of order—
        Bleak blows the blast ;—your hat has got a hole in't.
           So have your breeches.
           The Friend of Humanity and the Knife-Grinder.

722.   Story ! God bless you ! I have none to tell, Sir.   Ibid.

723.   *I* give thee sixpence ! I will see thee damned first.   Ibid.

724.   And finds, with keen discriminating sight,
        Black's not so black ;—nor white so *very* white.
                 New Morality, 199.

725.   But of all plagues, good Heaven, thy wrath can send,
        Save, save, oh save me from the *candid friend* !   Ibid., 210.

726. Here's to the Pilot that weathered the storm. [Pitt.]
              Song for the inauguration of the Pitt Club.

727.   In matters of commerce the fault of the Dutch
        Is offering too little and asking too much.
        The French are with equal advantage content,
        So we clap on Dutch bottoms just twenty per cent.
        Despatch to British Ambassador at the Hague, 31 Jan. 1826.

728. A sudden thought strikes me, let us swear an eternal friendship.   *The Rovers*, i. i.

729. I called the New World into existence to redress the balance of the Old.   *The King's Message*, 12 Dec. 1826.

CAREW, THOMAS, poet, 1595 ?— 1640

730.   He that loves a rosy cheek,
             Or a coral lip admires ;
           Or from star-like eyes doth seek
             Fuel to maintain his fires :
           As old Time makes these decay,
           So his flames must waste away.   *Disdain returned.*

731.   Then fly betimes, for only they
           Conquer Love, that run away.   *Conquest by Flight.*

CAREY, HENRY, poet, 1693 ?—4 Oct. 1743

732.   Namby Pamby's little rhymes, [Ambrose Phillips.]
        Little jingles, little chimes.   *Namby Pamby.*

733.   Of all the girls that are so smart,
                There's none like pretty Sally ;
            She is the darling of my heart,
                And she lives in our alley.   *Sally in our Alley.*

734.   Of all the days that's in the week
                I dearly love but one day—
            And that's the day that comes betwixt
                A Saturday and Monday.   *Ibid.*

735.   Aldeborontiphoscophornio !
            Where left you Chrononhotonthologos ?
                                Chrononhotonthologos, I. i.

CARLETON, WILL, U.S. poet, 21 Oct. 1845—18 Dec. 1912

736.   Things at home are crossways, and Betsey and I are out.
                                        Betsey and I are out.

CARLYLE, THOMAS, Scottish author, 4 Dec. 1795—4 Feb. 1881

737.   How does the poet speak to men, with power, but by being
still more a man than they ?   *Essays. Burns.*

738.   It can be said of him [Scott], when he departed, he took a
Man's life along with him. No sounder piece of British manhood was
put together in that eighteenth century of Time.
                                        Ibid., Sir Walter Scott.

739.   He who first shortened the labour of copyists by device of
Movable Types was disbanding hired armies, and cashiering most
Kings and Senates, and creating a whole new democratic world : he
had invented the art of printing.   *Sartor Resartus*, I. v

740.   Man is a tool-using animal.   Ibid.

741.   Be not the slave of words : is not the distant, the dead, while
I love it, and long for it, and mourn for it, here, in the genuine sense, as
truly as the floor I stand on ?   Ibid., viii.

742.   Do the duty which lies nearest thee, which thou knowest to
be a duty ! Thy second duty will already have become clearer.
                                        Ibid., II. ix.

743.   Produce ! Were it but the pitifulest infinitesimal fraction of a
product, produce it in God's name.   Ibid.

744.   ' Speech is silvern, Silence is golden ' ; or, as I might rather
express it, Speech is of Time, Silence is of Eternity.   Ibid., III. iii.

745.   A whiff of grapeshot.
                            History of the French Revolution, I. v. iii.

746.   The seagreen Incorruptible. [Robespierre.]   Ibid., II. IV. iv.

747.   The history of the world is but the biography of great men.
                    Heroes and Hero-Worship, i. *The Hero as Divinity.*

748.   The true university of these days is a collection of books.
                        Ibid., v. *The Hero as Man of Letters*

749.   The Dismal Science. [Political Economy.]
                        Latter-Day Pamphlets, I. *The Present Time.*

750. A Parliament speaking through reporters to Buncombe and the twenty-seven millions, mostly fools.   *Ibid.*, vi. *Parliaments.*

751. Work is the grand cure of all the maladies and miseries that ever beset mankind.

Rectorial Address at Edinburgh, 2 April, 1866.

752. The Public is an old woman. Let her maunder and mumble.

Journal, 1835.

753. The unspeakable Turk.   *Letter to G. Howard*, 24 Nov. 1876.

754.   So here hath been dawning
    Another blue Day :
Think, wilt thou let it
    Slip useless away ?   *To-day.*

755.   What is Hope ? A smiling rainbow
    Children follow through the wet ;
'Tis not here, still yonder, yonder :
    Never urchin found it yet.   *Cui Bono.*

756.   What is Man ? A foolish baby,
    Vainly strives, and fights, and frets ;
Demanding all, deserving nothing ;
    One small grave is what he gets.   Ibid.

CARNEY, JULIA A. FLETCHER, U.S. teacher, 1823–1908

757.   Little drops of water, little grains of sand,
Make the mighty ocean and the pleasant land.
So the little minutes, humble though they be,
Make the mighty ages of eternity.   *Little Things.*

[This has been wrongly attributed to E. C. Brewer, D. C. Colesworthy, Charles Mackay, and Frances S. Osgood.]

758.   Little deeds of kindness, little words of love,
Help to make earth happy, like the heaven above.

Ibid.

[Later reading of 2nd line, ' Make this earth an Eden.']

CARROLL, LEWIS (CHARLES LUTWIDGE DODGSON), mathematician and author, 27 Jan. 1832—14 Jan. 1898

759.   She has the bear's ethereal grace,
    The bland hyena's laugh,
The footstep of the elephant,
    The neck of the giraffe ;
I love her still, believe me,
    Though my heart its passion hides ;
' She's all my fancy painted her,'
    But oh ! *how much besides !*

College Rhymes. My Fancy.

760. ' What is the use of a book,' thought Alice, ' without pictures or conversations ? '   *Alice's Adventures in Wonderland*, i.

761. Curiouser and curiouser !   Ibid., ii.

762.   ' I'll be judge, I'll be jury,' said cunning old Fury ;
    ' I'll try the whole cause, and condemn you to death.'

Ibid., iii.

763.   ' You are old, Father William,' the young man said,
        'And your hair has become very white ;
      And yet you incessantly stand on your head—
        Do you think, at your age, it is right ? '   Ibid., v.

764.   ' In my youth,' Father William replied to his son,
        ' I feared it might injure the brain ;
      But now that I'm perfectly sure I have none,
        Why, I do it again and again.'   Ibid.

765.   He only does it to annoy,
        Because he knows it teases.   Ibid., vi.

766.   I speak severely to my boy,
        I beat him when he sneezes ;
      For he can thoroughly enjoy
        The pepper when he pleases !   Ibid.

767. Take care of the sense, and the sounds will take care of themselves.   Ibid., ix.

768. " Reeling and Writhing, of course, to begin with,' the Mock Turtle replied ; ' and then the different branches of Arithmetic—Ambition, Distraction, Uglification, and Derision.'   Ibid.

769.   When the sands are all dry, he is gay as a lark,
      And will talk in contemptuous tones of the Shark :
      But, when the tide rises and sharks are around,
      His voice has a timid and tremulous sound.   Ibid., x.

770.   Soup of the evening, beautiful soup !   Ibid.

771.   They told me you had been to her,
        And mentioned me to him :
      She gave me a good character,
        But said I could not swim.   Ibid., xii.

772.   Stating that he would not stand it,
      Stating in emphatic language
      What he'd be before he'd stand it.
        Phantasmagoria. Hiawatha's Photographing.

773.   Child of the pure unclouded brow
        And dreaming eyes of wonder !
        Through the Looking-Glass and What Alice
        found there, introduction.

774.   'Twas brillig, and the slithy toves
        Did gyre and gimble in the wabe
      All mimsy were the borogoves,
        And the mome raths outgrabe.
        Ibid., i. *Jabberwocky.*

775.   He left it dead, and with its head
        He went galumphing back.   Ibid.

776.   'And hast thou slain the Jabberwock ?
        Come to my arms, my beamish boy !
      O frabjous day ! Callooh ! Callay ! '
        He chortled in his joy.   Ibid

777. Curtsey while you're thinking what to say. It saves time.
        Ibid., ii.

778. ' You may call it " nonsense " if you like,' she [the Red Queen] said, ' but *I've* heard nonsense, compared with which that would be as sensible as a dictionary ! ' *Ibid.*

779.
  ' If seven maids with seven mops
   Swept it for half a year,
  Do you suppose,' the Walrus said,
   ' That they could get it clear ? '
  ' I doubt it,' said the Carpenter,
   And shed a bitter tear.
    Ibid., iv. *The Walrus and the Carpenter.*

780.
  ' The time has come,' the Walrus said,
   ' To talk of many things ;
  Of shoes—and ships—and sealing wax—
   Of cabbages—and kings—
  And why the sea is boiling hot—
   And whether pigs have wings.'   *Ibid.*

781.
  'A loaf of bread,' the Walrus said,
   ' Is what we chiefly need :
  Pepper and vinegar besides
   Are very good indeed.'   *Ibid.*

782.
  The Carpenter said nothing but
   ' The butter's spread too thick ! '   *Ibid.*

783.
  ' I weep for you,' the Walrus said :
   ' I deeply sympathise.'   *Ibid.*

784. The rule is, jam to-morrow and jam yesterday—but never jam to-day.   *Ibid.*, v.

785. Consider what a great girl you are. Consider what a long way you've come to-day. Consider what o'clock it is. Consider anything, only don't cry !   *Ibid.*

786. They gave it to me—for an un-birthday present.   *Ibid.* vi.

787.
  I said it very loud and clear ;
  I went and shouted in his ear.   *Ibid.*

788. I must have two, you know—to come and go. One to come, and one to go.   *Ibid.*, vii.

789. You might as well try to stop a Bandersnatch !   *Ibid.*

790. It's as large as life, and twice as natural !   *Ibid.*

791.
  I'll tell thee everything I can :
   There's little to relate.
  I saw an aged, aged man,
   A-sitting on a gate.
  'Who are you, aged man ? ' I said,
   'And how is it you live ? '
  And his answer trickled through my head
   Like water through a sieve.   *Ibid.* viii.

792.
  But I was thinking of a plan
   To dye one's whiskers green,
  And always use so large a fan
   That they could not be seen.   *Ibid.*

C

793.   He would answer to ' Hi ! ' or to any loud cry,
        Such as ' Fry me ! ' or ' Fritter my wig ! '
        To ' What-you-may-call-um ! ' or ' What-was-his-name ! '
        But especially ' Thing-um-a-jig ! '
                                        The Hunting of the Snark, fit i.

794.   His intimate friends called him ' Candle-ends,'
        And his enemies ' Toasted-cheese.'   Ibid.

795.   Then the bowsprit got mixed with the rudder sometimes.
                                                        Ibid., fit ii.

796.   Its habit of getting up late you'll agree
        That it carries too far when I say
        That it frequently breakfasts at five o'clock tea,
        And dines on the following day.   Ibid.

797.   I said it in Hebrew—I said it in Dutch—
        I said it in German and Greek :
        But I wholly forgot (and it vexes me much)
        That English is what you speak !   Ibid., fit iv.

798.   They sought it with thimbles, they sought it with care ;
        They pursued it with forks and hope ;
        They threatened its life with a railway share ;
        They charmed it with smiles and soap.   Ibid., fit v.

799.   ' Transportation for life ' was the sentence it gave,
        'And *then* to be fined forty pound.'   Ibid., fit vi.

800.   In the midst of the word he was trying to say,
        In the midst of his laughter and glee,
        He had softly and suddenly vanished away—
        For the Snark *was* a Boojum, you see.   Ibid., fit viii.

801.   He thought he saw a Banker's Clerk
        Descending from a bus :
        He looked again, and found it was
        A Hippopotamus :
        ' If this should stay to dine,' he said,
        ' There won't be much for us ! '
                                        Sylvie and Bruno, vii.

CARRUTH, WILLIAM HERBERT, U.S. poet, 5 April, 1859—15 Dec. 1924
802.   Some call it Evolution,
                And others call it God.
                                        Each in his own Tongue.

CARRYL, CHARLES EDWARD, U.S. author, 30 Dec. 1841—3 July, 1920
803.   A capital ship for an ocean trip
                Was the ' Walloping Window-blind.'
                No gale that blew dismayed her crew
                Or troubled the Captain's mind.
                                Davy and the Goblin, a Nautical Ballad.

CARTER, HENRY, author, died 30 July, 1806
804.   True patriots all ; for be it understood
        We left our country for our country's good.
                Prologue on opening the Theatre at Sydney, Botany Bay.

Cary, Phoebe, U.S. poetess, 4 Sept. 1824—31 July, 1871

805.   And though hard be the task,
                      ' Keep a stiff upper lip.'

Keep a Stiff Upper Lip.

Caswall, Edward, clergyman, 15 July, 1814—2 Jan. 1878

806.   Days and moments quickly flying
                      Blend the living with the dead ;
                  Soon shall you and I be lying
                      Each within our narrow bed.   *Hymn*.

807.   Jesus, the very thought of Thee
                      With sweetness fills my breast.   *Hymn*.

Cato, Marcus Porcius (' the Censor '), Roman statesman, 234–
    149 b.c.

    808. Delenda est Carthago.—Carthage must be destroyed.
              Words with which he ended every speech in the Senate.

Catullus, Gaius Valerius, Roman poet, 84–54 ? b.c.

809 Lugete, O Veneres Cupidinesque,
        Et quantumst hominum venustiorum.
        Passer mortuus est meae puellae,
        Passer, deliciae meae puellae.
        —Mourn, O Loves and Cupids, and all loveliest of mortals.
        My girl's sparrow is dead, the sparrow, my girl's pet.
                                            Carmina—Songs, iii.

810. Qui nunc it per iter tenebricosum
        Illuc, unde negant redire quemquam.
        —Which now goes along the dark path to that place whence they
            say none returns.   Ibid.

811. Vivamus, mea Lesbia, atque amemus,
        Rumoresque senum severiorum
        Omnes unius aestimemus assis.
        Soles occidere et redire possunt :
        Nobis cum semel occidit brevis lux
        Nox est perpetua una dormienda.
        —Let us live, my Lesbia, and love, and value the talk of over-
            serious old men at a single farthing. Suns can set and
            return ; for us, when once our brief day has gone, there is
            the sleep of one unending night.   Ibid., v.

812. Da mi basia mille, deinde centum,
        Dein mille altera, dein secunda centum,
        Deinde usque altera mille, deinde centum.
        —Give me a thousand kisses, then a hundred, then another
            thousand, then a second hundred, then yet another thousand,
            then a hundred.   Ibid.

813. Odi et amo. Quare id faciam, fortasse requiris.
          Nescio, sed fieri sentio et excrucior.
        —I hate and love. Why I do it, perhaps you ask. I know not,
            but I feel it and am tortured.   Ibid., lxxxv.

814. Multas per gentes et multa per aequora vectus
    Advenio has miseras, frater, ad inferias.
    —Passing through many peoples and over many seas I come
        brother, to these sad obsequies.   *Ibid., ci.*

815. Atque in perpetuum, frater, ave atque vale.
    —And for ever, brother, hail and farewell !   *Ibid.*

CAVELL, EDITH LOUISA, nurse, 4 Dec. 1865—12 Oct. 1915

816. Patriotism is not enough. I must have no hatred or bitterness
towards anyone.   *Before her execution by the Germans.*

CELANO, THOMAS OF, Italian mystic, died 1255 ?

817. Dies irae, dies illa, solvet saeclum in favilla.
    —Day of wrath, that day, the world shall dissolve in ashes.
                                    Hymn.

CENTLIVRE, SUSANNAH, actress and dramatist, 1667 ?—1 Dec. 1723

818. The real Simon Pure.   *A Bold Stroke for a Wife,* v. i.

CERVANTES SAAVEDRA, MIGUEL DE, Spanish novelist, baptised 9 Oct.
    1547, died 23 April, 1616.

819. El Caballero de la Triste Figura.—The Knight of the Rueful
    Countenance.   *Don Quixote,* I. xix.

820. Paciencia y barajar.—Patience, and shuffle the cards.
                                Ibid., II. xxiii.

821. Bien haya el que inventó el sueño, capa que cubre todos los
humanos pensamientos.—Blessed be he who invented sleep, a cloak
that covers all a man's thoughts.   *Ibid.,* lxviii.

CHAMBERLAIN, JOSEPH, statesman, 8 July, 1836—2 July, 1914

822. Provided that the City of London remains as it is at present,
the clearing-house of the world.
           Speech, Guildhall, London, 19 Jan. 1904.

823. Learn to think Imperially.   *Ibid.*

824. The day of small nations has long passed away. The day of
Empires has come.   *Speech, Birmingham,* 12 May, 1904.

CHAMBERS, CHARLES HADDON, dramatist, 22 April, 1860—28 March,
    1921

825. The long arm of coincidence.   *Captain Swift,* II·

CHANDLER, JOHN, clergyman, 16 June, 1806—1 July, 1876

826.   Conquering kings their titles take
        From the foes they captive make :
        Jesu, by a nobler deed,
        From the thousands He hath freed.
                      Hymn from the Latin.

CHAPMAN, ARTHUR, U.S. author, 25 June, 1873—4 Dec., 1935

827.   Out where the handclasp's a little stronger,
        Out where the smile dwells a little longer,
            That's where the West begins.
                                        Out where the West begins.

CHAPMAN, GEORGE, dramatist, 1559 ?—12 May, 1634

828.   Give me a spirit that on this life's rough sea
        Loves t'have his sails fill'd with a lusty wind,
        Even till his sail-yards tremble, his masts crack,
        And his rapt ship run on her side so low
        That she drinks water, and her keel ploughs air.
                    The Conspiracy of Charles, Duke of Byron, III. i.

829.   And let a scholar all Earth's volumes carry,
        He will be but a walking dictionary.   *Tears of Peace*, 265.

830. His [Homer's] naked Ulysses, clad in eternal fiction.
                    The Odysseys of Homer, epistle dedicatory.

CHARLES I, King, 19 Nov. 1600—30 Jan. 1649

  831. Never make a defence or apology before you be accused.
                    Letter to Lord Wentworth, 3 Sept. 1636.

CHARLES II, King, 29 May, 1630—6 Feb. 1685

  832. As good as a play !
                    On the Lords debating Lord Ross's Divorce Bill, 1670.

  833. I fear, gentlemen, I am an unconscionable time a-dying.
                    On his death-bed.

  834. Let not poor Nelly starve. [Of Nell Gwynn.]   Ibid.

CHATHAM, WILLIAM PITT, 1ST EARL OF, Prime Minister, 15 Nov. 1708—
        11 May, 1778

  835. The atrocious crime of being a young man . . . I shall neither
attempt to palliate nor deny.
                    Speech, House of Commons, 27 Jan. 1741.

  836. Confidence is a plant of slow growth in an aged bosom : youth
is the season of credulity.   Ibid., 14 Jan. 1766.

  837. Where law ends, tyranny begins.
                    Speech, House of Lords, 9 Jan. 1770.

  838. We have a Calvinistic creed, a Popish liturgy, and an Arminian
clergy.   Ibid., 19 May, 1772.

  839. If I were an American, as I am an Englishman, while a foreign
troop was landed in my country, I never would lay down my arms,—
never—never—never !   Ibid., 18 Nov. 1777.

  840. The poorest man may in his cottage bid defiance to all the
forces of the Crown. It may be frail—its roof may shake—the wind
may blow through it—the storm may enter—the rain may enter—
but the King of England cannot enter—all his force dares not cross the
threshold of the ruined tenement!   *Speech on the Excise Bill.*

CHATTERTON, THOMAS, poet, 20 Nov. 1752—24 Aug. 1770

841.   O sing unto my roundelay,
                        O drop the briny tear with me,
                        Dance no more at holy-day,
                          Like a running river be.
                              My love is dead,
                              Gone to his death-bed,
                            All under the willow-tree.   *Minstrel's Song.*

CHAUCER, GEOFFREY, poet, 1340 ?—25 Oct. 1400

842.   The lyf so short, the craft so long to lerne,
          Th' assay so hard, so sharp the conquering.
                            The Parlement of Foules, 1.

843.   Flee fro the prees, and dwelle with sothfastnesse.
                                      Truth, 1.

844.   O móral Gower, this booke I directe
          To thee.   *Troilus and Criseyde*, v. 1856.

845.   Of alle the floures in the mede,
          Than love I most these floures white and rede,
          Swiche as men callen daysies in our toun.
             The Legend of Good Women, Prologue, 41.

846.   Whan that Aprille with his shoures sote
          The droghte of Marche hath perced to the rote.
             The Canterbury Tales. Prologue, 1.

847.   And smale fowles maken melodye
          That slepen al the night with open yë.   Ibid., 9.

848.   And of his port as meke as is a mayde.   Ibid., 69.

849.   He was a verray parfit gentil knight.   Ibid., 72.

850.   He was as fresh as is the month of May.   Ibid., 92.

851.   Ful wel she song the service divyne,
          Entuned in hir nose ful semely ;
          And Frensh she spak ful faire and fetisly,
          After the scole of Stratford atte Bowe,
          For Frensh of Paris was to hir unknowe.   Ibid., 122.

852.   What sholde he studie, and make himselven wood,
          Upon a book in cloistre alwey to poure,
          Or swinken with his handes, and laboure,
          As Austin bit ?   How shal the world be served ?
          Lat Austin have his swink to him reserved.   Ibid., 184.

853.   A Clerk ther was of Oxenford also,
          That un-to logik hadde longe y-go.   Ibid., 285.

854.   For him was lever have at his beddes heed
          Twenty bokes, clad in blak or reed,
          Of Aristotle and his philosophye,
          Than robes riche, or fithele, or gay sautrye.   Ibid., 293.

855.   And gladly wold he lerne, and gladly teche.   Ibid., 308.

856.   No-wher so bisy a man as he ther nas,
          And yet he semed bisier than he was.   Ibid., 321.

857. It snewed in his hous of mete and drinke. *Ibid.*, 345.

858. With many a tempest hadde his berd been shake. *Ibid.*, 406.

859. His studie was but litel on the Bible. *Ibid.*, 438.

860. She was a worthy womman al hir lyve,
Housbondes at chirche-dore she hadde fyve,
Withouten other companye in youthe. *Ibid.*, 459.

861. But Cristes lore, and his apostles twelve,
He taughte, and first he folwed it himselve. *Ibid.*, 527.

862. And whan that he wel dronken hadde the wyn,
Than wolde he speke no word but Latyn. *Ibid.*, 637.

863. His walet lay biforn him in his lappe,
Bret-ful of pardoun come from Rome al hoot. *Ibid.*, 686.

864. The bisy larke, messager of day,
Saluëth in hir song the morwe gray ;
And fyry Phebus ryseth up so brighte,
That al the orient laugheth of the lighte.
Ibid., *The Knightes Tale*, 633.

865. The smyler with the knyf under the cloke. *Ibid.*, 1141.

866. Up roos the sonne, and up roos Emelye. *Ibid.*, 1415.

867. What is this world ? what asketh man to have ?
Now with his love, now in his colde grave
Allone, with-outen any companye. *Ibid.*, 1919.

868. Thou lokest as thou woldest finde an hare,
For ever up-on the ground I see thee stare.
Ibid., *Sir Thopas. Prologue*, 6.

869. This may wel be rym dogerel.
Ibid., *The Tale of Melibeus. Prologue*, 7.

CHEKHOV, ANTON PAVLOVITCH, Russian author, 17 Jan. 1860—2 July,
1904

870. Love, friendship, respect, do not unite people as much as a
common hatred for something. *Note-books*.

CHERRY, ANDREW, Irish dramatist, 11 Jan. 1762—12 Feb. 1812

871. Till next day,
There she lay,
In the Bay of Biscay, O !
The Bay of Biscay.

CHESTERFIELD, PHILIP DORMER STANHOPE, 4TH EARL OF, statesman,
22 Sept. 1694—24 March, 1773

872. Be wiser than other people if you can, but do not tell them so.
Letters to his Son, 19 Nov. 1745.

873. An injury is much sooner forgotten than an insult.
Ibid., 9 Oct. 1746.

874. Advice is seldom welcome ; and those who want it the most
always like it the least. *Ibid.*, 29 Jan. 1748.

875. A man of sense only trifles with them [women], plays with them, humours and flatters them, as he does with a sprightly and forward child ; but he neither consults them about, nor trusts them with, serious matters. *Ibid.*, 5 Sept. 1748.

876. Women are much more like each other than men : they have, in truth, but two passions, vanity and love. *Ibid.*, 19 Dec. 1749.

877. Tyrawley and I have been dead these two years ; but we don't choose to have it known. Boswell, *Life of Johnson*, an. 1773.

878. Give Dayrolles a chair. *Last Words.*

CHESTERTON, GILBERT KEITH, author, 29 May, 1874—14 June, 1936

879. For the front of the cover shows somebody shot,
And the back of the cover will tell you the plot.
Commercial Candour.

880. White founts falling in the courts of the sun,
And the Soldan of Byzantium is smiling as they run.
Lepanto.

881. Strong gongs groaning as the guns boom far,
Don John of Austria is going to the war. Ibid.

882. But the world is more full of glory
Than you can understand. *The Mortal Answers.*

883. Talk about the pews and steeples
And the Cash that goes therewith !
But the souls of Christian peoples . . .
Chuck it, Smith ! [F. E. Smith.]
Antichrist, or the Reunion of Christendom : An Ode.

884. And I dream of the days when work was scrappy,
And rare in our pockets the mark of the mint,
When we were angry and poor and happy,
And proud of seeing our names in print.
A Song of Defeat.

885. You never loved the sun in heaven as I have loved the rain.
The Last Hero.

886. The strangest whim has seized me . . . After all
I think I will not hang myself to-day.
A Ballade of Suicide.

887. And Noah he often said to his wife when he sat down to dine,
' I don't care where the water goes if it doesn't get into the
wine.' *Wine and Water.*

888. Before the Roman came to Rye or out to Severn strode,
The rolling English drunkard made the rolling English road.
The Rolling English Road.

889. For there is good news yet to hear and fine things to be seen,
Before we go to Paradise by way of Kensal Green. Ibid.

890. Tea, although an Oriental,
Is a gentleman at least ;
Cocoa is a cad and coward,
Cocoa is a vulgar beast.
The Song of Right and Wrong.

891.
Before the gods that made the gods
Had seen their sunrise pass,
The White Horse of the White Horse Vale
Was cut out of the grass.
The Ballad of the White Horse, I. 1.

892.
The devil's walking parody
Of all four-footed things. *The Donkey.*

893. There is a great deal of difference between the eager man who wants to read a book, and the tired man who wants a book to read.
Charles Dickens, v.

894. A good joke is the one ultimate and sacred thing which cannot be criticised. Our relations with a good joke are direct and even divine relations. *Preface to Dicken's Pickwick Papers.*

895. A man's good work is effected by doing what he does; a woman's by being what she is. *Robert Browning, ii.*

896. The two things that a healthy person hates most between heaven and hell are a woman who is not dignified and a man who is.
All Things considered. Cockneys and their Jokes.

897. If a thing is worth doing it is worth doing badly.
What's Wrong with the World. Folly and Female Education.

898. Hardy became a sort of village atheist brooding and blaspheming over the village idiot. *The Victorian Age in Literature, ii.*

CHEVALIER, ALBERT, actor, 21 March, 1861—10 July, 1923

899.
There ain't a lady in the land
As I'd swop for my dear old Dutch.
My Old Dutch.

CHOATE, RUFUS, U.S. statesman, 1 Oct. 1799—13 July, 1859

900. Its constitution the glittering and sounding generalities of natural right which make up the Declaration of Independence.
Letter to the Maine Whig Committee, 9 Aug. 1856.

CHORLEY, HENRY FOTHERGILL, musical critic, 15 Dec. 1808—16 Feb. 1872.

901.
God the All-terrible ! King, Who ordainest
Great winds Thy clarions, the lightnings Thy sword.
God the All-Terrible.

CHURCHILL, CHARLES, clergyman and poet, Feb. 1731—4 Nov. 1764

902. He mouths a sentence as curs mouth a bone. *The Rosciad, 322.*

903.
Be England what she will,
With all her faults, she is my country still.
The Farewell, 27.

904.
Apt alliteration's artful aid.
The Prophecy of Famine, 86

*C

905.   He for subscribers baits his hook.
              And takes your cash ; but where's the book ?
              No matter where ; wise fear, you know,
              Forbids the robbing of a foe ;
              But what, to serve our private ends,
              Forbids the cheating of our friends ?
[Of Dr. Johnson and his dictionary.]   *The Ghost*, III. 801.

CHURCHILL, SIR WINSTON LEONARD SPENCER, Prime Minister, 30 Nov.
    1874— 24 Jan. 1965

906. It cannot in the opinion of His Majesty's Government be
classified as slavery in the extreme acceptance of the word without some
risk of terminological inexactitude.
                              Speech, House of Commons, 22 Feb. 1906.

907. I would say to the House, as I have said to those who have
joined this Government : ' I have nothing to offer but blood, toil,
tears and sweat.'   Ibid., 13 May, 1940.

908. We shall not flag or fail. We shall go on to the end, we shall
fight in France, we shall fight on the seas and oceans, we shall fight
with growing confidence and growing strength in the air, we shall
defend our island, whatever the cost may be, we shall fight on the
beaches, we shall fight on the landing grounds, we shall fight in the
fields and in the streets, we shall fight in the hills ; we shall never
surrender.   Ibid.. 4 June, 1940.

909. Let us therefore brace ourselves to our duties, and so bear
ourselves that, if the British Empire and its Commonwealth last for a
thousand years, men will still say, ' This was their finest hour.'
                                                   Ibid., 18 June, 1940.

910. The gratitude of every home in our island, in our Empire, and
indeed throughout the world, except in the abodes of the guilty, goes
out to the British airmen who, undaunted by odds, unwearied in their
constant challenge and mortal danger, are turning the tide of the world
war by their prowess and by their devotion. Never in the field of
human conflict was so much owed by so many to so few.
                                                   Ibid., 20 Aug. 1940.

911. Undoubtedly this process means that these two great organisa-
tions of the English-speaking democracies, the British Empire and the
United States, will have to be somewhat mixed up together in some of
their affairs for mutual and general advantage. For my own part,
looking out upon the future, I do not view the process with any mis-
givings. I could not stop it if I wished ; no one can stop it. Like the
Mississippi, it just keeps rolling along. Let it roll. Let it roll on full
flood, inexorable, irresistible, benignant, to broader lands and better
days.   Ibid.

912. Give us the tools, and we will finish the job.
                                    Broadcast address, 9 Feb. 1941.

913. It becomes still more difficult to reconcile Japanese action with
prudence or even with sanity. What kind of a people do they think
we are ?   *Speech, U.S. Congress*, 26 Dec. 1941.

914. When I warned them [the French] that Britain would fight on alone whatever they did, their generals told their Prime Minister and his divided Cabinet, ' In three weeks England will have her neck wrung like a chicken.' Some chicken ; some neck.
> *Speech, Canadian Senate and House of Commons*, 30 Dec. 1941.

CIBBER, COLLEY, Poet Laureate, 6 Nov. 1671—12 Dec. 1757

915. Off with his head—so much for Buckingham !
> Shakespeare's *Richard III* (altered), IV. iii.

916. Conscience avaunt, Richard's himself again.   Ibid., v. iii.

917. Perish the thought !   Ibid., v

918. One had as good be out of the world as out of the fashion.
> *Love's Last Shift*, II.

919.   O say ! What is that thing called Light,
>   Which I can ne'er enjoy ?   *The Blind Boy*.

CICERO, MARCUS TULLIUS, Roman orator, 3 Jan. 106 B.C.—7 Dec. 43 B.C.

920. Silent enim leges inter arma.—For laws are dumb in the midst of arms.   *Pro Milone—On Behalf of Milo*, iv.

921. Salus populi suprema est lex.—The good of the people is the highest law.   *De Legibus—On Laws*, III. iii.

922. Quousque tandem abutere, Catilina, patientia nostra ?—How long, pray, will you abuse our patience, Catiline ?
> *In Catilinam—Against Catiline*, I. i.

923. O tempora ! O mores !—What times ! What ways of life !
> Ibid.

924. Abiit, excessit, evasit, erupit.—He departed, he withdrew, he escaped, he broke forth.   Ibid., II. i.

925. Spartam nactus es ; hanc orna.—Sparta is yours ; be an ornament to her.   *Epistolae ad Atticum—Letters to Atticus*, IV. vi.

926. Cedant arma togae, concedant laurea laudi.
>   —Let arms give place to the civic gown, and the laurel-wreath to praise.   *De Officiis—On Duties*, I. xxii.

927. O fortunatam natam me consule Romam !
>   —O lucky Roman State, born in my consulate !
> Juvenal, *Satires*, x. 122.

CLARE, JOHN, poet, 13 July, 1793—20 May, 1864

928.   Here sparrows build upon the trees,
>   And stockdove hides her nest ;
>   The leaves are winnowed by the breeze
>   Into a calmer rest :
>   The blackcap's song was very sweet,
>   That used the rose to kiss ;
>   It made the Paradise complete :
>   My early home was this.   *My Early Home*.

929. If life had a second edition, how I would correct the proofs.
> *Letter to a friend*.

CLARK, CHARLES HEBER, *see* Adeler, Max

CLARKE, McDONALD (THE ' MAD POET '), U.S. poet, 18 June, 1798—
5 March, 1842

930. Whilst twilight's curtain spreading far,
Was pinned with a single star.   *Death in Disguise,* 227.

CLAY, HENRY, U.S. statesman, 12 April, 1777—29 June, 1852

931. Sir, I would rather be right than be President.   *Speech,* 1850.

CLEMENS, SAMUEL LANGHORNE, *see* Twain, Mark

CLEVELAND, STEPHEN GROVER, U.S. President, 18 March, 1837—
24 June, 1908

932. Your every voter, as surely as your chief magistrate, exercises
a public trust.   *Inaugural Address,* 4 March, 1885.

933. However plenty silver dollars may become, they will not be
distributed as gifts among the people.
First Annual Message, 8 Dec. 1885.

CLIVE OF PLASSEY, ROBERT CLIVE, BARON, administrator, 29 Sept.
1725—22 Nov. 1774

934. By God, Mr. Chairman, at this moment I stand astonished at
my own moderation !
At Parliamentary inquiry into his conduct in India, 1773.

CLOUGH, ARTHUR HUGH, poet, 1 Jan. 1819—13 Nov. 1861

935. Grace is given of God, but knowledge is bought in the market.
The Bothie of Tober-na-Vuolich, iv.

936. Where lies the land to which the ship would go ?
Far, far ahead, is all her seamen know.
Where lies the Land.

937. Say not the struggle naught availeth,
The labour and the wounds are vain,
The enemy faints not, nor faileth,
And as things have been they remain.
Say not the Struggle naught availeth.

938. For while the tired waves, vainly breaking,
Seem here no painful inch to gain,
Far back, through creeks and inlets making,
Comes silent, flooding in, the main.   Ibid.

939. And not by eastern windows only,
When daylight comes, comes in the light;
In front, the sun climbs slow, how slowly,
But westward, look, the land is bright.   Ibid.

940. Thou shalt have one God only ; who
Would be at the expense of two ?
The Latest Decalogue.

941.   Thou shalt not kill ; but need'st not strive
            Officiously to keep alive.   Ibid.

COBBETT, WILLIAM, author, 9 March, 1762—18 June, 1835

  942. The great wen. [London.]   *Rural Rides*, 1821.

  943. To be poor and independent is very nearly an impossibility.
            Advice to Young Men, ii. *To a Young Man.*

COBORN, CHARLES (COLIN WHITTON McCALLUM), comedian, 4 Aug.
    1852—23 Nov. 1945

944.   Two lovely black eyes,
            Oh ! what a surprise !
            Only for telling a man he was wrong,
            Two lovely black eyes !   *Two Lovely Black Eyes.*

COCKBURN, ALICIA *or* ALISON RUTHERFORD, Scottish poetess, 8 Oct.
    1713—22 Nov. 1794

945.   I've seen the smiling
                Of Fortune beguiling ;
            I've felt all its favours, and found its decay :
                Sweet was its blessing,
                Kind its caressing ;
            But now 'tis fled—fled far away.
                            The Flowers of the Forest.

COKE, SIR EDWARD, Chief Justice, 1 Feb. 1552—3 Sept. 1634

  946. The gladsome light of jurisprudence.
            Institutes : Commentary upon Littleton. First Institute, epilogus.

  947. They [corporations] cannot commit treason, nor be outlawed,
nor excommunicate, for they have no souls.
            Case of Sutton's Hospital, 10 Rep. 32.

948.   Six hours in sleep, in law's grave study six,
            Four spend in prayer, the rest on Nature fix.   *Epigram.*

COLBY, FRANK MOORE, U.S. author, 10 Feb. 1865—3 March, 1925

  949. I have found some of the best reasons I ever had for remaining
at the bottom simply by looking at the men at the top.   *Essays*, II.

COLERIDGE, HARTLEY, author, 19 Sept. 1796—6 Jan. 1849

950.   She is not fair to outward view
                As many maidens be ;
            Her loveliness I never knew
                Until she smiled on me.
            O then I saw her eye was bright,
            A well of love, a spring of light.
                            Song. She is not Fair.

951.   Her very frowns are fairer far
            Than smiles of other maidens are.   Ibid.

Coleridge, Mary Elizabeth, authoress, 23 Sept. 1861—25 Aug. 1907

952. We were young, we were merry, we were very, very wise,
  And the door stood open at our feast,
 When there pass'd us a woman with the West in her eyes,
  And a man with his back to the East.   *Unwelcome.*

Coleridge, Samuel Taylor, poet, 21 Oct. 1772—25 July, 1834

953. It is an ancient Mariner,
   And he stoppeth one of three.
         The Ancient Mariner, part i.

954. He holds him with his glittering eye.   Ibid.

955. The bride hath paced into the hall,
   Red as a rose is she.   Ibid.

956. The ice was here, the ice was there,
   The ice was all around :
   It cracked and growled and roared and howled,
   Like noises in a swound.   Ibid.

957. Nor dim nor red, like God's own head,
   The glorious sun uprist.   Ibid., part ii.

958. The fair breeze blew, the white foam flew,
   The furrow followed free ;
   We were the first that ever burst
   Into that silent sea.   Ibid.

959. As idle as a painted ship
   Upon a painted ocean.   Ibid.

960. Water, water, everywhere.
   Nor any drop to drink.   Ibid.

961. The Night-mare Life-in-Death was she,
   Who thicks man's blood with cold. Ibid., part iii.

962. ' The game is done ! I've won ! I've won ! '
   Quoth she, and whistles thrice.   Ibid.

963. The sun's rim dips ; the stars rush out :
   At one stride comes the dark.   Ibid.

964. Till clomb above the eastern bar
   The hornèd moon, with one bright star
   Within the nether tip.   Ibid.

965. Alone, alone, all, all alone,
   Alone on a wide, wide sea ! Ibid., part iv.

966. The many men, so beautiful !
   And they all dead did lie ;
   And a thousand thousand slimy things
   Lived on ; and so did I.   Ibid.

967. The moving moon went up the sky,
   And nowhere did abide :
   Softly she was going up,
   And a star or two beside.   Ibid.

968. A spring of love gushed from my heart,
   And I blessed them unaware.   Ibid.

969.　Oh sleep ! it is a gentle thing,
　　　Beloved from pole to pole.　　　*Ibid.*, part v.

970.　A noise like of a hidden brook
　　　In the leafy month of June,
　　　That to the sleeping woods all night
　　　Singeth a quiet tune.　　　*Ibid.*

971.　Quoth he, ' The man hath penance done,
　　　And penance more will do.'　　　*Ibid.*

972.　Like one that on a lonesome road
　　　Doth walk in fear and dread,
　　　And having once turned round walks on,
　　　And turns no more his head ;
　　　Because he knows a frightful fiend
　　　Doth close behind him tread.　　　*Ibid.*, part vi.

973.　Brown skeletons of leaves that lag
　　　My forest brook along.　　　*Ibid.*, part vii.

974.　I pass like night from land to land ;
　　　I have strange power of speech.　　　*Ibid.*

975.　O Wedding-Guest ! this soul hath been
　　　Alone on a wide wide sea :
　　　So lonely 'twas, that God himself
　　　Scarce seemed there to be.　　　*Ibid.*

976.　He prayeth well, who loveth well
　　　Both man and bird and beast.　　　*Ibid.*

977.　He prayeth best who loveth best
　　　All things both great and small.　　　*Ibid.*

978.　A sadder and a wiser man,
　　　He rose the morrow morn.　　　*Ibid.*

979.　And the spring comes slowly up this way.
　　　　　　　　　　Christabel, part i.

980.　　　A sight to dream of, not to tell !　　　*Ibid.*

981.　Alas ! they had been friends in youth ;
　　　But whispering tongues can poison truth ;
　　　And constancy lives in realms above ;
　　　And life is thorny, and youth is vain ;
　　　And to be wroth with one we love
　　　Doth work like madness in the brain.　　　*Ibid.*, part ii.

982.　They stood aloof, the scars remaining,
　　　Like cliffs which had been rent asunder ;
　　　A dreary sea now flows between.　　　*Ibid.*

983.　In Xanadu did Kubla Khan
　　　A stately pleasure-dome decree :
　　　Where Alph, the sacred river, ran
　　　Through caverns measureless to man
　　　　Down to a sunless sea.　　　*Kubla Khan.*

984.　A savage place ! as holy and enchanted
　　　As e'er beneath a waning moon was haunted
　　　By woman wailing for her demon-lover.　　　*Ibid.*

985.　Five miles meandering with a mazy motion.　　　*Ibid.*

986.   Ancestral voices prophesying war.   *Ibid.*

987.   For he on honey-dew hath fed,
                    And drunk the milk of Paradise.   *Ibid.*

988. In the hexameter rises the fountain's silvery column :
In the pentameter aye falling in melody back.
The Ovidian Elegiac Metre.

989.   From his brimstone bed at break of day
        A-walking the Devil is gone,
      To visit his snug little farm the earth,
        And see how his stock goes on.
                      The Devil's Thoughts.

990.   His jacket was red and his breeches were blue,
      And there was a hole where the tail came through.
                                    Ibid.

991.   He saw a cottage with a double coach-house,
        A cottage of gentility :
      And the devil did grin, for his darling sin
        Is pride that apes humility.   *Ibid.*

992.   All thoughts, all passions, all delights,
        Whatever stirs this mortal frame,
      All are but ministers of Love,
        And feed his sacred flame.   *Love.*

993. All this long eve, so balmy and serene,
Have I been gazing on the western sky,
    And its peculiar tint of yellow green :
And still I gaze—and with how blank an eye !
And those thin clouds above, in flakes and bars,
That give away their motion to the stars ;
Those stars, that glide behind them or between,
Now sparkling, now bedimmed, but always seen :
Yon crescent moon, as fixed as if it grew
In its own cloudless, starless lake of blue ;
I see them all so excellently fair,
I see, not feel, how beautiful they are !   *Dejection : An Ode, 2.*

994. Trochee trips from long to short :
From long to long in solemn sort
Slow Spondee stalks ; strong foot ! yet ill able
Ever to come up with Dactyl trisyllable.
Iambics march from short to long ;
With a leap and a bound the swift Anapaests throng ;
One syllable long, with one short at each side,
Amphibrachys hastes with a stately stride ;
First and last being long, middle short, Amphimacer
Strikes his thundering hoofs like a proud high-bred racer.
                                  Metrical Feet.

995.   The Knight's bones are dust,
        And his good sword rust ;—
      His soul is with the saints, I trust. *The Knight's Tomb.*

996.   Verse, a breeze mid blossoms straying.
      Where Hope clung feeding, like a bee—
      Both were mine ! Life went a-maying
        With Nature, Hope, and Poesy,
        When I was young !   *Youth and Age.*

997.   I counted two and seventy stenches,
        All well defined, and several stinks.   *Cologne.*

998.   Stop, Christian passer-by !—Stop, child of God,
        And read with gentle breast. Beneath this sod
        A poet lies, or that which once seem'd he.
        O, lift one thought in prayer for S.T.C.   *Epitaph.*

999.   Swans sing before they die—'twere no bad thing
        Did certain persons die before they sing.
                      Epigram on a Volunteer Singer.

1000.   Clothing the palpable and familiar
        With golden exhalations of the dawn.
                The Death of Wallenstein, I. i.

1001.   A little child, dear brother Jem,
          That lightly draws its breath,
        And feels its life in every limb,
          What should it know of death ?
        Lines contributed to Wordsworth's *We are Seven.*

1002. Not the poem which we have *read*, but that to which we *return*, with the greatest pleasure, possesses the genuine power, and claims the name of *essential poetry*.   *Biographia Literaria,* i.

1003. Our myriad-minded Shakespeare.   Ibid., xv.

1004. I wish our clever young poets would remember my homely definitions of prose and poetry ; that is, prose=words in their best order ;—poetry=the *best* words in the best order.
                Table Talk, 12 July, 1827.

1005. The man's desire is for the woman ; but the woman's desire is rarely other than for the desire of the man.   Ibid., 23 July, 1827.

1006. Summer has set in with its usual severity.
        Quoted in Lamb's Letter to V. Novello, 9 May, 1826.

COLLINGS, JESSE, politician, 9 Jan. 1831—20 Nov. 1920

1007. Three acres and a cow.   *Land reform slogan,* 1885.

COLLINS, WILLIAM, poet, 25 Dec. 1721—12 June, 1759

1008.   How sleep the brave, who sink to rest
        By all their country's wishes blest !
              Ode written in the Year 1746.

1009.   By fairy hands their knell is rung,
        By forms unseen their dirge is sung ;
        There Honour comes, a pilgrim grey,
        To bless the turf that wraps their clay,
        And Freedom shall awhile repair
        To dwell a weeping hermit there !   Ibid.

1010.   If aught of oaten stop, or pastoral song
        May hope, O pensive Eve, to soothe thine ear.
                Ode to Evening.

1011.   Now air is hush'd, save where the weak-ey'd bat,
        With short shrill shriek flits by on leathern wing,
          Or where the beetle winds
         His small but sullen horn.   Ibid.

1012.   With eyes uprais'd, as one inspired.
                        Pale Melancholy sate retir'd.   *The Passions*, 57.

1013.   O Music, sphere-descended maid !   Ibid., 95.

1014.   To fair Fidele's grassy tomb
                   Soft maids and village hinds shall bring
                   Each op'ning sweet, of earliest bloom,
                      And rifle all the breathing Spring. *Dirge in Cymbeline.*

COLMAN, GEORGE (THE YOUNGER), dramatist, 21 Oct. 1762—17 Oct.
        1836

1015.   When taken,
                 To be well shaken.   *The Newcastle Apothecary.*

1016. Says he, ' I am a handsome man, but I'm a gay deceiver.'
                                          Unfortunate Miss Bailey.

COLTON, CHARLES CALEB, author, 1780 ?—28 April, 1832

   1017. Men will wrangle for religion ; write for it ; fight for it ; die
for it ; anything but—live for it.   *Lacon*, I. No. 25.

   1018. Imitation is the sincerest of flattery.   Ibid., No. 217.

   1019. Examinations are formidable even to the best prepared, for
the greatest fool may ask more than the wisest man can answer.
                                                Ibid., No. 322.

COLUM, PADRAIC, Irish author, 8 Dec. 1881—

1020.   Oh, to have a little house !
                 To own the hearth and stool and all !
                         An Old Woman of the Roads.

CONGREVE, WILLIAM, dramatist, 10 Feb. 1670—19 Jan. 1729

1021.   Thou liar of the first magnitude.
                                          Love for Love, II. v.

1022.   Music hath charms to soothe a savage breast,
                 To soften rocks, or bend a knotted oak.
                                          The Mourning Bride, I. i.

1023.   Heav'n has no rage like love to hatred turn'd,
                 Nor Hell a fury like a woman scorn'd.   Ibid., III. viii.

1024.   If there's delight in love, 'tis when I see
                 That heart, which others bleed for, bleed for me.
                                          The Way of the World, III. xii.

   1025. Let us be very strange and well-bred : Let us be as strange
as if we had been married a great while, and as well-bred as if we were
not married at all.   Ibid., IV. v.

1026.   Defer not till to-morrow to be wise,
                   To-morrow's sun to thee may never rise.
                                          Letter to Cobham.

Connell, James, Irish author, 1852—8 Feb. 1929

1027.   Then raise the scarlet standard high !
                 Beneath its shade we'll live and die !
                 Though cowards flinch, and traitors jeer,
                 We'll keep the Red Flag flying here !   *The Red Flag*.

Conrad, Joseph (Teodor Josef Konrad Korzeniowski), Anglo-
        Polish novelist, 3 Dec. 1857—3 Aug. 1924

1028. A work that aspires, however humbly, to the condition of
art should carry its justification in every line.
                              The Nigger of the Narcissus, preface.

1029. Women's rougher, simpler, more upright judgment embraces
the whole truth, which their tact, their mistrust of masculine idealism,
ever prevents them from speaking in its entirety.   *Chance*, I. v.

Constable, Henry, poet, 1562—9 Oct. 1613

1030.   Diaphenia, like the daffadowndilly,
                   White as the sun, fair as the lily,
                 Heigh-ho, how I do love thee !   *Diaphenia*.

Constant de Rebecque, Henri Benjamin, French politician, 25 Oct.
        1767—8 Dec. 1830

1031. Je ne suis pas la rose, mais j'ai vécu avec elle.—I am not the
rose, but I have lived with her.   *Attributed*.

Cook, Eliza, poetess, 24 Dec. 1818—23 Sept. 1889

1032.   I love it, I love it ; and who shall dare
                 To chide me from loving that old arm-chair ?
                                      The Old Arm-Chair.

Coolidge, Calvin, U.S. President, 4 July, 1872—5 Jan. 1933

1033. There is no right to strike against the public safety by anybody, anywhere, any time.
                     Telegram to Samuel Gompers, 14 Sept. 1919.

1034. They hired the money, didn't they ?
                              Of the Allies' war debts to U.S.

Cooper, Anthony Ashley, *see* Shaftesbury

Corbet, Richard, Bishop successively of Oxford and of Norwich,
        1582—28 July, 1635

1035.   Farewell, rewards and fairies,
                   Good housewives now may say,
                 For now foul sluts in dairies
                   Do fare as well as they.
                 And though they sweep their hearths no less
                   Than maids were wont to do,
                 Yet who of late for cleanliness
                   Finds sixpence in her shoe ?
                              Farewell, Rewards and Fairies.

CORNFORD, FRANCES CROFTS, poetess, 30 March 1886—19 Aug. 1960

1036.　　　O why do you walk through the fields in gloves,
　　　　　　　Missing so much and so much ?
　　　　　　O fat white woman whom nobody loves,
　　　　　　Why do you walk through the fields in gloves ?
　　　　　　　　　　　　　　　To a Lady seen from the Train.

CORNUEL, ANNE BIGOT DE, French wit, 1614—Feb. 1694

　　1037.　Il n'y a pas de héros pour un valet de chambre.—No man is a
hero to his valet.　　　　　　　*Letter of Mlle. Aïssé,* 13 Aug. 1728.

CORNWALL, BARRY, *see* Procter, Bryan Waller

CORY, WILLIAM JOHNSON, poet, 9 Jan. 1823—11 June, 1892

1038.　　　All beauteous things for which we live
　　　　　　　By laws of time and space decay.
　　　　　　But oh, the very reason why
　　　　　　I clasp them, is because they die.　*Mimnermus in Church*

1039.　　　Somewhere beneath the sun,
　　　　　　　These quivering heart-strings prove it,
　　　　　　Somewhere there must be one
　　　　　　Made for this soul, to move it.　　　　*Amaturus*

1040.　They told me, Heraclitus, they told me you were dead ;
　　　　　They brought me bitter news to hear and bitter tears to shed.
　　　　　I wept as I remembered how often you and I
　　　　　Had tired the sun with talking and sent him down the sky.
[Paraphrase from Callimachus.]　　　　　　　　*Heraclitus.*

1041.　Still are thy pleasant voices, thy nightingales, awake ;
　　　　　For Death, he taketh all away, but them he cannot take.
　　　　　　　　　　　　　　　　　　　　　　　Ibid.

COTTON, NATHANIEL, poet and doctor, 1705—2 Aug. 1788

1042.　　　Thus hand in hand through life we'll go ;
　　　　　　　Its checker'd paths of joy and woe
　　　　　　　　With cautious steps we'll tread.　　*The Fireside,* 13.

1043.　　　Yet still we hug the dear deceit.
　　　　　　　　　　　　　　Visions in Verse.　Content.

COUÉ, ÉMILE, French doctor, 26 Feb. 1857—2 July, 1926

　　1044.　Tous le jours, à tous points de vue, je vais de mieux en mieux.
—Every day, from every point of view, I am getting better and better.
　　　　　　　　　　　　　　　Formula for auto-suggestion.

COUSIN, VICTOR, French philosopher, 28 Nov. 1792—13 Jan. 1867
　　1045.　L'art pour l'art.—Art for art's sake.　*Sorbonne lectures,* xxii.

COWLEY, ABRAHAM, author, 1618—28 July, 1667

1046.　　　His *faith,* perhaps, in some nice tenets might
　　　　　　　Be wrong ; his *life,* I'm sure, was in the right.
　　　　　　　　　　　　　　　On the Death of Crashaw.

1047.
The thirsty earth soaks up the rain,
And drinks, and gapes for drink again ;
The plants suck in the earth, and are
With constant drinking fresh and fair.
From Anacreon. Drinking.

1048.
Fill all the glasses there, for why
Should every creature drink but I ?
Why, man of morals, tell me why ?   Ibid.

1049.
Love in her sunny eyes doth basking play ;
Love walks the pleasant mazes of her hair ;
Love does on both her lips for ever stray,
And sows and reaps a thousand kisses there :
In all her outward parts Love's always seen ;
But oh ! he never went within.   *The Change.*

1050. The monster London.
Essays in Verse and Prose, ii. *Of Solitude*, 11.

COWLEY, HANNAH, dramatist, 1743—11 March, 1809

1051. But what is woman ?—only one of Nature's agreeable
blunders.   *Who's the Dupe ?* II. ii.

1052. Five minutes ! Zounds ! I have been five minutes too late
all my lifetime !   *The Belle's Stratagem*, I. i.

COWPER, WILLIAM, poet, 15 Nov. 1731—25 April, 1800

1053.
No dancing bear was so genteel,
Or half so *dégagé*.   *On himself.*

1054.
There goes the parson, oh ! illustrious spark,
And there, scarce less illustrious, goes the clerk !
*On observing some Names of Little Note recorded in
the Biographica Britannica.*

1055.
Regions Caesar never knew
Thy posterity shall sway,
Where his eagles never flew,
None invincible as they.   *Boadicea : an Ode.*

1056.
Ages elaps'd ere Homer's lamp appear'd
And ages ere the Mantuan swan was heard :
To carry nature lengths unknown before,
To give a Milton birth, ask'd ages more.
Table Talk, 556.

1057.
How much a dunce that has been sent to roam
Excels a dunce that has been kept at home.
The Progress of Error, 415.

1058.
'Tis hard if all is false that I advance—
A fool must now and then be right, by chance.
Conversation, 95.

1059.
A moral, sensible, and well-bred man
Will not affront me, and no other can.   Ibid., 193

1060.   Pernicious weed ! whose scent the fair annoys,
Unfriendly to society's chief joys,
Thy worst effect is banishing for hours
The sex whose presence civilizes ours.   Ibid. 251.

1061.   I cannot talk with civet in the room,
A fine puss-gentleman that's all perfume.   Ibid. 283.

1062.   Absence of occupation is not rest,
A mind quite vacant is a mind distress'd.
                                    Retirement, 623.

1063. I praise the Frenchman, his remark was shrewd [La Bruyère.]
How sweet, how passing sweet, is solitude !
But grant me still a friend in my retreat,
Whom I may whisper—solitude is sweet.   Ibid., 739.

1064.   I am monarch of all I survey,
My right there is none to dispute.
        Verses supposed to be written by Alexander Selkirk.

1065.   O solitude ! where are the charms
That sages have seen in thy face ?   Ibid.

1066.   The path of sorrow, and that path alone,
Leads to the land where sorrow is unknown.
        An Epistle to a Protestant Lady in France.

1067. With outstretch'd hoe I slew him at the door,
And taught him NEVER TO COME THERE NO MORE.
[Of a viper that attacked three kittens.]   *The Colubriad.*

1068.   Toll for the brave—
The brave that are no more :
All sunk beneath the wave,
Fast by their native shore.
            On the Loss of the Royal George.

1069.   A land-breeze shook the shrouds,
And she was overset ;
Down went the Royal George
With all her crew complete   Ibid.

1070.   John Gilpin was a citizen
Of credit and renown.
A train-band captain eke was he
Of famous London town.   *John Gilpin.*

1071.   That, though on pleasure she was bent,
She had a frugal mind.   Ibid.

1072.   So, fair and softly, John he cried,
But John he cried in vain.   Ibid.

1073.   Away went Gilpin—who but he ?
His fame soon spread around—
He carries weight ! he rides a race !
'Tis for a thousand pound !

1074.   My hat and wig will soon be here—
They are upon the road.   Ibid.

1075.
> Said John—It is my wedding-day,
> And all the world would stare,
> If wife should dine at Edmonton,
> And I should dine at Ware !　　　*Ibid.*

1076.
> I sing the Sofa.
>
> *The Task*, I.   *The Sofa*, 1.

1077.
God made the country, and man made the town.

　　　　　　　　　　　　　　　　Ibid., 749.

1078.
> Oh for a lodge in some vast wilderness,
> Some boundless contiguity of shade,
> Where rumour of oppression and deceit,
> Of unsuccessful or successful war,
> Might never reach me more. *Ibid.*, II.   *The Timepiece*, 1.

1079.
> Slaves cannot breathe in England ; if their lungs
> Receive our air, that moment they are free ;
> They touch our country, and their shackles fall.
>
> *Ibid.*, 40.

1080.
> England, with all thy faults I love thee still,
> My country !　　　　　　　　　　　*Ibid.*, 206.

1081.
> There is a pleasure in poetic pains
> Which only poets know.　　　　*Ibid.*, 285.

1082.
> Variety's the very spice of life,
> That gives it all its flavour.　　　*Ibid.*, 606.

1083.
> I was a stricken deer, that left the herd
> Long since.　　　　*Ibid.*, III.   *The Garden*, 108.

1084.
Who loves a garden loves a greenhouse too.　　*Ibid.*, 566.

1085.
> Now stir the fire, and close the shutters fast,
> Let fall the curtains, wheel the sofa round,
> And while the bubbling and loud-hissing urn
> Throws up a steamy column, and the cups,
> That cheer but not inebriate, wait on each,
> So let us welcome peaceful ev'ning in.
>
> *Ibid.*, IV.   *The Winter Evening*, 36.

1086.
> O Winter, ruler of th' inverted year.   *Ibid.*, 120.

1087.
> With spots quadrangular of diamond form,
> Ensanguin'd hearts, clubs typical of strife,
> And spades, the emblem of untimely graves.
>
> *Ibid.*, 217.

1088.
> There is in souls a sympathy with sounds ;
> And, as the mind is pitch'd, the ear is pleas'd
> With melting airs, or martial, brisk, or grave :
> Some chord in unison with what we hear
> Is touch'd within us, and the heart replies.
>
> *Ibid.*, VI.   *The Winter Walk at Noon*, 1.

1089.
> Knowledge is proud that he has learn'd so much ;
> Wisdom is humble that he knows no more.   *Ibid.*, 96.

1090.
> Books are not seldom talismans and spells.   *Ibid.*, 98.

1091.
> I would not enter on my list of friends
> (Tho' grac'd with polish'd manners and fine sense,
> Yet wanting sensibility) the man
> Who needlessly sets foot upon a worm.   *Ibid.*, 560.

1092.   For public schools 'tis public folly feeds.   *Tirocinium*, 250.

1093.   An honest man, close-button'd to the chin,
Broadcloth without, and a warm heart within.
An Epistle to Joseph Hill, 62.

1094.   The poplars are fell'd, farewell to the shade
And the whispering sound of the cool colonnade.
The Poplar-Field.

1095.   O that those lips had language !   Life has pass'd
With me but roughly since I heard thee last.
On the Receipt of my Mother's Picture, 1.

1096.   By disappointment every day beguil'd,
Dupe of *to-morrow* even from a child.   *Ibid.*, 40.

1097.   For 'tis a truth well known to most,
That whatsoever thing is lost,
We seek it, ere it come to light,
In ev'ry cranny but the right.   *The Retired Cat*, 95.

1098.   Mary !   I want a lyre with other strings.
Sonnet to Mrs. Unwin.

1099.   But misery still delights to trace
Its semblance in another's case.   *The Castaway.*

1100.   Oh ! for a closer walk with God.   *Olney Hymns*, i.

1101.   What peaceful hours I once enjoy'd
How sweet their mem'ry still !
But they have left an aching void,
The world can never fill.   *Ibid.*

1102.   There is a fountain fill'd with blood
Drawn from Emmanuel's veins ;
And sinners, plung'd beneath that flood,
Lose all their guilty stains.   *Ibid.*, xv.

1103.   Can a woman's tender care
Cease, toward the child she bare ?
Yes, she may forgetful be,
Yet will I remember thee.   *Ibid.*, xviii.

1104.   God moves in a mysterious way,
His wonders to perform ;
He plants His footsteps in the sea,
And rides upon the storm.   *Ibid.*, xxxv.

1105.   Behind a frowning providence
He hides a smiling face.   *Ibid.*

CRABBE, GEORGE, poet and clergyman, 24 Dec. 1754—3 Feb. 1832

1106.   On Mincio's banks, in Caesar's bounteous reign,
If Tityrus found the Golden Age again,
Must sleepy bards the flattering dream prolong,
Mechanic echoes of the Mantuan song ?
From Truth and Nature shall we widely stray,
Where Virgil, not where Fancy, leads the way ?
The Village, i. 15.

[These lines were rewritten in this form by Dr. Johnson.]

1107.   Yes, thus the muses sing of happy swains,
Because the Muses never knew their pains :
They boast their peasants' pipes ; but peasants now
Resign their pipes and plod behind the plough.   *Ibid.*, 21.

1108.   By such examples taught, I paint the Cot,
As Truth will paint it, and as Bards will not.   *Ibid.*, 53.

1109.   Rank weeds, that every art and care defy,
Reign o'er the land and rob the blighted rye :
There thistles stretch their prickly arms afar,
And to the ragged infant threaten war ;
There poppies nodding, mock the hope of toil ;
There the blue bugloss paints the sterile soil ;
Hardy and high, above the slender sheaf,
The slimy mallow waves her silky leaf ;
O'er the young shoot the charlock throws a shade,
And clasping tares cling round the sickly blade.
   Ibid., 67.

1110.   Oh ! rather give me commentators plain,
Who with no deep researches vex the brain ;
Who from the dark and doubtful love to run,
And hold their glimmering tapers to the sun.
   The Parish Register, 1. introduction, 89.

1111.   Books cannot always please, however good ;
Minds are not ever craving for their food.
   The Borough, letter xxiv. *Schools*, 402.

1112.   Grave Jonas Kindred, Sybil Kindred's sire,
Was six feet high, and look'd six inches higher.
   Tales, **vi.** *The Frank Courtship*, 1.

1113.   When the coarse cloth she saw, with many a stain,
Soil'd by rude hinds who cut and came again.
   Ibid., vii. *The Widow's Tale*, 25.

1114.   The ring so worn, as you behold,
So thin, so pale, is yet of gold :
The passion such it was to prove ;
Worn with life's cares, love yet was love.
   His Mother's Wedding Ring.

CRAIK, DINAH MARIA MULOCK, authoress, 20 April, 1826—12 Oct. 1887

1115.   It's a bonnie bay at morning,
And bonnier at the noon,
But it's bonniest when the sun draps
And red comes up the moon ;
When the mist creeps o'er the Cumbraes,
And Arran peaks are grey,
And the great black hills, like sleepin' kings,
Sit grand roun' Rothesay Bay.   *Rothesay Bay.*

1116.   Could ye come back to me, Douglas, Douglas !
In the old likeness that I knew,
I would be so faithful, so loving, Douglas,
Douglas, Douglas, tender and true.   *Too Late.*

Crashaw 88 Cumberland

CRASHAW, RICHARD, poet, 1613 ?—21 Aug. 1649

1117.   Whoe'er she be
                      That not impossible she
                      That shall command my heart and me.
                              Wishes to his Supposed Mistress.

1118.   Where'er she lie
                      Locked up from mortal eye,
                      In shady leaves of destiny.   *Ibid.*

1119.   Life that dares send
                      A challenge to his end,
                      And when it comes say ' Welcome, Friend.'

                                                  Ibid.

1120.   Two walking baths ; two weeping motions ;
             Portable and compendious oceans.
                  Saint Mary Magdalene, or The Weeper, 19.

1121.   Nympha pudica Deum vidit, et erubuit.
           —The conscious water saw its God, and blushed.
               Epigrammata Sacra. Aquae in Vinum Versae.—
               Sacred Epigrams. The Water turned into Wine.
[Latin and translation both by Crashaw.]

CRAWFORD, FRANCIS MARION, U.S. novelist, 2 Aug. 1854—9 April, 1909

1122. What is charm ? It is what the violet has and the camelia has not.   *Children of the King,* v.

CROCKETT, DAVID, U.S. farmer, 17 Aug. 1786—6 March, 1836

1123. Don't shoot, colonel. I'll come down : I know I'm a gone coon.   *Story of a treed raccoon.*

CROMWELL, OLIVER, Lord Protector, 25 April, 1599—3 Sept. 1658

1124. I beseech you, in the bowels of Christ, think it possible you may be mistaken.
        Letter to the General Assembly of the Church of Scotland, 3 Aug.
        1650.

1125. What shall we do with this bauble ? There, take it away.
[Of the Mace.]   *When dismissing Parliament,* 20 April, 1653.

1126. It is not my design to drink or to sleep, but my design is to make what haste I can to be gone.   *Dying Words.*

CROSS, MRS., *see* Eliot, George

CROWNE, JOHN, dramatist, 1640 ?—1703 ?

1127. There is no hiding love from lover's eyes.
        The Destruction of Jerusalem, part I. IV. i.

CUMBERLAND, RICHARD, Bishop of Peterborough, 15 July, 1631—9 Oct. 1718

1128. It is better to wear out than to rust out.
        Bishop George Horne, *A Duty of Contending for the Faith.*

CUNNINGHAM, ALLAN, Scottish poet, 7 Dec. 1784—30 Oct. 1842

1129.   The sun rises bright in France,
            And fair sets he ;
         But he has tint the blythe blink he had
            In my ain countree.   *The Sun rises bright in France.*

1130.   A wet sheet and a flowing sea,
            A wind that follows fast,
         And fills the white and rustling sail,
            And bends the gallant mast.
                           A wet Sheet and a flowing Sea.

1131.   While the hollow oak our palace is,
            Our heritage the sea.   Ibid.

1132.   Wha the deil hae we got for a king,
         But a wee, wee German lairdie !
                           The Wee, Wee German Lairdie.

1133.   It's hame, and it's hame, hame fain wad I be,
         An' it's hame, hame, hame, to my ain countree !
                           Hame, Hame, Hame.
         [This and the preceding quotation are based on older poems.]

CURRAN, JOHN PHILPOT, Irish judge, 24 July, 1750—14 Oct. 1817

   1134. The condition upon which God hath given liberty to man is
eternal vigilance.
            Speech on the right of election of Lord Mayor of Dublin, 10 July,
            1790.

DANIEL, SAMUEL, Poet Laureate, 1562—14 Oct. 1619

1135.   Care-charmer Sleep, son of the sable Night,
         Brother to Death, in silent darkness born.
                           Sonnets to Delia, liv.

DANTE, ALIGHIERI, Italian poet, May, 1265—14 Sept. 1321

1136.   Lasciate ogni speranza, voi ch' entrate !
         —All hope abandon, ye who enter !
         La Divina Commedia—The Divine Comedy.   Inferno, iii. 9.

1137.   Questi non hanno speranza di morte.
         —These have not hope of death.   Ibid., 46.

1138.   Onorate l'altissimo poeta.
         —Honour the greatest poet.   Ibid., iv. 80.

1139.   Nessun maggior dolore,
         Che ricordarsi del tempo felice
         Nella miseria.
         —No greater sorrow that to recall in our misery
            the time when we were happy.   Ibid., v. 121.

1140.   E 'n la sua volontate è nostra pace.
         —And in His will is our peace.   *Paradiso*, iii. 85.

1141.   L'amor che move il sole e l'altre stelle.
         —The love that moves the sun and the other stars.
                           Ibid., xxxiii. 145.

DANTON, GEORGES JACQUES, French politician, 28 Dec. 1759—5 April, 1794.

1142. De l'audace, encore de l'audace, et toujours de l'audace !— Boldness, again boldness, and always boldness !
Speech to Legislative Committee of General Defence, 2 Sept. 1792.

DARWIN, CHARLES ROBERT, naturalist, 12 Feb. 1809—19 April, 1882

1143. I have called this principle, by which each slight variation, if useful, is preserved, by the term Natural Selection.
The Origin of Species, iii.

1144. The expression often used by Mr. Herbert Spencer, of the Survival of the Fittest, is more accurate, and is sometimes equally convenient. Ibid.

DARWIN, ERASMUS, scientist, 12 Dec. 1731—18 April, 1802

1145. Soon shall thy arm, unconquer'd steam ! afar
Drag the slow barge, or drive the rapid car ;
Or on wide-waving wings expanded bear
The flying chariot through the field of air.
The Botanic Garden, 1. i. 289.

D'AVENANT, SIR WILLIAM, Poet Laureate, Feb. 1606—7 April, 1668

1146. The lark now leaves his wat'ry nest
And, climbing, shakes his dewy wings. *Song.*

DAVIES, SIR JOHN, poet, baptised 16 April, 1569, died 7 Dec. 1626

1147. Wedlock, indeed, hath oft compared been
To public feasts, where meet a public rout,
Where they that are without would fain go in,
And they that are within would fain go out.
Contention betwixt a Wife, a Widow, and a Maid.

DAVIES, WILLIAM HENRY, poet, 3 July, 1871—26 Sept. 1940

1148. What is this life if, full of care,
We have no time to stand and stare. *Leisure.*

1149. Sweet stay-at-Home, sweet Well-content.
Sweet Stay-at-Home.

1150. A rainbow and a cuckoo's song
May never come together again ;
May never come
This side the tomb. *A Great Time.*

DAVIS, THOMAS OSBORNE, Irish poet, 14 Oct. 1814—16 Sept. 1845

1151. Come in the evening, or come in the morning,
Come when you're looked for, or come without warning.
The Welcome.

DECATUR, STEPHEN, U.S. naval commander, 5 Jan. 1779—22 March, 1820

1152. Our country ! In her intercourse with foreign nations may she always be in the right ; but our country, right or wrong.
Toast given at Norfolk, Virginia, April, 1816.

DEFFAND, MARIE ANNE DE VICHY-CHAMROND, MARQUISE DU, French authoress, 25 Dec. 1697—23 Sept. 1780.

1153. Il n'y a que le premier pas qui coûte.—It is only the first step which is troublesome.   *Letter to d'Alembert*, 7 July, 1763.

DEFOE, DANIEL, author, 1660 ?—26 April, 1731

1154. He bade me observe it, and I should always find, that the calamities of life were shared among the upper and lower part of mankind ; but that the middle station had the fewest disasters.
Robinson Crusoe, part 1.

1155.   Wherever God erects a house of prayer,
               The Devil always builds a chapel there ;
               And 'twill be found upon examination,
               The latter has the largest congregation.
                              The True-Born Englishman, I. I.

1156.   No danger can their daring spirit pall,
               Always provided that their belly's full.   Ibid., II. **13**

1157.   No panegyric need their praise record ;
               An Englishman ne'er wants his own good word.
                                                         Ibid., 152.

DEKKER, THOMAS, dramatist, 1570 ?—1641 ?

1158.   Art thou poor, yet hast thou golden slumbers ?
                    O sweet content !
               Art thou rich, yet is thy mind perplexed ?
                    O punishment !   *Patient Grissill*, 1.

1159.   To add to golden numbers, golden numbers.   Ibid.

1160.   Work apace, apace, apace, apace ;
               Honest labour bears a lovely face.   Ibid.

1161.   Golden slumbers kiss your eyes,
               Smiles awake you when you rise
               Sleep, pretty wantons, do not cry,
               And I will sing a lullaby.   Ibid., IV. ii.

1162.   The best of men
               That e'er wore earth about him was a sufferer ;
               A soft, meek, patient, humble, tranquil spirit,
               The first true gentleman that ever breathed.
                                   The Honest Whore, I. I. ii.

DE LA MARE, WALTER JOHN, poet, 25 April, 1873—22 June, 1956

1163.   Slowly, silently, now the moon
               Walks the night in her silver shoon.   *Silver.*

1164.   Softly along the road of evening,
                In a twilight dim with rose,
             Wrinkled with age, and drenched with dew,
                Old Nod, the shepherd, goes.   *Nod.*

1165.   Here lies a most beautiful Lady,
                Light of step and heart was she ;
             I think she was the most beautiful lady
                That ever was in the West Country.   *Epitaph.*

1166.   Look thy last on all things lovely
                Every hour.   *Farewell.*

1167.   Since that all things thou wouldst praise
             Beauty took from those who loved them
             In other days.   Ibid.

1168.   Oh, no man knows
                 Through what wild centuries
                 Roves back the rose.   *All that's Past.*

1169.   Far are the shades of Arabia
                Where the princes ride at noon.   *Arabia.*

1170.   ' Is there anybody there ? ' said the Traveller,
                Knocking on the moonlit door.   *The Listeners.*

DE MORGAN, AUGUSTUS, mathematician, 1806—18 March, 1871,

1171. Great fleas have little fleas upon their backs to bite 'em,
         And little fleas have lesser fleas, and so *ad infinitum.*
         And the great fleas themselves, in turn, have greater fleas
            to go on ;
         While these again have greater still, and greater still, and
            so on.   *A Budget of Paradoxes,* p. 377.

DENHAM, SIR JOHN, poet, 1615—10 March, 1669

1172.   O, could I flow like thee, and make thy stream
             My great example, as it is my theme !
             Though deep, yet clear ; though gentle, yet not dull ;
             Strong without rage ; without o'erflowing full.
     [Of the Thames.]   *Cooper's Hill,* 189.

DENMAN, THOMAS DENMAN, 1ST BARON, LORD CHIEF JUSTICE, 23 Feb.
         1779—22 Sept. 1854

1173. Trial by jury itself, instead of being a security to persons
who are accused, will be a delusion, a mockery, and a snare.
                        In O'Connell v. *the Queen,* 4 Sept. 1844.

DENNIS, JOHN, critic, 1657—6 Jan. 1734

1174. A man who could make so vile a pun would not scruple to
pick a pocket.   *Attributed.*

1175. They will not let my play run, and yet they steal my thunder !
             On hearing his own effects used in another play.

DE QUINCEY, THOMAS, author, 15 Aug. 1785—8 Dec. 1859

1176. If once a man indulge himself in murder, very soon he comes to think little of robbing ; and from robbing he next comes to drinking and Sabbath-breaking, and from that to incivility and procrastination.
Murder Considered as One of the Fine Arts.

1177. It is notorious that the memory strengthens as you lay burdens upon it, and becomes trustworthy as you trust it.
Confessions of an English Opium-Eater, part I.

DESCARTES, RENÉ, French philosopher, 31 March, 1596—11 Feb. 1650

1178. Cogito, ergo sum.—I think, therefore I am.
Discours de la Méthode—Discourse of Method.

DIBDIN, CHARLES, song writer, 4 March, 1745—25 July, 1814

1179.   There's a sweet little cherub that sits up aloft,
        To keep watch for the life of poor Jack.   *Poor Jack.*

1180.   And did you not hear of a jolly young waterman,
        Who at Blackfriar's Bridge used for to ply ?
        He feather'd his oars with such skill and dexterity,
        Winning each heart, and delighting each eye.
                            The Jolly Young Waterman.

1181.   Here, a sheer hulk, lies poor Tom Bowling,
              The darling of our crew ;
           No more he'll hear the tempest howling,
              For death has broach'd him to.   *Tom Bowling.*

1182.   Faithful below he did his duty,
              But now he's gone aloft.   Ibid.

1183.   Did you ever hear of Captain Wattle ?
        He was all for love, and a little for the bottle.
                            Captain Wattle and Miss Roe.

DIBDIN, THOMAS, dramatist, 21 March, 1771—16 Sept. 1841

1184.   O, it's a snug little island !
              A right little, tight little island !
                            The Snug Little Island.

DICKENS, CHARLES, novelist, 7 Feb. 1812—9 June, 1870

1185. He had used the word in its Pickwickian sense. [Blotton.]
Pickwick Papers, i.

1186. Not presume to dictate, but broiled fowl and mushrooms—capital thing !   [Jingle.]   Ibid., ii.

1187. Kent—apples, cherries, hops, and women. [Jingle.]   Ibid.

1188.   A rare old plant is the Ivy green.   *Song*, Ibid., vi·

1189. ' It wasn't the wine,' murmured Mr. Snodgrass, in a broken voice. ' It was the salmon.'   Ibid., viii.

1190. I wants to make your flesh creep. [Joe, the fat boy.]   Ibid·

1191.   Can I unmoved see thee dying
                          On a log,
                          Expiring frog !

Ode, Ibid., xv.

1192. Mr. Weller's knowledge of London was extensive and peculiar.
Ibid., xx.

1193. The wictim o' connubiality, as Blue Beard's domestic chaplain said, with a tear of pity, ven he buried him. [Sam Weller.]   Ibid.

1194. It's over, and can't be helped, and that's one consolation, as they always say in Turkey, ven they cuts the wrong man's head off. [Sam Weller.]   Ibid., xxiii.

1195. Dumb as a drum vith a hole in it. [Sam Weller.]   Ibid., xxv.

1196. Wen you're a married man, Samivel, you'll understand a good many things as you don't understand now ; but vether it's worth while goin' through so much to learn so little, as the charity-boy said ven he got to the end of the alphabet, is a matter o' taste. [Old Weller.]   Ibid. xxvii.

1197. A double glass o' the inwariable. [Old Weller.]   Ibid., xxxiii.

1198. She's a-swellin' wisibly before my wery eyes. [Old Weller.]
Ibid.

1199. ' Little to do, and plenty to get, I suppose ? ' said Sergeant Buzfuz with jocularity.
  ' Oh, quite enough to get, sir, as the soldier said ven they ordered him three hundred and fifty lashes,' replied Sam.
  ' You must not tell us what the soldier, or any other man, said, sir,' interposed the judge ; ' it's not evidence.'   Ibid, xxxiv.

1200. ' Yes, I have a pair of eyes,' replied Sam, ' and that's just it. If they wos a pair o' patent double million magnifyin' gas microscopes of hextra power, p'raps I might be able to see through a flight o' stairs and a deal door ; but bein' only eyes, you see, my wision's limited.'
Ibid.

1201. Vy worn't there a alleybi ! [Old Weller.]   Ibid.

1202. If he damned hisself in confidence, o' course that was another thing. [Old Weller.]   Ibid., xliii.

1203. Anythin' for a quiet life, as the man said wen he took the sitivation at the lighthouse. [Sam Weller.]   Ibid.

1204. Which is your partickler wanity ? [Sam Weller.]

Ibid., xlv.

1205. Oliver Twist has asked for more ! [Bumble.] *Oliver Twist*, ii.

1206. The Artful Dodger.   Ibid., viii.

1207. ' If the law supposes that,' said Mr. Bumble . . . ' the law is a ass—a idiot.'   Ibid., li.

1208. Here's richness ! [Squeers.]   *Nicholas Nickleby*, v.

1209. A demd, damp, moist, unpleasant body. [Mantalini.]
Ibid., xxxiv.

1210. She is come at last—at last—and all is gas and gaiters ! [The old gentleman.]   Ibid., xlix.

1211. My life is one demd horrid grind. [Mantalini.]   Ibid., lxiv.

1212. He has gone to the demnition bow-wows. [Mantalini.]   Ibid.

1213. Is the old min agreeable ?   [Dick Swiveller.]
The Old Curiosity Shop, ii.

1214. What is the odds so long as the fire of soul is kindled at the taper of conwiviality, and the wing of friendship never moults a feather ! [Dick Swiveller.]   Ibid.

1215. Codlin's the friend, not Short. [Codlin.]   Ibid., xix.

1216. ' There are strings,' said Mr. Tappertit, ' . . . in the human heart that had better not be wibrated.'   *Barnaby Rudge*, xxii.

1217. Any man may be in good spirits and good temper when he's well dressed.   There ain't much credit in that.   [Mark Tapley.]
Martin Chuzzlewit, v.

1218. Some credit in being jolly. [Mark Tapley.]   Ibid.

1219. With affection beaming in one eye, and calculation shining out of the other.   Ibid., viii.

1220. Let us be moral.   Let us contemplate existence. [Pecksniff.]
Ibid., ix.

1221. ' Mrs. Harris,' I says, ' leave the bottle on the chimley-piece, and don't ask me to take none, but let me put my lips to it when I am so dispoged.' [Mrs. Gamp.]   Ibid., xix.

1222. He'd make a lovely corpse. [Mrs. Gamp.]   Ibid., xxv.

1223. Our backs is easy ris.   We must be cracked-up, or they rises, and we snarls. . . . You'd better crack us up, you had ! [Chollop.]
Ibid., xxxiii.

1224. Oh Sairey, Sairey, little do we know wot lays afore us ! [Mrs. Gamp.]   Ibid., xl.

1225. ' Bother Mrs. Harris ! ' said Betsey Prig. . . . ' I don't believe there's no sich a person ! '   Ibid., xlix.

1226. ' But the words she spoke of Mrs. Harris, lambs could not forgive.   No, Betsey ! ' said Mrs. Gamp, in a violent burst of feeling, ' nor worms forget ! '   Ibid,

1227. In came Mrs. Fezziwig, one vast substantial smile.
A Christmas Carol, stave ii.

1228. ' God bless us every one ! ' said Tiny Tim.   Ibid., iii.

1229.   Oh, let us love our occupations,
                Bless the squire and his relations,
                Live upon our daily rations,
                And always know our proper stations.
The Chimes, 2nd quarter.

1230. He's tough, ma'am, tough, is J. B.   Tough, and devilish sly ! [Major Bagstock.]   *Dombey and Son*, vii.

1231. When found, make a note of. [Captain Cuttle.]   Ibid., xv.

1232. Train up a fig-tree in the way it should go, and when you are old sit under the shade of it. [Captain Cuttle.]   Ibid., xix.

1233. ' I am a lone lorn creetur,' were Mrs. Gummidge's words, . . . ' and everythink goes contrairy with me.'   *David Copperfield*, iii.

1234. She's been thinking of the old 'un ! [Mr. Peggotty.]
Ibid.

1235. Barkis is willin'. [Barkis.] Ibid., v.

1236. ' In case anything turned up,' which was his [Micawber's] favourite expression. Ibid., xi.

1237. I never will desert Mr. Micawber. [Mrs. Micawber.]
Ibid., xii.

1238. Annual income twenty pounds, annual expenditure nineteen nineteen six, result happiness. Annual income twenty pounds, annual expenditure twenty pounds ought and six, result misery. [Micawber.]
Ibid.

1239. ' I'm a very umble person. . . . My mother is likewise a very umble person. We live in a numble abode, Master Copperfield, but have much to be thankful for.' [Uriah Heep.] Ibid., xvi.

1240. ' I should be happy, myself, to propose two months, . . . but I have a partner, Mr. Jorkins. [Spenlow.] Ibid., xxiii.

1241. I'm Gormed—and I can't say no fairer than that ! [Mr. Peggotty.] Ibid., lxiii.

1242. A London particular. . . . A fog. [Guppy.]
Bleak House, iii.

1243. Educating the natives of Borrioboola-Gha, on the left bank of the Niger. [Mrs. Jellyby.] Ibid., iv.

1244. Not to put too fine a point upon it. [Snagsby.] Ibid., xi.

1245. He wos wery good to me, he wos. [Jo.] Ibid.

1246. ' It is,' says Chadband, ' the ray of rays, the sun of suns, the moon of moons, the star of stars. It is the light of Terewth.'
Ibid., xxv.

1247. Far better hang wrong fler than no fler. [The debilitated cousin of the Dedlocks.] Ibid., liii.

1248. Facts alone are wanted in life. [Gradgrind.]
Hard Times, I. i.

1249. Whatever was required to be done, the Circumlocution Office was beforehand with all the public departments in the art of perceiving—HOW NOT TO DO IT. *Little Dorrit*, I. x.

1250. Papa, potatoes, poultry, prunes, and prism, are all very good words for the lips : especially prunes and prism. [Mrs. General.]
Ibid., II. v

1251. It is a far, far better thing that I do, than I have ever done ; it is a far, far better rest that I go to, than I have ever known. [Sidney Carton.] *A Tale of Two Cities*, II. xv.

1252. Mr. Podsnap settled that whatever he put behind him he put out of existence. *Our Mutual Friend*, I. xi.

1253. The question about everything [with Podsnap] was, would it bring a blush to the cheek of a young person ? Ibid.

1254.
Who comes here ?
A Grenadier.
What does he want ?
A pot of beer. Ibid., II. ii.

DICKINSON, EMILY ELIZABETH, U.S. poetess, 10 Dec. 1830—15 May, 1886

1255. I asked no other thing,
No other was denied.
I offered Being for it ;
The mighty merchant smiled.

1256. Brazil ? He twirled a button,
Without a glance my way :
' But, madam, is there nothing else
That we can show to-day ? '

Poems, part I. *Life*, xii.

1257. How dreary to be somebody !
How public, like a frog
To tell your name the livelong day
To an admiring bog !   Ibid., xxvii.

1258. I never saw a moor,
I never saw the sea ;
Yet know I how the heather looks,
And what a wave must be.

Ibid., part IV. *Time and Eternity*, xvii.

1259. This quiet Dust was Gentlemen and Ladies,
And Lads and Girls ;
Was laughter and ability and sighing,
And frocks and curls.

Ibid., part v. *The Single Hound*, lxxiv.

DIDEROT, DENIS, French scholar, 5 Oct. 1713—30 July, 1784
1260. L'esprit de l'escalier.—Staircase wit (i.e. the retort which is thought of too late).
Paradoxe sur le Comédien.—The Paradox of the Comedian.

DILLON, WENTWORTH, *see* Roscommon, Earl of

DIONYSIUS OF HALICARNASSUS, Greek historian, 1st century B.C.
1261. Ἱστορία φιλοσοφία ἐστὶν ἐκ παραδειγμάτων.—History is philosophy derived from examples.
Ars Rhetorica.—Art of Rhetoric, XI. ii.

DISRAELI, BENJAMIN, 1ST EARL OF BEACONSFIELD, Prime Minister, 21 Dec. 1804—19 April, 1881

1262. I will sit down now, but the time will come when you will hear me.   *Maiden speech, House of Commons*, 7 Dec. 1837.

1263. The noble Lord is the Prince Rupert of Parliamentary discussion. [Lord Stanley.] *Speech, House of Commons*, 24 April, 1844.

1264. The right honourable gentleman caught the Whigs bathing, and walked away with their clothes. [Sir Robert Peel.]
Ibid., 28 Feb. 1845.

1265. The question is this : Is man an ape or an angel ? My lord, I am on the side of the angels.   Ibid., *Oxford*, 25 Nov. 1864.

1266. I believe that without party Parliamentary government is impossible.   Ibid., *Manchester*, 3 April, 1872.

1267. A university should be a place of light, of liberty, and of learning. *Ibid., House of Commons*, 11 March, 1873.

1268. He is a great master of gibes and flouts and jeers. [The Marquis of Salisbury.] *Ibid.*, 5 Aug. 1874.

1269. Lord Salisbury and myself have brought you back peace—but a peace I hope with honour. *Ibid.*, 16 July, 1878.

1270. A sophistical rhetorician, inebriated with the exuberance of his own verbosity. [Gladstone.]
Ibid., Knightsbridge, 27 July, 1878.

1271. Adventures are to the adventurous.
Ixion in Heaven, II. ii.

1272. No Government can be long secure without a formidable Opposition. *Coningsby*, II. i.

1273. Youth is a blunder ; Manhood a struggle ; Old Age a regret.
Ibid., III. i.

1274. London is a modern Babylon. *Tancred*, v. v.

1275. The gondola of London. [A hansom.] *Lothair*, xxvii.

1276. I have always thought that every woman should marry, and no man. *Ibid.*, xxx.

D'ISRAELI, ISAAC, antiquary, 11 May, 1766—19 Jan. 1848

1277. There is an art of reading, as well as an art of thinking, and an art of writing. *Literary Character*, xi.

DOBELL, SYDNEY THOMPSON, poet, 5 April, 1824—22 Aug. 1874

1278.   The murmur of the mourning ghost,
                That keeps the shadowy kine,
            ' Oh, Keith of Ravelston,
                The sorrows of thy line ! '   *A Nuptial Eve.*

DOBSON, HENRY AUSTIN, author, 18 Jan. 1840—2 Sept. 1921

1279.   Time goes, you say ?   Ah no !
            Alas, Time stays, *we* go.   *The Paradox of Time.*

1280.   The ladies of St. James's !
                They're painted to the eyes,
            Their white it stays for ever,
                Their red it never dies :
            But Phyllida, my Phyllida !
                Her colour comes and goes ;
            It trembles to a lily,—
                It wavers to a rose.   *The Ladies of St. James's.*

1281.   I intended an Ode,
            And it turn'd to a Sonnet.   *Urceus exit.*

DODDRIDGE, PHILIP, clergyman, 26 June, 1702—26 Oct. 1751

1282.　　　　Live while you live, the epicure would say,
　　　　　　And seize the pleasures of the present day ;
　　　　　　Live while you live, the sacred preacher cries,
　　　　　　And give to God each moment as it flies.
　　　　　　Lord, in my views let both united be ;
　　　　　　I live in pleasure when I live to thee.
　　　　　　　　　　Epigram on his Family Arms, ' Dum Vivimus
　　　　　　　　　　　　　　　Vivamus.'

1283.　　　　O God of Jacob, by whose hand
　　　　　　Thy people still are fed.　　　*Scripture Paraphases*, ii.
　　　　　　[Later altered to ' O God of Bethel.']

DODGE, MARY ABIGAIL, *see* Hamilton, Gail

DODGSON, CHARLES LUTWIDGE, *see* Carroll, Lewis

DONATUS, AELIUS, Roman grammarian, 4th century A.D.

　　1284.　Pereant qui ante nos nostra dixerunt.—Perish those who
have said our remarks before us.
　　　　　　　　　St. Jerome, *Commentary on Ecclesiastes*, i.

DONNE, JOHN, Dean of St. Paul's, 1571—31 March, 1631

1285.　　　　Go and catch a falling star,
　　　　　　Get with child a mandrake root,
　　　　　　Tell me, where all past years are,
　　　　　　Or who cleft the Devil's foot.　　　　　*Song.*

1286.　For God's sake hold your tongue and let me love.
　　　　　　　　　　　　　　　　　The Canonization.

1287.　　　　And whilst our souls negotiate there,
　　　　　　We like sepulchral statues lay ;
　　　　　　All day, the same our postures were,
　　　　　　And we said nothing, all the day.　　　*The Ecstasy.*

1288.　　　　I long to talk with some old lover's ghost,
　　　　　　Who died before the god of love was born.
　　　　　　　　　　　　　　　　　　Love's Deity.

1289.　　　　No spring nor summer beauty hath such grace
　　　　　　As I have seen in one autumnal face.
　　　　　　　　　　　　　Elegies, **ix.** *The Autumnal.*

1290.　　　　　　　Her pure and eloquent blood
　　　　　Spoke in her cheeks, and so distinctly wrought
　　　　　That one might almost say her body thought.
　　　　　　Of the Progress of the Soul. The Second Anniversary, 244.

DONNELLY, IGNATIUS, U.S. politician, 3 Nov. 1831—1 Jan. 1901

　　1291. The Democratic Party is like a mule—without pride of
ancestry or hope of posterity.　　　*Speech, Minnesota Legislature.*

DOOLEY, MR. (FINLEY PETER DUNNE), U.S. humorist, 10 July, 1867
　　　—30 June, 1919

　　1292.　Th' dead ar-re always pop'lar.　　　　　*On Charity.*

1293. Life'd not be worth livin' if we didn't keep our inimies.
On New Year's Resolutions.

1294. Vice . . . is a creature of such heejus mien. . . . that the more ye see it th' better ye like it. *The Crusade against Vice.*

DOSTOIEVSKY, FEODOR MIKHAILOVITCH, Russian novelist, 11 Nov. 1821—9 Feb. 1881

1295. Man is a pliable animal, a being who gets accustomed to everything. *The House of the Dead, I. ii.*

DOUDNEY, SARAH, authoress, 15 Jan. 1843—15 Dec. 1926

1296.　　　Listen to the water-mill ;
　　　Through the livelong day,
　　How the clicking of its wheel
　　　Wears the hours away !
　　　　　The Lesson of the Water-Mill.

1297.　　　And a proverb haunts my mind
　　　As a spell is cast—
　　' The mill cannot grind
　　　With the water that is past.' Ibid.

DOW, LORENZO, U.S. preacher, 16 Oct, 1777—2 Feb. 1834

1298. You can and you can't—You shall and you shan't—You will and you won't—You'll be damned if you do—And you'll be damned if you don't. [Defining Calvinism.]
Reflections on the Love of God.

DOWSON, ERNEST CHRISTOPHER, poet, 2 Aug. 1867—23 Feb. 1900

1299.　　　They are not long, the weeping and the laughter,
　　　　Love and desire and hate :
　　I think they have no portion in us after
　　　We pass the gate. *Vitae Summa Brevis.*

1300. And I was desolate and sick of an old passion.
Non sum qualis eram.

1301. I have been faithful to thee, Cynara ! in my fashion.
Ibid.

DOYLE, SIR ARTHUR CONAN, author, 22 May, 1859—7 July, 1930

1302. ' Wonderful ! ' I ejaculated. ' Commonplace,' said Holmes.
A Study in Scarlet, iii.

1303. An experience of women which extends over many nations and three separate continents. *The Sign of Four, ii.*

1304. You know my methods. Apply them. Ibid., vi.

1305. You see, but you do not observe.
The Adventures of Sherlock Holmes. A Scandal in Bohemia.

1306. The case has, in some respects, been not entirely devoid of interest. *Ibid., A Case of Identity.*

1307. Singularity is almost invariably a clue. The more featureless and commonplace a crime is, the more difficult it is to bring it home.
Ibid., The Boscombe Valley Mystery.

1308. A little monograph on the ashes of one hundred and forty different varieties of pipe, cigar, and cigarette tobacco. *Ibid.*

1309. A man should keep his little brain attic stocked with all the furniture that he is likely to use, and the rest he can put away in the lumber-room of his library, where he can get it if he wants it.
Ibid., The Five Orange Pips.

1310. It is my belief, Watson, founded upon my experience, that the lowest and vilest alleys of London do not present a more dreadful record of sin than does the smiling and beautiful countryside.
Ibid., The Copper Beeches.

1311. A long shot, Watson ; a very long shot !
The Memoirs of Sherlock Holmes. Silver Blaze.

1312. ' The curious incident of the dog in the night-time.'
' The dog did nothing in the night-time.'
' That was the curious incident,' remarked Sherlock Holmes.
Ibid.

1313. ' Excellent ! ' I cried. ' Elementary,' said he.
Ibid., The Crooked Man.

1314. He is the Napoleon of crime. *Ibid., The Final Problem.*

1315. But here, unless I am mistaken, is our client.
His Last Bow. Wisteria Lodge.

1316. The natives were Cucama Indians, an amiable but degraded race, with mental powers hardly superior to the average Londoner. [Professor Challenger.] *The Lost World, iv.*

1317.   What of the bow ?
        The bow was made in England :
        Of true wood, of yew wood,
        The wood of English bows.
The White Company. The Song of the Bow.

1318. The Grenadiers of Austria are proper men and tall.
Cremona.

DOYLE, SIR FRANCIS HASTINGS CHARLES, 2nd BARONET, poet, 21 Aug. 1810—8 June, 1888

1319.   Last night, among his fellow roughs,
          He jested, quaffed, and swore ;
        A drunken private of the Buffs,
          Who never looked before.
        To-day, beneath the foeman's frown,
          He stands in Elgin's place,
        Ambassador from Britain's crown,
          And type of all her race.
The Private of the Buffs.

1320.   Vain, mightiest fleets of iron framed ;
          Vain, those all-shattering guns ;
         Unless proud England keep, untamed,
          The strong heart of her sons. *Ibid.*

DRAKE, SIR FRANCIS, Admiral, 1540 ?—28 Jan. 1596

1321. There's plenty of time to win this game, and to thrash the Spaniards too.
>   *When the Armada was sighted as he was at bowls*, 20 July, 1588.

DRAYTON, MICHAEL, poet, 1563—23 Dec. 1631

1322.   Had in him those brave translunary things,
                     That the first poets had.   [Marlowe.]
>   *To Henry Reynolds, of Poets and Poesy*, 106.

1323.   For that fine madness still he did retain
                     Which rightly should possess a poet's brain.
>   Ibid., 109.

1324.   Fair stood the wind for France
                          When we our sails advance,
                          Nor now to prove our chance
                              Longer will tarry.   *The Ballad of Agincourt.*

1325.   O, when shall Englishmen
                          With such acts fill a pen,
                          Or England breed again
                              Such a King Harry ?   Ibid.

1326. Since there's no help, come let us kiss and part.
>   *Sonnets*, lxi.

1327.   Now at the last gasp of Love's latest breath,
                     When, his pulse failing, Passion speechless lies,
                     When Faith is kneeling by his bed of death,
                     And Innocence is closing up his eyes,
                     Now if thou wouldst, when all have given him over,
                     From death to life thou mightst him yet recover.   Ibid.

DRINKWATER, JOHN, author, 1 June, 1882—25 March, 1937

1328.   I never went to Mamble
                              That lies above the Teme,
                          So I wonder who's in Mamble,
                              And whether people seem
                          Who breed and brew along there
                              As lazy as the name.   *Mamble.*

1329.   And not a girl goes walking
                              Along the Cotswold lanes
                          But knows men's eyes in April
                              Are quicker than their brains.
>   *Cotswold Love.*

DRUMMOND, THOMAS, administrator, 10 Oct. 1797—15 April, 1840

1330. Property has its duties as well as its rights.
>   *Letter to the Earl of Donoughmore*, 22 May, 1838.

DRUMMOND, WILLIAM (OF HAWTHORNDEN), Scottish poet, 13 Dec. 1585—4 Dec. 1649

1331.   Phœbus, arise,
                          And paint the sable skies,
                          With azure, white, and red.   *Song.*

1332. Woods cut, again do grow,
       Bud doth the rose, and daisy, winter done,
       But we once dead no more do see the sun.   *Song.*

DRYDEN, JOHN, Poet Laureate, 9 Aug. 1631—1 May, 1700

1333. An horrid stillness first invades the ear,
       And in that silence we the tempest fear.
                                              Astraea Redux, 7.

1334. Whate'er he did was done with so much ease,
       In him alone 'twas natural to please.
                                 Absalom and Achitophel, I. 27.

1335. Of these the false Achitophel was first,
       A name to all succeeding ages curst.   Ibid., 150.

1336. A daring pilot in extremity,
       Pleased with the danger, when the waves went high
       He sought the storms ; but, for a calm unfit,
       Would steer too nigh the sands to boast his wit.   Ibid., 159.

1337. Great wits are sure to madness near allied,
       And thin partitions do their bounds divide.   Ibid., 163.

1338. Bankrupt of life, yet prodigal of ease.   Ibid., 168.

1339. And all to leave what with his toil he won
       To that unfeather'd two-legg'd thing, a son.   Ibid., 169.

1340. Resolv'd to ruin or to rule the state.   Ibid., 174.

1341. But wild ambition loves to slide, not stand,
       And fortune's ice prefers to virtue's land.   Ibid., 198.

1342. The wished occasion of the Plot he takes ;
       Some circumstances finds, but more he makes.   Ibid., 208.

1343. For politicians neither love nor hate.   Ibid., 223.

1344. The people's prayer, the glad diviner's theme,
       The young men's vision, and the old men's dream !
                                                        Ibid., 238.

1345. Than a successive title, long and dark,
       Drawn from the mouldy rolls of Noah's ark.   Ibid., 301.

1346. A man so various that he seem'd to be
       Not one, but all mankind's epitome :
       Stiff in opinions, always in the wrong,
       Was everything by starts and nothing long ;
       But in the course of one revolving moon,
       Was chymist, fiddler, statesman, and buffoon.   Ibid., 545.

1347. So over-violent or over-civil
       That every man with him was God or Devil.   Ibid, 557.

1348. In squandering wealth was his peculiar art ;
       Nothing went unrewarded but desert.
       Beggared by fools whom still he found too late,
       He had his jest, and they had his estate.   Ibid., 559.

1349. Did wisely from expensive sins refrain
       And never broke the Sabbath but for gain.   Ibid., 587.

*D

1350.   During his office treason was no crime,
         The sons of Belial had a glorious time.   *Ibid.*, 597.

1351.   His tribe were God Almighty's gentlemen.   *Ibid.*, 645.

1352.   Beware the fury of a patient man.   *Ibid.*, 1005.

1353.   Made still a blund'ring king of melody ;
         Spurr'd boldly on, and dash'd through thick and thin,
         Through sense and nonsense, never out nor in.
                                              Ibid., II. 413.

1354.   All human things are subject to decay,
         And, when fate summons, monarchs must obey.
                                              MacFlecknoe, 1.

1355.   The rest to some faint meaning make pretence,
         But Shadwell never deviates into sense.   *Ibid.*, 19.

1356.   And torture one poor word ten thousand ways.
                                              Ibid., 208.

1357.   She fear'd no danger, for she knew no sin.
                                  The Hind and the Panther, I. 4.

1358.   For truth has such a face and such a mien,
         As to be lov'd needs only to be seen.   *Ibid.*, 33.

1359.   By education most have been misled ;
         So they believe, because they so were bred,
         The priest continues what the nurse began,
         And thus the child imposes on the man.   *Ibid.*, III. 389.

1360.   For Tom the Second reigns like Tom the First.
                                  Epistle to Mr. Congreve, 48.

1361.   Be kind to my remains ; and O defend,
         Against your judgment, your departed friend !   *Ibid.*, 72.

1362.   Better to hunt in fields, for health unbought,
         Than fee the doctor for a nauseous draught.
         The wise, for cure, on exercise depend ;
         God never made his work for man to mend.
                                  To John Driden of Chesterton, 92.

1363.   Wit will shine
         Through the harsh cadence of a rugged line.
                                  To the Memory of Mr. Oldham, 15.

1364.   While yet a young probationer,
         And candidate of heav'n.
                                  To the Memory of Mrs. Killigrew, 15.

1365.   When rattling bones together fly
                  From the four corners of the sky.   *Ibid.*, 184.

1366.   Here lies my wife : here let her lie !
                  Now she's at rest, and so am I.
                                  Epitaph intended for Dryden's wife.

1367.   Three poets, in three distant ages born,
         Greece, Italy, and England did adorn.
         The first in loftiness of thought surpass'd ;
         The next, in majesty ; in both the last :
         The force of Nature could no further go,
         To make a third, she join'd the former two.
                                  Lines printed under a Portrait of Milton

1368.   From harmony, from heavenly harmony,
              This universal frame began :
          From harmony to harmony
          Through all the compass of the notes it ran,
          The diapason closing full in Man.
                              A Song for St. Cecilia's Day.

1369.   None but the brave deserves the fair. *Alexander's Feast,* 15.

1370.   With ravish'd ears
                   The monarch hears ;
                   Assumes the god,
                   Affects to nod,
              And seems to shake the spheres.   Ibid. 37.

1371.   Bacchus' blessings are a treasure,
                   Drinking is the soldier's pleasure ;
                   Rich the treasure,
                   Sweet the pleasure,
              Sweet is pleasure after pain.   Ibid., 56.

1372.   And thrice he routed all his foes, and thrice he slew the
              slain.   Ibid. 68.

1373.   Fallen, fallen, fallen, fallen,
                   Fallen from his high estate,
              And weltering in his blood.   Ibid., 77.

1374.   Sigh'd and look'd, and sigh'd again.   Ibid., 120.

1375.   And, like another Helen, fir'd another Troy.   Ibid., 154.

1376.   Oxford to him a dearer name shall be
          Than his own Mother University.
          Thebes did his green unknowing youth engage,
          He chooses Athens in his riper age.
                              Prologue to the University of Oxford.

1377.   For Art may err, but Nature cannot miss.
                              Fables. The Cock and the Fox, 452.

1378.   He trudg'd along unknowing what he sought,
          And whistled as he went, for want of thought.
                              Ibid., *Cymon and Iphigenia,* 84.

1379.   Of seeming arms to make a short essay,
          Then hasten to be drunk, the business of the day.   Ibid., 407.

1380.   Happy who in his verse can gently steer
          From grave to light, from pleasant to severe.
                              The Art of Poetry, i. 75.

1381.   Happy the man, and happy he alone,
              He who can call to-day his own :
              He who, secure within, can say,
          To-morrow, do thy worst, for I have liv'd to-day.
                              Imitation of Horace III. xxix. 65.

1382.   Not heav'n itself upon the past has pow'r ;
          But what has been, has been, and I have had my hour.
                              Ibid., 71.

1383. I can enjoy her while she's kind ;
       But when she dances in the wind,
       And shakes the wings, and will not stay,
       I puff the prostitute away.   [Of Fortune.]   *Ibid.*, 81

1384.   Pains of love be sweeter far
                    Than all other pleasures are.   *Tyrannic Love*, IV. i.

1385. But Shakespeare's magic could not copied be ;
       Within that circle none durst walk but he.
                                              The Tempest, prologue.

1386. I am as free as Nature first made man,
       Ere the base laws of servitude began,
       When wild in woods the noble savage ran.
                              The Conquest of Granada, part I. i. i.

1387. Forgiveness to the injured does belong ;
       For they ne'er pardon who have done the wrong.
                                          Ibid., part II. i. ii.

1388. When I consider life, 'tis all a cheat ;
       Yet, fool'd with hope, men favour the deceit ;
       Trust on, and think to-morrow will repay :
       To-morrow's falser than the former day ;
       Lies worse, and, while it says, we shall be blest
       With some new joys, cuts off what we possest.
       Strange cozenage ! None would live past years again,
       Yet all hope pleasure in what yet remain ;
       And from the dregs of life think to receive
       What the first sprightly running could not give.
                                              Aurengzebe, IV. i.

1389. Errors, like straws, upon the surface flow ;
       He who would search for pearls must dive below.
                                          All for Love, prologue.

1390. Men are but children of a larger growth.   *Ibid.*, IV. i.

1391.   There is a pleasure sure
       In being mad, which none but madmen know !
                                          The Spanish Friar, II. i.

1392. He was the man who of all modern, and perhaps ancient
poets, had the largest and most comprehensive soul. [Shakespeare.]
                                          Essay of Dramatic Poesy.

1393. He was naturally learn'd ; he needed not the spectacles of
books to read Nature ; he looked inwards, and found her there.
                                                            Ibid.

1394. He is many times flat, insipid ; his comic wit degenerating
into clenches, his serious swelling into bombast. But he is always
great when some occasion is presented to him.   *Ibid.*

1395. Here is God's plenty. [Of Chaucer's ' Canterbury Tales.']
                                                  Fables, preface.

1396. Cousin Swift, you will never be a poet.
                                          Johnson's Life of Swift.

DUDLEY, SIR HENRY BATE, clergyman and journalist, 25 Aug. 1745
    —1 Feb. 1824

1397. Wonders will never cease.   *Letter to Garrick*, 13 Sept. 1776.

DUFFERIN, COUNTESS OF, *see* Sheridan, Helen Selina

DUFFIELD, GEORGE, U.S. clergyman, 12 Sept. 1818—6 July, 1888
   1398. Stand up ! stand up for Jesus !   *Soldiers of the Cross.*

DUMAS, ALEXANDRE (THE ELDER), French novelist, 24 July, 1802—
    5 Dec. 1870

   1399. Cherchez la femme.—Look for the woman.
          Les Mohicans de Paris.—The Mohicans of Paris, III. x.

DU MAURIER, GEORGE LOUIS PALMELLA BUSSON, artist and novelist,
    6 March, 1834—6 Oct. 1896

   1400. I have no talent for making new friends, but oh, such a
genius for fidelity to old ones.   *Peter Ibbetson.*

   1401. I don't know much about his ability, but he's got a very
good bedside manner.   *Punch*, 15 March, 1884.

   1402.   A little work, a little play
          To keep us going—and so, good-day !
          A little warmth, a little light,
          Of love's bestowing—and so, good-night !
          A little fun, to match the sorrow
          Of each day's growing—and so, good-morrow !
          A little trust that when we die
          We reap our sowing ! and so—good-bye !
                       Trilby, part VIII.

DUNBAR, WILLIAM, Scottish poet, 1465 ?—1530 ?
   1403. All love is lost but upon God alone.
             The Merle and the Nightingale.

   1404.   Our plesance here is all vain glory,
          This fals world is but transitory,
          The flesh is bruckle, the Feynd is slee :—
          Timor Mortis conturbat me   *Lament for the Makaris.*

   1405. London, thou art the flower of cities all !   *London.*

DUNNE, FINLEY PETER, *see* Dooley, Mr.

DYER, SIR EDWARD, courtier, 1540—1607
   1406.   My mind to me a kingdom is ;
           Such present joys therein I find,
          That it excels all other bliss
           That earth affords or grows by kind :
          Though much I want which most would have,
          Yet still my mind forbids to crave.
             My Mind to me a Kingdom is.

DYER, JOHN, Welsh poet, baptised 13 Aug. 1699, buried 15 Dec.
    1757
   1407.   Ever charming, ever new,
          When will landscape tire the view ?
                    Grongar Hill, 5.

1408.   A little rule, a little sway,
                 A sunbeam in a winter's day,
                 Is all the proud and mighty have
                 Between the cradle and the grave.   Ibid., 89.

EDISON, THOMAS ALVA, U.S. scientist, 11 Feb. 1847—18 Oct. 1931

1409.   Genius is one per cent. inspiration and ninety-nine per cent.
perspiration.   *Newspaper interview.*

EDWARDS, OLIVER, lawyer, 1711–1791

1410.   You are a philosopher, Dr. Johnson.   I have tried too in my
time to be a philosopher ; but I don't know how, cheerfulness was
always breaking in.   Boswell's *Life of Johnson*, an. 1778.

EDWARDS, RICHARD, poet, 1523 ?—31 Oct. 1566

1411.   The falling out of faithful friends renewing is of love.
                                                       Amantium Irae.

ELIOT, GEORGE (MARY ANN *or* MARIAN EVANS, MRS. CROSS), novelist,
        22 Nov. 1819—22 Dec. 1880

1412.   Animals are such agreeable friends—they ask no questions,
they pass no criticisms.
                 Scenes of Clerical Life.   Mr. Gilfil's Love Story, vii.

1413.   It's but little good you'll do a-watering last year's crop.
                                                       Adam Bede, xviii.

1414.   We hand folks over to God's mercy, and show none ourselves.   Ibid., xlii.

1415.   The law's made to take care o' raskills.
                                          The Mill on the Floss, III. iv.

1416.   The happiest women, like the happiest nations, have no
history.   Ibid., VI. iii.

1417.   Men's men : gentle or simple, they're much of a muchness.
                                          Daniel Deronda, IV. xxxi.

1418.   O may I join the choir invisible
                 Of those immortal dead who live again
                 In minds made better by their presence.
                                                  The Choir Invisible.

ELIOT, THOMAS STEARNS, Anglo-American poet, 26 Sept. 1888—4 Jan.
       1965

1419.   When the evening is spread out against the sky
        Like a patient etherised upon a table.
                            The Love Song of J. Alfred Prufrock.

1420.   The yellow fog that rubs its back upon the window-panes.
                                                              Ibid.

1421.   I am aware of the damp souls of housemaids
        Sprouting despondently at area gates.
                                           Morning at the Window.

1422.   Wearily, as one would turn to nod good-bye to Rochefoucauld,
        If the street were time and he at the end of the street.
                                      The Boston Evening Transcript.

1423. O the moon shone bright on Mrs. Porter
And on her daughter
They wash their feet in soda water.

The Waste Land, III. *The Fire Sermon*.

1424. When lovely woman stoops to folly and
Paces about her room again, alone,
She smoothes her hair with automatic hand,
And puts a record on the gramophone.   Ibid.

1425. This is the way the world ends
Not with a bang but a whimper.   *The Hollow Men*.

1426. And when you reach the scene of crime—*Macavity's not there !*
Macavity : the Mystery Cat.

ELIZABETH, I, Queen. 7 Sept. 1533—24 March, 1603

1427. I know I have the body of a weak and feeble woman, but I
have the heart and stomach of a king, and of a king of England too.
Speech at Tilbury on the approach of the Spanish Armada, 1588.

1428. All my possessions for a moment of time.   *Last words*.

[See also Ralegh, Sir Walter.]

ELLERTON, JOHN, hymn-writer, 16 Dec. 1826—15 June, 1893

1429. Now the labourer's task is o'er ;
Now the battle-day is past ;
Now upon the farther shore
Lands the voyager at last.

Now the Labourer's Task.

ELLIOT, JEAN *or* JANE, Scottish poetess, 1727—29 March, 1805

1430. I've heard them lilting at our yowe-milking—
Lasses a-lilting before dawn of day ;
But now they are moaning on ilka green loaning—
The Flowers of the Forest are a' wede away.

The Flowers of the Forest.

ELLIOTT, CHARLOTTE, hymn-writer, 17 March, 1789—22 Sept. 1871

1431. Christian, seek not yet repose ;
Hear thy guardian angel say,
' Thou art in the midst of foes :
Watch and pray.'

Christian, seek not yet Repose.

ELLIOTT, EBENEZER, poet, 17 March, 1781—1 Dec. 1849

1432. When wilt thou save the people ?
Oh, God of mercy, when ?
Not kings and lords, but nations !
Not thrones and crowns, but men !

The People's Anthem.

ELLIS, GEORGE ('SIR GREGORY GANDER'), poet, 1753—10 April, 1815

1433.   Snowy, Flowy, Blowy,
                Showery, Flowery, Bowery,
                Hoppy, Croppy, Droppy,
                Breezy, Sneezy, Freezy.   *The Twelve Months.*

ELLIS, HENRY HAVELOCK, psychologist, 2 Feb. 1859—8 July, 1939

1434. The tide turns at low water as well as at high.
                    Impressions and Comments, i. 103.

EMERSON, RALPH WALDO, U.S. author, 25 May, 1803—27 April, 1882

1435. There is properly no history ; only biography.
                          Essays. History.

1436. A foolish consistency is the hobgoblin of little minds.
                      Ibid. Self-Reliance.

1437. To be great is to be misunderstood.   *Ibid.*

1438. All mankind love a lover.   *Ibid.|Love.*

1439. The only reward of virtue is virtue ; the only way to have a friend is to be one.   *Ibid. Friendship.*

1440. Beware when the great God lets loose a thinker on this planet.   *Ibid. Circles.*

1441. Nothing great was ever achieved without enthusiasm.
                                Ibid.

1442. Language is fossil poetry.   *Ibid. The Poet.*

1443. Every hero becomes a bore at last.
          Representative Men. Uses of Great Men.

1444. Give me health and a day, and I will make the pomp of emperors ridiculous.   *Nature*, iii.

1445. Hitch your wagon to a star.
          Society and Solitude. Civilisation.

1446. Never read any book that is not a year old.   *Ibid. Books.*

1447. If a man can write a better book, preach a better sermon, or make a better mouse-trap, than his neighbour, though he build his house in the woods, the world will make a beaten path to his door.
                            Attributed.

1448.   The hand that rounded Peter's dome,
                And groined the aisles of Christian Rome,
                Wrought in a sad sincerity ;
                Himself from God he could not free ;
                He builded better than he knew ;—
                The conscious stone to beauty grew.   *The Problem.*

1449.   Earth proudly wears the Parthenon
                As the best gem upon her zone.   *Ibid.*

1450.   The frolic architecture of the snow.   *The Snowstorm.*

1451.   Here once the embattled farmers stood,
                And fired the shot heard round the world.
      Hymn sung at the Completion of the Concord Monument.

1452.   So nigh is grandeur to our dust,
        So near is God to man,
    When Duty whispers low, *Thou must,*
        The youth replies, *I can.*   *Voluntaries*, iii.

1453.   If the red slayer thinks he slays,
        Or if the slain thinks he is slain,
    They know not well the subtle ways
        I keep, and pass, and turn again.   *Brahma.*

1454.   I am the doubter and the doubt,
        And I the hymn the Brahmin sings.   *Ibid.*

ENGLISH, THOMAS DUNN, U.S. author, 29 June, 1819—1 April, 1902

1455.   Don't you remember sweet Alice, Ben Bolt,—
        Sweet Alice whose hair was so brown,
    Who wept with delight when you gave her a smile,
        And trembled with fear at your frown ?   *Ben Bolt.*

ENNIUS, Roman poet, 239 ?—169 ? B.C.

1456.   Unus homo nobis cunctando restituit rem.
    —One man by delaying saved the State for us.   *Annals*, XII.
    [Of Quintus Fabius Maximus, Roman general.]

ERSKINE, HENRY, Scottish lawyer, 1 Nov. 1746—8 Oct. 1817

1457.   The rule of the road is a paradox quite,
        Both in riding and driving along ;
    If you keep to the left, you are sure to be right,
    If you keep to the right you are wrong.
        The Rule of the Road.

ESTIENNE, HENRI, French scholar, 1528—March, 1598

1458.   Si jeunesse savait ; si vieillesse pouvait.—If youth knew ;
if age could.   *Les Prémices*, Épigramme cxci.

EUCLID, Greek mathematician, about 300 B.C.

1459.   ὁ δὲ ἀπεκρίνατο, μὴ εἶναι βασιλικὴν ἀτραπὸν ἐπὶ γεωμετρίαν,—But he
answered that there was no royal road to geometry. [When Ptolemy
asked if there was not a shorter method.]
        Proclus, *Commentary on Euclid*, prologue G 20.

EURIPIDES, Greek dramatist, 484 ?—406 B.C.

1460.   Ἡ γλῶσσ' ὀμώμοχ', ἡ δὲ φρὴν ἀνώμοτος.—My tongue has sworn
it, but my mind's unsworn.   *Hippolytus*, 612.

1461.   Ἀσφαλὴς γάρ ἐστ' ἀμείνων ἢ θρασὺς στρατηλάτης.—A reliable
general is better than a dashing one.
        Phœnissae.—The Phœnician Maidens, 599.

1462.   Θάλασσα κλύζει πάντα τἀνθρώπων κακά.—The sea washes all
man's ills away.
    Iphigenia in Tauris—Iphigenia among the Tauri, 1193.

EUWER, ANTHONY HENDERSON, U.S. author, 11 Feb. 1877—

1463.   As a beauty I'm not a great star.
       Others are handsomer far ;
         But my face—I don't mind it
         Because I'm behind it ;
       It's the folks out in front that I jar.   *Limerick.*

EVANS, ABEL, cleric, 1679—18 Oct. 1737

1464.   Under this stone, Reader, survey
       Dead Sir John Vanbrugh's house of clay,
       Lie heavy on him, Earth, for he
       Laid many heavy loads on thee !
         Epitaph on Vanbrugh, architect and dramatist.

EVANS, MARY ANN OR MARIAN, *see* Eliot, George

EVELYN, JOHN, diarist, 31 Oct. 1620—27 Feb. 1706

1465. A studious decliner of honours and titles.
              Diary, introduction.

1466. I saw *Hamlet Prince of Denmark* played ; but now the old
plays begin to disgust this refined age.   Ibid., 26 Nov. 1661.

EVERETT, DAVID, U.S. author, 29 March, 1770—21 Dec. 1813

1467.   You'd scarce expect one of my age
       To speak in public on the stage ;
       And if I chance to fall below
       Demosthenes or Cicero,
       Don't view me with a critic's eye,
       But pass my imperfections by.
       Large streams from little fountains flow,
       Tall oaks from little acorns grow.
        Lines written for a School Declamation.

FABER, FREDERICK WILLIAM, cleric, 28 June, 1814—26 Sept. 1863

1468.   Angels of Jesus, angels of light,
       Singing to welcome the pilgrims of the night !
           Hark ! hark, my soul !

1469.   Small things are best ;
         Grief and unrest
       To rank and wealth are given ;
         But little things
         On little wings
       Bear little souls to heaven.
        Written in a Little Lady's Little Album.

FARMER, EDWARD, poet, 1809 ?—1876

1470. I have no pain, dear mother, now ; but, oh ! I am so dry :
   Just moisten poor Jim's lips once more ; and, mother, do
     not cry !   *The Collier's Dying Child.*

FARQUHAR, GEORGE, Irish dramatist, 1678—29 April, 1707.[*]

    1471. Lady Bountiful.   *The Beaux' Stratagem*, dramatis personæ.

    1472. I believe they talked of me, for they laughed consumedly.
                                   Ibid., III. i.

    1473. 'Twas for the good of my country that I should be abroad.
                                   Ibid., ii.

    1474. Spare all I have, and take my life.   Ibid., v. ii.

FERRIAR, JOHN, Scottish doctor, 21 Nov. 1761—4 Feb. 1815

    1475. Now cheaply bought for thrice their weight in gold.
            Illustrations of Sterne. Bibliomania, 65.

FEUERBACH, LUDWIG ANDREAS, German philosopher, 28 July, 1804—
    13 Sept. 1872

    1476. Der Mensch ist was er isst.—Man is what he eats.
        Preface to Moleschott's *Lehre der Nahrungsmittel für das Volk.*

FIELD, EUGENE, U.S. author, 2 or 3 Sept. 1850—4 Nov. 1895

    1477.   A little peach in the orchard grew.
                                   The Little Peach.

    1478.   So shut your eyes while mother sings
             Of wonderful sights that be,
       And you shall see the beautiful things
             As you rock on the misty sea
             Where the old shoe rocked the fishermen three,
                    Wynken,
                    Blynken,
                    And Nod.
                                     Dutch Lullaby.

    1479.   The little toy dog is covered with dust,
             But sturdy and staunch he stands ;
       And the little toy soldier is red with rust,
             And his musket moulds in his hands ;
       Time was when the little toy dog was new,
             And the soldier was passing fair ;
       And that was the time when our Little Boy Blue
             Kissed them and put them there.   *Little Boy Blue.*

    1480.   Where the Dinkey-Bird is singing
             In the Amfalula-Tree.   *The Dinkey-Bird.*

FIELDING, HENRY, author, 22 April, 1707—8 Oct. 1754

    1481. Love and scandal are the best sweeteners of tea.
                  Love in Several Masques. IV. xi.

    1482. All Nature wears one universal grin.
                    Tom Thumb the Great, I. i.

    1483. To sun myself in Huncamunca's eyes.   Ibid., iii.

1484.   Lo, when two dogs are fighting in the streets,
            With a third dog one of the two dogs meets ;
            With angry teeth he bites him to the bone,
            And this dog smarts for what that dog has done.

                                                            Ibid., vi.

1485.   Oh ! the roast beef of England,
                   And old England's roast beef.
                                      The Grub Street Opera, III. iii.

1486. Never trust the man who hath reason to suspect that you
know he hath injured you.   Jonathan Wild, III. iv.

1487. Thwackum was for doing justice, and leaving mercy to heaven.
                                                   Tom Jones, III. x.

1488. An amiable weakness.   Ibid., x. viii.

FISHER OF KILVERSTONE, JOHN ARBUTHNOT FISHER, 1ST BARON,
       admiral, 25 Jan. 1841—10 July, 1920

1489. Sack the lot !   Letter to the Times, 2 Sept. 1919.

FITZGERALD, EDWARD, translator, 31 March, 1809—14 June, 1883

1490.   Awake ! for Morning in the Bowl of Night
            Has flung the Stone that puts the Stars to flight,
                And Lo ! the Hunter of the East has caught
            The Sultán's Turret in a Noose of Light.
                                   Rubáiyát of Omar Khayyám, ed. I. 1.

1491.   Come, fill the Cup, and in the Fire of Spring
            The Winter Garment of Repentance fling :
                The Bird of Time has but a little way
            To fly—and Lo ! the Bird is on the Wing.   Ibid., 7.

1492.   Each Morn a thousand Roses brings, you say :
            Yes, but where leaves the Rose of Yesterday ?

                                                      Ibid., ed. IV. 9.

1493.   Here with a Loaf of Bread beneath the Bough,
            A Flask of Wine, a Book of Verse—and Thou
                Beside me singing in the Wilderness—
            And Wilderness is Paradise enow.   Ibid., ed. I. 11.

1494.   A Book of Verses underneath the Bough,
            A Jug of Wine, a Loaf of Bread—and Thou
                Beside me singing in the Wilderness—
            Oh, Wilderness were Paradise enow !   Ibid., ed. IV. 12.

1495.   Ah, take the Cash, and let the Credit go,
            Nor heed the rumble of a distant Drum !   Ibid., 13.

1496.   The Worldly Hope men set their Hearts upon
            Turns Ashes—or it prospers ; and anon,
                Like Snow upon the Desert's dusty Face
            Lighting a little Hour or two—is gone.   Ibid., ed. I. 14.

1497.   This batter'd Caravanserai
            Whose Doorways are alternate Night and Day.   Ibid., 16.

1498. They say the Lion and the Lizard keep
       The Courts where Jamshyd gloried and drank deep ;
         And Bahrám, that great Hunter—the Wild Ass
       Stamps o'er his Head, and he lies fast asleep.   Ibid., 17.

1499. I sometimes think that never blows so red
       The Rose as where some buried Caesar bled ;
         That every Hyacinth the Garden wears
       Dropt in its Lap from some once lovely Head.   Ibid., 18.

1500. *To-morrow ?*—Why, To-morrow I may be
       Myself with Yesterday's Sev'n Thousand Years.   Ibid., 20.

1501. Oh, come with old Khayyám, and leave the Wise
       To talk ; one thing is certain, that Life flies ;
         One thing is certain, and the Rest is Lies ;
       The Flower that once has blown for ever dies.   Ibid., 26.

1502. Myself when young did eagerly frequent
       Doctor and Saint, and heard great Argument
         About it and about : but evermore
       Came out by the same Door as in I went.   Ibid., 27.

1503. I came like Water, and like Wind I go.   Ibid., 28·

1504. Into this Universe, and *why* not knowing,
       Nor *whence*, like Water willy-nilly flowing :
         And out of it, as Wind along the Waste,
       I know not *whither*, willy-nilly blowing.   Ibid., 29.

1505. There was a Door to which I found no Key :
       There was a Veil past which I could not see.   Ibid., 32.

1506. One Moment in Annihilation's Waste,
       One Moment, of the Well of life to taste—
         The Stars are setting and the Caravan
       Starts for the Dawn of Nothing—Oh, make haste !   Ibid., 38.

1507. The Grape that can with Logic absolute
       The Two-and-Seventy jarring Sects confute.   Ibid, 43.

1508. 'Tis all a Chequer-board of Nights and Days
       Where Destiny with Men for Pieces plays :
         Hither and thither moves, and mates, and slays,
       And one by one back in the Closet lays.   Ibid., 49.

1509. The Ball no Question makes of Ayes or Noes,
       But Right or Left as strikes the Player goes ;
         And He that toss'd Thee down into the Field,
       He knows about it all—HE knows—HE knows !   Ibid., 50.

1510. The Moving Finger writes ; and, having writ,
       Moves on : nor all thy Piety nor Wit
         Shall lure it back to cancel half a Line,
       Nor all thy Tears wash out a Word of it.   Ibid., 51.

1511. And that inverted Bowl we call the Sky,
       Whereunder crawling coop't we live and die,
         Lift not thy hands to *It* for help—for It
       Rolls impotently on as Thou or I.   Ibid., 52.

1512.   Oh Thou, who didst with Pitfall and with Gin
        Beset the Road I was to wander in,
           Thou wilt not with Predestination round
        Enmesh me, and impute my Fall to Sin ?   *Ibid.*, 57.

1513.   Oh, Thou, who Man of baser Earth didst make,
        And who with Eden didst devise the Snake ;
           For all the Sin wherewith the Face of Man
        Is blacken'd, Man's Forgiveness give—and take !   *Ibid.*, 58.

1514.   Said one—' Folks of a surly Tapster tell,
        And daub his Visage with the Smoke of Hell ;
           They talk of some strict Testing of us—Pish !
        He's a Good Fellow, and 'twill all be well.'   *Ibid.*, 64.

1515.   I often wonder what the Vintners buy
        One half so precious as the Goods they sell.   *Ibid.*, 71.

1516.   Alas, that Spring should vanish with the Rose !
        That Youth's sweet-scented Manuscript should close !
                                            Ibid., 72.

1517.   Ah Love ! could thou and I with Fate conspire
        To grasp this sorry Scheme of Things entire,
           Would not we shatter it to bits—and then
        Re-mould it nearer to the Heart's Desire !
                                            Ibid., 73.

1518.   And when Thyself with shining Foot shall pass
        Among the Guests Star-scatter'd on the Grass,
           And in thy joyous Errand reach the Spot
        Where I made one—turn down an empty Glass !
                                            Ibid., 75.

1519. And when like her, O Saki, you shall pass.   *Ibid.*, ed. IV. 101.

1520. A Mr. Wilkinson, a clergyman.   *Line parodying Wordsworth.*

FITZSIMMONS, ROBERT, pugilist, 4 June, 1862—22 Oct. 1917
    1521. The bigger they come, the harder they fall.
           Before his fight with Jeffries in San Francisco, 25 July, 1902.

FLECKER, JAMES ELROY, poet, 5 Nov. 1884—3 Jan. 1915
1522.   A ship, an isle, a sickle moon—
           With few but with how splendid stars
          The mirrors of the sea are strewn
             Between their silver bars !
                        A Ship, an Isle, a Sickle Moon.

1523. For pines are gossip pines the wide world through.   *Brumana.*

1524. With her fair and floral air and the love that lingers there,
        And the streets where the great men go.   [Oxford.]
                                  The Dying Patriot.

1525. I have seen old ships sail like swans asleep
        Beyond the village which men still call Tyre.
                                    The Old Ships.

1526. Sweet to ride forth at evening from the wells,
        When shadows pass gigantic on the sand,
        And softly through the silence beat the bells
        Along the Golden Road to Samarkand.   *Hassan*, v. ii.

FLEMING, MARGARET, infant prodigy, 15 Jan. 1803—19 Dec. 1811

1527. A direful death indeed they had
       That would put any parent mad
       But she was more than usual calm
       She did not give a singel dam.   *Journal,* 29.

1528. I am now going to tell you the horrible and wretched plaege
that my multiplication table gives me ; the most devilish thing is
8 time 8 and 7 time 7 ; it is what nature itselfe cant endure.   Ibid., 47.

FLETCHER, ANDREW, Scottish patriot, 1655—Sept. 1716

1529. If a man were permitted to make all the ballads, he need not
care who should make the laws of a nation.
                 Letter to the Marquis of Montrose, and Others.

FLETCHER, JOHN, dramatist, born Dec. 1579, buried 29 Aug. 1625

1530. Care-charming Sleep, thou easer of all woes,
       Brother to Death, sweetly thyself dispose
       On this afflicted prince ; fall like a cloud
       In gentle showers ; give nothing that is loud
       Or painful to his slumbers ;—easy, light,
       And as a purling stream, thou son of night,
       Pass by his troubled senses ; sing his pain
       Like hollow murmuring wind or silver rain ;
       Into this prince gently, oh, gently slide,
       And kiss him into slumbers like a bride !
                                 Valentinian, V. ii.

1531. God Lyaeus, ever young,
       Ever honour'd, ever sung ;
       Stain'd with blood of lusty grapes,
       In a thousand lusty shapes.   Ibid., viii.

1532. Weep no more, nor sigh, nor groan ;
       Sorrow calls no time that's gone ;
       Violets plucked the sweetest rain
       Makes not fresh nor grow again.
                            The Queen of Corinth, III. ii.

1533.   Hence, all you vain delights,
        As short as are the nights
            Wherein you spend your folly !
        There's naught in this life sweet,
        If man were wise to see't,
            But only Melancholy,
            O sweetest Melancholy !
                            The Nice Valour, III. iii.

1534. Fountain heads and pathless groves,
       Places which pale passion loves.   Ibid.

1535. Man is his own star, and the soul that can
       Render an honest and a perfect man
       Commands all light, all influence, all fate.
       Nothing to him falls early, or too late.
       Our acts our angels are, or good or ill,
       Our fatal shadows that walk by us still.
                            Upon an Honest Man's Fortune

1536.   Primrose, first-born child of Ver,
                Merry springtime's harbinger,
                    With her bells dim.   *The Two Noble Kinsmen*, i. i.

FOCH, FERDINAND, Marshal of France, 2 Oct. 1851—20 March, 1929

1537. Mon centre cède, ma droite recule, situation excellente.
J'attaque !—My centre is yielding, my right is withdrawing.   Situation
excellent.   I shall attack.
                    Message to Joffre, First Battle of the Marne, Sept. 1914.

FOOTE, SAMUEL, dramatist, baptised 27 Jan. 1720, died 21 Oct. 1777

1538.   Born in a cellar . . . and living in a garret.   *The Author*, II.

1539. So she went into the garden to cut a cabbage leaf to make
an apple pie ; and at the same time a great she-bear, coming up the
street, pops its head into the shop.   ' What ! no soap ? '   So he died,
and she very imprudently married the barber ; and there were present
the Picninnies, and the Joblillies, and the Garyulies, and the Grand
Panjandrum himself, with the little round button at top, and they all
fell to playing the game of catch as catch can, till the gunpowder ran
out at the heels of their boots.   *Nonsense written as a memory test.*

FORD, JOHN, dramatist, baptised 17 April, 1586, died 1639 ?

1540. We can drink till all look blue.   *The Lady's Trial*, II. ii.

FORD, LENA GUILBERT, U.S. poetess, died 1918

1541. Keep the home fires burning, while your hearts are yearning,
            Though your lads are far away they dream of home ;
        There's a silver lining through the dark clouds shining,
            Turn the dark cloud inside out, till the boys come home.
                                Keep the Home Fires Burning.

FORGY, HOWELL MAURICE, U.S. naval chaplain, 18 Jan. 1908—

1542. Praise the Lord and pass the ammunition.
                                At Pearl Harbour, 7 Dec. 1941.

FOSS, SAM WALTER, U.S. librarian, 19 June, 1858—26 Feb. 1911

1543.   W'en you see a man in woe,
                Walk right up and say, ' hullo.'
                Say ' hullo ' and ' how d'ye do,'
                ' How's the world a-usin' you ? '   *Hullo.*

FOSTER, STEPHEN COLLINS, U.S. song-writer, 4 July, 1826—13 Jan.
    1864

1544.   The day goes by like a shadow o'er the heart,
                With sorrow where all was delight ;
            The time has come when the darkies have to part ;
                Then my old Kentucky home, good night !
                                My Old Kentucky Home.

1545.   'Way down upon de Swanee Ribber.
                                        The Old Folks at Home.

1546.   All up and down de whole creation,
            Sadly I roam,
        Still longing for de old plantation,
            And for de old folks at home.   Ibid.

1547.   Hard times, come again no more.   *Song.*

1548.   I'm coming, I'm coming,
        For my head is bending low,
        I hear the gentle voices calling
            ' Poor old Joe.'   *Poor old Joe.*

1549.   He had no wool on de top of his head,
        In de place where de wool ought to grow.   *Uncle Ned.*

FOUCHÉ, JOSEPH, Duke of Otranto, French politician, 29 May, 1763—
        25 Dec. 1820

    1550.   C'est plus qu'un crime ; c'est une faute.—It is worse than a
crime ; it is a blunder.
        Of the murder of the Duc d'Enghien by Napoleon in 1804.

FOX, CHARLES JAMES, statesman, 24 Jan. 1749—13 Sept. 1806

    1551.   How much the greatest event it is that ever happened in the
world ! and how much the best ! [The fall of the Bastille.]
                        Letter to Fitzpatrick, 30 July, 1789.

FRANCE, ANATOLE (JACQUES ANATOLE THIBAULT), French author,
        16 April, 1844—12 Oct. 1924

    1552.   Le bon critique est celui qui raconte les aventures de son
âme au milieu des chefs-d'œuvre.—The good critic is he who relates
the adventures of his soul among masterpieces.
                        La Vie littéraire—The Literary Life, preface.

FRANCIS I, King of France, 12 Sept. 1494—31 March, 1547

    1553.   Tout est perdu fors l'honneur.—All is lost except honour.
                Traditional words after defeat and capture at Pavia, 1525.

FRANKLIN, BENJAMIN, U.S. statesman and philosopher, 17 Jan. 1706—
        17 April, 1790

    1554.   Remember that time is money. *Advice to a Young Tradesman.*

    1555.   There never was a good war or a bad peace.
                        Letter to Josiah Quincy, 11 Sept. 1773.

    1556.   Yes, we must, indeed, all hang together, or, most assuredly,
we shall all hang separately.
                At signing of the Declaration of Independence, 4 July, 1776.

    1557.   He has paid dear, very dear, for his whistle.   *The Whistle.*

    1558.   He [the sun] gives light as soon as he rises. [Advocating
daylight saving.]   *An Economical Project.*

1559.　　　　　　　　　　Here Skugg lies snug
　　　　　　　　　　　　As a bug in a rug.
　　　　　　　　　Letter to Miss G. Shipley, 26 Sept. 1772.

FREDERICK II, THE GREAT, King of Prussia, 24 Jan. 1712—17 Aug.
　　　1786

　　1560.—Hunde, wollt ihr ewig leben ?—Dogs, would you live for
ever ?　　　　　　　*When the Guards hesitated, at Köln*, 18 June, 1757.

FREEMAN, JOHN, poet, 29 Jan. 1880—23 Sept. 1929

1561.　　　　　　　　It was the lovely moon—she lifted
　　　　　　　　　　Slowly her white brow among
　　　　　　　　　　Bronze cloud-waves that ebbed and drifted
　　　　　　　　　　Faintly, faintlier afar.　　　*It was the Lovely Moon.*

FREEMAN, THOMAS, epigrammatist, *fl.* 1614

1562.　　　　　　　　I love thee, Cornwall, and will ever,
　　　　　　　　　　　And hope to see thee once again !
　　　　　　　　　　For why ?—thine equal knew I never
　　　　　　　　　　　For honest minds and active men.
　　　　　　　　　　　　　　　　　　Encomion Cornubiae.

FRERE, JOHN HOOKHAM, 21 May, 1769—7 Jan. 1846

1563.　　　　　　The feather'd race with pinions skim the air—
　　　　　　　　　Not so the mackerel, and still less the bear !
　　　　　　　　　　　　　　　　　　Progress of Man, 34.

FROHMAN, CHARLES, U.S. theatrical manager, 17 June, 1860—7 May,
　　　1915

　　1564. Why fear death ?　It is the most beautiful adventure in life.
　　　　　　　　　　　　Before going down in the Lusitania.

FROST, ROBERT LEE, U.S. poet, 26 March, 1875—29 Jan. 1963

1565.　　　　　　　I'm going out to clean the pasture spring ;
　　　　　　　　　I'll only stop to rake the leaves away
　　　　　　　　　(And wait to watch the water clear, I may) :
　　　　　　　　　I shan't be gone long.—You come too.　　*The Pasture.*

1566.　　　　Something there is that doesn't love a wall.
　　　　　　　　　　　　　　　　　　Mending Wall.

1567.　　　　My apple trees will never get across
　　　　　　　And eat the cones under his pines, I tell him.
　　　　　　　He only says, ' Good fences make good neighbours.'
　　　　　　　　　　　　　　　　　　Ibid.

1568.　　　　　　　I shall be telling this with a sigh
　　　　　　　　　Somewhere ages and ages hence :
　　　　　　　　　Two roads diverged in a wood, and I—
　　　　　　　　　I took the one less travelled by,
　　　　　　　　　And that has made all the difference.
　　　　　　　　　　　　　　　　　　The Road not taken.

FULLER, THOMAS, cleric, June, 1608—16 Aug. 1661

1569. A little skill in antiquity inclines a man to Popery ; but depth in that study brings him about again to our religion.
The Holy and Profane State.   The True Church Antiquary.

1570. They that marry ancient people, merely in expectation to bury them, hang themselves in hope that one will come and cut the halter.   *Ibid. Of Marriage.*

1571. Light, God's eldest daughter, is a principal beauty in a building.   *Ibid. Of Building.*

1572. A proverb is much matter decocted into few words.
The History of the Worthies of England, ii.

GAINSBOROUGH, THOMAS, painter, baptised 14 May, 1727, died 2 Aug. 1788

1573. We are all going to heaven, and Van Dyck is of the company.
Last words.

GALILEI, GALILEO, Italian scientist, 15 Feb. 1564—8 Jan. 1642

1574. Eppur si muove.—Yet it does move.
Traditional words after being forced to recant his doctrine that the earth moves round the sun.

GANDER, SIR GREGORY, *see* Ellis, George

GARFIELD, JAMES ABRAM, U.S. President, 19 Nov. 1831—19 Sept. 1881

1575. Fellow citizens ! God reigns, and the Government at Washington still lives !   *Speech on the assassination of Lincoln,* 1865.

GARRICK, DAVID, actor, 19 Feb. 1717—20 Jan. 1779

1576.   Heart of oak are our ships,
             Heart of oak are our men :
                We always are ready,
                Steady, boys, steady !
             We'll fight and we'll conquer again and again.
Heart of Oak.

1577.   Here lies Nolly Goldsmith, for shortness call'd Noll,
             Who wrote like an angel, but talk'd like poor Poll.
Impromptu epitaph on Goldsmith.

1578.   A fellow-feeling makes one wondrous kind.
Prologue on quitting the Theatre, 1776.

GARRISON, WILLIAM LLOYD, U.S. reformer, 10 Dec. 1805—24 May, 1879

1579. I am in earnest—I will not equivocate—I will not excuse—I will not retreat a single inch—and I will be heard.
The Liberator, 1 Jan. 1832.

GARTH, SIR SAMUEL, doctor, 1661—18 Jan. 1719

1580.   Hard was their lodging, homely was their food ;
               For all their luxury was doing good.   *Claremont*, 148.

GASKELL, ELIZABETH CLEGHORN, novelist, 29 Sept. 1810—12 Nov. 1865

  1581. A man is *so* in the way in the house.   *Cranford*, i.

  1582. Bombazine would have shown a deeper sense of her loss.
                                                          Ibid., vii.

GAY, JOHN, poet, baptised 16 Sept. 1685, died 4 Dec. 1732

1583.   All in the Downs the fleet was moor'd.
                    Sweet William's Farewell to Black-eyed Susan, 1.

1584.   'Adieu ! ' she cries ; and wav'd her lily hand.   Ibid., 48.

1585.   Life is a jest ; and all things show it.
               I thought so once ; but now I know it.
                                                          My own Epitaph.

1586.   Where yet was ever found a mother,
               Who'd give her booby for another ?
                    Fables, I. iii.   *The Mother, the Nurse, and the Fairy*, 33.

1587.   And when a lady's in the case,
               You know, all other things give place.
                         Ibid., l.   *The Hare and many Friends*, 41.

1588.   O ruddier than the cherry !
                  O sweeter than the berry !
                     O nymph more bright
                     Than moonshine night,
                  Like kidlings blithe and merry !
                                                  Acis and Galatea, 11.

1589.   'Tis woman that seduces all mankind,
        By her we first were taught the wheedling arts.
                                            The Beggar's Opera, I. ii

1590.   By keeping men off, you keep them on.   Ibid., viii.

1591.   For on the rope that hangs my dear
                  Depends poor Polly's life.   Ibid., x.

1592.   If the heart of a man is deprest with cares,
        The mist is dispell'd when a woman appears.   Ibid., II. iii.

1593.   The fly that sips treacle is lost in the sweets.   Ibid., viii.

1594.   How happy could I be with either
                  Were t'other dear charmer away !   Ibid., xiii

1595.   One wife is too much for most husbands to hear
        But two at a time there's no mortal can bear. Ibid., III. xi.

1596.   The charge is prepar'd ; the lawyers are met ;
        The judges all rang'd (a terrible show !).   Ibid., xiii.

GEORGE II, King, 10 Nov. 1683—25 Oct. 1760

  1597. Oh ! he is mad, is he ?   Then I wish he would *bite* some other
of my generals.   *Of General Wolfe.*

1598. Non, j'aurai des maîtresses.—No, I shall have mistresses.
When the dying Queen urged him marry again.
[Her reply was 'Ah ! mon Dieu ! cela n'empêche pas.'—' Good Lord, that doesn't prevent it.']

GEORGE V, King, 3 June, 1865—20 Jan. 1936
1599. How is the Empire ? *Last words.*

GEORGE, HENRY, U.S. economist, 2 Sept. 1839—29 Oct. 1897
1600. A crank is a little thing that makes revolutions.
Attributed.

GIBBON, EDWARD, historian, 27 April, 1737—16 Jan. 1794
1601. History ; which is, indeed, little more than the register of the crimes, follies, and misfortunes of mankind.
Decline and Fall of the Roman Empire, iii.

1602. If a man were called to fix the period in the history of the world during which the condition of the human race was most happy and prosperous, he would, without hesitation, name that which elapsed from the death of Domitian to the accession of Commodus. Ibid.

1603. Corruption, the most infallible symptom of constitutional liberty. Ibid., xxi.

1604. In every deed of mischief he had a heart to resolve, a head to contrive, and a hand to execute. [Andronicus I.] Ibid., xlviii.

1605. I sighed as a lover, I obeyed as a son. *Autobiography.*

GIBBONS, THOMAS, dissenting minister, 31 May, 1720—22 Feb. 1785
1606. That man may last, but never lives,
Who much receives, but nothing gives ;
Whom none can love, whom none can thank,—
Creation's blot, creation's blank. *When Jesus dwelt.*

GIFFORD, RICHARD, cleric, 1725—1 March, 1807
1607. Verse softens toil, however rude the sound ;
She feels no biting pang the while she sings,
Nor, as she turns the giddy wheel around,
Revolves the sad vicissitude of things. *Comtemplation.*

GIFFORD, WILLIAM, editor of the ' Quarterly,' April, 1756—31 Dec. 1826
1608. His namby-pamby madrigals of love. *The Baviad*, 176·
1609. The ropy drivel of rheumatic brains. Ibid., 279.

GILBERT, SIR WILLIAM SCHWENCK, dramatist, 18 Nov. 1836—29 May, 1911
1610. There were captains by the hundred, there were baronets by dozens. *Bab Ballads. Ferdinando and Elvira.*
1611. Then I waved the turtle soup enthusiastically round me. Ibid.

1612.   Oh, I am a cook and a captain bold,
         And the mate of the *Nancy* brig,
         And a bo'sun tight, and a midshipmite,
         And the crew of the captain's gig.
                    Ibid. *The Yarn of the ' Nancy Bell.'*

1613.   Then they began to sing
              That extremely lovely thing
         ' *Scherzando ! ma non troppo, ppp.*'
                    Ibid. *The Story of Prince Agib.*

1614. The padre said, ' Whatever have you been and gone and
      done ? '
                    Ibid. *Gentle Alice Brown.*

1615.   She may very well pass for forty-three
         In the dusk, with a light behind her !
                                   Trial by Jury.

1616.   And many a burglar I've restored
         To his friends and his relations.   Ibid.

1617. Time was when Love and I were well acquainted.
                                   The Sorcerer, I.

1618. Fled gilded dukes and belted earls before me—
      Ah me, I was a pale young curate then !   Ibid.

1619.   Now to the banquet we press ;
              Now for the eggs and the ham ;
              Now for the mustard and cress,
              Now for the strawberry jam !   Ibid.

1620.   ' Though " Bother it," I may
              Occasionally say,
         I never use a big, big D.'
                    ' What, never ? '
                    ' No, never ! '
                    ' What, *never ?* '
                    ' Hardly ever ! '   *H.M.S. Pinafore*, I.

1621. And so do his sisters and his cousins and his aunts !   Ibid.

1622   When I was a lad I served a term
        As office boy to an Attorney's firm.
        I cleaned the windows and I swept the floor,
        And I polished up the handle of the big front door.
        I polished up that handle so carefullee
        That now I am the ruler of the Queen's Navee !   Ibid.

1623.   I always voted at my party's call,
        And I never thought of thinking for myself at all.   Ibid.

1624.   Things are seldom what they seem,
         Skim milk masquerades as cream.   Ibid., II.

1625.   He is an Englishman !
              For he himself has said it,
              And it's greatly to his credit,
         That he is an Englishman !   Ibid.

1626.   For he might have been a Roosian,
         A French, or Turk, or Proosian,
         Or perhaps Itali-an !   Ibid.

1627.   When constabulary duty's to be done,
           A policeman's lot is not a happy one.
                                             The Pirates of Penzance, ii.

1628.   When the enterprising burglar's not a-burgling.   Ibid.

1629.   If you're anxious for to shine in the high aesthetic line as a man
           of culture rare.   *Patience*, i.

1630.   The meaning doesn't matter if it's only idle chatter of a
           transcendental kind.   Ibid.

1631.   If this young man expresses himself in terms too deep for *me*,
           Why, what a very singularly deep young man this deep young
           man must be !   Ibid.

1632.   An attachment *à la* Plato for a bashful young potato, or a
           not-too-French French bean.   Ibid.

1633.   The consequence was he was lost to*tally*,
           And married a girl in the *corps de bally* !   Ibid., ii.

1634.   By no endeavour
                Can magnet ever
           Attract a Silver Churn !   Ibid.

1635.   A most intense young man,
                A soulful-eyed young man,
           An ultra-poetical, super-aesthetical,
                Out-of-the-way young man !   Ibid.

1636.   Francesca di Rimini, miminy, piminy,
           Je-ne-sais-quoi young man !
                                                                  Ibid.

1637.   A greenery-yallery, Grosvenor Gallery
           Foot-in-the-grave young man !   Ibid.

1638.   Bow, bow, ye lower middle classes !   *Iolanthe*, i.

1639.   A pleasant occupation for
           A rather susceptible Chancellor !   Ibid.

1640.   I often think it's comical
                How nature always does contrive
           That every boy and every gal
                That's born into the world alive
           Is either a little Liberal
                Or else a little Conservative.   Ibid., ii.

1641.   The House of Peers, throughout the war,
           Did nothing in particular
           And did it very well.   Ibid.

1642.   Politics we bar,
                   They are not our bent ;
                On the whole we are
                   Not intelligent.   *Princess Ida*, i.

1643   We will hang you, never fear,
           Most politely, most politely !   Ibid.

1644.   Man's a ribald—Man's a rake,
           Man is Nature's sole mistake !   Ibid., ii.

1645.   Oh, don't the days seem lank and long
                  When all goes right and nothing goes wrong,
                  And isn't your life extremely flat
                  With nothing whatever to grumble at !   Ibid., III.

  1646. Pooh-Bah (Lord High Everything Else).
                                        The Mikado, Dramatis Personae.

1647. I can trace my ancestry back to a protoplasmal primordial
             atomic globule.   Ibid., I.

1648. As some day it may happen that a victim must be found,
             I've got a little list—I've got a little list
         Of society offenders who might well be underground,
             And who never would be missed—who never would be
             missed !   Ibid.

1649.   My object all sublime
                        I shall achieve in time—
                  To let the punishment fit the crime.   Ibid., II.

1650.   I drew my snickersnee !

   1651. Something lingering, with boiling oil in it, I fancy.   Ibid.

   1652. Merely corroborative detail, intended to give artistic verisi-
militude to an otherwise bald and unconvincing narrative.   Ibid.

1653.   The flowers that bloom in the spring,
                                      Tra la,
                  Have nothing to do with the case.   Ibid.

   1654. All baronets are bad.   *Ruddigore*. I.

1655.   Cheerily carols the lark
                              Over the cot.
                        Merrily whistles the clerk
                              Scratching a blot.   Ibid.

   1656. Some word that teems with hidden meaning.—like ' Basing-
stoke.'   Ibid., II.

1657.   It's a song of a merryman, moping mum,
                  Whose soul was sad, and whose glance was glum,
                  Who sipped no sup, and who craved no crumb,
                  As he sighed for the love of a ladye.
                                        The Yeoman of the Guard, I.

1658.   He led his regiment from behind—
                  He found it less exciting.   *The Gondoliers*, I.

1659.   Of that there is no manner of doubt—
                  No probable, possible shadow of doubt—
                  No possible doubt whatever.   Ibid.

1660.   A taste for drink, combined with gout,
                  Had doubled him up for ever.   Ibid.

1661.   Oh, 'tis a glorious thing, I ween,
                  To be a regular Royal Queen !
                  No half-and-half affair, I mean,
                  But a right-down regular Royal Queen !   Ibid.

1662.   Take a pair of sparkling eyes.   Ibid., II.

1663.   When everyone is somebodee,
                        Then no one's anybody.   Ibid.

1664.
> There was an old man of St. Bees,
> Who was stung in the arm by a wasp.
> When asked, ' Does it hurt ? '
> He replied, ' No, it doesn't.
> I'm so glad it wasn't a hornet.' *Limerick.*

GILLILAN, STRICKLAND, U.S. journalist, 1869— 1954

1665.
> Bilin' down his repoort, wuz Finnigin !
> An' he writed this here : ' Muster Flannigan :
> Off ag'in, on ag'in,
> Gone ag'in.—Finnigin.' *Finnigin to Flannigan.*

GILMAN, CHARLOTTE PERKINS STETSON, U.S. author, 3 July, 1860—
11 Aug. 1935

1666.
> Cried all, ' Before such things can come,
> You idiotic child,
> *You must alter Human Nature ! '*
> And they all sat back and smiled. *Similar Cases.*

1667.
> I do not want to be a fly ;
> I want to be a worm ! *A Conservative.*

GLADSTONE, WILLIAM EWART, Prime Minister, 29 Dec. 1809—19 May,
1898

1668. Decision by majorities is as much an expedient as lighting
by gas. *Speech, House of Commons*, 21 Jan. 1858.

1669. These gentlemen [the Irish Land League] wish to march
through rapine to the disintegration and dismemberment of the
Empire. *Speech, Knowsley*, 27 Oct. 1881.

1670. An old parliamentary hand.
Speech, House of Commons, 21 Jan. 1886.

1671. All the world over, I will back the masses against the classes.
Speech, Liverpool, 28 June, 1886.

GLOUCESTER, WILLIAM HENRY, DUKE OF, 14 Nov. 1743—25 Aug. 1805

1672. Another damned, thick, square book ! Always scribble,
scribble, scribble ! Eh ! Mr. Gibbon ? *Attributed.*

GODLEY, ALFRED DENNIS, scholar, 22 Jan. 1856—27 June, 1925

1673.
> What is this that roareth thus ?
> Can it be a Motor Bus ?
> Yes, the smell and hideous hum
> Indicat Motorem Bum. *Motor Bus.*

E

GOETHE, JOHANN WOLFGANG VON, German poet, 28 Aug. 1749—
    22 March, 1832

1674. Kennst du das Land, wo die Zitronen blühn ?
      Im dunkeln Laub die Gold-Orangen glühn,
      Ein sanfter Wind vom blauen Himmel weht,
      Die Myrte still und hoch der Lorbeer steht.
      —Knowest thou the land where the lemon-trees bloom ? In the
          dark foliage the golden oranges gleam, a soft wind blows
          from the blue heavens, the myrtle is still and the laurel
          stands high.   *Wilhelm Meister*, III. i.

1675. Ohne Hast, aber ohn Rast.—Without haste, but without rest.
                                                                Motto.

1676. Mehr Licht !—More light !   *Attributed dying words.*

GOLDBERG, ISAAC, U.S. critic, 1 Nov. 1887—14 July, 1938

1677.   Diplomacy is to do and say
              The nastiest thing in the nicest way.   *The Reflex.*

GOLDSMITH, OLIVER, Irish poet, 10 Nov. 1728—4 April, 1774

1678.   The king himself has follow'd her,—
                When she has walk'd before.
                                    Elegy on Mrs. Mary Blaize.

1679.   The doctors found, when she was dead,—
                Her last disorder mortal.

1680.   A night-cap deck'd his brows instead of bay,
              A cap by night—a stocking all the day !
                          Description of an Author's Bedchamber.

1681.   Remote, unfriended, melancholy, slow.   *The Traveller*, I.

1682.   Where'er I roam, whatever realms to see,
              My heart untravell'd fondly turns to thee ;
              Still to my brother turns with ceaseless pain,
              And drags at each remove a lengthening chain.   Ibid., 7.

1683.   Such is the patriot's boast, where'er we roam,
              His first, best country ever is, at home.   Ibid., 73.

1684.   But winter ling'ring chills the lap of May.   Ibid., 172.

1685.   Laws grind the poor, and rich men rule the law.   Ibid., 386.

1686.   Taught by the Power that pities me,
                I learn to pity them.
                          Edwin and Angelina, or The Hermit.

1687.   Man wants but little here below,
                Nor wants that little long.   Ibid.

1688.   The naked every day he clad,
                When he put on his clothes.
                          Elegy on the Death of a Mad Dog.

1689.   The dog, to gain some private ends,
                Went mad, and bit the man.   Ibid.

1690.   The man recover'd of the bite,
                The dog it was that died.   Ibid.

1691.　　　　　　　When lovely woman stoops to folly,
　　　　　　　　　And finds too late that men betray,
　　　　　　　　What charm can soothe her melancholy,
　　　　　　　　　What art can wash her guilt away ?
　　　　　　　　The only art her guilt to cover,
　　　　　　　　　To hide her shame from every eye,
　　　　　　　　To give repentance to her lover,
　　　　　　　　　And wring his bosom, is—to die.
　　　　　　　　　　　Song. The Vicar of Wakefield, xxix.

1692. Sweet Auburn ! loveliest village of the plain.
　　　　　　　　　　　　　　The Deserted Village, 1.

1693. The hawthorn bush, with seats beneath the shade,
　　　 For talking age and whisp'ring lovers made.　　　　Ibid., 13.

1694. The bashful virgin's sidelong looks of love,
　　　 The matron's glance that would those looks reprove.　Ibid., 29.

1695. Ill fares the land, to hast'ning ills a prey,
　　　 Where wealth accumulates, and men decay :
　　　 Princes and lords may flourish, or may fade ;
　　　 A breath can make them, as a breath has made ;
　　　 But a bold peasantry, their country's pride,
　　　 When once destroy'd, can never be supplied.　　　　Ibid., 51.

1696. His best companions, innocence and health ;
　　　 And his best riches, ignorance of wealth.　　　　　Ibid., 61.

1697. How happy he who crowns in shades like these,
　　　 A youth of labour with an age of ease.　　　　　　Ibid., 99.
　　 [1st edition has ' How blest is he.']

1698. The watchdog's voice that bay'd the whisp'ring wind,
　　　 And the loud laugh that spoke the vacant mind.　　Ibid., 121.

1699. A man he was to all the country dear,
　　　 And passing rich with forty pounds a year.　　　　Ibid., 141.

1700. Wept o'er his wounds, or tales of sorrow done,
　　　 Shoulder'd his crutch, and show'd how fields were won.
　　　　　　　　　　　　　　　　　　　　　　Ibid., 157.

1701. Careless their merits, or their faults to scan,
　　　 His pity gave ere charity began.
　　　 Thus to relieve the wretched was his pride,
　　　 And e'en his failings lean'd to virtue's side.　　Ibid., 161.

1702. And, as a bird each fond endearment tries
　　　 To tempt its new-fledg'd offspring to the skies,
　　　 He tried each art, reprov'd each dull delay,
　　　 Allur'd to brighter worlds, and led the way.　　　Ibid., 167.

1703. Truth from his lips prevail'd with double sway,
　　　 And fools, who came to scoff, remain'd to pray.　Ibid., 179.

1704. Even children follow'd with endearing wile,
　　　 And pluck'd his gown, to share the good man's smile.
　　　　　　　　　　　　　　　　　　　　　　Ibid., 183.

1705. As some tall cliff, that lifts its awful form,
　　　 Swells from the vale, and midway leaves the storm,
　　　 Though round its breast the rolling clouds are spread,
　　　 Eternal sunshine settles on its head.　　　　　　Ibid., 189.

1706. A man severe he was, and stern to view ;
I knew him well, and every truant knew ;
Well had the boding tremblers learn'd to trace
The day's disasters in his morning face ;
Full well they laugh'd, with counterfeited glee,
At all his jokes, for many a joke had he ;
Full well the busy whisper, circling round,
Convey'd the dismal tidings when he frown'd ;
Yet he was kind ; or if severe in aught,
The love he bore to learning was in fault.   *Ibid.*, 197.

1707. In arguing too, the parson own'd his skill,
For e'en though vanquish'd, he could argue still ;
While words of learned length and thund'ring sound
Amazed the gazing rustics rang'd around,
And still they gaz'd, and still the wonder grew,
That one small head could carry all he knew.   *Ibid.*, 211.

1708. The white-wash'd wall, the nicely sanded floor,
The varnish'd clock that click'd behind the door ;
The chest contriv'd a double debt to pay,
A bed by night, a chest of drawers by day.   *Ibid.*, 227.

1709. The twelve good rules, the royal game of goose.   *Ibid.*, 232.

1710. Her modest looks the cottage might adorn,
Sweet as the primrose peeps beneath the thorn.   *Ibid.*, 329.

1711. In all the silent manliness of grief.   *Ibid.*, 384.

1712. Thou source of all my bliss, and all my woe.
That found'st me poor at first, and keep'st me so.   *Ibid.*, 413.

1713. Here lies our good Edmund, whose genius was such,
We scarcely can praise it, or blame it too much ;
Who, born for the Universe, narrow'd his mind,
And to party gave up what was meant for mankind.
[Edmund Burke.]   *Retaliation*, 29.

1714. Though equal to all things, for all things unfit,
Too nice for a statesman, too proud for a wit :
For a patriot, too cool ; for a drudge, disobedient ;
And too fond of the *right* to pursue the *expedient*.
[Same.]   *Ibid.*, 37.

1715. Here lies David Garrick, describe me, who can,
An abridgment of all that was pleasant in man.   *Ibid.*, 93.

1716. On the stage he was natural, simple, affecting ;
'Twas only that when he was off he was acting.   [Same.]
       Ibid., 101.

1717. He cast off his friends, as a huntsman his pack,
For he knew when he pleas'd he could whistle them back.
[Same.]   *Ibid.*, 107.

1718. Here Reynolds is laid, and to tell you my mind,
He has not left a better or wiser behind ;
His pencil was striking, resistless, and grand ;
His manners were gentle, complying, and bland.   *Ibid.*, 137.

1719. When they talk'd of their Raphaels, Correggios, and stuff,
       He shifted his trumpet, and only took snuff. [Same.]

Ibid., 145.

1720.   Hope, like the gleaming taper's light,
                   Adorns and cheers our way ;
                 And still, as darker grows the night,
                   Emits a brighter ray.   *The Captivity*, II.

1721. All our adventures were by the fire-side, and all our migra-
tions from the blue bed to the brown.   *The Vicar of Wakefield*, i.

1722. They would talk of nothing but high life, and high-lived
company, with other fashionable topics, such as pictures, taste,
Shakespeare, and the musical glasses.   *Ibid.*, ix.

1723. I love everything that's old ; old friends, old times, old
manners, old books, old wines.   *She Stoops to Conquer*, I.

1724. The very pink of perfection.   *Ibid.*

1725. In a concatenation accordingly.   *Ibid.*

1726. This is Liberty-hall, gentlemen.   *Ibid.*, II.

1727. There is no arguing with Johnson ; for when his pistol misses
fire, he knocks you down with the butt end of it.
                          Boswell's *Life of Johnson*, an. 1769.

1728. If you were to make little fishes talk, they would talk like
whales. [To Johnson.]   *Ibid.*, an. 1773.

GOLDWYN, SAMUEL, U.S. film producer, 27 Aug. 1882

    1729. Include me out.   *Attributed.*

GORDON, ADAM LINDSAY, Australian poet, 19 Oct. 1833—24 June, 1870

1730.   No game was ever worth a rap
                   For a rational man to play,
                 Into which no accident, no mishap,
                   Could possibly find its way.
                                 Ye Wearie Wayfarer, fytte 4.

1731.   Life is mostly froth and bubble,
                   Two things stand like stone,
                 Kindness in another's trouble,
                   Courage in your own.   *Ibid.*, fytte 8.

1732. I should live the same life over, if I had to live again ;
       And the chances are I go where most men go.
                                      The Sick Stockrider.

GORE-BOOTH, EVA SELENA, Irish poetess, 22 May, 1870—30 June, 1926

1733. But the little waves of Breffny have drenched my heart in
           spray,
         And the little waves of Breffny go stumbling through my ·
           soul.   *The Little Waves of Breffny.*

GOSCHEN, GEORGE JOACHIM GOSCHEN, 1ST VISCOUNT, statesman,
        10 Aug. 1831—7 Feb. 1907

1734. Our splendid isolation, as one of our colonial friends was good
enough to call it.   *Speech at Lewes*, 26 Feb. 1896.
[The phrase ' splendidly isolated ' was used by G. E. Foster and by
Sir Wilfred Laurier in the Canadian House of Commons earlier that
year.]

GRAHAM, HARRY JOCELYN CLIVE, author, 23 Dec. 1874—30 Oct. 1936
1735.   Father heard his children scream,
                   So he threw them in the stream,
                   Saying, as he drowned the third,
                   ' Children should be seen, not heard ! '
                              Ruthless Rhymes. The Stern Parent.

1736.   Billy, in one of his nice new sashes,
                   Fell in the fire and was burnt to ashes ;
                   Now, although the room grows chilly,
                   I haven't the heart to poke poor Billy.
                              Ibid. *Tender-Heartedness.*

GRAHAM, JAMES, *see* Montrose, Marquis of

GRAHAM, ROBERT (*later* CUNNINGHAME-GRAHAM), Scottish poet,
        1735 ?—1797 ?

1737.   If doughty deeds my lady please,
                   Right soon I'll mount my steed.   *If Doughty Deeds.*

GRAHAME, JAMES, Scottish poet, 22 April, 1765—14 Sept. 1811
1738.   Hail, Sabbath ! thee I hail, the poor man's day.
                                        The Sabbath, 29.

GRAHAME, KENNETH, author, 3 March, 1859—6 July, 1932
1739. The burglars vanished silently into the laurels, with horrid
implications !   *The Golden Age. The Burglars.*

1740. Believe me, my young friend, there is *nothing*—absolutely
nothing—half so much worth doing as simply messing about in boats.
                              The Wind in the Willows, i.

GRAINGER, JAMES, doctor, 1721 ?—16 Dec. 1766
1741. Now, Muse, let's sing of rats.   *The Sugar Cane.*
[Quoted by Boswell from the MS. Not in the printed version.]

GRANT, SIR ROBERT, Governor of Bombay, 1779—9 July, 1838
1742.   Our Shield and Defender, the Ancient of Days,
          Pavilioned in splendour, and girded with praise.
                              O worship the King.

GRANT, ULYSSES SIMPSON, U.S. President, 27 April, 1822—23 July,
        1885

1743. No terms except an unconditional and immediate surrender
can be accepted. I propose to move immediately upon your works.
                To General Buckner, Fort Donelson, 16 Feb. 1862.

1744. I propose to fight it out on this line, if it takes all summer.
                Despatch to Washington, 11 May, 1864.

GRAVES, ALFRED PERCEVAL, Irish author, 22 July, 1846—27 Dec. 1931

1745.   Och ! Father O'Flynn, you've the wonderful way wid you.
Father O'Flynn.

1746.   Checkin' the crazy ones,
               Coaxin' onaisy ones,
       Liftin' the lazy ones on wid the stick.   Ibid.

GRAY, THOMAS, poet, 26 Dec. 1716—30 July, 1771

1747.   Ye distant spires, ye antique towers.
Ode on a Distant Prospect of Eton College, 1.

1748.   They hear a voice in every wind,
        And snatch a fearful joy.   Ibid, 39.

1749.   Alas, regardless of their doom,
        The little victims play !
        No sense have they of ills to come,
        Nor care beyond to-day.   Ibid., 51.

1750.   To each his suff'rings : all are men,
        Condemn'd alike to groan ;
        The tender for another's pain,
        Th' unfeeling for his own.
        Yet ah ! why should they know their fate ?
        Since sorrow never comes too late,
        And happiness too swiftly flies.
        Thought would destroy their paradise.
        No more ; where ignorance is bliss,
        'Tis folly to be wise.   Ibid., 91.

1751.   Daughter of Jove, relentless power,
        Thou tamer of the human breast,
        Whose iron scourge and torturing hour
        The bad affright, afflict the best.   *Hymn to Adversity.*

1752.   What female heart can gold despise ?
        What cat's averse to fish ?
Ode on the Death of a Favourite Cat.

1753.   A fav'rite has no friend.   Ibid.

1754.   The curfew tolls the knell of parting day,
        The lowing herd winds slowly o'er the lea,
        The ploughman homeward plods his weary way,
        And leaves the world to darkness and to me.
Elegy written in a Country Churchyard, 1.

1755.   Now fades the glimmering landscape on the sight,
        And all the air a solemn stillness holds,
        Save where the beetle wheels his droning flight,
        And drowsy tinklings lull the distant folds.   Ibid., 5.

1756.   Each in his narrow cell for ever laid
        The rude forefathers of the hamlet sleep.   Ibid., 15.

1757.   The breezy call of incense-breathing morn.   Ibid., 17.

1758.   Let not ambition mock their useful toil,
        Their homely joys, and destiny obscure ;
        Nor grandeur hear with a disdainful smile,
        The short and simple annals of the poor.   Ibid., 29.

1759.   The boast of heraldry, the pomp of pow'r,
            And all that beauty, all that wealth e'er gave,
        Awaits alike th' inevitable hour,
            The paths of glory lead but to the grave.   *Ibid.*, 33.

1760.   Where through the long-drawn aisle and fretted vault
            The pealing anthem swells the note of praise.
                                                            Ibid., 39.

1761.   Can storied urn or animated bust
            Back to its mansion call the fleeting breath ?
        Can honour's voice provoke the silent dust,
            Or flatt'ry soothe the dull cold ear of death ?
                                                            Ibid., 41.

1762.   Hands, that the rod of empire might have sway'd,
            Or wak'd to ecstasy the living lyre.   *Ibid*, 47.

1763.   Full many a gem of purest ray serene
            The dark unfathom'd caves of ocean bear :
        Full many a flower is born to blush unseen,
            And waste its sweetness on the desert air.   *Ibid.*, 53.

1764.   Some village Hampden, that with dauntless breast
            The little tyrant of his fields withstood ;
        Some mute inglorious Milton here may rest,
            Some Cromwell guiltless of his country's blood.
                                                            Ibid., 57.

1765.   Forbade to wade through slaughter to a throne,
            And shut the gates of mercy on mankind.   *Ibid.* 67.

1766.   Far from the madding crowd's ignoble strife
            Their sober wishes never learn'd to stray ;
        Along the cool sequester'd vale of life
            They kept the noiseless tenor of their way.   *Ibid.*, 73.

1767.   For who to dumb forgetfulness a prey,
            This pleasing anxious being e'er resign'd,
        Left the warm precincts of the cheerful day,
            Nor cast one longing ling'ring look behind ?   *Ibid.*, 85.

1768.   Brushing with hasty steps the dews away
            To meet the sun upon the upland lawn.   *Ibid.*, 99.

1769.   Here rests his head upon the lap of earth
        A youth to fortune and to fame unknown.
        Fair Science frown'd not on his humble birth,
            And Melancholy mark'd him for her own.
                                                Ibid., *The Epitaph.*

1770.   Large was his bounty, and his soul sincere,
            Heav'n did a recompense as largely send :
        He gave to Mis'ry all he had, a tear,
            He gain'd from Heav'n ('twas all he wish'd) a friend.
                                                            Ibid

1771.   No farther seek his merits to disclose,
            Or draw his frailties from their dread abode,
        (There they alike in trembling hope repose),
            The bosom of his Father and his God.   Ibid.

1772.   Rich windows that exclude the light,
            And passages that lead to nothing.   *A Long Story*, 7.

1773. The meanest flowret of the vale,
       The simplest note that swells the gale,
       The common sun, the air, the skies,
       To him are opening paradise.
                Ode on the Pleasures arising from Vicissitude, 49.

1774. The bloom of young desire and purple light of love.
                              The Progress of Poesy, 41.

1775. Nor second he, that rode sublime
           Upon the seraph-wings of ecstasy,
           The secrets of th' abyss to spy.
       He pass'd the flaming bounds of place and time :
       The living throne, the sapphire-blaze.
       Where angels tremble while they gaze,
       He saw ; but blasted with excess of light,
       Closed his eyes in endless night. [Milton.]   Ibid., 95.

1776. Two coursers of ethereal race,
       With necks in thunder clothed, and long-resounding pace.
                                                   Ibid., 105

1777. Bright-eyed Fancy, hovering o'er,
       Scatters from her pictured urn
       Thoughts that breathe and words that burn.   Ibid., 108

1778. Beyond the limits of a vulgar fate,
       Beneath the good how far—but far above the great.
                                                   Ibid., 122.

1779.   Ruin seize thee, ruthless King !
           Confusion on thy banners wait.   *The Bard*, 1.

1780. Weave the warp, and weave the woof,
       The winding-sheet of Edward's race.   Ibid., 49.

1781. Fair laughs the morn, and soft the zephyr blows,
           While proudly riding o'er the azure realm
       In gallant trim the gilded vessel goes,
           Youth on the prow, and Pleasure at the helm.
                                                   Ibid., 71.

1782. Ye towers of Julius, London's lasting shame,
       With many a foul and midnight murther fed.
                                                   Ibid., 87.

1783.   Iron-sleet of arrowy shower
               Hurtles in the darkn'd air.
                                    The Fatal Sisters.

1784. Too poor for a bribe, and too proud to importune ;
       He had not the method of making a fortune.
                              Sketch of his own Character.

GREELEY, HORACE, U.S. journalist, 3 Feb. 1811—29 Nov. 1872
   1785. Go West, young man, and grow up with the country.
                              Hints toward Reform.

GREEN, MATTHEW, poet, 1696—1737
1786.   To cure the mind's wrong bias, Spleen,
               Some recommend the bowling-green ;
               Some, hilly walks ; all, exercise ;
               Fling but a stone, the giant dies
               Laugh and be well.   *The Spleen*, 89.

*E

GREENE, ALBERT GORTON, U.S. poet, 10 Feb. 1802—3 Jan. 1868

1787.   Old Grimes is dead ; that good old man
                   We never shall see more :
               He used to wear a long, black coat,
                   All button'd down before.   *Old Grimes.*

GREENE, ROBERT, author, July, 1558—3 Sept. 1592

1788.   Weep not, my wanton, smile upon my knee ;
                   When thou art old there's grief enough for thee.
                       Mother's wag, pretty boy,
                       Father's sorrow, father's joy.   *Sephestia's Song.*

GREGORY I., THE GREAT, Pope and Saint, 540 ?—10 March, 604

1789. Non Angli, sed angeli.—Not Angles, but angels.
               Traditional words on seeing English captives at Rome.

GRELLET, STEPHEN (ÉTIENNE DE GRELLET), Franco-American Quaker,
       2 Nov. 1773—16 Nov. 1855

1790. I expect to pass through this world but once.   Any good
thing therefore that I can do, or any kindness that I can show to any
fellow-creature, let me do it now ; let me not defer or neglect it, for I
shall not pass this way again.   *Attributed.*
[Authorship of this much disputed.]

GRENFELL, JULIAN HENRY FRANCIS, soldier, 3 March, 1888—26 May,
       1915

1791.   The fighting man shall from the sun
                   Take warmth, and life from the glowing earth ;
               Speed with the light-foot winds to run,
                   And with the trees to newer birth.   *Into Battle.*

GREY OF FALLODON, EDWARD, 1ST VISCOUNT, statesman, 25 April,
       1862—7 Sept. 1933

1792. The lamps are going out all over Europe ; we shall not see
them lit again in our lifetime.   *On the eve of war*, 3 Aug. 1914.

GRIFFIN, GERALD, Irish author, 12 Dec. 1803—12 June, 1840

1793.   Dear were her charms to me,
                   Dearer her laughter free,
                       Dearest her constancy,—
                           Eileen Aroon !   *Eileen Aroon.*

GUEDALLA, PHILIP, historian, 12 March, 1889–16 Dec. 1944

1794. The work of Henry James has always seemed divisible by a
simple dynastic arrangement into three reigns : James I, James II,
and the Old Pretender.   *Supers and Supermen.*

1795. The cheerful clatter of Sir James Barrie's cans as he went
round with the milk of human kindness.   *Some Critics.*

GUITERMAN, ARTHUR, U.S. author, 20 Nov., 1871—11 Jan. 1943

1796.   Bores of the dreariest hue,
                   Bringers of worry and care,
               Watch us respond to our cue,—
                 ' Exit, pursued by a bear.'
                                        The Shakespearean Bear.

GURNEY, DOROTHY FRANCES, poetess, 1858—1932

1797.   The kiss of the sun for pardon,
               The song of the birds for mirth,
             One is nearer God's Heart in a garden
               Than anywhere else on earth.   *God's Garden.*

HABBERTON, JOHN, U.S. author, 24 Feb. 1842—24 Feb. 1921
   1798. Want to shee the wheels go wound.   *Helen's Babies*, i.

HABINGTON, WILLIAM, 4 or 5 Nov. 1605—30 Nov. 1654

1799.   The starres, bright cent'nels of the skies.
                 Castara, I. *A Dialogue between Night and Araphil*, 3.

HAIG, DOUGLAS HAIG, EARL, 19 June, 1861—29 Jan. 1928

   1800. Every position must be held to the last man ; there must be
no retirement. With our backs to the wall, and believing in the justice
of our cause, each one of us must fight to the end.
                         Order to the British troops, 12 April, 1918.

HALE, EDWARD EVERETT, U.S. cleric, 3 April, 1822—10 June, 1909

1801.   To look up and not down,
                   To look forward and not back,
                   To look out and not in, and
                   To lend a hand.   *Ten Times One is Ten.*

HALE, SARAH JOSEPHA BUELL, U.S. author, 24 Oct. 1788—30 April,
         1879
1802.   Mary had a little lamb,
                   Its fleece was white as snow,
                   And everywhere that Mary went
                   The lamb was sure to go.   *Mary's Lamb.*

HALL, JOSEPH, Bishop of Norwich, 1 July, 1574—8 Sept. 1656

   1803. Moderation is the silken string running through the pearl
chain of all virtues.   *Christian Moderation*, Introduction.

HALLECK, FITZ-GREENE, U.S. poet, 8 July, 1790—19 Nov. 1867

1804.   Green be the turf above thee,
                   Friend of my better days !
                 None knew thee but to love thee,
                   Nor named thee but to praise.
                         On the Death of Joseph Rodman Drake.

HAMILTON, COUNT ANTHONY, soldier and author, 1646 ?—21 April, 1720

1805. Bélier, mon ami, lui dit le géant en l'interrompant, je ne comprends rien à tout cela. Si tu voulois bien commencer par le commencement, tu me ferois plaisir ; car tous ces récits qui commencent par le milieu ne font que m'embrouiller l'imagination.—' My dear Ram,' interrupted the giant, ' I have not the least notion what you are talking about. If you would have the kindness to begin at the beginning, I should be vastly obliged ; all these stories that begin in the middle simply fog my wits.' *Le Bélier—The Ram.*

HAMILTON, GAIL (MARY ABIGAIL DODGE), U.S. essayist, 31 March, 1833—17 Aug. 1896

1806. The total depravity of inanimate things. *Epigram.*

HAMILTON, WILLIAM, Scottish poet, 1704—25 March, 1754

1807.   Busk ye, busk ye, my bonny bonny bride,
             Busk ye, busk ye, my winsome marrow.
                                        The Braes of Yarrow.

HAMILTON, WILLIAM GERARD, politician, 28 Jan. 1729—16 July, 1796

1808. Johnson is dead.—Let us go to the next best :—there is nobody ; no man can be said to put you in mind of Johnson.
                              Boswell's *Life of Johnson*, an. 1784.

HANKEY, KATHERINE, hymn-writer, 1834—1911

1809.   Tell me the old, old story.   *The Old, Old Story.*

HARDENBERG, FRIEDRICH LEOPOLD VON, *see* Novalis

HARDY, THOMAS, author, 2 June, 1840—11 Jan. 1928

1810. A nice unparticular man.   *Far from the Madding Crowd*, viii.

1811. A lover without indiscretion is no lover at all.
                                        The Hand of Ethelberta, xx.

1812. Dialect words—those terrible marks of the beast to the truly genteel.   *The Mayor of Casterbridge*, xx.

1813. A little one-eyed blinking sort o' place.
                                        Tess of the D'Urbervilles, i.

1814. Always washing and never getting finished.   Ibid., iv.

1815. ' Justice ' was done, and the President of the Immortals (in Aeschylean phrase) had ended his sport with Tess.   Ibid., lix.

1816. Life's little ironies.   *Title of Volume.*

1817. Time and circumstance, which enlarge the views of most men, narrow the views of women almost invariably.   *Jude the Obscure*, vi.

1818.   When I came back from Lyonnesse
                 With magic in my eyes.
                                        When I set out for Lyonesse.

1819   What of the faith and fire within us
         Men who march away ?   *Men who march away.*

1820.   Only a man harrowing clods
         In a slow silent walk
     With an old horse that stumbles and nods
         Half asleep as they stalk.
            In Time of ' The Breaking of Nations.'

1821.   Yet this will go onward the same
            Though Dynasties pass.   Ibid.

1822.   When the Present has latched its postern behind my tremulous
       stay.   *Afterwards.*

   1823.   He was a man who used to notice such things.   Ibid.

1824.   This is the weather the cuckoo likes,
            And so do I.   *Weathers.*

HARE, MAURICE E., 1886—

1825.   There was a young man who said, ' Damn !
         At last I've found out what I am
            A creature that moves
            In determinate grooves,
         In fact not a bus but a tram.'   *Limerick.*

HARINGTON, SIR JOHN, author, 1561—20 Nov. 1612

1826.   Treason doth never prosper ; what's the reason ?
       For if it prosper, none dare call it treason.
            Epigrams, IV. 5.

HARRIS, CHARLES K., U.S. composer, 1 May, 1865—22 Dec. 1930

1827.   Many a heart is aching, if you could read them all,
       Many the hopes that have vanished, after the ball.
            After the Ball.

HARRIS, JOEL CHANDLER, U.S. author, 8 Dec. 1848—3 July, 1908

   1828.   Tar-Baby ain't sayin' nuthin', en Brer Fox, he lay low.
            Uncle Remus, ii.

   1829.   Ez soshubble ez a baskit er kittens.   Ibid., iii.

   1830.   Bred en bawn in a brier-patch, Brer Fox.   Ibid., iv.

   1831.   Lounjun 'roun' en suffer'n.   Ibid., xii.

   1832.   I'm de'f in one year, en I can't hear out'n de udder.
            Ibid., xix.

1833.   Oh, whar shill we go w'en de great day comes,
       Wid de blowin' er de trumpits en de bangin' er de drums ?
       How many po' sinners'll be kotched out late
       En find no latch ter de golden gate ?
            Uncle Remus. His Songs, i

HARTE, FRANCIS BRETT, U.S. author, 25 Aug. 1836—5 May, 1902

1834.   Which I wish to remark,
                  And my language is plain,
             That for ways that are dark
                And for tricks that are vain,
             The heathen Chinee is peculiar.

Plain Language from Truthful James.

1835.   With the smile that was childlike and bland.   Ibid.

1836. Then Abner Dean of Angels raised a point of order—when
      A chunk of old red sandstone took him in the abdomen,
      And he smiled a kind of sickly smile and curled up on the
          floor,
      And the subsequent proceedings interested him no more.

The Society upon the Stanislaus.

1837.   Do I sleep ?   Do I dream ?
                Do I wander and doubt ?
                Are things what they seem ?
                Or is visions about ?

Further Language from Truthful James.

1838.   If of all words of tongue and pen,
             The saddest are, ' It might have been,'
             More sad are these we daily see :
             ' It is, but hadn't ought to be.'

Mrs. Judge Jenkins.

HASKINS, MINNIE LOUISE, teacher and author, 12 May, 1875—
3 Feb. 1957

1839. And I said to the man who stood at the gate of the year:
'Give me a light that I may tread safely into the unknown.'
And he replied:
'Go out into the darkness and put your hand into the hand of God.
That shall be to you better than light and safer than a known way.'

God knows.

HAWES, STEPHEN, poet, died 1523 ?

1840.   For though the day be never so longe,
           At last the belles ringeth to evensonge.

Passetyme of Pleasure, xlii.

HAWKER, ROBERT STEPHEN, cleric, 3 Dec. 1803—15 Aug. 1875

1841.   And have they fixed the where and when ?
             And shall Trelawny die ?
          Here's twenty thousand Cornish men
             Will know the reason why ! *Song of the Western Men.*

HAWKINS, SIR ANTHONY HOPE, *see* Hope, Anthony

HAWTHORNE, NATHANIEL, U.S. author, 4 July, 1804—18 or 19 May, 1864

1842. Selfishness is one of the qualities apt to inspire love. This might be thought out at great length.   *American Note-Books*, 1840.

1843. Life is made up of marble and mud.

The House of the Seven Gables, ii

HAY, IAN (JOHN HAY BEITH), author, 17 April, 1876—22 Sept. 1952

1844. A good story is at present going the round of the clubs, . . .
anent a certain well-known but absent-minded Peer of the Realm.
The Right Stuff, iii.

1845. Funny peculiar, or funny ha-ha ?   *Housemaster*, III.

HAY, JOHN, U.S. author, 8 Oct. 1838—1 July, 1905

1846.   A keerless man in his talk was Jim,
               And an awkward hand in a row,
           He never flunked, and he never lied,—
               I reckon he never knowed how.   *Jim Bludso.*

HAZLITT, WILLIAM, essayist, 10 April, 1778—18 Sept. 1830

1847. The art of pleasing consists in being pleased.
The Round Table. On Manner.

1848. He [Coleridge] talked on for ever ; and you wished him to
talk on for ever.
Lectures on the English Poets. On the Living Poets.

1849. It is better to be able neither to read nor write than to be
able to do nothing else. *Table Talk. On the Ignorance of the Learned.*

1850. There is not a more mean, stupid, dastardly, pitiful, selfish,
spiteful, envious, ungrateful animal than the Public. It is the greatest
of cowards, for it is afraid of itself.
Ibid. *On Living to Oneself.*

1851. His worst is better than any other person's best.   [Scott.]
The Spirit of the Age. Sir Walter Scott.

1852. When I take up a work that I have read before (the oftener
the better) I know what I have to expect. The satisfaction is not
lessened by being anticipated.
The Plain Speaker. On reading Old Books.

1853. No young man believes he shall ever die.
On the Feeling of Immortality in Youth.

1854. As we advance in life, we acquire a keener sense of the value
of time. Nothing else, indeed, seems of any consequence ; and we
become misers in this respect.   Ibid.

HEBER, REGINALD, Bishop of Calcutta, 21 April, 1783—3 April, 1826

1855.   Failed the bright promise of your early day !   *Palestine.*

1856.   No hammers fell, no ponderous axes rung ;
             Like some tall palm the mystic fabric sprung.
             Majestic silence !   Ibid.

1857.   Brightest and best of the sons of the morning,
               Dawn on our darkness, and lend us thine aid.
Epiphany.

1858. When spring unlocks the flowers to paint the laughing soil.
Seventh Sunday after Trinity.

1859.   The Son of God goes forth to war,
                     A kingly crown to gain ;
                  His blood-red banner streams afar :
                     Who follows in His train ?
                                  The Son of God goes forth to War.

1860.   From Greenland's icy mountains,
                     From India's coral strand,
                  Where Afric's sunny fountains
                     Roll down their golden sand.   *Missionary Hymn.*

1861.   Though every prospect pleases,
                     And only man is vile.   Ibid.

1862.   The heathen in his blindness
                     Bows down to wood and stone.   Ibid.

HEMANS, FELICIA DOROTHEA, poetess, 25 Sept. 1793—16 May, 1835

1863.   The stately homes of England,
                     How beautiful they stand !
                  Amidst their tall ancestral trees,
                     O'er all the pleasant land.
                                          The Homes of England.

1864.   The boy stood on the burning deck,
                     Whence all but he had fled.   *Casabianca.*

1865.   There came a burst of thunder sound—
                     The boy—oh ! where was he ?   Ibid.

1866.   They grew in beauty, side by side,
                     They fill'd one home with glee ;—
                  Their graves are sever'd, far and wide,
                     By mount, and stream, and sea.
                                     The Graves of a Household.

1867.   Not there, not there, my child !   *The Better Land.*

1868.   Eye hath not seen it, my gentle boy !   Ibid.

HENLEY, WILLIAM ERNEST, author, 23 Aug. 1849—11 July, 1903

1869.   Far in the stillness a cat
                     Languishes loudly.   *In Hospital,* vii. *Vigil.*

1870.   Valiant in velvet, light in ragged luck,
          Most vain, most generous, sternly critical,
          Buffoon and poet, lover and sensualist :
          A deal of Ariel, just a streak of Puck,
          Much Anthony, of Hamlet most of all,
          And something of the Shorter-Catechist.   [R. L.
             Stevenson.]
                                  Ibid., xxv., *Apparition.*

1871.   Out of the night that covers me,
             Black as the Pit from pole to pole,
          I thank whatever gods may be
             For my unconquerable soul.
                     Echoes, iv. *In Memoriam R. T. Hamilton Bruce,
                        1846–99.*

| 1872. | Under the bludgeonings of chance
My head is bloody, but unbowed. | Ibid. |

1872. Under the bludgeonings of chance
    My head is bloody, but unbowed.   *Ibid.*

1873. I am the master of my fate :
    I am the captain of my soul.   *Ibid.*

1874. A late lark twitters from the quiet skies.
    Ibid., xxxv.   *In Memoriam Margaritae Sorori.*

1875. Or ever the knightly years were gone
    With the old world to the grave,
    I was a King in Babylon
    And you were a Christian Slave.
               Ibid., xxxvii.   *To W.A.*

1876. What have I done for you,
    England, my England ?
    What is there I would not do,
    England, my own ?
               Rhymes and Rhythms, xxv.

HENRI IV, King of France, 13 Dec. 1553—14 May, 1610

1877. Paris vaut bien une messe.—Paris is well worth a mass.
               Attributed.

1878. The wisest fool in Christendom.   [Of James I of England.]
               Ibid.

HENRY, O. (WILLIAM SYDNEY PORTER), U.S. author, 11 Sept. 1862—
    5 June, 1910

1879. If men knew how women pass the time when they are alone,
they'd never marry.   *Memoirs of a Yellow Dog.*
1880. Turn up the lights ; I don't want to go home in the dark.
               Last Words.

HENRY, PATRICK, U.S. statesman, 29 May, 1736—6 June, 1799

1881. Tarquin and Caesar each had his Brutus, Charles the First his
Cromwell, and George the Third (' Treason ! ' cried the Speaker)—*may
profit by their example.* If *this* be treason, make the most of it.
      Speech in Virginia House of Burgesses, 29 May, 1765.

1882. I am not a Virginian, but an American.
      Speech in First Continental Congress, 14 Oct. 1774.

1883. Is life so dear, or peace so sweet, as to be purchased at the
price of chains and slavery ? Forbid it, Almighty God ! I know not
what course others may take, but as for me, give me liberty, or give
me death !   *Speech in Virginia Convention*, 23 March, 1775.

HERBERT, SIR ALAN PATRICK, author and M.P., 24 Sept. 1890—

1884. Not huffy or stuffy, nor tiny or tall,
    But fluffy, just fluffy, with no brains at all.
               I like them Fluffy.

1885. Holy deadlock.   *Title of novel.*
1886. I regard the pub as a valuable institution.
      Letter to the Electors of Oxford University, 1935.

HERBERT, GEORGE, poet and cleric, born 3 April, 1593, buried 3 March,
        1633

1887.   Dare to be true : nothing can need a lie ;
             A fault which needs it most grows two thereby.
                                          The Church Porch, 77.

1888. Do all things like a man, not sneakingly :
       Think the king sees thee still ; for his King does. Ibid., 121.

1889.   Pulpits and Sundays, sorrow dogging sin,
                Afflictions sorted, anguish of all sizes,
             Fine nets and strategems to catch us in,
                Bibles laid open, millions of surprises.   *Sin.*

1890.   O day most calm, most bright.   *Sunday.*

1891.   Sweet day, so cool, so calm, so bright,
                The bridal of the earth and sky.   *Virtue.*

1892.   Sweet spring, full of sweet days and roses,
             A box where sweets compacted lie.   Ibid.

1893.   Only a sweet and virtuous soul,
             Like seasoned timber, never gives ;
             But though the whole world turn to coal,
                Then chiefly lives.   Ibid.

1894.   Love is swift of foot ;
                   Love's a man of war,
                      And can shoot,
                   And can hit from far.   *Discipline.*

1895. Do well, and right, and let the world sink.
             A Priest to the Temple or the Country Parson, xxix.

HERRICK, ROBERT, poet and cleric, baptised 24 Aug. 1591, buried
        15 Oct. 1674

1896. I sing of brooks, of blossoms, birds, and bowers :
       Of April, May, of June, and July flowers.
       I sing of maypoles, hock-carts, wassails, wakes,
       Of bridegrooms, brides, and of their bridal cakes.
       I write of youth, of love, and have access
       By these, to sing of cleanly-wantonness.
                        Hesperides. The Argument of his Book.

1897.   A sweet disorder in the dress
             Kindles in clothes a wantonness.
                                  Ibid. *Delight in Disorder.*

1898.   A winning wave (deserving note)
             In the tempestuous petticoat :
             A careless shoe-string, in whose tie
             I see a wild civility :
             Do more bewitch me, than when art
             Is too precise in every part.   Ibid.

1899.   Gather ye rosebuds while ye may,
                Old Time is still a-flying,
             And this same flower that smiles to-day
                To-morrow will be dying.
                        Ibid. *To the Virgins, to make much of Time.*

1900.   Bid me to live, and I will live
          Thy Protestant to be :
         Or bid me love, and I will give
          A loving heart to thee.
            Ibid. *To Anthea, who may command him any Thing.*

1901.   Fair daffodils, we weep to see
          You haste away so soon :
         As yet the early-rising sun
          Has not attain'd his noon.
                                        Ibid. *To Daffodils.*

1902.   Her pretty feet
               Like snails did creep
               A little out, and then,
               As if they started at bo-peep,
               Did soon draw in again.
                                        Ibid. *Upon her Feet.*

1903.   Her eyes the glow-worm lend thee,
         The shooting-stars attend thee
               And the elves also,
               Whose little eyes glow
         Like the sparks of fire, befriend thee.
                            Ibid. *The Night-piece, to Julia.*

1904.   Whenas in silks my Julia goes,
         Then, then, methinks, how sweetly flows
         That liquefaction of her clothes.
                            ιIbid. *Upon Julia's Clothes.*

1905. Attempt the end, and never stand to doubt ;
       Nothing's so hard but search will find it out.
                                        Ibid. *Seek and find.*

1906.   Here a little child I stand,
               Heaving up my either hand ;
               Cold as paddocks though they be,
               Here I lift them up to thee,
               For a benison to fall
               On our meat and on us all.   Amen.
                    Noble Numbers. Another Grace for a Child.

HESIOD, Greek poet, 8th century B.C.

1907. Πλέον ἥμισυ παντός—The half is more than the whole.
                                        Works and Days, 40.

HEYWOOD, JOHN, epigrammatist, 1497 ?—1580 ?

1908.   Let the world slide, let the world go :
               A fig for care, and a fig for woe !
               If I can't pay, why I can owe,
               And death makes equal the high and low.
                                        Be Merry Friends.

HEYWOOD, THOMAS, dramatist, 1572 ?—Aug. 1641

1909.   Pack clouds away and welcome day,
               With night we banish sorrow.
                                        Pack Clouds Away

HICKSON, WILLIAM EDWARD, nonconformist preacher, 7 Jan. 1803—22 March, 1870

1910.   Nor on this land alone—
                         But be God's mercies known
                         From shore to shore.
                         Lord, make the nations see
                         That men should brothers be,
                         And form one family
                         The wide world o'er.   *God bless our Native Land.*

[Sometimes used as a stanza of ' God Save the King.']

1911.   If at first you don't succeed,
                         Try, try again.   *Try and try again.*

HILL, AARON, poet, 10 Feb. 1685—8 Feb. 1750

1912.   First, then, a woman will, or won't, depend on't ;
        If she will do't, she will ; and there's an end on't.
        But if she won't, since safe and sound your trust is,
        Fear is affront, and jealousy injustice.   *Epilogue to Zara.*

1913.   Tender-handed stroke a nettle,
                             And it stings you for your pains ;
                         Grasp it like a man of mettle,
                             And it soft as silk remains.

                         'Tis the same with common natures :
                             Use 'em kindly, they rebel ;
                         But be rough as nutmeg-graters,
                             And the rogues obey you well.
                         Verses written on a window in Scotland.

HIPPOCLIDES, Greek notable, 6th century B.C.

1914.   Οὐ φροντὶς Ἱπποκλείδῃ—Hippoclides does not care.
                                        Herodotus, VI. 129.

HIPPOCRATES, Greek doctor, 460 ?—357 ? B.C.

1915.   Ὁ βίος βραχύς, ἡ δὲ τέχνη μακρή—Life is short and art is long.
                                        Aphorisms, I. I.

[Commonly quoted in Latin, 'Ars longa, vita brevis.']

HOBBES, THOMAS, philosopher, 5 April, 1588—4 Dec. 1679

1916.   For words are wise men's counters, they do but reckon by them ; but they are the money of fools.   *Leviathan*, I. iv.

1917.   Sudden glory is the passion which maketh those grimaces called laughter.   Ibid., vi.

1918.   No arts ; no letters ; no society ; and which is worst of all, continual fear and danger of violent death ; and the life of man solitary, poor, nasty, brutish, and short.   Ibid, xiii.

HOCH, EDWARD WALLIS, U.S. politician, 17 March, 1849—2 June, 1925

1919.   There is so much good in the worst of us,
                         And so much bad in the best of us,
                         That it hardly becomes any of us
                         To talk about the rest of us.   *Good and Bad*

HODGSON, RALPH, poet, 9 Sept. 1871—3 Nov. 1962

1920.
Time, you old gipsy man,
  Will you not stay,
Put up your caravan
  Just for one day ?
Time, You Old Gipsy Man.

1921.
Wondering, listening,
Listening, wondering,
Eve with a berry
Halfway to her lips. *Eve.*

HOFFMAN, AUGUST HEINRICH, VON FALLERSLEBEN, German poet and philologist, 2 April, 1798—19 Jan. 1874

1922. Deutschland, Deutschland über alles.—Germany, Germany over all. *Song.*

HOGG, JAMES (THE ETTRICK SHEPHERD), Scottish poet, baptised 9 Dec. 1770, died 21 Nov. 1835

1923.
Bonny Kilmeny gaed up the glen. *Kilmeny, 1.*

1924.
Cam ye by Athol, lad wi' the philabeg ?
Bonnie Prince Charlie.

1925.
Bird of the wilderness,
Blithesome and cumberless,
Sweet be thy matin o'er moorland and lea !
  Emblem of happiness,
  Blest is thy dwelling-place—
O to abide in the desert with thee ! *The Skylark.*

1926.
My love she's but a lassie yet. *Song.*

1927.
Where the pools are bright and deep,
Where the grey trout lies asleep,
Up the river and o'er the lea,
That's the way for Billy and me. *A Boy's Song.*

HOLLAND, SIR RICHARD, Scottish poet, fl. 1450

1928.
O Dowglas, O Dowglas, tendir and trewe !
Buke of the Howlat, 31.

HOLMES, OLIVER WENDELL, U.S. author, 29 Aug. 1809—7 Oct. 1894

1929.
Ay, tear her tattered ensign down !
  Long has it waved on high,
And many an eye has danced to see
  That banner in the sky.
Old Ironsides.

1930.
Nail to the mast her holy flag,
  Set every threadbare sail,
And give her to the god of storms,
  The lightning and the gale. **Ibid.**

1931.
Their discords sting through Burns and Moore
Like hedgehogs dressed in lace. *The Music-Grinders.*

1932.   And silence, like a poultice, comes
             To heal the blows of sound.   Ibid.

1933.   And, since, I never dare to write
             As funny as I can.
                                        The Height of the Ridiculous.

1934.   When the last reader reads no more.
                                                The Last Reader.

1935.   The freeman casting with unpurchased hand
             The vote that shakes the turrets of the land.
                                        Poetry, a Metrical Essay.

1936.   Have you heard of the wonderful one-horse shay,
             That was built in such a logical way
             It ran a hundred years to a day ?
                                        The Deacon's Masterpiece.

1937. A thought is often original, though you have uttered it a
hundred times.   *The Autocrat of the Breakfast Table,* i.

1938. The axis of the earth sticks out visibly through the centre
of each and every town or city.   Ibid, vi.

1939. The world's great men have not commonly been scholars,
nor its scholars great men.   Ibid.

HOME, JOHN, Scottish poet, 21 Sept. 1722—5 Sept. 1808

1940.   My name is Norval ; on the Grampian hills
             My father feeds his flocks ; a frugal swain,
             Whose constant cares were to increase this store,
             And keep his only son, myself, at home.   *Douglas,* II. i.

1941.   Like Douglas conquer, or like Douglas die.   Ibid., v. i.

HOMER, Greek poet, about 900 B.C.

1942. Μῆνιν ἄειδε, θεά, Πηληϊάδεω Ἀχιλῆος.
       —Sing, goddess, the wrath of Achilles, son of Peleus.
                                                  Iliad, i. 1.

1943. Βῆ δ᾽ ἀκέων παρὰ θῖνα πολυφλοίσβοιο θαλάσσης.
       —He went in silence along the shore of the loud-sounding sea.
                                                  Ibid., 34.

1944. Τὸν δ᾽ ἀπαμειβόμενος προσέφη πόδας ὠκὺς Ἀχιλλεύς.
       —And swift-footed Achilles answered him and said.
                                                  Ibid., 84.

1945. Ἔπεα πτερόεντα.
       —Winged words.   Ibid., 201.

1946. Ἐπὶ οἴνοπα πόντον.
       —Over the wine-dark sea.   Ibid., 350.

1947. Ποῖόν σε ἔπος φύγεν ἕρκος ὀδόντων ;
       —What a word has escaped the barrier of thy teeth !
                                                  Ibid., iv. 350.

1948. Οἵη περ φύλλων γενεή, τοίη δὲ καὶ ἀνδρῶν.
       —As the generation of leaves, so also is that of men.
                                                  Ibid., vi. 146.

1949. Αἰὲν ἀριστεύειν καὶ ὑπείροχον ἔμμεναι ἄλλων.
—Always to excel, and be distinguished above others.
Ibid., 208.

1950. 'Αλλ' ἤτοι μὲν ταῦτα θεῶν ἐν γούνασι κεῖται.
—But verily these things lie on the knees of the gods.
Ibid., xvii. 514.

1951 Πολλῶν δ' ἀνθρώπων ἴδεν ἄστεα καὶ νόον ἔγνω.
—Many were the men whose cities he saw and whose mind he
learned. *Odyssey*, i. 4.

1952 Ἧμος δ' ἠριγένεια φάνη ῥοδοδάκτυλος ἠώς.
—But when rosy-fingered dawn, child of the morning, appeared.
Ibid., ii. 1.

1953 Ἑξῆς δ' ἑζόμενοι πολιὴν ἅλα τύπτον ἐρετμοῖς.
—And sitting in order they smote the hoary sea with their oars.
Ibid., ix. 104.

1954. Τέτλαθι δή, κραδίη · καὶ κύντερον ἄλλο ποτ' ἔτλης.
—Bear, O my heart ; thou hast borne yet a harder thing.
Ibid., xx. 18.

HOOD, THOMAS, poet, 23 May, 1799—3 May, 1845

1955.   They went and told the sexton and
The sexton toll'd the bell.   *Faithless Sally Brown.*

1956.   Ben Battle was a soldier bold,
And used to war's alarms :
But a cannon-ball took off his legs,
So he laid down his arms !   *Faithless Nelly Gray.*

1957.   For here I leave my second leg
And the Forty-Second Foot !   Ibid.

1958.   Spring it is cheery,
Winter is dreary,
Green leaves hang, but the brown must fly ;
When he's forsaken,
Wither'd and shaken,
What can an old man do but die ?   *Ballad.*

1959.   I remember, I remember,
The house where I was born,
The little window where the sun
Came peeping in at morn.
I remember, I remember.

1960.   I remember, I remember,
The fir trees dark and high ;
I used to think their slender tops
Were close against the sky :
It was a childish ignorance,
But now 'tis little joy
To know I'm farther off from heav'n
Than when I was a boy.   Ibid.

1961.   Two stern-faced men set out from Lynn
Through the cold and heavy mist,
And Eugene Aram walked between
With gyves upon his wrist.
The Dream of Eugene Aram.

1962.   Boughs are daily rifled
                      By the gusty thieves,
                      And the Book of Nature
                      Getteth short of leaves.   *The Seasons.*

1963.   Our very hopes belied our fears,
                      Our fears our hopes belied—
                      We thought her dying when she slept,
                      And sleeping when she died !   *The Death-Bed.*

1964.   Seem'd washing his hands with invisible soap,
          In imperceptible water.
                            Miss Kilmansegg. Her Christening.

1965.   With fingers weary and worn,
            With eyelids heavy and red,
          A woman sat, in unwomanly rags,
            Plying her needle and thread—
                Stitch ! stitch ! stitch !
          In poverty, hunger, and dirt,
          And still with a voice of dolorous pitch
          She sang the ' Song of the Shirt ' !   *The Song of the Shirt.*

1966.   It is not linen you're wearing out
            But human creatures' lives.   Ibid.

1967.   Oh ! God ! that bread should be so dear,
            And flesh and blood so cheap.   Ibid.

1968.   My tears must stop, for every drop
            Hinders needle and thread !   Ibid.

1969.   But evil is wrought by want of thought,
            As well as want of heart.   *The Lady's Dream.*

1970.   One more Unfortunate,
                      Weary of breath,
                      Rashly importunate,
                      Gone to her death !

                      Take her up tenderly,
                      Lift her with care ;
                      Fashioned so slenderly,
                      Young, and so fair.   *The Bridge of Sighs.*

1971.   Alas ! for the rarity
                      Of Christian charity
                      Under the sun !   Ibid.

HOOKER, RICHARD, theologian, 1554 ?—2 Nov. 1600

     1972. To live by one man's will became the cause of all men's
misery.   *Ecclesiastical Polity,* I.

HOPE, ANTHONY (SIR ANTHONY HOPE HAWKINS), novelist, 9 Feb.
     1863—8 July, 1933

     1973. ' Bourgeois,' I observed, ' is an epithet which the riff-raff
apply to what is respectable, and the aristocracy to what is decent.'
                          Dolly Dialogues, xvii.
     1974. His foe was folly and his weapon wit.
                          On memorial to W. S. Gilbert.

HOPE, LAURENCE (ADELA FLORENCE NICOLSON), poetess, 9 April, 1865—4 Oct. 1904

1975.   Less than the dust beneath thy chariot wheel.
                              Indian Love Lyrics. Less than the Dust.

1976.   Pale hands I loved beside the Shalimar,
          Where are you now ?   Who lies beneath your spell ?
                              Ibid. *Pale Hands I loved.*

HOPKINS, GERARD MANLEY, poet and cleric, 28 July, 1844—8 June, 1889

1977.   The world is charged with the grandeur of God.
                              God's Grandeur.

1978. Glory be to God for dappled things—
          For skies of couple-colour as a brindled cow ;
          For rose-moles all in stipple upon trout that swim.
                              Pied Beauty.

1979.   Margaret, are you grieving
          Over Goldengrove unleaving ?
          Leaves, like the things of man, you
          With your fresh thoughts care for, can you ?
                              Spring and Fall : to a young child.

1980.   What would the world be, once bereft
          Of wet and of wildness ?   Let them be left,
          O let them be left, wildness and wet ;
          Long live the weeds and wilderness yet.   *Inversnaid.*

HOPKINSON, JOSEPH, U.S. Judge, 12 Nov. 1770—15 Jan. 1842

1981.   Hail, Columbia ! happy land !
          Hail, ye heroes ! heaven-born band !
            Who fought and bled in Freedom's cause.
                              Hail, Columbia.

HORACE (QUINTUS HORATIUS FLACCUS), Roman poet, 8 Dec. 65 B.C.— 27 Nov. 8 B.C.

1982.   Mutato nomine de te
          Fabula narratur.
          —Change the name, and the story is told about you.
                              Satires, I. i. 69.

1983.   Hoc genus omne.
          —All this sort.   Ibid., ii. 2.

1984.   Faenum habet in cornu.
          —He is dangerous (*lit.* He has hay on his horn). Ibid., iv. 34.

1985.   Ad unguem
          Factus homo.
          —A highly accomplished person (*lit.* made to the nail,
            from the testing of marble work by drawing the nail
            over it).   Ibid., v. 32.

1986.   Sic me servavit Apollo.
          —So Apollo preserved me.   Ibid., ix. 78.

1987 Carpe diem, quam minimum credula postero.
  —Seize the present day, trusting the morrow as little as
   may be.   *Odes*, I. xi. 8.

1988. Integer vitae scelerisque purus.
  —The man of upright life and pure from guilt.   Ibid., xxii. 1.

1989.   Neque semper arcum
  Tendit Apollo.
  —Nor does Apollo always keep his bow strung.   Ibid., II. x. 19.

1990. Eheu fugaces, Postume, Postume,
  Labunter anni.
  —Alas, Postumus, Postumus, the fleeting years glide past.
                Ibid., xiv. 1.

1991. Odi profanum vulgus et arceo.
  —I hate the vulgar throng and drive them from me.
                Ibid., III. i. 1.

1992. Dulce et decorum est pro patria mori.
  —It is a sweet and glorious thing to die for one's country.
                Ibid., ii. 13.

1993. Si fractus illabatur orbis
  Impavidum ferient ruinae.
  —If the heavens were to break and fall, the ruins would
   strike him undismayed.   Ibid., iii. 7

1994. Exegi monumentum aere perennius.
  —I have completed a memorial more lasting than brass.
                Ibid., xxx. 1.

1995. Vixere fortes ante Agamemnona
  Multi.
  —Many brave men lived before Agamemnon.   Ibid., IV. ix. 25.

1996.   Rem facias, rem
  Si possis, recte, si non, quocumque modo rem.
  —Make money, money, honestly if you can ; if not, by any
   means at all, make money.   *Epistles*, I. i. 66.

1997. Quidquid delirant reges plectuntur Achivi.
  —Whatever madness the kings commit, the Greeks suffer
   for it.   Ibid., ii. 14.

1998. Dimidium facti qui coepit habet.
  —He who has begun has half done.   Ibid., 40.

1999. Rusticus expectat dum defluat amnis.
  —Like the yokel, waits for the river to flow away.   Ibid., 42.

2000. Semper avarus eget.
  —The miser is always in want.   Ibid., 56.

2001. Ira furor brevis est.
  —Anger is a short madness.   Ibid., 62.

2002. Naturam expelles furca, tamen usque recurret.
  —Though you drive nature out with a pitchfork, she will
   ever return.   Ibid., x. 24.

2003. Caelum, non animum, mutant qui trans mare currunt.
  —They change their climate, not their soul, who run beyond
   the sea.   Ibid., xi. 27.

2004. Genus irritabile vatum.
—The touchy race of poets. *Ibid.*, II. ii. 102.

2005. Brevis esse laboro,
Obscurus fio.
—I struggle to be brief, and become obscure. *Ars Poetica*, 25.

2006. Parturiunt montes, nascetur ridiculus mus.
—The mountains are in labour ; there will be born a ridiculous
mouse. *Ibid.*, 139.

2007. Laudator temporis acti.
—Praiser of times past. *Ibid.*, 173.

2008. Exemplaria Graeca
Nocturna versate manu, versate diurna.
—Con the pages of Greek models day and night. *Ibid.*, 268.

2009. Indignor, quandoque bonus dormitat Homerus.
—I think it shame when the worthy Homer nods. *Ibid.* 359.

HOUGHTON, RICHARD MONCKTON MILNES, 1ST BARON, poet and
politician, 19 June, 1809—11 Aug. 1885

2010. But on and up, where Nature's heart
Beats strong amid the hills.
Tragedy of the Lac de Gaube, 2

2011. But the beating of my own heart
Was all the sound I heard. *The Brookside.*

2012. A fair little girl sat under a tree,
Sewing as long as her eyes could see ;
Then smoothed her work, and folded it right,
And said, ' Dear work, good-night, good-night.'
Good-Night and Good-Morning.

HOUSMAN, ALFRED EDWARD, scholar and poet, 26 March, 1859—
30 April, 1936

2013. Loveliest of trees, the cherry now
Is hung with bloom along the bough.
A Shropshire Lad, ii.

2014. Clay lies still, but blood's a rover. Ibid., iv. *Reveille.*

2015. When I was one-and-twenty
I heard a wise man say,
' Give crowns and pounds and guineas
But not your heart away.' Ibid., xiii.

2016. To-day, the road all runners come,
Shoulder-high we bring you home,
And set you at your threshold down,
Townsman of a stiller town.
Ibid., xix. *To an Athlete dying Young.*

2017. And silence sounds no worse than cheers
After death has stopped the ears. Ibid.

2018. They carry back bright to the coiner the mintage of man,
The lads that will die in their glory and never be old.
Ibid., xxiii.

2019. Dust's your wages, son of sorrow,
But men may come to worse than dust. *Ibid.*, xliv.

2020. By brooks too broad for leaping
The lightfoot boys are laid. *Ibid.*, liv.

2021. And malt does more than Milton can
To justify God's ways to man.
Ale, man, ale's the stuff to drink
For fellows whom it hurts to think. *Ibid.*, lxii.

2022. Pass me the can, lad ; there's an end of May.
Last Poems, ix.

2023. May will be fine next year as like as not :
Oh ay, but then we shall be twenty-four. *Ibid.*

2024. The fairies break their dances
And leave the printed lawn. *Ibid.*, xxi.

2025. The pence are here and here's the fair,
But where's the lost young man ? *Ibid.*, xxxv.

2026. These, in the day when heaven was falling,
The hour when earth's foundations fled,
Followed their mercenary calling
And took their wages and are dead.
Ibid, xxxviii. *Epitaph on an Army of Mercenaries.*

2027. Even when poetry has a meaning, as it usually has, it may be
inadvisable to draw it out. . . . Perfect understanding will sometimes
almost extinguish pleasure.
The Name and Nature of Poetry.

HOWARD, HENRY, *see* Surrey, Earl of

HOWARTH, ELLEN CLEMENTINE, U.S. author, 20 May, 1827—1899
2028. 'Tis but a little faded flower. *Song.*

HOWE, JULIA WARD, U.S. reformer, 27 May, 1819—17 Oct. 1910.
2029. Mine eyes have seen the glory of the coming of the Lord ;
He is trampling out the vintage where the grapes of wrath
stored ;
He hath loosed the fateful lightning of His terrible, swift
sword ;
His truth is marching on. *Battle Hymn of the Republic.*
2030. In the beauty of the lilies Christ was born across the sea. *Ibid.*

HOWELLS, WILLIAM DEAN, U.S. author, 1 March, 1837—11 May, 1920
2031. Tossing his mane of snows in wildest eddies and tangles,
Lion-like March cometh in, hoarse, with tempestuous
breath. *Earliest Spring.*

HOWITT, MARY, author, 12 March, 1799—30 Jan. 1888
2032. ' Will you walk into my parlour ? ' said a spider to a fly :
' 'Tis the prettiest little parlour that ever you did spy ;
The way into my parlour is up a winding stair,
And I have many curious things to show when you are
there.' *The Spider and the Fly.*

HOYLE, EDMOND, writer on whist, 1672—29 Aug. 1769
    2033. When in doubt, win the trick.
Whist. Twenty-four Short Rules for Learners.

HUBBARD, ELBERT, U.S. author, 19 June, 1856—7 May, 1915
    2034. Life is just one damned thing after another.
A Thousand and One Epigrams, 137.

HUGHES, THOMAS, novelist, 20 Oct. 1822—22 March, 1896
    2035. Life isn't all beer and skittles ; but beer and skittles, or something better of the same sort, must form a good part of every Englishman's education.   <i>Tom Brown's Schooldays</i>, I. ii.

HUME, DAVID, Scottish historian, 26 April, 1711—25 Aug., 1776
    2036. Avarice, the spur of industry.   <i>Essays. Of Civil Liberty.</i>
    2037. Custom, then, is the great guide of human life.
Inquiry concerning Human Understanding, v. i.

HUNT, GEORGE WILLIAM, song-writer, 1829 ?—3 March, 1904
    2038. We don't want to fight, but by jingo if we do,
        We've got the ships, we've got the men, we've got the money
            too.   <i>Song.</i>

HUNT, JAMES HENRY LEIGH, author, 19 Oct. 1784—28 Aug. 1859
    2039. Where the light woods go seaward from the town.
The Story of Rimini, i. 18.
  2040.   The two divinest things this world has got,
        A lovely woman in a rural spot !   Ibid., iii. 257.
  2041.   Abou Ben Adhem (may his tribe increase)
        Awoke one night from a deep dream of peace.
Abou Ben Adhem.
  2042.   Write me as one who loves his fellow men.   Ibid.
  2043.   And lo ! Ben Adhem's name led all the rest.   Ibid.
  2044.   Green little vaulter in the sunny grass.
To the Grasshopper and the Cricket.
  2045.   Jenny kissed me when we met,
        Jumping from the chair she sat in.   <i>Rondeau.</i>
    2046. This Adonis in loveliness was a corpulent man of fifty. [The Prince Regent.]   <i>The Examiner</i>, 22 March, 1812.

HUTCHESON, FRANCIS, Scottish philosopher, 8 Aug. 1694—1746
    2047. That action is best, which procures the greatest happiness for the greatest numbers.
Inquiry into the Original of our Ideas of Beauty and Virtue,
II. iii. 8.

HUXLEY, ALDOUS LEONARD, novelist, 26 July, 1894—22 Nov. 1963
    2048. There are not enough <i>bon mots</i> in existence to provide any industrious conversationalist with a new stock for every social occasion.
Point Counter Point, vii.

HUXLEY, THOMAS HENRY, scientist, 4 May, 1825—29 June, 1895

2049. The great end of life is not knowledge but action.

Technical Education.

2050. It is the customary fate of new truths to begin as heresies and to end as superstitions. *The Coming of Age of the Origin of Species.*

IBSEN, HENRIK JOHAN, Norwegian dramatist, 20 March, 1828—28 May, 1906

2051. You should never put on your best trousers when you go out to fight for freedom and truth. *An Enemy of the People,* v.

2052. With vine leaves in his hair. *Hedda Gabler,* II.

INGE, CHARLES, cleric, 20th century

2053.   This very remarkable man
             Commends a most practical plan :
                 You can do what you want
                 If you don't think you can't,
             So don't think you can't think you can.

On Monsieur Coué.

INGE, WILLIAM RALPH, Dean of St. Paul's, 6 June, 1860—26 Feb. 1954

2054. Public opinion, a vulgar, impertinent, anonymous tyrant who deliberately makes life unpleasant for anyone who is not content to be the average man.

Outspoken Essays, 1st series. *Our Present Discontents.*

2055. The modern town-dweller has no God and no Devil ; he lives without awe, without admiration, without fear. Ibid.

2056. A man may build himself a throne of bayonets, but he cannot sit on it. Marchant, *Wit and Wisdom of Dean Inge,* 108.

2057. The nations which have put mankind and posterity most in their debt have been small States—Israel, Athens, Florence, Elizabethan England. Ibid., 181.

INGELOW, JEAN, poetess, 17 March, 1820—20 July, 1897

2058.   But two are walking apart for ever,
             And wave their hands for a mute farewell. *Divided.*

2059.   Play uppe ' The Brides of Enderby.'
             The High Tide on the Coast of Lincolnshire, 1571.

INGERSOLL, ROBERT GREEN, U.S. lawyer, 11 Aug. 1833—21 July, 1899

2060. An honest God is the noblest work of man. *Gods,* I.

INGRAM, JOHN KELLS, Irish economist, 7 July, 1823—1 May, 1907

2061.   Who fears to speak of Ninety-eight ?
                     Who blushes at the name ?
                 When cowards mock the patriot's fate,
                     Who hangs his head for shame ?

The Memory of the Dead.

IRVING, WASHINGTON, U.S. author, 3 April, 1783—28 Nov. 1859

2062. The almighty dollar, that great object of universal devotion throughout our land, seems to have no genuine devotees in these peculiar villages.   *Wolfert's Roost. The Creole Village.*

2063. A sharp tongue is the only edged tool that grows keener with constant use.   *The Sketch-Book. Rip Van Winkle.*

2064. They who drink beer will think beer.   Ibid. *Stratford.*

JACKSON, HELEN HUNT, U.S. author, 15 Oct. 1830—12 Aug. 1885

2065.   Oh, write of me, not ' Died in bitter pains,'
            But ' Emigrated to another star ! '   *Emigravit.*

JAMES I, King, 19 June, 1566—27 March, 1625

2066. A custom loathsome to the eye, hateful to the nose, harmful to the brain, dangerous to the lungs, and in the black, stinking fume thereof nearest resembling the horrible Stygian smoke of the pit that is bottomless.   *A Counterblast to Tobacco.*

2067. No bishop, no king.   *Attributed.*

JAMES, HENRY, U.S. author, 15 April, 1843—28 Feb. 1916

2068. He was worse than provincial—he was parochial. [Thoreau.]
                    Life of Nathaniel Hawthorne, iv.

2069. The time-honoured bread-sauce of the happy ending.
                    Theatricals, 2nd series.

JEFFERSON, THOMAS, U.S. President, 13 April, 1743—4 July, 1826

2070. The God who gave us life gave us liberty at the same time.
                    Summary View of the Rights of British America.

2071. We hold these truths to be self-evident,—that all men are created equal ; that they are endowed by their Creator with certain unalienable rights ; that among these are life, liberty, and the pursuit of happiness.   *Declaration of Independence.*

2072. Error of opinion may be tolerated when reason is left free to combat it.   *First Inaugural Address,* 4 March, 1801.

2073. Peace, commerce, and honest friendship with all nations,— entangling alliances with none.   Ibid.

JEFFREY, FRANCIS, LORD, Scottish lawyer and critic, 23 Oct. 1773— 26 Jan. 1850

2074.   Here lies the preacher, judge, and poet, Peter,
            Who broke the laws of God, and man, and metre.
                    On Peter Robinson.

2075. This will never do. [On Wordsworth's *Excursion.*]
                    Edinburgh Review, Nov. 1814.

JEROME, JEROME KLAPKA, author, 2 May, 1859—14 June, 1927

2076. I like work ; it fascinates me. I can sit and look at it for hours. I love to keep it by me : the idea of getting rid of it nearly breaks my heart. *Three Men in a Boat*, xv.

2077. Love is like the measles ; we all have to go through it.
Idle Thoughts of an Idle Fellow. On Being in Love.

JERROLD, DOUGLAS WILLIAM, author, 3 Jan. 1803—8 June, 1857

2078. Love's like the measles—all the worse when it comes late in life. *A Philanthropist.*

2079. Earth is here [in Australia] so kind, that just tickle her with a hoe and she laughs with a harvest. *A Land of Plenty.*

JOHNSON, LIONEL PIGOT, poet, 15 March, 1867—4 Oct. 1902

2080.   The saddest of all kings
          Crowned, and again discrowned.
          By the Statue of King Charles at Charing Cross.

2081.   There Shelley dreamed his white Platonic dreams. *Oxford.*

JOHNSON, Philander Chase, U.S. journalist, 6 Feb. 1866—18 May, 1939

2082. Cheer up, the worst is yet to come. *Shooting Stars.*

JOHNSON, ROSSITER, U.S. author, 27 Jan. 1840—3 Oct. 1931

2083.   O for a lodge in a garden of cucumbers !
          O for an iceberg or two at control !
          O for a vale which at midday the dew cumbers !
          O for a pleasure trip up to the Pole!
          Ninety-nine in the Shade.

JOHNSON, SAMUEL, lexicographer, 18 Sept. 1709—13 Dec. 1784

2084.   Here falling houses thunder on your head,
          And here a female atheist talks you dead.   *London,* 17.

2085.   Of all the griefs that harass the distress'd,
          Sure the most bitter is a scornful jest.   Ibid., 166.

2086.   This mournful truth is ev'rywhere confess'd,
          Slow rises worth by poverty depress'd.   Ibid., 176.

2087.   Prepare for death if here at night you roam,
          And sign your will before you sup from home.   Ibid., 224.

2088.   Let observation with extensive view
          Survey mankind from China to Peru.
          The Vanity of Human Wishes, 1.

2089.   There mark what ills the scholar's life assail,
          Toil, envy, want, the patron, and the jail.   Ibid., 159.

2090.   He left the name, at which the world grew pale,
          To point a moral, or adorn a tale.   Ibid., 221.

2091. In life's last scene what prodigies surprise,
       Fears of the brave, and follies of the wise !
       From Marlb'rough's eyes the streams of dotage flow,
       And Swift expires a driv'ler and a show.   *Ibid.*, 315.

2092. Must helpless man, in ignorance sedate,
       Roll darkling down the torrent of his fate ?   *Ibid.*, 345.

2093. When Learning's triumph o'er her barb'rous foes
       First rear'd the Stage, immortal Shakespeare rose ;
       Each change of many-colour'd life he drew,
       Exhausted worlds, and then imagin'd new :
       Existence saw him spurn her bounded reign,
       And panting Time toil'd after him in vain.
            Prologue at the Opening of the Theatre in Drury Lane, 1.

2094. For we that live to please, must please to live.   *Ibid.*, 54.

2095.   I put my hat upon my head
                    And walk'd into the Strand,
                 And there I met another man
                    Whose hat was in his hand.
                 Parodies of the Hermit of Warkworth, ii.

       [Another version is :—
                 As with my hat upon my head
                    I walk'd along the Strand,
                 I there did meet another man
                    With his hat in his hand.]

2096. Phrase that time has flung away,
       Uncouth words in disarray :
       Trickt in antique ruff and bonnet,
       Ode and elegy and sonnet.
            Lines written in Ridicule of Thomas Warton's Poems.

2097. If the man who turnips cries,
       Cry not when his father dies,
       'Tis a proof that he had rather
       Have a turnip than his father.
            Burlesque of Lines by Lope de Vega.

2098. How small, of all that human hearts endure,
       That part which laws or kings can cause or cure,
       Still to ourselves in every place consign'd,
       Our own felicity we make or find :
       With secret course, which no loud storms annoy,
       Glides the smooth current of domestic joy.
            Added to Goldsmith's *Traveller*, 429.

2099. That trade's proud empire hastes to swift decay,
       As ocean sweeps the laboured mole away ;
       While self-dependent power can time defy,
       As rocks resist the billows and the sky.
            Added to Goldsmith's *Deserted Village*, 427.

2100. No place affords a more striking conviction of the vanity of human hopes, than a public library   *The Rambler*, 23 March, 1751.

2101. I am not yet so lost in lexicography, as to forget that words are the daughters of earth, and that things are the sons of heaven.
            Dictionary of the English Language, preface.

F

2102. *Lexicographer*—A writer of dictionaries, a harmless drudge.

Ibid., definitions.

2103. *Oats*—A grain, which in England is generally given to horses, but in Scotland supports the people.   Ibid.

2104. *Patron*—Commonly a wretch who supports with insolence, and is paid with flattery.   Ibid,

2105. *Pension*—An allowance made to anyone without an equivalent. In England it is generally understood to mean pay given to a state hireling for treason to his country.   Ibid.

2106. Ye who listen with credulity to the whispers of fancy, and pursue with eagerness the phantoms of hope ; who expect that age will perform the promises of youth, and that the deficiencies of the present day will be supplied by the morrow ; attend to the history of Rasselas, Prince of Abyssinia.   *Rasselas*, i.

2107. Marriage has many pains, but celibacy has no pleasures.

Ibid., xxvi.

2108. The stream of time, which is continually washing the dissoluble fabricks of other poets, passes without injury by the adamant of Shakespeare.   *Edition of Shakespeare*, preface.

2109. That man is little to be envied whose patriotism would not gain force upon the plain of Marathon, or whose piety would not grow warmer among the ruins of Iona.

Journey to the Western Islands. Inch Kenneth.

2110. Whoever wishes to attain an English style, familiar but not coarse, and elegant but not ostentatious, must give his days and nights to the volumes of Addison.   *Lives of the English Poets. Addison.*

2111. To be of no church is dangerous. Religion, of which the rewards are distant, and which is animated only by Faith and Hope, will glide by degrees out of the mind, unless it be invigorated and reimpressed by external ordinances, by stated calls to worship, and the salutary influence of example.   Ibid. *Milton.*

2112. That stroke of death, which has eclipsed the gaiety of nations, and impoverished the public stock of harmless pleasure. [Garrick's death.]   Ibid. *Edmund Smith.*

2113. Nullum quod tetigit non ornavit.—He touched nothing that he did not adorn.   *Epitaph on Goldsmith.*

2114. Sir, we are a nest of singing birds. [Pembroke College, Oxford.]   Boswell's *Life of Johnson*, an. 1730.

2115. Like the Monument. [When asked how he felt on the ill success of his tragedy, *Irene.*]   Ibid., an. 1749.

2116. A man may write any time, if he will set himself doggedly to it.   Ibid., an. 1750.

2117. Wretched un-idea'd girls.   Ibid., an. 1753

2118. This man I thought had been a lord among wits, but I find he is only a wit among lords. [Lord Chesterfield.]   Ibid., an. 1754.

2119. They teach the morals of a whore, and the manners of a dancing master. [Lord Chesterfield's *Letters.*]   Ibid.

2120. Is not a Patron, my Lord, one who looks with unconcern on a man struggling for life in the water, and when he has reached ground, encumbers him with help ? The notice which you have been pleased to take of my labours, had it been early, had been kind ; but it has been delayed till I am indifferent, and cannot enjoy it ; till I am solitary, and cannot impart it ; till I am known, and do not want it.

Ibid., *Letter to Lord Chesterfield*, 1755.

2121. Ignorance, Madam, pure ignorance. [When asked why he defined *pastern* as ' the knee of a horse ' in his dictionary.]

Ibid., an. 1755.

2122. A man, Sir, should keep his friendship in constant repair.

Ibid.

2123. Being in a ship is being in jail, with the chance of being drowned. . . . A man in a jail has more room, better food, and commonly better company. Ibid., an. 1759.

2124. That, Sir, I find, is what a very great many of your country-men cannot help. [When Boswell said that he could not help coming from Scotland.] Ibid., an. 1763.

2125. Another charge was, that he did not love clean linen ; and I have no passion for it. [Of Kit Smart.] Ibid.

2126. You *may* abuse a tragedy, though you cannot write one. You may scold a carpenter who has made you a bad table, though you cannot make a table. It is not your trade to make tables. Ibid.

2127. Consider, Sir, how insignificant this will appear a twelve-month hence. Ibid.

2128. The noblest prospect which a Scotchman ever sees, is the high road that leads him to England. Ibid.

2129. A man ought to read just as inclination leads him ; for what he reads as a task will do him little good. Ibid.

2130. If he does really think that there is no distinction between virtue and vice, why, Sir, when he leaves our houses let us count our spoons. Ibid.

2131. Sir, a woman's preaching is like a dog's walking on his hinder legs. It is not done well ; but you are surprised to find it done at all.

Ibid.

2132. For my part I mind my belly very studiously and very care-fully ; for I look upon it, that he who does not mind his belly, will hardly mind anything else. Ibid.

2133. It was not for me to bandy civilities with my sovereign.

Ibid., an. 1767.

2134. Sir, we *know* our will is free, and *there's* an end on't.

Ibid., an. 1769.

2135. It matters not how a man dies, but how he lives. Ibid.

2136. That fellow seems to me to possess but one idea, and that is a wrong one. Ibid., an. 1770.

2137. Why, Sir, if you were to read Richardson for the story, your impatience would be so much fretted that you would hang yourself.

Ibid., an. 1772

2138. Much may be made of a Scotchman, if he be *caught* young.
Ibid.

2139. No, Sir, do *you* read books *through* ? [When asked if he had read a new book through.]   Ibid., an. 1773.

2140. My dear Sir, never accustom your mind to mingle virtue and vice. The woman's a whore, and there's an end on't.   Ibid.

2141. There are few ways in which a man can be more innocently employed than in getting money.   Ibid., an. 1775.

2142. A man will turn over half a library to make one book.   Ibid.

2143. Patriotism is the last refuge of a scoundrel.   Ibid.

2144. Knowledge is of two kinds. We know a subject ourselves, or we know where we can find information upon it.   Ibid.

2145. In lapidary inscriptions a man is not upon oath.   Ibid.

2146. There is nothing which has yet been contrived by man, by which so much happiness is produced as by a good tavern or inn.
Ibid., an. 1776.

2147. No man but a blockhead ever wrote except for money.   Ibid.

2148. Sir, you have but two topics, yourself and me, and I am sick of both.   Ibid.

2149. Sir, it is not so much to be lamented that Old England is lost, as that the Scotch have found it.   Ibid.

2150. If I had no duties, and no reference to futurity, I would spend my life in driving briskly in a postchaise with a pretty woman.
Ibid., an. 1777.

2151. Depend upon it, Sir, when a man knows he is to be hanged in a fortnight, it concentrates his mind wonderfully.   Ibid.

2152. No, Sir, when a man is tired of London he is tired of life ; for there is in London all that life can afford.   Ibid.

2153. All argument is against it ; but all belief is for it. [Of the appearance of men's spirits after death.]   Ibid., an. 1778.

2154. All censure of a man's self is oblique praise. It is in order to show how much he can spare.   Ibid.

2155. Claret is the liquor for boys ; port for men ; but he who aspires to be a hero must drink brandy.   Ibid., an. 1779.

2156. Worth seeing ? yes ; but not worth going to see. [Of the Giant's Causeway.]   Ibid.

2157. Greek, Sir, is like lace ; every man gets as much of it as he can.   Ibid., an. 1780.

2158. Sir, I have two very cogent reasons for not printing any list of subscribers ; —one, that I have lost all the names,—the other, that I have spent all the money. [Anecdote of 1763, referring to his edition of Shakespeare.]   Ibid., an. 1781.

2159. My dear friend, clear your *mind* of cant. You may *talk* as other people do : you may say to a man, ' Sir, I am your most humble servant.' You are *not* his most humble servant.   Ibid., an. 1783.

2160. It might as well be ' Who drives fat oxen should himself be fat.' [Parodying the line from Brooke's *Earl of Essex*, ' Who rules o'er freemen should himself be free.']   Ibid., an. 1784.

2161. Sir, I have found you an argument ; but I am not obliged to find you an understanding.   *Ibid.*

2162. Preserve me from unseasonable and immoderate sleep.
Prayers and Meditations.

2163. Books that you may carry to the fire, and hold readily in your hand, are the most useful after all.
Hawkins, *Apophthegms, Sentiments, Opinions.*

2164. Dictionaries are like watches ; the worst is better than none, and the best cannot be expected to go quite true.
Mrs. Piozzi, *Anecdotes of Johnson.*

2165. Difficult do you call it, Sir ? I wish it were impossible. [Of the performance of a celebrated violinist.]   W. Seward, *Anecdotes.*

JONES, JOHN PAUL, Scottish adventurer who became U.S. naval officer, 6 July, 1747—18 July, 1792

2166. I have not yet begun to fight.
When summoned to surrender, as his ship was sinking, 1779.

JONES, SIR WILLIAM, oriental scholar, 28 Sept. 1746—27 April, 1794

2167.   Seven hours to law, to soothing slumber seven,
Ten to the world allot, and all to Heaven.
In place of Sir E. Coke's lines, No. 948.

JONSON, BEN, Poet Laureate, 1572—6 Aug. 1637

2168.   Underneath this stone doth lie
As much beauty as could die ;
Which in life did harbour give
To more virtue than doth live.
Epitaph on Elizabeth, L.H.

2169.   Drink to me only with thine eyes,
And I will pledge with mine ;
Or leave a kiss but in the cup,
And I'll not look for wine.   *To Celia.*

2170.   Have you seen but a bright lily grow,
Before rude hands have touch'd it ?
Have you mark'd but the fall o' the snow
Before the soil hath smutch'd it ?

    .   .   .   .   .

O so white ! O so soft ! O so sweet is she !
Celebration of Charis, iv. *Her Triumph.*

2171.   Soul of the age !
The applause ! delight ! the wonder of our stage !
My Shakespeare, rise ; I will not lodge thee by
Chaucer, or Spenser, or bid Beaumont lie
A little further, to make thee a room.
To the Memory of Shakespeare.

2172. Or sporting Kyd, or Marlowe's mighty line.   Ibid.

2173. And though thou hadst small Latin, and less Greek.   Ibid.

2174. He was not of an age, but for all time.   Ibid.

2175.   Sweet Swan of Avon !   Ibid.

2176.   It is not growing like a tree
                    In bulk, doth make men better be.
                            A Pindaric Ode on the Death of Sir H. Morison.

2177.   Queen and huntress, chaste and fair,
                        Now the sun is laid to sleep,
                    Seated in thy silver chair,
                            State in wonted manner keep :
                                Hesperus entreats thy light,
                                Goddess excellently bright.
                                            Cynthia's Revels, v. iii.

2178.   Still to be neat, still to be drest,
                    As you were going to a feast.
                            Epicoene ; or The Silent Woman, i. i.

2179.   I remember the players have often mentioned it as an honour
in Shakespeare that in his writing (whatsoever he penned) he never
blotted out a line.   My answer hath been ' Would he had blotted a
thousand.'   *Timber, or Discoveries made upon Men and Matters.*

2180.   For I loved the man, and do honour his memory, on this side
idolatry, as much as any.   Ibid.

JULIAN THE APOSTATE (FLAVIUS CLAUDIUS JULIANUS), Roman
        Emperor, 331—26 June, 363

2181 . Vicisti, Galilaee.—Thou has conquered, O Galilean.
                                            Attributed dying words.

JUNIUS (pseudonym of writer never identified), *fl.* 1770.

2182.   The liberty of the press is the *Palladium* of all the civil,
political, and religious rights of an Englishman.
                                            Letters, dedication.

JUNOT, ANDOCHE, Marshal of France, 23 Oct. 1771—29 July, 1813

2183.   Moi je suis mon ancêtre.—I am my own ancestor.
                                            When created Duke of Abrantes.

JUVENAL (DECIMUS JUNIUS JUVENALIS), Roman satirist, A.D. 60 ?—
        140 ?

2184.   Quidquid agunt homines, votum timor ira voluptas
        Gaudia discursus, nostri farrago libelli est.
            —Whatever men do, wishes, fears, anger, pleasures, joys,
                goings to and fro, is the medley of my book.
                                            Satires, i. 85.
2185.   Nemo repente fuit turpissimus.
            —No one ever became thoroughly bad all at once.
                                            Ibid., ii. 83.
2186.   Res angusta domi.
            —Straitened means at home.   Ibid., iii. 165.
2187.   Rara avis in terris nigroque simillima cycno.
            —A rare bird on the earth and very like a black swan.
                                            Ibid., vi. 165

2188.   Hoc volo, sic jubeo, sit pro ratione voluntas.
      —This is my wish, thus I command. Let my will take
        the place of reason.   Ibid., 223.

2189.   Quis custodiet ipsos
      Custodes ?
      —Who is to guard the guards themselves ?   Ibid., 347.

2190.   Scribendi cacoethes.
        —The itch for writing.   Ibid., vii. 52.

2191.   Crambe repetita.
        —Cabbage served up again.   Ibid., 154.

2192.   Nobilitas sola est atque unica virtus.
      —Virtue is the sole and only nobility.   Ibid., viii. 20.

2193.   Panem et circenses.
        —Bread and games.   Ibid., **x.** 81.

2194.   Mens sana in corpore sano.
       —A sound mind in a sound body.   Ibid., 356.

KANT, IMMANUEL, German philosopher, 22 April, 1724—12 Feb. 1804

2195. Ich soll niemals anders verfahren, als so, dass ich auch wollen könne, meine Maxime solle ein allgemeines Gesetz werden.—I am never to act otherwise than so that I could also will that my maxim should become a universal law.
      Grundlegung zur Metaphysik der Sitten.—Foundations of a
      Metaphysic of Morals, i.

KARR, JEAN BAPTISTE ALPHONSE, French novelist, 24 Nov. 1808—30 Sept. 1890

2196. Plus ça change, plus c'est la même chose.—The more it changes the more it is the same thing.   *Les Guêpes,* Jan. 1849.

2197. Si l'on veut abolir la peine de mort en ce cas, que MM. les assassins commencent.—If it is intended to abolish the death penalty in this case, let the gentlemen who do the murders take the first step.
      Ibid.

KEATS, JOHN, poet, 29 or 31 Oct. 1795—23 Feb. 1821

2198.   Here are sweet peas, on tip-toe for a flight.
      I stood tip-toe upon a Little Hill.

2199.   To one who has been long in city pent,
        'Tis very sweet to look into the fair
        And open face of heaven.
      To one who has been long.

2200.   Much have I travell'd in the realms of gold,
      And many goodly states and kingdoms seen.
      On first looking into Chapman's Homer.

2201.   Then felt I like some watcher of the skies
      When a new planet swims into his ken;
    Or like stout Cortez when with eagle eyes
      He star'd at the Pacific—and all his men
    Look'd at each other with a wild surmise—
      Silent, upon a peak in Darien.   Ibid.

2202. They sway'd about upon a rocking-horse,
And thought it Pegasus. *Sleep and Poetry*, 186.

2203. A thing of beauty is a joy for ever :
Its loveliness increases ; it will never
Pass into nothingness ; but still will keep
A bower quiet for us, and a sleep
Full of sweet dreams, and health, and quiet breathing.
Endymion, I. I.

2204. Love in a hut, with water and a crust,
Is—Love, forgive us !—cinders, ashes, dust ;
Love in a palace is perhaps at last
More grievous torment than a hermit's fast. *Lamia*, ii. I.

2205. Philosophy will clip an angel's wings. Ibid,. 234.

2206. So the two brothers and their murder'd man
Rode past fair Florence. *Isabella*, 27.

2207. St. Agnes' Eve—Ah, bitter chill it was !
The owl, for all his feathers, was a-cold.
The Eve of St. Agnes, I.

2208. The silver, snarling trumpets 'gan to chide. Ibid., 4.

2209. As though a rose should shut, and be a bud again.
Ibid., 27.

2210. A heap
Of candied apple, quince, and plum, and gourd ;
With jellies soother than the creamy curd,
And lucent syrops, tinct with cinnamon ;
Manna and dates, in argosy transferr'd
From Fez ; and spiced dainties, every one,
From silken Samarcand to cedar'd Lebanon. Ibid., 30.

2211. My heart aches, and a drowsy numbness pains
My sense, as though of hemlock I had drunk.
Ode to a Nightingale, I.

2212. O for a beaker full of the warm South,
Full of the true, the blushful Hippocrene,
With beaded bubbles winking at the brim,
And purple-stainèd mouth ;
That I might drink, and leave the world unseen,
And with thee fade away into the forest dim. Ibid., 2.

2213. Where youth grows pale, and spectre-thin, and dies.
Ibid., 3.

2214. Away ! away ! for I will fly to thee,
Not charioted by Bacchus and his pards,
But on the viewless wings of Poesy,
Though the dull brain perplexes and retards. Ibid., 4.

2215. I cannot see what flowers are at my feet,
Nor what soft incense hangs upon the boughs. Ibid., 5.

2216. Darkling I listen ; and for many a time
I have been half in love with easeful Death. Ibid., 6.

2217.   Thou wast not born for death, immortal Bird !
        No hungry generations tread thee down ;
        The voice I hear this passing night was heard
        In ancient days by emperor and clown :
        Perhaps the self-same song that found a path
        Through the sad heart of Ruth, when, sick for home,
        She stood in tears amid the alien corn ;
        The same that oft-times hath
        Charm'd magic casements, opening on the foam
        Of perilous seas, in faery lands forlorn.   Ibid, 7.

2218.   Thou still unravish'd bride of quietness,
        Thou foster-child of silence and slow time.
                            Ode on a Grecian Urn, I

2219.   Heard melodies are sweet but those unheard
        Are sweeter ; therefore, ye soft pipes, play on ;
        Not to the sensual ear, but, more endear'd,
        Pipe to the spirit ditties of no tone.   Ibid, 2.

2220.   For ever wilt thou love, and she be fair !   Ibid.

2221.   ' Beauty is truth, truth beauty,'—that is all
        Ye know on earth, and all ye need to know.   Ibid., 5.

2222.   And there shall be for thee all soft delight
        That shadowy thought can win,
        A bright torch, and a casement ope at night,
        To let the warm Love in !   *Ode to Psyche,* 64.

2223.   Ever let the fancy roam,
                    Pleasure never is at home.   *Fancy,* 1.

2224.   Where's the eye, however blue,
                    Doth not weary ? Where's the face
                    One would meet in every place ?
                    Where's the voice, however soft,
                    One would hear so very oft ?   Ibid., 72.

2225.   Bards of Passion and of Mirth,
                    Ye have left your souls on earth !
                    Have ye souls in heaven too,
                    Double lived in regions new ?
                    Ode (written in a volume of Beaumont and Fletcher), 1.

2226.   Souls of poets dead and gone,
                    What Elysium have ye known,
                    Happy field or mossy cavern
                    Choicer than the Mermaid Tavern ?
                            Lines on the Mermaid Tavern, 1.

2227.   Season of mists and mellow fruitfulness,
        Close bosom-friend of the maturing sun.
                            To Autumn, 1.

2228.   Sometimes whoever seeks abroad may find
        Thee sitting careless on a granary floor,
        Thy hair soft-lifted by the winnowing wind.   Ibid., 2.

*F

2229.   Deep in the shady sadness of a vale
Far sunken from the healthy breath of morn,
Far from the fiery noon, and eve's one star,
Sat grey-hair'd Saturn, quiet as a stone,
Still as the silence round about his lair ;
Forest on forest hung about his head
Like cloud on cloud.   *Hyperion*, I. I.

2230.   As when, upon a tranced summer night,
Those green-rob'd senators of mighty woods,
Tall oaks, branch-charmed by the earnest stars,
Dream, and so dream all night without a stir.   Ibid., 72.

2231.   When I have fears that I may cease to be
Before my pen has glean'd my teeming brain.
    Sonnet. When I have Fears.

2232.   In a drear-nighted December,
Too happy, happy tree,
Thy branches ne'er remember
Their green felicity.
    Stanzas. In a Drear-nighted December.

2233.   O what can ail thee, knight-at-arms,
Alone and palely loitering ?
The sedge has wither'd from the lake,
And no birds sing.   *La Belle Dame sans Merci*, I.
[Another version of line I is :—
Ah, what can ail thee, wretched wight.]

2234.   Bright star, would I were steadfast as thou art—
Not in lone splendour hung aloft the night
And watching, with eternal lids apart,
Like nature's patient, sleepless Eremite,
The moving waters at their priestlike task
Of pure ablution round earth's human shores.
    Sonnet. Bright Star.

2235. The imagination of a boy is healthy, and the mature imagination of a man is healthy ; but there is a space of life between, in which the soul is in a ferment, the character undecided, the way of life uncertain, the ambition thick-sighted : thence proceeds mawkishness.
    Endymion, preface

2236. O for a life of sensations rather than of thoughts !
    Letter to Benjamin Bailey, 22 Nov. 1817.

2237. Poetry should surprise by a fine excess, and not by singularity ; it should strike the reader as a wording of his own highest thoughts, and appear almost a remembrance.
    Letter to John Taylor, 27 Feb. 1818.

2238. Here lies one whose name was writ in water.
    Epitaph for himself.

KEBLE, JOHN, cleric and professor of poetry, 25 April, 1792—29 March, 1866

2239.   We need not bid, for cloister'd cell,
Our neighbour and our work farewell.
    The Christian Year. Morning.

2240.	The trivial round, the common task,
	Will furnish all we ought to ask.

Ibid.

2241.	Abide with me from morn till eve,
	For without Thee I cannot live;
	Abide with me when night is nigh,
	For without Thee I dare not die.

Ibid. Evening.

2242.	The voice that breathed o'er Eden,
	That earliest wedding day.

Holy Matrimony.

KEMBLE, JOHN PHILIP, actor, 1 Feb. 1757—26 Feb. 1823

2243.	I give thee all—I can no more,
	Tho' poor the offering be;
	My heart and lute are all the store
	That I can bring to thee.

Lodoiska III. i.

2244.	Perhaps it was right to dissemble your love,
	But—Why did you kick me downstairs?

An Expostulation.

KEMPIS, THOMAS À, Augustinian monk, 1379?—1471?

2245. Sic transit gloria mundi.—So passes away the glory of the world. *De Imitatione Christi—On the Imitation of Christ*, iii. 6.

KEN *or* KENN, THOMAS, bishop, July, 1637—19 March, 1711

2246.	Awake my soul, and with the sun
	The daily stage of duty run.

Morning Hymn.

2247. Praise God, from whom all blessings flow.
Morning and Evening Hymn.

KENNEDY, JOHN FITZGERALD, U.S. President, 29 May 1917—22 Nov. 1963

2248. Let us never negotiate out of fear. But let us never fear to negotiate. *Inaugural Address*, 20 Jan. 1961.

KERR, ORPHEUS C., *see* Newell, Robert Henry

KETHE, WILLIAM, Protestant cleric, died 1608 ?

2249.	All people that on earth do dwell,
	Sing to the Lord with cheerful voice.

Psalm 100.

KEY, FRANCIS SCOTT, U.S. lawyer, 1 Aug. 1779—11 Jan. 1843

2250. Oh, say, can you see, by the dawn's early light,
What so proudly we hailed at the twilight's last gleaming ?
Whose broad stripes and bright stars, through the perilous fight,
O'er the ramparts we watched, were so gallantly streaming ;
And the rocket's red glare, the bombs bursting in air,
Gave proof through the night that our flag was still there ;
Oh, say, does that star-spangled banner yet wave
O'er the land of the free and the home of the brave ?
The Star-Spangled Banner.

KILMER, JOYCE, U.S. poet, 6 Dec. 1886—30 July, 1918

2251.   I think that I shall never see
         A poem lovely as a tree.   *Trees.*

2252.   Poems are made by fools like me,
         But only God can make a tree.   Ibid.

KING, BENJAMIN FRANKLIN, U.S. humorist, 1857—1894

2253.   Nothing to do but work,
            Nothing to eat but food,
         Nothing to wear but clothes
            To keep one from going nude.   *The Pessimist.*

KING, STODDARD, U.S. author, 19 Aug. 1889—13 June, 1933

2254.   There's a long, long trail a-winding
            Into the land of my dreams.   *The Long Long Trail.*

KINGSLEY, CHARLES, cleric and author, 12 June, 1819—23 Jan. 1875

2255.   O Mary, go and call the cattle home
              Across the sands of Dee.   *The Sands of Dee.*

2256.   Three fishers went sailing away to the west.
                                            The Three Fishers.

2257.   For men must work, and women must weep,
         And the sooner it's over, the sooner to sleep.   Ibid.

2258.   Airly Beacon, Airly Beacon ;
            Oh the pleasant sight to see
         Shires and towns from Airly Beacon,
            While my love climbed up to me !   *Airly Beacon.*

2259.   Be good, sweet maid, and let who will be clever ;
         Do noble things, not dream them, all day long :
         And so make life, death, and that vast for-ever
              One grand, sweet song.   *A Farewell.*
         [Another version is :—
         Be good, sweet maid, and let who can be clever ;
         Do lovely things, not dream them, all day long.]

2260.   Oh ! that we two were maying.
                             The Saint's Tragedy, II. ix.

2261.   Young blood must have its course, lad,
            And every dog his day.
                       The Water Babies. Young and Old.

2262.   God grant you find one face there,
            You loved when all was young.   Ibid.

2263.   I once had a sweet little doll, dears,
            The prettiest doll in the world ;
         Her cheeks were so red and so white, dears,
            And her hair was so charmingly curled.
                               Ibid. *My Little Doll.*

2264.   Yet for old sakes' sake she is still, dears,   Ibid.
            The prettiest doll in the world.

2265.   Do the work that's nearest,
                       Though it's dull at whiles,
                     Helping, when you meet them,
                        Lame dogs over stiles.   *The Invitation.*

KIPLING, RUDYARD, author, 30 Dec. 1865—18 Jan. 1936

2266. Don't dance or ride with General Bangs—a most immoral
          man.   *A Code of Morals.*

2267.   For sixty takes to seventeen,
                       Nineteen to forty-nine.   *My rival.*

2268. And a woman is only a woman, but a good Cigar is a Smoke.
                                                          The Betrothed.

2269. Something lost behind the Ranges. Lost and waiting for
          you. Go !   *The Explorer.*

2270. Who hath desired the Sea ?—the sight of salt water un-
          bounded—
      The heave and the halt and the hurl and the crash of the
          comber wind-hounded ?   *The Sea and the Hills.*

2271. So and no otherwise—so and no otherwise—hillmen desire
          their Hills.   Ibid.

2272. There's never a law of God or man runs north of Fifty-Three.
                                          The Rhyme of the Three Sealers.

2273. Predestination in the stride o' yon connectin'-rod.
                                                   McAndrew's Hymn.

2274. For you muddled with books and pictures, an' china an'
          etchin's an' fans,
      And your rooms at college was beastly—more like a whore's
          than a man's.   *The ' Mary Gloster.'*

2275. Stiff-necked Glasgow beggar ! I've heard he's prayed for my
          soul,
      But he couldn't lie if you paid him, and he'd starve before
          he stole.   Ibid.

2276. The Liner she's a lady, an' she never looks nor 'eeds—
      The Man-o'-War's 'er 'usband, an' 'e gives 'er all she needs.
                                               The Liner she's a Lady.

2277.   You have heard the beat of the off-shore wind,
              And the thresh of the deep-sea rain ;
         You have heard the song—how long ? how long ?
              Pull out on the trail again !   *The Long Trail.*

2278. Pull out, pull out, on the Long Trail—the trail that is always
          new !   Ibid.

2279.   Fair is our lot—O goodly is our heritage !
                                              A Song of the English.

2280.   We have fed our sea for a thousand years
              And she calls us, still unfed,
         Though there's never a wave of all her waves
              But marks our English dead.   *The Song of the Dead,* ii

2281.   If blood be the price of admiralty,
          Lord God, we ha' paid in full !   *Ibid.*

2282.   Daughter am I in my mother's house,
          But mistress in my own.   *Our Lady of the Snows.*

2283.   Winds of the World, give answer ! They are whimpering to
              and fro—
          And what should they know of England who only England
              know ?   *The English Flag.*

2284.   Never was isle so little, never was sea so lone,
          But over the scud and the palm-trees an English flag has
              flown.   *Ibid.*

2285.   And those that were good shall be happy : they shall sit in a
              golden chair ;
          They shall splash at a ten-league canvas with brushes of
              comet's hair.   *When Earth's Last Picture is painted.*

2286.   And each, in his separate star,
          Shall draw the Thing as he sees It for the God of Things as
              They are !   *Ibid.*

2287.   Oh, East is East, and West is West, and never the twain
              shall meet,
          Till Earth and Sky stand presently at God's great Judgment
              Seat.   *The Ballad of East and West.*

2288.   He trod the ling like a buck in spring, and he looked like a
              lance in rest.   *Ibid.*

2289.   Then ye returned to your trinkets ; then ye contented your
              souls
          With the flannelled fools at the wicket or the muddied oafs at
              the goals.   *The Islanders.*

2290.   Take up the White Man's Burden.
                                      The White Man's Burden.

2291.   Your new-caught, sullen peoples,
                  Half devil and half child.   *Ibid.*

2292.   God of our fathers, known of old,
                  Lord of our far-flung battle-line.   *Recessional.*

2293.   The tumult and the shouting dies ;
                      The Captains and the Kings depart ;
                  Still stands Thine ancient sacrifice,
                      An humble and a contrite heart.
                  Lord God of Hosts, be with us yet,
                  Lest we forget—lest we forget !   *Ibid.*

2294.   Such boastings as the Gentiles use
                  Or lesser breeds without the Law.   *Ibid.*

2295.   In a ram-you-damn-you liner with a brace of bucking screws.
                                              The Three-Decker.

2296.   Till the Devil whispered behind the leaves, ' It's pretty but
              is it art ? '   *The Conundrum of the Workshops.*

2297.   There are nine and sixty ways of constructing tribal lays,
          And every single one of them is right.   *In the Neolithic Age.*

2298.   When 'Omer smote 'is bloomin' lyre,
      He'd 'eard men sing by land an' sea ;
    An' what he thought 'e might require,
      'E went an' took—the same as me !
                      When 'Omer smote 'is Bloomin' Lyre.

2299. For the sin ye do by two and two ye must pay for one by one.
                                                      Tomlinson.

2300. The female of the species is more deadly than the male.
                                    The Female of the Species.

2301.   And all unseen
    Romance brought up the nine-fifteen.   *The King.*

2302. They have cast their burden upon the Lord, and—the Lord
      He lays it on Martha's Sons !   *The Sons of Martha.*

2303. Then it's Tommy this, an' Tommy that, an' ' Tommy, 'ow's
      yer soul ? '
    But it's ' Thin red line of 'eroes ' when the drums begin to
      roll.   *Tommy.*

2304. We aren't no thin red 'eroes, nor we aren't no blackguards
      too,
    But single men in barricks, most remarkable like you.   Ibid.

2305. So 'ere's *to* you, Fuzzy-Wuzzy, at your 'ome in the Soudan ;
    You're a pore benighted 'eathen but a first-class fightin' man.
                                      Fuzzy-Wuzzy.

2306. 'E's all 'ot sand an' ginger when alive,
      An' 'e's generally shammin' when 'e's dead.   Ibid.

2307. The uniform 'e wore
    Was nothin' much before,
    An' rather less than 'arf o' that be'ind.   *Gunga Din.*

2308.   Though I've belted you and flayed you,
      By the livin' Gawd that made you,
    You're a better man than I am, Gunga Din.   Ibid.

2309. When you're wounded and left on Afghanistan's plains,
    And the women come out to cut up what remains,
    Jest roll to your rifle and blow out your brains
      An' go to your Gawd like a soldier.
                            The Young British Soldier.

2310. On the road to Mandalay,
    Where the flyin'-fishes play,
    An' the dawn comes up like thunder outer China 'crost the
      Bay !   *Mandalay.*

2311. But that's all shove be'ind me—long ago an' fur away,
    An' there ain't no buses runnin' from the Bank to Mandalay.
                                          Ibid.

2312. Ship me somewheres east of Suez, where the best is like the
      worst,
    Where there aren't no Ten Commandments an' a man can raise
      a thirst.   Ibid.

2313.   Back to the Army again, sergeant,
            Back to the Army again.
                          Back to the Army again.

2314. But to stand an' be still to the *Birkenhead* drill is a damn'
    tough bullet to chew,
    An' they done it, the Jollies—'Er Majesty's Jollies—soldier
    an' sailor too !   *Soldier an' Sailor too.*

2315.   An' I learned about women from 'er !   *The Ladies.*

2316.   When you get to a man in the case,
        They're like as a row of pins—
      For the Colonel's Lady an' Judy O'Grady
      Are sisters under their skins.   Ibid

2317.   For to admire an' for to see,
        For to be'old this world so wide—
      It never done no good to me,
        But I can't drop it if I tried !   *For to admire.*

2318. Duke's son—cook's son—son of a hundred kings—
    (Fifty thousand horse and foot going to Table Bay !)
  Each of 'em doing his country's work
    (and who's to look after their things ?)
  Pass the hat for your credit's sake,
      and pay—pay—pay !   *The Absent-Minded Beggar.*

2319. Boots—boots—boots—boots—movin' up and down again !
                          Boots.

2320.   The bachelor may risk 'is 'ide
        To 'elp you when you're downed ;
      But the married man will wait beside
        Till the ambulance comes round. *The Married Man.*

2321.   Of all the trees that grow so fair,
        Old England to adorn,
      Greater are none beneath the Sun
        Than Oak, and Ash, and Thorn.   *A Tree Song.*

2322.   My new-cut ashlar takes the light
      Where crimson-blank the windows flare.
                  My New-cut Ashlar.

2323. Mithras, God of the Morning, our trumpets waken the Wall !
                A Song to Mithras.

2324.   Nine hundred and ninety-nine can't bide
      The shame or mocking or laughter,
      But the Thousandth Man will stand by your side
      To the gallows-foot—and after !   *The Thousandth Man.*

2325.   Down to Gehenna or up to the Throne,
      He travels the fastest who travels alone.
                  The Winners.

2326. In telegraphic sentences, half nodded to their friends,
  They hint a matter's inwardness—and there the matter ends.
  And while the Celt is talking from Valencia to Kirkwall,
  The English—ah, the English !—don't say anything at all.
                  The Puzzler.

2327. And the end of the fight is a tombstone white with the name
    of the late deceased,
  And the epitaph drear : 'A fool lies here who tried to hustle
    the East.'   *Chapter Headings. The Naulahka.*

2328. If you can keep your head when all about you
    Are losing theirs and blaming it on you.   *If——.*

2329. If you can meet with Triumph and Disaster
    And treat those two impostors just the same.   Ibid.

2330. If you can talk with crowds and keep your virtue,
    Or walk with Kings—nor lose the common touch.
        Ibid.

2331. If you can fill the unforgiving minute
    With sixty seconds' worth of distance run,
    Yours is the Earth and everything that's in it,
    And—which is more—you'll be a Man, my son ¡   Ibid

2332. Brother and Sisters, I bid you beware
    Of giving your heart to a dog to tear.
        The Power of the Dog.

2333.   We get the hump—
        Cameelious hump—
    The hump that is black and blue !
        Just So Verses. How the Camel got his Hump.

2334. The cure for this ill is not to sit still,
    Or frowst with a book by the fire ;
    But to take a large hoe and a shovel also,
    And dig till you gently perspire.   Ibid.

2335.   And I'd like to roll to Rio
        Some day before I'm old.
        Ibid. The Beginning of the Armadilloes.

2336.   We must go back with Policeman Day—
    Back from the City of Sleep.   *The City of Sleep.*

2337. But you the unhoodwinked wave shall test—the immediate
    gulf condemn—
    Except ye owe the Fates a jest, be slow to jest with them.
        Poseidon's Law.

2338. Splendaciously mendacious rolled the Brass-bound Man
    ashore.   Ibid.

2339. Watch the wall, my darling, while the Gentlemen go by !
        A Smuggler's Song.

2340. And when your back stops aching and your hands begin to
    harden,
    You will find yourself a partner in the Glory of the Garden.
        The Glory of the Garden.

2341. Take my word for it, the silliest woman can manage a clever
man ; but it needs a very clever woman to manage a fool.
        Plain Tales from the Hills. Three and —an Extra.

2342. But that is another story.   Ibid.

2343. Never praise a sister to a sister, in the hope of your compli-
ments reaching the proper ears.   Ibid. *False Dawn.*

2344. Nice but nubbly.   *Just-So Stories. How the Whale got his*
        Throat.

2345. A man of infinite-resource-and-sagacity.   Ibid.

2346. An Elephant's Child—who was full of 'satiable curtiosity.

Ibid. *The Elephant's Child.*

2347. This is too butch for be.   Ibid.

2348. 'Tisn't beauty, so to speak, nor good talk necessarily. It's just IT.   *Traffics and Discoveries. Mrs. Bathurst.*

KNOX, JOHN, Scottish reformer, 1505—24 Nov. 1572

2349. The First Blast of the Trumpet Against the Monstrous Regiment of Women.   *Title of pamphlet,* 1558.

KNOX, RONALD ARBUTHNOT, cleric, 17 Feb. 1888—24 Aug. 1957

2350.   There once was a man who said, ' God
                 Must think it exceedingly odd
                     If he finds that this tree
                     Continues to be
                 When there's no one about in the Quad.'   *Limerick.*
[The following reply was written by an unknown author :—
                 Dear Sir,
                     Your astonishment's odd :
                 I am always about in the Quad.
                     And that's why the tree
                     Will continue to be,
                 Since observed by
                     Yours faithfully,
                                     God.]

KNOX, WILLIAM, Scottish poet, 17 Aug, 1789—12 Nov. 1825

2351.   Oh why should the spirit of mortal be proud !
                                                     Mortality, 1.

LA COSTE, MARIE RAVENEL DE, U.S. poetess, 1849—1936

2352.   Tenderly bury the fair young dead,
                     Pausing to drop on his grave a tear ;
                 Carve on the wooden slab at his head,
                 ' Somebody's darling slumbers here.'
                                     Somebody's Darling.

LAMB, CHARLES, essayist, 10 Feb. 1775—27 Dec. 1834

2353. The human species, according to the best theory I can form of it, is composed of two distinct races, *the men who borrow,* and *the men who lend.*   *Essays of Elia. The Two Races of Men.*

2354. A clear fire, a clean hearth, and the rigour of the game.

Ibid. *Mrs. Battle's Opinions on Whist.*

2355. Coleridge holds that man cannot have a pure mind who refuses apple-dumplings. I am not certain but he is right.

Ibid. *Grace before Meat.*

2356. ' Presents,' I often say, ' endear Absents.'

Ibid. *A Dissertation upon Roast Pig.*

2357. I can read anything which I call a *book*. There are things in that shape which I cannot allow for such. In this catalogue of *books which are no books—biblia a-biblia*—I reckon Court Calendars, Directories, Pocket Books, Draught Boards bound and lettered at the back, Scientific Treatises, Almanacks ; Statues at Large ; the works of Hume, Gibbon, Robertson, Beattie, Soame Jenyns, and, generally, all those volumes which ' no gentleman's library should be without ' : the Histories of Flavius Josephus (that learned Jew), and Paley's Moral Philosophy.

Last Essays of Elia. Detached Thoughts on Books and Reading.

2358. Things in books' clothing. Ibid.

2359. It [a pun] is a pistol let off at the ear ; not a feather to tickle the intellect.

Ibid. *Popular Fallacies. That the Worst Puns are the Best.*

2360. An Oxford scholar, meeting a porter who was carrying a hare through the streets, accosts him with this extraordinary question, ' Prithee, friend, is that thy own hare, or a wig ? ' Ibid.

2361. An archangel a little damaged. [Coleridge.]

Letter to Wordsworth, 26 April, 1816.

2362. The greatest pleasure I know, is to do a good action by stealth and to have it found out by accident.

Table Talk by the late Elia. The Athenaeum, 4 Jan. 1834.

2363. I have had playmates, I have had companions,
In my days of childhood, in my joyful schooldays
All, all are gone, the old familiar faces.

The Old Familiar Faces.

2364. Who first invented work, and bound the free
And holyday-rejoicing spirit down
To the ever-haunting importunity
Of business in the green fields, and the town—
To plough, loom, anvil, spade—and oh ! most sad,
To that dry drudgery at the desk's dead wood ? *Work.*

2365. Thou straggler into loving arms,
Young climber up of knees,
When I forget thy thousand ways,
Then life and all shall cease.

Parental Recollections.

Lamb, William, *see* Melbourne, Viscount

Lampton, William James, journalist, 1859—30 May, 1917

2366. Same old slippers,
Same old rice,
Same old glimpse of
Paradise. *June Weddings.*

Landon, Letitia Elizabeth (Mrs. Maclean), poetess, 14 Aug. 1802—15 Oct. 1838

2367. As beautiful as woman's blush,—
As evanescent too. *Apple Blossoms.*

LANDOR, WALTER SAVAGE, author, 30 Jan. 1775—17 Sept. 1864

2368.　　　　Ah, what avails the sceptred race !
　　　　　　Ah, what the form divine.　　　　　*Rose Aylmer.*

2369.　　　　Rose Aylmer, whom these wakeful eyes
　　　　　　　May weep, but never see,
　　　　　　A night of memories and of sighs
　　　　　　　I consecrate to thee.　　　　　　　　*Ibid.*

2370.　　　　Browning !　Since Chaucer was alive and hale,
　　　　　　No man hath walk'd along our roads with step
　　　　　　So active, so inquiring eye, or tongue
　　　　　　So varied in discourse.　　*To Robert Browning.*

2371.　　I strove with none, for none was worth my strife ;
　　　　　　Nature I loved ; and next to Nature, Art ;
　　　　　I warm'd both hands before the fire of life ;
　　　　　　It sinks, and I am ready to depart.　　*I strove with None.*

2372.　　　　Stand close around, ye Stygian set,
　　　　　　　With Dirce in one boat convey'd !
　　　　　　Or Charon, seeing, may forget
　　　　　　　That he is old, and she a shade.　　　　　*Dirce.*

2373.　　Proud word you never spoke, but you will speak
　　　　　　Four not exempt from pride some future day.
　　　　　Resting on one white hand a warm wet cheek
　　　　　Over my open volume you will say,
　　　　　　' This man loved *me* ! ' then rise and trip away.
　　　　　　　　　　　　Proud Word you never spoke.

2374.　　　　George the First was always reckoned
　　　　　　Vile, but viler George the Second ;
　　　　　　And what mortal ever heard
　　　　　　Any good of George the Third ?
　　　　　　When from earth the Fourth descended
　　　　　　God be praised, the Georges ended !　　*Epigram.*

　　2375. I shall dine late ; but the dining-room will be well lighted,
the guests few and select.
　　　Imaginary Conversations. Archdeacon Hare and Walter Landor.

LANE, GEORGE MARTIN, U.S. professor of Latin, 24 Dec. 1823—30 June,
　　1897

2376.　　The waiter roars it through the hall :
　　　　　' We don't give bread with one fish-ball ! '　*One Fish-ball.*

LANG, ANDREW, Scottish author, 31 March 1844—20 July, 1912

2377.　　　St. Andrews by the Northern Sea,
　　　　　A haunted town it is to me.　　　　*Almae Matres.*

2378.　　　There's a joy without canker or cark,
　　　　　　There's a pleasure eternally new,
　　　　　'Tis to gloat on the glaze and the mark
　　　　　　Of china that's ancient and blue.
　　　　　　　　　　　　Ballade of Blue China.

2379.　　　The surge and thunder of the Odyssey.
　　　　　　　　　　　　　　The Odyssey.

2380.   *I* am the batsman and the bat,
                I am the bowler and the ball,
                The umpire, the pavilion cat,
                    The roller, pitch, and stumps, and all.   *Brahma.*
        [Parody of Emerson, No. 1454.]

LANGHORNE, JOHN, cleric and poet, March, 1735—1 April, 1779

2381.   Cold on Canadian hills or Minden's plain,
                Perhaps that parent mourn'd her soldier slain ;
                Bent o'er her babe, her eye dissolv'd in dew,
                The big drops mingling with the milk he drew,
                Gave the sad presage of his future years,
                The child of misery, baptis'd in tears.
                                           The Country Justice, I. 161.

LANGLAND, WILLIAM, priest and poet, 1332 ?—1400 ?

2382.   In a somer seson whan soft was the sonne.
                    The Vision of William concerning Piers the Plowman,
                    B Text, prologue, 1.

LANIER, SIDNEY, U.S. poet, 3 Feb. 1842—7 Sept. 1881

2383.   Into the woods my Master went,
                Clean forspent, forspent.
                Into the woods my Master came,
                Forspent with love and shame.
                But the olives they were not blind to Him ;
                The little grey leaves were kind to Him ;
                The thorn-tree had a mind to Him
                When into the woods He came.
                                   A Ballad of Trees and the Master.

LANIGAN, GEORGE THOMAS, U.S. journalist, 10 Dec. 1845—5 Feb. 1886

2384.   For the Ahkoond I mourn,
                    Who wouldn't ?
                He strove to disregard the message stern,
                    But he Ahkoodn't.
                                   Threnody for the Ahkoond of Swat.

LA ROCHEFOUCAULD-LIANCOURT, FRANÇOIS ALEXANDRE FRÉDÉRIC,
        DUC DE, 11 Jan. 1747—24 March, 1827

    2385. Non, Sire, c'est une révolution.—No, Sire, it is a revolution.
            *When Louis XVI asked ' Is it a revolt ? ' on getting news of
            the fall of the Bastille,* 1789.

LATIMER, HUGH, Bishop of Worcester, 1485 ?—16 Oct. 1555

    2386. Be of good comfort, Master Ridley, and play the man ; we
shall this day light such a candle by God's grace in England, as I trust
shall never be put out.
            As he and Ridley were being burned at Oxford for heresy.

LAUDER, SIR HARRY, Scottish comedian, 4 Aug. 1870—26 Feb, 1950

2387.   I love a lassie.   *Song.*

2388.   Roamin' in the gloamin'.   *Song.*

2389.   If you can say ' It's a braw bricht moonlicht nicht '
         Y're a' richt, ye ken.   *Just a Wee Deoch-an-doris.*

LAWRENCE, DAVID HERBERT, author, 11 Sept. 1885—2 March, 1930

2390.   I never saw a wild thing
                         Sorry for itself.   *Self-Pity.*

LAWRENCE, THOMAS EDWARD (LAWRENCE OF ARABIA), soldier, 15 Aug.
         1888—19 May, 1935

2391.   I loved you, so I drew these tides of men into my hands and
wrote my will across the sky in stars.
                         The Seven Pillars of Wisdom, dedication.

LAZARUS, EMMA, U.S. poetess, 22 July, 1849—19 Nov. 1887

2392.   Give me your tired, your poor,
            Your huddled masses yearning to breathe free,
            The wretched refuse of your teeming shore,
            Send these, the homeless, tempest-tossed, to me :
            I lift my lamp beside the golden door.
                                        The New Colossus.

    [Lines inscribed on the Statue of Liberty.]

LEACOCK, STEPHEN BUTLER, Anglo-Canadian economist and humorist,
         30 Dec. 1869—28 March, 1944

2393.   Lord Ronald said nothing ; he flung himself from the room,
flung himself upon his horse, and rode madly off in all directions.
                    Nonsense Novels.   Gertrude the Governess.

2394.   Then he too Ajax on the one hand leaped (or possibly jumped)
into the fight wearing on the other hand yes certainly a steel corslet
(or possibly a bronze under-tunic) and on his head of course yes without
doubt he had a helmet with a tossing plume taken from the mane (or
perhaps extracted from the tail) of some horse which once fed along
the banks of the Scamander (and it sees the herd and raises its head
and paws the ground).   *Behind and Beyond. Homer and Humbug.*
    [Parody of Homer.]

2395.   The up-to-date clean-shaven snoopopathic man. . . . How one
would enjoy seeing a man—a real one with Nevada whiskers and long
boots—land him one solid kick from behind.
                         Further Foolishness. The Snoopopaths.

2396.   The salesman should select from his wardrobe (or from his
straw valise) a suit of plain, severe design, attractive and yet simple,
good and yet bad, long and at the same time short, in other words,
something that is expensive but cheap.
                    The Garden of Folly.   The Perfect Salesman.

LEAR, EDWARD, author and artist, 12 May, 1812—29 Jan. 1888

2397.   ' How pleasant to know Mr. Lear ! '
               Who has written such volumes of stuff !
            Some think him ill-tempered and queer,
               But a few think him pleasant enough.
                                          Nonsense Songs, preface.

2398.   There was an old man with a beard,
            Who said, ' It is just as I feared !
               Two Owls and a Hen
               Four Larks and a Wren
            Have all built their nests in my beard.'
                                          Book of Nonsense.

2399.   The Owl and the Pussy-Cat went to sea
               In a beautiful pea-green boat,
            They took some honey, and plenty of money,
               Wrapped up in a five-pound note.
                                          The Owl and the Pussy-Cat.

2400.   Far and few, far and few,
               Are the lands where the Jumblies live ;
            Their heads are green, and their hands are blue,
               And they went to sea in a sieve.   *The Jumblies.*
            [Also occurs in *The Dong with a Luminous Nose.*]

2401.   Ploffskin, Pluffskin, Pelican jee,
            We think no Birds so happy as we !
            Plumpskin, Ploshkin, Pelican jill,
            We think so then, and we thought so still.
                                          The Pelican Chorus.

2402.   On the Coast of Coromandel
               Where the early pumpkins blow,
                  In the middle of the woods
               Lived the Yonghy-Bonghy-Bò.
            Two old chairs and half a candle,—
            One old jug without a handle,—
               These were all his worldly goods.
                     The Courtship of the Yonghy-Bonghy-Bò.

2403.   He has gone to fish, for his Aunt Jobiska's
            Runcible cat with crimson whiskers.
                                          The Pobble who has no Toes.

2404.   And she said,—' It's a fact the whole world knows.
            That Pobbles are happier without their toes.'   Ibid.

2405. Who, or why, or which, or *what*, is the Akond of SWAT ?
                                          The Akond of Swat.

LEASE, MARY ELIZABETH, U.S. lecturer, 11 Sept. 1853—29 Oct. 1933

2406. Kansas had better stop raising corn and begin raising hell.
                                          Attributed.

LEE, HENRY, U.S. soldier, 29 Jan. 1756—25 March, 1818

2407. First in war, first in peace, and first in the hearts of his
countrymen.
            Resolution on Washington, House of Representatives, Dec. 1799.

LEE, NATHANIEL, dramatist, born 1653 ?—buried 6 May, 1692

2408. Then he will talk—good gods, how he will talk !
The Rival Queens or the Death of Alexander the Great, I. iii.

2409. When Greeks joined Greeks, then was the tug of war !
Ibid., IV. ii.

LE GALLIENNE, RICHARD, poet, 20 Jan. 1866—14 Sept. 1947

2410. She's somewhere in the sunlight strong,
Her tears are in the falling rain,
She calls me in the wind's soft song,
And with the flowers she comes again. *Song*.

2411. What of the darkness ? Is it very fair ?
What of the Darkness.

LEIGH, HENRY SAMBROOKE, author, 29 March, 1837—16 June, 1883

2412. In form and feature, face and limb,
I grew so like my brother
That folks got taking me for him,
And each for one another. *The Twins*.

2413. And when I died—the neighbours came
And buried brother John ! Ibid.

2414. I know where little girls are sent
For telling taradiddles. *Only Seven*.

LELAND, CHARLES GODFREY, U.S. author, 15 Aug. 1824—20 March, 1903

2415. Hans Breitmann gife a barty—
Where ish dat barty now ?
Hans Breitmann's Party.

2416. All goned afay mit de Lager Beer—
Afay in de Ewigkeit ! Ibid.

LENIN (VLADIMIR ILITCH ULIANOV), Russian statesman, 22 April, 1870—21 Jan. 1924

2417. It is true that liberty is precious—so precious that it must be rationed. *Attributed*.

L'ESTRANGE, SIR ROGER, pamphleteer, 17 Dec. 1616—11 Dec. 1704

2418. Though this may be play to you, 'tis death to us.
Fables from Several Authors, 398.

LEWIS, DAVID, Welsh poet, born 1683 ?—buried 8 April, 1760

2419 And when with envy Time transported
Shall think to rob us of our joys,
You'll in your girls again be courted,
And I'll go wooing in my boys. *Song to Winfreda*.
[Authorship uncertain. Wrongly attributed to J. G. Cooper.]

LINCOLN, ABRAHAM, U.S. President, 12 Feb. 1809—15 April, 1865

2420. In giving freedom to the slave we assure freedom to the free,—honourable alike in what we give and what we preserve.
Annual Message to Congress, 1 Dec. 1862.

2421. That this nation, under God, shall have a new birth of freedom, and that government of the people, by the people, for the people, shall not perish from the earth.
Address, Gettysburg, 19 Nov. 1863.

2422. I claim not to have controlled events, but confess plainly that events have controlled me. *Letter to A. G. Hodges*, 4 Apr. 1864.

2423. I have not permitted myself, gentlemen, to conclude that I am the best man in the country ; but I am reminded in this connection of a story of an old Dutch farmer, who remarked to a companion once that it was not best to swap horses when crossing a stream.
Reply to National Union League, 9 June, 1864.

2424. With malice towards none ; with charity for all ; with firmness in the right, as God gives us to see the right, let us strive on to finish the work we are in ; to bind up the nation's wounds ; to care for him who shall have borne the battle, and for his widow and his orphan—to do all which may achieve and cherish a just and lasting peace among ourselves and with all nations.
Second Inaugural Address, 4 March, 1865.

2425. The Lord prefers common-looking people. That is the reason He makes so many of them. J. Morgan, *Our Presidents*, vi.

2426. People who like this sort of thing will find this the sort of thing they like. *Criticism of an unreadably sentimental book.*

LINDSAY, NICHOLAS VACHEL, U.S. poet, 10 Nov. 1879—5 Dec. 1931

2427.   The banjos rattled, and the tambourines
            Jing-jing-jingled in the hands of Queens !
General Booth enters Heaven.

2428.   Then I saw the Congo, creeping through the black,
            Cutting through the jungle with a golden track.
The Congo, 1.

LINLEY, GEORGE, composer, 1798—10 Sept. 1865

2429.   Ever of thee I'm fondly dreaming.   *Ever of Thee.*

2430.   Tho' lost to sight, to mem'ry dear
            Thou ever wilt remain.   *Song.*
[The first line is older and of unknown origin.]

LIVY (TITUS LIVIUS), Roman historian, 59 B.C.—A.D. 17

2431. Vae victis.—Woe to the vanquished.
History of Rome, v. xlviii.

LLOYD GEORGE, DAVID LLOYD GEORGE, 1ST EARL, Prime Minister, 17 Jan. 1863—26 March, 1945.

2432. What is our task? To make Britain a fit country for heroes to live in. *Speech, Wolverhampton*, 24 Nov. 1918.

LOCKE, JOHN, philosopher, 29 Aug. 1632—28 Oct. 1704

2433. All men are liable to error ; and most men are, in many points, by passion or interest, under temptation to it.

Essay on the Human Understanding, xx. 17.

LOCKER-LAMPSON, FREDERICK, poet, 29 May, 1821—30 May, 1895

2434.   And many are afraid of God—
                And more of Mrs. Grundy.   *The Jester's Plea.*

LODGE, THOMAS, author, 1558 ?–1625

2435.   Love in my bosom, like a bee,
                    Doth suck his sweet.   *Love in my Bosom.*

2436.   Heigh-ho, would she were mine !   *Rosaline.*

LONGFELLOW, HENRY WADSWORTH, U.S. poet, 27 Feb. 1807—24 March, 1882

2437.   Tell me not, in mournful numbers,
                Life is but an empty dream !
            For the soul is dead that slumbers,
                And things are not what they seem.

2438.   Life is real ! Life is earnest !
                And the grave is not its goal ;
            Dust thou art, to dust returnest,
                Was not spoken of the soul.   *A Psalm of Life.*

2439.   Art is long, and Time is fleeting,
                And our hearts, though stout and brave,
            Still, like muffled drums, are beating
                Funeral marches to the grave.   Ibid.

2440.   Trust no future, howe'er pleasant !
                Let the dead Past bury its dead !
            Act, act in the living present !
                Heart within, and God o'erhead !   Ibid.

2441.   Lives of great men all remind us
                We can make our lives sublime,
            And, departing, leave behind us
                Footprints on the sands of time.   Ibid.

2442.   Let us, then, be up and doing,
                With a heart for any fate ;
            Still achieving, still pursuing,
                Learn to labour and to wait.   Ibid.

2443.   There is a Reaper whose name is Death,
                And, with his sickle keen,
            He reaps the bearded grain at a breath,
                And the flowers that grow between.
                                   The Reaper and the Flowers.

2444.   It was the schooner Hesperus,
                That sailed the wintry sea ;
            And the skipper had taken his little daughter,
                To bear him company.   *The Wreck of the Hesperus.*

2445.   Blue were her eyes as the fairy-flax.   *Ibid.*

2446.   Under a spreading chestnut tree
      The village smithy stands ;
      The smith, a mighty man is he,
        With large and sinewy hands ;
      And the muscles of his brawny arms
       Are strong as iron bands.
                    The Village Blacksmith.

2447.   His brow is wet with honest sweat,
      He earns whate'er he can,
      And looks the whole world in the face,
       For he owes not any man.   *Ibid.*

2448.   Something attempted, something done,
      Has earned a night's repose.   *Ibid.*

2449.   Standing with reluctant feet,
      Where the brook and river meet,
      Womanhood and childhood fleet !   *Maidenhood.*

2450.   The shades of night were falling fast,
      As through an Alpine village passed
      A youth, who bore, 'mid snow and ice,
      A banner with the strange device,
       Excelsior !   *Excelsior.*

2451.   Beside the ungather'd rice he lay,
      His sickle in his hand.   *The Slave's Dream.*

2452.   Between the dark and the daylight,
      When the night is beginning to lower,
      Comes a pause in the day's occupations,
      That is known as the Children's Hour.
                    The Children's Hour.

2453.   And the night shall be filled with music,
      And the cares that infest the day
      Shall fold their tents like the Arabs,
      And as silently steal away.   *The Day is Done.*

2454.   I shot an arrow into the air,
      It fell to earth, I knew not where.
                    The Arrow and the Song.

2455.   And the song, from beginning to end,
      I found again in the heart of a friend.   *Ibid.*

2456.   Though the mills of God grind slowly, yet they grind
      exceeding small ;
   Though with patience He stands waiting, with exactness
      grinds He all.   *Retribution.*

2457.   This is the forest primeval.   *Evangeline*, prelude.

2458.   Silently one by one, in the infinite meadows of heaven
   Blossomed the lovely stars, the forget-me-nots of the angels.
                    Ibid., i. iii.

2459.   Build me straight, O worthy Master !
      Staunch and strong, a goodly vessel,
      That shall laugh at all disaster,
      And with wave and whirlwind wrestle !
                    The Building of the Ship.

2460.   Thou too, sail on, O Ship of State!
          Sail on, O Union, strong and great!
          Humanity with all its fears,
          With all its hopes of future years,
          Is hanging breathless on thy fate!   Ibid.

2461.   ' Wouldst thou '—so the helmsman answered,—
              ' Learn the secret of the sea ?
          ' Only those who brave its dangers
              Comprehend its mystery ! '   *The Secret of the Sea.*

2462.   As unto the bow the cord is,
          So unto the man is woman,
          Though she bends him, she obeys him,
          Though she draws him, yet she follows,
          Useless each without the other !
                                        The Song of Hiawatha, x.

2463. Archly the maiden smiled, and with eyes overrunning with
          laughter,
      Said, in a tremulous voice, ' Why don't you speak for your-
              self, John ? '   *The Courtship of Miles Standish,* III.

2464.   The heights by great men reached and kept
              Were not attained by sudden flight,
          But they, while their companions slept,
              Were toiling upward in the night.
                              The Ladder of Saint Augustine.

2465.   A boy's will is the wind's will,
          And the thoughts of youth are long, long thoughts.
                                                My Lost Youth.

2466.   A Lady with a Lamp shall stand
              In the great history of the land,
              A noble type of good,
              Heroic womanhood.   *Santa Filomena.*

2467. Ships that pass in the night, and speak each other in passing,
      Only a signal shown and a distant voice in the darkness ;
      So on the ocean of life we pass and speak one another,
      Only a look and a voice ; then darkness again and a silence.
              Tales of a Wayside Inn, III.   *The Theologian's Tale.
              Elizabeth,* iv.

2468.   There was a little girl
                  Who had a little curl
              Right in the middle of her forehead ;
                  And when she was good
                  She was very, very good,
              But when she was bad she was horrid.
                                        There was a Little Girl.

Loos, Anita (Mrs. John Emerson), U.S. author, 26 April, 1893—

    2469. Kissing your hand may make you feel very good but a diamond
bracelet lasts forever.
                        Gentlemen prefer Blondes, caption to frontispiece.

    [The passage, in chapter iv, has ' very very good ' and ' a diamond
and safire bracelet.']

Louis XIV, King of France, 16 Sept., 1638—1 Sept. 1715
    2470. L'État, c'est moi.—I am the State.   *Attributed.*

LOVELACE, RICHARD, 1618–1658
2471.   I could not love thee, Dear, so much
              Loved I not Honour more.
                    To Lucasta, on going to the Wars.

2472.   Stone walls do not a prison make,
              Nor iron bars a cage ;
            Minds innocent and quiet take
              That for an hermitage :
            If I have freedom in my love
              And in my soul am free,
            Angels alone, that soar above,
              Enjoy such liberty,   *To Althea from Prison.*

LOVELL, MARIA ANNE, dramatist, 16 July, 1803—2 April, 1877
2473.   Two souls with but a single thought,
              Two hearts that beat as one.
                  Ingomar the Barbarian, II.
[Translated from the German of Von Münch Bellinghausen.]

LOVEMAN, ROBERT, U.S. author, 11 April, 1864—10 July, 1923
2474.   It is not raining rain to me,
              It's raining violets.   *April Rain.*

LOVER, SAMUEL, Irish author, 24 Feb. 1797—6 July, 1868
2475.   Reproof on her lip, but a smile in her eye. *Rory O'More,* I.

    2476. When once the itch of literature comes over a man, nothing
can cure it but the scratching of a pen.   *Handy Andy,* xxxvi.

LOWELL, JAMES RUSSELL, U.S. author, 22 Feb. 1819—12 Aug, 1891
2477. Once to every man and nation comes the moment to decide,
    In the strife of Truth with Falsehood, for the good or evil side.
                      The Present Crisis.

2478.   And what is so rare as a day in June ?
            Then, if ever, come perfect days ;
            Then Heaven tries the earth if it be in tune,
              And over it softly her warm ear lays.
              The Vision of Sir Launfal, I. prelude.

2479.   An' you've gut to git up airly
            Ef you want to take in God.
                The Biglow Papers, 1st series, i.

2480. He's been true to *one* party,—an' thet is himself.
            Ibid., iii. *What Mr. Robinson Thinks.*

2481.   I *don't* believe in princerple,
            But oh I *du* in interest.
             Ibid., vi. *The Pious Editor's Creed.*

2482.   I scent which pays the best, an' then
                    Go into it baldheaded.   Ibid.

2483.   God makes sech nights, all white and still,
                Fur'z you can look or listen.
                            Ibid., 2nd series, *The Courtin'*.

2484.   All kin' o' smily round the lips
                    An' teary round the lashes.   Ibid.

  2485. There is no good in arguing with the inevitable. The only
argument available with an east wind is to put on your overcoat.
                            Democracy and Addresses.

LOWRY, ROBERT, U.S. minister, 12 March, 1826—25 Nov. 1899

2486.   Yes, we'll gather at the river,
                    The beautiful, the beautiful river,
                Gather with the saints at the river
                    That flows from the throne of God.
                            Shall we gather at the River ?

LUCAN (MARCUS ANNAEUS LUCANUS), Roman poet, A.D. 39–65

2487. Victrix causa deis placuit, sed victa Catoni.
        —The victorious cause was pleasing to the Gods, but the
            vanquished to Cato.   *Pharsalia,* 128.

2488. Magni nominis umbra.
        —The shadow of a mighty name.   *Ibid.,* 135.

LUCRETIUS (TITUS LUCRETIUS CARUS), Roman poet, 99 ?–55 ? B.C.

2489. Suave, mari magno turbantibus aequora ventis,
        E terra magnum alterius spectare laborem.
            —It is pleasant, when the sea is high and the winds are dashing
                the waves about, to watch from the land the struggles
                of another.
                    De Rerum Natura—On the Nature of Things, II. I.

LUTHER, MARTIN, German reformer, 10 Nov. 1483—18 Feb. 1546

  2490. Wenn ich gewisst hätte, dass so viel Teufel auf mich gezielet
hätten, als Ziegel auf den Dächern waren zu Worms, wäre ich dennoch
eingeritten.—If I had known that as many devils would set on me as
there are tiles on the roofs in Worms, still I would have gone there.
                            On approaching Worms, April, 1521.

  2491. Hier stehe ich ! Ich kann nicht anders, Gotte helfe mir !
Amen.—Here I stand. I can do no otherwise, God help me ! Amen.
                    Speech at Diet of Worms, 18 April, 1521.

  2492. Esto peccator et pecca fortiter, sed fortius fide et gaude in
Christo.—Be a sinner and sin stoutly, but more stoutly trust and
rejoice in Christ.   *Letter to Melanchthon.*

LYDGATE, JOHN, poet, 1370 ?—1451 ?

  2493. Sithe off oure language he was the lodesterre. [Chaucer.]
                    The Fall of Princes, prologue, 252

LYLY, JOHN, author, born 1554 ?—buried 30 Nov. 1606

2494.   Cupid and my Campaspe play'd
           At cards for kisses : Cupid paid.   *Campaspe*, III. v.

2495.   None but the lark so shrill and clear !
           Now at heaven's gates she claps her wings,
           The morn not waking till she sings.   *Ibid.*, v. i.

LYTE, HENRY FRANCIS, hymn-writer, 1 June, 1793—20 Nov. 1847

2496.   Abide with me : fast falls the eventide ;
           The darkness deepens ; Lord, with me abide :
           When other helpers fail, and comforts flee,
           Help of the helpless, O abide with me.

2497.   Swift to its close ebbs out life's little day ;
           Earth's joys grow dim, its glories pass away ;
           Change and decay in all around I see :
           O Thou Who changest not, abide with me.   *Abide with me.*

LYTTELTON, GEORGE LYTTELTON, 1ST BARON, politician, 17 Jan
      1709—22 Aug. 1773

2498.   Where none admire, 'tis useless to excel ;
           Where none are beaux, 'tis vain to be a belle.
                          Soliloquy of a Beauty in the Country.

LYTTON, EDWARD GEORGE EARLE LYTTON BULWER-LYTTON, 1ST
      BARON, author, 25 May, 1803—18 Jan. 1873

2499.   Beneath the rule of men entirely great,
           The pen is mightier than the sword.   *Richelieu*, II. ii.

2500.   In the lexicon of youth, which fate reserves
           For a bright manhood, there is no such word
           As—*fail*.   Ibid.

2501.   The brilliant chief, irregularly great,
           Frank, haughty, rash,—the Rupert of debate.
                                          The New Timon, I. 6.

2502.   Revolutions are not made with rose-water.
                                          The Parisians, v. vii.

LYTTON, EDWARD ROBERT BULWER-LYTTON, 1ST EARL OF (OWEN
      MEREDITH), 8 Nov. 1831—24 Nov. 1891

2503. Genius does what it must, and Talent does what it can.
                          Last Words of a Sensitive Second-Rate Poet.

MACAULAY, THOMAS BABINGTON MACAULAY, BARON, author, 25 Oct.
      1800–28 Dec. 1859

2504. The dust and silence of the upper shelf.   *Essays. Milton.*

2505. Out of his surname they have coined an epithet for a knave.
And out of his Christian name a synonym for the Devil.
                                          Ibid. *Machiavelli.*

2506. The gallery in which the reporters sit has become a fourth
estate of the realm.   Ibid. *Hallam's Constitutional History.*

2507. We take this to be, on the whole, the worst similitude in the world. In the first place, no stream meanders, or can possibly meander, level with its fount. In the next place, if streams did meander level with their founts, no two motions can be less like each other than that of meandering level and that of mounting upwards. [Referring to No. 2941 *infra*.] *Ibid. Mr. Robert Montgomery's Poems.*

2508. We know of no spectacle so ridiculous as the British public in one of its periodical fits of morality.
Ibid. Moore's Life of Lord Byron.

2509. With the dead there is no rivalry. In the dead there is no change. Plato is never sullen. Cervantes is never petulant. Demosthenes never comes unseasonably. Dante never stays too long. No difference of political opinion can alienate Cicero. No heresy can excite the horror of Bossuet. *Ibid. Lord Bacon.*

2510. Every schoolboy knows who imprisoned Montezuma, and who strangled Atahualpa. *Ibid. Lord Clive.*

2511. She [the Roman Catholic Church] may still exist in undiminished vigour when some traveller from New Zealand shall, in the midst of a vast solitude, take his stand on a broken arch of London Bridge to sketch the ruins of St. Paul's.
Ibid. Ranke's History of the Popes.

2512. The Chief Justice was rich, quiet, and infamous.
Ibid. Warren Hastings.

2513. The great Proconsul. *Ibid.*

2514. In order that he might rob a neighbour whom he had promised to defend, black men fought on the coast of Coromandel, and red men scalped each other by the Great Lakes of North America.
Ibid. Frederic the Great.

2515. He was a rake among scholars, and a scholar among rakes. [Richard Steele.] *Ibid. Aikin's Life of Addison.*

2516. The Puritan hated bear-baiting, not because it gave pain to the bear, but because it gave pleasure to the spectators.
History of England, I. ii.

2517. There were gentlemen and there were seamen in the navy of Charles the Second. But the seamen were not gentlemen ; and the gentlemen were not seamen. *Ibid., iii.*

2518. Lars Porsena of Clusium
By the Nine Gods he swore
That the great house of Tarquin
Should suffer wrong no more.
Lays of Ancient Rome. Horatius, 1.

2519. Then out spake brave Horatius,
The Captain of the Gate :
" To every man upon this earth
Death cometh soon or late.
And how can a man die better
Than facing fearful odds,
For the ashes of his fathers,
And the temples of his gods ? " *Ib., 27.*

2520.
> Then none was for a party ;
> Then all were for the State ;
> Then the great man helped the poor,
> And the poor man loved the great :
> Then lands were fairly portioned ;
> Then spoils were fairly sold ;
> The Romans were like brothers
> In the brave days of old.   *Ib.*, 32.

2521.
> Was none who would be foremost
> To lead such dire attack :
> For those behind cried " Forward ! "
> And those before cried " Back ! "   *Ibid.*, 50.

2522.
> O Tiber ! father Tiber !
> To whom the Romans pray,
> A Roman's life, a Roman's arms,
> Take thou in charge this day !   *Ibid.*, 58.

2523.
> And even the ranks of Tuscany
> Could scarce forbear to cheer.   *Ibid.*, 60.

2524.
> How well Horatius kept the bridge
> In the brave days of old.   *Ibid.*, 70.

2525.
> In lordly Lacedaemon,
> The city of two kings.
>   Ibid. *The Battle of Lake Regillus*, 2.

2526.
> These be the great Twin Brethren
> To whom the Dorians pray.   *Ibid.*, 40.

2527. Press where ye see my white plume shine, amidst the
      ranks of war,
      And be your oriflamme to-day the helmet of Navarre.   *Ivry.*

2528. Night sank upon the dusky beach, and on the purple sea,
      Such night in England ne'er had been, nor e'er again
      shall be.   *The Armada.*

McCRAE, JOHN, Canadian doctor and poet, 30 Nov. 1872—28 Jan.
     1918
2529.
> In Flanders fields the poppies blow
> Between the crosses, row on row.
>   *In Flanders Fields.*

McCREERY, JOHN LUCKEY, U.S. journalist, 21 or 31 Dec. 1835—
     6 Sept. 1906
2530.
> There is no death !   The stars go down
> To rise upon some other shore,
> And bright in heaven's jewelled crown
> They shine for evermore.   *There is no Death.*

MacDONALD, GEORGE, Scottish author, 10 Dec. 1824—18 Sept. 1905
2531.
> Alas ! how easily things go wrong !
> A sigh too much, or a kiss too long,
> And there follows a mist and a weeping rain,
> And life is never the same again.   *Phantastes*, xix.

G

2532.   Where did you come from, baby dear ?
             Out of the everywhere into here.   *Baby.*

2533.   Where did you get your eyes so blue ?
             Out of the sky as I came through.   Ibid.

MACKAY, CHARLES, Scottish journalist and song-writer, 27 March, 1814—24 Dec. 1889

2534.   The coin is spurious, nail it down.   *John Littlejohn.*

2535.   Old Tubal Cain was a man of might,
                 In the days when the earth was young.

                                                        Tubal Cain.

2536. There's a good time coming, boys.   *The Good Time Coming.*

2537. Cheer, boys ! cheer !   *Song.*

MACKINTOSH, SIR JAMES, Scottish philosopher, 24 Oct. 1765—30 May, 1832

   2538. The Commons, faithful to their system, remained in a wise and masterly inactivity.   *Vindiciae Gallicae.*
   2539. The frivolous work of polished idleness.
             Dissertation on Ethical Philosophy. Remarks on Thomas Brown.

MACKLIN, CHARLES, Irish actor and dramatist, 1697 ?—11 July, 1797

   2540. The law is a sort of hocus-pocus science, that smiles in yer face while it picks yer pocket ; and the glorious uncertainty of it is of mair use to the professors than the justice of it.

                                              Love à la Mode, II. i.

MACLEAN, MRS., *see* Landon, Letitia Elizabeth

McLENNAN, MURDOCH, Scottish minister, 1701–1783

2541. There's some say that we wan, some say that they wan,
             Some say that nane wan at a', man ;
         But one thing I'm sure, that at Sheriffmuir
             A battle there was which I saw, man :
         And we ran, and they ran, and they ran, and we ran,
             And we ran ; and they ran awa', man.   *Sheriffmuir.*

MACLEOD, NORMAN, Scottish minister, 3 June, 1812—16 June, 1872

2542.   Courage, brother ! do not stumble,
                     Though thy path be dark as night ;
                 There's a star to guide the humble :
                     " Trust in God, and do the right."

                                                      Trust in God.

MACMAHON, MARIE EDMÉ PATRICE MAURICE DE, Duke of Magenta, Marshal of France, 13 July, 1808—17 Oct. 1893

   2543. J'y suis. j'y reste.—Here I am, here I stay.
                             At the siege of Sevastopol, Sept. 1855.

MacNally, Leonard, Irish dramatist, 1752—13 Feb. 1820

2544.   On Richmond Hill there lives a lass,
                  More sweet than May day morn,
               Whose charms all other maids surpass,
                  A rose without a thorn.
               This lass so neat, with smiles so sweet,
                  Has won my right good will,
               I'd crowns resign to call thee mine,
          .   Sweet lass of Richmond Hill.
                                       The Lass of Richmond Hill.

Madden, Samuel, Irish author, 23 Dec. 1686—31 Dec. 1765
2545. Words are men's daughters, but God's sons are things.
                                       Boulter's Monument, 377.
          [Said to have been inserted by Dr. Johnson.]

Maeterlinck, Maurice, Count, Belgian author, 29 Aug. 1862—
   2546. Il n'y a pas de morts.—There are no dead.
                           L'Oiseau Bleu.—The Blue Bird, iv. ii.

Mahony, Francis Sylvester, *see* Prout, Father

Maistre, Joseph Marie, Comte de, French author, 1 April, 1754—
   26 Feb. 1821

2547. Toute nation a le gouvernement qu'elle mérite.—Every
nation has the government it deserves.
                           Letter from St. Petersburg, 27 Aug. 1811.

Malory, Sir Thomas, author, *fl.* 1470

2548. Thou wert never matched of earthly knight's hand ; and thou
wert the courteoust knight that ever bare shield ; and thou wert the
truest friend to thy lover that ever bestrad horse ; and thou wert
the truest lover of a sinful man that ever loved woman ; and thou
wert the kindest man that ever struck with sword ; and thou wert the
goodliest person that ever came among press of knights ; and thou
wert the meekest man and the gentlest that ever ate in hall among
ladies ; and thou wert the sternest knight to thy mortal foe that
ever put spear in the rest.   [Lancelot.]   *Morte D'Arthur*, xxi. xiii.

Mangan, James Clarence, Irish poet, 1 May, 1803—20 June, 1849
2549.   My dark Rosaleen !   *Dark Rosaleen.*
2550.   The fair hills of Éire, O.   *Title of Poem.*

Mann, Horace, U.S. educationist, 4 May, 1796—2 Aug. 1859

2551. Lost, yesterday, somewhere between sunrise and sunset, two
golden hours, each set with sixty diamond minutes.   No reward is
offered, for they are gone for ever.   *Lost, Two Golden Hours.*

2552. Be ashamed to die until you have won some victory for
humanity.   *Commencement Address, Antioch College*, 1859.

Manners, John, *see* Rutland, Duke of

MANNYNG, ROBERT (ROBERT OF BRUNNE), poet, 1264?—1340?.

2553. A gode womman is mannys blys. *Handlyng Synne.*

MARCY, WILLIAM LEARNED, U.S. Secretary for War, 12 Dec. 1786—
4 July, 1857

2554. They see nothing wrong in the rule that to the victors belong
the spoils of the enemy. *Speech, U.S. Senate,* Jan. 1832.

MARKHAM, EDWIN, U.S. poet, 23 April, 1852—7 March, 1940

2555.   Bowed by the weight of centuries he leans
           Upon his hoe and gazes on the ground,
           The emptiness of ages in his face,
           And on his back the burden of the world.
                                 The Man with the Hoe.

2556.   He drew a circle that shut me out—
           Heretic, rebel, a thing to flout.
           But Love and I had the wit to win :
           We drew a circle that took him in. *Outwitted.*

MARLOWE, CHRISTOPHER, dramatist, 1564—1 June, 1593

2557. From jigging veins of rhyming mother wits,
        And such conceits as clownage keeps in pay,
        We'll lead you to the stately tent of war,
        Where you shall hear the Scythian Tamburlaine
        Threatening the world with high astounding terms,
        And scourging kingdoms with his conquering sword.
                         Tamburlaine, part I. Prologue.

2558.   Our swords shall play the orator for us. Ibid.. I. ii.

2559. " And ride in triumph through Persepolis ! "
        Is it not brave to be a king, Techelles ?
        Usumcasane and Theridamas,
        Is it not passing brave to be a king,
        " And ride in triumph through Persepolis '' ?
                                        Ibid., II. v.

2560. If all the pens that ever poets held
        Had fed the feeling of their masters' thoughts,
        And every sweetness that inspired their hearts,
        Their minds, and muses on admirèd themes ;
        If all the heavenly quintessence they still
        From their immortal flowers of poesy,
        Wherein, as in a mirror, we perceive
        The highest reaches of a human wit ;
        If these had made one poem's period,
        And all combined in beauty's worthiness,
        Yet should there hover in their restless heads
        One thought, one grace, one wonder, at the least,
        Which into words no virtue can digest. Ibid., v. i.

2561. Now walk the angels on the walls of Heaven,
        As sentinels to warn th' immortal souls
        To entertain divine Zenocrate. Ibid., part II. II. iv.

2562. Holla, ye pampered jades of Asia !
        What ! can ye draw but twenty miles a day ! Ibid., IV. iv.

2563. Was this the face that launched a thousand ships
And burnt the topless towers of Ilium ?
Sweet Helen, make me immortal with a kiss.
Her lips suck forth my soul ; see where it flies !—
Come, Helen, come, give me my soul again.
Here will I dwell, for Heaven is in these lips,
And all is dross that is not Helena.   *Doctor Faustus*, xiv.

2564. Oh, thou art fairer than the evening air
Clad in the beauty of a thousand stars.   Ibid.

2565. Now hast thou but one bare hour to live,
And then thou must be damned perpetually !
Stand still, you ever-moving spheres of Heaven
That time may cease, and midnight never come.   Ibid., xvi.

2566. *O lente, lente currite noctis equi !*
The stars move still, time runs, the clock will strike,
The Devil will come, and Faustus must be damned.
O, I'll leap up to my God ! Who pulls me down ?
See, see where Christ's blood streams in the firmament !   Ibid.

2567. Ugly hell, gape not ! come not, Lucifer !
I'll burn my books ! Ah Mephistophilis !   Ibid.

2568. Cut is the branch that might have grown full straight,
And burnèd is Apollo's laurel bough,
That sometime grew within this learnèd man.   Ibid.

2569. Infinite riches in a little room.   *The Jew of Malta*, I. i.

2570. My men, like satyrs grazing on the lawns,
Shall with their goat-feet dance the antic hay.
                                                Edward II, I. i.

2571. It lies not in our power to love or hate,
For will in us is over-ruled by fate.
When two are stripped, long ere the course begin,
We wish that one should lose, the other win ;
And one especially do we affect
Of two gold ingots, like in each respect :
The reason no man knows ; let it suffice,
What we behold is censured by our eyes.
Where both deliberate, the love is slight :
Who ever loved, that loved not at first sight ?
                                    Hero and Leander, I. 167.

2572. Come live with me and be my love,
And we will all the pleasures prove
That hills and valleys, dales and fields,
Woods, or steepy mountain yields.
                        The Passionate Shepherd to his Love.

2573.   By shallow rivers, to whose falls
               Melodious birds sing madrigals.   Ibid.

MARMION, SHACKERLEY, dramatist, Jan. 1603—Jan. 1639

2574. What find you better or more honourable than age ? Take
the preheminence of it in everything : in an old friend, in old wine,
in an old pedigree.   *The Antiquary*, II. i.

MARQUIS, DONALD ROBERT PERRY, U.S. poet, 29 July, 1878—29 Dec.
1937

2575.   A little while with grief and laughter,
     And then the day will close ;
    The shadows gather . . . what comes after
     No man knows.   *A Little While.*

2576.   it s cheerio
    my deario
    that pulls a
    lady through *archy and mehitabel cheerio my deario*
[Archy, a cockroach, cannot do punctuation or capitals.]

2577. To stroke a platitude until it purrs like an epigram.
              The Sun Dial.

MARRIOTT, JOHN, poet and clergyman, 1780—31 March, 1825

2578.   In a Devonshire lane as I trotted along
    T'other day, much in want of a subject for song ;
    Thinks I to myself, I have hit on a strain—
    Sure marriage is much like a Devonshire lane.
            The Devonshire Lane.

MARRYAT, FREDERICK, captain in the Navy and novelist, 10 July,
1792—9 Aug. 1848

2579. If you please, ma'am, it was a very little one. [Excusing
her illegitimate baby.]   *Midshipman Easy*, iii.

2580. All zeal, Mr. Easy.   Ibid., ix.

MARTIAL (MARCUS VALERIUS MARTIALIS), Roman poet, 40 ?—104 ?

2581. Non amo te, Sabidi, nec possum dicere quare :
    Hoc tantum possum dicere, non amo te.
    —I do not love you, Sabidius, and I cannot say why :
    this only I can say, I do not love you. *Epigrams*, I. xxxii.

2582.   Bonosque
   Soles effugere atque abire sentit,
   Qui nobis pereunt et imputantur.
   —And he feels that the good days are flying and passing away,
   those days that perish and are put down to our account.
             Ibid., V. xx.

MARVELL, ANDREW, poet and M.P., 31 March, 1621—18 Aug. 1678

2583.   Where the remote Bermudas ride,
    In the ocean's bosom unespied.   *Bermudas.*

2584.   The orange bright,
    Like golden lamps in a green night.   Ibid.

2585.   And all the way, to guide their chime,
    With falling oars they kept the time.   Ibid.

2586.   Had we but world enough, and time,
    This coyness, Lady, were no crime.
          To his Coy Mistress.

2587. But at my back I always hear
Time's winged chariot hurrying near;
And yonder all before us lie
Deserts of vast eternity.   Ibid.

2588. The grave's a fine and private place,
But none, I think, do there embrace.   Ibid.

2589. Stumbling on melons, as I pass,
Ensnared with flowers, I fall on grass.
                        Thoughts in a Garden.

2590. Annihilating all that's made
To a green thought in a green shade.   Ibid.

2591. Casting the body's vest aside,
My soul into the boughs does glide.   Ibid.

2592. The inglorious arts of peace.
        A Horatian Ode upon Cromwell's Return from Ireland.

2593. He nothing common did, or mean,
Upon that memorable scene,
But with his keener eye
The axe's edge did try.   Ibid.

MARX, HEINRICH KARL, German socialist, 5 May, 1818—14 March, 1883

2594. Die Religion . . . ist das Opium des Volkes.—Religion
. . . is the opium of the people.
        *Kritik der Hegelschen Rechtsphilosophie—Critique of the
        Hegelian Philosophy of Right*, introduction.

MARY I, QUEEN, 18 Feb. 1516—17 Nov. 1558

2595. When I am dead and opened, you shall find " Calais " lying
in my heart.   Holinshed's *Chronicles*, III. 1160.

MASEFIELD, JOHN, Poet Laureate, 1 June, 1878—12 May, 1967

2596. Theirs be the music, the colour, the glory, the gold;
Mine be a handful of ashes, and a mouthful of mould.
Of the maimed, of the halt and the blind in the rain and
    the cold—
Of these shall my songs be fashioned, my tales be told.
                        A Consecration.

2597. I must go down to the seas again, to the lonely sea and
    the sky,
And all I ask is a tall ship and a star to steer her by.
                        Sea-Fever.

2598. And all I ask is a merry yarn from a laughing fellow-
    rover,
And quiet sleep and a sweet dream when the long trick's
    over.   Ibid.

2599. Dirty British coaster with a salt-caked smoke stack
Butting through the Channel in the mad March days,
With a cargo of Tyne coal,
Road-rail, pig-lead,
Firewood, iron-ware, and cheap tin trays.   *Cargoes.*

2600. But I'm for toleration and for drinking at an inn,
      Says the old bold mate of Henry Morgan.
Captain Stratton's Fancy.

2601. I have seen dawn and sunset on moors and windy hills
      Coming in solemn beauty like slow old tunes of Spain.
Beauty.

2602. But the loveliest things of beauty God ever has showed to
      me,
      Are her voice, and her hair, and eyes, and the dear red
      curve of her lips.   Ibid.

2603. Laugh and be merry, remember, better the world with a
      song,
      Better the world with a blow in the teeth of a wrong.
      Laugh, for the time is brief, a thread the length of a span.
      Laugh and be proud to belong to the old proud pageant
      of man.   *Laugh and be Merry.*

2604.   And he who gives a child a treat
        Makes joy-bells ring in Heaven's street,
        And he who gives a child a home
        Builds palaces in Kingdom come.
The Everlasting Mercy.

MASON, WILLIAM, poet, 12 Feb. 1724—7 April, 1797

  2605. The fattest hog of Epicurus' sty.   *An Heroic Epistle,* 24.

MASSINGER. PHILIP, dramatist, 1583—March 1640

2606. Her goodness does disdain comparison,
      And, but herself, admits no parallel.
The Duke of Milan, IV. iii.

2607. He that would govern others, first should be
      The master of himself.   *The Bondman,* I. iii.

2608. The devil turned precisian !
A New Way to pay Old Debts, I. i.

2609. Some undone widow sits upon mine arm,
      And takes away the use of 't ; and my sword,
      Glued to my scabbard with wronged orphans' tears,
      Will not be drawn.   Ibid., v. i.

2610. Death hath a thousand doors to let out life.
      I shall find one.   *A Very Woman,* v. iv.

MAULE, SIR WILLIAM HENRY, judge, 25 April, 1788—16 Jan. 1858

  2611. My lords, we are vertebrate animals, we are mammalia !
My learned friend's manner would be intolerable in Almighty God
to a black beetle.
In law court, opposing counsel being Sir Cresswell Cresswell.

MAXWELL, JAMES CLERK, scientist, 13 June, 1831—5 Nov. 1879

2612.   Gin a body meet a body
                 Flyin' through the air,
             Gin a body hit a body,
                 Will it fly ? and where ?
             Ilka impact has its measure,
                 Ne'er a ane hae I,
             Yet a' the lads they measure me,
                 Or, at least they try.   *Rigid Body Sings.*

MEE, WILLIAM, poet, 1788—29 May, 1862

2613.   She's all my fancy painted her ;
             She's lovely, she's divine.   *Alice Gray.*

MELBOURNE, WILLIAM LAMB, 2ND VISCOUNT, Prime Minister, 15 March,
        1779—24 Nov. 1848

2614. I wish I was as cocksure of anything as Tom Macaulay is of
everything.   *Attributed.*

2615. Things have come to a pretty pass when religion is allowed
to invade the sphere of private life.   Ibid.

MENANDER, Greek dramatist, 342 ?–291 ? B.C.

2616. Φθείρουσιν ἤθη χρήσθ' ὁμιλίαι κακαί.
        —Evil communications corrupt good manners.   *Thais.*

MENCKEN, HENRY LOUIS, U.S. critic, 12 Sept. 1880—29 Jan. 1956

2617. The great artists of the world are never Puritans, and seldom
even ordinarily respectable.   *Prejudices*, I. xvi.

2618. To be in love is merely to be in a state of perpetual anaesthesis
—to mistake an ordinary young man for a Greek god or an ordinary
young woman for a goddess.   Ibid.

MEREDITH, GEORGE, author, 12 Feb. 1828—18 May, 1909

2619.   I've studied men from my topsy-turvy
             Close, and, I reckon, rather true.
             Some are fine fellows : some, right scurvy :
             Most, a dash between the two.   *Juggling Jerry.*

2620.   She is steadfast as a star,
                 And yet the maddest maiden :
             She can wage a gallant war,
                 And give the peace of Eden.   *Marian.*

2621.   And if I drink oblivion of a day,
             So shorten I the stature of my soul.

                                            Modern Love, xii.

2622.   Ah, what a dusty answer gets the soul
             When hot for certainties in this our life !   Ibid., l.

2623.   Into the breast that gives the rose,
             Shall I with shuddering fall ?
                     Ode to the Spirit of Earth in Autumn.

*G

2624.   Sweet as Eden is the air,
                         And Eden-sweet the ray.   *Woodland Peace.*

2625. Under yonder beech-tree single on the green-sward,
           Couched with her arms behind her golden head,
       Knees and tresses folded to slip and ripple idly,
           Lies my young love sleeping in the shade.
                                                  Love in the Valley.

2626. She whom I love is hard to catch and conquer,
           Hard, but O the glory of the winning were she won !   Ibid.

2627. When her mother tends her before the laughing mirror,
           Tying up her laces, looping up her hair.   Ibid.

2628. Like the swinging May-cloud that pelts the flowers with
           hailstones
       Off a sunny border, she was made to bruise and bless.   Ibid.

2629. Lovely are the curves of the white owl sweeping
           Wavy in the dusk lit by one large star.
       Lone on the fir-branch, his rattle-note unvaried,
           Brooding o'er the gloom, spins the brown eve-jar.   Ibid.

2630. Brave in her shape, and sweeter unpossessed.   Ibid.

2631. Pure from the night, and splendid for the day.   Ibid.

2632.   The song seraphically free
                         Of taint of personality.   *The Lark Ascending.*

2633.   Enter those enchanted woods,
                         You who dare.   *The Woods of Westermain.*

2634. Around the ancient track marched, rank on rank,
           The army of unalterable law.   *Lucifer in Starlight.*

2635.   Thence had he the laugh
                    . . . broad as ten thousand beeves
                    At pasture !   *The Spirit of Shakespeare.*

2636. I expect that Woman will be the last thing civilised by Man.
                              The Ordeal of Richard Feverel, i.

2637. He has a leg.   *The Egoist*, ii.

2638. A dainty rogue in porcelain,   Ibid., v.

2639. Cynicism is intellectual dandyism.   Ibid., vii.

2640. A Phoebus Apollo turned fasting friar.   Ibid., x.

2641. Men may have rounded Seraglio Point : they have not yet
doubled Cape Turk.   *Diana of the Crossways*, i.

2642. 'Tis Ireland gives England her soldiers, her generals too.
                                                  Ibid., ii.

2643. Ah could eat hog a solid hower ! [Andrew Hedger.] Ibid., viii.

2644. " But how divine is utterance ! " she said. "As we to the
brutes, poets are to us."   Ibid., xvi.

2645. None of your dam punctilio.   *One of our Conquerors*, i.

MERRITT, DIXON LANIER, U.S. journalist, 9 July, 1879—1954

2646.
A rare old bird is the pelican,
His beak holds more than his belican.
He can take in his beak
Enough food for a week.
I'm darned if I know how the helican! *Limerick.*

MEYNELL, ALICE CHRISTIANA GERTRUDE, authoress, 22 Sept. 1847—
27 Nov. 1922

2647.
Thou art like silence unperplexed,
A secret and a mystery
Between one footfall and the next. *To the Beloved.*

2648.
I must not think of thee; and, tired yet strong,
I shun the thought that lurks in all delight—
The thought of thee—and in the blue Heaven's height,
And in the sweetest passage of a song. *Renouncement.*

2649.
She walks—the lady of my delight—
A shepherdess of sheep.
Her flocks are thoughts. She keeps them white;
She guards them from the steep. *The Shepherdess.*

2650.
Flocks of the memories of the day draw near
The dovecot doors of sleep. *At Night.*

MICKLE, WILLIAM JULIUS, Scottish poet, 28 Sept. 1735—28 Oct. 1788

2651.
The dews of summer night did fall,
The moon, sweet regent of the sky,
Silver'd the walls of Cumnor Hall,
And many an oak that grew thereby.
Cumnor Hall.

MIDDLETON, RICHARD BARHAM, author, 28 Oct. 1882—1 Dec. 1911

2652.
Why are her eyes so bright, so bright,
Why do her lips control
The kisses of a summer night
When I would love her soul? *Any Lover, Any Lass.*

MIDDLETON, THOMAS, dramatist, 18 April, 1580—4 July, 1627

2653.
Black spirits and white, red spirits and grey,
Mingle, mingle, mingle, you that mingle may!
The Witch, IV. iii.

2654.
By many a happy accident.
No Wit, No Help, like a Woman's, IV. i.

MIDLANE, ALBERT, hymn-writer, 23 Jan. 1825—27 Feb. 1909

2655.
There's a Friend for little children
Above the bright blue sky,
A Friend who never changes,
Whose love can never die. *Hymn.*

MILL, JOHN STUART, philosopher, 20 May, 1806—8 May, 1873

2656. When the object is to raise the permanent condition of a people, small means do not merely produce small effects ; they produce no effect at all. *The Principles of Political Economy*, II. xiii. 4.

2657. The liberty of the individual must be thus far limited ; he must not make himself a nuisance to other people. *Liberty*, iii.

2658. Unearned increment. *Dissertations and Discussions*, IV. 299.

MILLAY, EDNA ST. VINCENT (MRS. EUGEN JAN BOISSEVAIN), U.S. poetess, 22 Feb. 1892—19 Oct. 1950

2659.   My candle burns at both ends ;
          It will not last the night ;
          But, ah, my foes, and oh, my friends—
          It gives a lovely light, *Figs from Thistles. First Fig.*

2660. Safe upon the solid rock the ugly houses stand :
       Come and see my shining palace built upon the sand !
          Ibid. *Second Fig.*

2661. I will be the gladdest thing under the sun !
       I will touch a hundred flowers and not pick one.
          Afternoon on a Hill.

2662.   And if I loved you Wednesday,
             Well, what is that to you ?
          I do not love you Thursday—
             So much is true. *Thursday.*

2663.   And, " One thing there's no getting by—
          I've been a wicked girl," said I ;
          " But if I can't be sorry, why,
             I might as well be glad ! " *The Penitent.*

MILLER, WILLIAM, Scottish poet, August, 1810—20 August, 1872

2664. Wee Willie Winkie rins through the town,
       Upstairs and downstairs in his nicht-gown,
       Tirling at the window, crying at the lock,
       "Are the weans in their bed, for it's now ten o'clock ? "
          Wee Willie Winkie.

MILLS, JOHN, banker, 16 Dec. 1821—26 Sept. 1896

2665.   Life's race well run,
          Life's work well done,
          Life's victory won,
             Now cometh rest. *Epitaph.*
[There are various alternative versions, and authorship has been claimed for E. H. Parker, a U.S. doctor who used the lines in his funeral ode on President Garfield.]

MILMAN, HENRY HART, Dean of St. Paul's and historian, 10 Feb. 1791 —24 Sept. 1868

2666. And the cold marble leapt to life a god.
          The Belvidere Apollo.

MILNE, ALAN ALEXANDER, author, 18 Jan. 1882—31 Jan. 1956

2667.   I do like a little bit of butter to my bread.
                    When we were very Young.   The King's Breakfast.

2668.   James James
                        Morrison Morrison
                        Weatherby George Dupree
                        Took great
                        Care of his Mother
                        Though he was only three.
                                        Ibid. *Disobedience.*

MILNES, RICHARD MONCKTON, *see* Houghton, Baron

MILTON, JOHN, poet, 9 Dec. 1608—8 Nov. 1674

2669.   Let us with a gladsome mind
        Praise the Lord, for he is kind,
            For his mercies ay endure,
            Ever faithful, ever sure.   *Psalm* 136.

2670.   It was the winter wild,
            While the Heav'n-born child
        All meanly wrapt in the rude manger lies.
                        On the Morning of Christ's Nativity, 29.

2671.   No war, or battle's sound
        Was heard the world around.   Ibid., 53.

2672.   While birds of calm sit brooding on the charmèd wave.
                                                       Ibid., 68.

2673.   Time will run back, and fetch the age of gold.   Ibid., 135.

2674.   The oracles are dumb.   Ibid., 173.

2675.   No nightly trance, or breathed spell,
        Inspires the pale-eyed priest from the prophetic cell.
                                                       Ibid., 179.

2676.   So when the sun in bed,
            Curtain'd with cloudy red,
        Pillows his chin upon an orient wave.   Ibid., 229.

2677.   Blest pair of Sirens, pledges of Heav'n's joy,
        Sphere-born harmonious sisters, Voice and Verse.
                                        At a Solemn Music, 1.

2678.   What needs my Shakespeare for his honour'd bones,
        The labour of an age in piled stones,
        Or that his hallow'd relics should be hid
        Under a star-y-pointing pyramid ?
        Dear son of memory, great heir of fame,
        What need'st thou such weak witness of thy name ?
                                        On Shakespeare.

2679.   O nightingale, that on yon bloomy spray
            Warbl'st at eve, when all the woods are still.
                        Sonnet. To the Nightingale.

2680.   How soon hath Time, the subtle thief of youth,
            Stoln on his wing my three and twentieth year !
            Sonnet. On his being arrived to the Age of twenty-three.

2681.   All is, if I have grace to use it so,
    As ever in my great Taskmaster's eye.   *Ibid.*

2682.   Hence, loathed Melancholy.   *L'Allegro*, 1.

2683.   Haste thee, nymph, and bring with thee
    Jest, and youthful jollity,
    Quips, and cranks, and wanton wiles,
    Nods, and becks, and wreathed smiles.   *Ibid.*, 25.

2684.   Sport that wrinkled Care derides,
    And Laughter holding both his sides.
    Come, and trip it as you go,
    On the light fantastic toe.   *Ibid.*, 31.

2685.   The mountain nymph, sweet Liberty.   *Ibid.*, 36.

2686.   To hear the lark begin his flight,
    And singing startle the dull night,
    From his watch-tower in the skies,
    Till the dappled dawn doth rise.   *Ibid.*, 41.

2687.   While the cock with lively din
    Scatters the rear of darkness thin,
    And to the stack, or the barn-door,
    Stoutly struts his dames before.   *Ibid.*, 49.

2688.   Right against the eastern gate
    Where the great sun begins his state.   *Ibid.*, 59.

2689.   Meadows trim with daisies pied,
    Shallow brooks, and rivers wide ;
    Towers and battlements it sees
    Bosom'd high in tufted trees,
    Where perhaps some beauty lies,
    The cynosure of neighbouring eyes.   *Ibid.*, 75.

2690.   Of herbs, and other country messes,
    Which the neat-handed Phyllis dresses.   *Ibid.*, 85.

2691.   Then to the spicy nut-brown ale.   *Ibid.*, 100.

2692.   Tower'd cities please us then,
    And the busy hum of men.   *Ibid.*, 117.

2693.   With store of ladies, whose bright eyes
    Rain influence, and judge the prize
    Or wit or arms.   *Ibid.*, 121.

2694.   Such sights as youthful poets dream
    On summer eves by haunted stream ;
    Then to the well-trod stage anon,
    If Jonson's learned sock be on,
    Or sweetest Shakespeare, Fancy's child,
    Warble his native wood-notes wild.   *Ibid.*, 129.

2695.   And ever, against eating cares,
    Lap me in soft Lydian airs,
    Married to immortal verse
    Such as the meeting soul may pierce
    In notes, with many a winding bout
    Of linked sweetness long drawn out.   *Ibid.*, 135.

2696. The melting voice through mazes running,
Untwisting all the chains that tie
The hidden soul of harmony. *Ibid.*, 142.

2697. Hence, vain deluding joys,
The brood of Folly without father bred.
Il Penseroso, 1.

2698. The gay motes that people the sunbeams. *Ibid.*, 8.

2699. Sober, steadfast, and demure. *Ibid.*, 32.

2700. And looks commercing with the skies,
Thy rapt soul sitting in thine eyes. *Ibid.*, 39.

2701. And add to these retired Leisure,
That in trim gardens takes his pleasure. *Ibid.*, 49.

2702. Sweet bird, that shunn'st the noise of folly,
Most musical, most melancholy. *Ibid.*, 61.

2703. To behold the wand'ring moon,
Riding near her highest noon,
Like one that had been led astray
Through the heaven's wide pathless way ;
And oft, as if her head she bow'd,
Stooping through a fleecy cloud. *Ibid.*, 67.

2704. Oft, on a plat of rising ground,
I hear the far-off curfew sound,
Over some wide-water'd shore,
Swinging slow with sullen roar. *Ibid.*, 73.

2705. Where glowing embers through the room
Teach light to counterfeit a gloom,
Far from all resort of mirth,
Save the cricket on the hearth. *Ibid.*, 79.

2706. Sometime let gorgeous Tragedy
In sceptred pall come sweeping by,
Presenting Thebes, or Pelops' line,
Or the tale of Troy divine. *Ibid.*, 97.

2707. Or bid the soul of Orpheus sing
Such notes as, warbled to the string,
Drew iron tears down Pluto's cheek. *Ibid.*, 105.

2708. Or call up him that left half told
The story of Cambuscan bold. *Ibid.*, 109.

2709. Where more is meant than meets the ear. *Ibid.*, 120.

2710. En ling on the rustling leaves
With minute drops from off the eaves. *Ibid.*, 129.

2711. But let my due feet never fail
To walk the studious cloister's pale,
And love the high embowed roof,
With antique pillars massy proof,
And storied windows richly dight,
Casting a dim religious light.
There let the pealing organ blow
To the full-voiced quire below. *Ibid.*, 155.

2712.   Under the shady roof
        Of branching elm star-proof.   *Arcades*, 88.

2713.   Above the smoke and stir of this dim spot,
        Which men call Earth.   *Comus*, 5.

2714.   An old and haughty nation proud in arms.   Ibid., 33.

2715.   These my sky robes spun out of Iris' woof.   Ibid., 83.

2716.   The star that bids the shepherd fold.   Ibid., 93.

2717.   Midnight shout and revelry,
        Tipsy dance and jollity.   Ibid., 103.

2718.   And, on the tawny sands and shelves,
        Trip the pert fairies and the dapper elves.   Ibid., 117.

2719.   Ere the blabbing eastern scout,
        The nice Morn on the Indian steep
        From her cabin'd loop-hole peep.   Ibid., 138.

2720.   When the grey-hooded Even
        Like a sad votarist in palmer's weed,
        Rose from the hindmost wheels of Phoebus' wain.
                                                        Ibid., 188

2721.   O welcome, pure-eyed Faith, white-handed Hope,
        Thou hovering angel girt with golden wings.   Ibid., 213.

2722.   I took it for a faery vision
        Of some gay creatures of the element,
        That in the colours of the rainbow live,
        And play i' the plighted clouds.   Ibid., 298.

2723.   I know each lane, and every alley green,
        Dingle, or bushy dell, of this wild wood,
        And every bosky bourn from side to side,
        My daily walks and ancient neighbourhood.   Ibid., 311.

2724.   With thy long levell'd rule of streaming light. Ibid., 340.

2725.   Virtue could see to do what virtue would
        By her own radiant light, though sun and moon
        Were in the flat sea sunk.   Ibid., 373.

2726.   He that has light within his own clear breast
        May sit i' th' centre and enjoy bright day,
        But he that hides a dark soul and foul thoughts
        Benighted walks under the midday sun ;
        Himself is his own dungeon.   Ibid., 381.

2727.   'Tis chastity, my brother, chastity :
        She that has that is clad in complete steel.   Ibid., 420.

2728.   Some say no evil thing that walks by night
        In fog, or fire, by lake, or moorish fen,
        Blue meagre hag, or stubborn unlaid ghost,
        That breaks his magic chains at curfew time,
        No goblin, or swart faery of the mine,
        Hath hurtful power o'er true virginity.   Ibid., 432.

2729.   How charming is divine philosophy !
        Not harsh, and crabbed as dull fools suppose,
        But musical as is Apollo's lute,
        And a perpetual feast of nectar'd sweets,
        Where no crude surfeit reigns.   Ibid., 476.

2730.	And fill'd the air with barbarous dissonance.	Ibid., 550.
2731.	I was all ear, And took in strains that might create a soul Under the ribs of death.	Ibid., 560.
2732.	If this fail, The pillar'd firmament is rottenness, And earth's base built on stubble.	Ibid., 597.
2733.	The dull swain Treads on it daily with his clouted shoon.	Ibid., 634.
2734.	Those budge doctors of the Stoic fur.	Ibid., 707.
2735.	It is for homely features to keep home, They had their name thence ; coarse complexions And cheeks of sorry grain will serve to ply The sampler, and to tease the huswife's wool. What need a vermeil-tinctured lip for that, Love-darting eyes, or tresses like the morn ?	Ibid., 748.
2736.	Sabrina fair, Listen where thou art sitting Under the glassy, cool, translucent wave, In twisted braids of lilies knitting The loose train of thy amber-dropping hair.	Ibid., 859.
2737.	Mortals that would follow me, Love virtue, she alone is free, She can teach ye how to climb Higher than the sphery chime ; Or, if virtue feeble were, Heaven itself would stoop to her.	Ibid., 1018.
2738.	Yet once more, O ye laurels, and once more Ye myrtles brown, with ivy never sere, I come to pluck your berries harsh and crude, And with forc'd fingers rude, Shatter your leaves before the mellowing year.	*Lycidas*, 1.
2739.	He knew Himself to sing, and build the lofty rhyme.	Ibid., 10.
2740.	Without the meed of some melodious tear.	Ibid., 14.
2741.	Under the opening eyelids of the morn.	Ibid., 26.
2742.	But, O the heavy change, now thou art gone, Now thou art gone, and never must return !	Ibid., 37.
2743.	The gadding vine.	Ibid., 40.
2744.	And strictly meditate the thankless Muse.	Ibid., 66.
2745.	To sport with Amaryllis in the shade, Or with the tangles of Neaera's hair.	Ibid., 69.
2746.	Fame is the spur that the clear spirit doth raise (That last infirmity of noble mind) To scorn delights, and live laborious days ; But the fair guerdon when we hope to find, And think to burst out into sudden blaze, Comes the blind Fury with th' abhorred shears And slits the thin-spun life.	Ibid., 70

2747.   Fame is no plant that grows on mortal soil.   Ibid., 78.

2748.   Last came, and last did go
             The Pilot of the Galilean lake,
             Two massy keys he bore of metals twain
             (The golden opes, the iron shuts amain).   Ibid., 108.

2749. Blind mouths ! that scarce themselves know how to hold
       A sheep-hook.   Ibid., 119.

2750.   And, then they list, their lean and flashy songs
             Grate on their scrannel pipes of wretched straw ;
             The hungry sheep look up, and are not fed,
             But, swoln with wind and the rank mist they draw,
             Rot inwardly, and foul contagion spread.   Ibid., 123.

2751.   But that two-handed engine at the door
             Stands ready to smite once, and smite no more. Ibid., 130.

2752.   Throw hither all your quaint enamell'd eyes,
             That on the green turf suck the honied showers
             And purple all the ground with vernal flowers.
             Bring the rathe primrose that forsaken dies,
             The tufted crow-toe, and pale jessamine,
             The white pink, and the pansy freak'd with jet,
             The glowing violet,
             The musk-rose, and the well-attir'd woodbine,
             With cowslips wan that hang the pensive head,
             And every flower that sad embroidery wears :
             Bid amaranthus all his beauty shed,
             And daffadillies fill their cups with tears,
             To strew the laureate hearse where Lycid lies.
                                                             Ibid., 139.

2753.   So sinks the day-star in the ocean bed,
             And yet anon repairs his drooping head,
             And tricks his beams, and with new-spangled ore
             Flames in the forehead of the morning sky.   Ibid., 168.

2754.   At last he rose, and twitch'd his mantle blue :
             To-morrow to fresh woods, and pastures new.   Ibid., 192.

2755.   Captain or Colonel, or Knight in arms.
                     Sonnet. When the Assault was intended to the City.

2756.   The great Emathian conqueror bid spare
         The house of Pindarus, when temple and tower
         Went to the ground.   Ibid.

2757.   Killed with report that old man eloquent.
                     Sonnet. To the Lady Margaret Ley.

2758.   That would have made Quintilian stare and gasp.
                 *Sonnet.   On the Detraction which followed upon my
                 writing certain Treatises.*

2759.   License they mean when they cry liberty.
                                     Sonnet. On the same.

2760.   Avenge, O Lord, thy slaughter'd saints, whose bones
         Lie scatter'd on the Alpine mountains cold.
                     Sonnet. On the late Massacre in Piedmont.

2761.   When I consider how my light is spent,
          Ere half my days, in this dark world and wide,
          And that one talent which is death to hide
        Lodg'd with me useless, though my soul more bent
        To serve therewith my Maker, and present
          My true account, lest He returning chide,
          Doth God exact day-labour, light denied,
        I fondly ask : but Patience, to prevent
        That murmur, soon replies, God doth not need
          Either man's work or His own gifts ; who best
          Bear His mild yoke, they serve Him best : His state
        Is kingly.   Thousands at His bidding speed
          And post o'er land and ocean without rest :
          They also serve who only stand and wait.
                              Sonnet.   On his Blindness.

2762.   Methought I saw my late espousèd Saint.
                              Sonnet.   On his Deceased Wife.

2763.   New Presbyter is but old Priest writ large.
                *Sonnet.   On the New Forcers of Conscience under the
                    Long Parliament.*

2764.   Peace hath her victories
          No less renowned than war.
                Sonnet.   To the Lord General Cromwell, May, 1652.

2765.   Of Man's first disobedience, and the fruit
        Of that forbidden tree, whose mortal taste
        Brought death into the world, and all our woe,
        With loss of Eden, till one greater Man
        Restore us, and regain the blissful seat,
        Sing, heav'nly Muse.   *Paradise Lost*, I. I.

2766.   Things unattempted yet in prose or rhyme.   Ibid., 16.

2767.   What in me is dark
        Illumine, what is low raise and support ;
        That to the highth of this great argument
        I may assert eternal Providence,
        And justify the ways of God to men.   Ibid., 22.

2768.   As far as angels' ken.   Ibid., 59.

2769.   Yet from those flames
        No light, but rather darkness visible
        Serv'd only to discover sights of woe,
        Regions of sorrow, doleful shades, where peace
        And rest can never dwell, hope never comes
        That comes to all.   Ibid., 62.

2770.   What though the field be lost ?
        All is not lost ; th' unconquerable will,
        And study of revenge, immortal hate,
        And courage never to submit or yield :
        And what is else not to be overcome ?   Ibid., 105.

2771.   To be weak is miserable
        Doing or suffering.   Ibid., 157.

2772.   And out of good still to find means of evil.   Ibid., 165.

2773.   Farewell happy fields
        Where joy for ever dwells : Hail horrors, hail. Ibid., 249.

2774.	The mind is its own place, and in itself Can make a heav'n of hell, a hell of heav'n.	Ibid., 254.
2775.	Better to reign in hell, than serve in heav'n.	Ibid., 263.
2776.	His spear, to equal which the tallest pine Hewn on Norwegian hills, to be the mast Of some great ammiral, were but a wand, He walk'd with to support uneasy steps Over the burning marl.	Ibid., 292.
2777.	Thick as autumnal leaves that strow the brooks In Vallombrosa, where th' Etrurian shades High overarch'd imbower.	Ibid., 302.
2778.	Busiris and his Memphian chivalry.	Ibid., 307.
2779.	Awake, arise, or be for ever fall'n !	Ibid., 330.
2780.	And when night Darkens the streets, then wander forth the sons Of Belial, flown with insolence and wine.	Ibid., 500.
2781.	Th' imperial ensign, which, full high advanc'd, Shone like a meteor, streaming to the wind.	Ibid., 536.
2782.	Sonorous metal blowing martial sounds : At which the universal host up sent A shout that tore hell's concave, and beyond Frighted the reign of Chaos and old Night.	Ibid., 540.
2783.	Anon they move In perfect phalanx to the Dorian mood Of flutes and soft recorders.	Ibid., 549
2784.	What resounds In fable or romance of Uther's son Begirt with British and Armoric knights ; And all who since, baptis'd or infidel, Jousted in Aspramont or Montalban, Damasco, or Marocco, or Trebisond, Or whom Biserta sent from Afric shore When Charlemain with all his peerage fell In Fontarabbia.	Ibid., 579.
2785.	His form had yet not lost All her original brightness, nor appear'd Less than archangel ruined, and th' excess Of glory obscur'd.	Ibid., 591.
2786.	The sun . . . In dim eclipse disastrous twilight sheds On half the nations, and with fear of change Perplexes monarchs.	Ibid., 594.
2787.	Thrice he assay'd, and thrice in spite of scorn, Tears, such as angels weep, burst forth.	Ibid., 619.
2788.	Who overcomes By force, hath overcome but half his foe.	Ibid., 648.
2789.	Let none admire That riches grow in hell ; that soil may best Deserve the precious bane.	Ibid., 690.

2790.
        How he fell
From heav'n, they fabl'd, thrown by angry Jove
Sheer o'er the crystal battlements : from morn
To noon he fell, from noon to dewy eve,
A summer's day ; and with the setting sun
Dropt from the zenith like a falling star,
On Lemnos th' Aegean isle.   Ibid., 740.

2791.
         Faery elves,
Whose midnight revels, by a forest side
Or fountain some belated peasant sees,
Or dreams he sees, while overhead the moon
Sits arbitress.   Ibid., 781.

2792.
High on a throne of royal state, which far
Outshone the wealth of Ormus and of Ind,
Or where the gorgeous East with richest hand
Showers on her kings barbaric pearl and gold,
Satan exalted sat, by merit rais'd
To that bad eminence.   Ibid., II. 1.

2793.
My sentence is for open war : of wiles
More unexpert, I boast not.   Ibid., 51.

2794.
       When the scourge
Inexorably, and the torturing hour
Calls us to penance.   Ibid., 90.

2795.
Which if not victory is yet revenge.   Ibid., 105.

2796.
Belial, in act more graceful and humane ;
A fairer person lost not heav'n ; he seemed
For dignity compos'd and high exploit :
But all was false and hollow ; though his tongue
Dropt manna, and could make the worse appear
The better reason, to perplex and dash
Maturest counsels.   Ibid., 109.

2797.
      For who would lose,
Though full of pain, this intellectual being,
Those thoughts that wander through eternity,
To perish rather, swallowed up and lost
In the wide womb of uncreated night,
Devoid of sense and motion ?   Ibid., 146.

2798.
His red right hand.   Ibid., 174.

2799.
Unrespited, unpitied, unreprived,
Ages of hopeless end.   Ibid., 185.

2800.
     The never-ending flight
Of future days.   Ibid., 221.

2801.
       With grave
Aspect he rose, and in his rising seem'd
A pillar of state ; deep on his front engraven
Deliberation sat and public care ;
And princely counsel in his face yet shone
Majestic though in ruin.   Ibid., 300.

2802.
And through the palpable obscure find out
His uncouth way.   Ibid., 406.

2803. Long is the way
And hard, that out of hell leads up to light. Ibid., 432.

2804. Others apart sat on a hill retir'd
In thoughts more elevate, and reason'd high
Of providence, foreknowledge, will, and fate,
Fix'd fate, free will, foreknowledge absolute,
And found no end, in wand'ring mazes lost. Ibid., 557.

2805. Vain wisdom all, and false philosophy. Ibid., 565.

2806. A gulf profound as that Serbonian bog,
Betwixt Damiata and Mount Casius old,
Where armies whole have sunk : the parching air
Burns frore, and cold performs th' effect of fire. Ibid., 592.

2807. O'er many a frozen, many a fiery Alp,
Rocks, caves, lakes, fens, bogs, dens, and shades of death.
Ibid., 620.

2808. Gorgons and Hydras, and Chimaeras dire. Ibid., 628.

2809. The other shape,
If shape it might be call'd that shape had none
Distinguishable in member, joint, or limb,
Or substance might be call'd that shadow seem'd,
For each seem'd either ; black it stood as night,
Fierce as ten furies, terrible as hell,
And shook a dreadful dart ; what seem'd his head
The likeness of a kingly crown had on. Ibid., 666.

2810. Whence and what art thou, execrable shape ? Ibid., 681.

2811. Incens'd with indignation Satan stood
Unterrifi'd, and like a comet burn'd,
That fires the length of Ophiuchus huge
In th' arctic sky, and from his horrid hair
Shakes pestilence and war. Ibid., 707.

2812. Their fatal hands
No second stroke intend. Ibid., 712.

2813. So frown'd the mighty combatants, that hell
Grew darker at their frown. Ibid., 719.

2814. On a sudden open fly
With impetuous recoil and jarring sound
Th' infernal doors, and on their hinges grate
Harsh thunder. Ibid., 879.

2815. For hot, cold, moist, and dry, four champions fierce,
Strive here for mastery. Ibid., 898.

2816. So eagerly the fiend
O'er bog or steep, through strait, rough, dense, or rare,
With head, hands, wings, or feet pursues his way,
And swims or sinks, or wades, or creeps, or flies.
Ibid., 947.

2817. With ruin upon ruin, rout on rout,
Confusion worse confounded. Ibid., 995.

2818. So he with difficulty and labour hard
Mov'd on, with difficulty and labour he. Ibid., 1021.

2819. Hail, holy light, offspring of heav'n first-born. Ibid., III. 1.

2820.   Those other two equall'd with me in fate,
        So were I equall'd with them in renown,
        Blind Thamyris and blind Maeonides,
        And Tiresias and Phineus, prophets old.   Ibid., 33.

2821.   Thus with the year
        Seasons return, but not to me returns
        Day, or the sweet approach of ev'n or morn,
        Or sight of vernal bloom, or summer's rose,
        Or flocks, or herds, or human face divine ;
        But cloud instead, and ever-during dark
        Surrounds me, from the cheerful ways of men
        Cut off, and for the book of knowledge fair
        Presented with a universal blank
        Of nature's works to me expung'd and ras'd,
        And wisdom at one entrance quite shut out.   Ibid., 40.

2822.   Dark with excessive bright.   Ibid., 380.

2823.   Eremites and friars,
        White, black and grey, with all their trumpery.
                                                               Ibid., 474.

2824.   Into a Limbo large and broad, since called
        The Paradise of Fools, to few unknown.   Ibid., 495.

2825.   At whose sight all the stars
        Hide their diminished heads.   Ibid. IV. 34.

2826.   Me miserable ! which way shall I fly
        Infinite wrath, and infinite despair ?
        Which way I fly is hell ; myself am hell ;
        And in the lowest deep a lower deep
        Still threat'ning to devour me opens wide,
        To which the hell I suffer seems a heav'n.   Ibid., 73.

2827.   So farewell hope, and with hope farewell fear,
        Farewell remorse : all good to me is lost ;
        Evil, be thou my good.   Ibid., 108.

2828.   Sabean odours from the spicy shore
        Of Araby the blest.   Ibid., 162.

2829   Thence up he flew, and on the Tree of Life,
        The middle tree and highest there that grew,
        Sat like a cormorant.   Ibid., 194.

2830.   A heaven on earth.   Ibid., 208.

2831.   Flowers of all hue, and without thorn the rose.   Ibid., 256.

2832.   For contemplation he and valour form'd,
        For softness she and sweet attractive grace,
        He for God only, she for God in him :
        His fair large front and eye sublime declar'd
        Absolute rule.   Ibid., 297.

2833   Implied
        Subjection, but requir'd with gentle sway,
        And by her yielded, by him best receiv'd,
        Yielded with coy submission, modest pride,
        And sweet reluctant amorous delay.   Ibid., 307.

2834.   Adam the goodliest man of men since born
          His sons, the fairest of her daughters Eve.   Ibid., 323.

2835.   Imparadis'd in one another's arms.   Ibid., 506.

2836.   Now came still evening on, and twilight grey
          Had in her sober livery all things clad ;
          Silence accompanied, for beast and bird,
          They to their grassy couch, these to their nests
          Were slunk, all but the wakeful nightingale ;
          She all night long her amorous descant sung ;
          Silence was pleas'd : now glow'd the firmament
          With living sapphires : Hesperus, that led
          The starry host, rode brightest, till the moon
          Rising in clouded majesty, at length
          Apparent queen unveil'd her peerless light,
          And o'er the dark her silver mantle threw.   Ibid., 598.

2837.   With thee conversing I forget all time,
          All seasons and their change, all please alike.
          Sweet is the breath of morn, her rising sweet,
          With charm of earliest birds ; pleasant the sun
          When first on this delightful land he spreads
          His orient beams, on herb, tree, fruit, and flower,
          Glist'ring with dew ; fragrant the fertile earth
          After soft showers ; and sweet the coming on
          Of grateful evening mild, then silent night
          With this her solemn bird and this fair moon,
          And these the gems of heav'n, her starry train.
                                                          Ibid., 639.

2838.   Eas'd the putting off
          These troublesome disguises which we wear.   Ibid., 739.

2839.   Hail wedded love, mysterious law, true source
          Of human offspring, sole propriety
          In Paradise of all things common else.   Ibid., 750.

2840.   Him thus intent Ithuriel with his spear
          Touch'd lightly ; for no falsehood can endure
          Touch of celestial temper.   Ibid., 810.

2841.   Not to know me argues yourselves unknown.   Ibid., 830.

2842.   Abash'd the devil stood
          And felt how awful goodness is, and saw
          Virtue in her shape how lovely.   Ibid., 846.

2843.   But wherefore thou alone ?   Wherefore with thee
          Came not all hell broke loose ?   Ibid., 917.

2844.   Like Teneriff or Atlas unremov'd.   Ibid., 987.

2845.   Now morn her rosy steps in th' eastern clime
          Advancing, sow'd the earth with orient pearl,
          When Adam wak'd, so custom'd, for his sleep
          Was aery light, from pure digestion bred.   Ibid., v. 1.

2846.   My fairest, my espous'd, my latest found,
          Heav'n's last best gift, my ever new delight.   Ibid., 18.

2847.   Best image of myself and dearer half.   Ibid., 95.

2848.   These are thy glorious words, Parent of Good ! Ibid., 153.

2849. Him first, him last, him midst, and without end.
Ibid., 165.

2850. A wilderness of sweets.
Ibid., 294.

2851. So saying, with dispatchful looks in haste
She turns, on hospitable thoughts intent.
Ibid., 331.

2852. No fear lest dinner cool.
Ibid., 396.

2853. Thrones, dominations, princedoms, virtues, powers.
Ibid., 601.

2854. So spake the seraph Abdiel, faithful found
Among the faithless, faithful only he.
Ibid., 893.

2855. All night the dreadless angel unpursu'd
Through heav'n's wide champain held his way, till morn,
Wak'd by the circling hours, with rosy hand
Unbarr'd the gates of light.
Ibid., VI. 1.

2856.   Arms on armour clashing bray'd
Horrible discord, and the madding wheels
Of brazen chariots rag'd ; dire was the noise
Of conflict.
Ibid., 209.

2857. He onward came ; far off his coming shone.
Ibid., 768.

2858. More safe I sing with mortal voice, unchang'd
To hoarse or mute, though fall'n on evil days,
On evil days though fall'n, and evil tongues.
Ibid., VII. 24.

2859.   Still govern thou my song,
Urania, and fit audience find, though few.
Ibid., 30.

2860. The angel ended, and in Adam's ear
So charming left his voice, that he awhile
Thought him still speaking, still stood fix'd to hear.
Ibid., VIII. 1.

2861. Liquid lapse of murmuring streams.
Ibid., 263.

2862. And feel that I am happier than I know.
Ibid., 282.

2863. Grace was in all her steps, heav'n in her eye,
In every gesture dignity and love.
Ibid., 488.

2864. Her virtue and the conscience of her worth,
That would be woo'd, and not unsought be won.
Ibid., 502.

2865.   The amorous bird of night
Sung spousal, and bid haste the evening star
On his hill top, to light the bridal lamp.
Ibid., 518.

2866.   So absolute she seems
And in herself complete, so well to know
Her own, that what she wills to do or say,
Seems wisest, virtuousest, discreetest, best.
Ibid., 547.

2867. Accuse not Nature, she hath done her part ;
Do thou but thine.
Ibid., 561.

2868. To whom the angel with a smile that glow'd
Celestial rosy red, love's proper hue.
Ibid., 618.

2869. Since first this subject for heroic song
Pleas'd me long choosing, and beginning late.

Ibid., IX. 25.

2870. The serpent subtlest beast of all the field. *Ibid.*, 86.

2871. For solitude sometimes is best society,
And short retirement urges sweet return. *Ibid.*, 249.

2872. As one who long in populous city pent,
Where houses thick and sewers annoy the air.

Ibid., 445.

2873.   Hope elevates, and joy
Brightens his crest. *Ibid.*, 633.

2874. God so commanded, and left that command
Sole daughter of his voice. *Ibid.*, 652.

2875. Earth felt the wound, and Nature from her seat
Sighing through all her works gave signs of woe,
That all was lost. *Ibid.*, 782.

2876. O fairest of creation, last and best
Of all God's works, creature in whom excell'd
Whatever can to sight or thought be form'd
Holy, divine, good, amiable, or sweet !
How art thou lost, how on a sudden lost,
Defac'd, deflower'd, and now to death devote ? *Ibid.*, 896.

2877.   A pillar'd shade
High overarch'd, and echoing walks between. *Ibid.*, 1106.

2878.   Yet shall I temper so
Justice with mercy, as may illustrate most
Them fully satisfied, and thee appease. *Ibid.*, X. 77.

2879. Demoniac frenzy, moping melancholy,
And moon-struck madness. *Ibid.*, XI. 485.

2880. And over them triumphant Death his dart
Shook, but delay'd to strike, though oft invok'd
With vows, as their chief good, and final hope. *Ibid.*, 491.

2881. So may'st thou live, till like ripe fruit thou drop
Into thy mother's lap. *Ibid.*, 535.

2882. Nor love thy life, nor hate ; but what thou liv'st
Live well, how long or short permit to heav'n. *Ibid.*, 553.

2883. A bevy of fair women. *Ibid.*, 582.

2884. The brazen throat of war had ceased to roar,
All now was turn'd to jollity and game,
To luxury and riot, feast and dance. *Ibid.*, 713.

2885. Some natural tears they dropp'd, but wip'd them soon ;
The world was all before them, where to choose
Their place of rest, and Providence their guide :
They hand in hand with wand'ring steps and slow,
Through Eden took their solitary way. *Ibid.*, XII. 645.

2886.   Satan, bowing low
His grey dissimulation, disappear'd.

Paradise Regained, I. 497.

2887.
> Beauty stands
> In the admiration only of weak minds
> Led captive.

Ibid., II. 220.

2888.
> Of fairy damsels met in forest wide
> By knights of Logres, or of Lyones,
> Lancelot or Pelleas, or Pellenore.

Ibid., 359.

2889.
> Of whom to be disprais'd were no small praise.

Ibid., III. 56.

2890.
> Syene, and where the shadow both way falls,
> Meroe, Nilotic isle.

Ibid., IV. 70.

2891.
> The childhood shows the man,
> As morning shows the day.

Ibid., 220.

2892.
> Athens, the eye of Greece, mother of arts
> And eloquence.

Ibid., 240.

2893.
> See there the olive grove of Academe,
> Plato's retirement, where the Attic bird
> Trills her thick-warbl'd notes the summer long.

Ibid., 244.

2894.
> Thence to the famous orators repair,
> Those ancient, whose resistless eloquence
> Wielded at will that fierce democratie,
> Shook the arsenal and fulmin'd over Greece,
> To Macedon, and Artaxerxes' throne.

Ibid., 267.

2895.
> Deep vers'd in books and shallow in himself.

Ibid., 327.

2896.
> Till morning fair
> Came forth with pilgrim steps in amice grey.

Ibid., 426.

2897.
> He unobserv'd
> Home to his mother's house private return'd.

Ibid., 638.

2898.
> A little onward lend thy guiding hand
> To these dark steps, a little further on.

Samson Agonistes, 1.

2899.
> Eyeless in Gaza at the mill with slaves.

Ibid., 41.

2900.
> O dark, dark, dark, amid the blaze of noon,
> Irrecoverably dark, total eclipse
> Without all hope of day.

Ibid., 80.

2901.
> Just are the ways of God,
> And justifiable to men ;
> Unless there be who think not God at all.

Ibid., 293.

2902.
> What boots it at one gate to make defence
> And at another to let in the foe ?

Ibid., 560.

2903.
> But who is this, what thing of sea or land ?
> Female of sex it seems,
> That so bedeck'd, ornate, and gay,
> Comes this way sailing
> Like a stately ship
> Of Tarsus, bound for th' isles
> Of Javan or Gadier,
> With all her bravery on, and tackle trim,
> Sails fill'd, and streamers waving,
> Courted by all the winds that hold them play,
> An amber scent of odorous perfume
> Her harbinger.

Ibid., 710.

2904.   He's gone, and who knows how he may report
         Thy words by adding fuel to the flame ?   Ibid., 1350.

2905.   For evil news rides post, while good news baits.
                                                         Ibid., 1538.

2906.   Nothing is here for tears, nothing to wail
         Or knock the breast, no weakness, no contempt,
         Dispraise, or blame, nothing but well and fair,
         And what may quiet us in a death so noble.   Ibid., 1721.

2907.   Calm of mind, all passion spent.   Ibid., 1758.

2908. A poet soaring in the high region of his fancies with his
garland and singing robes about him.
                    The Reason of Church Government, II. Introduction.

2909. By labour and intent study (which I take to be my portion
in this life) joined with the strong propensity of nature, I might perhaps
leave something so written to after times, as they should not willingly
let it die.   Ibid.

2910. He who would not be frustrate of his hope to write well
hereafter in laudable things ought himself to be a true poem.
                                        Apology for Smectymnus.

2911. Truth is as impossible to be soiled by any outward touch as
the sunbeam.   *The Doctrine and Discipline of Divorce.*

2912. To which [rhetoric] poetry would be made subsequent, or
indeed rather precedent, as being less subtle and fine, but more simple,
sensuous and passionate.   *Tractate of Education.*

2913. As good almost kill a man as kill a good book ; who kills
a man kills a reasonable creature, God's image ; but he who destroys
a good book kills reason itself, kills the image of God, as it were in the
eye.   *Areopagitica.*

2914. A good book is the precious life-blood of a master spirit,
embalmed and treasured up on purpose to a life beyond life.   Ibid.

2915. I cannot praise a fugitive and cloistered virtue, unexercised
and unbreathed, that never sallies out and sees her adversary, but
slinks out of the race, where that immortal garland is to be run for,
not without dust and heat.   Ibid.

2916. Our sage and serious poet Spenser.   Ibid.

2917. Lords and Commons of England, consider what nation it is
whereof ye are and whereof ye are the governors : a nation not slow
and dull, but of a quick, ingenious, and piercing spirit, acute to invent,
subtle and sinewy to discourse, not beneath the reach of any point the
highest that human capacity can soar to.   Ibid.

2918. Now once again, by all concurrence of signs and by the
general instinct of holy and devout men, as they daily and solemnly
express their thoughts, God is decreeing to begin some new and great
period in his Church, even to the reforming of Reformation itself.
What does He then but reveal himself to his servants, and as his manner
is, first to his Englishmen ?   Ibid.

2919. Methinks I see in my mind a noble and puissant nation
rousing herself like a strong man after sleep, and shaking her invincible
locks.   Methinks I see her as an eagle mewing her mighty youth, and
kindling her undazzled eyes at the full midday beam.   Ibid.

2920.   Let her and Falsehood grapple; who ever knew Truth put to the worse in a free and open encounter?   *Ibid.*

2921.   Rhyme being no necessary adjunct or true ornament of poem or good verse, in longer works especially, but the invention of a barbarous age, to set off wretched matter and lame metre.
The Verse.   Preface to Paradise Lost, 1668.

MOLIÈRE (JEAN BAPTISTE POQUELIN), French dramatist, 15 Jan. 1622—
         —17 Feb. 1673.

2922.   Nous avons changé tout cela.—We have changed all that.
Le Médecin malgré lui—The Doctor in spite of himself, II. vi.

2923.   Il y a plus de quarante ans que je dis de la prose sans que j'en susse rien.—For more than forty years I have been talking prose without knowing it.
Le Bourgeois Gentilhomme—The Citizen turned Gentleman, II. iv.

2924.   Que diable allait-il faire dans cette galère?—What the devil should he be doing in that galley?
Les Fourberies de Scapin—The Knavery of Scapin, II. vii.

MONKHOUSE, WILLIAM COSMO, art critic and poet, 18 March, 1840—
         2 July, 1901

2925.   There was an old party of Lyme,
                   Who married three wives at one time.
                     When asked, "Why the third?"
                     He replied, "One's absurd,
                   And bigamy, sir, is a crime!"   *Limerick.*

MONRO, HAROLD EDWARD, poet, 14 March, 1879—16 March, 1932

2926.   Silence is scattered like a broken glass,
                 The minutes prick their ears and run about,
              Then one by one subside again and pass
                 Sedately in, monotonously out.   *Solitude.*

2927.   She nestles over the shining rim,
                 Buries her chin in the creamy sea;
              Her tail hangs loose; each drowsy paw
                 Is doubled under each bending knee.   *Milk for the Cat.*

MONSELL, JOHN SAMUEL BEWLEY, Irish priest, 2 March, 1811—9 April,
         1875

2928.   Fight the good fight
                   With all thy might;
                 Christ is thy strength, and Christ thy right.
                                              Fight of Faith.

MONTAGU, LADY MARY WORTLEY, authoress, baptised 26 May, 1689,
         died 21 Aug. 1762

2929.   Le this great maxim be my virtue's guide,—
              In part she is to blame that has been tried:
              He comes too near that comes to be denied.
                 [Last line from Overbury, No. 3080]   *The Lady's Resolve.*

2930. And we meet, with champagne and a chicken, at last.
The Lover.

2931.   Be plain in dress, and sober in your diet ;
             In short, my deary ! kiss me, and be quiet.
A Summary of Lord Lyttelton's Advice.

2932.   Satire should, like a polished razor keen,
             Wound with a touch that's scarcely felt or seen.
To the Imitator of the First Satire of Horace, Book II.

2933. This world consists of men, women, and Herveys.
Letters, I. 67.

MONTAIGNE, MICHAEL EYQUEM DE, French essayist, 28 Feb. 1533—
13 Sept. 1592

2934. Quand je me jouë à ma chatte, qui scait, si elle passe son
temps de moy plus que je ne fay d'elle ?—When I play with my cat,
who knows whether I do not make her more sport than she makes me ?
Essais, II. xii.

2935. Peu d'hommes ont esté admiréz par leurs domestiques.—Few
men have been admired by their servants.   Ibid., III. ii.

2936. Miserable à mon gré, qui n'a chez soy, où estre à soy : où se
faire particulierement la cour : où se cacher.—Miserable, to my thinking,
is he who in his home has no place where he can be his sole company;
where he can invite his mind ; where he can lurk secure.   Ibid., iii.

2937. Il en advient ce qui se voit aux cages, les oyseaux qui en sont
dehors, desperent d'y entrer ; et d'un pareil soing en sortir, ceux qui
sont au dedans.—It happens as with cages : the birds outside despair
to get in, and those inside despair of getting out. [Of marriage.]
Ibid., v.

2938. Tout le monde me recognoist en mon livre, et mon livre en
moy.—All the world knows me in my book, and my book in me.
Ibid.

MONTGOMERY, JAMES, poet, 4 Nov. 1771—30 April, 1854

2939.   Here in the body pent,
                     Absent from Him I roam,
                  Yet nightly pitch my moving tent
                     A day's march nearer home.
At Home in Heaven.

MONTGOMERY, ROBERT, clergyman and poet, 1807—3 December, 1855

2940. The solitary monk who shook the world.
Luther. Man's Need and God's Supply, 68.

2941. The soul aspiring pants its source to mount
       As streams meander level with their fount.
The Omnipresence of the Deity, I. 339.

MONTROSE, JAMES GRAHAM, 1ST MARQUIS OF, Scottish soldier, 1612—
    21 May, 1650

2942.   He either fears his fate too much,
                      Or his deserts are small,
                   That dares not put it to the touch,
                      To gain or lose it all.   *My Dear and Only Love.*
   [An alternative version is :—
                   That puts it not unto the touch
                   To win or lose it all.]

2943.   I'll make thee glorious by my pen,
                   And famous by my sword.   Ibid.

MOORE, EDWARD, dramatist, 22 March, 1712—1 March, 1757

2944.   I am rich beyond the dreams of avarice.
                                            The Gamester, II. ii.

MOORE, GEORGE, Irish author, 24 Feb. 1852—21 Jan. 1933

   2945. Acting is therefore the lowest of the arts, if it is an art at all.
                                            Mummer-Worship.

   2946. All reformers are bachelors.   *The Bending of the Bough*, I.

MOORE, JULIA A., U.S. poetess, 1847–1920

2947.   ' Lord Byron ' was an Englishman
                   A poet I believe,
                  His first works in old England
                   Was poorly received.
                  Perhaps it was ' Lord Byron's ' fault
                   And perhaps it was not.
                  His life was full of misfortunes,
                   Ah, strange was his lot.
                              Sketch of Lord Byron's Life.

MOORE, THOMAS, Irish poet, 28 May, 1779—25 Feb. 1852

2948.   How shall we rank thee upon glory's page ?
        Thou more than soldier and just less than sage.
                                            To Thomas Hume.

2949.   Row, brothers, row, the stream runs fast,
        The Rapids are near and the daylight's past.
                                            A Canadian Boat Song.

2950.   A Persian's Heav'n is easily made,
        'Tis but black eyes and lemonade.   *Intercepted Letters*, vi.

2951.   Go where glory waits thee,
                   But, while fame elates thee,
                   Oh ! still remember me.
                  Irish Melodies. Go where Glory waits thee.

2952.   When he, who adores thee, has left but the name
        Of his faults and his sorrows behind.
                              Ibid. *When he who adores thee.*

2953.
> The harp that once through Tara's halls
> > The soul of music shed,
> Now hangs as mute on Tara's walls,
> > As if that soul were fled.
> > > Ibid. *The Harp that once through Tara's Halls.*

2954.
> Rich and rare were the gems she wore,
> > And a bright gold ring on her wand she bore.
> > > Ibid. *Rich and Rare were the Gems she wore.*

2955.
> There is not in the wide world a valley so sweet
> As that vale in whose bosom the bright waters meet.
> > Ibid. *The Meeting of the Waters.*

2956.
> Believe me, if all those endearing young charms,
> > Which I gaze on so fondly to-day.
> > > Ibid. *Believe me, if all those endearing Young Charms.*

2957.
> No, the heart that has truly lov'd never forgets,
> > But as truly loves on to the close,
> As the sun-flower turns on her god, when he sets,
> > The same look which she turn'd when he rose.   Ibid.

2958.
> And to know, when far from the lips we love,
> > We've but to make love to the lips we are near.
> > > Ibid. *'Tis Sweet to think.*

2959.
> But there's nothing half so sweet in life
> > As love's young dream.   Ibid. *Love's Young Dream.*

2960.
> Lesbia hath a beaming eye,
> > But no one knows for whom it beameth.
> > > Ibid. *Lesbia hath a Beaming Eye.*

2961.
> Eyes of most unholy blue !
> > Ibid. *By that Lake whose Gloomy Shore.*

2962.
> She is far from the land where her young hero sleeps,
> > And lovers are round her, sighing :
> But coldly she turns from their gaze, and weeps,
> > For her heart in his grave is lying.
> > > Ibid. *She is far from the Land.*

2963.
> 'Tis the last rose of summer
> > Left blooming alone ;
> All her lovely companions
> > Are faded and gone.
> > > Ibid. *The Last Rose of Summer.*

2964.
> Then awake !—the heavens look bright, my dear,
> 'Tis never too late for delight, my dear,
> > And the best of all ways
> > To lengthen our days,
> Is to steal a few hours from the night, my dear !
> > > Ibid. *The Young May Moon.*

2965.
> The Minstrel Boy to the war is gone,
> > In the ranks of death you'll find him ;
> His father's sword he has girded on,
> > And his wild harp slung behind him.
> > > Ibid. *The Minstrel Boy.*

2966.
> You may break, you may shatter the vase, if you will,
> But the scent of the roses will hang round it still.
> > Ibid. *Farewell !—But whenever you welcome the Hour.*

2967.   The time I've lost in wooing,
           In watching and pursuing
               The light, that lies
               In woman's eyes.
           Had been my heart's undoing.
                           Ibid. *The Time I've lost in wooing.*

2968.   My only books
               Were woman's looks,
           And folly's all they've taught me.   Ibid.

2969.   Oft, in the stilly night,
               Ere Slumber's chain has bound me,
           Fond Memory brings the light
               Of other days around me ;
                   The smiles, the tears,
                   Of boyhood's years,
           The words of love then spoken ;
                   The eyes that shone,
                   Now dimm'd and gone,
           The cheerful hearts now broken !
                       National Airs.   Oft in the Stilly Night.

2970.   I feel like one
               Who treads alone
           Some banquet-hall deserted,
               Whose lights are fled,
               Whose garlands dead,
           And all but he departed !   Ibid.

2971.   Oh ! ever thus, from childhood's hour,
               I've seen my fondest hopes decay ;
           I never lov'd a tree or flow'r,
               But 'twas the first to fade away.
           I never nurs'd a dear gazelle,
               To glad me with its soft black eye,
           But when it came to know me well,
               And love me, it was sure to die !
                       Lalla Rookh.   The Fire-Worshippers, I. 279.

2972. " Come, come," said Tom's father, " at your time of life,
           There's no longer excuse for thus playing the rake—
       It is time you should think, boy, of taking a wife "—
           " Why, so it is, father—whose wife shall I take ? "
                               A Joke Versified.

   2973.   The minds of some of our own statesmen, like the pupil of
the human eye, contract themselves the more, the stronger light
there is shed upon them.   *Corruption and Intolerance*, preface.

MORDAUNT, THOMAS OSBERT, 1730—1809
2974.   Sound, sound the clarion, fill the fife,
                   Throughout the sensual world proclaim,
               One crowded hour of glorious life
                   Is worth an age without a name.
                       Verses written during the War, 1756–1763.
                       [Quoted as anonymous by Scott in *Old
                       Mortality*, xxxiii.   " To all " being put for
                       " Throughout."]

   H

More, Hannah, authoress, 2 Feb. 1745—7 Sept., 1833

2975.   He liked those literary cooks
                 Who skim the cream of others' books;
                 And ruin half an author's graces
                 By plucking *bon-mots* from their places.

Florio, 123.

More, Sir Thomas, Lord Chancellor and Saint, 7 Feb., 1478—6 July, 1535

2976.   For men use, if they have an evil tourne, to write it in marble: and whoso doth us a good tourne we write it in dust.   *Richard III.*

2977.   Is not this house [the Tower of London] as nigh heaven as mine own?   Roper, *Life of Sir Thomas More*, 83.

2978.   I pray you, Master Lieutenant, see me safe up, and for my coming down let me shift for myself.

Words on mounting the scaffold.

Morehead, John Motley, U.S. statesman, 4 July, 1796—27 Aug. 1866

2979.   It's a long time between drinks.
                 Remark to the Governor of South Carolina when Morehead was Governor of North Carolina.

Morell, Thomas, author, 18 March, 1703—19 Feb. 1784

2980.   See, the conquering hero comes!
                 Sound the trumpets, beat the drums!

Joshua, part iii.
                 [Lines wrongly ascribed to Nathaniel Lee.]

Morley, Christopher Darlington, U.S. author, 5 May, 1890—28 March, 1957.

2981.   There is no prince or prelate
                 I envy—no, not one.
                 No evil can befall me—
                     By God, I have a son!   *Secret Laughter.*

Morley, John, Viscount, 24 Dec. 1838—23 Sept. 1932

2982.   Literature, the most seductive, the most deceiving, the most dangerous of professions.   *Burke*, i.

2983.   Every man of us has all the centuries in him, though their operations be latent, dim, and very various.

Life of Gladstone, ii. vi.

2984.   The great business of life is, to be, to do, to do without, and to depart.   *Address on aphorisms, Edinburgh*, Nov. 1887.

Morris, Charles, song-writer, 1745—11 July, 1838

2985.   Solid men of Boston, make no long orations;
                 Solid men of Boston, banish strong potations.

Billy Pitt and the Farmer.

2986.   If one must have a villa in summer to dwell,
                 Oh, give me the sweet shady side of Pall Mall!

The Contrast.

MORRIS, GEORGE POPE, U.S. journalist and poet, 10 Oct. 1802—
        6 July, 1864

2987.   Woodman, spare that tree !
                         Touch not a single bough !
                         In youth it sheltered me,
                         And I'll protect it now.
                                    Woodman, spare that Tree.

2988.   A song for our banner ! The watchword recall
                Which gave the Republic her station :
             ' United we stand, divided we fall ! '
                It made and preserves us a nation !
             The union of lakes, the union of lands,
                The union of States none can sever,
             The union of hearts, the union of hands,
                And the flag of our Union for ever !
                                    The Flag of our Union.

MORRIS, WILLIAM, artist and poet, 24 March, 1834—3 Oct. 1896

2989. Pray but one prayer for me 'twixt thy closed lips,
         Think but one thought of me up in the stars.
                                    Summer Dawn.

2990. And ever she sung from noon to noon,
       Two red roses across the moon.
                                Two Red Roses across the Moon.

2991. My lady seems of ivory
       Forehead, straight nose, and cheeks that be
       Hollow'd a little mournfully.
                 Beata mea Domina !   *Praise of my Lady.*

2992. I know a little garden close
       Set thick with lily and red rose,
       Where I would wander if I might
       From dewy dawn to dewy night,
       And have one with me wandering.
                            The Life and Death of Jason, IV. 577.

2993. The idle singer of an empty day.
                            The Earthly Paradise. An Apology.

2994. Dreamer of dreams, born out of my due time,
         Why should I strive to set the crooked straight ?   Ibid.

2995. Love is enough : though the world be a-waning,
         And the woods have no voice but the voice of complaining,
           Though the sky be too dark for dim eyes to discover
         The gold-cups and daisies fair blooming thereunder.
                                    Love is enough, i.

2996. Wilt thou do the deed and repent it ? thou hadst better
           never been born :
       Wilt thou do the deed and exalt it ? then thy fame
           shall be outworn :
       Thou shalt do the deed and abide it, and sit on thy throne
           on high.
       And look on to-day and to-morrow as those that never
           die.   *Sigurd the Volsung,* ii. 10.

MORTON, THOMAS, dramatist, 1764 ?—28 March, 1838

2997. Push on—keep moving.   *A Cure for the Heartache*, II. i.

2998. Approbation from Sir Hubert Stanley is praise indeed.
Ibid., v. ii.

2999. Always ding, dinging Dame Grundy into my ears—what will Mrs. Grundy say ?   What will Mrs. Grundy think ?
Speed the Plough, I. i.

Moss, THOMAS, poet and clergyman, 1740 ?—6 Dec. 1808

3000.   A pamper'd menial forc'd me from the door.   *The Beggar*, 15.

MOTHERWELL, WILLIAM, Scottish poet, 13 Oct. 1797—1 Nov. 1835

3001.   I've wandered east, I've wandered west,
                    Through mony a weary way ;
               But never, never can forget
                    The love o' life's young day.   *Jeanie Morrison.*

MOTLEY, JOHN LOTHROP, U.S. historian, 15 April, 1814—29 May, 1877

3002. Give us the luxuries of life, and we will dispense with its necessities.   O. W. Holmes's *Autocrat of the Breakfast Table*, vi.

MULOCK, DINAH MARIA, *see* Craik

MUNRO, HECTOR HUGH, *see* Saki

MUNRO, NEIL, Scottish author, 3 June, 1864—22 Dec. 1930

3003. It was chust sublime.   *The Vital Spark. Wee Teeny.*

MUNSTER, ERNST FRIEDRICH HERBERT, COUNT VON, Hanoverian politician, 1766–1839

3004. Absolutism tempered by assassination.   [Description of the Russian Constitution.]   *Letter.*

MURPHY, ARTHUR, Irish dramatist, 27 Dec. 1727—18 June, 1805

3005.   Above the vulgar flight of common souls.   *Zenobia*, v. i.

MYERS, FREDERIC WILLIAM HENRY, author, 6 Feb. 1843—17 Jan. 1901

3006. Christ, I am Christ's, and let the name suffice you ;
             Aye, for me, too, it greatly hath sufficed.
       Lo, with no winning words would I entice you,
             Paul hath no honour and no friend but Christ.   *Saint Paul.*

NAIRNE, CAROLINA OLIPHANT, BARONESS, Scottish poetess, 16 Aug. 1766—26 Oct. 1845

3007.   I'm wearin' awa' John,
      Like snaw-wreaths in thaw, John;
      I'm wearin' awa'
        To the land o' the leal.
      There's nae sorrow there, John;
      There's neither cauld nor care, John;
      The day's aye fair
        In the land o' the leal.   *The Land o' the Leal.*

3008.   The Laird o' Cockpen he's proud and he's great,
    His mind is ta'en up with the things o' the State.
                     The Laird o' Cockpen.

3009.   Favour wi' wooin' was fashous to seek.   Ibid.

3010.   A penniless lass wi' a lang pedigree.   Ibid.

3011.   Oh, Charlie is my darling, my darling, my darling,
    Oh, Charlie is my darling, the young Chevalier.
                     Charlie is my Darling.

3012.   Wi' a hundred pipers an' a', an' a'.
                     The Hundred Pipers.

3013.   Better lo'ed ye canna be,
      Will ye no come back again?
              Will ye no come back again?

NAPIER, SIR CHARLES JAMES, soldier and administrator, 10 Aug. 1782—29 Aug. 1853

  3014.   Peccavi. [I have sinned = I have Sind.]
      Punning dispatch after victory of Hyderabad in Sind, 1843.

NAPOLEON BONAPARTE, Emperor of France, 15 Aug. 1769—5 May, 1821

  3015.   Soldats, songez que, du haut de ces pyramides, quarante siècles vous contemplent.—Soldiers, consider that, from the summit of these pyramids, forty centuries look down upon you.
      Speech before the Battle of the Pyramids, 21 July, 1798.

  3016.   Du sublime au ridicule il n'y a qu'un pas.—From the sublime to the ridiculous there is only one step.
      After the retreat from Moscow, 1812.

  3017.   La carrière ouverte aux talents.—The career open to talents.
      On St. Helena, 1817.

  3018.   L'Angleterre est une nation de boutiquiers.—England is a nation of shopkeepers.   *Attributed.*

  3019.   Tout soldat français porte dans sa giberne le bâton de maréchal de France.—Every French soldier carries in his cartridge-pouch the baton of a marshal of France.   Ibid.

NASH, OGDEN U.S. poet, 19 Aug. 1902—

3020.   I think that I shall never see
      A billboard lovely as a tree.   *Song of the Open Road.*

3021.   A girl who is bespectacled,
          She may not get her nectacled.
               Lines written to console those Ladies distressed by
               the Lines ' Men seldom make Passes, etc.'

3022. I sit in an office at 244 Madison Avenue,
       And say to myself You have a responsible job, havenue ?
                                        Spring comes to Murray Hill.

3023. But the old men know when an old man dies.   *Old Men.*

NASH *or* NASHE, THOMAS, author, November, 1567—1601

3024. Spring, the sweet spring, is the year's pleasant king ;
       Then blooms each thing, then maids dance in a ring,
       Cold doth not sting, the pretty birds do sing :
            Cuckoo, jug-jug, pu-we, to-witta-woo !   *Spring.*

3025.   Brightness falls from the air ;
          Queens have died young and fair ;
          Dust hath closed Helen's eye.
                    A Lament in Time of Plague.

NEALE, JOHN MASON, clergyman and author, 24 Jan. 1818—6 Aug.
       1866

3026.   Jerusalem the golden,
             With milk and honey blest,
          Beneath thy contemplation
             Sink heart and voice oppressed.
                    Hymn from the Latin of Bernard of Morlaix.

3027.   Brief life is here our portion.   *Hymn from same.*

3028.   Art thou weary, art thou languid,
             Art thou sore distressed.   *Hymn from the Greek.*

3029.   Christian, dost thou see them
             On the holy ground,
          How the troops of Midian
             Prowl and prowl around.   *Hymn from same.*

3030.   Good King Wenceslas looked out
             On the Feast of Stephen ;
          When the snow lay round about,
             Deep and crisp and even.   *Good King Wenceslas.*

3031.   Bring me flesh and bring me wine,
             Bring me pine-logs hither.   Ibid.

NELSON, HORATIO NELSON, VISCOUNT, admiral, 29 Sept. 1758—21 Oct.
       1805

   3032. Westminster Abbey or victory !
                    At Battle of Cape St. Vincent, 14 Feb. 1797.

   3033. It is warm work ; and this day may be the last to any of us at
a moment. But mark you ! I would not be elsewhere for thousands.
                    At Battle of Copenhagen, 2 April, 1801.

   3034. I really do not see the signal !
                    Ibid. (*putting the telescope to his blind eye*).

3035. England expects that every man will do his duty.
Signal from flagship at Trafalgar, 21 Oct. 1805.

3036. Thank God, I have done my duty. *Dying words.*

NERO (NERO CLAUDIUS CAESAR), Roman Emperor, 15 Dec. 37—9 June, 68

3037. Qualis artifex pereo!—What an artist perishes in me!
Dying words.

NESBIT, EDITH (MRS. HUBERT BLAND), authoress, 19 Aug. 1858—4 May, 1924

3038. The chestnut's proud, and the lilac's pretty,
The poplar's gentle and tall,
But the plane tree's kind to the poor dull city—
I love him best of all. *Child's Song in Spring.*

NEWBOLT, SIR HENRY JOHN, poet, 6 June, 1862—19 April, 1938

3039. Take my drum to England, hang et by the shore,
Strike et when your powder's runnin' low;
If the Dons sight Devon, I'll quit the port o' Heaven,
An' drum them up the Channel as we drummed
them long ago. *Drake's Drum.*

3040. All night long in a dream untroubled of hope
He brooded, clasping his knees. *He fell among Thieves.*

3041. To set the cause above renown,
To love the game beyond the prize,
To honour, while you strike him down,
The foe that comes with fearless eyes. *Clifton Chapel.*

3042. 'Qui procul hinc,' the legend's writ,—
The frontier-grave is far away—
'Qui ante diem periit:
Sed miles, sed pro patria.' Ibid.
[Who died far from here, before his time, but as a
soldier, for his country.]

3043. A bumping pitch and a blinding light,
An hour to play and the last man in. *Vitaï Lampada.*

3044. The sand of the desert is sodden red,—
Red with the wreck of a square that broke;—
The Gatling's jammed and the Colonel dead,
And the regiment blind with dust and smoke.
The river of death has brimmed his banks,
And England's far, and Honour a name,
But the voice of a schoolboy rallies the ranks:
'Play up! play up! and play the game!' Ibid.

NEWELL, ROBERT HENRY ('ORPHEUS C. KERR'), U.S. author, 13 Dec. 1836—July, 1901

3045. Dog Hollow, in the Green Mount State,
Was his first stopping-place;
And then Skunk's Misery displayed
Its sweetness and its grace.
The American Traveller.

NEWLAND, ABRAHAM, banker, 23 April, 1730—21 Nov. 1807

3046.   Beneath this stone old Abraham lies ;
               Nobody laughs and nobody cries.
               Where he is gone and how he fares,
               Nobody knows, and nobody cares.

                                        His own epitaph.

NEWMAN, JOHN HENRY, CARDINAL, 21 Feb. 1801—11 Aug. 1890

3047.   Lead, kindly Light, amid the encircling gloom,
                    Lead Thou me on ;
               The night is dark, and I am far from home ;
                    Lead Thou me on.
               Keep Thou my feet ; I do not ask to see
               The distant scene,—one step enough for me.

                                        Lead Kindly Light.

3048.   And with the morn those angel faces smile
               Which I have loved long since, and lost awhile.

                                                      Ibid.

NEWTON, SIR ISAAC, scientist, 25 Dec. 1642—20 March, 1727

3049. I do not know what I may appear to the world, but to myself
I seem to have been only like a boy playing on the sea-shore, and
diverting myself in now and then finding a smoother pebble or a
prettier shell than ordinary, whilst the great ocean of truth lay all
undiscovered before me.   Brewster's *Memoirs of Newton*, II. xxvii.

3050. O Diamond ! Diamond ! thou little knowest the mischief
done !   *To a dog that destroyed papers representing years of work.*

NEWTON, JOHN, clergyman, 24 July, 1725—21 Dec. 1807

3051.   Glorious things of thee are spoken,
                    Zion, city of our God.   *Hymn.*

NICOLSON, ADELA FLORENCE, *see* Hope, Laurence

NOBLES, MILTON, U.S. actor and dramatist, 28 Sept. 1847—14 June,
          1924
3052.   The villain still pursued her.   *The Phœnix*, I. iii.

NOEL, THOMAS, poet, 11 May, 1799—16 May, 1861

3053.   Rattle his bones over the stones ;
               He's only a pauper, whom nobody owns !

                                        The Pauper's Drive.

NORRIS, JOHN, clergyman, 1657—1711

3054.   How fading are the joys we dote upon,—
                    Like apparitions seen and gone :
               But those which soonest take their flight,
                    Are the most exquisite and strong,
               Like angels' visits, short and bright ;
                    Mortality's too weak to bear them long.

                                        The Parting, 19.

NORTON, CAROLINE ELIZABETH SARAH, poetess, 1808—15 June, 1877

3055. My beautiful, my beautiful ! that standest meekly by,
  With thy proudly-arched and glossy neck, and dark and
   fiery eye !
  Fret not to roam the desert now, with all thy winged
   speed :
  I may not mount on thee again !—thou'rt sold, my Arab
   steed !   *The Arab's Farewell to his Steed.*

NOVALIS (FRIEDRICH LEOPOLD VON HARDENBERG), German author,
  2 May, 1772—25 March, 1801

 3056. Gott-trunkener Mensch.—A God-intoxicated man.
               Said of Spinoza.

NOYES, ALFRED, author, 16 Sept. 1880—28 June, 1958

3057. Apes and ivory, skulls and roses, in junks of old Hong-
  Kong,
  Gliding over a sea of dreams to a haunted shore of song.
              Apes and Ivory.

3058. Calling as he used to call, faint and far away,
  In Sherwood, in Sherwood, about the break of day.
                Sherwood.

3059. There's a barrel-organ carolling across a golden street
  In the City as the sun sinks low. *The Barrel-Organ.*

3060. Come down to Kew in lilac-time, in lilac-time, in lilac-
  time ;
   Come down to Kew in lilac-time (it isn't far from
    London !)
  And you shall wander hand in hand with love in summer's
   wonderland ;
   Come down to Kew in lilac-time (it isn't far from
    London !)   Ibid.

3061. The wind was a torrent of darkness among the gusty
   trees,
  The moon was a ghostly galleon tossed upon cloudy seas,
  The road was a ribbon of moonlight over the purple moor,
  And the highwayman came riding—
     Riding—riding—
  The highwayman came riding, up to the old inn-door.
             The Highwayman, i.

3062. Down to the valley she came, for far and far below in the
   dreaming meadows
   Pleaded ever the Voice of voices, calling his love by
    her golden name ;
  So she arose from her home in the hills, and down through
    the blossoms that danced with their shadows,
   Out of the blue of the dreaming distance, down to
    the heart of her lover she came.
          Orpheus and Eurydice, i.

3063.   God, how the dead men
       Grin by the wall,
       Watching the fun
       Of the Victory Ball.   *A Victory Dance.*

 *H

OAKELEY, FREDERICK, priest, 5 Sept. 1802—29 Jan. 1880

3064.   O come, all ye faithful,
                     Joyful and triumphant,
                     O come ye, O come ye to Bethlehem.
                                Hymn from Latin Adeste Fideles.

O'CASEY, SEAN, Irish dramatist, 30 March 1880—18 Sept. 1964

   3065. The whole world is in a state of chassis.
                                Juno and the Paycock, I. i.

OGILVY, JAMES, 1ST EARL OF SEAFIELD, Lord Chancellor of Scotland,
      1664—15 Aug. 1730

   3066. Now there's ane end of ane old sang.
                                At the Act of Union of the Parliaments.

O'KEEFFE, JOHN, Irish dramatist, 24 June, 1747—4 Feb. 1833

3067.   Amo, amas, I love a lass,
                     As cedar tall and slender ;
                     Sweet cowslip's grace
                     Is her nominative case,
                     And she's of the feminine gender.
                                Agreeable Surprise, II. ii.

O'KELLY, DENNIS, racehorse owner, 1720 ?—28 Dec. 1787

   3068. It will be Eclipse first, the rest nowhere.
                                At Epsom, 3 May, 1769.

OLDHAM, JOHN, poet, 9 Aug. 1653—9 Dec. 1683

   3069. Racks, gibbets, halters, were their arguments.
                  Satires upon the Jesuits, I. *Garnet's Ghost*, 176.

OLDYS, WILLIAM, antiquary, 14 July, 1696—15 April, 1761

3070.   Busy, curious, thirsty fly,
                     Drink with me, and drink as I.
                                Busy, Curious, Thirsty Fly.

OMAR KHAYYÀM, *see* FitzGerald, Edward

O'NEILL, MOIRA (MRS. N. H. SKRINE), Irish authoress, 1864—

3071.   Over here in England I'm helpin' wi' the hay,
          An' I wisht I was in Ireland the livelong day ;
          Weary on the English hay, an' sorra take the wheat.
          Och ! Corrymeela an' the blue sky over it.
                                Corrymeela.

OPIE, JOHN, painter, May, 1761—9 April, 1807

   3072. I mix them with my brains, sir.
                     When asked with what he mixed his colours.

ORCZY, EMMUSKA *or* EMMA MAGDALENA ROSALIA MARIE JOSEPHA BARBARA, BARONESS (MRS. MONTAGU BARSTOW), Anglo-Hungarian novelist, 23 Sept. 1865—12 Nov. 1947

3073.   We seek him here, we seek him there,
          Those Frenchies seek him everywhere.
          Is he in heaven?—Is he in hell?
          That demmed, elusive Pimpernel?
                    The Scarlet Pimpernel, xii.

O'REILLY, JOHN BOYLE, Irish author, 28 June, 1844—10 Aug. 1890

3074.   You may grind their souls in the self-same mill,
          You may bind them, heart and brow;
          But the poet will follow the rainbow still,
          And his brother will follow the plough.
                    The Rainbow's Treasure.

3075.   The organised charity, scrimped and iced,
      In the name of a cautious, statistical Christ.   *In Bohemia.*

O'SHAUGHNESSY, ARTHUR WILLIAM EDGAR, poet, 14 March, 1844—30 Jan. 1881

3076.   We are the music-makers,
          And we are the dreamers of dreams,
          Wandering by lone sea-breakers,
          And sitting by desolate streams;
          World-losers and world-forsakers,
          On whom the pale moon gleams:
          Yet we are the movers and shakers
          Of the world for ever, it seems.   *Ode.*

3077.   One man with a dream, at pleasure,
          Shall go forth and conquer a crown:
          And three with a new song's measure
          Can trample an empire down.   Ibid.

OTWAY, THOMAS, dramatist, 3 March, 1652—14 April, 1685

3078.   O woman! lovely woman! Nature made thee
      To temper man: we had been brutes without you;
      Angels are painted fair, to look like you;
      There's in you all that we believe of heaven,—
      Amazing brightness, purity, and truth,
      Eternal joy, and everlasting love.   *Venice Preserved*, I. i.

3079.   What mighty ills have not been done by woman!
      Who was't betrayed the Capitol? A woman!
      Who lost Mark Antony the world? A woman!
      Who was the cause of a long ten years' war,
      And laid at last old Troy in ashes? Woman!
      Destructive, damnable, deceitful woman!
                    The Orphan, III. i.

OVERBURY, SIR THOMAS, poet, 1581—15 Sept. 1613

3080.   In part to blame is she
      Which hath without consent been only tried;
      He comes too near that comes to be denied.   *A Wife*, 26.

Ovid (Publius Ovidius Naso), Roman poet, 20 March, 43 b.c.—17 a.d.

3081. Forsitan et nostrum nomen miscebitur istis.
       —Perhaps our name too will be mingled with these.
                                               Ars Amatoria, iii. 339.

3082. Medio tutissimus ibis.
       —You will go most safely in the middle.
                                               Metamorphoses, ii. 137.

3083.   Video meliora, proboque ;
       Deteriora sequor.
       —I see better things and approve them ; I follow the worse.
                                               Ibid., vii. 20.

3084. Tempus edax rerum.
       —Time, the devourer of things.   Ibid. xv. 234.

Owen, John, Welsh epigrammatist, 1560 ?–1622

3085.   God and the doctor we alike adore
            But only when in danger, not before ;
            The danger o'er, both are alike requited,
            God is forgotten, and the doctor slighted.   *Epigrams*.

Owen, Robert, social reformer, 14 May, 1771—17 Nov. 1858

3086. All the world is queer save thee and me, and even thou art
a little queer.
                On separating from his business partner, William Allen,
                1828.

Oxenstierna, Axel Gustafsson, Count, Swedish Chancellor,
       16 June, 1583—28 Aug. 1654.

3087. Behold, my son, with how little wisdom the world is governed.
                                               Letter to his son, 1648.

Oxford Edward de Vere, 17th Earl of, poet, 2 April, 1550—
       24 June, 1604.

3088.   If women could be fair and yet not fond.
                                               Women's Changeableness.

Oxford and Asquith, Earl of, *see* Asquith

Paine, Thomas, political pamphleteer, 29 Jan. 1737—8 June, 1809
       3089. These are the times that try men's souls.
                                               The American Crisis, No. 1.

       3090. The final event to himself [Mr. Burke] has been that, as he
rose like a rocket, he fell like the stick.
                Letter to the Addressers on the Late Proclamation, 1792.

       3091. The sublime and the ridiculous are often so nearly related,
that it is difficult to class them separately. One step above the sublime makes the ridiculous ; and one step above the ridiculous makes
the sublime again.   *The Age of Reason*, ii. 20.

PALAFOX Y MELZI, JOSÉ DE, DUKE OF SARAGOSSA, Spanish soldier, 1780—15 Feb. 1847

   3092. Guerra al cuchillo.—War to the knife.
                Reply when summoned to surrender Saragossa, 1808.

PALEY, WILLIAM, ARCHDEACON OF CARLISLE, July, 1743—25 May, 1805

   3093. Who can refute a sneer ?   *Moral Philosophy,* v. **ix.**

PARKER, DOROTHY (MRS. ALAN CAMPBELL), U.S. authoress, 22 Aug. 1893—7 June, 1967

   3094. Where's the man could ease a heart
        Like a satin gown ?   *The Satin Dress.*

   3095. Four be the things I'd been better without :
        Love, curiosity, freckles, and doubt.   *Inventory.*

   3096.   Guns aren't lawful ;
                 Nooses give ;
                 Gas smells awful ;
                 You might as well live.   *Résumé.*

   3097.   Down from Caesar past Joynson-Hicks
                 Echoes the warning, ever new ;
             Though they're trained to amusing tricks,
                 Gentler, they, than the pigeon's coo,
                 Careful, son, of the cursed two—
             Either one is a dangerous pet ;
                 Natural history proves it true—
             Women and elephants never forget.
                 Ballade of Unfortunate Mammals.

   3098.   Excuse my dust.   *Her own epitaph.*

PARKER, MARTIN, ballad-monger, died 1656 ?

   3099.   Ye gentlemen of England
                 That live at home at ease,
                 Ah ! little do you think upon
                 The dangers of the seas.
                 Ye Gentlemen of England.

PARNELL, THOMAS, poet, 1679—Oct. 1718

   3100. Still an angel appear to each lover beside,
        But still be a woman to you.   *When thy Beauty appears.*

   3101. Remote from man, with God he passed the days,
        Prayer all his business, all his pleasure praise.
                        The Hermit, 5.

   3102. We call it only pretty Fanny's way.
                An Elegy to an Old Beauty, 34.

PARR, SAMUEL, schoolmaster, 26 Jan. 1747—6 March, 1825

   3103. Ay, now that the old lion is dead, every ass thinks he may kick at him.   Boswell's *Life of Johnson,* an. 1784.

PASCAL, BLAISE, French author, 19 June, 1623—19 Aug. 1662

3104. Le nez de Cléopâtre : s'il eût été plus court, toute la face de la terre aurait changé.—If Cleopatra's nose had been shorter, the whole face of the world would have been changed.

Pensées, sect. ii. 162.

3105. Le cœur a ses raisons que la raison ne connaît point.—The heart has its reasons of which reason knows nothing.

Ibid., sect. iv. 277

PATER, WALTER HORATIO, author, 4 Aug. 1839—30 July, 1894

3106. She is older than the rocks among which she sits ; like the vampire, she has been dead many times, and learned the secrets of the grave ; and has been a diver in deep seas, and keeps their fallen day about her ; and trafficked for strange webs with Eastern merchants : and, as Leda, was the mother of Helen of Troy, and, as Saint Anne, the mother of Mary ; and all this has been to her but as the sound of lyres and flutes, and lives only in the delicacy with which it has moulded the changing lineaments, and tinged the eyelids and the hands. [Mona Lisa].   *The Renaissance. Leonardo da Vinci.*

3107. All art constantly aspires towards the condition of music.

Ibid. Giorgione.

3108. To burn always with this hard, gemlike flame, to maintain this ecstasy, is success in life.   *Ibid. Conclusion.*

3109. In truth all art does but consist in the removal of surplusage, from the last finish of the gem-engraver blowing away the last particles of invisible dust, back to the earliest divination of the finished work to be, lying somewhere, according to Michelangelo's fancy, in the rough-hewn block of stone.   *Appreciations. Style.*

PATMORE, COVENTRY KERSEY DIGHTON, poet, 23 July, 1823—26 Nov. 1896

3110.   Ah, wasteful woman, she who may
                    On her sweet self set her own price,
               Knowing man cannot choose but pay,
                    How has she cheapened paradise ;
               How given for nought her priceless gift,
                    How spoil'd the bread and spill'd the wine,
               Which, spent with due, respective thrift,
                    Had made brutes men, and men divine.
                         The Angel in the House, i. iii. prelude 3, *Unthrift.*

3111.   ' I saw you take his kiss ! '   ' Tis true.'
               ' O, modesty ! '   ' Twas strictly kept :
               He thought me asleep ; at least, I knew
                    He thought I thought he thought I slept.'
                              Ibid., viii. prelude 3, *The Kiss.*

3112.   Why, having won her, do I woo ?
                    Because her spirit's vestal grace
               Provokes me always to pursue,
                    But, spirit-like, eludes embrace.
                         Ibid., xii. prelude 1, *The Married Lover.*

3113. My little Son, who look'd from thoughtful eyes
          And moved and spoke in quiet grown-up wise.
                         The Unknown Eros, i. x. *The Toys.*

3114. If I were dead, you'd sometimes say, ' Poor Child ! '
                             Ibid., xiv. *If I were Dead.*

3115.   This is to say, my dear Augusta,
                We've had another awful buster :
                Ten thousand Frenchmen sent below !
                Thank God from whom all blessings flow.
             Epigram on message sent by King William of
                      Prussia to his Queen, Aug. 1870.

PAYNE, JOHN HOWARD, U.S. actor and dramatist, 9 June, 1791—
    9 April, 1852
3116. Mid pleasures and palaces though we may roam,
      Be it ever so humble, there's no place like home.
            Clari, the Maid of Milan. Home, Sweet Home.

PEACOCK, THOMAS LOVE, author, 18 Oct. 1785—23 Jan. 1866
3117.   Seamen three ! what men be ye ?
             Gotham's three Wise Men we be.
        Whither in your bowl so free ?
             To rake the moon from out the sea.
        The bowl goes trim.   The moon doth shine,
        And our ballast is old wine.
            Nightmare Abbey, xi. *The Men of Gotham.*

3118.   The mountain sheep are sweeter,
               But the valley sheep are fatter ;
               We therefore deemed it meeter
               To carry off the latter.
            The Misfortunes of Elphin, xi. *The War Song*
                    of Dinas Vawr.

PEEL, SIR ROBERT, 2ND BARONET, Prime Minister, 5 Feb. 1788—
    2 July, 1850
  3119. It takes three generations to make a gentleman.
                                  Attributed.

PEELE, GEORGE, dramatist, 1558 ?—1597 ?
3120. Fair and fair, and twice so fair,
      As fair as any may be ;
      The fairest shepherd on our green,
        A love for any lady.   *The Arraignment of Paris,* I. ii.
3121. My merry, merry, merry roundelay
      Concludes with Cupid's curse,—
      They that do change old love for new,
        Pray gods they change for worse !   *Ibid.*
3122. His golden locks time hath to silver turn'd ;
      O time too swift, O swiftness never ceasing !
      His youth 'gainst time and age hath ever spurn'd,
        But spurn'd in vain ; youth waneth by increasing.
                   Polyhymnia. Sonnet.
3123. His helmet now shall make a hive for bees,
      And, lovers' sonnets turn'd to holy psalms,
      A man-at-arms must now serve on his knees,
        And feed on prayers, which are age's alms.   *Ibid.*

PEMBROKE, HENRY HERBERT, 10TH EARL OF, 3 July, 1734—26 Jan.
1794

3124. Dr. Johnson's sayings would not appear so extraordinary,
were it not for his *bow-wow way*.

Boswell's *Life of Johnson*, an. 1775, note.

PENN, WILLIAM, founder of Pennsylvania, 14 Oct. 1644—30 July, 1718

3125. No pain, no palm ; no thorns, no throne ; no gall, no glory ;
no cross, no crown.   *No Cross, No Crown.*

PEPYS, SAMUEL, diarist, 23 Feb. 1633—26 May, 1703

3126. And so to bed.   *Diary*, 6 May, 1660, *et passim.*

3127. This morning came home my fine camlet cloak, with gold
buttons, and a silk suit, which cost me much money, and I pray God to
make me able to pay for it.   Ibid., 1 July, 1660.

3128. My wife, who, poor wretch, is troubled with her lonely life.

Ibid., 19 Dec. 1662.

3129. Went to hear Mrs. Turner's daughter play on the harpsichon ;
but, Lord ! it was enough to make any man sick to hear her ; yet was
I forced to commend her highly.   Ibid., 1 May, 1663.

3130. Saw a wedding in the church . . . and strange to see what
delight we married people have to see these poor fools decoyed into
our condition.   Ibid., 25 Dec. 1665.

3131. Home, and, being washing-day, dined upon cold meat.

Ibid., 4 April, 1666.

3132. To church ; and with my mourning, very handsome, and new
periwig, make a great show.   Ibid., 31 March, 1667.

PERICLES, Greek statesman, 493 ?—429 B.C.

3133. Φιλοκαλοῦμεν τε γὰρ μετ' εὐτελείας καὶ φιλοσοφοῦμεν ἄνευ μαλακίας.
—For we are lovers of the beautiful without extravagance, and cultivate
our minds without effeminacy.   Thucydides, II. xl.

3134. 'Ανδρῶν γὰρ ἐπιφανῶν πᾶσα γῆ τάφος.—For to famous men the
whole earth is a sepulchre.   Ibid., xliii.
[Both quotations from his Funeral Oration over the Athenian dead
in the first year of the Peloponnesian War, 431 B.C.]

PERRONET, EDWARD, Methodist preacher, 1726—2 Jan. 1792
3135.   All hail, the power of Jesus' name !
                   Let angels prostrate fall ;
                   Bring forth the royal diadem,
                   To crown Him Lord of all.

Hymn on the Resurrection.

PERSIUS (AULUS PERSIUS FLACCUS), Roman poet, 4 Dec. A.D. 34—
24 Nov. 62

3136. Virtutem videant, intabescantque relicta.
           —Let them look on Virtue, and pine away because they have
           abandoned her.   *Satires*, iii. 38.

3137. Venienti occurrite morbo.
           —Meet the disease as it approaches.   Ibid., 64.

PÉTAIN, HENRI PHILIPPE, Marshal of France, 24 April, 1856—23 July, 1951

3138. Ils ne passeront pas.—They shall not pass.

> *At the defence of Verdun*, 1916.

PETRONIUS ARBITER, Roman satirist, died A.D. 65

3139. Horatii curiosa felicitas.—The studied felicity of Horace.

> *Satyricon*, cxviii.

PHELPS, EDWARD JOHN, U.S. lawyer and diplomat, 11 July, 1822—9 March, 1900

3140. The man who makes no mistakes does not usually make anything.   *Speech at Mansion House, London*, 24 Jan. 1899.

PHILIPS, AMBROSE, poet and M.P., 1675?—18 June, 1749

3141.   The flowers, anew, returning seasons bring!
         But beauty faded has no second spring.

> *The First Pastoral*, 55.

PHILIPS, JOHN, poet, 30 Dec. 1676—15 Feb. 1709

3142.   Happy the man who, void of cares and strife,
         In silken or in leathern purse retains
         A Splendid Shilling.   *The Splendid Shilling*, 1.

PHILLIPS, STEPHEN, poet, 28 July, 1864—9 Dec. 1915

3143.   A man not old, but mellow, like good wine.

> *Ulysses*, III. ii.

PHILLIPS, WENDELL, U.S. reformer, 29 Nov. 1811—2 Feb. 1884

3144. One on God's side is a majority.

> *Speech at Brooklyn*, 1 Nov. 1859.

PHILLPOTTS, EDEN, author, 4 Nov. 1862—29 Dec. 1960

3145.   Then old man's talk o' the days behind 'e,
           Your darter's youngest darter to mind 'e;
           A li'l dreamin', a li'l dyin':
           A li'l lew corner o' airth to lie in.   *Man's Days*.

3146. He never went out of bounds at all, from fear and also from goodness, but cheefly from fear.

> *The Human Boy Again. The Qwarry*.

PINDAR, Greek poet, 522?—442 ? B.C.

3147. Ἄριστον μὲν ὕδωρ.
       —Water is best.   *Olympian Odes*, i.

3148. Αἴ τε λιπαραὶ καὶ ἰοστέφανοι καὶ ἀοίδιμοι,
       Ἑλλάδος ἔρεισμα, κλειναὶ Ἀθᾶναι, δαιμόνιον πτολίεθρον.
       —Shining and violet-crowned and celebrated in song, bulwark of Greece, famous Athens, divine city.   *Fragment*.

PINDAR, PETER, *see* Wolcot, John

PINERO, SIR ARTHUR WING, dramatist, 24 May, 1855—23 Nov. 1934

3149. From forty to fifty a man is at heart either a stoic or a satyr.
The Second Mrs. Tanqueray, I.

PITT, WILLIAM, Prime Minister, 28 May, 1759—23 Jan. 1806

3150. Necessity is the plea for every infringement of human freedom.
It is the argument of tyrants ; it is the creed of slaves.
Speech, House of Commons, 18 Nov. 1783.

3151. England has saved herself by her exertions ; and will, as I
trust, save Europe by her example.
Speech, Lord Mayor's Banquet, 9 Nov. 1805.

3152. Roll up that map [of Europe] ; it will not be wanted these ten
years. *On hearing of the battle of Austerlitz.*

3153. O my country ! how I leave my country ! [*Or* how I love my
country !] *Last words, by common account.*

3154. I think I could eat one of Bellamy's veal pies.
Last words, according to an old waiter.

PITT, WILLIAM, *see* Chatham, Earl of

PITT, WILLIAM, dockyard official, 1790 ?—1840

3155.   One night came on a hurricane,
               The sea was mountains rolling,
           When Barney Buntline turned his quid,
               And said to Billy Bowling :
           'A strong nor'-wester's blowing, Bill ;
               Hark ! don't ye hear it roar now !
           Lord help 'em, how I pities them
               Unhappy folks on shore now ! '
                             The Sailor's Consolation.

POE, EDGAR ALLAN, U.S. author, 19 Jan. 1809—7 Oct. 1849

3156.   All that we see or seem
           Is but a dream within a dream.
                             A Dream Within a Dream.

3157. I was a child and she was a child,
               In this kingdom by the sea,
           But we loved with a love that was more than love—
               I and my Annabel Lee—
           With a love that the winged seraphs of heaven
               Coveted her and me. *Annabel Lee.*

3158. Once upon a midnight dreary, while I pondered, weak and
               weary,
           Over many a quaint and curious volume of forgotten lore,
           While I nodded, nearly napping, suddenly there came a
               tapping,
           As of someone gently rapping. *The Raven.*

3159. Deep into the darkness peering, long I stood there, wondering,
        fearing,
    Doubting, dreaming dreams no mortal ever dared to dream
        before.   Ibid.

3160. Take thy beak from out my heart, and take thy form from
        off my door !
    Quoth the Raven, " Nevermore."   Ibid.

3161.   Helen, thy beauty is to me
          Like those Nicaean barks of yore,
        That gently, o'er a perfumed sea,
          The weary, wayworn wanderer bore
        To his own native shore.

3162.   On desperate seas long wont to roam,
          Thy hyacinth hair, thy classic face,
        Thy Naiad airs, have brought me home
          To the glory that was Greece
        And the grandeur that was Rome.   *To Helen.*

POMPADOUR, JEANNE ANTOINETTE POISSON LE NORMANT D'ÉTIOLES,
    MARQUISE DE, mistress of Louis XV, 29 Dec. 1721—15 April,
    1764

    3163. Après nous le déluge.—After us the deluge.
                After the battle of Rossbach, 5 Nov. 1757.

POOLE, JOHN, dramatist, born 1786 ?, buried 10 Feb. 1872
    3164. I hope I don't intrude.   *Paul Pry,* I. ii.

POPE, ALEXANDER, poet, 21 May, 1688—30 May, 1744

3165.   Happy the man, whose wish and care
          A few paternal acres bound,
        Content to breathe his native air
          In his own ground.   *Ode on Solitude*

3166.   Thus let me live, unseen, unknown,
          Thus unlamented let me die,
         Steal from the world, and not a stone
          Tell where I lie.   Ibid.

3167. Where'er you walk, cool gales shall fan the glade,
    Trees, where you sit, shall crowd into a shade :
    Where'er you tread, the blushing flowers shall rise
    And all things flourish where you turn your eyes.
                Pastorals. Summer, 73.

3168. 'Tis with our judgments as our watches, none
    Go just alike, yet each believes his own.
                Essay on Criticism, 9.

3169. Pride, the never-failing vice of fools.   Ibid., 204.

3170. A little learning is a dangerous thing ;
    Drink deep, or taste not the Pierian spring :
    There shallow draughts intoxicate the brain,
    And drinking largely sobers us again.   Ibid., 215.

3171. Hills peep o'er hills, and Alps on Alps arise !   Ibid., 232.

3172. Whoever thinks a faultless piece to see,
Thinks what ne'er was, nor is, nor e'er shall be.   *Ibid.*, 253.

3173. True wit is nature to advantage dress'd,
What oft was thought, but ne'er so well express'd.   *Ibid.*, 297.

3174. Words are like leaves ; and where they most abound,
Much fruit of sense beneath is rarely found.   *Ibid.*, 309.

3175. Such labour'd nothings, in so strange a style,
Amaze th' unlearn'd, and make the learned smile.   *Ibid.*, 326.

3176. Be not the first by whom the new are tried,
Nor yet the last to lay the old aside.   *Ibid.*, 335.

3177.   Some to church repair
Not for the doctrine, but the music there.   *Ibid.*, 342.

3178. These equal syllables alone require,
Though oft the ear the open vowels tire ;
While expletives their feeble aid do join ;
And ten low words oft creep in one dull line.   *Ibid.*, 344.

3179. Where'er you find ' the cooling western breeze,'
In the next line, it ' whispers through the trees ' :
If crystal streams ' with pleasing murmurs creep,'
The reader's threaten'd (not in vain) with ' sleep ' :
Then, at the last and only couplet fraught
With some unmeaning thing they call a thought,
A needless Alexandrine ends the song,
That, like a wounded snake, drags its slow length along.
          Ibid., 350.

3180. True ease in writing comes from art, not chance,
As those move easiest who have learn'd to dance.
'Tis not enough no harshness gives offence,
The sound must seem an echo to the sense :
Soft is the strain when zephyr gently blows,
And the smooth stream in smoother numbers flows ;
But when loud surges lash the sounding shore,
The hoarse, rough verse should like a torrent roar.
When Ajax strives some rock's vast weight to throw,
The line too labours, and the words move slow :
Not so when swift Camilla scours the plain,
Flies o'er the' unbending corn, and skims along the main.
          Ibid., 362.

3181. For fools admire, but men of sense approve.   *Ibid.*, 391.

3182. But let a lord once own the happy lines,
How the wit brightens ! how the style refines !   *Ibid.*, 420.

3183. To err is human, to forgive, divine.   *Ibid.*, 525.

3184. The bookful blockhead, ignorantly read,
With loads of learned lumber in his head.   *Ibid.*, 612.

3185. For fools rush in where angels fear to tread.   *Ibid.*, 625.

3186. What dire offence from amorous causes springs,
What mighty contests rise from trivial things,
I sing.   *The Rape of the Lock*, i. 1.

3187. And all Arabia breathes from yonder box.   *Ibid.*, 134.

3188. On her white breast a sparkling cross she wore,
Which Jews might kiss, and infidels adore. *Ibid.*, ii. 7.

3189. If to her share some female errors fall,
Look on her face, and you'll forget them all. *Ibid.*, 17.

3190. Fair tresses man's imperial race insnare,
And beauty draws us with a single hair. *Ibid.*, 27.

3191. Here thou, great Anna ! whom three realms obey,
Dost sometimes counsel take—and sometimes tea. *Ibid.*, iii. 7.

3192. At every word a reputation dies. *Ibid.* 16.

3193. The hungry judges soon the sentence sign,
And wretches hang that jurymen may dine. *Ibid.*, 21.

3194. ' Let spades be trumps ! ' she said, and trumps they were.
Ibid., 46.

3195. Coffee, which makes the politician wise,
And see through all things with his half-shut eyes. *Ibid.*, 117.

3196. The meeting points the sacred hair dissever
From the fair head, for ever, and for ever ! *Ibid.*, 153.

3197. Not louder shrieks to pitying heaven are cast,
When husbands or when lap-dogs breathe their last. *Ibid.*, 157.

3198. Sir Plume, of amber snuff-box justly vain,
And the nice conduct of a clouded cane. *Ibid.*, iv. 123.

3199. Charms strike the sight, but merit wins the soul. *Ibid.*, v. 34.

3200. A brave man struggling in the storms of fate,
And greatly falling with a falling State.
Prologue to Addison's Cato, 21.

3201. Proud Nimrod first the bloody chase began,
A mighty hunter, and his prey was man.
Windsor Forest, 61.

3202. Nor fame I slight, nor for her favours call ;
She comes unlook'd for, if she comes at all.
The Temple of Fame, 513.

3203. Achilles' wrath, to Greece the direful spring
Of woes unnumber'd, heavenly goddess, sing !
Homer's Iliad, i. 1.

3204. She moves a goddess, and she looks a queen.
Ibid., iii. 1.

3205. True friendship's laws are by this rule exprest,
Welcome the coming, speed the parting guest.
Homer's Odyssey, xv. 83.

3206. What beckoning ghost along the moonlight shade
Invites my steps, and points to yonder glade ?
Elegy to the Memory of an Unfortunate Lady, 1.

3207. Ambition first sprung from your blest abodes,
The glorious fault of angels and of gods. *Ibid.*, 13.

3208. By foreign hands thy dying eyes were closed,
By foreign hands thy decent limbs composed,
By foreign hands thy humble grave adorn'd,
By strangers honour'd, and by strangers mourn'd. *Ibid.*, 51.

3209. So peaceful rests, without a stone, a name,
What once had beauty, titles, wealth, and fame.
How loved, how honour'd once, avails thee not,
To whom related, or by whom begot ;
A heap of dust alone remains of thee,
'Tis all thou art, and all the proud shall be !   *Ibid.*, 69.

3210. Speed the soft intercourse from soul to soul,
And waft a sigh from Indus to the Pole.
                                        Eloisa to Abelard, 57.

3211. Love, free as air, at sight of human ties,
Spreads his light wings, and in a moment flies.   *Ibid.*, 75.

3212. And love th' offender, yet detest th' offence.   *Ibid.*, 192.

3213. How happy is the blameless vestal's lot !
The world forgetting, by the world forgot.   *Ibid.*, 207.

3214. One thought of thee puts all the pomp to flight,
Priests, tapers, temples, swim before my sight.   *Ibid.*, 273.

3215. He best can paint them who shall feel them most.   *Ibid.*, 366.

3216. Such were the notes thy once-loved poet sung,
Till death untimely stopp'd his tuneful tongue.
                                Epistle to Robert Earl of Oxford, 1.

3217. Poetic justice, with her lifted scale,
Where, in nice balance, truth with gold she weighs,
And solid pudding against empty praise.
                                        The Dunciad, i. 52.

3218. Now night descending, the proud scene was o'er,
But lived, in Settle's numbers, one day more.   *Ibid.*, 89.

3219. While pensive poets painful vigils keep,
Sleepless themselves to give their readers sleep.   *Ibid.*, 93.

3220. Next, o'er his books his eyes began to roll,
In pleasing memory of all he stole.   *Ibid.*, 127.

3221. And gentle Dulness ever loves a joke.   *Ibid.*, ii. 34.

3222. Lo ! where Maeotis sleeps, and hardly flows
The freezing Tanais through a waste of snows.   *Ibid.*, iii. 87.

3223. All crowd, who foremost shall be damned to fame.   *Ibid.*, 158.

3224. Silence, ye wolves ! while Ralph to Cynthia howls,
And makes night hideous—Answer him, ye owls !   *Ibid.*, 165.

3225. A wit with dunces, and a dunce with wits.   *Ibid.*, iv. 90.

3226. The right divine of kings to govern wrong.   *Ibid.*, 188.

3227. Stretch'd on the rack of a too easy chair.   *Ibid.*, 342.

3228. Even Palinurus nodded at the helm.   *Ibid.*, 614.

3229. Religion blushing veils her sacred fires,
And unawares morality expires.
Nor public flame, nor private, dares to shine,
Nor human spark is left, nor glimpse divine !
Lo ! thy dread empire, Chaos ! is restor'd ;
Light dies before thy uncreating word ;
Thy hand, great Anarch ! lets the curtain fall,
And universal darkness buries all.   *Ibid.*, 649.

3230. Awake, my St. John ! leave all meaner things
   To low ambition and the pride of kings.
   Let us (since life can little more supply
   Than just to look about us, and to die)
   Expatiate free o'er all this scene of man ;
   A mighty maze ! but not without a plan.
                                    Essay on Man.   Epistle i. 1.

3231. Eye Nature's walks, shoot folly as it flies,
   And catch the manners living as they rise :
   Laugh where we must, be candid where we can ;
   But vindicate the ways of God to man.   Ibid., 13.

3232. Heaven from all creatures hides the book of Fate.   Ibid., 77.

3233. Who sees with equal eye, as God of all,
   A hero perish, or a sparrow fall,
   Atoms or systems into ruin hurl'd,
   And now a bubble burst, and now a world.   Ibid., 87.

3234. Hope springs eternal in the human breast :
   Man never is, but always to be blest.   Ibid., 95.

3235. Lo, the poor Indian ! whose untutor'd mind
   Sees God in clouds, or hears Him in the wind ;
   His soul proud science never taught to stray
   Far as the solar walk or milky way.   Ibid., 99.

3236. But thinks, admitted to that equal sky,
   His faithful dog shall bear him company.   Ibid., 111.

3237. Why has not man a microscopic eye ?
   For this plain reason, man is not a fly.   Ibid., 193.

3238. Die of a rose in aromatic pain.   Ibid., 200.

3239. The spider's touch, how exquisitely fine !
   Feels at each thread, and lives along the line. Ibid., 217.

3240. All are but parts of one stupendous whole,
   Whose body Nature is, and God the soul.   Ibid., 267.

3241. Warms in the sun, refreshes in the breeze,
   Glows in the stars, and blossoms in the trees. Ibid., 271.

3242. All nature is but art, unknown to thee ;
   All chance, direction which thou canst not see ;
   All discord, harmony not understood ;
   All partial evil, universal good :
   And, spite of pride, in erring reason's spite,
   One truth is clear, Whatever is, is right.   Ibid., 289.

3243. Know then thyself, presume not God to scan,
   The proper study of mankind is man.   Ibid., Epistle ii. 1.

3244. Chaos of thought and passion, all confused ;
   Still by himself abused or disabused ;
   Created half to rise, and half to fall ;
   Great lord of all things, yet a prey to all ;
   Sole judge of truth, in endless error hurl'd :
   The glory, jest, and riddle of the world !   Ibid., 13.

3245. Vice is a monster of so frightful mien,
   As, to be hated, needs but to be seen ;
   Yet seen too oft, familiar with her face,
   We first endure, then pity, then embrace.   Ibid., 217.

3246. Behold the child, by nature's kindly law,
      Pleased with a rattle, tickled with a straw :
      Some livelier plaything gives his youth delight,
      A little louder, but as empty quite :
      Scarfs, garters, gold, amuse his riper stage,
      And beads and prayer-books are the toys of age :
      Pleased with this bauble still, as that before ;
      Till tired he sleeps, and life's poor play is o'er.   Ibid., 275.

3247. For forms of government let fools contest ;
      What'er is best administer'd is best :
      For modes of faith let graceless zealots fight ;
      He can't be wrong whose life is in the right :
      In faith and hope the world will disagree,
      But all mankind's concern is charity.   Ibid., Epistle iii. 303.

3248. O happiness ! our being's end and aim !
      Good, pleasure, ease, content ! whate'er thy name :
      That something still which prompts th' eternal sigh,
      For which we bear to live, or dare to die.
                                             Ibid., Epistle iv. 1.

3249. Order is heaven's first law.   Ibid., 49.

3250. Worth makes the man, and want of it the fellow :
      The rest is all but leather or prunella.   Ibid., 203

3251. What can ennoble sots, or slaves, or cowards ?
      Alas ! not all the blood of all the Howards.   Ibid., 215.

3252. An honest man's the noblest work of God.   Ibid., 248.

3253. And more true joy Marcellus exiled feels,
      Than Caesar with a senate at his heels.   Ibid., 257.

3254. If parts allure thee, think how Bacon shined,
      The wisest, brightest, meanest of mankind :
      Or, ravish'd with the whistling of a name,
      See Cromwell, damn'd to everlasting fame !   Ibid., 281.

3255. Slave to no sect, who takes no private road,
      But looks through nature up to nature's God.   Ibid., 331.

3256. Form'd by thy converse happily to steer
      From grave to gay, from lively to severe.   Ibid., 379.

3257. Thou wert my guide, philosopher, and friend.   Ibid., 390.

3258. To observations which ourselves we make,
      We grow more partial for the observer's sake.
                                   Moral Essays. Epistle i. 11.

3259. Like following life through creatures you dissect,
      You lose it in the moment you detect.   Ibid., 29.

3260. 'Tis from high life high characters are drawn,
      A saint in crape is twice a saint in lawn.   Ibid., 135.

3261. 'Tis education forms the common mind,
      Just as the twig is bent, the tree's inclined.   Ibid., 149.

3262. " Odious ! in woollen ! 'twould a saint provoke ! "
      (Were the last words that poor Narcissa spoke).   Ibid., 246.

3263. " One would not, sure, be frightful when one's dead—
      And—Betty—give this cheek a little red."   Ibid., 250.

3264. And you, brave Cobham, to the latest breath,
Shall feel your ruling passion strong in death.   **Ibid.**, 262.

3265. Whether the charmer sinner it, or saint it,
If folly grow romantic, I must paint it.   Ibid., Epistle ii. 15.

3266. Choose a firm cloud before it fall, and in it
Catch, ere she change, the Cynthia of this minute.   Ibid., 19.

3267. Fine by defect, and delicately weak.   Ibid., 43.

3268. With too much quickness ever to be taught :
With too much thinking to have common thought.   Ibid., 97.

3269. Virtue she finds too painful an endeavour,
Content to dwell in decencies for ever.   Ibid., 163.

3270. Men, some to business, some to pleasure take ;
But every woman is at heart a rake.   Ibid., 215.

3271. See how the world its veterans rewards !
A youth of frolics, an old age of cards.   Ibid., 243.

3272. She who ne'er answers till a husband cools,
Or, if she rules him, never shows she rules ;
Charms by accepting, by submitting sways,
Yet has her humour most when she obeys.   Ibid., 261.

3273. And mistress of herself, though China fall.   Ibid., 268.

3274. Woman's at best a contradiction still.   Ibid,. 270.

3275. Who shall decide when doctors disagree ?   Ibid., Epistle iii. 1.

3276. But thousands die, without or this or that,
Die, and endow a college or a cat.   Ibid., 95.

3277. The ruling passion, be it what it will,
The ruling passion conquers reason still.   Ibid., 153.

3278. Rise, honest muse ! and sing the Man of Ross.   Ibid., 250.

3279. Where London's column, pointing at the skies
Like a tall bully, lifts the head and lies.   Ibid., 339

3280. To rest, the cushion and soft dean invite,
Who never mentions hell to ears polite.   Ibid., Epistle iv. 149.

3281. Statesman, yet friend to truth ! of soul sincere,
In action faithful, and in honour clear ;
Who broke no promise, served no private end,
Who gained no title, and who lost no friend.
        Ibid., Epistle v. *To Mr. Addison*, 67.

3282. Shut, shut the door, good John ! fatigued, I said ;
Tie up the knocker, say I'm sick, I'm dead.
        Epistle to Dr. Arbuthnot or Prologue to the Satires, 1.

3283. Fire in each eye, and papers in each hand.
They rave, recite, and madden round the land,   Ibid., 5.

3284. Is there a parson, much bemused in beer,
A maudlin poetess, a rhyming peer,
A clerk, foredoom'd his father's soul to cross,
Who pens a stanza, when he should engross ?   Ibid., 15.

3285. Fired that the house reject him, ' 'Sdeath ! I'll print it,
And shame the fools.'   Ibid., 61.

3286. No creature smarts so little as a fool.   Ibid., 84.

3287. Destroy his fib or sophistry—in vain !
      The creature's at his dirty work again.   Ibid., 91.

3288. As yet a child, nor yet a fool to fame,
      I lisp'd in numbers, for the numbers came.   Ibid., 127.

3289. This long disease, my life.   Ibid., 132.

3290. And he, whose fustian's so sublimely bad
      It is not poetry, but prose run mad.   Ibid., 187.

3291.   Were there one whose fires
      True genius kindles, and fair fame inspires ;
      Blest with each talent, and each art to please,
      And born to write, converse, and live with ease ;
      Should such a man, too fond to rule alone,
      Bear, like the Turk, no brother near the throne,
      View him with scornful, yet with jealous eyes,
      And hate for arts that caused himself to rise ;
      Damn with faint praise, assent with civil leer,
      And, without sneering, teach the rest to sneer ;
      Willing to wound, and yet afraid to strike,
      Just hint a fault, and hesitate dislike ;
      Alike reserved to blame, or to commend,
      A timorous foe, and a suspicious friend ;
      Dreading e'en fools, by flatterers besieged,
      And so obliging, that he ne'er obliged ;
      Like Cato, give his little senate laws,
      And sit attentive to his own applause ;
      While wits and Templars every sentence raise,
      And wonder with a foolish face of praise—
      Who but must laugh, if such a man there be ?
      Who would not weep, if Atticus were he ?   Ibid., 193.

3292. Cursed be the verse, how well soe'er it flow,
      That tends to make one worthy man my foe.   Ibid., 283.

3293. Satire or sense, alas ! can Sporus feel,
      Who breaks a butterfly upon a wheel ?   Ibid., 307.

3294. This painted child of dirt, that stinks and stings.   Ibid., 310.

3295. Eternal smiles his emptiness betray,
      As shallow streams run dimpling all the way.   Ibid., 315.

3296. Wit that can creep, and pride that licks the dust.   Ibid., 333.

3297. The lines are weak, another's pleased to say,
      Lord Fanny spins a thousand such a day.
          Satires and Epistles of Horace Imitated, Bk. II.   Satire i. 6.

3298. The feast of reason and the flow of soul.   Ibid., 128.

3299. One simile, that solitary shines
      In a dry desert of a thousand lines.
                               Ibid., Bk. II. Epistle i. 111.

3300. Waller was smooth ; but Dryden taught to join
      The varying verse, the full-resounding line,
      The long majestic march and energy divine.   Ibid., 267.

3301. Even copious Dryden wanted, or forgot,
      The last and greatest art, the art to blot.   Ibid., 280.

3302. The many-headed monster of the pit.   Ibid., 305.

3303. The vulgar boil, the learned roast an egg.   Ibid., Epistle ii. 85.

3304. Do good by stealth, and blush to find it fame.
        Epilogue to the Satires, dialogue i. 136.

3305.   Vain was the chief's, the sage's pride !
    They had no poet, and they died.
        Imitations of Horace, Odes, iv. ix.

3306.   Teach me to feel another's woe,
        To hide the fault I see ;
      That mercy I to others show
        That mercy show to me.   *The Universal Prayer.*

3307.   Heaven, as its purest gold, by tortures tried !
    The saint sustain'd it, but the woman died.
        Epitaph on Mrs. Corbet.

3308.   Of manners gentle, of affections mild ;
    In wit, a man ; simplicity, a child :
    With native humour tempering virtuous rage,
    Form'd to delight at once and lash the age.
        Epitaph on Mr. Gay.

3309.   Nature and Nature's laws lay hid in night :
    God said, ' Let Newton be ! ' and all was light.
        Epitaph intended for Sir Isaac Newton.

3310.   ' Has she no faults, then (Envy says), sir ? '
      Yes, she has one, I must aver :
    When all the world conspires to praise her,
      The woman's deaf, and does not hear.
        On a Certain Lady at Court.

3311. Dear, damn'd, distracting town, farewell !
        A Farewell to London, 1.

3312.   You beat your pate and fancy wit will come :
    Knock as you please, there's nobody at home.   *Epigram.*

3313.   I am his Highness' dog at Kew ;
      Pray tell me, sir, whose dog are you ?
    On the Collar of a Dog which I gave to his Royal Highness.

3314. I never knew any man in my life who could not bear another's misfortunes perfectly like a Christian.

        Thoughts on Various Subjects.

3315. When men grow virtuous in their old age, they only make a sacrifice to God of the devil's leavings.   Ibid.

3316. ' Blessed is the man who expects nothing, for he shall never be disappointed ' was the ninth beatitude which a man of wit . . . added to the eighth.   *Letter to Wm. Fortescue*, 23 Sept. 1725.

POPE, WALTER, astronomer, 1630 ?—25 June, 1714

3317. If I live to be old, for I find I go down,
    Let this be my fate : in a country town
    May I have a warm house with a stone at the gate,
    And a cleanly young girl to rub my bald pate.
      May I govern my passion with an absolute sway,
      And grow wiser and better as my strength wears away,
      Without gout or stone, by a gentle decay.
        The Old Man's Wish.

PORSON, RICHARD, Professor of Greek, 25 Dec. 1759—25 Sept. 1808

3318.   When Dido found Aeneas would not come,
          She mourned in silence, and was Di-do-dum.
                              Epigram on Latin gerunds.

3319.   I went to Strasburg, where I got drunk
          With that most learn'd professor, Brunck.
          I went to Wortz, where I got more drunken
          With that more learn'd professor. Ruhnken.
                    Richard Porson, by M. L. Clarke, p. 16

3320.   The Germans in Greek
               Are sadly to seek ;
               Not five in five score,
               But ninety-five more ;
               All ; save only Hermann,
               And Hermann's a German.   Ibid., p. 69.

PORTER, WILLIAM SYDNEY, *see* Henry, O.

PRAED, WINTHROP MACKWORTH, poet, 26 July, 1802—15 July, 1839

3321. Some lie beneath the churchyard stone,
          And some before the Speaker.   *Schools and Schoolfellows.*

3322. Tom Mill was used to blacken eyes
          Without the fear of sessions ;
       Charles Medlar loathed false quantities
          As much as false professions ;
       Now Mill keeps order in the land,
          A magistrate pedantic ;
       And Medlar's feet repose unscanned
          Beneath the wide Atlantic.   Ibid.

3323. He must walk—like a god of old story
          Come down from the home of his rest ;
       He must smile—like the sun in his glory
          On the buds he loves ever the best ;
       And oh ! from its ivory portal
          Like music his soft speech must flow !—
       If he speak, smile, or walk like a mortal,
          My own Araminta, say " No ! "   *A Letter of Advice.*

3324. His talk was like a stream, which runs
          With rapid change from rocks to roses :
       It slipped from politics to puns,
          It passed from Mahomet to Moses ;
       Beginning with the laws which keep
          The planets in their radiant courses,
       And ending with some precept deep
          For dressing eels, or shoeing horses.   *The Vicar.*

3325. The ice of her Ladyship's manners,
          The ice of his Lordship's champagne.
                         Good-night to the Season.

PRIMROSE, ARCHIBALD PHILIP, *see* Rosebery, Earl of

PRIOR, MATTHEW, poet and diplomatist, 21 July, 1664—18 Sept.
1721

3326. The merchant, to secure his treasure,
            Conveys it in a borrow'd name :
        Euphelia serves to grace my measure ;
            But Chloe is my real flame.   *An Ode.*

3327. Be to her virtues very kind ;
        Be to her faults a little blind ;
        Let all her ways be unconfin'd ;
        And clap your padlock—on her mind.

                                        An English Padlock, 78.

3328. The end must justify the means.   *Hans Carvel*, 67.

3329. To John I ow'd great obligation ;
        But John unhappily thought fit
        To publish it to all the nation :
            Sure John and I are more than quit.   *Epigram.*

3330. No longer shall the bodice, aptly lac'd
        From thy full bosom to thy slender waist,
        That air and harmony of shape express,
        Fine by degrees, and beautifully less.   *Henry and Emma*, 427.

3331. Abra was ready ere I call'd her name ;
        And, though I call'd another, Abra came.
                    Solomon on the Vanity of the World, ii. 362.

3332. For hope is but the dream of those that wake.   Ibid., iii. 102.

3333. Cur'd yesterday of my disease,
        I died last night of my physician.
                            The Remedy Worse than the Disease.

3334. For, as our different ages move,
            'Tis so ordain'd (would Fate but mend it !),
        That I shall be past making love
            When she begins to comprehend it.
                    *To a Child of Quality, Five Years Old. The Author
                        then Forty.*

3335.   Nobles and heralds, by your leave,
            Here lies what once was Matthew Prior ;
        The son of Adam and of Eve :
            Can Bourbon or Nassau claim higher ?   *Epitaph*

PROCTER, ADELAIDE ANN, poetess, 30 Oct. 1825—2 Feb. 1864

3336.   Seated one day at the organ,
            I was weary and ill at ease.   *A Lost Chord.*

3337.   But I struck one chord of music,
            Like the sound of a great Amen.   Ibid.

PROCTER, BRYAN WALLER (' BARRY CORNWALL '), poet, 21 Nov.
1787—5 Oct. 1874

3338.   The sea ! the sea ! the open sea !
            The blue, the fresh, the ever free !   *The Sea.*

3339.   I'm on the sea !   I'm on the sea !
        I am where I would ever be,
        With the blue above and the blue below,
        And silence wheresoe'er I go.   *Ibid.*

3340.   I never was on the dull, tame shore
        But I loved the great sea more and more.   *Ibid.*

PROUT, FATHER (FRANCIS SYLVESTER MAHONY), Irish author, 1804—
18 May, 1866

3341.   'Tis the bells of Shandon,
             That sound so grand on
             The pleasant waters
                Of the River Lee.   *The Bells of Shandon.*

PROWSE, WILLIAM JEFFREY, poet, 6 May, 1836—17 April, 1870

3342.   Though the latitude's rather uncertain,
          And the longitude also is vague,
        The persons I pity who know not the city,
          The beautiful city of Prague.   *The City of Prague.*

PUTNAM, ISRAEL, U.S. General, 7 Jan. 1718—29 May, 1790

3343.   Don't one of you fire until you see the white of their eyes.
                              At Bunker Hill, 17 June, 1775.

QUARLES, FRANCIS, poet, baptised 8 May, 1592, died 8 Sept. 1644

3344.   Sweet Phosphor, bring the day ;
         Light will repay
         The wrongs of night ;
           Sweet Phosphor, bring the day !
                           Emblems, I. xiv.

3345.   Be wisely worldly, be not worldly wise.   *Ibid.*, II. ii.

3346.   My soul, sit thou a patient looker-on ;
        Judge not the play before the play is done :
        Her plot hath many changes ; every day
        Speaks a new scene ; the last act crowns the play.
                     Epigram. Respice Finem.

3347.   We'll cry both arts and learning down,
         And hey ! then up go we !
           The Shepherd's Oracles. Song of Anarchus.

QUILLER-COUCH, SIR ARTHUR THOMAS, Professor of English, 21 Nov.
1863—12 May, 1944

3348.   Know you her secret none can utter ?
         —Hers of the Book, the tripled Crown ?
        Still on the spire the pigeons flutter ;
          Still by the gateway haunts the gown ;
        Still on the street from corbel and gutter,
          Faces of stone look down.   *Alma Mater.*

3349. It was bellows to mend with Roberts—starred three for a
             penalty kick:
         But he chalked his cue and gave 'em the butt, and Oom Paul
             marked the trick—
         'Offside—No Ball—and at fourteen all! Mark Cock! and two
             for his nob!'
         When W. G. ran clean through his lee and beat him twice
             with a lob.   *The Famous Ballad of the Jubilee Cup.*

3350.   The lion is the beast to fight,
                       He leaps along the plain,
                       And if you run with all your might
                       He runs with all his mane.   *Sage Counsel.*

    3351. To be, or the contrary? Whether the former or the latter
be preferable would seem to admit of some difference of opinion; the
answer in the present case being of an affirmative or of a negative
character according as to whether one elects on the one hand to mentally
suffer the disfavour of fortune, albeit in an extreme degree, or on the
other to boldly envisage adverse conditions in the prospect of eventually
bringing them to a conclusion. [Hamlet's soliloquy jargonised.]
                                   The Art of Writing, lecture v.

QUINCY, JOSIAH, U.S. politician, 4 Feb. 1772—1 July, 1864

    3352. If this Bill [for the admission of Orleans Territory as a State]
passes, it is my deliberate opinion that it is virtually a dissolution of
the Union; that it will free the States from their moral obligation;
and, as it will be the right of all, so it will be the duty of some, definitely
to prepare for a separation,—amicably if they can, violently if they
must.   *Abridged Congressional Debates*, 14 Jan. 1811.

RABELAIS, FRANÇOIS, French author, 1494?—9 April, 1553?

    3353. L'appétit vient en mangeant.—Appetite comes with eating.
                                             Works, I. v.

    3354. Je m'en vais chercher un grand peut-être.—I go in quest of a
great Perhaps.   *Traditional deathbed saying.*

    3355. Tirez le rideau, la farce est jouée.—Ring down the curtain,
the farce is played.   Ibid.

RACINE, JEAN, French dramatist, Dec. 1639—21 April, 1699

3356.   Ce n'est plus une ardeur dans mes veines cachée;
         C'est Vénus toute entière à sa proie attachée.
         —It is no longer a passion hidden in my veins; it is Venus's
         very self fastened on her prey.   *Phèdre*, I. iii.

RALEGH *or* RALEIGH, SIR WALTER, soldier and author, 1552?—29 Oct.
             1618

3357.   If all the world and love were young,
                 And truth in every shepherd's tongue,
                 These pretty pleasures might me move
                 To live with thee, and be thy love.
                      The Nymph's reply to the Passionate Shepherd.

3358. Silence in love bewrays more woe
    Than words, though ne'er so witty ;
A beggar that is dumb, you know,
    May challenge double pity.   *The Silent Lover.*

3359. As you came from the holy land
    Of Walsinghame,
Met you not with my true love
    By the way as you came ?   *Walsinghame.*

3360. How shall I know your true love,
    That have met many a one
As I went to the holy land,
    That have come, that have gone.   Ibid.

3361. Give me my scallop-shell of quiet,
    My staff of faith to walk upon,
My scrip of joy, immortal diet,
    My bottle of salvation,
My gown of glory, hope's true gage,
And thus I'll take my pilgrimage.   *The Pilgrimage.*

3362. Methought I saw the grave where Laura lay.
           Verses to Edmund Spenser.

3363. Go, Soul, the body's guest,
    Upon a thankless arrant ;
Fear not to touch the best,
    The truth shall be thy warrant :
Go, since I needs must die,
And give the world the lie.   *The Lie.*

3364. Fain would I climb, yet fear I to fall.
    *Said to have been written on a window-pane in the
        presence of Queen Elizabeth, who wrote under-
        neath :—*
If thy heart fails thee, climb not at all.

3365. Even such is Time, that takes in trust
    Our youth, our joys, our all we have,
And pays us but with earth and dust ;
    Who in the dark and silent grave,
When we have wander'd all our ways,
Shuts up the story of our days ;
But from this earth, this grave, this dust,
My God shall raise me up, I trust.
        Written the night before his death.

3366. O eloquent, just, and mightie Death ! whom none could advise, thou hast perswaded ; what none hath dared, thou hast done ; and whom all the world hath flattered, thou only hast cast out of the world and despised : thou hast drawne together all the farre stretched greatnesse, all the pride, crueltie, and ambition of men, and covered it all over with these two narrow words, *Hic jacet !*
        Historie of the World, Bk. v. part i. *ad fin.*

3367. So the heart be right, it is no matter which way the head lieth.   *When laying his head on the block.*

RALEIGH, SIR WALTER ALEXANDER, Professor of English, 6 Sept. 1861
——13 May, 1922

3368.   I wish I loved the Human Race;
                     I wish I loved its silly face;
                     I wish I liked the way it walks;
                     I wish I liked the way it talks;
                     And when I'm introduced to one
                     I wish I thought *What Jolly Fun!*
                          Laughter from a Cloud. Wishes of an Elderly
                                Man.

3369. In an examination those who do not wish to know ask questions
of those who cannot tell.   Ibid. *Some Thoughts on Examinations.*

RAMSAY, ALLAN, Scottish poet, 15 Oct. 1686——7 Jan. 1758
3370.   Farewell to Lochaber, and farewell my Jean,
             Where heartsome with thee I hae mony day been;
             For Lochaber no more, Lochaber no more,
             We'll maybe return to Lochaber no more.
                                            Lochaber No More.

RANDALL, JAMES RYDER, U.S. poet, 1 Jan. 1839——14 Jan. 1908
3371.   The despot's heel is on thy shore,
                          Maryland!
                     His torch is at thy temple door,
                          Maryland!
                     Avenge the patriotic gore
                     That fleck'd the streets of Baltimore,
                     And be the battle queen of yore,
                          Maryland, my Maryland!
                                       Maryland, My Maryland.

RANKIN, JEREMIAH EAMES, U.S. Minister, 2 Jan. 1828——28 Nov. 1904
3372.   God be with you till we meet again.   *Hymn.*

READE, CHARLES, novelist, 8 June, 1814——11 April, 1884
3373. Courage, camarade! Le diable est mort.——Courage, comrade!
The devil is dead.   *The Cloister and the Hearth*, xxiv.

REMARQUE, ERICH MARIA (ERICH PAUL REMARK), German author,
        22 June, 1898——
3374. Im Westen nichts Neues.——All quiet on the Western front [*lit.*
No news in the West].   *Title of novel.*

REYNOLDS, FREDERIC, dramatist, 1 Nov. 1764——16 April, 1841
3375. How goes the enemy? [Said by Mr. Ennui, 'the time-
killer.']   *The Dramatist*, I.

REYNOLDS, SIR JOSHUA, portrait-painter, 16 July, 1723——23 Feb. 1792
3376. If you have great talents, industry will improve them: if you
have but moderate abilities, industry will supply their deficiency.
                                            Discourses, ii.
3377. A mere copier of nature can never produce anything great.
                                            Ibid., iii.

I

RHOADES, James, author, 9 April, 1841—16 March, 1923

3378.   Is he gone to a land of no laughter,
                The man who made mirth for us all ?
                              On the Death of Artemus Ward.

RHODES, CECIL JOHN, South African statesman, 5 July, 1853—26
    March, 1902

    3379. The unctuous rectitude of my countrymen.
                      Speech at Port Elizabeth, 24 Dec. 1896.

    3380. Educational relations make the strongest tie.
                      Will, establishing the Rhodes Scholarships.

    3381. So little done, so much to do.   *Last words.*

RHODES, WILLIAM BARNES, banker and dramatist, 25 Dec. 1772—
    1 Nov. 1826

3382.   ' Who dares this pair of boots displace,
                Must meet Bombastes face to face.'
                Thus do I challenge all the human race.
                                   Bombastes Furioso, iv.

RHYS, ERNEST PERCIVAL, Welsh author, 17 July, 1859—25 May, 1946

3383. Wales England wed ; so I was bred. 'Twas merry London gave
        me breath.
            I dreamt of love, and fame : I strove. But Ireland taught me
            love was best :
        And Irish eyes and London cries, and streams of Wales may
            tell the rest.
    What more than these I ask'd of Life I am content to have from
        Death.   *An Autobiography.*

RICE, GRANTLAND, U.S. author, 1 Nov. 1880—1954

3384. For when the One Great Scorer comes to write against your
        name,
            He marks—not that you won or lost—but how you played the
            game.   *Alumnus Football.*

RICE, SIR STEPHEN, Irish judge, 1637—16 Feb. 1715

    3385. I will drive a coach and six through the Act of Settlement.
                      Macaulay's *History of England*, xii.

RICHARDSON, ROBERT, Australian poet, 7 Jan. 1850—4 Oct. 1901

3386.   Warm summer sun, shine friendly here ;
                Warm western wind, blow kindly here ;
                Green sod above, rest light, rest light—
                Good-night, Annette ! Sweetheart, good-night !
                                            Annette.

RILEY, JAMES WHITCOMB, U.S. poet, 7 Oct. 1849—22 July, 1916

3387. Onc't there was a little boy wouldn't say his pray'rs—
An' when he went to bed at night, away up stairs,
His mammy heerd him holler, an' his daddy heerd him bawl,
An' when they turn't the kivvers down, he wasn't there at
all !
An' they seeked him in the rafter-room, an' cubby-hole, an'
press,
An' seeked him up the chimbly-flue, an' ever'wheres, I guess ;
But all they ever found was thist his pants an' roundabout !
An' the Gobble-uns'll git you
Ef you
Don't
Watch
Out ! *Little Orphant Annie.*

ROCHE, SIR BOYLE, Irish politician, 1743—5 June, 1807

3388. What has posterity done for us ?
Speech in Irish Parliament, 1780.

3389. Mr. Speaker, I smell a rat ; I see him forming in the air and
darkening the sky ; but I'll nip him in the bud. *Attributed.*

ROCHESTER, JOHN WILMOT, 2ND EARL OF, poet, 10 April, 1647—
26 July, 1680

3390. Here lies a great and mighty king,
Whose promise none relies on ;
He never said a foolish thing,
Nor ever did a wise one.
Written on Charles II's bedchamber door.
[There are various versions, the first two lines being commonly
given as :—
Here lies our sovereign lord the king,
Whose word no man relies on.]

3391. For pointed satire I would Buckhurst choose,
The best good man with the worst-natured muse.
An Allusion to Horace, Satire x. Bk. I.

3392. A merry monarch, scandalous and poor.
On the King.

3393. For all men would be cowards if they durst.
A Satire Against Mankind.

3394. I cannot change, as others do,
Though you unjustly scorn,
Since that poor swain that sighs for you,
For you alone was born ;
No, Phillis, no, your heart to move
A surer way I'll try,—
And to revenge my slighted love
Will still love on, and die. *Constancy.*

RODGER, ALEXANDER, Scottish poet, 16 July, 1784—26 Sept. 1846

3395.   My mither men't my auld breeks,
          And wow, but they were duddy !
          And sent me to get Mally shod
          At Robin Tamson's smiddy.
                                        Robin Tamson's Smiddy.

ROGERS, SAMUEL, poet, 30 July, 1763—18 Dec. 1855

3396.   Oh ! she was good as she was fair.
          None—none on earth above her !
          As pure in thought as angels are,
          To know her was to love her.   *Jacqueline,* i. 68.

3397.   But there are moments which he calls his own.
          Then, never less alone than when alone,
          Those that he loved so long and sees no more,
          Loved and still loves—not dead—but gone before,
          He gathers round him.   *Human Life,* 755.

3398.   Mine be a cot beside the hill ;
          A beehive's hum shall soothe my ear ;
          A willowy brook, that turns a mill,
          With many a fall shall linger near.   *A Wish.*

3399.   That very law which moulds a tear
          And bids it trickle from its source,
          That law preserves the earth a sphere
          And guides the planets in their course.   *On a Tear.*

3400.   Ward has no heart, they say, but I deny it :
        He has a heart, and gets his speeches by it.
                                      Epigram upon Lord Dudley.

ROLAND DE LA PLATIÈRE, MARIE JEANNE PHLIPON, MADAME, French
     revolutionary, 18 March, 1754—8 Nov. 1793

   3401. O Liberté ! comme on t'a jouée !—O Liberty ! how thou hast
been played with ! [*Or* O Liberté ! que de crimes on commet en ton
nom !—O Liberty ! what crimes are committed in thy name !]
        At execution, viewing the statue of Liberty from the scaffold.

ROOSEVELT, FRANKLIN DELANO, U.S. President, 30 Jan. 1882—12
     April, 1945

   3402. The forgotten man at the bottom of the economic pyramid.
                              Broadcast address, 7 April, 1932.

   3403. I pledge you—I pledge myself—to a new deal for the American
people.   *Speech at Convention, Chicago,* 2 July, 1932.

   3404. In the field of world policy I would dedicate this nation to the
policy of the good neighbour. *First Inaugural Address,* 4 March, 1933.

ROOSEVELT, THEODORE, U.S. President, 27 Oct. 1858—6 Jan. 1919

   3405. I wish to preach, not the doctrine of ignoble ease, but the
doctrine of the strenuous life.
                   Speech, Hamilton Club, Chicago, 10 April, 1899.

3406. There is a homely adage which runs, ' Speak softly and carry a big stick ; you will go far.' If the American nation will speak softly and yet build and keep at a pitch of the highest training a thoroughly efficient navy, the Monroe Doctrine will go far.
Speech, Minnesota State Fair, 2 Sept. 1901.

3407. A man who is good enough to shed his blood for his country is good enough to be given a square deal afterward. More than that no man is entitled to, and less than that no man shall have.
Speech, Springfield, Illinois, 4 July, 1903.

3408. No man is justified in doing evil on the ground of expediency.
The Strenuous Life. Latitude and Longitude Among Reformers.

ROSCOMMON, WENTWORTH DILLON, 4TH EARL OF, Irish author, 1633 ?— Jan. 1685

3409. And choose an author as you choose a friend.
Essay on Translated Verse, 96.

3410. Immodest words admit of no defence,
For want of decency is want of sense. Ibid., 113.

ROSEBERY, ARCHIBALD PHILIP PRIMROSE, 5TH EARL OF, Prime Minister, 7 May, 1847—21 May, 1929

3411. There is no need for any nation, however great, leaving the Empire, because the Empire is a Commonwealth of Nations.
Speech at Adelaide, 18 Jan. 1884.

3412. It is beginning to be hinted that we are a nation of amateurs.
Rectorial Address, Glasgow, 16 Nov. 1900.

3413. I must plough my furrow alone.
Speech, City of London Liberal Club, 19 July, 1901.

ROSS, ALEXANDER, Scottish poet, 13 April, 1699—20 May, 1784

3414. Woo'd, and married, and a',
Married, and woo'd, and a' !
And was she nae very weel aff,
That was woo'd, and married, and a' ?
Woo'd, and Married, and A'.

ROSSETTI, CHRISTINA GEORGINA, poetess, 5 Dec. 1830—29 Dec. 1894

3415. Rest, rest, for evermore
Upon a mossy shore ;
Rest, rest at the heart's core
Till time shall cease :
Sleep that no pain shall wake,
Night that no morn shall break
Till joy shall overtake
Her perfect peace. *Dream Land.*

3416. My heart is like a singing bird
Whose nest is in a watered shoot ;
My heart is like an apple-tree
Whose boughs are bent with thick-set fruit ;
My heart is like a rainbow shell
That paddles in a halcyon sea ;
My heart is gladder than all these
Because my love is come to me. *A Birthday.*

3417.   Remember me when I am gone away,
               Gone far away into the silent land.   *Remember.*

3418.   Better by far that you should forget and smile
               Than that you should remember and be sad.   *Ibid.*

3419.   When I am dead, my dearest,
                   Sing no sad songs for me ;
               Plant thou no roses at my head,
                   Nor shady cypress tree :
               Be the green grass above me
                   With showers and dewdrops wet ;
               And if thou wilt, remember,
                   And if thou wilt, forget.   *Song.*

3420.   Does the road wind up-hill all the way ?
               Yes, to the very end.   *Up-Hill.*

ROSSETTI, DANTE GABRIEL, poet, 12 May, 1828—9 April, 1882

3421.   The blessed damozel leaned out
                   From the gold bar of Heaven ;
               Her eyes were deeper than the depth
                   Of waters stilled at even ;
               She had three lilies in her hand,
                   And the stars in her hair were seven.
                               The Blessed Damozel.

3422.   Her hair that lay along her back
               Was yellow like ripe corn.   *Ibid.*

3423.   As low as where this earth
           Spins like a fretful midge.   *Ibid.*

3424.   And the souls mounting up to God
               Went by her like thin flames.   *Ibid.*

3425.   ' We two,' she said, ' will seek the groves
                   Where the lady Mary is,
               With her five handmaidens, whose names
                   Are five sweet symphonies,
               Cecily, Gertrude, Magdalen,
                   Margaret and Rosalys.'   *Ibid.*

3426.   Look in my face : my name is Might-have-been ;
           I am also called No-more, Too-late, Farewell.
                  The House of Life. A Superscription.

3427.   Was it a friend or foe that spread these lies ?
           Nay, who but infants question in such wise ?
           'Twas one of my most intimate enemies.   *Fragment.*

ROUGET DE LISLE, CLAUDE JOSEPH, French author, 10 May, 1760—
    26 June, 1836

3428. Allons, enfants de la patrie,
        Le jour de gloire est arrivé.
        —Come, children of our country, the day of glory has arrived.
                                The Marseillaise.

ROUSSEAU, JEAN JACQUES, French author, 28 June, 1712—2 July, 1778

3429. L'homme est né libre, et partout il est dans les fers.—Man is born free, and everywhere he is in fetters. *Du contrat social*, i.

ROUTH, MARTIN JOSEPH, President of Magdalen College, Oxford, 18 Sept. 1755—22 Dec. 1854

3430. Always verify your references. *Attributed.*

ROWE, NICHOLAS, Poet Laureate, baptised 30 June, 1674, died 6 Dec. 1718

3431. At length the morn and cold indifference came.
The Fair Penitent, i. i.

3432. Is this that haughty, gallant, gay Lothario ? Ibid., v. i.

RUSKIN, JOHN, art critic and author, 8 Feb. 1819—20 Jan. 1900

3433. It is far more difficult to be simple than to be complicated, far more difficult to sacrifice skill and cease exertion in the proper place, than to expend both indiscriminately.
Modern Painters, I. i. iii. 5.

3434. To see clearly is poetry, prophecy, and religion, all in one.
Ibid., III. iv. xvi. 28.

3435. All travelling becomes dull in exact proportion to its rapidity.
Ibid., xvii. 24.

3436. Mountains are the beginning and the end of all natural scenery. Ibid., IV. v. xx. i.

3437. The purest and most thoughtful minds are those which love colour the most. *The Stones of Venice*, II. v. 30.

3438. There is no wealth but life. *Unto this Last*, 77.

3439. Life being very short, and the quiet hours of it few, we ought to waste none of them in reading valueless books.
Sesame and Lilies, preface.

3440. Engraving, then, is, in brief terms, the Art of Scratch.
Ariadne Florentina, lecture i.

3441. I have seen, and heard, much of Cockney impudence before now ; but never expected to hear a coxcomb ask two hundred guineas for flinging a pot of paint in the public's face. [On Whistler's ' Nocturne in Black and Gold.'] *Fors Clavigera*, letter lxxix.

3442. Trust thou thy Love : if she be proud, is she not sweet ?
Trust thou thy Love : if she be mute, is she not pure ?
Lay thou thy soul full in her hands, low at her feet ;
Fail, Sun and Breath !—yet, for thy peace, she shall endure.
Trust Thou Thy Love.

RUSSELL, GEORGE WILLIAM, *see* Æ

RUSSELL, JOHN RUSSELL, 1ST EARL, Prime Minister, 18 Aug. 1792—
    28 May, 1878

3443. Among the defects of the Bill, which were numerous, one
provision was conspicuous by its presence and another by its absence.
                        Address to his constituents, 7 April, 1859.

3444. One man's wit, and all men's wisdom.
                        Definition of a proverb.
[Sometimes quoted as ' The wisdom of many and the wit of one.']

RUTILIUS NAMATIANUS, CLAUDIUS, Roman poet, 5th century A.D.
3445. Urbem fecisti quod prius orbis erat.
    —Thou has made a city what was a world before. [Of Rome.]
                        De Reditu Suo—On his Return, i. 66.

RUTLAND, JOHN JAMES ROBERT MANNERS, 7TH DUKE OF, politician,
    13 Dec. 1818—4 Aug. 1906
3446.   Let wealth and commerce, laws and learning die,
             But leave us still our old nobility.
                        England's Trust, iii. 227.

SAKI (HECTOR HUGH MUNRO), author, 18 Dec. 1870—14 Nov. 1916

3447. The cook was a good cook, as cooks go ; and as cooks go she
went.   *Reginald. Reginald on Besetting Sins.*

3448. Waldo is one of those people who would be enormously
improved by death.   *Beasts and Super-Beasts. The Feast of Nemesis.*

SALLUST (GAIUS SALLUSTIUS CRISPUS), Roman historian, 86–35 B.C.

3449. Alieni appetens, sui profusus.—Coveting other men's wealth,
lavish of his own.   *Bellum Catilinae—The War of Catiline*, v.

3450. Idem velle atque idem nolle, ea demum firma amicitia est.—
To desire the same and to reject the same, that indeed is true friendship.
                        Ibid., xx.

SALVANDY, NARCISSE ACHILLE, COMTE DE, French statesman, 11 June,
    1795—15 Dec. 1856
3451. Nous dansons sur un volcan.—We are dancing on a volcano.
    *At a fete given by the Duke of Orleans to the King of Naples
        before the revolution in* 1830.

SANDBURG, CARL, U.S. poet, 6 Jan. 1878—22 July, 1967
3452   The fog comes
                            on little cat feet.   *Fog.*

SARGENT, EPES, U.S. author, 27 Sept. 1813—30 Dec. 1880
3453.   A life on the ocean wave,
                          A home on the rolling deep.   *Song.*

SASSOON, SIEGFRIED LORRAINE, author, 8 Sept. 1886—1 Sept. 1967
3454. Everyone suddenly burst out singing.   *Everyone Sang.*

SAVAGE, RICHARD, poet, 1697 ?—1 Aug. 1743

3455.   He lives to build, not boast, a generous race :
          No tenth transmitter of a foolish face.   *The Bastard*, 7.

SCHILLER, JOHANN CHRISTOPH FRIEDRICH VON, German author,
     10 Nov. 1759—9 May, 1805

  3456. Mit der Dummheit kämpfen Götter selbst vergebens.—With
stupidity the gods themselves struggle in vain.
          Die Jungfrau von Orleans—The Maid of Orleans, III. vi.

SCHNECKENBURGER, MAX, German song-writer, 17 Feb. 1819—3 May,
     1849

3457. Lieb' Vaterland, magst ruhig sein,
          Fest steht und treu die Wacht am Rhein !
          —Dear Fatherland, you may be secure ; firm and true stands
               the watch on the Rhine !
                    Die Wacht am Rhein—The Watch on the Rhine.

SCOTT, ALEXANDER, Scottish poet, 1525 ?—1584 ?

3458.   They would have all men bound and thrall
          To them, and they for to be free.   *Of Womankind*, 49.

SCOTT, ROBERT FALCON, Antarctic explorer, 6 June, 1868—March, 1912

  3459. We are in a desperate state, feet frozen, etc. No fuel and a
long way from food, but it would do your heart good to be in our tent,
to hear our songs and the cheery conversation.
                    Farewell letter to Sir J. M. Barrie.

SCOTT, SIR WALTER, BARONET, Scottish author, 15 Aug. 1771—
     21 Sept. 1832

3460.   The way was long, the wind was cold,
          The Minstrel was infirm and old ;
          His wither'd cheek, and tresses grey,
          Seem'd to have known a better day.
                    The Lay of the Last Minstrel, introduction, 1.

3461.   If thou would'st view fair Melrose aright,
          Go visit it by the pale moonlight.   Ibid., ii. 1.

3462.   In peace, Love tunes the shepherd's reed ;
          In war, he mounts the warrior's steed ;
          In halls, in gay attire is seen ;
          In hamlets, dances on the green.
          Love rules the court, the camp, the grove,
          And men below, and saints above :
          For love is heaven, and heaven is love.   Ibid., 10.

3463.   The meeting of these champions proud
          Seem'd like the bursting thundercloud.   Ibid., iii. 5.

3464.   Her blue eyes sought the west afar,
          For lovers love the western star.   Ibid., 24.

     *I

3465.	Call it not vain ; they do not err,
	　Who say, that when the Poet dies,
	Mute Nature mourns her worshipper,
	　And celebrates his obsequies.
	　　　　　　　　　　　　　　Ibid., **v**. 1.

3466.	True love's the gift which God has given
	To man alone beneath the heaven :
	　It is not fantasy's hot fire,
	　　Whose wishes, soon as granted, fly ;
	　It liveth not in fierce desire,
	　　With dead desire it doth not die ;
	It is the secret sympathy,
	The silver link, the silken tie,
	Which heart to heart, and mind to mind,
	In body and in soul can bind.
	　　　　　　　　　　　　　　Ibid., 13.

3467.	Breathes there the man, with soul so dead,
	Who never to himself hath said,
	　This is my own, my native land !
	Whose heart hath ne'er within him burn'd,
	As home his footsteps he hath turn'd,
	　From wandering on a foreign strand !
	If such there breathe, go, mark him well ;
	For him no Minstrel raptures swell ;
	High though his titles, proud his name,
	Boundless his wealth as wish can claim ;
	Despite those titles, power, and pelf,
	The wretch, concentred all in self,
	Living, shall forfeit fair renown,
	And, doubly dying, shall go down
	To the vile dust, from whence he sprung,
	Unwept, unhonour'd, and unsung.
	　　　　　　　　　　　　　　Ibid. vi. 1.

3468.	O Caledonia ! stern and wild,
	Meet nurse for a poetic child !
	Land of brown heath and shaggy wood,
	Land of the mountain and the flood,
	Land of my sires !
	　　　　　　　　　　　　　　Ibid., 2.

3469.	That day of wrath, that dreadful day,
	When heaven and earth shall pass away.
	　　　　　　　Ibid., 31. *Hymn for the Dead.*

3470.	His square-turn'd joints, and strength of limb,
	Show'd him no carpet knight so trim,
	But in close fight a champion grim,
	　In camps a leader sage.
	　　　　　　　　　　　　　Marmion, i. 5.

3471.	Just at the age 'twixt boy and youth,
	When thought is speech, and speech is truth.
	　　　　　　　　　　Ibid., ii. introduction.

3472.	In the lost battle,
	　Borne down by the flying,
	Where mingles war's rattle
	　With groans of the dying.
	　　　　　　　　　　　　　　Ibid., iii. 11.

3473. Such dusky grandeur cloth'd the height,
       Where the huge Castle holds its state,
           And all the steep slope down,
       Whose ridgy back heaves to the sky,
       Pil'd deep and massy, close and high,
           Mine own romantic town.   [Edinburgh.]   Ibid.. iv. 30.

3474. The gallant Frith the eye might note,
       Whose islands on its bosom float,
           Like emeralds chas'd in gold.   Ibid.

3475. Cried ' Where's the coward that would not dare
           To fight for such a land ! '   Ibid.

3476. O, young Lochinvar is come out of the west,
       Through all the wide Border his steed was the best.
                               Ibid., v. 12. *Lochinvar.*

3477. So faithful in love, and so dauntless in war,
       There never was knight like the young Lochinvar.   Ibid.

3478. He staid not for brake, and he stopp'd not for stone,
       He swam the Eske river where ford there was none.   Ibid.

3479. For a laggard in love, and a dastard in war,
       Was to wed the fair Ellen of brave Lochinvar.   Ibid.

3480. With a smile on her lips, and a tear in her eye.   Ibid.

3481. Fierce he broke forth. 'And dar'st thou then
       To beard the lion in his den,
           The Douglas in his hall ? '   Ibid., vi. 14.

3482. O what a tangled web we weave,
       When first we practise to deceive.   Ibid., 17.

3483. O Woman ! in our hours of ease,
       Uncertain, coy, and hard to please,
       And variable as the shade
       By the light quivering aspen made ;
       When pain and anguish wring the brow
       A ministering angel thou !   Ibid., 30.

3484. ' Charge, Chester, charge ! On, Stanley, on ! '
       Were the last words of Marmion.   Ibid.. 32.

3485. O, for a blast of that dread horn,
       On Fontarabian echoes borne.   Ibid., 33.
       [*Rob Roy*, ii. has ' O for the voice of that wild horn.']

3486. The stubborn spear-men still made good
       Their dark impenetrable wood,
       Each stepping where his comrade stood,
           The instant that he fell.   Ibid., 34.

3487. The stag at eve had drunk his fill,
       Where danced the moon on Monan's rill.
                           The Lady of the Lake, i. 1.

3488. Woe worth the chase, woe worth the day,
       That costs thy life, my gallant grey !   Ibid., 9.

3489. In listening mood, she seem'd to stand,
       The guardian Naiad of the strand.   Ibid., 17.

3490. And ne'er did Grecian chisel trace
       A Nymph, a Naiad, or a Grace
       Of finer form, or lovelier face !
                                          Ibid., 18.

3491. A foot more light, a step more true,
       Ne'er from the heath-flower dash'd the dew ;
       E'en the slight harebell raised its head,
       Elastic from her airy tread.   *Ibid.*

3492. On his bold visage middle age
       Had slightly press'd its signet sage,
       Yet had not quench'd the open truth
       And fiery vehemence of youth ;
       Forward and frolic glee was there,
       The will to do, the soul to dare.   *Ibid.* 21.

3493. Soldier, rest ! thy warfare o'er,
       Dream of fighting fields no more :
       Sleep the sleep that knows not breaking,
       Morn of toil, nor night of waking.   *Ibid.* 31.

3494. Hail to the Chief who in triumph advances !
                           Ibid., ii. 19. *Boat Song.*

3495. Speed, Malise, speed ! the dun deer's hide
       On fleeter foot was never tied.   *Ibid.*, iii. 13.

3496. Like the dew on the mountain,
          Like the foam on the river,
       Like the bubble on the fountain,
          Thou art gone, and for ever !   *Ibid.*, 16. *Coronach.*

3497. These are Clan-Alpine's warriors true ;
       And, Saxon,—I am Roderick Dhu !   *Ibid.*, v. 9.

3498. Come one, come all ! this rock shall fly
       From its firm base as soon as I.   *Ibid.* 10.

3499. And the stern joy which warriors feel
       In foemen worthy of their steel.   *Ibid.*

3500. O, Brignal banks are wild and fair,
          And Greta woods are green,
       And you may gather garlands there
          Would grace a summer queen.   *Rokeby*, iii. 16.

3501. A weary lot is thine, fair maid.   *Ibid.*, 28.

3502. O ! many a shaft, at random sent,
       Finds mark the archer little meant !
       And many a word, at random spoken,
       May soothe or wound a heart that's broken !
                           The Lord of the Isles, v. 18.

3503. But answer came there none.
                           The Bridal of Triermain, iii. 10.

3504. O hush thee, my babie, thy sire was a knight,
       Thy mother a lady, both lovely and bright.
                           Lullaby of an Infant Chief.

3505.   Come as the winds come, when
              Forests are rended,
            Come as the waves come, when
              Navies are stranded.   *Pibroch of Donuil Dhu.*

3506.   Twist ye, twine ye ! even so
          Mingle human bliss and woe.
                    Guy Mannering, iii. *The Spindle Song.*

3507.   Come fill up my cup, come fill up my can,
          Come saddle my horses, and call up my man ;
          Come open your gates, and let me gae free,
          I daurna stay langer in bonny Dundee.   *Rob Roy*, xxiii.
     [Slightly different version in *The Doom of Devorgoil*, II. i.]

3508.   Proud Maisie is in the wood,
                  Walking so early ;
               Sweet Robin sits on the bush,
                  Singing so rarely.   *The Heart of Midlothian*, xl.

3509.   Look not thou on beauty's charming,
          Sit thou still when kings are arming,
          Taste not when the wine-cup glistens,
          Speak not when the people listens,
          Stop thine ear against the singer,
          From the red gold keep thy finger ;
          Vacant heart and hand and eye,
          Easy live and quiet die.   *The Bride of Lammermoor*, ii.

3510.   When Israel, of the Lord beloved,
               Out of the land of bondage came,
          Her fathers' God before her moved,
               An awful guide in smoke and flame.
                    Ivanhoe, xxxix. *Rebecca's Hymn.*

3511.   March, march, Ettrick and Teviotdale,
               Why the deil dinna ye march forward in order ?
          March, march, Eskdale and Liddesdale,
               All the Blue Bonnets are bound for the Border.
                    The Monastery, xxv. *Border March.*

3512.   The lark, his lay who thrill'd all day,
               Sits hush'd his partner nigh ;
          Breeze, bird, and flower confess the hour,
               But where is County Guy ?   *Quentin Durward*, iv.

3513.   Come weal, come woe, we'll gather and go,
               And live or die with Charlie.   *Redgauntlet*, xi.

3514.   ' Pro-di-gi-ous ! ' exclaimed Dominie Samson.
                    Guy Mannering, xiv.

3515.   Among the sea of upturned faces.   *Rob Roy*, xx.

3516. My foot is on my native heath, and my name is MacGregor !
                    Ibid., xxxiv.

3517. Jock, when ye hae naething else to do, ye may be aye sticking
     in a tree ; it will be growing, Jock, when ye're sleeping.
                    The Heart of Midlothian, viii.

3518. It's ill speaking between a fou man and a fasting.
                    Redgauntlet letter xi. *Wandering Willie's Tale.*

3519. [Miss Austen] had a talent for describing the involvements and feelings and characters of ordinary life which is to me the most wonderful I ever met with.   The Big Bow-Wow strain I can do myself like any now going ; but the exquisite touch which renders ordinary commonplace things and characters interesting, from the truth of the description and the sentiment, is denied to me.

Journal, 14 March, 1826.

SCOTT, WILLIAM, BARON STOWELL, lawyer, 17 Oct. 1745—28 Jan. 1836
   3520. A dinner lubricates business.

Boswell's *Life of Johnson* (1835 edition), an. 1781.

   3521. The elegant simplicity of the three per cents.

Campbell's *Lives of the Lord Chancellors*, **x.** ccxii.

SEAFIELD, EARL OF, *see* Ogilvy

SEARS, EDMUND HAMILTON, U.S. clergyman, 6 April, 1810—16 Jan. 1876
3522.   It came upon the midnight clear,
                  That glorious song of old.   *The Angels' Song.*

SEDLEY, SIR CHARLES, dramatist, 1639 ?—20 Aug. 1701
3523.   When change itself can give no more,
              'Tis easy to be true.   *Reasons for Constancy.*
3524.   Love still has something of the sea
              From whence his mother rose.
                     Love still has something of the Sea.
3525.   Phyllis is my only joy,
              Faithless as the winds or seas,
              Sometimes cunning, sometimes coy,
              Yet she never fails to please.   *Phyllis.*

SEEGER, ALAN, soldier and poet, 22 June, 1888—4 July, 1916
3526.   I have a rendezvous with Death
              At some disputed barricade.
                   I have a Rendezvous with Death.

SELDEN, JOHN, jurist, 16 Dec. 1584—30 Nov. 1654
   3527. Old friends are best.   King James used to call for his old shoes ; they were easiest for his feet.   *Table Talk. Friends.*

   3528. Commonly we say a judgment falls upon a man for something in him we cannot abide.   Ibid., *Judgments.*

   3529. Ignorance of the law excuses no man ; not that all men know the law, but because 'tis an excuse every man will plead, and no man can tell how to refute him.   Ibid., *Law.*

   3530. Pleasures are all alike, simply considered in themselves. He that takes pleasure to hear sermons enjoys himself as much as he that hears plays.   Ibid. *Pleasure.*

   3531. A King is a thing men have made for their own sakes, for quietness' sake. Just as in a family one man is appointed to buy the meat.   Ibid. *Of a King.*

SEWARD, THOMAS, clergyman, 1708—4 March, 1790

3532.   Seven wealthy towns contend for Homer dead,
          Through which the living Homer begg'd his bread.

Attributed.

SEWARD, WILLIAM HENRY, U.S. statesman, 16 May, 1801—10 Oct.
          1872

   3533. There is a higher law than the Constitution.

Speech in U.S. Senate, 11 March, 1850.

SHADWELL, THOMAS, Poet Laureate, 1642 ?—19 Nov. 1692
   3534. I'll do't instantly, in the twinkling of a bed-staff.

The Virtuoso, I. i.

SHAFTESBURY, ANTHONY ASHLEY COOPER, 3RD EARL OF, philosopher,
          26 Feb. 1671—4 Feb. 1713

   3535. 'Twas the saying of an ancient sage, that humour was the only
test of gravity ; and gravity, of humour. For a subject which would
not bear raillery was suspicious ; and a jest which would not bear a
serious examination was certainly false wit.

Characteristicks. Essay on the Freedom of Wit and Humour, 5.
   [The sage was Gorgias, in Aristotle, *Rhetoric*, III. xviii.]

SHAKESPEARE, WILLIAM, dramatist, baptised 26 April, 1564, died
          23 April, 1616

   [The text used in the following quotations is that of Clark and
Wright's *Cambridge Shakespeare* as reproduced in the Globe Edition
of 1911. The plays are arranged in what the latest authorities consider
to be the order of composition, and are followed by the poems. For
convenience of reference, an alphabetical index of the works is given
below.]

KING HENRY VI, PART I.

3536 Hung be the heavens with black, yield day to night !
King Henry VI, part I, I. i. 1.

3537. Unbidden guests
Are often welcomest when they are gone. Ibid., II. ii. 55.

3538. Between two hawks, which flies the higher pitch ;
Between two dogs, which hath the deeper mouth ;
Between two blades, which bears the better temper ;
Between two horses, which doth bear him best ;
Between two girls, which hath the merriest eye ;
I have perhaps some shallow spirit of judgment ;
But in these nice sharp quillets of the law,
Good faith, I am no wiser than a daw. Ibid., iv. II.

3539. She's beautiful and therefore to be woo'd ;
She is a woman, therefore to be won. Ibid., v. iii. 78.

KING HENRY VI, PART II.

3540. Could I come near your beauty with my nails,
I'd set my ten commandments in your face.
King Henry VI, part II. I. iii. 144.

3541. Smooth runs the water where the brook is deep. Ibid., III. i. 53.

3542. What stronger breastplate than a heart untainted ?
Thrice is he arm'd that hath his quarrel just,
And he but naked, though lock'd up in steel,
Whose conscience with injustice is corrupted. Ibid., ii. 232.

3543. The gaudy, blabbing and remorseful day
Is crept into the bosom of the sea. Ibid., IV. i. I.

3544. There shall be in England seven halfpenny loaves sold for a penny : the three-hooped pot shall have ten hoops ; and I will make it a felony to drink small beer. Ibid., ii. 71.

3545. Is not this a lamentable thing, that the skin of an innocent lamb should be made parchment ? that parchment, being scribbled o'er, should undo a man ? Ibid., 84.

3546. Sir, he made a chimney in my father's house, and the bricks are alive at this day to testify it. Ibid., 156.

3547. Thou hast most traitorously corrupted the youth of the realm in erecting a grammar school ; and whereas, before, our forefathers had no other books but the score and tally, thou hast caused printing to be used, and, contrary to the king, his crown and dignity, thou hast built a paper-mill. Ibid., vii. 35.

3548. Away with him, away with him ! he speaks Latin. Ibid., 62.

KING HENRY VI., PART III.

3549. O tiger's heart wrapt in a woman's hide !
King Henry VI, part III. I. iv. 137.

3550. Didst thou never hear
That things ill got had ever bad success ?
And happy always was it for that son
Whose father for his hoarding went to hell ? Ibid., II, ii. 45.

KING HENRY VI, PART III.

3551. O God ! methinks it were a happy life,
To be no better than a homely swain ;
To sit upon a hill, as I do now,
To carve out dials quaintly, point by point,
Thereby to see the minutes how they run,
How many make the hour full complete ;
How many hours bring about the day ;
How many days will finish up the year ;
How many years a mortal man may live.   Ibid., v. 21.

3552. Gives not the hawthorn-bush a sweeter shade
To shepherds looking on their silly sheep,
Than doth a rich embroider'd canopy
To kings that fear their subjects' treachery ?   Ibid., 42.

3553. My crown is in my heart, not on my head ;
Not deck'd with diamonds and Indian stones,
Nor to be seen : my crown is called content.   Ibid., III. i. 62.

3554. A little fire is quickly trodden out ;
Which, being suffer'd, rivers cannot quench.   Ibid., IV. viii. 7.

3555. Suspicion always haunts the guilty mind ;
The thief doth fear each bush an officer.   Ibid., v. vi. 11.

3556. Down, down to hell ; and say I sent thee thither.   Ibid., 67.

KING RICHARD III.

3557. Now is the winter of our discontent
Made glorious summer by the sun of York.
                    King Richard III, I. i. 1.

3558. Our stern alarums changed to merry meetings,
Our dreadful marches to delightful measures.
Grim-visaged war hath smooth'd his wrinkled front.   Ibid., 7.

3559. I, that am curtail'd of this fair proportion,
Cheated of feature by dissembling nature,
Deform'd, unfinish'd, sent before my time
Into this breathing world, scarce half made up,
And that so lamely and unfashionable
That dogs bark at me as I halt by them.   Ibid., 18.

3560. In this weak piping time of peace.   Ibid., 24.

3561. I am determined to prove a villain.   Ibid., 30.

3562. Was ever woman in this humour woo'd ?
Was ever woman in this humour won ?   Ibid., ii. 228.

3563. And thus I clothe my naked villainy
With old odd ends stolen out of holy writ ;
And seem a saint, when most I play the devil.   Ibid., iii. 336.

3564. O, I have pass'd a miserable night,
So full of ugly sights, of ghastly dreams,
That, as I am a Christian faithful man,
I would not spend another such a night,
Though 'twere to buy a world of happy days,
So full of dismal terror was the time !   Ibid., iv. 2.

KING RICHARD III.

3565. Lord, Lord ! methought,what pain it was to drown !
What dreadful noise of waters in mine ears !
What ugly sights of death within mine eyes !
Methought I saw a thousand fearful wrecks ;
Ten thousand men that fishes gnaw'd upon ;
Wedges of gold, great anchors, heaps of pearl,
Inestimable stones, unvalued jewels,
All scatter'd in the bottom of the sea :
Some lay in dead men's skulls ; and, in those holes
Where eyes did once inhabit, there were crept,
As 'twere in scorn of eyes, reflecting gems,
Which woo'd the slimy bottom of the deep,
And mock'd the dead bones that lay scatter'd by.   Ibid., 21.

3566. So wise so young, they say, do never live long.   Ibid., III. i. 79.

3567. High-reaching Buckingham grows circumspect.   Ibid., IV. ii. 31.

3568. Their lips were four red roses on a stalk,
Which in their summer beauty kiss'd each other.   Ibid., iii. 12.

3569. The sons of Edward sleep in Abraham's bosom.   Ibid., 38.

3570. An honest tale speeds best being plainly told.   Ibid., iv. 358.

3571. Harp not on that string.   Ibid., 364.

3572. True hope is swift, and flies with swallow's wings ;
Kings it makes gods, and meaner creatures kings.
                                                    Ibid., v. ii. 23.

3573. The king's name is a tower of strength.   Ibid., iii. 12.

3574. O coward conscience, how dost thou afflict me !   Ibid., 179.

3575. My conscience hath a thousand several tongues,
And every tongue brings in a several tale,
And every tale condemns me for a villain.   Ibid., 193.

3576. A horse ! a horse ! my kingdom for a horse !   Ibid., iv. 7 and 13.

3577. Slave, I have set my life upon a cast,
And I will stand the hazard of the die :
I think there be six Richmonds in the field.   Ibid., 9.

THE COMEDY OF ERRORS

3578. The pleasing punishment that women bear.
                        The Comedy of Errors, I. i. 47.

3579. A wretched soul, bruised with adversity.   Ibid., II. i. 34.

3580. They brought one Pinch, a hungry lean-faced villain,
A mere anatomy, a mountebank,
A threadbare juggler and a fortune-teller,
A needy, hollow-eyed, sharp-looking wretch,
A living-dead man.   Ibid., v. i. 237.

TITUS ANDRONICUS

3581. Sweet mercy is nobility's true badge
                        Titus Andronicus, I. i. 119.

3582. She is a woman, therefore may be woo'd;
She is a woman, therefore may be won;
She is Lavinia, therefore must be loved.
What, man ! more water glideth by the mill
Than wots the miller of ; and easy it is
Of a cut loaf to steal a shive, we know.   *Ibid.*, II. i. 82.

3583. Come, and take choice of all my library,
And so beguile thy sorrow.   *Ibid.*, IV. i. 34.

3584. The eagle suffers little birds to sing,
And is not careful what they mean thereby.   *Ibid.*, iv. 83.

3585. If one good deed in all my life I did,
I do repent it from my very soul.   *Ibid.*, V. iii. 189.

THE TAMING OF THE SHREW

3586. As Stephen Sly and old John Naps of Greece
And Peter Turph and Henry Pimpernell
And twenty more such names and men as these
Which never were nor no man ever saw.
The Taming of the Shrew, induction, ii. 95.

3587. No profit grows where is no pleasure ta'en :
In brief, sir, study what you most affect.   *Ibid.*, I. i. 39.

3588. 'Tis a very excellent piece of work, madam lady : would 'twere
done !   *Ibid.*, 258.

3589. I must dance bare-foot on her wedding day
And for your love to her lead apes in hell.   *Ibid.*, ii. 33.

3590. This is the way to kill a wife with kindness.   *Ibid.*, IV. i. 211.

3591. And as the sun breaks through the darkest clouds,
So honour peereth in the meanest habit.   *Ibid.*, iii. 175.

3592. A woman moved is like a fountain troubled,
Muddy, ill-seeming, thick, bereft of beauty.   *Ibid.*, V. ii. 142.

3593. Such duty as the subject owes the prince
Even such a woman oweth to her husband.   *Ibid.*, 155.

THE TWO GENTLEMEN OF VERONA

3594. Home-keeping youth have ever homely wits.
The Two Gentlemen of Verona, I. i. 2.

3595. I have no other but a woman's reason ;
I think him so because I think him so.   *Ibid.*, ii. 23.

3596. Put forth their sons to seek preferment out :
Some to the wars, to try their fortune there ;
Some to discover islands far away ;
Some to the studious universities.   *Ibid.*, iii. 6.

3597. O, how this spring of love resembleth
The uncertain glory of an April day !   *Ibid.*, 84.

3598. He makes sweet music with the enamell'd stones,
Giving a gentle kiss to every sedge
He overtaketh in his pilgrimage.   *Ibid.*, II. vii. 28.

THE TWO GENTLEMEN OF VERONA

3599. Except I be by Sylvia in the night,
There is no music in the nightingale. *Ibid.*, III. i. 178.

3600. A man I am cross'd with adversity. *Ibid.*, IV. i. 12.

3601. Who is Sylvia ? what is she,
That all our swains commend her ? *Ibid.*, ii. 39.

3602. Is she kind as she is fair ?
For beauty lives with kindness. *Ibid.*, 44.

3603. How use doth breed a habit in a man. *Ibid.*, V. iv. 1.

3604. O heaven ! were man
But constant, he were perfect. *Ibid.*, 110.

LOVE'S LABOUR'S LOST

3605. Spite of cormorant devouring Time.
Love's Labour's Lost, I. i. 4.

3606. Why, all delights are vain ; but that most vain,
Which with pain purchased doth inherit pain. *Ibid.*, 72.

3607. Light seeking light doth light of light beguile. *Ibid.*, 77.

3608. Study is like the heaven's glorious sun
That will not be deep-search'd with saucy looks :
Small have continual plodders ever won
Save base authority from others' books. *Ibid.*, 84.

3609. At Christmas I no more desire a rose
Than wish a snow in May's new-fangled mirth. *Ibid.*, 105.

3610. Devise, wit ; write, pen ; for I am for whole volumes in folio.
Ibid., ii. 192

3611. Remuneration ! O, that's the Latin word for three farthings.
Ibid., III. i. 140.

3612. A very beadle to a humorous sigh. *Ibid.*, 177.

3613. This wimpled, whining, purblind, wayward boy ;
This senior-junior, giant-dwarf, Dan Cupid ;
Regent of love-rhymes. lord of folded arms,
The anointed sovereign of sighs and groans.
Liege of all loiterers and malcontents. *Ibid.*, 181.

3614. He hath never fed of the dainties that are bred in a book ;
he hath not eat paper, as it were ; he hath not drunk ink.
Ibid., IV. ii. 25.

3615. A lover's eyes will gaze an eagle blind ;
A lover's ear will hear the lowest sound,
When the suspicious head of theft is stopp'd :
Love's feeling is more soft and sensible
Than are the tender horns of cockled snails ;
Love's tongue proves dainty Bacchus gross in taste :
For valour, is not Love a Hercules,
Still climbing trees in the Hesperides ?
Subtle as Sphinx ; as sweet and musical
As bright Apollo's lute, strung with his hair ;
And when Love speaks, the voice of all the gods
Make heaven drowsy with the harmony. *Ibid.*, iii. 334.

3616. From women's eyes this doctrine I derive :
     They sparkle still the right Promethean fire ;
     They are the books, the arts, the academes,
     That show, contain, and nourish all the world.   Ibid., 350.

3617. He draweth out the thread of his verbosity finer than the
staple of his argument.   Ibid., v. i. 18.

3618. Priscian a little scratched, 'twill serve.   Ibid., 31.

3619. They have been at a great feast of languages, and stolen the
scraps.   Ibid., 39.

3620. In the posteriors of this day, which the rude multitude call
the afternoon.   Ibid., 94.

3621. In russet yeas and honest kersey noes.   Ibid., ii. 413.

3622.   A jest's prosperity lies in the ear
     Of him that hears it, never in the tongue
     Of him that makes it.   Ibid., 871.

3623.   When daisies pied and violets blue
       And lady-smocks all silver-white
     And cuckoo-buds of yellow hue
       Do paint the meadows with delight,
     The cuckoo then, on every tree,
     Mocks married men ; for thus sings he,
          Cuckoo ;
     Cuckoo, cuckoo : O word of fear,
     Unpleasing to a married ear.   Ibid., 904.

3624. The words of Mercury are harsh after the songs of Apollo.
    Ibid., 940.

3625 A pair of star-cross'd lovers.   *Romeo and Juliet*, prologue, 6.

3626. I do not bite my thumb at you, sir, but I bite my thumb, sir.
    Ibid., I. i. 57.

3627. Gregory, remember thy swashing blow.   Ibid., 69.

3628.   An hour before the worshipp'd sun
     Peer'd forth the golden window of the east.   Ibid., 125.

3629. Saint-seducing gold.   Ibid., 220.

3630. When well apparell'd April on the heel
     Of limping winter treads.   Ibid., ii. 27.

3631.   One fire burns out another's burning,
     One pain is lessen'd by another's anguish.   Ibid., 46.

3632. Thou wilt fall backward when thou comest to age. Ibid., iii. 56.

3633. That book in many's eyes doth share the glory,
     That in gold clasps locks in the golden story.   Ibid., 91.

3634. For I am proverb'd with a grandsire phrase.   Ibid., iv. 37.

3635. O, then, I see Queen Mab hath been with you.
　　　She is the fairies' midwife, and she comes
　　　In shape no bigger than an agate-stone
　　　On the fore-finger of an alderman,
　　　Drawn with a team of little atomies
　　　Athwart men's noses as they lie asleep ;
　　　Her waggon-spokes made of long spinners' legs,
　　　The cover of the wings of grasshoppers,
　　　The traces of the smallest spider's web,
　　　The collars of the moonshine's watery beams,
　　　Her whip of cricket's bone, the lash of film,
　　　Her waggoner a small grey-coated gnat,
　　　Not half so big as a round little worm
　　　Prick'd from the lazy finger of a maid ;
　　　Her chariot is an empty hazel-nut
　　　Made by the joiner squirrel or old grub,
　　　Time out o' mind the fairies' coachmakers.
　　　And in this state she gallops night by night
　　　Through lovers' brains, and then they dream of love ;
　　　O'er courtiers' knees, that dream of court'sies straight,
　　　O'er lawyers' fingers, who straight dream on fees,
　　　O'er ladies' lips, who straight on kisses dream.　　　Ibid., 53.

3636. 　　　　　　　True, I talk of dreams,
　　　Which are but children of an idle brain,
　　　Begot of nothing but vain fantasy.　　　Ibid., 96.

3637. For you and I are past our dancing days.　　　Ibid., v. 33.

3638. O, she doth teach the torches to burn bright !
　　　It seems she hangs upon the cheek of night
　　　Like a rich jewel in an Ethiope's ear ;
　　　Beauty too rich for use, for earth too dear !　　　Ibid., 46.

3639. We have a trifling foolish banquet towards.　　　Ibid., 124.

3640. Young Adam Cupid, he that shot so trim,
　　　When King Cophetua loved the beggar-maid.　　　Ibid., ii. i. 13.

3641. He jests at scars that never felt a wound.　　　Ibid., ii. 1.

3642. See, how she leans her cheek upon her hand !
　　　O, that I were a glove upon that hand,
　　　That I might touch that cheek !　　　Ibid., 23.

3643. O Romeo, Romeo ! wherefore art thou Romeo ?　　　Ibid., 33.

3644. What's in a name ? that which we call a rose
　　　By any other name would smell as sweet.　　　Ibid., 43.

3645. 　　　　　　At lovers' perjuries,
　　　They say, Jove laughs.　　　Ibid., 92

3646. But trust me, gentlemen, I'll prove more true
　　　Than those that have more cunning to be strange.　　　Ibid., 100.

3647. *Romeo.* Lady, by yonder blessed moon I swear
　　　　　That tips with silver all these fruit-tree tops—
　　　Juliet. O, swear not by the moon, the inconstant moon,
　　　　　That monthly changes in her circled orb,
　　　　　Lest that thy love prove likewise variable.　　　Ibid., 107.

ROMEO AND JULIET

3648. The God of my idolatry. Ibid., 114.

3649. It is too rash, too unadvised, too sudden ;
Too like the lightning, which doth cease to be
Ere one can say ' It lightens.' Ibid., 118.

3650. Love goes toward love, as schoolboys from their books,
But love from love, toward school with heavy looks.
Ibid., 156.

3651. How silver-sweet sound lovers' tongues by night,
Like softest music to attending ears ! Ibid., 166.

3652. Good night, good night ! parting is such sweet sorrow,
That I shall say good night till it be morrow. Ibid., 185.

3653. For nought so vile that on the earth doth live
But to the earth some special good doth give,
Nor aught so good but strain'd from that fair use
Revolts from true birth, stumbling on abuse :
Virtue itself turns vice, being misapplied ;
And vice sometimes by action dignified. Ibid., iii. 17.

3654. Care keeps his watch in every old man's eye,
And where care lodges, sleep will never lie. Ibid., 35.

3655. O flesh, flesh, how art thou fishified ! Ibid., iv. 39.

3656. I am the very pink of courtesy. Ibid., 61.

3657. These violent delights have violent ends. Ibid., vi. 9.

3658. Too swift arrives as tardy as too slow. Ibid., 15.

3659. Here comes the lady : O, so light a foot
Will ne'er wear out the everlasting flint. Ibid., 16.

3660. A word and a blow. Ibid., III. i. 43.

3661. A plague o' both your houses. Ibid., 94 and 103.

3662. No, 'tis not so deep as a well, nor so wide as a church-door ;
but 'tis enough, 'twill serve. Ibid., 99.

3663. Gallop apace, you fiery-footed steeds,
Towards Phoebus' lodging : such a waggoner
As Phaethon would whip you to the west,
And bring in cloudy night immediately.
Spread thy close curtain, love-performing night,
That runaways' eyes may wink, and Romeo
Leap to these arms, untalk'd of and unseen. Ibid., ii. 1.

3664. Give me my Romeo ; and, when he shall die,
Take him and cut him out in little stars,
And he will make the face of heaven so fine
That all the world will be in love with night
And pay no worship to the garish sun. Ibid., 21.

3665. Adversity's sweet milk, philosophy. Ibid., iii. 55.

3666. Night's candles are burnt out, and jocund day
Stands tiptoe on the misty mountain tops. Ibid., v. 9.

3667. Villain and he be many miles asunder. Ibid., 82.

3668. A beggarly account of empty boxes. Ibid., v. i. 45.

3669. My poverty, but not my will, consents.   Ibid., 75.

3670.   Beauty's ensign yet
Is crimson in thy lips and in thy cheeks,
And death's pale flag is not advanced there.   Ibid., iii. 94.

3671.   Eyes, look your last !
Arms, take your last embrace !   Ibid., 112.

3672. Old John of Gaunt, time-honour'd Lancaster.
                King Richard II., I. i. 1.

3673. A jewel in a ten-times-barr'd-up chest
Is a bold spirit in a loyal breast.
Mine honour is my life ; both grow in one ;
Take honour from me, and my life is done.   Ibid., 180.

3674. We were not born to sue, but to command.   Ibid., 196.

3675. That which in mean men we intitle patience
Is pale cold cowardice in noble breasts.   Ibid., ii. 33.

3676. The daintiest last, to make the end most sweet.   Ibid., iii. 68.

3677. Truth hath a quiet breast.   Ibid., 96.

3678.   This must my comfort be,
The sun that warms you here shall shine on me.   Ibid., 144.

3679. How long a time lies in one little word !   Ibid., 213.

3680. Things sweet to taste prove in digestion sour.   Ibid., 236.

3681. All places that the eye of heaven visits
Are to the wise man ports and happy havens.   Ibid., 275.

3682. O, who can hold a fire in his hand
By thinking on the frosty Caucasus ?
Or cloy the hungry edge of appetite
By bare imagination of a feast ?
Or wallow naked in December snow
By thinking on fantastic summer's heat ?
O, no ! the apprehension of the good
Gives but a greater feeling to the worse.   Ibid., 294.

3683. Methinks I am a prophet new inspired
And thus expiring do foretell of him :
His rash fierce blaze of riot cannot last,
For violent fires soon burn out themselves ;
Small showers last long, but sudden storms are short ;
He tires betimes that spurs too fast betimes.   Ibid., II. i. 31.

3684. This royal throne of kings, this scepter'd isle,
This earth of majesty, this seat of Mars,
This other Eden, demi-paradise,
This fortress built by Nature for herself
Against infection and the hand of war,
This happy breed of men, this little world,
This precious stone set in the silver sea,
Which serves it in the office of a wall
Or as a moat defensive to a house,
Against the envy of less happier lands,
This blessed plot, this earth, this realm, this England. Ibid., 40.

3685. England, bound in with the triumphant sea,
Whose rocky shore beats back the envious siege
Of watery Neptune, is now bound in with shame,
With inky blots and rotten parchment bonds :
That England, that was wont to conquer others,
Hath made a shameful conquest of itself.   Ibid., 61.

3686. Can sick men play so nicely with their names ?   Ibid., 84.

3687. I am a stranger here in Gloucestershire :
These high wild hills and rough uneven ways
Draws out our miles and makes them wearisome.   Ibid., iii. 3.

3688. I count myself in nothing else so happy
As in a soul remembering my good friends.   Ibid., 46.

3689. Evermore thanks, the exchequer of the poor.   Ibid., 65.

3690. Things past redress are now with me past care.   Ibid., 171.

3691. Eating the bitter bread of banishment.   Ibid., III. i. 21.

3692. Not all the water in the rude rough sea
Can wash the balm from an anointed king.   Ibid., ii. 54.

3693. O, call back yesterday, bid time return.   Ibid., 69.

3694.   Of comfort no man speak :
Let's talk of graves, of worms and epitaphs ;
Make dust our paper and with rainy eyes
Write sorrow on the bosom of the earth,
Let's choose executors and talk of wills.   Ibid., 144.

3695. For God's sake let us sit upon the ground
And tell sad stories of the death of kings :
How some have been deposed ; some slain in war ;
Some haunted by the ghosts they have deposed ;
Some poison'd by their wives ; some sleeping kill'd ;
All murder'd : for within the hollow crown
That rounds the mortal temples of a king
Keeps Death his court and there the antic sits,
Scoffing his state and grinning at his pomp,
Allowing him a breath, a little scene,
To monarchize, be fear'd and kill with looks,
Infusing him with self and vain conceit,
As if this flesh which walls about our life
Were brass impregnable, and humour'd thus
Comes at the last and with a little pin
Bores through his castle wall, and farewell king !   Ibid., 155.

3696. What must the king do now ? must he submit ?
The king shall do it : must he be deposed ?
The king shall be contented : must he lose
The name of king ? o' God's name, let it go :
I'll give my jewels for a set of beads,
My gorgeous palace for a hermitage,
My gay apparel for an almsman's gown,
My figured goblets for a dish of wood,
My sceptre for a palmer's walking-staff,
My subjects for a pair of carved saints
And my large kingdom for a little grave,
A little little grave, an obscure grave.   Ibid., iii. 143.

3697. If I dare eat, or drink, or breathe, or live,
I dare meet Surrey in a wilderness,
And spit upon him, whilst I say he lies,
And lies, and lies. Ibid., IV. i. 73.

3698. And there at Venice gave
His body to that pleasant country's earth
And his pure soul unto his captain Christ,
Under whose colours he had fought so long. Ibid., 97.

3699. Peace shall go sleep with Turks and infidels. Ibid., 139.

3700. You may my glories and my state depose,
But not my griefs ; still am I king of those. Ibid., 192.

3701. I am sworn brother, sweet,
To grim Necessity, and he and I
Will keep a league till death. Ibid., V. i. 20.

3702. As in a theatre the eyes of men,
After a well-graced actor leaves the stage,
Are idly bent on him that enters next,
Thinking his prattle to be tedious. Ibid., ii. 23.

3703. How sour sweet music is,
When time is broke and no proportion kept !
So is it with the music of men's lives. Ibid., V. 42.

A MIDSUMMER NIGHT'S DREAM

3704. But earthlier happy is the rose distill'd,
Than that which withering on the virgin thorn
Grows, lives and dies in single blessedness.
A Midsummer Night's Dream, I. i. 76.

3705. For aught that I could ever read,
Could ever hear by tale or history,
The course of true love never did run smooth. Ibid., 132.

3706. O hell ! to choose love by another's eyes. Ibid., 140.

3707. Swift as a shadow, short as any dream ;
Brief as the lightning in the collied night,
That, in a spleen, unfolds both heaven and earth,
And ere a man hath power to say ' Behold ! '
The jaws of darkness do devour it up :
So quick bright things come to confusion. Ibid., 144.

3708. Love looks not with the eyes, but with the mind ;
And therefore is wing'd Cupid painted blind. Ibid., 234.

3709. Masters, spread yourselves. Ibid., ii. 16.

3710. A part to tear a cat in. Ibid., 31.

3711. This is Ercles' vein. Ibid., 42.

3712. I am slow of study. Ibid., 69.

3713. I will roar you as gently as any sucking dove ; I will roar you
as 'twere any nightingale. Ibid., 84.

3714. A proper man, as one shall see in a summer's day. Ibid., 88.

3715. Since once I sat upon a promontory,
       And heard a mermaid on a dolphin's back
       Uttering such dulcet and harmonious breath
       That the rude sea grew civil at her song
       And certain stars shot madly from their spheres,
       To hear the sea-maid's music.   Ibid., II. i. 149.

3716. And the imperial votaress passed on,
       In maiden meditation, fancy-free.
       Yet mark's I where the bolt of Cupid fell :
       It fell upon a little western flower,
       Before milk-white, now purple with love's wound,
       And maidens call it love-in-idleness.   Ibid., 163.

3717. I'll put a girdle round about the earth
       In forty minutes.   Ibid., 175.

3718. I know a bank where the wild thyme blows,
       Where oxlips and the nodding violet grows,
       Quite over-canopied with luscious woodbine,
       With sweet musk-roses and with eglantine. Ibid., 249.

3719. A lion among ladies, is a most dreadful thing ; for there is
not a more fearful wild-fowl than your lion living.   Ibid., III. i. 31.

3720. A calendar, a calendar ! look in the almanac ; find out
moonshine, find out moonshine.   Ibid., 54.

3721. What hempen homespuns have we swaggering here ?   Ibid., 79.

3722. Bless thee, Bottom ! bless thee ! thou are translated.
                                                  Ibid., 121.

3723. Lord, what fools these mortals be !   Ibid., ii. 115

3724.   So we grew together,
       Like to a double cherry, seeming parted,
       But yet an union in partition ;
       Two lovely berries moulded on one stem.   Ibid., 208.

3725. She was a vixen when she went to school ;
       And though she be but little, she is fierce.   Ibid., 324.

3726. I have a reasonable good ear in music. Let's have the tongs
and the bones.   Ibid., IV. i. 30.

3727. I have an exposition of sleep come upon me.   Ibid., 41.

3728. My hounds are bred out of the Spartan kind,
       So flew'd, so sanded, and their heads are hung
       With ears that sweep away the morning dew ;
       Crook-knee'd, and dew-lapp'd like Thessalian bulls ;
       Slow in pursuit, but match's in mouth like bells.   Ibid., 123.

3729. The lunatic, the lover and the poet
       Are of imagination all compact.   Ibid., v. i. 7.

3730.   The lover, all as frantic,
       Sees Helen's beauty in a brow of Egypt :
       The poet's eye, in a fine frenzy rolling,
       Doth glance from heaven to earth, from earth to heaven ;
       And as imagination bodies forth
       The forms of things unknown, the poet's pen
       Turns them to shapes and gives to airy nothing
       A local habitation and a name.   Ibid., 10.

A MIDSUMMER NIGHT'S DREAM

3731. Or in the night, imagining some fear,
How easy is a bush supposed a bear !   *Ibid.*, 21.

3732. Very tragical mirth.   *Ibid.*, 57.

3733. That is the true beginning of our end.   *Ibid.*, 111.

3734. Whereat, with blade, with bloody blameful blade,
He bravely broach'd his boiling bloody breast.   *Ibid.*, 147.

3735. The best in this kind are but shadows ; and the worst are
no worse, if imagination amend them.   *Ibid.*, 214.

3736. The iron tongue of midnight hath told twelve.   *Ibid.*, 370.

KING JOHN

3737. Lord of thy presence and no land beside.   *King John*, I. i. 137.

3738. For new-made honour doth forget men's names.   *Ibid.*, 187.

3739. For courage mounteth with occasion.   *Ibid.*, II. i. 82.

3740. Saint George, that swinged the dragon, and e'er since
Sits on his horse back at mine hostess' door.   *Ibid.*, 288.

3741. Zounds ! I was never so bethumped with words
Since first I call'd my brother's father dad.   *Ibid.*, 466.

3742.   Here I and sorrows sit ;
Here is my throne, bid kings come bow to it.   *Ibid.*, III. i. 73.

3743. Thou wear a lion's hide ! doff it for shame,
And hang a calf's-skin on those recreant limbs.   *Ibid.*, 128.

3744. Grief fills the room up of my absent child,
Lies in his bed, walks up and down with me,
Puts on his pretty looks, repeats his words,
Remembers me of all his gracious parts,
Stuffs out his vacant garments with his form.   *Ibid.*, iv. 93.

3745. Life is as tedious as a twice-told tale,
Vexing the dull ear of a drowsy man.   *Ibid.*, 108.

3746.   When Fortune means to men most good,
She looks upon them with a threatening eye.   *Ibid.*, 119.

3747. Heat me these irons hot.   *Ibid.*, IV. i. 1.

3748. To gild refined gold, to paint the lily,
To throw a perfume on the violet,
To smooth the ice, or add another hue
Unto the rainbow, or with taper-light
To seek the beauteous eye of heaven to garnish,
Is wasteful and ridiculous excess.   *Ibid.*, ii. 11.

3749. And oftentimes excusing of a fault
Doth make the fault the worse by the excuse.   *Ibid.*, 30.

3750. Another lean unwashed artificer.   *Ibid.*, 201.

3751. How oft the sight of means to do ill deeds
Makes deeds ill done !   *Ibid.*, 219.

3752. This England never did, nor never shall,
Lie at the proud foot of a conqueror,
But when it first did help to wound itself.   *Ibid.*, V. vii. 112.

3753. Come the three corners of the world in arms,
And we shall shock them.   Nought shall make us rue,
If England to itself do rest but true.   *Ibid.*, 116.

3754. Nature hath framed strange fellows in her time :
Some that will evermore peep through their eyes
And laugh like parrots at a bag-piper,
And other of such vinegar aspect
That they'll not show their teeth in way of smile,
Though Nestor swear the jest be laughable.
The Merchant of Venice, I. i. 51

3755. I hold the world but as the world, Gratiano ;
A stage where every man must play a part,
And mine a sad one.   Ibid., 77

3756. Why should a man, whose blood is warm within,
Sit like his grandsire cut in alabaster ?   Ibid., 83.

3757. There are a sort of men whose visages
Do cream and mantle like a standing pond.   Ibid., 88.

3758. As who should say ' I am Sir Oracle,
And when I ope my lips let no dog bark ! '   Ibid., 93.

3759. Gratiano speaks an infinite deal of nothing, more than any
man in all Venice. His reasons are as two grains of wheat hid in two
bushels of chaff : you shall seek all day ere you find them, and when you
have them, they are not worth the search.   Ibid., 114.

3760. In my school-days, when I had lost one shaft,
I shot his fellow of the self-same flight
The self-same way with more advised watch,
To find the other forth, and by adventuring both
I oft found both.   Ibid., 140.

3761. They are as sick that surfeit with too much as they that
starve with nothing.   Ibid., ii. 5.

3762. If to do were as easy as to know what were good to do,
chapels had been churches and poor men's cottages princes' palaces.
Ibid., 13.

3763. God made him, and therefore let him pass for a man.
Ibid., 60.

3764. I dote on his very absence.   Ibid., 119.

3765. Ships are but boards, sailors but men : there be land-rats and
water-rats, water-thieves and land-thieves.   Ibid., iii. 22.

3766. How like a fawning publican he looks !
I hate him for he is a Christian,
But more for that in low simplicity
He lends out money gratis and brings down
The rate of usance here with us in Venice.
If I can catch him once upon the hip,
I will feed fat the ancient grudge I bear him.   Ibid., 42.

3767. Even there where merchants most do congregate.   Ibid., 50.

3768. The devil can cite Scripture for his purpose.   Ibid., 99.

3769. A goodly apple rotten at the heart :
O, what a goodly outside falsehood hath !   Ibid., 102.

3770. Still have I borne it with a patient shrug,
For sufferance is the badge of all our tribe.   Ibid., 110.

THE MERCHANT OF VENICE

3771. You call me misbeliever, cut-throat dog,
And spit upon my Jewish gaberdine.   Ibid., 112.

3772. Shall I bend low and in a bondman's key,
With bated breath and whispering humbleness.   Ibid., 124.

3773. O father Abram, what these Christians are,
Whose own hard dealings teaches them suspect
The thoughts of others !   Ibid., 161.

3774. I like not fair terms and a villain's mind. Ibid., 181.

3775. Mislike me not for my complexion,
The shadow'd livery of the burnish'd sun.   Ibid., ii. i. 1.

3776. O heavens, this is my true-begotten father !   Ibid., ii. 37.

3777. It is a wise father that knows his own child.   Ibid., 80.

3778. There is some ill a-brewing towards my rest,
For I did dream of money-bags to-night.   Ibid., v. 17.

3779. And the vile squealing of the wry-neck'd fife. Ibid., 30.

3780.   All things that are,
Are with more spirit chased than enjoy'd.   Ibid., vi. 12.

3781. But love is blind and lovers cannot see
The pretty follies that themselves commit.   Ibid., 36.

3782. What, must I hold a candle to my shames ?   Ibid., 41.

3783. My daughter ! O my ducats ! O my daughter !
Fled with a Christian ! O my Christian ducats ! Ibid., viii. 15.

3784. Let him look to his bond.   Ibid., iii. i. 49, 50 and 52.

3785. I am a Jew. Hath not a Jew eyes ? hath not a Jew hands,
organs, dimensions, senses, affections, passions ?   Ibid., 62.

3786. The villainy you teach me, I will execute, and it shall go hard
but I will better the instruction.   Ibid., 76.

3787. I would not have given it for a wilderness of monkeys.
Ibid., 127.

3788.   He makes a swan-like end,
Fading in music.   Ibid., ii. 44.

3789. Tell me where is fancy bred,
Or in the heart or in the head ?
How begot, how nourished ?   Ibid., 63.

3790. In law, what plea so tainted and corrupt
But, being season'd with a gracious voice,
Obscures the show of evil ? In religion,
What damned error, but some sober brow
Will bless it and approve it with a text ?   Ibid. 75.

3791. There is no vice so simple but assumes
Some mark of virtue on his outward parts.   Ibid., 81.

3792. Thus ornament is but the guilded shore
To a most dangerous sea ; the beauteous scarf
Veiling an Indian beauty ; in a word,
The seeming truth which cunning times put on
To entrap the wisest.   Ibid., 97.

THE MERCHANT OF VENICE

3793.   An unlesson'd girl, unschool'd, unpractised ;
Happy in this, she is not yet so old
But she may learn.   Ibid. 161.

3794. Here are a few of the unpleasant'st words
That ever blotted paper.   Ibid., 254.

3795. I never did repent for doing good,
Nor shall not now.   Ibid., iv. 10.

3796.   I'll not answer that :
But, say, it is my humour.   Ibid., IV. i. 42.

3797. A harmless necessary cat.   Ibid., 55.

3798. What, wouldst thou have a serpent sting thee twice ?   Ibid., 69.

3799. The quality of mercy is not strain'd,
It droppeth as the gentle rain from heaven
Upon the place beneath : it is twice blest ;
It blesseth him that gives and him that takes :
'Tis mightiest in the mightiest : it becomes
The throned monarch better than his crown ;
His sceptre shows the force of temporal power,
The attribute to awe and majesty,
Wherein doth sit the dread and fear of kings ;
But mercy is above this sceptred sway ;
It is enthroned in the hearts of kings,
It is an attribute to God himself ;
And earthly power doth then show likest God's
When mercy seasons justice.   Therefore, Jew,
Though justice be thy plea, consider this,
That, in the course of justice, none of us
Should see salvation : we do pray for mercy ;
And that same prayer doth teach us all to render
The deeds of mercy.   Ibid., 184.

3800. Wrest once the law to your authority :
To do a great right, do a little wrong.   Ibid., 215.

3801. A Daniel come to judgment ! yea, a Daniel !   Ibid., 223.

3802. 'Tis not in the bond.   Ibid., 262.

3803. For, as thou urgest justice, be assured
Thou shalt have justice, more than thou desirest.   Ibid., 315.

3804. A second Daniel, a Daniel, Jew !
Now, infidel, I have thee on the hip.   Ibid., 333.

3805. I thank thee, Jew, for teaching me that word.   Ibid., 341.

3806. You take my house when you do take the prop
That doth sustain my house ; you take my life
When you do take the means whereby I live.   Ibid.. 375.

3807. He is well paid that is well satisfied.   Ibid., 415.

3808. You taught me first to beg ; and now methinks
You teach me how a beggar should be answer'd.   Ibid., 439.

THE MERCHANT OF VENICE

3809.   How sweet the moonlight sleeps upon this bank !
Here will we sit and let the sounds of music
Creep in our ears : soft stillness and the night
Become the touches of sweet harmony.
Sit, Jessica.   Look how the floor of heaven
Is thick inlaid with patines of bright gold :
There's not the smallest orb which thou behold'st
But in his motion like an angel sings,
Still quiring to the young-eyed cherubins ;
Such harmony is in immortal souls ;
But whilst this muddy vesture of decay
Doth grossly close us in, we cannot hear it.   Ibid., v. I. 54.

3810.   I am never merry when I hear sweet music.   Ibid., 69.

3811.   The man that hath no music in himself,
Nor is not moved with concord of sweet sounds,
Is fit for treasons, stratagems, and spoils ;
The motions of his spirit are dull as night
And his affections dark as Erebus :
Let no such man be trusted.   Ibid., 83.

3812.   How far that little candle throws his beams !
So shines a good deed in a naughty world.   Ibid., 90.

3813.   How many things by season season'd are
To their right praise and true perfection !   Ibid., 107.

KING HENRY IV., PART I.

3814.   So shaken as we are, so wan with care.
King Henry IV. part I. i. i. 1.

3815.   In those holy fields
Over whose acres walk'd those blessed feet
Which fourteen hundred years ago were nail'd
For our advantage on the bitter cross.   Ibid., 24.

3816.   Let us be Diana's foresters, gentlemen of the shade, minions
of the moon.   Ibid., ii. 28.

3817.   What, in thy quips and thy quiddities ?   Ibid., 50.

3818.   Old father antic the law.   Ibid., 69.

3819.   Thou hast damnable iteration, and art indeed able to corrupt
a saint.   Ibid., 101.

3820.   'Tis my vocation, Hal ; 'tis no sin for a man to labour in
his vocation.   Ibid., 117.

3821.   There's neither honesty, manhood, nor good fellowship in
thee.   Ibid., 155.

3822.   Farewell, thou latter spring ! farewell, All-hallown summer!
Ibid., 177.

3823.   If all the year were playing holidays,
To sport would be as tedious as to work.   Ibid., 227.

3824.   A certain lord, neat and trimly dress'd,
Fresh as a bridegroom ; and his chin new reap'd
Show'd like a stubble-land at harvest-home ;
He was perfumed like a milliner ;
And 'twixt his finger and his thumb he held
A pouncet-box, which ever and anon
He gave his nose and took't away again.   Ibid., iii. 33.

3825.   And as the soldiers bore dead bodies by,
He call'd them untaught knaves, unmannerly,
To bring a slovenly unhandsome corse
Betwixt the wind and his nobility.   Ibid., 42.

3826.   He made me mad
To see him shine so brisk and smell so sweet
And talk so like a waiting-gentlewoman
Of guns and drums and wounds,—God save the mark !—
And telling me the sovereign'st thing on earth
Was parmaceti for an inward bruise ;
And that it was great pity, so it was,
This villainous salt-petre should be digg'd
Out of the bowels of the harmless earth,
Which many a good tall fellow had destroy'd
So cowardly ; and but for these vile guns,
He would himself have been a soldier.   Ibid., 53.

3827.   The blood more stirs
To rouse a lion than to start a hare !   Ibid., 197.

3828.   By heaven, methinks it were an easy leap,
To pluck bright honour from the pale-faced moon,
Or dive into the bottom of the deep,
Where fathom-line could never touch the ground,
And pluck up drowned honour by the locks.   Ibid., 201.

3829.   Why, what a candy deal of courtesy
This fawning greyhound then did proffer me !   Ibid. 251.

3830.   I know a trick worth two of that.   Ibid., ii. i. 40.

3831.   I am bewitched with the rogue's company. If the rascal
have not given me medicines to make me love him, I'll be hanged.
       Ibid., ii. 18.

3832.   It would be argument for a week, laughter for a month and
a good jest for ever.   Ibid., 100.

3833.   Falstaff sweats to death,
And lards the lean earth as he walks along.   Ibid., 117.

3834.   Out of this nettle, danger, we pluck this flower, safety.
       Ibid., iii. 10.

3835.   Our plot is as good a plot as ever was laid ; our friends true
and constant ; a good plot, good friends, and full of expectation ;
an excellent plot, very good friends.   Ibid., 18.

3836.   I could brain him with his lady's fan.   Ibid., 25.

3837.   A Corinthian, a lad of mettle, a good boy.   Ibid., iv. 13.

K

3838. I am not yet of Percy's mind, the Hotspur of the north ; he that kills me some six or seven dozen of Scots at a breakfast, washes his hands, and says to his wife, ' Fie upon this quiet life ! I want work.'
                                                                        Ibid., 114.

3839. A plague of all cowards, I say.   Ibid., 128.

3840. There live not three good men unhanged in England ; and one of them is fat and grows old.   Ibid., 142.

3841. Call you that backing of your friends ? A plague upon such backing !   Ibid., 165.

3842. I am a Jew else, an Ebrew Jew.   Ibid., 198.

3843. I have peppered two of them ; two I am sure I have paid, two rogues in buckram suits. I tell thee what, Hal, if I tell thee a lie, spit in my face, call me horse. Thou knowest my old ward ; here I lay, and thus I bore my point. Four rogues in buckram let drive at me——.   Ibid., 211.

3844. O monstrous ! eleven buckram men grown out of two !
                                                                        Ibid., 243.

3845. Three misbegotten knaves in Kendal green.   Ibid., 245.

3846. Give you a reason on compulsion ! if reasons were as plentiful as blackberries, I would give no man a reason upon compulsion, I.
                                                                        Ibid., 263.

3847. Mark now, how a plain tale shall put you down.   Ibid., 281.

3848. No more of that, Hal, an thou lovest me !   Ibid., 312.

3849. A plague of sighing and grief ! it blows a man up like a bladder.   Ibid., 365.

3850. I will do it in King Cambyses' vein.   Ibid., 426.

3851. That reverend vice, that grey iniquity, that father ruffian, that vanity in years.   Ibid., 499.

3852. Banish plump Jack, and banish all the world.   Ibid., 527.

3853. O monstrous ! but one half-pennyworth of bread to this intolerable deal of sack !   Ibid., 591.

3854. I am not in the roll of common men.   Ibid., iii. i. 43.

3855. *Glendower.* I can call spirits from the vasty deep.
  Hotspur. Why, so can I, and so can any man ;
  But will they come when you do call for them ?   Ibid., 53.

3856. O, while you live, tell truth and shame the devil !   Ibid., 62.

3857. I had rather be a kitten and cry mew
Than one of these same metre ballad-mongers.   Ibid., 130.

3858.   Mincing poetry :
'Tis like the forced gait of a shuffling nag.   Ibid., 134.

3859. But in the way of bargain, mark ye me,
I'll cavil on the ninth part of a hair.   Ibid., 139.

3860. And such a deal of skimble-skamble stuff.   Ibid., 154.

3861. I understand thy kisses and thou mine,
And that's a feeling disputation.   Ibid., 205.

3862. And those musicians that shall play to you
Hang in the air a thousand leagues from hence.   Ibid., 226.

3863. Swear me, Kate, like a lady as thou art,
A good mouth-filling oath. Ibid., 258.

3864. A fellow of no mark nor likelihood. Ibid., ii. 45.

3865. The skipping king, he ambled up and down
With shallows jesters and rash bavin wits. Ibid., 60.

3866. He was but as the cuckoo is in June,
Heard, not regarded. Ibid., 75.

3867. Company, villainous company, hath been the spoil of me.
Ibid., iii. 10.

3868. Shall I not take mine ease at mine inn ? Ibid., 92.

3869. That daff'd the world aside,
And bid it pass. Ibid., IV. i. 96.

3870. I saw young Harry, with his beaver on,
His cuisses on his thighs, gallantly arm'd,
Rise from the ground like feather'd Mercury,
And vaulted with such ease into his seat,
As if an angel dropp'd down from the clouds,
To turn and wind a fiery Pegasus
And witch the world with noble horsemanship. Ibid., 104.

3871. Doomsday is near ; die all, die merrily. Ibid., 134.

3872. The cankers of a calm world and a long peace. Ibid., ii. 32.

3873. There's but a shirt and a half in all my company ; and the
half shirt is two napkins tacked together and thrown over the shoulders
like a herald's coat without sleeves. Ibid., 46.

3874. Food for powder, food for powder ; they'll fill a pit as well
as better. Ibid., 71.

3875. I would 'twere bed-time, Hal, and all well. Ibid., v. i. 125.

3876. Honour pricks me on. Yea, but how if honour prick me off
when I come on ? how then ? Can honour set a leg ? no : or an arm ?
no : or take away the grief of a wound ? no. Honour hath no skill in
surgery, then ? no. What is honour ? a word. What is in that word
honour ? what is that honour ? air. A trim reckoning ! Who hath it ?
he that died o' Wednesday. Doth he feel it ? no. Doth he hear it ?
no. 'Tis insensible, then ? Yea, to the dead. But will it not live with
the living ? no. Why ? detraction will not suffer it. Therefore I'll none
of it. Honour is a mere scutcheon : and so ends my catechism.
Ibid., 131.

3877. The time of life is short !
To spend that shortness basely were too long. Ibid., ii. 82.

3878. Two stars keep not their motion in one sphere. Ibid., 65.

3879. What, old acquaintance ! could not all this flesh
Keep in a little life ? Poor Jack, farewell !
I could have better spared a better man. Ibid., iv. 102.

3880. Full bravely has thou flesh'd
Thy maiden sword. Ibid., 133.

3881. Lord, Lord, how this world is given to lying ! Ibid., 150.

3882. I'll purge, and leave sack, and live cleanly as a nobleman
should do. Ibid., 168.

3883.   Even such a man, so faint, so spiritless,
        So dull, so dead in look, so woe-begone,
        Drew Priam's curtain in the dead of night,
        And would have told him half his Troy was burnt.
                            King Henry IV, part II. i. i. 70.

3884.   Yet the first bringer of unwelcome news
        Hath but a losing office, and his tongue
        Sounds ever after as a sullen bell,
        Remember'd tolling a departed friend.   Ibid., 100.

3885.   I am not only witty in myself, but the cause that wit is in
other men.   Ibid., ii. 11.

3886.   A rascally yea-forsooth knave.   Ibid., 42.

3887.   We that are in the vaward of our youth.   Ibid., 198.

3888.   For my voice, I have lost it with halloing and singing of
anthems.   Ibid., 212.

3889.   It was alway yet the trick of our English nation, if they have
a good thing, to make it too common.   Ibid., 241.

3890.   If I do, fillip me with a three-man beetle.   Ibid., 255.

3891.   I can get no remedy against this consumption of the purse :
borrowing only lingers and lingers it out, but the disease is incurable.
                                                        Ibid., 264.

3892.   An habitation giddy and unsure
        Hath he that buildeth on the vulgar heart.   Ibid., iii. 89.

3893.   Past and to come seem best ; things present worst.   Ibid., 108.

3894.   Away, you scullion ! you rampallian ! you fustilarian ! I'll
tickle your catastrophe.   Ibid., ii. i. 65.

3895.   He hath eaten me out of house and home.   Ibid., 80.

3896.   Thou didst swear to me upon a parcel-gilt goblet, sitting in
my Dolphin-chamber, at the round table, by a sea-coal fire, upon
Wednesday in Wheeson week.   Ibid., 93.

3897.   Let the end try the man.   Ibid., ii. 50.

3898.   He was indeed the glass
        Wherein the noble youth did dress themselves. Ibid., iii. 21.

3899.   I beseek you now, aggravate your choler.   Ibid., iv. 175.

3900.   By my troth, captain, these are very bitter words.   Ibid., 184.

3901.   Is it not strange that desire should so many years outlive
performance.   Ibid., 286.

3902.   O sleep, O gentle sleep,
        Nature's soft nurse, how have I frighted thee,
        That thou no more wilt weigh my eyelids down
        And steep my senses in forgetfulness ?   Ibid., III. i 5

3903.   Wilt thou upon the high and giddy mast
        Seal up the ship-boy's eyes, and rock his brains
        In cradle of the rude imperious surge
        And in the visitation of the winds,
        Who take the ruffian billows by the top,
        Curling their monstrous heads and hanging them
        With deafening clamour in the slippery clouds,
        That, with the hurly, death itself awakes ?   Ibid., 18.

KING HENRY IV., PART II.

3904. With all appliances and means to boot.   Ibid., 29.

3905. Uneasy lies the head that wears a crown.   Ibid., 31.

3906. Death, as the Psalmist saith, is certain to all ; all shall die.
How a good yoke of bullocks at Stamford fair ?   Ibid., ii. 41-

3907. Accommodated ; that is, when a man is, as they say, accommodated ; or when a man is, being, whereby a' may be thought to be
accommodated ; which is an excellent thing.   Ibid., 85.

3908. We have heard the chimes at midnight.   Ibid., 228.

3909. A man can die but once.   Ibid., 250.

3910. Lord, Lord, how subject we old men are to this vice of lying !
                                                       Ibid., 325.

3911. Against ill chances men are ever merry ;
But heaviness foreruns the good event.   Ibid., IV. ii. 81.

3912. A peace is of the nature of a conquest ;
For then both parties nobly are subdued,
And neither party loser.   Ibid., 89.

3913. He hath a tear for pity and a hand
Open as day for melting charity.   Ibid., iv. 31.

3914. O polish'd perturbation ! golden care !
That keep'st the ports of slumber open wide
To many a watchful night !   Ibid., v. 23.

3915. Thy wish was father, Harry, to that thought.   Ibid., 93.

3916.   Commit
The oldest sins the newest kind of ways.   Ibid., 126.

3917. A joint of mutton, and any pretty little tiny kickshaws.
                                                Ibid., v. i. 28.

3918. Not Amurath an Amurath succeeds,
But Harry Harry.   Ibid., ii. 48.

3919. A foutre for the world and worldlings base !
I speak of Africa and golden joys.   Ibid., iii. 103.

3920. Under which king, Besonian ? speak, or die.   Ibid., 119.

3921. I know thee not, old man : fall to thy prayers ;
How ill white hairs become a fool and jester ! Ibid., v. 51.

MUCH ADO ABOUT NOTHING

3922. He hath indeed better bettered expectation.
                          Much Ado about Nothing, I. i. 15.

3923. He is a very valiant trencher-man.   Ibid., 51.

3924. There's a skirmish of wit between them.   Ibid., 63.

3925. He wears his faith but as the fashion of his hat. Ibid., 75.

3926. My dear Lady Disdain.   Ibid., 119.

3927. Benedick the married man.   Ibid., 270.

3928. I have a good eye, uncle ; I can see a church by daylight.
                                                Ibid., II. i. 86.

3929. Speak low, if you speak love.   Ibid., 103.

3930. Friendship is constant in all other things
       Save in the office and affairs of love :
       Therefore all hearts in love use their own tongues ;
       Let every eye negotiate for itself
       And trust no agent.   Ibid., 182.

       3931. Silence is the perfectest herald of joy : I were but little happy,
if I could say how much.   Ibid., 316.

       3932. There was a star danced, and under that was I born.
                                                     Ibid., 349.

       3933. Is it not strange that sheeps' guts should hale souls out of
men's bodies ?   Ibid., iii. 61.

3934. Sigh no more, ladies, sigh no more,
       Men were deceivers ever,
       One foot on sea and one on shore,
       To one thing constant never.   Ibid,. 64.

       3935. Sits the wind in that corner ?   Ibid., 102.

       3936. Shall quips and sentences and these paper bullets of the brain
awe a man from the career of his humour ? No, the world must be
peopled. When I said I would die a bachelor, I did not think I should
live till I were married.   Ibid., 248.

       3937. Disdain and scorn ride sparkling in her eyes.   Ibid., iii. i. 51.

       3938. Taming my wild heart to thy loving hand.   Ibid., 112.

       3939. Everyone can master a grief but he that has it.   Ibid., ii. 28.

       3940. Are you good men and true ?   Ibid., iii. 1.

       3941. To be a well-favoured man is the gift of fortune ; but to write
and read comes by nature.   Ibid., 14.

       3942. *Second Watch.* How if a' will not stand ?
       Dogberry. Why, then, take no note of him, but let him go ; and
presently call the rest of the watch together and thank God you are
rid of a knave.   Ibid., 27.

       3943. For the watch to babble and talk is most tolerable and not
to be endured.   Ibid., 36.

       3944. The most peaceable way for you, if you do take a thief, is to
let him show himself what he is and steal out of your company.
                                                     Ibid., 61.

       3945. I thank God I am as honest as any man living that is an old
man and no honester than I.   Ibid., v. 15.

       3946. Comparisons are odorous.   Ibid., 18.

       3947. If I were as tedious as a king, I could find it in my heart to
bestow it all of your worship.   Ibid., 23.

       3948. A good old man, sir ; he will be talking : as they say, When
the age is in, the wit is out.   Ibid., 37.

       3949. O, what men dare do ! what men may do ! what men daily do,
not knowing what they do !   Ibid., iv. i. 19.

3950.   I have mark's
       A thousand blushing apparitions
       To start into her face, a thousand innocent shames
       In angel whiteness beat away those blushes.   Ibid., 160.

MUCH ADO ABOUT NOTHING

3951.   For it so falls out
        That what we have we prize not to the worth
        Whiles we enjoy it, but being lack'd and lost,
        Why, then we rack the value, then we find
        The virtue that possession would not show us
        While it was ours.   Ibid., 219.

3952.   The idea of her life shall sweetly creep
        Into his study of imagination,
        And every lovely organ of her life
        Shall come apparell'd in more precious habit,
        More moving-delicate and full of life,
        Into the eye and prospect of his soul,
        Than when she lived indeed.   Ibid., 226.

    3953. Masters, it is proved already that you are little better than
false knaves ; and it will go near to be thought so shortly.   Ibid., ii. 22.

    3954. Flat burglary as ever was committed.   Ibid., 52.

    3955. O villain ! thou wilt be condemned into everlasting redemp-
tion for this.   Ibid., 58.

    3956. O that he were here to write me down an ass !   Ibid., 77.

    3957   A fellow that hath had losses, and one that hath two gowns
and everything handsome about him.   Ibid., 87

3958. Patch grief with proverbs.   Ibid., v. i. 17.

3959. For there was never yet philosopher
       That could endure the toothache patiently.   Ibid., 35.

    3960. I was not born under a rhyming planet.   Ibid., ii. 40.

3961. Done to death by slanderous tongues.   Ibid., iii. 3.

KING HENRY V.

3962. O for a Muse of fire, that would ascend
       The brightest heaven of invention.
                            King Henry V., prologue, 1.

3963.   Can this cockpit hold
       The vasty fields of France ? or may we cram
       Within this wooden O the very casques
       That did affright the air at Agincourt ?   Ibid., 11.

3964. Consideration, like an angel, came,
       And whipp'd the offending Adam out of him.   Ibid., I. i. 28.

3965. Turn him to any cause of policy,
       The Gordian knot of it he will unloose,
       Familiar as his garter : that, when he speaks,
       The air, a charter'd libertine, is still.   Ibid., 45.

3966. And make her chronicle as rich with praise
       As is the ooze and bottom of the sea
       With sunken wreck and sunless treasuries.   Ibid., ii. 163.

3967.   For so work the honey-bees,
                Creatures that by a rule in nature teach
                The act of order to a peopled kingdom.
                They have a king and officers of sorts ;
                Where some, like magistrates, correct at home,
                Others, like merchants, venture trade abroad,
                Others, like soldiers, armed in their stings,
                Make boot upon the summer's velvet buds,
                Which pillage they with merry march bring home
                To the tent-royal of their emperor ;
                Who, busied in his majesty, surveys
                The singing masons building roofs of gold,
                The civil citizens kneading up the honey,
                The poor mechanic porters crowding in
                Their heavy burdens at the narrow gate,
                The sad-eyed justice, with his surly hum,
                Delivering o'er to executors pale
                The lazy yawning drone.   Ibid., 187.

3968.   As 'tis ever common
                That men are merriest when they are from home.   Ibid., 271.

3969. Now all the youth of England are on fire,
        And silken dalliance in the wardrobe lies.

                                             Ibid., II. prologue, 1.

3970. I dare not fight ; but I will wink and hold out mine iron.
                                             Ibid., i. 7.

3971. Though patience be a tired mare, yet she will plod.   Ibid., 26.

3972. Base is the slave that pays.   Ibid., 100.

3973. He's in Arthur's bosom, if ever man went to Arthur's bosom.
A' made a finer end and went away an it had been any christom child ;
a' parted even just between twelve and one, even at the turning o' the
tide ; for after I saw him fumble with the sheets and play with flowers
and smile upon his fingers' ends, I knew there was but one way ; for
his nose was as sharp as a pen, and a' babbled of green fields.

                                             Ibid., iii. 9.

3974. Now I, to comfort him, bid him a' should not think of God ; I
hoped there was no need to trouble himself with any such thoughts yet.
                                             Ibid., 21.

3975. Trust none.
        For oaths are straws, men's faiths are wafer-cakes,
        And hold-fast is the only dog, my duck.   Ibid., 52.

3976. Self-love, my liege, is not so vile a sin
        As self-neglecting.   Ibid., iv. 74.

3977. Once more unto the breach, dear friends, once more ;
        Or close the wall up with our English dead.
        In peace there's nothing so becomes a man
        As modest stillness and humility :
        But when the blast of war blows in our ears,
        Then imitate the action of the tiger ;
        Stiffen the sinews, summon up the blood,
        Disguise fair nature with hard-favour'd rage.   Ibid., III. i. 1.

3978.   On, on, you noblest English,
Whose blood is fet from fathers of war-proof !
Fathers that, like so many Alexanders,
Have in these parts from morn till even fought
And sheathed their swords for lack of argument.   Ibid. 17.

3979. I see you stand like greyhounds in the slips,
Straining upon the start.   Ibid., 31.

3980. Men of few words are the best men.   Ibid., ii. 38.

3981. I thought upon one pair of English legs
Did march three Frenchmen.   Ibid., vi. 158.

3982. From camp to camp through the foul womb of night
The hum of either army stilly sounds,
That the fix'd sentinels almost receive
The secret whispers of each other's watch :
Fire answers fire, and through their paly flames
Each battle sees the other's umber'd face ;
Steed threatens steed, in high and boastful neighs
Piercing the night's dull ear ; and from the tents
The armourers, accomplishing the knights,
With busy hammers closing rivets up,
Give dreadful note of preparation.   Ibid., IV. prologue, 1.

3983. There is some soul of goodness in things evil,
Would men observingly distil it out.   Ibid., i. 4.

3984. Every subject's duty is the king's ; but every subject's soul
is his own.   Ibid., 185.

3985. Who with a body fill'd and vacant mind,
Gets him to rest, cramm'd with distressful bread.   Ibid., 286.

3986.   O that we now had here
But one ten thousand of those men in England
That do no work to-day !   Ibid., iii. 16.

3987. If we are mark'd to die, we are enow
To do our country loss ; and if to live,
The fewer men, the greater share of honour.   Ibid., 20.

3988. But if it be a sin to covet honour,
I am the most offending soul alive.   Ibid., 28.

3989. This day is call'd the feast of Crispian.
He that outlives this day, and comes safe home,
Will stand a tip-toe when this day is named,
And rouse him at the name of Crispian.   Ibid., 40.

3990.   Then shall our names,
Familiar in his mouth as household words,
Harry the king, Bedford and Exeter,
Warwick and Talbot, Salisbury and Gloucester,
Be in their flowing cups freshly remember'd.   Ibid., 51.

3991. We few, we happy few, we band of brothers.   Ibid., 60.

3992. And gentlemen in England now a-bed
Shall think themselves accursed they were not here,
And hold their manhoods cheap whiles any speaks
That fought with us upon Saint Crispin's day.   Ibid., 64.
*K

KING HENRY V.

3993. There is occasions and causes why and wherefore in all things.
Ibid., v. i. 3.

3994. All hell shall stir for this. *Ibid.*, 72.

3995. For these fellows of infinite tongue, that can rhyme themselves into ladies' favours, they do always reason themselves out again.
Ibid., ii. 162.

3996. If he be not fellow with the best king, thou shalt find the best king of good fellows. *Ibid.*, 260.

JULIUS CAESAR

3997. As proper men as ever trod upon's neat's leather.
Julius Caesar, I. i. 28.

3998. You blocks, you stones, you worse than senseless things !
Ibid., 40.

3999. Beware the ides of March. *Ibid.*, ii. 19.

4000. I am not gamesome : I do lack some part
Of that quick spirit that is in Antony. *Ibid.*, 28.

4001. Set honour in one eye and death i' the other,
And I will look on both indifferently. *Ibid.*, 86.

4002. Well, honour is the subject of my story.
I cannot tell what you and other men
Think of this life ; but, for my single self,
I had as lief not be as live to be
In awe of such a thing as I myself. *Ibid.*, 92.

4003. Caesar said to me ' Darest thou, Cassius, now
Leap in with me into this angry flood,
And swim to yonder point ? ' Upon the word,
Accoutred as I was, I plunged in
And bade him follow. *Ibid.*, 102.

4004. Ye gods, it doth amaze me
A man of such a feeble temper should
So get the start of the majestic world
And bear the palm alone. *Ibid.*, 128.

4005. Why, man, he doth bestride the narrow world
Like a Colossus, and we petty men
Walk under his huge legs and peep about
To find ourselves dishonourable graves.
Men at some time are masters of their fates :
The fault, dear Brutus, is not in our stars,
But in ourselves, that we are underlings. *Ibid.*, 135.

4006. Conjure with 'em,
Brutus will start a spirit as soon as Caesar.
Now in the name of all the gods at once,
Upon what meat doth this our Caesar feed,
That he is grown so great ? Age, thou art shamed !
Rome, thou hast lost the breed of noble bloods ! *Ibid.*, 146

4007. There was a Brutus once that would have brook'd
The eternal devil to keep his state in Rome
As easily as a king. *Ibid.*, 159.

JULIUS CAESAR

4008. Let me have men about me that are fat ;
Sleek-headed men and such as sleep o' nights :
Yond Cassius has a lean and hungry look ;
He thinks too much : such men are dangerous.   Ibid., 192

4009. He is a great observer and he looks
Quite through the deeds of men.   Ibid., 202.

4010. Seldom he smiles, and smiles in such a sort
As if he mock'd himself and scorn'd his spirit
That could be moved to smile at any thing.   Ibid., 205.

4011.   Lowliness is young ambition's ladder,
Whereto the climber-upward turns his face ;
But when he once attains the upmost round,
He then unto the ladder turns his back,
Looks in the clouds, scorning the base degrees
By which he did ascend.   Ibid., II. i. 21.

4012. Between the acting of a dreadful thing
And the first motion, all the interim is
Like a phantasma, or a hideous dream :
The Genius and the mortal instruments
Are then in council ; and the state of man,
Like to a little kingdom, suffers then
The nature of an insurrection.   Ibid., 63.

4013. For he will never follow any thing
That other men begin.   Ibid., 151.

4014. A dish fit for the gods.   Ibid. 173.

4015. But when I tell him he hates flatterers,
He says he does, being then most flattered.   Ibid., 207.

4016. You are my true and honourable wife,
As dear to me as are the ruddy drops
That visit my sad heart.   Ibid., 288.

4017. Fierce fiery warriors fought upon the clouds,
In ranks and squadrons and right form of war.   Ibid., ii. 19.

4018. When beggars die, there are no comets seen ;
The heavens themselves blaze forth the death of princes.   Ibid., 30.

4019. Cowards die many times before their deaths ;
The valiant never taste of death but once.   Ibid., 32.

4020. How hard it is for women to keep counsel.   Ibid., iv. 9.

4021. But I am constant as the northern star,
Of whose true-fix'd and resting quality
There is no fellow in the firmament.   Ibid., III. i. 60.

4022. Why, he that cuts off twenty years of life
Cuts off so many years of fearing death.   Ibid., 101.

4023.   How many ages hence
Shall this our lofty scene be acted over
In states unborn and accents yet unknown !   Ibid., 111.

4024. O mighty Caesar ! dost thou lie so low ?
Are all thy conquests, glories, triumphs, spoils,
Shrunk to this little measure ?   Ibid., 148.

4025. The choice and master spirits of this age.   Ibid., 163.

4026. Though last, not least in love.   Ibid., 189.

4027. O, pardon me, thou bleeding piece of earth,
      That I am meek and gentle with these butchers !
      Thou art the ruin of the noblest man
      That ever lived in the tide of times.   Ibid., 254.

4028. Cry ' Havoc,' and let slip the dogs of war.   Ibid., 273.

4029. As Caesar loved me, I weep for him ; as he was fortunate, I
rejoice at it ; as he was valiant, I honour him ; but as he was ambitious,
I slew him.   There is tears for his love ; joy for his fortune ; honour
for his valour ; and death for his ambition.   Ibid., ii. 27.

4030. Friends, Romans, countrymen, lend me your ears ;
      I come to bury Caesar, not to praise him.
      The evil that men do lives after them ;
      The good is oft interred with their bones.   Ibid., 78.

4031. For Brutus is an honourable man ;
      So are they all, all honourable men.   Ibid., 87.

4032. When that the poor have cried, Caesar hath wept :
      Ambition should be made of sterner stuff.   Ibid., 96.

4033. O judgment ! thou art fled to brutish beasts,
      And men have lost their reason.   Ibid., 109.

4034. But yesterday the word of Caesar might
      Have stood against the world ; now lies he there,
      And none so poor to do him reverence.   Ibid., 123.

4035. If you have tears, prepare to shed them now.   Ibid., 173.

4036. See what a rent the envious Casca made.   Ibid., 179.

4037. This was the most unkindest cut of all.   Ibid., 187.

4038. Ingratitude, more strong than traitors' arms,
      Quite vanquish'd him : then burst his mighty heart.
                                                          Ibid., 189.

4039. O, what a fall was there, my countrymen !   Ibid., 194.

4040. I am no orator, as Brutus is ;
      But, as you know me all, a plain blunt man.   Ibid., 221.

4041. For I have neither wit, not words, nor worth,
      Action, not utterance, nor the power of speech,
      To stir men's blood : I only speak right on.   Ibid., 225.

4042.   Put a tongue
      In every wound of Caesar that should move
      The stones of Rome to rise and mutiny.   Ibid., 232.

4043. Tear him for his bad verses, tear him for his bad verses.
                                                          Ibid., iii. 34.

4044. This is a slight unmeritable man,
      Meet to be sent on errands.   Ibid., iv. i. 12.

4045. When love begins to sicken and decay,
      It useth an enforced ceremony.
      There are no tricks in plain and simple faith.   Ibid., ii. 20.

JULIUS CAESAR

4046.   You yourself
Are much condemn'd to have an itching palm.   Ibid., iii. 9.

4047. I had rather be a dog, and bay the moon,
Than such a Roman.   Ibid., 27.

4048. Away, slight man !   Ibid., 37.

4049. There is no terror, Cassius, in your threats,
For I am arm'd so strong in honesty
That they pass by me as the idle wind,
Which I respect not.   Ibid., 66.

4050. A friend shou.d bear his friend's infirmities,
But Brutus makes mine greater than they are.   Ibid., 86.

4051. Check'd like a bondman ; all his faults observed,
Set in a note-book, learn'd, and conn'd by rote,
To cast into my teeth.   Ibid., 97.

4052. There is a tide in the affairs of men,
Which, taken at the flood, leads on to fortune ;
Omitted, all the voyage of their life
Is bound in shallows and in miseries.
On such a full sea are we now afloat ;
And we must take the current when it serves,
Or lose our ventures.   Ibid., 218.

4053. But for your words, they rob the Hybla bees,
And leave them honeyless.   Ibid., v. i. 34.

4054. For ever, and for ever, farewell, Cassius !
If we do meet again, why, we shall smile ;
If not, why then, this parting was well made.   Ibid., 117.

4055.   O, that a man might know
The end of this day's business ere it come !   Ibid., 123.

4056. The last of all the Romans, fare thee well ! Ibid., iii. 99.

4057. This was the noblest Roman of them all.   Ibid., v. 68.

4058. His life was gentle, and the elements
So mix'd in him that Nature might stand up,
And say to all the world ' This was a man ! '   Ibid., 73.

AS YOU LIKE IT

4059. Fleet the time carelessly, as they did in the golden world.
As You Like It, I. i. 124.

4060. How now, wit ! whither wander you ?   Ibid., ii. 60.

4061. Well said : that was laid on with a trowel.   Ibid., 112.

4062. My pride fell with my fortunes.   Ibid., 264.

4063. *Celia.* Not a word ?
Rosalind. Not one to throw at a dog.   Ibid. iii. 2.

4064. O, how full of briers is this working-day world ! Ibid., 12.

4065. Beauty provoketh thieves sooner than gold.   Ibid., 112.

4066. We'll have a swashing and a martial outside,
As many other mannish cowards have
That do outface it with their semblances.   Ibid., 122.

4067. Sweet are the uses of adversity,
Which, like the toad, ugly and venomous,
Wears yet a precious jewel in its head :
And this our life exempt from public haunt
Finds tongues in trees, books in the running brooks,
Sermons in stones and good in everything. Ibid., II. i 1.

4068. The big round tears
Coursed one another down his innocent nose
In piteous chase. Ibid., 38.

4069. Thou makest a testament
As worldlings do, giving thy sum of more
To that which had too much. Ibid., 47.

4070. Sweep on, you fat and greasy citizens. Ibid., 55.

4071. For in my youth I never did apply
Hot and rebellious liquors to my blood. Ibid., iii. 48.

4072. Therefore my age is as a lusty winter,
Frosty, but kindly. Ibid., 52.

4073. O good old man, how well in thee appears
The constant service of the antique world,
When service sweat for duty, not for meed !
Thou art not for the fashion of these times,
When none will sweat but for promotion. Ibid. 56.

4074. Ay, now am I in Arden ; the more fool I ; when I was at
home, I was in a better place : but travellers must be content.
Ibid., iv. 16.

4075. If thou remember'st not the slightest folly
That ever love did make thee run into,
Thou hast not loved. Ibid., 34.

4076. We that are true lovers run into strange capers. Ibid., 54.

4077. Under the greenwood tree
Who loves to lie with me,
And turn his merry note
Unto the sweet bird's throat,
Come hither, come hither, come hither :
Here shall he see
No enemy
But winter and rough weather. Ibid., v. 1.

4078. I can suck melancholy out of a song, as a weasel sucks eggs.
Ibid., 12.

4079. Who doth ambition shun
And loves to live i' the sun,
Seeking the food he eats,
And pleased with what he gets. Ibid., 40.

4080. And rail'd on Lady Fortune in good terms,
In good set terms. Ibid., vii. 16.

4081. Call me not fool till heaven hath sent me fortune. Ibid., 19.

4082. And then he drew a dial from his poke,
And, looking on it with lack-lustre eye,
Says very wisely, ' It is ten o'clock :
Thus we may see,' quoth he, ' how the world wags.' Ibid., 20.

4083. And so, from hour to hour, we ripe and ripe,
And then, from hour to hour, we rot and rot ;
And thereby hangs a tale.   Ibid., 26.

4084. My lungs began to crow like chanticleer,
That fools should be so deep-contemplative,
And I did laugh sans intermission
An hour by his dial.   Ibid., 30.

4085. Motley's the only wear.   Ibid., 34.

4086. And says, if ladies be but young and fair,
They have the gift to know it : and in his brain,
Which is as dry as the remainder biscuit
After a voyage, he doth strange places cramm'd
With observation, the which he vents
In mangled forms   Ibid., 37.

4087.   I must have liberty
Withal, as large a charter as the wind,
To blow on whom I please.   Ibid., 47.

4088. The ' why ' is plain as way to parish church. Ibid., 52.

4089.   Whate'er you are
That in this desert inaccessible,
Under the shade of melancholy boughs,
Lose and neglect the creeping hours of time.   Ibid., 109.

4090.   All the world's a stage,
And all the men and women merely players :
They have their exits and their entrances ;
And one man in his time plays many parts,
His acts being seven ages.   At first the infant,
Mewling and puking in the nurses' arms.
And then the whining school-boy, with his satchel
And shining morning face, creeping like snail
Unwillingly to school.   And then the lover,
Sighing like furnace, with a woeful ballad
Made to his mistress' eyebrow.   Then a soldier,
Full of strange oaths and bearded like the pard,
Jealous in honour, sudden and quick in quarrel,
Seeking the bubble reputation
Even in the cannon's mouth.   And then the justice,
In fair round belly with good capon lined,
With eyes severe and beard of formal cut,
Full of wise saws and modern instances ;
And so he plays his part.   The sixth stage shifts
Into the lean and slipper'd pantaloon,
With spectacles on nose and pouch on side,
His youthful hose, well saved, a world too wide
For his shrunk shank ; and his big manly voice
Turning again towards childish treble, pipes
And whistles in his sound.   Last scene of all,
That ends this strange eventful history,
Is second childishness and mere oblivion,
Sans teeth, sans eyes, sans taste, sans everything. Ibid., 139.

4091.   Blow, blow, thou winter wind,
              Thou art not so unkind
                  As man's ingratitude ;
              Thy tooth is not so keen,
              Because thou art not seen,
                Although thy breath be rude.   *Ibid.*, 174.

4092. Most friendship is feigning, most loving mere folly.   *Ibid.*, 181.

4093. The fair, the chaste and unexpressive she.   *Ibid.*, III. ii. 10.

4094. Hast any philosophy in thee, shepherd ?   *Ibid.*, 22.

4095. He that wants money, means and content is without three good friends.   *Ibid.*, 25.

4096. Truly thou art damned, like an ill-roasted egg all on one side.   *Ibid.*, 38.

4097. This is the very false gallop of the verses.   *Ibid.*, 119.

4098. O wonderful, wonderful, and most wonderful ! and yet again wonderful, and after that, out of all hooping !   *Ibid.*, 201.

4099. Speak, sad brow and true maid.   *Ibid.*, 227.

4100. Do you not know I am a woman ? when I think, I must speak.   *Ibid.*, 263.

4101. I do desire we may be better strangers.   *Ibid.*, 275.

4102. *Jacques.* What stature is she of ?
       Orlando. Just as high as my heart.   *Ibid.* 285.

4103. Time travels in divers paces with divers persons. I'll tell you who Time ambles withal, who Time trots withal, who Time gallops withal and who he stands still withal.   *Ibid.*, 325

4104. Every one fault seeming monstrous till his fellow-fault came to match it.   *Ibid.*, 372.

4105. Truly, I would the gods had made thee poetical.   *Ibid.*, iii. 16.

4106. I am not a slut, though I thank the gods I am foul.   *Ibid.*, 38.

4107. If ever,—as that ever may be near,—
      You meet in some fresh cheek the power of fancy,
      Then shall you know the wounds invisible
      That love's keen arrows make.   *Ibid.*, iv. 28.

4108.   Down on your knees,
      And thank heaven, fasting, for a good man's love.   *Ibid.*, 57.

4109. Dead shepherd, now I find thy saw of might,
     ' Who ever loved that loved not at first sight ? '
    [Quoting Marlowe's ' Hero and Leander.' See No. 2571.]

4110. It is a melancholy of mine own, compounded of many simples, extracted from many objects, and indeed the sundry contemplation of my travels, in which my often rumination wraps me in a most humorous sadness.   *Ibid.*, IV. i. 16.

4111. I had rather have a fool to make me merry than experience to make me sad.   *Ibid.*, 28.

4112. Very good orators, when they are out, they will spit.
                               ibid., 75.

4113. Men have died from time to time and worms have eaten them, but not for love. Ibid., 106.

4114. Men are April when they woo, December when they wed : maids are May when they are maids, but the sky changes when they are wives. Ibid., 147.

4115. The horn, the horn, the lusty horn
Is not a thing to laugh to scorn. Ibid., ii. 18.

4116. Chewing the food of sweet and bitter fancy. Ibid., iii. 102.

4117. It is meat and drink to me to see a clown. Ibid., v. i. 11.

4118. No sooner met but they looked, no sooner looked but they loved, no sooner loved but they sighed, no sooner sighed but they asked one another the reason, no sooner knew the reason but they sought the remedy. Ibid., ii. 36.

4119. O, how bitter a thing it is to look into happiness through another man's eyes ! Ibid., 47.

4120. It is to be all made of sighs and tears.

.   .   .   .   .

It is to be all made of faith and service.

.   .   .   .   .

It is to be all made of fantasy,
All made of passion and all made of wishes,
All adoration, duty, and observance,
All humbleness, all patience and impatience,
All purity, all trial, all observance. [Of love.] Ibid. 90.

4121. It was a lover and his lass,
With a hey, and a ho, and a hey nonino,
That o'er the green corn-field did pass
In the spring time, the only pretty ring time,
When birds do sing, hey ding a ding, ding :
Sweet lovers love the spring. Ibid., iii. 17.

4122. An ill-favoured thing, sir, but mine own. Ibid., iv. 60.

4123. O Sir, we quarrel in print, by the book ; as you have books for good manners : I will name you the degrees. The first, the Retort Courteous ; the second, the Quip Modest ; the third, the Reply Churlish ; the fourth, the Reproof Valiant ; the fifth, the Countercheck Quarrelsome ; the sixth, the Lie with Circumstance ; the seventh, the Lie Direct. Ibid. 94.

4124. Your If is the only peace-maker ; much virtue in If. Ibid., 107.

4125. He uses his folly like a stalking-horse and under the presentation of that he shoots his wit. Ibid., 111.

4126. If it be true that good wine needs no bush, 'tis true that a good play needs no epilogue. Ibid., epilogue, 3.

TWELFTH NIGHT

4127. If music be the food of love, play on ;
Give me excess of it, that, surfeiting,
The appetite may sicken, and so die.
That strain again ! it had a dying fall :
O, it came o'er my ear like the sweet sound,
That breathes upon a bank of violets,
Stealing and giving odour ! *Twelfth Night*, I. i. 1.

4128. I am sure care's an enemy to life. Ibid., iii. 2.

4129. Speaks three or four languages word for word without book.
Ibid., 27.

4130. I am a great eater of beef and I believe that does harm to
my wit. Ibid., 89.

4131. Wherefore are these things hid ? Ibid., 133.

4132. Is it a world to hide virtues in ? Ibid., 140.

4133. Many a good hanging prevents a bad marriage. Ibid., v. 20.

4134. Good my mouse of virtue, answer me. Ibid., 69.

4135. 'Tis beauty truly blent, whose red and white
Nature's own sweet and cunning hand laid on. Ibid., 257.

4136. Make me a willow cabin at your gate,
And call upon my soul within the house ;
Write loyal cantons of contemned love
And sing them loud even in the dead of night ;
Halloo your name to the reverberate hills
And make the babbling gossip of the air
Cry out ' Olivia ! ' Ibid., 287.

4137. Farewell, fair cruelty. Ibid., 307.

4138. Not to be a-bed after midnight is to be up betimes.
Ibid., II. iii. 1.

4139. O mistress mine, where are you roaming ?
O, stay and hear ; your true love's coming,
That can sing both high and low :
Trip no further, pretty sweeting ;
Journeys end in lovers meeting,
Every wise man's son doth know. Ibid., 40.

4140. In delay there lies no plenty ;
Then come kiss me, sweet and twenty,
Youth's a stuff will not endure. Ibid., 51.

4141. He does it with a better grace, but I do it more natural.
Ibid., 88.

4142. *Sir Toby.* Dost thou think, because thou art virtuous, there
shall be no more cakes and ale ?
Clown. Yes, by Saint Anne, and ginger shall be hot i' the
mouth too. Ibid., 123.

4143. My purpose is, indeed, a horse of that colour. Ibid., 181.

4144. It gives a very echo to the seat
Where Love is throned. Ibid., iv. 21.

4145. Let still the woman take
An elder than herself ; so wears she to him,
So sways she level in her husband's heart :
For, boy, however we do praise ourselves,
Our fancies are more giddy and unfirm,
More longing, wavering, sooner lost and worn,
Than women's are. Ibid., 30.

4146. Then let thy love be younger than thyself,
Or thy affection cannot hold the bent. Ibid., 37

4147. The spinsters and the knitters in the sun
And the free maids that weave their thread with bones
Do use to chant it : it is silly sooth,
And dallies with the innocence of love,
Like the old age.   Ibid., 45.

4148. Come away, come away, death,
  And in sad cypress let me be laid ;
Fly away, fly away, breath ;
  I am slain by a fair cruel maid.
My shroud of white, stuck all with yew,
  O, prepare it !
My part of death, no one so true
  Did share it.   Ibid., 52.

4149. *Duke.* And what's her history ?
   Viola. A blank, my lord. She never told her love,
  But let concealment, like a worm i' the bud,
  Feed on her damask cheek : she pined in thought,
  And with a green and yellow melancholy
  She sat like patience on a monument,
  Smiling at grief.   Ibid., 112.

4150. I am all the daughters of my father's house,
And all the brothers too.   Ibid., 123.

4151. Be not afraid of greatness : some are born great, some achieve
greatness and some have greatness thrust upon 'em. Ibid., v. 156.

4152. O world, how apt the poor are to be proud. Ibid., iii. i. 138.

4153. O, what a deal of scorn looks beautiful
In the contempt and anger of his lip !   Ibid., 157.

4154. Love sought is good, but given unsought is better. Ibid., 168.

4155. Let there be gall enough in thy ink, though thou write with
a goose-pen, no matter.   Ibid., ii. 51.

4156. I think we do know the sweet Roman hand. Ibid., iv. 30.

4157. Why, this is very midsummer madness   Ibid., 61.

4158. If this were played upon a stage now, I could condemn it as
an improbable fiction.   Ibid., 140.

4159. Still you keep o' the windy side of the law. Ibid., 181.

4160. Fare thee well ; and God have mercy upon one of our souls.
He may have mercy upon mine ; but my hope is better, and so look
to thyself.   Ibid., 183.

4161. An I thought he had been valiant and so cunning in fence,
I'ld have seen him damned ere I'ld have challenged him. Ibid., 311.

4162. Out of my lean and low ability
I'll lend you something.   Ibid., 378.

4163. I hate ingratitude more in a man
Than lying, vainness, babbling, drunkenness,
Or any taint of vice whose strong corruption
Inhabits our frail blood.   Ibid., 388.

4164. *Clown.* What is the opinion of Pythagoras concerning wild fowl ?

Malvolio. That the soul of our grandam might haply inhabit a bird. Ibid., IV. ii. 54.

4165. Thus the whirligig of time brings in his revenges.

Ibid., v. i. 384.

4166. When that I was and a little tiny boy,
With hey, ho, the wind and the rain,
A foolish thing was but a toy,
For the rain it raineth every day. Ibid., 398.

HAMLET

4167. For this relief much thanks. *Hamlet*, I. i. 8.

4168. But in the gross and scope of my opinion,
This bodes some strange eruption to our state. Ibid., 67.

4169. Whose sore task
Does not divide the Sunday from the week. Ibid., 75.

4170. This sweaty haste
Doth make the night joint-labourer with the day. Ibid., 78.

4171. In the most high and palmy state of Rome,
A little ere the mightiest Julius fell,
The graves stood tenantless and the sheeted dead
Did squeak and gibber in the Roman streets. Ibid., 113.

4172. We do it wrong, being so majestical,
To offer it the show of violence. Ibid., 143.

4173. And then it started like a guilty thing
Upon a fearful summons. Ibid., 148.

4174. Whether in sea or fire, in earth or air,
The extravagant and erring spirit hies
To his confine. Ibid., 153.

4175. Some say that ever 'gainst that season comes
Wherein our Saviour's birth is celebrated,
The bird of dawning singeth all night long :
The nights are wholesome ; then no planets strike,
No fairy takes, nor witch hath power to charm,
So hallow'd and so gracious is the time. Ibid., 158.

4176. But, look, the morn, in russet mantle clad,
Walks o'er the dew of yon high eastward hill. Ibid., 166.

4177. With an auspicious and a dropping eye,
With mirth in funeral and with dirge in marriage,
In equal scale weighing delight and dole. Ibid., ii. 11.

4178. A little more than kin, and less than kind. Ibid., 65.

4179. Thou know'st 'tis common ; all that lives must die,
Passing through nature to eternity. Ibid., 72.

4180. Seems, madam ! nay, it is ; I know not ' seems.'
'Tis not alone my inky cloak, good mother,
Nor customary suits of solemn black. Ibid., 76.

4181. But I have that within which passeth show ;
These but the trappings and the suits of woe.

Ibid., 85.

4182. O, that this too too solid flesh would melt,
Thaw and resolve itself into a dew !
Or that the Everlasting had not fix'd
His canon 'gainst self-slaughter ! O God ! God !
How weary, stale, flat and unprofitable,
Seem to me all the uses of this world !

Ibid., 129.

4183. So excellent a king ; that was, to this,
Hyperion to a satyr ; so loving to my mother
That he might not beteem the winds of heaven
Visit her face too roughly.

Ibid., 139.

4184.   Why, she would hang on him,
As if increase of appetite had grown
By what it fed on.

Ibid., 143.

4185. Frailty, thy name is woman !

Ibid., 146.

4186. A beast, that wants discourse of reason.

Ibid., 150.

4187. It is not nor it cannot come to good.

Ibid., 158.

4188. Thrift, thrift, Horatio ! the funeral baked meats
Did coldly furnish forth the marriage tables.

Ibid., 180.

4189. In my mind's eye, Horatio.

Ibid., 185.

4190. He was a man, take him for all in all,
I shall not look upon his like again.

Ibid., 187.

4191. In the dead vast and middle of the night.

Ibid., 198.

4192. A countenance more in sorrow than in anger.

Ibid., 232.

4193. While one with moderate haste might tell a hundred.

Ibid., 238.

4194. A sable silver'd.

Ibid., 242.

4195. Give it an understanding, but no tongue.

Ibid., 249.

4196. Foul play.

Ibid., 256.

4197. His greatness weigh'd, his will is not his own ;
For he himself is subject to his birth :
He may not, as unvalued persons do,
Carve for himself ; for on his choice depends
The safety and the health of this whole state.

Ibid., iii. 17.

4198. The chariest maid is prodigal enough,
If she unmask her beauty to the moon :
Virtue itself 'scapes not calumnious strokes :
The canker galls the infants of the spring,
Too oft before their buttons be disclosed,
And in the morn and liquid dew of youth
Contagious blastments are most imminent.

Ibid., 36.

4199. Do not, as some ungracious pastors do,
Show me the steep and thorny way to heaven ;
Whiles, like a puff'd and reckless libertine,
Himself the primrose path of dalliance treads,
And recks not his own rede.

Ibid., 47.

4200. And these few precepts in thy memory
See thou character. Give thy thoughts no tongue,
Nor any unproportion'd thought his act.
Be thou familiar, but by no means vulgar.
Those friends thou hast, and their adoption tried,
Grapple them to thy soul with hoops of steel.   Ibid., 58.

4201.   Beware
Of entrance to a quarrel, but being in,
Bear't that the opposed may beware of thee.
Give every man thy ear, but few thy voice ;
Take each man's censure, but reserve thy judgment.
Costly thy habit as thy purse can buy,
But not express'd in fancy ; rich, not gaudy ;
For the apparel oft proclaims the man.   Ibid., 65.

4202. Neither a borrower nor a lender be ;
For loan oft loses both itself and friend,
And borrowing dulls the edge of husbandry.
This above all : to thine own self be true,
And it must follow as the night the day,
Thou canst not then be false to any man.   Ibid., 75.

4203. Ay, springes to catch woodcocks.   Ibid., 115·

4204. Be somewhat scanter of your maiden presence.   Ibid., 121.

4205. *Hamlet.* The air bites shrewly ; it is very cold.
Horatio. It is a nipping and an eager air.   Ibid., iv. 1.

4206. But to my mind, though I am native here
And to the manner born, it is a custom
More honour'd in the breach than the observance.   Ibid., 14.

4207. Angels and ministers of grace defend us !
Be thou a spirit of health or goblin damn'd,
Bring with thee airs from heaven or blasts from hell,
Be thy intents wicked or charitable,
Thou comest in such a questionable shape
That I will speak to thee.   Ibid., 39.

4208. Hath oped his ponderous and marble jaws.   Ibid., 50.

4209.   What may this mean,
That thou, dead corse, again in complete steel
Revisit'st thus the glimpses of the moon,
Making night hideous ?   Ibid., 51.

4210.   Look, with what courteous action
It waves you to a more removed ground.   Ibid., 60.

4211. I do not set my life at a pin's fee ;
And for my soul, what can it do to that,
Being a thing immortal as itself ?   Ibid., 65.

4212.   Unhand me, gentlemen ;
By heaven, I'll make a ghost of him that lets me !   Ibid., 84.

4213. Something is rotten in the state of Denmark.   Ibid., 90.

4214.   But that I am forbid
To tell the secrets of my prison-house,
I could a tale unfold whose lightest word
Would harrow up thy soul, freeze thy young blood,
Make thy two eyes, like stars, start from their spheres,
Thy knotted and combined locks to part,
And each particular hair to stand an end,
Like quills upon the fretful porpentine :
But this eternal blazon must not be
To ears of flesh and blood.   List, list O list !   Ibid., **v**. 13.

4215. Murder most foul, as in the best it is ;
But this most foul, strange and unnatural.   Ibid., 27.

4216.   O my prophetic soul !
My uncle !   Ibid., 40.

4217. O Hamlet, what a falling-off was there !   Ibid., 47

4218. But soft ! methinks I scent the morning air.   Ibid., 58.

4219. Cut off even in the blossoms of my sin,
Unhousel'd, disappointed, unaneled,
No reckoning made, but sent to my account
With all my imperfections on my head.   Ibid., 76.

4220.   Leave her to heaven
And to those thorns that in her bosom lodge,
To prick and sting her.   Ibid., 86.

4221. The glow-worm shows the matin to be near,
And 'gins to pale his uneffectual fire.   Ibid., 89

4222.   While memory holds a seat
In this distracted globe.   Remember thee !
Yea, from the table of my memory
I'll wipe away all trivial fond records,
All saws of books, all forms, all pressures past,
That youth and observation copied there.   Ibid., 97.

4223. O villain, villain, smiling, damned villain !
My tables,—meet it is I set it down,
That one may smile, and smile, and be a villain ;
At least I'm sure it may be so in Denmark.   Ibid., 106.

4224. There needs no ghost, my lord, come from the grave
To tell us this.   Ibid., 125.

4225. Wild and whirling words.   Ibid., 133.

4226. There are more things in heaven and earth, Horatio,
Than are dreamt of in your philosophy.   Ibid., 166.

4227. Rest, rest, perturbed spirit !   Ibid., 182.

4228. The time is out of joint : O cursed spite,
That ever I was born to set it right.   Ibid., 189.

4229. Brevity is the soul of wit.   Ibid., **ii**. ii. 90.

4230. More matter, with less art.   Ibid., 95.

4231. That he is mad, 'tis true : 'tis true 'tis pity ;
And pity 'tis 'tis true.   Ibid., 97.

4232.   Doubt thou the stars are fire ;
                  Doubt that the sun doth move ;
                  Doubt truth to be a liar ;
                  But never doubt I love.   Ibid., 116.

4233. Still harping on my daughter.   Ibid., 188.

4234. *Polonius.* What do you read, my lord ?
       Hamlet. Words, words, words.   Ibid., 193.

4235. Though this be madness, yet there is method in't. Ibid., 207.

4236. On fortune's cap we are not the very button.   Ibid., 233.

4237. There is nothing either good or bad, but thinking makes it so.   Ibid., 255.

4238. Beggar that I am, I am even poor in thanks.   Ibid., 271.

4239. It goes so heavily with my disposition that this goodly frame, the earth, seems to me a sterile promontory, this most excellent canopy, the air, look you, this brave o'erhanging firmament, this majestical roof fretted with golden fire, why, it appears no other thing to me than a foul and pestilent congregation of vapours. What a piece of work is a man ! how noble in reason ! how infinite in faculty ! in form and moving how express and admirable ! in action how like an angel ! in apprehension how like a God ! the beauty of the world ! the paragon of animals ! And yet, to me, what is this quintessence of dust ? man delights not me : no, nor woman neither.   Ibid., 304.

4240. I am but mad north-north-west : when the wind is southerly I know a hawk from a handsaw.   Ibid., 397.

4241. The best actors in the world, either for tragedy, comedy, history, pastoral, pastoral-comical, historical-pastoral, tragical-historical, tragical-comical-historical-pastoral, scene individable, or poem unlimited : Seneca cannot be too heavy, nor Plautus too light.
                                          Ibid., 415.

4242. Come, give us a taste of your quality.   Ibid., 451.

4243. The play, I remember, pleased not the million ; 'twas caviare to the general.   Ibid., 456.

4244. The mobled queen.   Ibid., 525.

4245. They are the abstract and brief chronicles of the time. [The players.]   Ibid., 548.

4246. Use every man after his desert, and who should 'scape whipping ?   Ibid., 555.

4247. O, what a rogue and peasant slave am I !   Ibid., 576.

4248. What's Hecuba to him or he to Hecuba,
       That he should weep for her ?   Ibid., 585.

4249. But I am pigeon-liver'd and lack gall
       To make oppression bitter.   Ibid., 605.

4250. Must, like a whore, unpack my heart with words,
       And fall a-cursing, like a very drab,
       A scullion !   Ibid., 614.

4251.   The play's the thing
       Wherein I'll catch the conscience of the king. Ibid.. 633.

4252.   With devotion's visage
          And pious action we do sugar o'er
          The devil himself.   Ibid., III. i. 47.

4253.   To be or not to be : that is the question :
          Whether 'tis nobler in the mind to suffer
          The slings and arrows of outrageous fortune,
          Or to take arms against a sea of troubles,
          And by opposing end them ?   To die : to sleep ;
          No more ; and by a sleep to say we end
          The heart-ache and the thousand natural shocks
          That flesh is heir to, 'tis a consummation
          Devoutly to be wished.   To die, to sleep :
          To sleep : perchance to dream : ay, there's the rub ;
          For in that sleep of death what dreams may come
          When we have shuffled off this mortal coil,
          Must give us pause ; there's the respect
          That makes calamity of so long life ;
          For who would bear the whips and scorns of time,
          The oppressor's wrong, the proud man's contumely,
          The pangs of despised love, the law's delay,
          The insolence of office and the spurns
          That patient merit of the unworthy takes,
          When he himself might his quietus make
          With a bare bodkin ? who would fardels bear,
          To grunt and sweat under a weary life,
          But that the dread of something after death,
          The undiscover'd country from whose bourn
          No traveller returns, puzzles the will
          And makes us rather bear those ills we have
          Than fly to others that we know not of ?
          Thus conscience does make cowards of us all ;
          And thus the native hue of resolution
          Is sicklied o'er with the pale cast of thought,
          And enterprises of great pitch and moment
          With this regard their currents turn awry,
          And lose the name of action.   Ibid., 56.

4254.   Nymph, in thy orisons
          Be all my sins remember'd.   Ibid., 89.

4255.   Take these again ; for to the noble mind
          Rich gifts wax poor when givers prove unkind. Ibid., 100.

  4256. Get thee to a nunnery.   Ibid., 122.

  4257. What should such fellows as I do crawling between earth and
heaven ?   Ibid., 130.

  4258. Be thou as chaste as ice, as pure as snow, thou shalt not
escape calumny.   Ibid., 140.

  4259. I have heard of your paintings too, well enough ; God has
given you one face, and you make yourselves another.   Ibid., 148.

4260.   O, what a noble mind is here o'erthrown !
          The courtier's, soldier's, scholar's, eye, tongue, sword ;
          The expectancy and rose of the fair state,
          The glass of fashion and the mould of form,
          The observed of all observers, quite, quite down ! Ibid., 158.

4261.   Now see that noble and most sovereign reason,
      Like sweet bells jangled, out of tune and harsh.   Ibid., 165.

4262. Speak the speech, I pray you, as I pronounced it to you, trippingly on the tongue : but if you mouth it, as many of your players do, I had as lief the town-crier spoke my lines. Nor do not saw the air too much with your hand, thus, but use all gently.   Ibid., ii. 1.

4263. Tear a passion to tatters, to very rags, to split the ears of the groundlings.   Ibid., 11.

4264. It out-herods Herod.   Ibid., 16.

4265. Suit the action to the word, the word to the action ; with this special observance, that you o'erstep not the modesty of nature.
                                      Ibid., 20.

4266. The purpose of playing, whose end, both at the first and now, was and is, to hold, as 'twere, the mirror up to nature.   Ibid., 24.

4267. I have thought some of nature's journeymen had made men and not made them well, they imitated humanity so abominably.
                                        Ibid., 38.

4268.   A man that fortune's buffets and rewards
         Hast ta'en with equal thanks.   Ibid., 72.

4269.   Give me that man
         That is not passion's slave, and I will wear him
         In my heart's core, ay, in my heart of heart,
         As I do thee.   Ibid., 72.

4270.   And my imaginations are as foul
         As Vulcan's stithy.   Ibid., 88

4271. Here's metal more attractive.   Ibid., 116.

4272. This is miching mallecho ; it means mischief.   Ibid., 147.

4273. *Ophelia.* 'Tis brief, my lord.
      Hamlet. As woman's love.   Ibid., 164.

4274. The lady doth protest too much, methinks.   Ibid., 240.

4275. Let the galled jade wince, our withers are unwrung. Ibid., 253.

4276. What, frighted with false fire !   Ibid., 277.

4277.   Why, let the stricken deer go weep,
        The hart ungalled play ;
      For some must watch, while some must sleep :
        So runs the world away.   Ibid., 282.

4278. The proverb is something musty.   Ibid., 359.

4279. It will discourse most eloquent music.   Ibid., 374.

4280. You would pluck out the heart of my mystery.   Ibid., 381.

4281. Very like a whale.   Ibid., 399.

4282. They fool me to the top of my bent.   Ibid., 401.

4283. 'Tis now the very witching time of night,
      When churchyards yawn and hell itself breathes out
      Contagion to this world.   Ibid., 406.

4284. I will speak daggers to her, but use none.   Ibid., 414.

HAMLET

4285. O, my offence is rank, it smells to heaven ;
It hath the primal eldest curse upon't,
A brother's murder. *Ibid., iii. 36.*

4286. May one be pardon'd and retain the offence ? *Ibid., 56.*

4287.   'Tis not so above ;
There is no shuffling, there the action lies
In his true nature ; and we ourselves compell'd,
Even to the teeth and forehead of our faults,
To give in evidence. *Ibid., 60.*

4288.   About some act
That has no relish of salvation in't. *Ibid., 91.*

4289. My words fly up, my thoughts remain below :
Words without thoughts never to heaven go. *Ibid., 97.*

4290. How now ! a rat ? Dead, for a ducat, dead ! *Ibid., iv. 23.*

4291. As false as dicers' oaths. *Ibid., 45.*

4292. Look here, upon this picture, and on this,
The counterfeit presentment of two brothers.
See, what a grace was seated on this brow ;
Hyperion's curls ; the front of Jove himself ;
An eye like Mars, to threaten and command ;
A station like the herald Mercury
New-lighted on a heaven-kissing hill ;
A combination and a form indeed,
Where every god did seem to set his seal,
To give the world assurance of a man. *Ibid., 53.*

4293. You cannot call it love ; for at your age
The hey-day in the blood is tame, it's humble,
And waits upon the judgment. *Ibid., 68.*

4294. A cutpurse of the empire and the rule,
That from a shelf the precious diadem stole,
And put it in his pocket ! *Ibid., 99.*

4295. A king of shreds and patches. *Ibid., 102.*

4296. This is the very coinage of your brain. *Ibid., 137.*

4297. My pulse, as yours, doth temperately keep time,
And makes as healthful music : it is not madness
That I have utter'd : bring me to the test. *Ibid., 140.*

4298. Lay not the flattering unction to your soul. *Ibid., 145.*

4299. Assume a virtue, if you have it not. *Ibid., 160.*

4300. I must be cruel, only to be kind. *Ibid., 178*

4301. For 'tis the sport to have the enginer
Hoist with his own petar. *Ibid., 206.*

4302.   Diseases desperate grown
By desperate appliance are relieved,
Or not at all. *Ibid., iv. iii. 9.*

4303. A certain convocation of politic worms are e'en at him.
Ibid., 21.

4304. A man may fish with the worm that hath eat of a king, and
eat of the fish that hath fed of that worm *Ibid., 28.*

4305. How all occasions do inform against me,
And spur my dull revenge ! What is a man,
If his chief good and market of his time
Be but to sleep and feed ? a beast, no more.
Sure, he that made us with such large discourse,
Looking before and after, gave us not
That capability and god-like reason
To fust in us unused.   Ibid, iv. 32.

4306.   Some craven scruple
Of thinking too precisely on the event.   Ibid., 40.

4307.   Rightly to be great
Is not to stir without great argument,
But greatly to find quarrel in a straw
When honour's at the stake.   Ibid., 53

4308. So full of artless jealousy is guilt,
It spills itself in fearing to be spilt.   Ibid., v. 19.

4309. How should I your true love know
      From another one ?
By his cockle hat and staff,
      And his sandal shoon.   Ibid., 23.

4310. We know what we are, but know not what we may be.
                                               Ibid., 42.

4311. When sorrows come, they come not single spies,
      But in battalions.   Ibid., 78.

4312. There's such divinity doth hedge a king,
      That treason can but peep to what it would.   Ibid., 123.

4313. To hell, allegiance ! vows, to the blackest devil !
      Conscience and grace, to the profoundest pit !
      I dare damnation.   Ibid., 131.

4314. There's rosemary, that's for remembrance ; pray, love,
remember : and there is pansies, that's for thoughts.   Ibid., 175.

4315. You must wear your rue with a difference.   Ibid., 183.

4316. A very riband in the cap of youth.   Ibid., vii. 78.

4317. One woe doth tread upon another's heel,
      So fast they follow.   Ibid., 164.

4318. Cudgel thy brains no more about it.   Ibid., v. i. 63.

4319. Has this fellow no feeling of his business ?   Ibid., 73.

4320. The hand of little employment hath the daintier sense.
                                               Ibid., 77.

4321. How absolute the knave is ! we must speak by the card, or
equivocation will undo us.   Ibid., 148.

4322. The age is grown so picked that the toe of the peasant comes
so near the heel of the courtier, he galls his kibe.   Ibid., 151.

4323. Alas, poor Yorick ! I knew him, Horatio : a fellow of infinite
jest, of most excellent fancy.   Ibid., 202.

4324. Where be your gibes now ? your gambols ? your songs ? your
flashes of merriment, that were wont to set the table in a roar.
                                               Ibid., 208.

HAMLET

4325. To what base uses we may return, Horatio ! Why may not imagination trace the noble dust of Alexander, till he find it stopping a bung-hole ?
Ibid., 223

4326.   Imperious Caesar, dead and turn'd to clay,
         Might stop a hole to keep the wind away.   Ibid., 236.

4327.   Lay her i' the earth :
         And from her fair and unpolluted flesh
         May violets spring.   Ibid., 261.

4328.   A ministering angel shall my sister be.   Ibid., 264.

4329.   Sweets to the sweet : farewell.   Ibid., 266.

4330.   I thought thy bride-bed to have deck'd, sweet maid,
         And not have strew'd thy grave.   Ibid., 268.

4331.   For, though I am not splenetive and rash,
         Yet have I in me something dangerous.   Ibid., 284.

4332.   Nay, an thou'lt mouth,
         I'll rant as well as thou.   Ibid., 306.

4333.   Let Hercules himself do what he may,
         The cat will mew and dog will have his day.   Ibid., 314.

4334.   There's a divinity that shapes our ends,
         Rough-hew them how we will.   Ibid., ii. 10.

4335.   It did me yeoman's service.   Ibid., 36.

4336.   Into a towering passion.   Ibid., 80.

4337. What imports the nomination of this gentleman ?   Ibid., 133.

4338. His purse is empty already ; all's golden words are spent.
Ibid., 136.

4339. The phrase would be more german to the matter.   Ibid., 165.

4340. Not a whit, we defy augury ; there's a special providence in the fall of a sparrow.
Ibid., 230.

4341.   A hit, a very palpable hit.   Ibid., 292.

4342.   This fell sergeant, death,
         Is strict in his arrest.   Ibid., 347.

4343.   Report me and my cause aright.   Ibid., 350.

4344.   If thou didst ever hold me in thy heart,
         Absent thee from felicity awhile,
         And in this harsh world draw thy breath in pain,
         To tell my story.   Ibid., 357.

4345.   The rest is silence.   Ibid., 369.

4346.   Now cracks a noble heart. Good-night, sweet prince :
         And flights of angels sing thee to thy rest !   Ibid., 370.

THE MERRY WIVES OF WINDSOR
4347. I will make a Star-chamber matter of it.
The Merry Wives of Windsor, I. i. 1.

4348. I had rather than forty shillings I had my Book of Songs and Sonnets here.
Ibid., 205.

THE MERRY WIVES OF WINDSOR

4349.   ' Convey ' the wise it call.   ' Steal ! ' foh !   a fico for the phrase !
                    Ibid., iii. 32.

4350.   Here will be an old abusing of God's patience and the king's English.
                    Ibid., iv. 5.

4351.   We burn daylight.   *Ibid.*, II. i. 54.

4352.   Faith, thou hast some crotchets in thy head.   *Ibid.*, 159.

4353.   Why, then the world's mine oyster,
   Which I with sword will open.   *Ibid.*, ii. 2.

4354.   I cannot tell what the dickens his name is.   *Ibid.*, III. ii. 19.

4355.   O, what a world of vile ill-favour'd faults
   Look handsome in three hundred pounds a-year !
                    Ibid., iv. 32.

4356.   I have a kind of alacrity in sinking.   *Ibid.*, v. 13.

4357.   As good luck would have it.   *Ibid.*, 84.

4358.   The rankest compound of villainous smell that ever offended nostril.
                    Ibid., 93.

4359.   A man of my kidney.   *Ibid.*, 117.

4360.   Vengeance of Jenny's case !   *Ibid.*, IV. i. 64.

4361.   They say there is divinity in odd numbers, either in nativity, chance or death.
                    Ibid., v. i. 3.

TROILUS AND CRESSIDA

4362.   I have had my labour for my travail.
       Troilus and Cressida, I. i. 71.

4363.   Women are angels, wooing :
   Things won are done ;   joy's soul lies in the doing.
   That she beloved knows nought that knows not this :
   Men prize the thing ungain'd more than it is.   *Ibid.*, ii. 312.

4364.   The baby figure of the giant mass
   Of things to come at large.   *Ibid.*, iii. 345.

4365.   I am giddy ;   expectation whirls me round.
   The imaginary relish is so sweet
   That it enchants my sense.   *Ibid.*, III. ii. 19.

4366.   To be wise and love
   Exceeds man's might.   *Ibid.*, 163.

4367.   Welcome ever smiles,
   And farewell goes out sighing.   *Ibid.*, iii. 168.

4368.   One touch of nature makes the whole world kin.   *Ibid.*, 175.

4369.   And give to dust that is a little gilt
   More laud than gilt o'erdusted.   *Ibid.*, 178.

4370.   And, like a dew-drop from the lion's mane,
   Be shook to air.   *Ibid.*, 224.

4371.   There's language in her eye, her cheek, her lip,
   Nay, her foot speaks ;   her wanton spirits look out
   At every joint and motive of her body.   *Ibid.*, IV. v. 55.

4372.   Now they are clapper-clawing one another.   *Ibid.*, v. iv. 1.

4373.   Love all, trust a few,
Do wrong to none : be able for thine enemy
Rather in power than use, and keep thy friend
Under thy own life's key : be check'd for silence,
But never tax'd for speech.

All's Well that ends well, I. i. 73

4374.   'Twere all one
That I should love a bright particular star
And think to wed it, he is so above me.   Ibid., 96.

4375.   The hind that would be mated by the lion
Must die for love.   Ibid., 102.

4376.   Our remedies oft in ourselves do lie,
Which we ascribe to heaven : the fated sky
Gives us free scope, only doth backward pull
Our slow designs when we ourselves are dull.   Ibid., 231.

4377.   Oft expectation fails and most oft there
Where most it promises, and oft it hits
Where hope is coldest and despair most fits.   Ibid., II. i. 145.

4378.   From lowest place when virtuous things proceed,
The place is dignified by the doer's deed.   Ibid., iii. 132

4379.   A young man married is a man that's marr'd.   Ibid., 315

4380. The web of our life is of a mingled yarn, good and ill together
                                                Ibid., IV. iii. 83

4381.   There's place and means for every man alive.   Ibid., 375

4382.   Praising what is lost
Makes the remembrance dear   Ibid., v. iii. 19.

4383.   Heaven doth with us as we with torches do,
Not light them for themselves ; for if our virtues
Did not go forth of us, 'twere all alike
As if we had them not.   Spirits are not finely touch'd
But to fine issues.   *Measure for Measure*, I. i. 33.

4384.   I hold you as a thing ensky'd and sainted.   Ibid., iv. 34.

4385.   A man whose blood
Is very snow-broth ; one who never feels
The wanton stings and motions of the sense.   Ibid., 57.

4386.   Our doubts are traitors
And make us lose the good we oft might win
By fearing to attempt.   Ibid., 77.

4387.   The jury, passing on the prisoner's life,
May in the sworn twelve have a thief or two
Guiltier than him they try.   Ibid., II. i. 19.

4388.   Some rise by sin, and some by virtue fall.   Ibid., 38.

4389.   This will last out a night in Russia.
When nights are longest there.   Ibid., 139.

4390.   Condemn the fault, and not the actor of it ?   Ibid., ii. 37.

4391.   No ceremony that to great ones 'longs,
        Not the king's crown, nor the deputed sword,
        The marshal's truncheon, nor the judge's robe,
        Become them with so half as good a grace
        As mercy does.   Ibid., 59.

4392.   Why, all the souls that were were forfeit once ;
        And He that might the vantage best have took
        Found out the remedy. How would you be,
        If He, which is the top of judgment, should
        But judge you as you are ?   Ibid., 73.

4393.   O, it is excellent
        To have a giant's strength ; but it is tyrannous
        To use it like a giant.   Ibid., 107.

4394.   But man, proud man,
        Drest in a little brief authority,
        Most ignorant of what he's most assured,
        His glassy essence, like an angry ape,
        Play such fantastic tricks before high heaven
        As make the angels weep.   Ibid., 117.

4395.   That in the captain's but a choleric word,
        Which in the soldier is flat blasphemy.   Ibid., 130.

4396.   The miserable have no other medicine
        But only hope.   Ibid., III. i. 2.

4397.   Be absolute for death ; either death or life
        Shall thereby be the sweeter. Reason thus with life :
        If I do lose thee, I do lose a thing
        That none but fools would keep : a breath thou art,
        Servile to all the skyey influences.   Ibid., 5.

4398.   Palsied eld.   Ibid., 36.

4399.   The sense of death is most in apprehension ;
        And the poor beetle, that we tread upon,
        In corporal sufferance finds a pang as great
        As when a giant dies.   Ibid., 78.

4400.   If I must die,
        I will encounter darkness as a bride,
        And hug it in mine arms.   Ibid., 83.

4401.   Ay, but to die, and go we know not where ;
        To lie in cold obstruction and to rot ;
        This sensible warm motion to become
        A kneaded clod ; and the delighted spirit
        To bathe in fiery floods, or to reside
        In thrilling region of thick-ribbed ice ;
        To be imprison'd in the viewless winds,
        And blown with restless violence round about
        The pendent world !   Ibid., 118.

4402.   The weariest and most loathed worldly life
        That age, ache, penury and imprisonment
        Can lay on nature is a paradise
        To what we fear of death.   Ibid., 129.

4403.   Virtue is bold, and goodness never fearful.   Ibid., 215.

4404. There, at the moated grange, resides this dejected Mariana.

Ibid., 277.

4405. Take, O, take those lips away
    That so sweetly were forsworn ;
And those eyes, the break of day,
    Lights that do mislead the morn :
But my kisses bring again, bring again ;
Seals of love, but seal'd in vain, seal'd in vain.

Ibid., IV. i. 1.

4406. Every true man's apparel fits your thief. *Ibid.,* ii. 46.

4407. A forted residence 'gainst the tooth of time
And razure of oblivion. *Ibid.,* v. i. 12.

4408. They say, best men are moulded out of faults ;
And, for the most, become much more the better
For being a little bad. *Ibid.,* 444.

OTHELLO

4409. A fellow almost damn'd in a fair wife;
That never set a squadron in the field,
Nor the divisions of a battle knows
More than a spinster. *Othello,* I. i. 21.

4410. The bookish theoric. *Ibid.,* 24.

4411. But I will wear my heart upon my sleeve
For daws to peck at. *Ibid.,* 64.

4412. You are one of those that will not serve God, if the devil bid
you. *Ibid.,* 107.

4413. Your daughter and the Moor are now making the beast with
two backs. *Ibid.,* 117.

4414. The wealthy curled darlings of our nation. *Ibid.,* ii. 68.

4415. Most potent, grave, and reverend signiors,
My very noble and approved good masters. *Ibid.,* iii. 76.

4416. The very head and front of my offending
Hath this extent, no more. *Ibid.,* 80

4417.   Rude am I in my speech,
And little bless'd with the soft phrase of peace ;
For since these arms of mine had seven years' pith,
Till now some nine moons wasted, they have used
Their dearest action in the tented field. *Ibid.,* 81.

4418. I will a round unvarnish'd tale deliver
Of my whole course of love. *Ibid.,* 90.

4419.   A maiden never bold ;
Of spirit so still and quiet, that her motion
Blush'd at herself. *Ibid.,* 94.

4420. Wherein I spake of most disastrous chances,
Of moving accidents by flood and field,
Of hairbreadth 'scapes i' th' imminent deadly breach.

Ibid., 134.

4421.   Antres vast and deserts idle,
Rough quarries, rocks and hills whose heads touch
    heaven. *Ibid.,* 140.

L

OTHELLO

4422. And of the Cannibals that each other eat,
The Anthropophagi and men whose heads
Do grow beneath their shoulders. *Ibid.,* 143.

4423. My story being done,
She gave me for my pains a world of sighs :
She swore, in faith, 'twas strange, 'twas passing strange,
'Twas pitiful, 'twas wondrous pitiful :
She wish'd she had not heard it, yet she wish'd
That heaven had made her such a man : she thank'd me,
And bade me, if I had a friend that loved her,
I should but teach him how to tell my story,
And that would woo her. Upon this hint I spake :
She loved me for the dangers I had pass'd,
And I loved her that she did pity them.
This only is the witchcraft I have used. *Ibid.,* 158.

4424. I do perceive here a divided duty. *Ibid.,* 181.

4425. To mourn a mischief that is past and gone
Is the next way to draw new mischief on. *Ibid.,* 204.

4426. The robb'd that smiles steals something from the thief.
Ibid., 208.

4427. The tyrant custom, most grave senators,
Hath made the flinty and steel couch of war
My thrice-driven bed of down. *Ibid.,* 230.

4428. Put money in thy purse. *Ibid.,* 345.

4429. The food that to him now is as luscious as locusts, shall be
to him shortly as bitter as coloquintida. *Ibid.,* 354.

4430. Framed to make women false. *Ibid.,* 404.

4431. I am not merry ; but I do beguile
The thing I am, by seeming otherwise. *Ibid.,* II. i. 122.

4432. To suckle fools and chronicle small beer. *Ibid.,* 161.

4433. O most lame and impotent conclusion ! *Ibid.,* 162.

4434. I have very poor and unhappy brains for drinking : I could
wish courtesy would invent some other custom of entertainment.
Ibid., iii. 34.

4435. Potations pottle-deep. *Ibid.,* 57.

4436. And let me the canakin clink ;
A soldier's a man ;
A life's but a span ;
Why, then, let a soldier drink. *Ibid.,* 72.

4437. Silence that dreadful bell : it frights the isle
From her propriety. *Ibid,,* 175.

4438. But men are men ; the best sometimes forget. *Ibid.,* 241.

4439. Cassio, I love thee ;
But never more be officer of mine. *Ibid.,* 248.

4440. Reputation, reputation, reputation ! O, I have lost my reputation ! I have lost the immortal part of myself, and what remains is
bestial. *Ibid.,* 262.

4441. O God, that men should put an enemy in their mouths to steal away their brains !
Ibid., 292.

4442. Come, come, good wine is a good familiar creature, if it be well used.
Ibid., 313.

4443.   How poor are they that have not patience !
          What wound did ever heal but by degrees ?
Ibid., 376.

4444.   Excellent wretch ! Perdition catch my soul,
          But I do love thee ! and when I love thee not,
          Chaos is come again.
Ibid., III. iii. 90.

4445.   Good name in man and woman, dear my lord,
          Is the immediate jewel of their souls :
          Who steals my purse steals trash ; 'tis something,
               nothing ;
          'Twas mine, 'tis his, and has been slave to thousands ;
          But he that filches from me my good name
          Robs me of that which not enriches him
          And makes me poor indeed.
Ibid., 155.

4446.   O, beware, my lord, of jealousy ;
          It is the green-eyed monster which doth mock
          The meat it feeds on.
Ibid., 164.

4447.   I am declined
          Into the vale of years.
Ibid., 265.

4448.   O curse of marriage,
          That we can call these delicate creatures ours,
          And not their appetites ! I had rather be a toad,
          And live upon the vapour of a dungeon,
          Than keep a corner in the thing I love
          For others' uses.
Ibid., 268.

4449.   Trifles light as air
          Are to the jealous confirmations strong
          As proofs of holy writ.
Ibid., 322.

4450.   Not poppy, nor mandragora,
          Nor all the drowsy syrups of the world,
          Shall ever medicine thee to that sweet sleep
          Which thou owedst yesterday.
Ibid., 330.

4451.   He that is robb'd, not wanting what is stol'n,
          Let him not know't, and he's not robb'd at all.
Ibid., 342.

4452.   O, now for ever
          Farewell the tranquil mind ! farewell content !
          Farewell the plumed troop, and the big wars
          That make ambition virtue ! O. farewell !
          Farewell the neighing steed, and the shrill trump,
          The spirit-stirring drum, the ear-piercing fife,
          The royal banner, and all quality,
          Pride, pomp and circumstance of glorious war !
          And, O you mortal engines, whose rude throats
          The immortal Jove's dread clamours counterfeit,
          Farewell ! Othello's occupation's gone !
Ibid., 347.

4453. Be sure of it ; give me the ocular proof.
Ibid., 360.

4454. No hinge nor loop
To hang a doubt on.   Ibid., 365.

4455. On horror's head horrors accumulate.   Ibid., 370.

4456. Take note, take note, O world,
To be direct and honest is not safe.   Ibid., 377.

4457. But this denoted a foregone conclusion.   Ibid., 428.

4458. Like to the Pontic sea,
Whose icy current and compulsive course
Ne'er feels retiring ebb, but keeps due on
To the Propontic and the Hellespont,
Even so my bloody thoughts, with violent pace,
Shall ne'er look back, ne'er ebb to humble love,
Till that a capable and wide revenge
Swallow them up.   Ibid., 453.

4459. I would have him nine years a-killing.   Ibid., IV. i. 188.

4460. But yet the pity of it, Iago ! O Iago, the pity of it, Iago !
                                                         Ibid., 206.

4461. But, alas, to make me
A fixed figure for the time of scorn
To point his slow unmoving finger at.   Ibid., ii. 53.

4462. O thou weed,
Who art so lovely fair and smell'st so sweet
That the sense aches at thee, would thou hadst ne'er been
                born !   Ibid., 67.

4463. O heaven, that such companions thou'ldst unfold,
And put in every honest hand a whip
To lash the rascals naked through the world.   Ibid., 141.

4464. 'Tis neither here not there.   Ibid., iii. 59.

4465. He hath a daily beauty in his life
That makes me ugly.   Ibid., v. i. 19.

4466. This is the night
That either makes me or fordoes me quite.   Ibid., 128.

4467. It is the cause, it is the cause, my soul,—
Let me not name it to you, you chaste stars !—
It is the cause.   Ibid., ii. 1.

4468. Put out the light, and then put out the light ;
If I quench thee, thou flaming minister,
I can again thy former light restore,
Should I repent me ; but once put out thy light,
Thou cunning pattern of excelling nature,
I know not where is that Promethean heat
That can thy light relume.   Ibid., 7.

4469. Had all his hairs been lives, my great revenge
Had stomach for them all.   Ibid., 74.

4470. She was too fond of her most filthy bargain.   Ibid., 157.

4471. Curse his better angel from his side
And fall to reprobation.   Ibid., 208.

4472. Every puny whisper gets my sword.   *Ibid.*, 244.

4473. Here is my journey's end, here is my butt,
And very sea-mark of my utmost sail.   *Ibid.*, 267.

4474. Soft you ; a word or two before you go.
I have done the state some service, and they know't.
No more of that. I pray you, in your letters,
Speak of me as I am ; nothing extenuate,
Nor set down aught in malice : then must you tell
Of one that loved not wisely but too well ;
Of one not easily jealous, but being wrought
Perplex'd in the extreme ; of one whose hand,
Like the base Indian, threw a pearl away
Richer than all his tribe ; of one whose subdued eyes,
Albeit unused to the melting mood,
Drop tears as fast as the Arabian trees
Their medicinal gum. Set you down this ;
And say besides, that in Aleppo once,
Where a malignant and a turban'd Turk
Beat a Venetian and traduced the state,
I took by the throat the circumcised dog,
And smote him, thus.   *Ibid.*, 338.

4475. *Lear.* So young, and so untender ?
Cordelia. So young, my lord, and true.   *King Lear*, I. i. 108.

4476. A still-soliciting eye.   *Ibid.*, 234.

4477. These late eclipses in the sun and moon portend no good to us.
    Ibid., ii. 112.

4478. This is the excellent foppery of the world, that, when we are
sick in fortune,—often the surfeit of our own behaviour,—we make
guilty of our disasters the sun, the moon, and the stars: as if we were
villains by necessity ; fools by heavenly compulsion ; knaves, thieves,
and treachers, by spherical predominance ; drunkards, liars, and
adulterers, by an enforced obedience of planetary influence ; and all
that we are evil in, by a divine thrusting on.   *Ibid.*, 129.

4479. My cue is villainous melancholy, with a sigh like Tom o'
Bedlam.   *Ibid.*, 147.

4480. Ingratitude, thou marble-hearted fiend,
More hideous when thou show'st thee in a child
Than the sea-monster !   *Ibid.*, iv. 281.

4481. How sharper than a serpent's tooth it is
To have a thankless child.   *Ibid.*, 310.

4482. Striving to better, oft we mar what's well.   *Ibid.*, 369.

4483. Thou whoreson zed ! thou unnecessary letter !
    Ibid., II. ii. 69.

4484. I have seen better faces in my time
Than stands on any shoulder that I see
Before me at this instant.   *Ibid.*, 99.

4485. Fortune, good night : smile once more ; turn thy wheel !
    Ibid., 180.

KING LEAR

4486.   Hysterica passio, down, thou climbing sorrow,
       Thy element's below.   Ibid., iv. 57.

4487.   That sir which serves and seeks for gain,
          And follows but for form,
       Will pack when it begins to rain,
          And leave thee in the storm.   Ibid., 79.

4488.   You are old ;
       Nature in you stands on the very verge
       Of her confine.   Ibid., 148.

4489.   And let not women's weapons, water-drops,
       Stain my man's cheeks !   Ibid., 280.

4490.   Blow, winds, and crack your cheeks ! rage ! blow !
       You cataracts and hurricanoes, spout
       Till you have drench'd our steeples, drown'd the cocks !
       You sulphurous and thought-executing fires,
       Vaunt-couriers to oak-cleaving thunderbolts,
       Singe my white head ! And thou, all-shaking thunder,
       Smite flat the thick rotundity o' the world !
       Crack nature's moulds, all germens spill at once,
       That make ungrateful man !   Ibid., III. ii. 1.

4491.   I tax you not, you elements, with unkindness.   Ibid., 16.

4492.   A poor, infirm, weak, and despised old man.   Ibid., 20.

4493.   There was never yet fair woman but she made mouths in a
glass.   Ibid., 35.

4494.   Things that love night
       Love not such nights as these ; the wrathful skies
       Gallow the very wanderers of the dark.   Ibid., 42.

4495.   I am a man
       More sinn'd against than sinning.   Ibid., 59.

4496.   O, that way madness lies ; let me shun that.   Ibid., iv. 21.

4497.   Poor naked wretches, whersoe'er you are,
       That bide the pelting of this pitiless storm,
       How shall your houseless heads and unfed sides,
       Your loop'd and window'd raggedness, defend you
       From seasons such as these ?   Ibid., 28.

4498.   Take physic, pomp ;
       Expose thyself to feel what wretches feel.   Ibid., 33.

4499.   Out-paramoured the Turk.   Ibid., 94.

4500.   'Tis a naughty night to swim in.   Ibid., 115.

4501.   The green mantle of the standing pool.   Ibid., 139.

4502.   But mice and rats and such small deer,
       Have been Tom's food for seven long year.   Ibid., 144.

4503.   The prince of darkness is a gentleman.   Ibid., 148.

4504.   Poor Tom's a-cold.   Ibid., 152.

4505.   I'll talk a word with this same learned Theban.   Ibid., 162.

4506.   Child Rowland to the dark tower came,
His word was still,—Fie, foh, and fum.
I smell the blood of a British man.   Ibid., 187.

4507.   The little dogs and all,
Tray, Blanch, and Sweet-heart, see, they bark at me.
                                                       Ibid., vi. 65.

4508.   Mastiff, greyhound, mongrel grim,
Hound or spaniel, brach or lym,
Or bobtail tike or trundle-tail.   Ibid., 71.

4509.   The worst is not
So long as we can say ' This is the worst.'   Ibid., IV. i. 29.

4510.   As flies to wanton boys, are we to gods,
They kill us for their sport.   Ibid., 38.

4511.   You are not worth the dust which the rude wind
Blows in your face.   Ibid., ii. 30.

4512.   Wisdom and goodness to the vile seem vile :
Filths savour but themselves.   Ibid., 38.

4513.   Patience and sorrow strove
Who should express her goodliest.   Ibid., iii. 18.

4514.   It is the stars,
The stars above us, govern our conditions.   Ibid., 34.

4515.   How fearful
And dizzy 'tis to cast one's eyes so low !
The crows and choughs that wing the midway air
Show scarce so gross as beetles : half way down
Hangs one that gathers samphire, dreadful trade !
The fishermen, that walk upon the beach,
Appear like mice ; and yond tall anchoring bark,
Diminish'd to her cock ; her cock, a buoy
Almost too small for sight : the murmuring surge
That on the unnumber'd idle pebbles chafes,
Cannot be heard so high.   Ibid., vi. 11.

4516.   Ay, every inch a king.   Ibid. 109.

4517.   The wren goes to 't, and the small gilded fly
Does lecher in my sight.   Ibid., 114.

4518.   Give me an ounce of civet, good apothecary, to sweeten my
imagination.   Ibid., 132.

4519.   See how yond justice rails upon yond simple thief. Hark, in
thine ear : change places ; and handy-dandy, which is the justice,
which is the thief ?   Ibid., 155.

4520.   Through tatter'd clothes small vices do appear ;
Robes and furr'd gowns hide all.   Ibid., 168.

4521.   Mine enemy's dog,
Though he had bit me, should have stood that night
Against my fire.   Ibid., vii. 36.

4522.   I am a very foolish fond old man,
Fourscore and upward, not an hour more or less ;
And, to deal plainly,
I fear I am not in my perfect mind.   Ibid., 60.

4523.   Men must endure
Their going hence, even as their coming hither :
Ripeness is all.   Ibid., v. ii. 9.

4524.   Come, let's away to prison :
We two alone will sing like birds i' the cage :
When thou dost ask me blessing, I'll kneel down,
And ask of thee forgiveness : so we'll live,
And pray, and sing, and tell old tales, and laugh
At gilded butterflies, and hear poor rogues
Talk of court news ; and we'll talk with them too,
Who loses and who wins ; who's in, who's out ;
And take upon's the mystery of things,
As if we were God's spies.   Ibid., iii. 8.

4525.   Upon such sacrifices, my Cordelia,
The gods themselves throw incense.   Ibid., 20.

4526.   The gods are just, and of our pleasant vices
Make instruments to plague us.   Ibid., 170.

4527.   The wheel is come full circle.   Ibid., 174.

4528.   Her voice was ever soft,
Gentle and low, an excellent thing in woman.   Ibid., 272.

4529.   I have seen the day, with my good biting falchion
I would have made them skip.   Ibid., 276.

4530.   And my poor fool is hang'd ! No, no, no life !
Why should a dog, a horse, a rat, have life,
And thou no breath at all ? Thou'lt come no more,
Never, never, never, never, never !   Ibid,. 305.

4531.   Vex not his ghost : O, let him pass ! he hates him much
That would upon the rack of this tough world
Stretch him out longer.   Ibid., 313.

4532.   *First Witch.* When shall we three meet again
        In thunder, lightning, or in rain ?
    Second Witch. When the hurly-burly's done,
        When the battle's lost and won.   *Macbeth,* I. i. 1.

4533.   Fair is foul, and foul is fair.   Ibid., 11.

4534.   What bloody man is that ?   Ibid., ii. 1.

4535.   Sleep shall neither night nor day
Hang upon his pent-house lid ;
He shall live a man forbid :
Weary se'nnights nine times nine
Shall he dwindle, peak and pine.   Ibid., iii. 19.

4536.   The weird sisters.   Ibid., 32.

4537.   What are these
So wither'd and so wild in their attire,
That look not like the inhabitants o' the earth,
And yet are on't ?   Ibid., 39.

4538.   If you can look into the seeds of time,
And say which grain will grow and which will not.   Ibid. 58.

4539.   Stands not within the prospect of belief.   Ibid., 7.

MACBETH

4540. The earth hath bubbles, as the water has,
And these are of them. Ibid., 79.

4541. The insane root
That takes the reason prisoner. Ibid., 84.

4542. And oftentimes, to win us to our harm,
The instruments of darkness tell us truths,
Win us with honest trifles, to betray's
In deepest consequence. Ibid., 123

4543. Why do I yield to that suggestion
Whose horrid image doth unfix my hair
And makes my seated heart knock at my ribs
Against the use of nature ? Present fears
Are less than horrible imaginings. Ibid., 134.

4544. Come what come may,
Time and the hour runs through the roughest day. Ibid., 146.

4545. Nothing in his life
Became him like the leaving it ; he died
As one that had been studied in his death
To throw away the dearest thing he owed,
As 'twere a careless trifle. Ibid., iv. 7.

4546. There's no art
To find the mind's construction in the face ;
He was a gentleman on whom I built
An absolute trust. Ibid., 11.

4547. Yet I do fear thy nature ;
It is too full o' the milk of human kindness. Ibid., v. 17.

4548. What thou wouldst highly,
That wouldst thou holily ; wouldst not play false,
And yet wouldst wrongly win. Ibid., 21.

4549. That no compunctions visitings of nature
Shake my fell purpose. Ibid., 46.

4550. Your face, my thane, is as a book where men
May read strange matters. Ibid., 63.

4551. Look like the innocent flower,
But be the serpent under't. Ibid., 66

4552. This castle hath a pleasant seat ; the air
Nimbly and sweetly recommends itself
Unto our gentle senses. Ibid., vi. 1.

4553. Coign of vantage. Ibid., 7.

4554. If it were done when 'tis done, then 'twere well
It were done quickly : if the assassination
Could trammel up the consequence, and catch
With his surcease success ; that but this blow
Might be the be-all and the end-all here,
But here, upon this bank and shoal of time,
We'ld jump the life to come. Ibid., vii. 1.

4555. We but teach
Bloody instructions, which, being taught, return
To plague the inventor : this even-handed justice
Commends the ingredients of our poison'd chalice
To our own lips. Ibid., 8

*L

4556.   Besides, this Duncan
Hath borne his faculties so meek, hath been
So clear in his great office, that his virtues
Will plead like angels, trumpet-tongued, against
The deep damnation of his taking-off ;
And pity, like a naked new-born babe,
Striding the blast, or heaven's cherubim, horsed
Upon the sightless couriers of the air,
Shall blow the horrid deed in every eye.   Ibid., 16.

4557.   I have no spur
To prick the sides of my intent, but only
Vaulting ambition, which o'erleaps itself
And falls on the other.   Ibid., 25.

4558.   I have bought
Golden opinions from all sorts of people.   Ibid., 32.

4559.   Letting I ' dare not ' wait upon ' I would,'
Like the poor cat i' the adage.   Ibid., 44.

4560.   I dare do all that may become a man ;
Who dares do more is none.   Ibid., 46.

4561.   I have given suck, and know
How tender 'tis to love the babe that milks me :
I would, while it was smiling in my face,
Have pluck'd my nipple from his boneless gums,
And dash'd the brains out, had I so sworn as you
Have done to this.   Ibid., 54.

4562.   *Macbeth.*   If we should fail ?
Lady Macbeth.   We fail !
But screw your courage to the sticking-place,
And we'll not fail.   Ibid., 59.

4563.   Memory, the warder of the brain.   Ibid., 65.

4564.   Away, and mock the time with fairest show :
False face must hide what the false heart doth know.
                                                   Ibid., 81.

4565.   There's husbandry in heaven ;
Their candles are all out.   Ibid., ii. i. 4.

4566.   Merciful powers,
Restrain in me the cursed thoughts that nature
Gives way to in repose.   Ibid., 7.

4567.   Shut up
In measureless content.   Ibid., 15.

4568.   Is this a dagger which I see before me,
The handle toward my hand ? Come, let me clutch thee.
I have thee not, and yet I see thee still.
Art thou not, fatal vision, sensible
To feeling as to sight ? or art thou but
A dagger of the mind, a false creation,
Proceeding from the heat-oppressed brain ?   Ibid., 33

4569.   Thou sure and firm-set earth,
Hear not my steps, which way they walk, for fear
The very stones prate of my whereabout.   Ibid., 56.

4570. Hear it not, Duncan ; for it is a knell
That summons thee to heaven or to hell.   Ibid., 63.

4571. It was the owl that shriek'd, the fatal bellman
Which gave the stern'st good-night.   Ibid., ii. 3.

4572.   The attempt and not the deed
Confounds us.   Ibid., 11.

4573. Consider it not so deeply.   Ibid., 30.

4574. I had most need of blessing, and ' Amen '
Stuck in my throat.   Ibid., 32.

4575.   These deeds must not be thought
After these ways ; so, it will make us mad.   Ibid., 33.

4576. Methought I heard a voice cry ' Sleep no more !
Macbeth does murder sleep ', the innocent sleep,
Sleep that knits up the ravell'd sleave of care,
The death of each day's life, sore labour's bath,
Balm of hurt minds, great nature's second course,
Chief nourisher in life's feast.   Ibid., 35.

4577.   Infirm of purpose !
Give me the daggers.   Ibid. 52.

4578. Will all great Neptune's ocean wash this blood
Clean from my hand ?   No, this my hand will rather
The multitudinous seas incarnadine,
Making the green one red.   Ibid., 60.

4579. Go the primrose way to the everlasting bonfire. Ibid., iii. 23.

4580. The labour we delight in physics pain.   Ibid., 54.

4581. Confusion now hath made his masterpiece !
Most sacrilegious murder hath broke ope
The Lord's anointed temple, and stole thence
The life o' the building.   Ibid., 71.

4582. Shake off this downy sleep, death's counterfeit,
And look on death itself !   Ibid., 81.

4583. The wine of life is drawn, and the mere lees
Is left this vault to brag of.   Ibid., 100.

4584. Who can be wise, amazed, temperate and furious,
Loyal and neutral, in a moment ?   Ibid., 113.

4585. A falcon, towering in her pride of place,
Was by a mousing owl hawk'd at and kill'd.   Ibid., iv. 12.

4586. I must become a borrower of the night
For a dark hour or twain.   Ibid., III. i. 26.

4587. *First Murderer.*   We are men, my liege.
Macbeth.   Ay, in the catalogue ye go for men ;
As hounds and greyhounds, mongrels, spaniels, curs,
Shoughs, water-rugs and demiwolves are clept
All by the name of dogs.   Ibid., 91.

4588.   I am one, my liege,
Whom the vile blows and buffets of the world
Have so incensed that I am reckless what
I do to spite the world.   Ibid., 108.

4589.   Things without all remedy
Should be without regard : what's done is done. *Ibid.,* ii. 11.

4590.   We have scotch'd the snake, not kill'd it.   *Ibid.,* 13.

4591.   Duncan is in his grave ;
After life's fitful fever he sleeps well
Treason has done his worst : nor steel, nor poison,
Malice domestic, foreign levy, nothing,
Can touch him further.   *Ibid.,* 22.

4592.   But in them nature's copy's not eterne.   *Ibid.,* 38.

4593.   The shard-borne beetle with his drowsy hums
Hath rung night's yawning peal.   *Ibid.,* 42.

4594.   A deed of dreadful note.   *Ibid.,* 44.

4595.   Be innocent of the knowledge, dearest chuck,
Till thou applaud the deed.   *Ibid.,* 45.

4596.   Light thickens ; and the crow
Makes wing to the rooky wood :
Good things of day begin to droop and drowse ;
Whiles night's black agents to their preys do rouse. *Ibid.,* 50.

4597.   Things bad begun make strong themselves by ill. *Ibid.,* 55.

4598.   Now spurs the lated traveller apace
To gain the timely inn.   *Ibid.,* iii. 6.

4599.   But now I am cabin'd, cribb'd, confined, bound in
To saucy doubts and fears.   *Ibid.,* iv. 24.

4600.   Now, good digestion wait on appetite,
And health on both !   *Ibid.,* 38.

4601.   Thou canst not say I did it : never shake
Thy gory locks at me.   *Ibid.,* 50.

4602.   The air-drawn dagger.   *Ibid.,* 62.

4603.   The time has been,
That, when the brains were out, the man would die,
And there an end ; but now they rise again,
With twenty mortal murders on their crowns,
And push us from our stools.   *Ibid.,* 78.

4604.   What man dare, I dare :
Approach thou like the rugged Russian bear,
The arm'd rhinocerus, or the Hyrcan tiger ;
Take any shape but that, and my firm nerves
Shall never tremble.   *Ibid.,* 99.

4605.   Hence, horrible shadow !
Unreal mockery, hence !   *Ibid.,* 106.

4606.   You have displaced the mirth, broke the good meeting,
With most admired disorder.   *Ibid.,* 109.

4607.   Stand not upon the order of your going,
But go at once.   *Ibid.,* 119.

4608.   *Macbeth.*   What is the night ?
Lady Macbeth.   Almost at odds with morning, which is which.
                                                    Ibid., 126.

4609.   I am in blood
       Stepp'd in so far that, should I wade no more,
       Returning were as tedious as go o'er.   Ibid., 136.

4610.   Double, double, toil and trouble ;
       Fire burn and cauldron bubble.   Ibid., IV. i. 10.

4611.   By the pricking of my thumbs,
   · Something wicked this way comes.
            Open, locks,
               Whoever knocks !   Ibid., 44.

4612.   How now, you secret, black, and midnight hags !   Ibid., 48.

4613.   A deed without a name.   Ibid., 49.

4614.   But yet I'll make assurance double sure,
       And take a bond of fate.   Ibid., 83.

4615.   Macbeth shall never vanquished be until
       Great Birnam wood to high Dunsinane hill
       Shall come against him.   Ibid., 92.

4616.   What, will the line stretch out to the crack of doom ?
                     Ibid., 117.

4617.   When our actions do not,
       Our fears do make us traitors.   Ibid., ii. 3.

4618.   Angels are bright still, though the brightest fell.
                     Ibid., iii. 22.

4619.   Pour the sweet milk of concord into hell,
       Uproar the universal peace, confound
       All unity on earth.   Ibid., 98.

4620.   Stands Scotland where it did ?   Ibid., 164.

4621.   Give sorrow words : the grief that does not speak
       Whispers the o'erfrought heart and bids it break.   Ibid., 209.

4622.   What, all my pretty chickens and their dam
       At one fell swoop ?   Ibid., 218.

4623.   *Malcolm.*   Dispute it like a man.
       Macduff.   I shall do so ;
       But I must also feel it as a man :
       I cannot but remember such things were,
       That were most precious to me.   Ibid., 220.

4624.   O, I could play the woman with mine eyes
       And braggart with my tongue !   Ibid., 230.

4625.   Out, damned spot ! out, I say !   Ibid., v. i. 39.

4626.   Fie, my lord, fie ! a soldier, and afeard ?   Ibid., 41.

4627.   Yet who would have thought the old man to have had so
much blood in him.   Ibid., 44.

4628.   All the perfumes of Arabia will not sweeten this little hand.
                     Ibid., 57.

4629.   The devil damn thee black, thou cream-faced loon !
       Where got'st thou that goose look ?   Ibid., iii. 11.

4630. I have lived long enough : my way of life
Is fall'n into the sear, the yellow leaf :
And that which should accompany old age,
As honour, love, obedience, troops of friends,
I must not look to have ; but, in their stead,
Curses, not loud but deep, mouth-honour, breath,
Which the poor heart would fain deny, and dare not. Ibid., 22.

4631. Canst thou not minister to a mind diseased,
Pluck from the memory a rooted sorrow,
Raze out the written troubles of the brain
And with some sweet oblivious antidote
Cleanse the stuff'd bosom of that perilous stuff
Which weighs upon the heart ? Ibid., 40.

4632. Throw physic to the dogs ; I'll none of it. Ibid., 47.

4633. I would applaud thee to the very echo,
That should applaud again. Ibid., 53.

4634. Hang out our banners on the outward walls :
The cry is still ' They come.' Ibid., v. 1.

4635. The time has been, my senses would have cool'd
To hear a night-shriek ; and my fell of hair
Would at a dismal treatise rouse and stir
As life were in't : I have supp'd full with horrors ;
Direness, familiar to my slaughterous thoughts,
Cannot once start me. Ibid., 10.

4636. To-morrow, and to-morrow, and to-morrow,
Creeps in this petty pace from day to day
To the last syllable of recorded time,
And all our yesterdays have lighted fools
The way to dusty death. Out, out, brief candle !
Life's but a walking shadow, a poor player
That struts and frets his hour upon the stage
And then is heard no more : it is a tale
Told by an idiot, full of sound and fury,
Signifying nothing. Ibid., 19.

4637. I 'gin to be aweary of the sun. Ibid., 49.

4638. Blow wind ! come, wrack !
At least we'll die with harness on our back. Ibid., 51.

4639. They have tied me to a stake ; I cannot fly,
But, bear-like, I must fight the course. Ibid., vii. 1.

4640. I bear a charmed life. Ibid., viii. 12.

4641. And be these juggling fiends no more believed,
That palter with us in a double sense ;
That keep the word of promise to our ear,
And break it to our hope. Ibid., 19.

4642. Live to be the show and gaze o' the time. Ibid., 24.

4643. Lay on, Macduff,
And damn'd be him that first cries ' Hold, enough ! ' Ibid., 33.

ANTONY AND CLEOPATRA

4644. There's beggary in the love that can be reckon'd.
Antony and Cleopatra, I. i. 15.

4645. In nature's infinite book of secrecy
A little can I read.   Ibid., ii. 9.

4646. The nature of bad news infects the teller.   Ibid., 99.

4647. Where's my serpent of old Nile ?   Ibid., v. 25.

4648.   My salad days,
When I was green in judgment.   Ibid., 73.

4649. The barge she sat in, like a burnish'd throne,
Burn'd on the water : the poop was beaten gold ;
Purple the sails, and so perfumed that
The winds were love-sick with them ; the oars were silver,
Which to the tune of flutes kept stroke, and made
The water which they beat to follow faster,
As amorous of their strokes.   For her own person,
It beggar'd all description.   Ibid., ii. 196.

4650.   I saw her once
Hop forty paces through the public street ;
And having lost her breath, she spoke, and panted,
That she did make defect perfection,
And, breathless, power breathe forth.   Ibid., 233.

4651. Age cannot wither her, nor custom stale
Her infinite variety.   Ibid., 240.

4652. Though it be honest, it is never good
To bring bad news.   Ibid., v. 85.

4653. Come, thou monarch of the vine
Plumpy Bacchus with pink eyne !   Ibid., vii. 120.

4654. Who does i' the wars more than his captain can,
Becomes his captain's captain : and ambition,
The soldier's virtue, rather makes choice of loss,
Than gain which darkens him.   Ibid., III. i. 21.

4655. Celerity is never more admired
Than by the negligent.   Ibid., vii. 25

4656.   He wears the rose
Of youth upon him.   Ibid., xiii. 20.

4657. I found you as a morsel cold upon
Dead Caesar's trencher.   Ibid., 116.

4658. Let's have one other gaudy night.   Ibid., 183.

4659. To business that we love we rise betime,
And go to't with delight.   Ibid., IV. iv. 20.

4660.   I have yet
Room for six scotches more.   Ibid., vii. 9.

4661. Sometime we see a cloud that's dragonish ·
A vapour sometime like a bear or lion,
A tower'd citadel, a pendent rock,
A forked mountain, or blue promontory
With trees upon't.   Ibid., xiv. 2

ANTONY AND CLEOPATRA

4662. Unarm, Eros ; the long day's task is done,
And we must sleep. Ibid., 35.

4663. I am dying, Egypt, dying ; only
I here importune death awhile, until
Of many thousand kisses the poor last
I lay upon thy lips. Ibid., xv. 18.

4664. O, wither'd is the garland of the war,
The soldier's pole is fall'n : young boys and girls
Are level now with men ; the odds is gone,
And there is nothing left remarkable
Beneath the visiting moon. Ibid., 64.

4665. What's brave, what's noble,
Let's do it after the high Roman fashion,
And make death proud to take us. Ibid., 86.

4666. His legs bestrid the ocean : his rear'd arm
Crested the world : his voice was propertied
As all the tuned spheres, and that to friends ;
But when he meant to quail and shake the orb,
He was as rattling thunder. For his bounty,
There was no winter in't ; an autumn 'twas
That grew the more by reaping : his delights
Were dolphin-like ; they show'd his back above
The elements they lived in : in his livery
Walk'd crowns and crownets ; realms and islands were
As plates dropp'd from his pocket. Ibid., v. ii. 82.

4667. Finish, good lady ; the bright day is done,
And we are for the dark. Ibid., 193.

4668. I shall see
Some squeaking Cleopatra boy my greatness Ibid., 219.

4669. His biting is immortal ; those that do die of it seldom or
never recover. Ibid., 247.

4670. I wish you joy o' the worm. Ibid., 281.

4671. Give me my robe, put on my crown ; I have
Immortal longings in me. Ibid., 283.

4672. If thou and nature can so gently part,
The stroke of death is as a lover's pinch
Which hurts, and is desired. Ibid., 297.

4673. Dost thou not see my baby at my breast,
That sucks the nurse asleep ? Ibid., 312.

4674. Now boast thee, death, in thy possession lies
A lass unparallel'd. Downy windows, close ;
And golden Phœbus never be beheld
Of eyes again so royal ! Ibid., 318.

4675. It is well done, and fitting for a princess
Descended of so many royal kings. Ibid., 329.

CORIOLANUS

4676. My gracious silence, hail !   *Coriolanus*, II. i. 192.

4677.   Look, sir, my wounds !
I got them in my country's service, when
Some certain of your brethren roar's and ran
From the noise of our own drums.   Ibid., iii. 57.

4678.   Bid them wash their faces
And keep their teeth clean.   Ibid., 66.

4679.   I thank you for your voices : thank you :
Your most sweet voices.   Ibid., 179.

4680. Hear you this Triton of the minnows ? mark you
His absolute ' shall ' ?   Ibid., III. i. 89.

4681. His nature is too noble for the world :
He would not flatter Neptune for his trident,
Or Jove for's power to thunder.   Ibid., 255.

4682. You common cry of curs ! whose breath I hate
As reek o' the rotten fens, whose loves I prize
As the dead carcasses of unburied men
That do corrupt my air, I banish you !   Ibid., iii. 120.

4683.   O, a kiss
Long as my exile, sweet as my revenge !   Ibid., v. iii. 44.

4684.   Chaste as the icicle
That's curdied by the frost from purest snow
And hangs on Diana's temple.   Ibid., 65.

4685. If you have writ your annals true, 'tis there,
That, like an eagle in a dovecot, I
Flutter'd your Volscians in Corioli :
Alone I did it.   Ibid., vi. 114.

TIMON OF ATHENS

4686. But flies an eagle flight, bold and forth on,
Leaving no tract behind.   *Timon of Athens*, I. i. 49.

4687. 'Tis not enough to help the feeble up,
But to support him after.   Ibid., 107.

4688. I wonder men dare trust themselves with men.   Ibid., ii. 44.

4689. Here's that which is too weak to be a sinner, honest water,
which ne'er left man i' the mire.   Ibid., 59.

4690.   I'll example you with thievery :
The sun's a thief, and with his great attraction
Robs the vast sea : the moon's an arrant thief,
And her pale fire she snatches from the sun :
The sea's a thief, whose liquid surge resolves
The moon into salt tears : the earth's a thief,
That feeds and breeds by a composture stolen
From general excrement : each thing's a thief.
          Ibid., IV. iii. 438.

4691. See where she comes, apparell'd like the spring !
Pericles, I. i. 12.

4692. 'Tis time to fear when tyrants seem to kiss. Ibid., ii. 79.

4693. *Third Fisherman.* Master, I marvel how the fishes live in the sea.
First Fisherman. Why, as men do a-land ; the great ones eat up the little ones. Ibid., II. i. 29.

4694. No, I will rob Tellus of her weed,
To strew thy green with flowers : the yellows, blues,
The purple violets, and marigolds,
Shall as a carpet hang upon thy grave,
While summer days do last. Ay me ! poor maid,
Born in a tempest, when my mother died,
This world to me is like a lasting storm,
Whirring me from my friends. Ibid., IV. i. 14.

4695. Hark, hark ! the lark at heaven's gate sings,
And Phœbus 'gins arise,
His steeds to water at those springs
On chaliced flowers that lies ;
And winking Mary-buds begin
To ope their golden eyes :
With every thing that pretty is,
My lady sweet, arise. *Cymbeline*, II. iii. 21.

4696. There be many Caesars,
Ere such another Julius. Britain is
A world by itself ; and we will nothing pay
For wearing our own noses. Ibid., III. i. 11.

4697. The natural bravery of your isle, which stands
As Neptune's park, ribbed and paled in
With rocks unscaleable and roaring waters. Ibid., 18.

4698. Prouder than rustling in unpaid-for silk. Ibid., iii. 24.

4699. Slander,
Whose edge is sharper than the sword, whose tongue
Outvenoms all the worms of Nile, whose breath
Rides on the posting winds and doth belie
All corners of the world. Ibid., iv. 35.

4700. I have not slept one wink. Ibid., 103.

4701. Weariness
Can snore upon the flint, when resty sloth
Finds the down pillow hard. Ibid., vi. 33.

4702. With fairest flowers
Whilst summer lasts and I live here, Fidele,
I'll sweeten thy sad grave : thou shalt not lack
The flower that's like thy face, pale primrose, nor
The azured harebell, like thy veins, no, nor
The leaf of eglantine, whom not to slander,
Out-sweeten'd not thy breath. Ibid., IV. ii. 220.

4703. Thersites' body is as good as Ajax',
      When neither are alive.   Ibid., 252.

4704. Fear no more the heat o' the sun,
        Nor the furious winter's rages ;
      Thou thy worldly task hast done,
        Home art gone, and ta'en thy wages :
      Golden lads and girls all must,
      As chimney-sweepers, come to dust.   Ibid., 258.

4705. The sceptre, learning, physic, must
      All follow this, and come to dust.   Ibid., 268.

4706. Fear no more the lightning-flash,
        Nor the all-dreaded thunder-stone ;
      Fear not slander, censure rash ;
        Thou hast finish'd joy and moan :
      All lovers young, all lovers must
      Consign to thee, and come to dust.   Ibid., 270.

THE WINTER'S TALE

4707. Two lads that thought there was no more behind
      But such a day to-morrow as to-day,
      And to be boy eternal.   *The Winter's Tale,* I. ii. 63.

4708. We were as twinn'd lambs that did frisk i' the sun,
      And bleat the one at the other : what we changed
      Was innocence for innocence : we knew not
      The doctrine of ill-doing, nor dream'd
      That any did.   Ibid., 67.

4709. A sad tale's best for winter.   Ibid., II. i. 25.

4710. The silence often of pure innocence
      Persuades when speaking fails.   Ibid., ii. 41.

4711.   What's gone and what's past help
      Should be past grief.   Ibid., III. ii. 223.

  4712. Exit, pursued by a bear.   Ibid., iii. 58, *stage direction.*

  4713. I would there were no age between sixteen and three-and-
twenty, or that youth would sleep out the rest ; for there is nothing
in the between but getting wenches with child, wronging the ancientry,
stealing, fighting.   Ibid., 59.

4714. When daffodils begin to peer,
        With heigh ! the doxy over the dale,
      Why, then comes in the sweet o' the year ;
        For the red blood reigns in the winter's pale.   Ibid., IV. iii. 1.

4715. A snapper-up of unconsidered trifles.   Ibid., 26.

4716. Jog on, jog on, the foot-path way,
        And merrily hent the stile-a :
      A merry heart goes all the day,
        Your sad tires in a mile-a.   Ibid., 132.

4717. For you there's rosemary and rue ; these keep
      Seeming and savour all the winter long.   Ibid., iv. 74.

4718.   Here's flowers for you ;
Hot lavender, mints, savory, marjoram ;
The marigold, that goes to bed wi' the sun
And with him rises weeping : these are flowers
Of middle summer, and I think they are given
To men of middle age.   *Ibid.*, 103.

4719.   O Proserpina,
For the flowers now, that frighted thou let'st fall
From Dis's waggon ! daffodils
That come before the swallow dares, and take
The winds of March with beauty ; violets dim,
But sweeter than the lids of Juno's eyes
Or Cytherea's breath ; pale primroses,
That die unmarried, ere they can behold
Bright Phœbus in his strength—a malady
Most incident to maids ; bold oxlips and
The crown imperial ; lilies of all kinds,
The flower-de-luce being one !   *Ibid.*, 116.

4720   What you do
Still betters what is done. When you speak, sweet,
I'ld have you do it ever : when you sing,
I'ld have you buy and sell so, so give alms,
Pray so ; and, for the ordering your affairs,
To sing them too : when you do dance, I wish you
A wave o' the sea, that you might ever do
Nothing but that ; move still, still so,
And own no other function.   *Ibid.*, 135.

4721.   Good sooth, she is
The queen of curds and cream.   *Ibid.*, 160.

4722. I think there is not half a kiss to choose
Who loves another best.   *Ibid.*, 175.

4723. Lawn as white as driven snow. *Ibid.*, 220.

4724. Will you buy any tape,
   Or lace for your cape,
My dainty duck, my dear-a ?
   Any silk, any thread,
   Any toys for your head,
Of the new'st and finest, finest wear-a ? *Ibid.*, 322.

4725. The selfsame sun that shines upon his court
Hides not his visage from our cottage but
Looks on alike.   *Ibid.*, 454.

4726. Let me have no lying : it becomes none but tradesmen.
           Ibid., 743.

4727. He hath no drowning mark upon him ; his complexion is
perfect gallows.   *The Tempest*, I. i. 32.

4728. In the dark backward and abysm of time. *Ibid.*, ii. 50.

4729.   Like one,
Who having into truth, by telling of it,
Made such a sinner of his memory,
To credit his own lie.   *Ibid.*, 99.

4730.   My library
Was dukedom large enough.   *Ibid.*, 109.

4731. Knowing I loved my books, he furnish'd me
From mine own library with volumes that
I prize above my dukedom.   *Ibid.*, 166.

4732. From the still-vex'd Bermoothes.   *Ibid.*, 229.

4733. I will be correspondent to command
And do my spiriting gently.   *Ibid.*, 297.

4734. You taught me language ; and my profit on't
Is, I know how to curse. The red plague rid you
For learning me your language !   *Ibid.*, 363.

4735.   Come unto these yellow sands,
           And then take hands :
        Courtsied when you have and kiss'd
           The wild waves whist.   *Ibid.*, 376.

4736.   Full fathom five thy father lies ;
           Of his bones are coral made ;
        Those are pearls that were his eyes :
           Nothing of him that doth fade
        But doth suffer a sea-change
        Into something rich and strange.   *Ibid.*, 396.

4737. The fringed curtains of thine eye advance
And say what thou seest yond.   *Ibid.*, 408.

4738.   At the first sight
They have changed eyes.   *Ibid.*, 440.

4739. Fie, what a spendthrift is he of his tongue !   *Ibid.*, II. i. 24.

4740. They'll take suggestion as a cat laps milk.   *Ibid.*, 288.

4741. A very ancient and fish-like smell.   *Ibid.*, ii. 27.

4742. Misery acquaints a man with strange bedfellows.   *Ibid.*, 41.

4743. Well, here's my comfort. (*Drinks*.)   *Ibid.*, 47.

4744.   No more dams I'll make for fish ;
           Nor fetch in firing
           At requiring :
        Nor scrape trencher, nor wash dish :
           'Ban, 'Ban, Cacaliban
           Has a new master : get a new man.   *Ibid.*, 184.

4745.   For several virtues
Have I liked several women ; never any
With so full soul, but some defect in her
Did quarrel with the noblest grace she owed
And put it to the foil.   *Ibid.*, III. i. 42.

4746. *Ferdinand.* Here's my hand.
     Miranda. And mine, with my heart in't.   *Ibid.*, 89.

4747. I am in case to justle a constable.   *Ibid.*, ii. 30.

4748. He that dies pays all debts.   Ibid., 140.

4749. Be not afeard ; the isle is full of noises,
       Sounds and sweet airs, that give delight and hurt not.
                                                       Ibid., 144.

4750. Our revels now are ended.   These our actors,
       As I foretold you, were all spirits and
       Are melted into air, into thin air :
       And, like the baseless fabric of this vision,
       The cloud-capp'd towers, the gorgeous palaces,
       The solemn temples, the great globe itself,
       Yea, all which it inherit, shall dissolve
       And, like this insubstantial pageant faded,
       Leave not a rack behind.   We are such stuff
       As dreams are made on, and our little life
       Is rounded with a sleep.   Ibid., IV. i. 148.

4751. I do begin to have bloody thoughts.   Ibid., 220.

4752. With foreheads villainous low.   Ibid., 250.

4753. Ye elves of hills, brooks, standing lakes and groves,
       And ye that on the sands with printless foot
       Do chase the ebbing Neptune and do fly him
       When he comes back.   Ibid., v. i. 33.

4754. And deeper that did ever plummet sound
       I'll drown my book.   Ibid., 56.

4755.   Where the bee sucks, there suck I :
           In a cowslip's bell I lie ;
           There I couch when owls do cry.
           On the bat's back I do fly
           After summer merrily.
       Merrily, merrily shall I live now
       Under the blossom that hangs on the bough.   Ibid., 88.

4756. How beauteous mankind is !   O brave new world,
       That has such people in't !   Ibid., 183.

4757.   'Tis better to be lowly born,
       And range with humble livers in content,
       Than to be perk'd up in a glistering grief,
       And wear a golden sorrow.   *King Henry VIII.* II. iii. 19.
           [A commonly accepted theory of the play's authorship
           gives this passage to Shakespeare and all those below to
           Fletcher.]

4758. Orpheus with his lute made trees,
       And the mountain tops that freeze,
          Bow themselves when he did sing.   Ibid., III. i. 3.

4759. Heaven is above all yet ; there sits a judge
       That no king can corrupt.   Ibid., 100.

KING HENRY VIII.

4760. Farewell! a long farewell to all my greatness!
This is the state of man : to-day he puts forth
The tender leaves of hopes ; to-morrow blossoms,
And bears his blushing honours thick upon him ;
The third day comes a frost, a killing frost,
And, when he thinks, good easy man, full surely
His greatness is a-ripening, nips his root,
And then he falls, as I do.   Ibid., ii. 351.

4761. Vain pomp and glory of this world, I hate ye :
I feel my heart new open'd.   O, how wretched
Is that poor man that hangs on princes' favours !
There is, betwixt that smile we would aspire to,
That sweet aspect of princes, and their ruin,
More pangs and fears than wars or women have :
And when he falls, he falls like Lucifer,
Never to hope again.   Ibid., 365.

4762. A peace above all earthly dignities,
A still and quiet conscience.   Ibid., 379.

4763. Cromwell, I charge thee, fling away ambition :
By that sin fell the angels.   Ibid., 440.

4764. Love thyself last : cherish those hearts that hate thee ;
Corruption wins not more than honesty.
Still in thy right hand carry gentle peace,
To silence envious tongues.   Be just, and fear not :
Let all the ends thou aim'st at be thy country's,
Thy God's, and truth's.   Ibid., 443.

4765. Had I but served my God with half the zeal
I served my king, he would not in mine age
Have left me naked to mine enemies.   Ibid., 455.

4766. He gave his honours to the world again,
His blessed part to heaven, and slept in peace.   Ibid., IV. ii. 29.

4767. So may he rest ; his faults lie gently on him.   Ibid., 31.

4768.   He was a man
Of an unbounded stomach.   Ibid., 33.

4769. Men's evil manners live in brass ; their virtues
We write in water.   Ibid., 45.

4770. He was a scholar, and a ripe and good one ;
Exceeding wise, fair-spoken, and persuading :
Lofty and sour to them that loved him not ;
But to those men that sought him sweet as summer.   Ibid., 51.

4771. Those twins of learning that he raised in you,
Ipswich and Oxford.   Ibid., 58.

POEMS

4772. Hunting he loved, but love he laugh'd to scorn.
Venus and Adonis, 4.

4773. Bid me discourse, I will enchant thine ear,
Or, like a fairy, trip upon the green,
Or, like a nymph, with long dishevell'd hair,
Dance on the sands, and yet no footing seen :
  Love is a spirit all compact of fire,
  Not gross to sink, but light, and will aspire.   Ibid., 145

4774. Round-hoof'd, short-jointed, fetlocks shag and long,
Broad breast, full eye, small head and nostril wide,
High crest, short ears, straight legs and passing strong,
Thin mane, thick tail, broad buttock, tender hide :
    Look, what a horse should have he did not lack,
    Save a proud rider on so proud a back.   *Ibid.*, 295.

4775. Love comforteth like sunshine after rain,
But Lust's effect is tempest after sun ;
Love's gentle spring doth always fresh remain,
Lust's winter comes ere summer half be done :
    Love surfeits not, Lust like a glutton dies ;
    Love is all truth, Lust full of forged lies.   *Ibid.*, 799.

4776. Lo, here the gentle lark, weary of rest,
From his moist cabinet mounts up on high,
And wakes the morning.   *Ibid.*, 853.

4777. Beauty itself doth of itself persuade
The eyes of men without an orator.
    The Rape of Lucrece, 29.

4778. For greatest scandal waits on greatest state.   *Ibid.*, 1006.

4779. To the onlie begetter of these insuing sonnets.
    Sonnets, dedication.

4780. From fairest creatures we desire increase,
That thereby beauty's rose might never die.   *Ibid.*, i.

4781. Thou art thy mother's glass, and she in thee
Calls back the lovely April of her prime.   *Ibid.*, iii.

4782. And stretched metre of an antique song.   *Ibid.*, xvii.

4783. Shall I compare thee to a summer's day ?
Thou art more lovely and more temperate :
Rough winds do shake the darling buds of May,
And summer's lease hath all too short a date.   *Ibid.*, xviii.

4784. But thy eternal summer shall not fade.   *Ibid.*

4785. The painful warrior famoused for fight,
After a thousand victories once foil'd,
Is from the book of honour razed quite,
And all the rest forgot for which he toil'd.   *Ibid.*, xxv.

4786. When in disgrace with fortune and men's eyes
I all alone beweep my outcast state.   *Ibid.*, xxix.

4787. Wishing me like to one more rich in hope,
Featur'd like him, like him with friends possess'd,
Desiring this man's art and that man's scope,
With what I most enjoy contented least.   *Ibid.*

4788. When to the sessions of sweet silent thought
I summon up remembrance of things past,
I sigh the lack of many a thing I sought,
And with old woes new wail my dear time's waste :
Then can I drown an eye, unused to flow,
For precious friends hid in death's dateless night,
And weep afresh love's long since cancell'd woe,
And moan the expense of many a vanish'd sight.   *Ibid.*, xxx.

4789. But if the while I think on thee, dear friend,
     All losses are restored and sorrows end.   Ibid.

4790. Full many a glorious morning have I seen
     Flatter the mountain-tops with sovereign eye,
     Kissing with golden face the meadows green,
     Gilding pale streams with heavenly alchemy.   Ibid., xxxiii.

4791. Why didst thou promise such a beauteous day
     And make me travel forth without my cloak ?   Ibid., xxxiv.

4792. Not marble, nor the gilded monuments
     Of princes, shall outlive this powerful rhyme.   Ibid., lv.

4793. Being your slave, what should I do but tend
     Upon the hours and times of your desire ?
     I have no precious time at all to spend,
     Nor services to do, till you require.
     Nor dare I chide the world-without-end hour
     Whilst I, my sovereign, watch the clock for you,
     Nor think the bitterness of absence sour
     When you have bid your servant once adieu.   Ibid., lvii.

4794. So true a fool is love that in your will,
     Though you do any thing, he thinks no ill.   Ibid.

4795. Like as the waves make towards the pebbled shore,
     So do our minutes hasten to their end.   Ibid., lx.

4796. When I have seen the hungry ocean gain
     Advantage on the kingdom of the shore.   Ibid., lxiv

4797. Tired with all these, for restful death I cry.   Ibid., lxvi.

4798. And art made tongue-tied by authority,
     And folly doctor-like controlling skill,
     And simple truth miscall'd simplicity,
     And captive good attending captain ill.   Ibid.

4799. That time of year thou mayst in me behold
     When yellow leaves, or none, or few, do hang
     Upon those boughs which shake against the cold,
     Bare ruin'd choirs, where late the sweet birds sang.
     In me thou see'st the twilight of such day
     As after sunset fadeth in the west,
     Which by and by black night doth take away,
     Death's second self, that seals up all in rest.   Ibid., lxxiii.

4800. Was it the proud full sail of his great verse,
     Bound for the prize of all too precious you.   Ibid., lxxxvi.

4801. Farewell ! thou art too dear for my possessing,
     And like enough thou know'st thy estimate.   Ibid., lxxxvii.

4802. Thus have I had thee, as a dream doth flatter,
     In sleep a king, but waking no such matter.   Ibid.

4803. Ah, do not, when my heart hath 'scaped this sorrow,
     Come in the rearward of a conquer'd woe ;
     Give not a windy night a rainy morrow,
     To linger out a purposed overthrow.   Ibid., xc.

4804. They that have power to hurt and will do none,
       That do not do the thing they most do show,
       Who, moving others, are themselves as stone.
       Unmoved, cold, and to temptation slow,
       They rightly do inherit heaven's graces
       And husband nature's riches from expense ;
       They are the lords and owners of their faces,
       Others, but stewards of their excellence.   Ibid., xciv.

4805. For sweetest things turn sourest by their deeds ;
       Lilies that fester smell far worse than weeds.   Ibid.

4806. From you have I been absent in the spring,
       When proud-pied April dress'd in all his trim
       Hath put a spirit of youth in every thing.   Ibid., xcviii.

4807. To me, fair friend, you never can be old,
       For as you were when first your eye I eyed,
       Such seems your beauty still.   Three winters cold
       Have from the forests shook three summers' pride,
       Three beauteous springs to yellow autumn turn'd.   Ibid., civ.

4808. Ah ! yet doth beauty, like a dial-hand,
       Steal from his figure and no pace perceived.   Ibid.

4809. When in the chronicle of wasted time
       I see descriptions of the fairest wights,
       And beauty making beautiful old rhyme
       In praise of ladies dead and lovely knights.   Ibid., cvi.

4810. O, never say that I was false of heart,
       Though absence seem'd my flame to qualify.   Ibid., cix.

4811. Alas, 'tis true I have gone here and there
       And made myself a motley to the view.   Ibid., cx.

4812.   My nature is subdued
       To what it works in, like the dyer's hand.   Ibid., cxi.

4813. Let me not to the marriage of true minds
       Admit impediments.   Love is not love
       Which alters when it alteration finds.   Ibid., cxvi.

4814. Love's not Time's fool, though rosy lips and cheeks
       Within his bending sickle's compass come.   Ibid.

4815. The expense of spirit in a waste of shame
       Is lust in action ; and till action, lust
       Is perjured, murderous, bloody, full of blame,
       Savage, extreme, rude, cruel, not to trust.   Ibid., cxxix.

4816. Mad, in pursuit and in possession so ;
       Had, having, and in quest to have, extreme ;
       A bliss in proof, and proved, a very woe ;
       Before, a joy proposed ; behind, a dream.
          All this the world well knows ; yet none knows well
          To shun the heaven that leads men to this hell.   Ibid.

4817. That full star that ushers in the even.   Ibid., cxxxii.

4818. Two loves I have of comfort and despair,
       Which like two spirits do suggest me still :
       The better angel is a man right fair,
       The worser spirit a woman colour'd ill.   Ibid., cxliv.

4819. Crabbed age and youth cannot live together :
Youth is full of pleasance, age is full of care ;
Youth like summer morn, age like winter weather ;
Youth like summer brave, age like winter bare.
The Passionate Pilgrim, xii.

4820. Good friend, for Jesu's sake forbear
To dig the dust enclosed here.
Blest be the man that spares these stones,
And curst be he that moves my bones. *His own epitaph.*

SHAW, GEORGE BERNARD, Irish dramatist, 26 July, 1856—2 Nov. 1950.

4821. We have no more right to consume happiness without producing it than to consume wealth without producing it. *Candida*, I.

4822. I'm only a beer teetotaller, not a champagne teetotaller
Ibid., III.

4823. We don't bother much about dress and manners in England, because as a nation we don't dress well and we've no manners.
You never can tell, I.

4824. When we want to read of the deeds that are done for love, whither do we turn ? To the murder column.
Three Plays for Puritans, preface.

4825. When a stupid man is doing something he is ashamed of, he always declares that it is his duty. *Caesar and Cleopatra*, III.

4826. A lifetime of happiness ! No man alive could bear it ; it would be hell on earth. *Man and Superman*, I.

4827. You think that you are Ann's suitor ; that you are the pursuer and she the pursued ; that it is your part to woo, to persuade, to prevail, to overcome. Fool : it is you who are the pursued, the marked-down quarry, the destined prey. Ibid., II.

4828. There are two tragedies in life. One is not to get your heart's desire. The other is to get it. Ibid., IV.

4829. Do not do unto others as you would they should do unto you. Their tastes may not be the same.
Ibid., *Maxims for Revolutionists*, 227.

4830. Marriage is popular because it combines the maximum of temptation with the maximum of opportunity. Ibid., 231.

4831. The reasonable man adapts himself to the world : the unreasonable one persists in trying to adapt the world to himself. Therefore all progress depends on the unreasonable man. Ibid., 238.

4832. Home is the girl's prison and the woman's workhouse.
Ibid., 240.

4833. Every man over forty is a scoundrel. Ibid., 242.

4834. A man is like a phonograph with half a dozen records. You soon get tired of them all ; and yet you have to sit at table whilst he reels them off to every new visitor. *Getting Married.*

4835. Not bloody likely.   *Pygmalion*, II.

4836. With the single exception of Homer, there is no eminent writer, not even Sir Walter Scott, whom I can despise so entirely as I despise Shakespeare when I measure my mind against his.
Dramatic Opinions and Essays, II. 52.

SHEALE, RICHARD, ballad-writer, 16th century
4837. For when his legs were smitten off,
      He fought upon his stumps.   *Ballad of Chevy Chase*, II. x.

SHEFFIELD, JOHN, *see* Buckingham and Normanby, 1st Duke of

SHELLEY, PERCY BYSSHE, poet, 4 Aug. 1792—8 July, 1822
4838. How wonderful is Death,
      Death and his brother Sleep.   *Queen Mab*, I.

4839. With hue like that when some great painter dips
      His pencil in the gloom of earthquake and eclipse.
The Revolt of Islam, v. 23.

4840. My name is Ozymandias, king of kings:
      Look on my works, ye Mighty, and despair!   *Ozymandias*.

4841.   Most wretched men
      Are cradled into poetry by wrong,
      They learn in suffering what they teach in song.
Julian and Maddalo, 543.

4842. I could lie down like a tired child
         And weep away the life of care
         Which I have borne and yet must bear
      Till death like sleep might steal on me.
Stanzas written in Dejection, near Naples.

4843. Men of England, wherefore plough
      For the lords who lay ye low?
      Wherefore weave with toil and care
      The rich robes your tyrants wear?
Song to the Men of England.

4844. O wild West Wind, thou breath of Autumn's being,
      Thou, from whose unseen presence the leaves dead
      Are driven, like ghosts from an enchanter fleeing.
Ode to the West Wind, I.

4845. Thou who didst waken from his summer dreams
      The blue Mediterranean, where he lay,
      Lulled by the coil of his crystalline streams.   Ibid., 3.

4846.   O, wind,
      If Winter comes, can Spring be far behind?   Ibid., 5.

4847. I arise from dreams of thee
      In the first sweet sleep of night,
      When the winds are breathing low,
      And the stars are shining bright.   *The Indian Serenade*.

4848. Nothing in the world is single;
         All things by a law divine
         In one spirit meet and mingle.
         Why not I with thine?   *Love's Philosophy*.

4849. Hell is a city much like London—
    A populous and a smoky city.
                  Peter Bell the Third, III. *Hell*, 1.

4850. When a man marries, dies, or turns Hindoo,
    His best friends hear no more of him.
                  Letter to Maria Gisborne, 235.

4851. A Sensitive Plant in a garden grew,
    And the young winds fed it with silver dew.
                  The Sensitive Plant, I. 1.

4852. That orbed maiden with white fire laden,
      Whom mortals call the moon,
    Glides glimmering o'er my fleece-like floor,
      By the midnight breezes strewn.   *The Cloud.*

4853. I am the daughter of earth and water,
      And the nursling of the sky ;
    I pass through the pores of the ocean and shores ;
      I change, but I cannot die.   Ibid.

4854. Hail to thee, blithe spirit !
    Bird thou never wert.   *To a Skylark.*

4855. And singing still dost soar, and soaring ever singest.   Ibid.

4856. Like an unbodied joy whose race is just begun.   Ibid.

4857.   We look before and after
        And pine for what is not :
        Our sincerest laughter
          With some pain is fraught ;
    Our sweetest songs are those that tell of saddest thought.   Ibid.

4858. I fear thy kisses, gentle maiden,
      Thou needest not fear mine ;
    My spirit is too deeply laden
      Ever to burden thine.   *To——. I fear thy Kisses.*

4859. I dreamed that, as I wandered by the way,
      Bare winter suddenly was changed to spring,
    And gentle odours led my steps astray,
      Mixed with a sound of waters murmuring.   *The Question.*

4860. There grew pied wind-flowers and violets,
      Daisies, those pearled Arcturi of the earth,
    The constellated flower that never sets.   Ibid.

4861.   Art thou pale for weariness
    Of climbing heaven and gazing on the earth,
      Wandering companionless
    Among the stars that have a different birth,—
    And ever changing, like a joyless eye
    That finds no object worth its constancy ?   *To the Moon.*

4862. As long as skies are blue, and fields are green,
    Evening must usher night, night urge the morrow,
    Month follow month with woe, and year wake year to sorrow.
                       Adonais, 21.

4863. A pardlike spirit beautiful and swift.   Ibid., 32.

4864.   He has outsoared the shadow of our night ;
         Envy and calumny and hate and pain,
         And that unrest which men miscall delight,
         Can touch him not and torture not again ;
         From the contagion of the world's slow stain
         He is secure, and now can never mourn
         A heart grown cold, a head grown grey in vain.   *Ibid.,* 40.

4865.   He is a portion of the loveliness
         Which once he made more lovely.   *Ibid.,* 43.

4866.   The One remains, the many change and pass ;
         Heaven's light forever shines, Earth's shadows fly ;
         Life, like a dome of many-coloured glass,
         Stains the white radiance of eternity.   *Ibid.,* 52.

4867.   The soul of Adonais, like a star,
         Beacons from the abode where the Eternal are.   *Ibid.,* 55.

4868.   Swiftly walk over the western wave,
            Spirit of Night !   *To Night.*

4869.   Music, when soft voices die,
         Vibrates in the memory—
         Odours, when sweet violets sicken,
         Live within the sense they quicken.
                    To——.   Music, when Soft voices die.

4870.   Rarely, rarely, comest thou,
                     Spirit of Delight !   *Song.*

4871.   The desire of the moth for the star,
            Of the night for the morrow,
         The devotion to something afar
            From the sphere of our sorrow.
                    To——.   One Word is too often profaned.

4872.   When the lamp is shattered
         The light in the dust lies dead—
            When the cloud is scattered
         The rainbow's glory is shed.
            When the lute is broken,
         Sweet tones are remembered not ;
            When the lips have spoken,
         Loved accents are soon forgot.
                    Lines : When the Lamp is shattered.

4873.   Forms more real than living man,
         Nurslings of immortality !   *Prometheus Unbound,* I. 737.

4874.   All love is sweet,
         Given or returned.   Common as light is love,
         And its familiar voice wearies not ever.

         They who inspire it are most fortunate,
         As I am now ; but those who feel it most
         Are happier still.   *Ibid.,* II. v. 40.

4875. The world's great age begins anew,
      The golden years return,
    The earth doth like a snake renew
      Her winter weeds outworn :
    Heaven smiles, and faiths and empires gleam,
    Like wrecks of a dissolving dream.   *Hellas*, 1060.

4876. Oh, cease ! must hate and death return ?
      Cease ! must men kill and die ?
    Cease ! drain not to its dregs the urn
      Of bitter prophecy.
    The world is weary of the past,
    Oh, might it die or rest at last !   Ibid., 1096.

4877. Poetry is the record of the best and happiest moments of
the happiest and best minds.   *A Defence of Poetry*.

4878. Poets are the unacknowledged legislators of the world.   Ibid.

4879. It might make one in love with death, to think that one
should be buried in so sweet a place.   *Adonais*, preface.

SHERIDAN, HELEN SELINA, Countess of Dufferin, 1807—13 June,
    1867

4880. I'm sitting on the stile, Mary,
      Where we sat, side by side.
                The Lament of the Irish Emigrant.

4881. They say there's bread and work for all,
      And the sun shines always there—
    But I'll not forget old Ireland,
      Were it fifty times as fair !   Ibid.

SHERIDAN, PHILIP HENRY, U.S. General, 6 March, 1831—5 Aug.
    1888

4882. If I owned Texas and Hell, I would rent out Texas and live
in Hell.   *At officers' mess, Fort Clark, Texas*, 1855.

SHERIDAN, RICHARD BRINSLEY, dramatist and politician, 30 Oct.
    1751—7 July, 1816

4883. Illiterate him, I say, quite from your memory.   [Mrs.
Malaprop.]   *The Rivals*, I. ii.

4884. 'Tis safest in matrimony to begin with a little aversion.
[Same.]   Ibid.

4885. A progeny of learning.   [Same.]   Ibid.

4886. If I reprehend anything in this world, it is the use of my
oracular tongue, and a nice derangement of epitaphs.   [Same.]
                Ibid., III. iii.

4887. As headstrong as an allegory on the banks of the Nile.
[Same.]

4888. No caparisons, miss, if you please.   Caparisons don't become
a young woman.   [Same.]   Ibid., IV. ii.

4889. You are not like Cerberus, three gentlemen at once, are
you ?   [Same.]   Ibid.

4890. My valour is certainly going !—it is sneaking off !—I feel it oozing out as it were at the palms of my hands !   Ibid., v. iii.

4891. I own the soft impeachment. [Mrs. Malaprop.]   Ibid.

4892. Had I a heart for falsehood framed,
       I ne'er could injure you.   *The Duenna*, I. v.

4893. You shall see them on a beautiful quarto page, where a neat rivulet of text shall meander through a meadow of margin.
       The School for Scandal, I. i.

4894. Here's to the maiden of bashful fifteen ;
       Here's to the widow of fifty ;
       Here's to the flaunting extravagant quean,
       And here's to the housewife that's thrifty.
             Let the toast pass,—
             Drink to the lass,
       I'll warrant she'll prove an excuse for the glass.

                                   Ibid., III. iii.

4895. An   unforgiving   eye,   and   a   damned   disinheriting
countenance !   Ibid., IV. i.

4896. No scandal about Queen Elizabeth, I hope ?
                                   The Critic, II. i.

4897. The Spanish fleet thou canst not see—because
       —It is not yet in sight !   Ibid., ii.

4898. All that can be said is, that two people happened to hit on the same thought—and Shakespeare made use of it first, that's all.
                                   Ibid., III. i.

4899. An oyster may be crossed in love !   Ibid.

4900. You write with ease, to show your breeding,
       But easy writing's curst hard reading.   *Clio's Protest.*

4901. The Right Honourable gentleman is indebted to his memory for his jests, and to his imagination for his facts.
       Replying to Mr. Dundas, in the House of Commons.

SHIRLEY, JAMES, dramatist, born 18 Sept. 1596, buried 29 Oct. 1666

4902. The glories of our blood and state
       Are shadows, not substantial things ;
       There is no armour against fate ;
       Death lays his icy hand on kings :
             Sceptre and crown
             Must tumble down,
       And in the dust be equal made
       With the poor crooked scythe and spade.
             The Contention of Ajax and Ulysses, iii.

4903. Only the actions of the just
       Smell sweet, and blossom in their dust.   Ibid.

SIDNEY, SIR PHILIP, soldier, statesman, and poet, 30 Nov. 1554—
       17 Oct. 1586

4904. My true love hath my heart and I have his,
       By just exchange one for the other given.   *Arcadia*, III.

4905. Have I caught my heav'nly jewel.
                                   Astrophel and Stella, song ii.

4906. ' Fool ! ' said my Muse to me, ' look in thy heart, and write.'

Ibid., sonnet i.

4907. With how sad steps, O Moon, thou climb'st the skies !
How silently, and with how wan a face !   Ibid., sonnet xxxi.

4908. Come Sleep ! O Sleep, the certain knot of peace,
 The baiting-place of wit, the balm of woe,
The poor man's wealth, the prisoner's release,
 Th' indifferent judge between the high and low.

Ibid., sonnet xxxix.

4909. With a tale forsooth he cometh unto you, with a tale which
holdeth children from play, and old men from the chimney corner.
The Defence of Poesy.

4910. Thy necessity is yet greater than mine.
*On giving his water-bottle to a wounded soldier, when he himself
had received his death wound at the battle of Zutphen, 22 Sept.
1586.*

SIMONIDES OF CEOS, Greek poet, 556 ?—468 ? B.C.

4911. Ὦ ξεῖν', ἀγγειλον Λακεδαιμονίοις ὅτι τῇδε
 κείμεθα, τοῖς κείνων ῥήμασι πειθόμενοι.
—Stranger, tell the Lacedaemonians that we lie here obedient
to their orders.
Epitaph on the Spartan dead at Thermopylae.

SKELTON, JOHN, poet, 1460 ?—21 June, 1529

4912.   With solace and gladness,
       Much mirth and no madness,
       All good and no badness ;
       So joyously,
       So maidenly,
       So womanly
       Her demeaning.
To Mistress Margaret Hussey.

4913.   Steadfast of thought,
       Well made, well wrought,
       Far may be sought,
       Ere that ye can find
       So courteous, so kind,
       As merry Margaret,
       This midsummer flower,
       Gentle as falcon,
       Or hawk of the tower.   Ibid.

SMART, CHRISTOPHER, poet, 11 April, 1722—21 May, 1771

4914. Strong is the lion—like a coal
    His eyeball—like a bastion's mole
     His chest against his foes.   *Song to David,* 76.

4915. And now the matchless deed's achiev'd,
    Determined, dared, and done.   Ibid., 84.

M

SMILES, SAMUEL, social reformer, 23 Dec. 1812—16 April, 1904

4916. We often discover what *will* do, by finding out what will not do ; and probably he who never made a mistake never made a discovery.
Self-Help, xi.

4917. A place for everything, and everything in its place.
Thrift, v.

SMITH, ADAM, Scottish political economist, 5 June, 1723—17 July, 1790

4918. To found a great empire for the sole purpose of raising up a people of customers may at first sight appear a project fit only for a nation of shopkeepers. It is, however, a project altogether unfit for a nation of shopkeepers ; but extremely fit for a nation whose Government is influenced by shopkeepers.   *Wealth of Nations*, II. IV. vii. 3.

SMITH, ALEXANDER, Scottish poet, 31 Dec. 1830—5 Jan. 1867

4919. Like a pale martyr in his shirt of fire.   *A Life Drama*, ii.

4920.   In winter, when the dismal rain
                  Came down in slanting lines,
              And Wind, that grand old harper, smote
                  His thunder-harp of pines.   Ibid.

SMITH, ARABELLA EUGENIA, U.S. teacher, 1844—24 July, 1916

4921. If I should die to-night,
      My friends would look upon my quiet face,
      Before they laid it in its resting-place,
      And deem that death had left it almost fair.
If I should die to-night.

SMITH, F. E., *see* Birkenhead, 1st Earl of

SMITH, GOLDWIN, historian, 13 Aug. 1823—7 June, 1910

4922. King Nebuchadnezzar was turned out to grass
      With oxen, horses and the savage ass.
      The King surveyed the unaccustomed fare
      With an inquiring but disdainful air
      And murmured as he cropped the unwonted food,
      ' It may be wholesome but it is not good.'
Lines parodying Newdigate Prize poems.

SMITH, HORACE, parodist, 31 Dec. 1779—12 July, 1849

4923. Who makes the quartern loaf and Luddites rise ?
      Who fills the butchers' shops with large blue flies ?
                              [Parody of W. T. Fitzgerald.]
Rejected Addresses, i. *Loyal Effusion.*

4924. ' What are they fear'd on ? fools ! 'od rot 'em ! '
      Were the last words of Higginbottom.   [Parody of Scott.]
Ibid., ix. *A Tale of Drury Lane.*

4925. In the name of the Prophet—figs !
Ibid., x. *Johnson's Ghost.*

SMITH, JAMES, parodist, 10 Feb. 1775—24 Dec. 1839

4926. I saw them go : one horse was blind,
　　　　The tails of both hung down behind,
　　　　　　Their shoes were on their feet.　　[Parody of Wordsworth.]
　　　　　　　　　　　　　　　　　Rejected Addresses, ii. *The Baby's Début*.

4927. John Richard William Alexander Dwyer
　　　　Was footman to Justinian Stubbs, Esquire.
　　　　　　　　　　　　　　　　　[Parody of Crabbe.]
　　　　　　　　　　　　　　　　　Ibid., xvii. *The Theatre*.

SMITH, JOHN, GOVERNOR OF VIRGINIA, baptised 9 Jan. 1580, died
　　　21 June, 1631

4928. Why should the brave Spanish soldier brag, The sun never
sets in the Spanish dominions, but ever shineth on one part or other
we have conquered for our king ?
　　　　　　　　　Advertisements for the Unexperienced Planters, xv.

SMITH. LANGDON, U.S. journalist, 4 Jan. 1858—1908

4929. When you were a tadpole and I was a fish,
　　　　In the Palaeozoic time.　　　　　　　　　*Evolution*.

SMITH, LOGAN PEARSALL, Anglo-American author, 18 Oct. 1865—
　　　2 March, 1946

4930. There are two things to aim at in life : first, to get what
you want ; and, after that, to enjoy it.　Only the wisest of mankind
achieve the second.　　　　*Afterthoughts*, i. *Life and Human Nature*.

4931. A best-seller is the gilded tomb of a mediocre talent.
　　　　　　　　　　　　　　　　　Ibid., v. *Art and Letters*.

4932. People say that life is the thing, but I prefer reading.
　　　　　　　　　　　　　　　　　Ibid., vi. *Myself*.

SMITH, SAMUEL FRANCIS, U.S. clergyman, 21 Oct. 1808—16 Nov.
　　　1895

4933.　　　　　　　My country, 'tis of thee,
　　　　　　　　　Sweet land of liberty,
　　　　　　　　　　Of thee I sing :
　　　　　　　　　Land where my fathers died,
　　　　　　　　　Land of the pilgrims' pride,
　　　　　　　　　From every mountain-side
　　　　　　　　　　Let freedom ring.　　　　　　　　*America*.

SMITH, SYDNEY, clergyman, 3 June, 1771—22 Feb. 1845

4934. We shall generally find that the triangular person has got
into the square hole, the oblong into the triangular, and a square
person has squeezed himself into the round hole.
　　　　　　　　　　　　　Sketches of Moral Philosophy, ix.

4935. The motto I proposed for the [*Edinburgh*] *Review* was :
Tenui musam meditamur avena—' We cultivate literature upon a
little oatmeal.'　　　　　　　　　　　　　*Works*, i. preface.

4936. The attempt of the Lords to stop the progress of reform reminds me very forcibly of the great storm of Sidmouth, and of the conduct of the excellent Mrs. Partington on that occasion.

Speech, Taunton, 11 Oct. 1831.

4937. I have no relish for the country ; it is a kind of healthy grave.

Letter to Miss G. Harcourt, 1838.

4938. Poverty is no disgrace to a man, but it is confoundedly inconvenient.   *Wit and Wisdom of Rev. Sydney Smith,* 89.

4939. It requires a surgical operation to get a joke well into a Scotch understanding.

Lady Holland's *A Memoir of the Rev. Sydney Smith,* i. ii.

4940. I heard him speak disrespectfully of the Equator.   Ibid.

4941. That garret of the earth—that knuckle-end of England— that land of Calvin, oatcakes, and sulphur. [Scotland.]   Ibid.

4942. As the French say, there are three sexes,—men, women, and clergymen.   Ibid., ix.

4943. Heat, ma'am ! It was so dreadful here, that I found there was nothing left for it but to take off my flesh and sit in my bones.

Ibid.

4944. Live always in the best company when you read.   Ibid., x.

4945. He [Macaulay] has occasional flashes of silence, that make his conversation perfectly delightful.   Ibid.

4946. I never read a book before reviewing it ; it prejudices a man so.   H. Pearson, *The Smith of Smiths,* iii.

4947. Serenely full, the epicure would say,
Fate cannot harm me,—I have dined to-day.

Recipe for Salad.

SMOLLETT, TOBIAS GEORGE, Scottish novelist, baptised 19 March, 1721, died 17 Sept. 1771

4948. He was formed for the ruin of our sex.

Roderick Random, xxii.

4949. Hark ye, Clinker, you are a most notorious offender. You stand convicted of sickness, hunger, wretchedness, and want.

Humphrey Clinker, letter to Sir Watkin Phillips, 24 May.

4950. The Great Cham of literature, Samuel Johnson.

Letter to John Wilkes, 16 March, 1759.

SOLON, Greek lawgiver, 640 ?—558 ? B.C.

4951. Γηράσκω δ' αἰεὶ πολλὰ διδασκόμενος.
—But I grow old always learning many things.

Plutarch, *Solon,* xxxi.

SOMERVILLE, WILLIAM, poet, 2 Sept. 1675—17 July, 1742

4952.   The chase, the sport of kings ;
Image of war, without its guilt.   *The Chase,* i. 13.

SOPHOCLES, Greek dramatist, 495 ?—406 B.C.

4953. Πολλὰ τὰ δεινὰ κοὐδὲν ἀνθρώπου δεινότερον πέλει.
         —Wonders are many, and nothing is more wonderful than man.
                                                    Antigone, 332.

4954. Ἔρως ἀνίκατε μάχαν.
         —Love, unconquered in battle.   Ibid., 781.

4955. Ἔφη αὐτὸς μὲν οἵους δεῖ ποιεῖν, Εὐριπίδην δὲ οἷοι εἰσίν.
—I portray men as they ought to be portrayed, but Euripides portrays
them as they are.   Aristotle, *Poetics*, xxv.

SOUTHERNE, THOMAS, dramatist, 1660—22 May, 1746

    4956. Pity's akin to love.   *Oroonoko*, II. ii.

SOUTHEY, ROBERT, Poet Laureate, 12 Aug. 1774—21 March, 1843

4957.   How beautiful is night !
         A dewy freshness fills the silent air ;
         No mist obscures, nor cloud, nor speck, nor stain,
              Breaks the serene of heaven.
                                        Thalaba the Destroyer, I. I.

4958. And Sleep shall obey me,
         And visit thee never,
         And the Curse shall be on thee
              For ever and ever.   *The Curse of Kehama*, II. 14.

4959. My days among the Dead are past ;
         Around me I behold,
         Where'er these casual eyes are cast,
         The mighty minds of old ;
         My never-failing friends are they,
         With whom I converse day by day.
         [Written in his library.] *My Days among the Dead are Past.*

4960.   How does the water
                    Come down at Lodore ?
                                            The Cataract of Lodore.

4961.   It was a summer evening,
                 Old Kaspar's work was done,
               And he before his cottage door
                 Was sitting in the sun,
               And by him sported on the green
               His little grandchild Wilhelmine.
                                            The Battle of Blenheim.

4962.   ' But what good came of it at last ? '
                 Quoth little Peterkin.
               ' Why, that I cannot tell,' said he,
               ' But 'twas a famous victory.'   Ibid.

4963. Till the vessel strikes with a shivering shock,—
         ' Oh Christ ! it is the Inchcape Rock !'   *The Inchcape Rock.*

4964. Sir Ralph the Rover tore his hair ;
         He curst himself in his despair.   Ibid

4965. You are old, Father William, the young man cried,
    The few locks which are left you are grey ;
You are hale, Father William, a hearty old man,
    Now tell me the reason, I pray.   *The Old Man's Comforts.*

4966. From his brimstone bed at break of day
    A walking the Devil is gone,
To look at his little snug farm of the World,
    And see how his stock went on.   *The Devil's Walk,* 1.

4967. His coat was red and his breeches were blue,
And there was a hole where his tail came through.   Ibid., 3.

4968. He pass'd a cottage with a double coach-house,
    A cottage of gentility !
And he own'd with a grin
That his favourite sin
    Is pride that apes humility.   Ibid., 8.

4969. Blue, darkly deeply beautifully blue,
    In all its rich variety of shades.
                   Madoc in Wales, v. *Lincoya,* 102.

  4970. The Satanic School.   *The Vision of Judgment,* preface.

  4971. The march of intellect.
     Colloquies on the Progress and Prospects of Society, xiv.

SOUTHWELL, ROBERT, Jesuit and poet, 1561 ?—21 Feb. 1595

4972. As I in hoary winter's night stood shivering in the snow,
Surprised I was with sudden heat which made my heart to glow ;
And lifting up a fearful eye to view what fire was near,
A pretty Babe all burning bright did in the air appear.
                          The Burning Babe.

SPENCER, HERBERT, philosopher, 27 April, 1820—8 Dec. 1903

  4973. Education has for its object the formation of character.
                     Social Statics, II. xvii. 4.

  4974. No one can be perfectly free till all are free ; no one can be
perfectly moral till all are moral ; no one can be perfectly happy till
all are happy.   *Ibid.,* IV. xxx. 16.

  4975. Science is organised knowledge.   *Education,* ii.

  4976. Survival of the fittest.
    Principles of Biology, III. xii. *Indirect Equilibration,* 165,
    et passim.

  4977. The Republican form of government is the highest form of
government ; but because of this it requires the highest type of human
nature—a type nowhere at present existing.
                    Essays. The Americans.

SPENCER, WILLIAM ROBERT, poet, 1769—24 Oct. 1834

4978. Too late I stayed—forgive the crime ;
    Unheeded flew the hours ;
How noiseless falls the foot of Time
    That only treads on flowers !
                 Lines to Lady Anne Hamilton.

SPENSER, EDMUND, Poet Laureate, 1552?—16 Jan. 1599

4979. To Kerke the narre, from God more farre,
    Has bene an old-sayd sawe,
  And he, that strives to touch a starre,
    Oft stombles at a strawe.
          The Shepheard's Calender, Julye, 97.

4980. A gentle Knight was pricking on the plaine.
          The Faerie Queene, I. i. 1.

4981. And on his breast a bloodie Crosse he bore,
  The deare remembrance of his dying Lord.   Ibid., 2.

4982. The noblest mind the best contentment has. Ibid., 35.

4983. A bold bad man.   Ibid., 37.

4984.   Her angels face
  As the great eye of heaven, shyned bright,
  And made a sunshine in the shady place.   Ibid., iii. 4.

4985. Sleepe after toyle, port after stormie seas,
  Ease after warre, death after life, does greatly please.
              Ibid., ix. 40.

4986. The Squyre of Dames.   Ibid., III. vii. 51.

4987. How over that same dore was likewise writ,
  Be bolde, be bolde, and every where *Be bold.*

     .   .   .   .   .

  Another yron dore, on which was writ,
  Be not too bold.   Ibid., xi. 54.

4988. Dan Chaucer, well of English undefyled,
  On Fames eternall beadroll worthie to be fyled.
             Ibid., IV., ii. 32.

4989. Full little knowest thou, that hast not tride,
  What hell it is in suing long to bide :
  To loose good dayes, that might be better spent ;
  To wast long nights in pensive discontent ;
  To speed to day, to be put back to morrow ;
  To feed on hope, to pine with feare and sorrow ;
  To have thy Princes grace, yet want her Peeres ;
  To have thy asking, yet waite manie yeares;
  To fret thy soule with crosses and with cares ;
  To eate thy heart through comfortlesse dispaires ;
  To fawne, to crowche, to waite, to ride, to ronne,
  To spend, to give, to want, to be undonne,
  Unhappie wight, borne to disastrous end,
  That doth his life in so long tendance spend !
         Mother Hubbards Tale, 895.

4990. What more felicitie can fall to creature
  Then to enjoy delight with libertie. *Muiopotmos*, 209.

4991. For of the soule the bodie forme doth take ;
  The soule is forme, and doth the bodie make.
      An Hymn in Honour of Beautie, 132.

4992. The woods shall to me answer, and my Eccho ring.
          Epithalamion, 18.

4993. Sweet Themmes ! runne softly, till I end my Song.

Prothalamion, 18.

4994. At length they all to mery London came,
To mery London, my most kyndly Nurse.   Ibid., 127.

4995. I was promis'd on a time,
To have reason for my rhyme ;
From that time unto this season,
I received nor rhyme nor reason.

Lines on his promised pension.

SPOONER, WILLIAM ARCHIBALD, Warden of New College, Oxford,
22 July, 1844—29 Aug. 1930

4996. Kinquering Congs their titles take.

Announcing hymn in New College chapel, 1879.

4997. Let us drink to the queer old Dean.   *Attributed.*

4998. Sir, you have tasted two whole worms ; you have hissed all
my mystery lectures and been caught fighting a liar in the quad ; you
will leave by the next town drain.   Ibid.

[The first of the above is said to be the only genuine
' spoonerism,' all others being invented.]

SPRING-RICE, SIR CECIL ARTHUR, diplomatist, 27 Feb. 1859—14 Feb.
1918

4999. I vow to thee, my country—all earthly things above—
Entire and whole and perfect the service of my love.

I vow to thee, my Country.

5000. And her ways are ways of gentleness, and all her paths are
peace.   Ibid.

SQUIRE, SIR JOHN COLLINGS, author, 2 April, 1884—20 Dec. 1958

5001. It did not last : the Devil howling *Ho*,
Let Einstein be, restored the status quo.

Answer to Pope's couplet on Newton, No. 3309.

5002. But I'm not so think as you drunk I am.

Ballade of Soporific Absorption.

STANLEY, SIR HENRY MORTON, explorer, 29 June, 1841—10 May,
1904

5003. Dr. Livingstone, I presume ?

On meeting him at Ujiji, Central Africa, 10 Nov. 1871.

STANTON, CHARLES E., U.S. soldier, 1859—1933

5004. Lafayette, we are here.

*Address on behalf of the American Expeditionary Force, at
the tomb of Lafayette*, 4 *July*, 1917.

[Often wrongly attributed to General Pershing.]

STANTON, EDWIN MCMASTERS, U.S. statesman, 19 Dec. 1814—
       24 Dec. 1869

   5005. Now he belongs to the ages.
                                     At the deathbed of President Lincoln.

STANTON, FRANK LEBBY, U.S. author, 22 Feb. 1857—7 Jan. 1927

5006.   Sweetes' li'l' feller—
                            Everybody knows ;
                         Dunno what ter call 'im,
                            But he mighty lak' a rose !
                                         Sweetes' Li'l' Feller.

STEELE, SIR RICHARD, Irish author, baptised 12 March, 1672, died
       1 Sept. 1729

   5007. Though her mien carries much more invitation than command,
to behold her is an immediate check to loose behaviour ; to love her
is a liberal education.   *The Tatler*, 49.

   5008. The insupportable labour of doing nothing.   Ibid., 54.

   5009. Reading is to the mind what exercise is to the body.
                                                        Ibid., 147.

   5010. Will Honeycomb calls these over-offended ladies the out-
rageously virtuous.   *The Spectator*, 266.

STEPHEN, JAMES KENNETH, parodist, 25 Feb. 1859—3 Feb. 1892

5011. Two voices are there : one is of the deep ;
       It learns the storm-cloud's thunderous melody,
       Now roars, now murmurs with the changing sea,
       Now bird-like pipes, now closes soft in sleep ;
       And one is of an old half-witted sheep
       Which bleats articulate monotony,
       And indicates that two and one are three,
       That grass is green, lakes damp, and mountains steep :
       And, Wordsworth, both are thine.
                                 Lapsus Calami.   A Sonnet.

5012. When the Rudyards cease from Kipling
          And the Haggards Ride no more.   Ibid., *To R. K.*

5013. Ah ! Matt. ; old age has brought to me
       Thy wisdom, less thy certainty ;
       The world's a jest, and joy's a trinket :
       I knew that once : but now—I think it.
                                 Ibid., *Senex to Matt. Prior.*

STERNE, LAURENCE, clergyman and author, 24 Nov. 1713—18 March,
       1768

   5014. Go, poor devil, get thee gone ; why should I hurt thee ?
This world surely is wide enough to hold both thee and me.
[Uncle Toby to the fly.]   *Tristram Shandy*, II. xii.

   5015. ' Our armies swore terribly in Flanders,' cried my Uncle
Toby, ' but nothing to this.'   Ibid., III. xi.
   *M

5016. Of all the cants which are canted in this canting world, though the cant of hypocrites may be the worst, the cant of criticism is the most tormenting !   Ibid., xii.

5017. ' He shall not die, by G——,' cried my uncle Toby.—The Accusing Spirit, which flew up to heaven's chancery with the oath, blushed as he gave it in ; and the Recording Angel, as he wrote it down, dropped a tear upon the word, and blotted it out for ever.
Ibid., VI. viii.

5018. ' They order,' said I, ' this matter better in France.'
A Sentimental Journey, i.

5019. ' God tempers the wind,' said Maria, ' to the shorn lamb.'
Ibid., Maria.

STEVENS, GEORGE ALEXANDER, author, 1710—6 Sept. 1784

5020.   Cease, rude Boreas, blustering railer !
                 List, ye landsmen, all to me ;
                 Messmates, hear a brother sailor
                 Sing the dangers of the sea.   The Storm.

STEVENSON, ROBERT LOUIS, Scottish author, 13 Nov. 1850—3 Dec. 1894

5021. In marriage, a man becomes slack and selfish, and undergoes a fatty degeneration of his moral being.   Virginibus Puerisque, i.

5022. Times are changed with him who marries ; there are no more by-path meadows, where you may innocently linger, but the road lies long and straight and dusty to the grave.   Ibid., ii.

5023. To marry is to domesticate the Recording Angel. Once you are married, there is nothing left for you, not even suicide, but to be good.   Ibid.

5024. The cruellest lies are often told in silence.   Ibid., iv.

5025. Old and young, we are all on our last cruise.
Ibid., Crabbed Age and Youth.

5026. For God's sake give me the young man who has brains enough to make a fool of himself !   Ibid.

5027. Books are good enough in their own way, but they are a mighty bloodless substitute for life.   Ibid., An Apology for Idlers.

5028. Extreme busyness, whether at school or college, kirk or market, is a symptom of deficient vitality.   Ibid.

5029. There is no duty we so much underrate as the duty of being happy.   Ibid.

5030. Even if the doctor does not give you a year, even if he hesitates about a month, make one brave push and see what can be accomplished in a week.   Ibid., Aes Triplex.

5031. To travel hopefully is a better thing than to arrive, and the true success is to labour.   Ibid., El Dorado.

5032. I have thus played the sedulous ape to Hazlitt, to Lamb, to Wordsworth, to Sir Thomas Browne, to Defoe, to Hawthorne, to Montaigne, to Baudelaire and to Obermann.
Memories and Portraits, iv.

5033. A Penny Plain and Twopence Coloured. *Ibid.*

5034. Here lies one who meant well, tried a little, failed much :—
surely that may be his epitaph, of which he need not be ashamed.
Across the Plains. A Christmas Sermon.

5035. Give us grace and strength to forbear and to persevere.
Give us courage and gaiety and the quiet mind, spare us to our friends,
soften to us our enemies. *Prayer.*

5036.   Fifteen men on the Dead Man's Chest—
      Yo-ho-ho, and a bottle of rum !
    Drink and the devil had done for the rest—
      Yo-ho-ho, and a bottle of rum ! *Treasure Island,* i.

5037. Tip me the black spot. *Ibid.,* iii.

5038. Am I no a bonny fighter ? [Alan Breck.] *Kidnapped,* x.

5039. Nothing like a little judicious levity. [Michael Finsbury.]
The Wrong Box, vii.

[Written by Stevenson and his stepson Lloyd Osborne.]

5040.   In winter I get up at night
    And dress by yellow candle-light.
    In summer, quite the other way,
    I have to go to bed by day.
A Child's Garden of Verses : Bed in Summer.

5041.   A child should always say what's true,
    And speak when he is spoken to,
    And behave mannerly at table :
    At least as far as he is able.
Ibid., Whole Duty of Children.

5042.   When I am grown to man's estate
    I shall be very proud and great,
    And tell the other girls and boys
    Not to meddle with my toys. *Ibid., Looking Forward.*

5043. The pleasant land of counterpane.
The Land of Counterpane.

5044.   The friendly cow, all red and white,
      I love with all my heart :
    She gives me cream with all her might
      To eat with apple-tart. *Ibid., The Cow.*

5045. The world is so full of a number of things,
I'm sure we should all be as happy as kings.
Ibid., Happy Thought.

5046. And ever again, in the wink of an eye,
Painted stations whistle by.
Ibid., From a Railway Carriage.

5047.   Go, little book, and wish to all,
    Flowers in the garden, meat in the hall,
    A bin of wine, a spice of wit,
    A house with lawns enclosing it,
    A living river by the door,
    A nightingale in the sycamore ! *Underwoods,* I. *Envoy.*

5048. Under the wide and starry sky,
Dig the grave and let me lie.
Glad did I live and gladly die,
    And I laid me down with a will.

5049. This be the verse you grave for me :
Here he lies where he longed to be ;
Home is the sailor, home from sea,
    And the hunter home from the hill.   Ibid., *Requiem.*

5050. If I have faltered more or less
In my great task of happiness.   Ibid., *The Celestial Surgeon.*

5051. Lord, thy most pointed pleasure take
And stab my spirit broad awake ;
Or, Lord, if too obdurate I,
Choose thou, before that spirit die,
A piercing pain, a killing sin,
And to my dead heart run them in !   Ibid.

5052. The untented Kosmos my abode,
    I pass, a wilful stranger :
My mistress still the open road
    And the bright eyes of danger.   Ibid., *Youth and Love.*

5053. I will make you brooches and toys for your delight
Of bird-song at morning and star-shine at night.   Ibid., xi.

5054. In the highlands, in the country places,
Where the old plain men have rosy faces,
And the young fair maidens
    Quiet eyes.   Ibid., xvi.

5055. Trusty, dusky, vivid, true,
With eyes of gold and bramble-dew,
Steel-true and blade-straight,
The great artificer
    Made my mate.   Ibid. *My Wife.*

5056. Blows the wind to-day, and the sun and the rain are flying,
    Blows the wind on the moors to-day and now,
Where about the graves of the martyrs the whaups are crying,
    My heart remembers how !   Ibid., *To S. R. Crockett.*

STEVENSON, WILLIAM, Fellow of Christ's College, Cambridge, 1530 ?
    —1575

5057.   I cannot eat but little meat,
        My stomach is not good ;
    But sure I think that I can drink
        With him that wears a hood.
    Though I go bare, take ye no care,
        I am nothing a-cold :
    I stuff my skin so full within
        Of jolly good ale and old.
    Back and side go bare, go bare,
        Both foot and hand go cold ;
    But belly, God send thee good ale enough,
        Whether it be new or old.
                Gammer Gurton's Needle, II. song.
        [The authorship of this is disputed.]

STIRLING, EARL OF, *see* Alexander, Sir William

STONE, SAMUEL JOHN, clergyman, 25 April, 1839—19 Nov. 1900

5058.   The Church's one foundation
                   Is Jesus Christ her Lord.

STOWE, HARRIET ELIZABETH BEECHER, U.S. authoress, 14 June
        1811—1 July, 1896

5059. ' Never was born ! ' persisted Topsy ; ' never had no father,
nor mother, nor nothin'. I was raised by a speculator.'
                                     Uncle Tom's Cabin, **xx.**

5060. ' Do you know who made you ? ' ' Nobody, as I knows on,'
said the child, with a short laugh. . . . ' I 'spect I grow'd. Don't
think nobody never made me.'   Ibid.

5061. I's wicked—I is. I's mighty wicked, anyhow. I can't help
it.   Ibid.

STOWELL, BARON, *see* Scott, William

SUCKLING, SIR JOHN, poet, baptised 10 Feb. 1609, died 1642

5062. Her feet beneath her petticoat
      Like little mice, stole in and out,
          As if they fear'd the light.   *Ballad upon a Wedding.*

5063. Her lips were red, and one was thin,
      Compar'd to that was next her chin
          (Some bee had stung it newly).   Ibid.

5064. Why so pale and wan, fond lover ?
      Prithee, why so pale ?
      Will, when looking well can't move her,
          Looking ill prevail ?   *Aglaura*, IV. i. *song.*

5065. Quit, quit, for shame, this will not move,
      This cannot take her ;
      If of herself she will not love,
      Nothing can make her :
          The Devil take her !   Ibid.

5066. Out upon it, I have loved
      Three whole days together
      And am like to love three more,
          If it prove fair weather.   *A Poem with the Answer.*

SURREY, HENRY HOWARD, Earl of, 1517 ?—21 Jan. 1547

5067. The soote season, that bud and bloom forth brings,
      With green hath clad the hill, and eke the vale.
                                     Description of Spring.

5068. But oft the words come forth awry of him that loveth well.
      Description of the Fickle Affections, Pangs, and Slights of Love.

SURTEES, ROBERT SMITH, sporting novelist, 1803—16 March, 1864

5069. Full o' beans and benevolence !   *Handley Cross*, xxvii

5070. Hellish dark, and smells of cheese !   Ibid., l.

5071. There is no secret so close as that between a rider and his horse.   *Mr. Sponge's Sporting Tour*, xxxi.

5072. The only infallible rule we know is, that the man who is always talking about being a gentleman never is one.   *Ask Mamma*, i.

SWIFT, JONATHAN, Dean of St. Patrick's, Irish satirist, 30 Nov. 1667 —19 Oct. 1745

5073. Read all the prefaces of Dryden,
For them our critics much confide in,
(Tho' merely writ at first for filling
To raise the volume's price, a shilling).   *On Poetry*, 251.

5074. Hobbes clearly proves that every creature
Lives in a state of war by nature.   Ibid., 319.

5075. So, naturalists observe, a flea
Hath smaller fleas that on him prey ;
And these have smaller fleas to bite 'em,
And so proceed *ad infinitum*.   Ibid., 337.

5076. Yet malice never was his aim ;
He lash'd the vice, but spared the name ;
No individual could resent,
Where thousands equally were meant.
On the Death of Dr. Swift, 512.

5077. The two noblest of things, which are sweetness and light.
The Battle of the Books, preface.

5078. He [the Emperor] is taller by almost the breadth of my nail than any of his court, which alone is enough to strike an awe into the beholders.   *Gulliver's Travels. Voyage to Lilliput*, ii.

5079. And he gave it for his opinion, that whoever could make two ears of corn or two blades of grass to grow upon a spot of ground where only one grew before, would deserve better of mankind, and do more essential service to his country, than the whole race of politicians put together.   Ibid., *Voyage to Brobdingnag*, vii.

5080. He had been eight years upon a project for extracting sunbeams out of cucumbers, which were to be put into vials hermetically sealed, and let out to warm the air in raw inclement summers.
Ibid., *Voyage to Laputa*, v.

5081. I said the thing which was not.
Ibid., *Voyage to the Houyhnhms*, iii.

5082. I have been assured by a very knowing American of my acquaintance in London, that a young healthy child well nursed is at a year old a most delicious, nourishing, and wholesome food, whether stewed, roasted, baked, or boiled, and I make no doubt that it will equally serve in a fricassee, or a ragout.

A Modest Proposal for preventing the Children of Ireland from being a Burden to their Parents or Country.

5083. The reason why so few marriages are happy, is, because young ladies spend their time in making nets, not in making cages.
Thoughts on Various Subjects.

5084. A nice man is a man of nasty ideas. Ibid.

5085. Proper words in proper places, make the true definition of a style. *Letter to a young clergyman,* 9 Jan. 1720.

5086. Not die here in a rage, like a poisoned rat in a hole.
Letter to Bolingbroke, 21 March, 1729.

5087. Good God ! what a genius I had when I wrote that book. [Of ' The Tale of a Tub.']
Walter Scott, *Memoirs of Jonathan Swift,* ii.

5088. I shall be like that tree, I shall die at the top. Ibid., vii.

5089. Ubi saeva indignatio ulterius cor lacerare nequit.—Where fierce indignation can no more tear his heart.
Inscription on Swift's grave.

SWINBURNE, ALGERNON CHARLES, poet, 5 April, 1837—10 April, 1909

5090. I have put my days and dreams out of mind,
Days that are over, dreams that are done.
The Triumph of Time.

5091. The strong sea-daisies feast on the sun. Ibid.

5092. I will go back to the great sweet mother,
Mother and lover of men, the sea.
I will go down to her, I and no other,
Close with her, kiss her and mix her with me. Ibid.

5093. I shall never be friends again with roses. Ibid.

5094. Let us go hence, my songs ; she will not hear.
A Leave-taking.

5095. I have lived long enough, having seen one thing, that love hath an end;
Goddess and maiden and queen, be near me now and befriend.
Hymn to Proserpine.

5096. Yea, is not even Apollo, with hair and harpstring of gold,
A bitter God to follow, a beautiful God to behold ? Ibid.

5097. Thou hast conquered, O pale Galilean ; the world has grown grey from Thy breath. Ibid.

5098. Kissing her hair I sat against her feet. *Rondel.*

5099. Change in a trice
The lilies and languors of virtue
For the raptures and roses of vice. *Dolores.*

5100. O splendid and sterile Dolores,
Our Lady of Pain. Ibid.

5101. From too much love of living,
From hope and fear set free,
We thank with brief thanksgiving
Whatever gods may be
That no life lives for ever ;
That dead men rise up never ;
That even the weariest river
Winds somewhere safe to sea.

The Garden of Proserpine.

5102. Shall I strew on thee rose or rue or laurel ?

Ave atque vale. In memory of Charles Baudelaire.

5103. Glory to Man in the Highest ! for Man is the master of things.

Hymn of Man.

5104. Maiden, and mistress of the months and stars
Now folded in the flowerless fields of heaven.

Atalanta in Calydon.

5105. When the hounds of spring are on winter's traces,
The mother of months in meadow or plain
Fills the shadows and windy places
With lisp of leaves and ripple of rain. Ibid., *Chorus.*

5106. And in green underwood and cover
Blossom by blossom the spring begins. Ibid.

5107 He weaves, and is clothed with derision ;
Sows, and he shall not reap ;
His life is a watch or a vision
Between a sleep and a sleep. Ibid.

5108. Hope thou not much, and fear thou not at all.

Hope and Fear.

SYMONDS, JOHN ADDINGTON, critic, 5 Oct. 1840—19 April, 1893

5109. These things shall be ! A loftier race
Than e'er the world hath known, shall rise,
With flame of freedom in their souls
And light of knowledge in their eyes.

New and Old. A Vista.

SYMONS, ARTHUR, poet and critic, 28 Feb. 1865—22 Jan. 1945

5110. I have ever held that the rod with which popular fancy invests criticism is properly the rod of divination : a hazel-switch for the discovery of buried treasure, not a birch-twig for the castigation of offenders. *An Introduction to the Study of Browning*, preface.

TACITUS, CORNELIUS, Roman historian, 55 ?—117 ?

5111. Omne ignotum pro magnifico est.—Everything unknown is taken as marvellous. *Agricola*, xxx.

5112. Ubi solitudinem faciunt, pacem appellant.—Where they make a desert, they call it peace. Ibid.

5113. Felix . . . opportunitate mortis.—Fortunate in the occasion of his death. Ibid., xlv.

5114. Omnium consensu capax imperii nisi imperasset.—Would by all have been reckoned competent to rule, had he not been emperor.
[Of Galba.] *Histories*, I. xlix.

5115. Sine ira et studio.—Without rancour or partiality.
Annals, I. i.

TALFOURD, SIR THOMAS NOON, judge and author, 26 May, 1795—13 March, 1854

5116. 'Tis a little thing
To give a cup of water ; yet its draught
Of cool refreshment, drain'd by fever'd lips,
May give a shock of pleasure to the frame
More exquisite than when nectarean juice
Renews the life of joy in happiest hours. *Ion*, I. ii.

TALLEYRAND–PÉRIGORD, CHARLES MAURICE DE, French statesman, 13 Feb. 1754—17 May, 1838

5117. C'est le commencement de la fin.—It is the beginning of the end. *Remark to Napoleon after battle of Leipzig*, 18 Oct. 1813.

5118. Vous ne jouez donc pas le whist, monsieur ? Hélas ! quelle triste vieillesse vous vous preparez !—You do not then play whist, sir ? Alas, what a sad old age you are preparing for yourself !
When reproached for his addiction to cards.

5119. Ils n'ont rien appris, ni rien oublié.—They have learned nothing and forgotten nothing. *Attributed.*

5120. Pas trop de zèle.—Not too much zeal. Ibid.

5121. Noir comme le diable,
Chaud comme l'enfer,
Pur comme un ange,
Doux comme l'amour.
—Black as the devil,
Hot as hell,
Pure as an angel,
Sweet as love. *Recipe for coffee.*

TANNAHILL, ROBERT, Scottish poet, 3 June, 1774—17 May, 1810

5122. She's modest as ony, and blithe as she's bonny ;
For guileless simplicity marks her its ain :
And far be the villain, divested of feeling,
Wha'd blight in its bloom the sweet flower o' Dumblane.
The Flower o' Dumblane.

5123. When gloamin treads the heels o' day,
And birds sit courin on the spray,
Alang the flow'ry hedge I stray,
To meet mine ain dear somebody.
Mine ain Dear Somebody.

TATE, NAHUM, Irish author, Poet Laureate, 1652—12 Aug. 1715

5124. Permit the transports of a British Muse,
And pardon raptures that yourselves infuse.
As Poet Laureate to the Parliament, 1701.

TAYLOR, ANN (MRS. GILBERT), poetess, 30 Jan. 1782—20 Dec. 1866

5125. Who ran to help me when I fell,
And would some pretty story tell,
Or kiss the place to make it well ?
My Mother. *Original Poems. My Mother.*

5126. Meddlesome Matty. Ibid., Title.

5127. I thank the goodness and the grace
Which on my birth have smiled,
And made me, in these Christian days,
A happy English child.
Hymns for Infant Minds. A Child's Hymn of Praise.

TAYLOR, BAYARD, U.S. author, 11 Jan. 1825—19 Dec. 1878

5128. Till the sun grows cold,
And the stars are old,
And the leaves of the Judgment Book unfold.
Bedouin Song.

TAYLOR, SIR HENRY, author, 18 Oct. 1800—27 March, 1886

5129. The world knows nothing of its greatest men.
Philip Van Artefelde, part I. i. v.

5130. He that lacks time to mourn, lacks time to mend. Ibid.

5131. Such souls,
Whose sunken visitations daze the world,
Vanish like lightning, but they leave behind
A voice that in the distance far away
Wakens the slumbering ages. Ibid., vii.

TAYLOR, JANE, poetess, 23 Sept. 1783—13 April, 1824

5132. Twinkle, twinkle, little star,
How I wonder what you are !
Up above the world so high,
Like a diamond in the sky !
Rhymes for the Nursery. The Star.

TAYLOR, JEREMY, Bishop of Down and Connor, baptised 15 Aug.
1613, died 13 Aug. 1667

5133. The sun reflecting upon the mud of strands and shores is
unpolluted in his beam. *Holy Living*, i. 3.

5134. Desperate by too quick a sense of constant infelicity.
Holy Dying, i. 5.

5135. He that loves not his wife and children, feeds a lioness at
home and broods a nest of sorrows. *Sermons. Married Love.*

TEASDALE, SARA (MRS. ERNST B. FILSINGER), U.S. poetess, 8 Aug. 1884
—29 Jan. 1933

5136. When I am dead and over me bright April
Shakes out her rain-drenched hair. *I shall not care.*

5137. Redbud, buckberry,
        Wild plum-tree
        And proud river sweeping
        Southward to the sea.   *Redbirds.*

5138. Strephon's kiss was lost in jest,
        Robin's lost in play,
        But the kiss in Colin's eyes
        Haunts me night and day.   *The Look.*

TEMPLE, SIR WILLIAM, statesman and author, 1628—27 Jan. 1699
    5139. When all is done, human life is, at the greatest and the best,
but like a froward child, that must be played with and humoured a
little to keep it quiet till it falls asleep, and then the care is over.
                                        Essay on Poetry.

TENNYSON, ALFRED TENNYSON, 1ST BARON, Poet Laureate, 6 Aug.
    1809—6 Oct. 1892

5140. Her court was pure ; her life serene ;
        God gave her peace ; her land reposed ;
        A thousand claims to reverence closed
        In her as Mother, Wife, and Queen.   *To the Queen.*

5141. Airy, fairy Lilian.   *Lilian.*

5142. She only said, ' My life is dreary,
        He cometh not,' she said ;
        She said, ' I am aweary, aweary,
        I would that I were dead ! '   *Mariana.*

5143. Dower'd with the hate of hate, the scorn of scorn,
            The love of love.   *The Poet.*

5144. He thought to quell the stubborn hearts of oak,
        Madman !   *Buonaparte.*

5145. A happy bridesmaid makes a happy bride.   *The Bridesmaid.*

5146. To many-tower'd Camelot.   *The Lady of Shalott,* i.

5147. ' The curse is come upon me,' cried
        The Lady of Shalott.   Ibid., iii.

5148. Across the walnuts and the wine.   *The Miller's Daughter.*

5149. O mother Ida, many-fountained Ida,
        Dear mother Ida, hearken ere I die.   *Oenone,* 22.

5150. Self-reverence, self-knowledge, self-control.
        These three alone lead life to sovereign power.   Ibid., 142.

5151. Her manners had not that repose
        Which stamps the caste of Vere de Vere.
                                    Lady Clara Vere de Vere.

5152. Kind hearts are more than coronets,
        And simple faith than Norman blood.   Ibid.

5153. You must wake and call me early, call me early, mother dear ;
        To-morrow 'ill be the happiest time of all the glad New Year ;
        Of all the glad New Year, mother, the maddest merriest day ;
        For I'm to be Queen o' the May, mother, I'm to be Queen o'
        the May.   *The May Queen.*

5154.   A land
In which it seemed always afternoon.   *The Lotos-Eaters.*

5155. Music that gentlier on the spirit lies,
Than tir'd eyelids upon tir'd eyes.   Ibid., *Choric Song,* i.

5156. The spacious times of great Elizabeth.
                  A Dream of Fair Women, 7.

5157. A daughter of the gods, divinely tall,
And most divinely fair.   Ibid., 87.

5158. A land of settled government,
    A land of just and old renown,
      Where freedom slowly broadens down
From precedent to precedent.   *You ask me why.*

5159. She stood, a sight to make an old man young.
             The Gardener's Daughter, 140.

5160. In teacup-times of hood and hoop,
Or while the patch was worn.   *The Talking Oak,* 16.

5161. And drunk delight of battle with my peers,
Far on the ringing plains of windy Troy.   *Ulysses,* 16.

5162. I am a part of all that I have met.   Ibid., 18.

5163. To follow knowledge like a sinking star,
Beyond the utmost bound of human thought.   Ibid., 31.

5164. To strive, to seek, to find, and not to yield.   Ibid., 70.

5165. The woods decay, the woods decay and fall,
The vapours weep their burthen to the ground,
Man comes and tills the field and lies beneath,
And after many a summer dies the swan.   *Tithonus,* 1.

5166. The Gods themselves cannot recall their gifts.   Ibid., 49.

5167. In the Spring a livelier iris changes on the burnish'd dove ;
In the Spring a young man's fancy lightly turns to thoughts of
    love.   *Locksley Hall,* 19.

5168. He will hold thee, when his passion shall have spent its novel
    force,
Something better than his dog, a little dearer than his horse.
                          Ibid., 49.

5169.   This is truth the poet sings,
That a sorrow's crown of sorrow is remembering happier things.
                          Ibid., 75.

5170. Heard the heavens fill with shouting, and there rain'd a ghastly
    dew
From the nations' airy navies grappling in the central blue.
                          Ibid., 123.

5171. Till the war-drum throbb'd no longer, and the battle-flags
    were furl'd,
In the Parliament of man, the Federation of the world.
                          Ibid., 127.

5172. Knowledge comes, but wisdom lingers.   Ibid., 141.

5173. Woman is the lesser man, and all thy passions, match'd with mine,
    Are as moonlight unto sunlight, and as water unto wine.
                Ibid., 151.

5174. Let the great world spin for ever down the ringing grooves
    of change.   *Ibid.*, 182.

5175. Better fifty years of Europe than a cycle of Cathay.
                 Ibid., 184.

5176. And o'er the hills, and far away,
    Beyond their utmost purple rim,
    Beyond the night, across the day,
    Thro' all the world she follow'd him.   *The Departure.*

5177. Make Thou my spirit pure and clear
    As are the frosty skies,
    Or this first snowdrop of the year
    That in my bosom lies.   *St. Agnes' Eve.*

5178. My strength is as the strength of ten,
    Because my heart is pure.   *Sir Galahad.*

5179. O plump head-waiter at The Cock
    To which I most resort,
    How goes the time ?   'Tis five o'clock.
    Go fetch a pint of port.
        Will Waterproof's Lyrical Monologue, 1.

5180. Cophetua sware a royal oath :
    ' This beggar maid shall be my queen ! '   *The Beggar Maid.*

5181. He clasps the crag with crooked hands.   *The Eagle.*

5182. The wrinkled sea beneath him crawls.   *Ibid.*

5183. God made Himself an awful rose of dawn.
        The Vision of Sin, iii. and v.

5184. Break, break, break,
    On thy cold grey stones, O Sea !
    And I would that my tongue could utter
    The thoughts that arise in me.   *Break, break, break.*

5185. And the stately ships go on
    To their haven under the hill ;
    But O for the touch of a vanish'd hand,
    And the sound of a voice that is still !   *Ibid.*

5186. But the tender grace of a day that is dead
    Will never come back to me.   *Ibid.*

5187. The myriad shriek of wheeling ocean-fowl,
    The league-long roller thundering on the reef.
        Enoch Arden, 579.

5188. And when they buried him the little port
    Had seldom seen a costlier funeral.   *Ibid.*, 910.

5189.   I chatter, chatter, as I flow
        To join the brimming river,
    For men may come and men may go,
        But I go on for ever.   *The Brook.*

5190.   What does little birdie say
        In her nest at peep of day ?   *Sea Dreams,* 281.

5191. With prudes for proctors, dowagers for deans,
And sweet girl-graduates in their golden hair.
The Princess, prologue, 141.

5192. A rosebud set with little wilful thorns,
And sweet as English air could make her, she. Ibid., 153.

5193. And blessings on the falling out
That all the more endears,
When we fall out with those we love
And kiss again with tears ! Ibid., ii. *song.*

5194. Jewels five words long
That on the stretch'd forefinger of all Time
Sparkle for ever. Ibid., 355.

5195. Sweet and low, sweet and low,
Wind of the western sea. Ibid., iii. *song.*

5196. The splendour falls on castle walls
And snowy summits old in story :
The long light shakes across the lakes,
And the wild cataract leaps in glory.
Blow, bugle, blow, set the wild echoes flying,
Blow, bugle ; answer, echoes, dying, dying, dying.
Ibid., iv. *song*

5197. The horns of Elfland faintly blowing. Ibid.

5198. Tears, idle tears, I know not what they mean,
Tears from the depth of some divine despair
Rise in the heart, and gather to the eyes,
In looking on the happy Autumn fields,
And thinking of the days that are no more. Ibid., *song.*

5199. Dear as remember'd kisses after death,
And sweet as those by hopeless fancy feign'd
On lips that are for others ; deep as love,
Deep as first love, and wild with all regret ;
O Death in Life, the days that are no more. Ibid.

5200. O Swallow, Swallow, flying, flying South. Ibid., *song.*

5201. O tell her, Swallow, thou that knowest each,
That bright and fierce and fickle is the South,
And dark and true and tender is the North. Ibid.

5202. Thy voice is heard thro' rolling drums,
That beat to battle where he stands. Ibid., *song.*

5203. Man is the hunter ; woman is his game. Ibid., v. 147.

5204. Home they brought her warrior dead :
She nor swoon'd, nor utter'd cry :
All her maidens, watching, said,
' She must weep or she will die.' Ibid., vi. *song.*

5205. Rose a nurse of ninety years,
Set his child upon her knee—
Like summer tempest came her tears—
' Sweet my child, I live for thee.' Ibid

5206. Ask me no more : the moon may draw the sea. Ibid., vii. *song.*

5207. Come down, O maid, from yonder mountain height.
Ibid., 177.

5208. Myriads of rivulets hurrying thro' the lawn,
The moan of doves in immemorial elms,
And murmuring of innumerable bees.
Ibid., 205.

5209. Not once or twice in our rough island-story,
The path of duty was the way to glory :
He that walks it, only thirsting
For the right, and learns to deaden
Love of self, before his journey closes,
He shall find the stubborn thistle bursting
Into glossy purples, which outredden
All voluptuous garden-roses.
Ode on the Death of the Duke of Wellington, vii.

5210. Half a league, half a league,
Half a league onward,
All in the valley of Death
Rode the six hundred.
The Charge of the Light Brigade.

5211. Some one had blunder'd.
Ibid.

5212. Theirs not to make reply,
Theirs not to reason why,
Theirs but to do and die.
Ibid.

5213. Cannon to right of them,
Cannon to left of them,
Cannon in front of them
Volley'd and thunder'd.
Ibid.

5214. Sea-king's daughter from over the sea,
Alexandra !
A Welcome to Alexandra.

5215. And the parson made it his text that week, and he said like-
wise,
That a lie which is half a truth is ever the blackest of lies,
That a lie which is all a lie may be met and fought with out-
right,
But a lie which is part a truth is a harder matter to fight.
The Grandmother, 8.

5216. Bessy Marris's barne ! tha knaws she laäid it to meä.
Mowt a beän, mayhap, for she wur a bad un, sheä.
Northern Farmer. Old Style.

5217. Doänt thou marry for munny, but goä wheer munny is !
Northern Farmer. New Style.

5218. All along the valley, stream that flashest white.
In the Valley of Cauteretz.

5219. Speak to Him thou for He hears, and Spirit with Spirit can
meet—
Closer is He than breathing, and nearer than hands and feet.
The Higher Pantheism.

5220. Flower in the crannied wall,
   I pluck you out of the crannies,
   I hold you here, root and all, in my hand,
   Little flower—but *if* I could understand
   What you are, root and all, and all in all,
   I should know what God and man is.
          Flower in the Crannied Wall.

5221. O mighty-mouth'd inventor of harmonies,
   O skill'd to sing of Time or Eternity,
    God-gifted organ-voice of England,
    Milton, a name to resound for ages. *Milton. Alcaics.*

5222. O you chorus of indolent reviewers. *Hendecasyllabics.*

5223. I hold it truth, with him who sings
    To one clear harp in divers tones,
    That men may rise on stepping-stones
   Of their dead selves to higher things. *In Memoriam*, i.

5224. I do but sing because I must,
   And pipe but as the linnets sing. Ibid., xxi.

5225. The Shadow cloak'd from head to foot,
   Who keeps the keys of all the creeds. Ibid., xxiii.

5226. 'Tis better to have loved and lost
   Than never to have loved at all. Ibid., xxvii.

5227. O yet we trust that somehow good
    Will be the final goal of ill. Ibid., liv.

5228.   But what am I ?
    An infant crying in the night :
    An infant crying for the light :
    And with no language but a cry. Ibid.

5229. Nature, red in tooth and claw. Ibid., lvi.

5230. So many worlds, so much to do,
    So little done, such things to be. Ibid., lxxiii.

5231. When rosy plumelets tuft the larch,
    And rarely pipes the mounted thrush ;
    Or underneath the barren bush
   Flits by the sea-blue bird of March. Ibid., xci.

5232. There lives more faith in honest doubt,
   Believe me, than in half the creeds. Ibid., xcvi.

5233. Ring out the old, ring in the new,
    Ring, happy bells, across the snow :
    The year is going, let him go ;
   Ring out the false, ring in the true. Ibid., cvi.

5234. Ring out old shapes of foul disease ;
    Ring out the narrowing lust of gold ;
    Ring out the thousand wars of old,
   Ring in the thousand years of peace. Ibid.

5235. And thus he bore without abuse
    The grand old name of gentleman. Ibid., cxi.

5236. Move upward, working out the beast,
   And let the ape and tiger die. Ibid., cxviii.

5237. One God, one law, one element,
And one far-off divine event,
To which the whole creation moves. Ibid., conclusion.

5238. Faultily faultless, icily regular, splendidly null.
Maud, I. ii.

5239. That oil'd and curl'd Assyrian bull. Ibid., vi. 6.

5240. O let the solid ground
Not fail beneath my feet
Before my life has found
What some have found so sweet. Ibid., xi. 1.

5241. Birds in the high Hall-garden
When twilight was falling,
Maud, Maud, Maud, Maud,
They were crying and calling. Ibid., xii. 1.

5242. I know the way she went
Home with her maiden posy.
For her feet have touch'd the meadows
And left the daisies rosy. Ibid., 6.

5243. Gorgonised me from head to foot
With a stony British stare. Ibid., xiii. 2.

5244. Rosy is the West,
Rosy is the South,
Roses are her cheeks,
And a rose her mouth. Ibid., xvii.

5245. There is none like her, none. Ibid., xviii. 1.

5246. Come into the garden, Maud,
For the black bat, night, has flown,
Come into the garden, Maud,
I am here at the gate alone. Ibid., xxii. 1.

5247. Queen rose of the rosebud garden of girls. Ibid., 9.

5248. She is coming, my own, my sweet;
Were it ever so airy a tread,
My heart would hear her and beat,
Were it earth in an earthy bed;
My dust would hear her and beat,
Had I lain for a century dead;
Would start and tremble under her feet,
And blossom in purple and red. Ibid., 11.

5249. O that 'twere possible
After long grief and pain
To find the arms of my true love
Round me once again! Ibid., II. iv. 1.

5250. Wearing the white flower of a blameless life,
Before a thousand peering littlenesses,
In that fierce light that beats upon a throne.
Idylls of the King, dedication.

5251. Clothed in white samite, mystic, wonderful.
Ibid., *The Coming of Arthur*, 284.
[Also *The Passing of Arthur*, 199.]

5252. From the great deep to the great deep he goes. Ibid., 410.

5253.   Lightly was her slender nose
        Tip-tilted like the petal of a flower.
                              Ibid., Gareth and Lynette, 576.

5254. It is the little rift within the lute,
        That by and by will make the music mute,
        And ever widening slowly silence all.
                            Ibid., Merlin and Vivien, 388.

5255. Defaming and defacing, till she left
        Not even Lancelot brave, nor Galahad clean.   *Ibid.*, 802.

5256. For men at most differ as Heaven and earth,
        But women, worst and best, as Heaven and Hell.   *Ibid.*, 812.

5257. Elaine the fair, Elaine the lovable,
        Elaine, the lily maid of Astolat.
                           Ibid., Lancelot and Elaine, 1.

5258.   To me
        He is all fault who hath no fault at all :
        For who loves me must have a touch of earth.   *Ibid.*, 131.

5259.   In me there dwells
        No greatness, save it be some far-off touch
        Of greatness to know well I am not great.   *Ibid.*, 447.

5260. His honour rooted in dishonour stood,
        And faith unfaithful kept him falsely true.   *Ibid.*, 871.

5261. He makes no friend who never made a foe.   *Ibid.*, 1082.

5262. Too late, too late ! ye cannot enter now.
                                Ibid., Guinevere, 168.

5263. To reverence the King, as if he were
        Their conscience, and their conscience as their King,
        To break the heathen and uphold the Christ,
        To ride abroad redressing human wrongs,
        To speak no slander, no, nor listen to it.   *Ibid.*, 465.

5264. To love one maiden only, cleave to her,
        And worship her by years of noble deeds,
        Until they won her.   *Ibid.*, 472.

5265. We needs must love the highest when we see it.   *Ibid.*, 655.

5266. I found Him in the shining of the stars,
        I mark'd Him in the flowering of His fields,
        But in His ways with men I find Him not.
                     Ibid., The Passing of Arthur, 9.

5267. So all day long the noise of battle roll'd
        Among the mountains by the winter sea.   *Ibid.*, 170.

5268. Authority forgets a dying king.   *Ibid.*, 289.

5269. When every morning brought a noble chance,
        And every chance brought out a noble knight.   *Ibid.*, 398.

5270. The old order changeth, yielding place to new,
        And God fulfils himself in many ways,
        Lest one good custom should corrupt the world.   *Ibid.*, 408.

5271. If thou shouldst never see my face again,
        Pray for my soul.   More things are wrought by prayer
        Than this world dreams of.   Wherefore, let thy voice
        Rise like a fountain for me night and day.   *Ibid.*, 414.

5272. For so the whole round earth is every way
Bound by gold chains about the feet of God. *Ibid.*, 422.

5273. To the island-valley of Avilion ;
Where falls not hail, or rain, or any snow,
Nor ever wind blows loudly ; but it lies
Deep-meadow'd, happy, fair with orchard lawns,
And bowery hollows crown'd with summer sea. *Ibid.*, 427.

5274. And the sun went down, and the stars came out far over the
summer sea. *The Revenge*, ix.

5275. God of battles, was ever a battle like this in the world before ?
Ibid.

5276. Sink me the ship, Master Gunner—sink her, split her in twain !
Fall into the hands of God, not into the hands of Spain !
Ibid., xi.

5277. All the charm of all the Muses often flowering in a lonely word.
To Virgil.

5278. I salute thee, Mantovano, I that loved thee since my day began,
Wielder of the stateliest measure ever moulded by the lips of
man. *Ibid.*

5279. Row us out from Desenzano, to your Sirmione row !
So they row'd, and there we landed—' O venusta Sirmio ! '
' *Frater ave atque vale.*'

5280. Follow the Gleam. *Merlin and the Gleam.*

5281. Sunset and evening star,
And one clear call for me !
And may there be no moaning of the bar,
When I put out to sea. *Crossing the Bar.*

5282. Twilight and evening bell,
And after that the dark !
And may there be no sadness of farewell
When I embark. *Ibid.*

5283. I hope to see my Pilot face to face
When I have crost the bar. *Ibid.*

TERENCE (PUBLIUS TERENTIUS AFER), Roman dramatist, 195?—159
B.C.

5284. Hinc illae lacrimae.
—Hence these tears. *Andria—The Maid of Andros*, 126.

5285. Davus sum, non Oedipus.
—I'm Davus, not Oedipus. [i.e. I can't solve riddles.]
Ibid., 194.

5286. Amantium irae amoris integratio est.
—The quarrels of lovers are the renewal of love.
Heauton Timoroumenos—The Self-Tormentor, 77.

5287. Quot homines, tot sententiae.
—So many men, so many opinions. *Phormio*, 454.

TERTULLIAN (QUINTUS SEPTIMIUS FLORENS TERTULLIANUS), Roman
    theologian, A.D. 150 ?—220 ?

5288. Certum est quia impossibile est.—It is certain because it is
impossible.
> *De Carne Christi—Concerning the Flesh of Christ*, II. v.
> [Commonly misquoted ' Credo quia impossibile '—' I
> believe because it is impossible.']

THACKERAY, WILLIAM MAKEPEACE, novelist, 18 July, 1811—
    24 Dec. 1863

5289. Fashnable fax and polite annygoats.
> *The Yellowplush Papers*, part I. title.

5290. There are some meannesses which are too mean even for
man—woman, lovely woman alone, can venture to commit them.
> *A Shabby-Genteel Story*, iii.

5291. This I set down as a positive truth. A woman with fair
opportunities and without an absolute hump, may marry whom she
likes. *Vanity Fair*, iv.

5292. Them's my sentiments. Ibid., xxi.

5293. Darkness came down on the field and city : and Amelia was
praying for George, who was lying on his face, dead, with a bullet
through his heart. Ibid., xxxii.

5294. I think I could be a good woman if I had five thousand a
year. Ibid., xxxvi.

5295. Ah ! Vanitas Vanitatum ! Which of us is happy in this
world ? Which of us has his desire ? or, having it, is satisfied ?—
Come, children, let us shut up the box and the puppets, for our play
is played out. Ibid., last words.

5296. Remember, it's as easy to marry a rich woman as a poor
woman. *Pendennis*, xxviii.

5297. 'Tis strange what a man may do, and a woman yet think
him an angel. *Henry Esmond*, vii.

5298. The true pleasure of life is to live with your inferiors.
> *The Newcomes*, ix.

5299. What money is better bestowed than that of a schoolboy's
tip ? Ibid., xvi.

5300. As the last bell struck, a peculiar sweet smile shone over
his face, and he lifted up his head a little, and quickly said, ' Adsum ! '
and fell back. It was the word we used at school, when names were
called ; and lo, he, whose heart was as that of a little child, had answered
to his name, and stood in the presence of The Master. Ibid., lxxx.

5301. Dick [Idle] only began by playing pitch-and-toss on a tombstone. . . . From pitch-and-toss he proceeded to manslaughter, if
necessary : to highway robbery ; to Tyburn and the rope there.
> *Roundabout Papers. Turnbridge Toys.*

5302.   Little we fear
         Weather without,
         Sheltered about
         The Mahogany Tree.   *The Mahogany Tree*

5303. Charlotte, having seen his body
    Borne before her on a shutter,
    Like a well-conducted person,
    Went on cutting bread-and-butter.   *The Sorrows of Werther.*

5304. Ho, pretty page, with the dimpled chin,
    That never has known the barber's shear,
    All your wish is woman to win,
    This is the way that boys begin,—
      Wait till you come to Forty Year.   *The Age of Wisdom.*

5305. There were three sailors of Bristol City
    Who took a boat and went to sea.   *Little Billee.*

5306. There was gorging Jack and guzzling Jimmy,
    And the youngest he was little Billee.   Ibid.

THAYER, ERNEST LAWRENCE, U.S. poet, 14 Aug. 1863—21 Aug. 1940

5307. Oh, somewhere in this favoured land the sun is shining bright ;
    The band is playing somewhere, and somewhere hearts are light,
    And somewhere men are laughing, and little children shout,
    But there is no joy in Mudville—great Casey has struck out.
                               Casey at the Bat.

THEOCRITUS, Greek poet, 3rd century B.C

5308. Ἔαρ θ' ὁρόωσα Νύχεια.
    —And Nycheia with Spring in her eyes.   *Idylls*, xiii. 45.

THIBAULT, JACQUES ANATOLE, *see* France, Anatole

THOMAS, PHILIP EDWARD, poet, 3 March, 1878—9 April, 1917

5309. If I should ever by chance grow rich
    I'll buy Codham, Cockridden, and Childerditch,
    Roses, Pyrgo, and Lapwater,
    And let them all to my elder daughter.
                  If I should ever by Chance.

THOMPSON, FRANCIS, poet, 18 Dec. 1859—13 Nov. 1907

5310. The hills look over on the South,
    And southward dreams the sea ;
    And with the sea-breeze hand in hand
    Came innocence and she.   *Daisy.*

5311. Summer set lip to earth's bosom bare,
    And left the flushed print in a poppy there.   *The Poppy.*

5312. Look for me in the nurseries of Heaven.   *To my Godchild.*

5313. I fled Him, down the nights and down the days ;
    I fled Him, down the arches of the years ;
    I fled Him, down the labyrinthine ways
      Of my own mind, and in the mist of tears
    I hid from Him, and under running laughter.
                 The Hound of Heaven.

5314. Virtue may unlock hell, or even
A sin turn in the wards of Heaven
(As ethics of the text-book go),
So little men their own deeds know.
Epilogue to ' A Judgment in Heaven.'

5315.   Thou canst not stir a flower
Without troubling of a star.   *The Mistress of Vision.*

5316. O world invisible, we view thee,
O world intangible, we touch thee,
O world unknowable, we know thee.   *The Kingdom of God.*

5317.   Upon thy so sore loss
Shall shine the traffic of Jacob's ladder
Pitched betwixt Heaven and Charing Cross.   Ibid.

5318. Know you what it is to be a child ? . . . It is to believe in
love, to believe in loveliness, to believe in belief ; it is to be so little
that the elves can reach to whisper in your ear ; it is to turn pumpkins
into coaches, and mice into horses, lowness into loftiness, and nothing
into everything, for each child has its fairy godmother in its own soul.
Shelley.

5319. The universe is his box of toys. He dabbles his fingers in
the day-fall. He is gold-dusty with tumbling amidst the stars. He
makes bright mischief with the moon. [Of Shelley.]   Ibid.

THOMPSON, WILLIAM HEPWORTH, Master of Trinity College, Cambridge,
27 March, 1810—1 Oct. 1886

5320. We're none of us infallible—not even the youngest among us.
Remark to a Junior Fellow.

THOMSON, JAMES, Scottish poet, 11 Sept. 1700—27 Aug. 1748

5321. Come, gentle Spring, ethereal mildness, come.
The Seasons. Spring, 1.

5322. Delightful task ! to rear the tender thought,
To teach the young idea how to shoot.   Ibid., 1152.

5323. An elegant sufficiency, content
Retirement, rural quiet, friendship, books,
Ease and alternate labour, useful life,
Progressive virtue, and approving Heaven !   Ibid., 1161.

5324. Or sighed and looked unutterable things.   Ibid., *Summer,* 1188.

5325. While Autumn nodding o'er the yellow plain
Comes jovial on.   Ibid., *Autumn,* 2.

5326.   Loveliness
Needs not the foreign aid of ornament,
But is when unadorned adorned the most.   Ibid., 204.

5327.   There studious let me sit,
And hold high converse with the mighty dead—
Sages of ancient time, as gods revered.   Ibid., *Winter,* 431.

5328. The kiss, snatched hasty from the sidelong maid.   Ibid., 625.

5329. A pleasing land of drowsyhed it was :
    Of dreams that wave before the half-shut eye ;
    And of gay castles in the clouds that pass,
    For ever flushing round a summer sky.
                    The Castle of Indolence, i. 6.

5330. A little, round, fat, oily man of God.   Ibid., 69.

5331. Oh ! Sophonisba, Sophonisba, Oh !   *Sophonisba*, III. ii.
    [Altered after the second edition to
      O Sophonisba ! I am wholly thine.]

5332. When Britain first, at Heaven's command,
    Arose from out the azure main,
    This was the charter of the land,
      And guardian angels sung this strain—
        ' Rule, Britannia, rule the waves ;
      Britons never will be slaves.'   *Alfred : a Masque*, II. v.
    [Authorship also claimed for David Mallet, who collaborated
    with Thomson in the masque.]

THOMSON, JAMES, Scottish poet, 23 Nov. 1834—3 June, 1882

5333. As we rush, as we rush in the train,
    The trees and the houses go wheeling back,
    But the starry heavens above that plain
    Come flying on our track.   *Sunday at Hampstead*, x.

5334. Give a man a pipe he can smoke,
    Give a man a book he can read :
    And his home is bright with a calm delight,
    Though the room be poor indeed.   *Gifts.*

5335. The City is of Night ; perchance of Death,
    But certainly of Night.   *The City of Dreadful Night.*

THOREAU, HENRY DAVID, U.S. essayist, 12 July, 1817—6 May, 1862

5336. The mass of men lead lives of quiet desperation.
                  Walden. Economy.

5337. I have lived some thirty years on this planet, and I have
yet to hear the first syllable of valuable or even earnest advice from
my seniors.   Ibid.

5338. Beware of all enterprises that require new clothes.   Ibid.

5339. Simplify, simplify.   Ibid., *Where I lived and what I lived for.*

5340. I never found the companion that was so companionable
as solitude.   Ibid., *Solitude.*

5341. Love your life, poor as it is. You may perhaps have some
pleasant, thrilling, glorious hours, even in a poorhouse.
                Ibid., *Conclusion.*

5342. Some circumstantial evidence is very strong, as when you
find a trout in the milk.   *Journal*, 11 Nov. 1854.

5343. That man is the richest whose pleasures are the cheapest.
                Ibid., 11 March, 1856.

THORPE, ROSE HARTWICK, U.S. authoress, 18 July, 1850—19 July, 1939

5344. As she climbed the dusty ladder on which fell no ray of light,—
Up and up, her white lips saying, ' Curfew shall not ring
to-night.'   *Curfew must not ring to-night.*

THRING, GODFREY, clergyman, 25 March, 1823—13 Sept. 1903

5345. Fierce raged the tempest o'er the deep.   *Hymn.*

THUCYDIDES, Greek historian, 460 ?—400 ? B.C.

5346. Κτῆμα ἐς ἀεί—A possession for ever.   *History*, I. xxii.

THURLOW, EDWARD THURLOW, 2nd Baron, poet, 10 June, 1781—
4 June, 1829

5347. Did you ever expect a corporation to have a conscience,
when it has no soul to be damned, and no body to be kicked ?
Attributed.

TICKELL, THOMAS, poet, 1686—23 April, 1740

5348. There taught us how to live ; and (oh ! too high
The price for knowledge) taught us how to die.
On the Death of Mr. Addison, 81.

5349.   I hear a voice you cannot hear,
Which says I must not stay ;
I see a hand you cannot see,
Which beckons me away.   *Colin and Lucy.*

TILLOTSON, JOHN ROBERT, Archbishop of Canterbury, baptised
10 Oct. 1630, died 22 Nov. 1694

5350. If God were not a necessary Being of himself, He might
almost seem to be made for the use and benefit of men.   *Sermon* 93.

TOBIN, JOHN, dramatist, 28 Jan. 1770—8 Dec. 1804

5351. The man who lays his hand upon a woman,
Save in the way of kindness, is a wretch
Whom 'twere gross flattery to name a coward.
The Honeymoon, II. i.

TOLSTOY, COUNT LEO NIKOLAIEVICH, Russian author, 9 Sept. 1828
—21 Nov. 1910

5352. Pure and complete sorrow is as impossible as pure and complete joy.   *War and Peace*, XV. i.

5353. All happy families resemble one another ; every unhappy
family is unhappy in its own way.   *Anna Karenina*, I. i.

TOPLADY, AUGUSTUS MONTAGUE, clergyman, 4 Nov. 1740—14 Aug.
1778

5354.   Rock of Ages, cleft for me,
                     Let me hide myself in Thee.   *Rock of Ages.*

TRAHERNE, THOMAS, poet, 1637 ?—27 Sept. 1674

5355. You never enjoy the world aright, till the sea itself floweth
in your veins, till you are clothed with the heavens, and crowned with
the stars.   *Centuries of Meditation*, i. 29.

5356. The Men ! O what venerable and reverend creatures did the
aged seem ! Immortal Cherubims ! And the young men glittering
and sparkling Angels, and maids strange seraphic pieces of life and
beauty ! Boys and girls tumbling in the street, and playing, were
moving jewels.   Ibid., iii. 3.

TRAILL, HENRY DUFF, author, 14 Aug. 1842—21 Feb. 1900

5357. Look in my face. My name is Used-to-was ;
      I am also called Played-out and Done-to-death,
      And It-will-wash-no-more.   *After Dilettante Concetti*, viii.
          [Parody of D. G. Rossetti, No. 3426.]

TRAPP, JOSEPH, Professor of Poetry at Oxford, Nov. 1679—22 Nov.
1747

5358. The King, observing with judicious eyes,
      The state of both his universities,
      To Oxford sent a troop of horse, and why ?
      That learned body wanted loyalty ;
      To Cambridge books, as very well discerning
      How much that loyal body wanted learning.
          Epigram on George I's donation of a library to Cambridge.
              [Sir William Browne's answer is No. 322 *supra.*]

TRENCH, FREDERIC HERBERT, Irish poet, 26 Nov. 1865—11 June,
1923

5359. Come let us make love deathless, thou and I.
                                              To Ardilia, vi.

5360. But when Night is on the hills, and the great Voices
          Roll in from sea,
      By starlight and by candlelight and dreamlight
          She comes to me.
              Ibid., ix. *She comes not when Noon is on the Roses.*

5361. O dreamy, gloomy, friendly Trees.   *Poem.*

TRENCH, RICHARD CHENEVIX, Archbishop of Dublin, 5 Sept. 1807—
28 March, 1886

5362. England, we love thee better than we know.   *Gibraltar.*

TROLLOPE, ANTHONY, novelist, 24 April, 1815—6 Dec. 1882

5363. Not only humble but umble, which I look upon to be the
comparative, or, indeed, superlative degree.   *Doctor Thorne*, iv.
    N

5364. A man who desires to soften another man's heart, should always abuse himself. In softening a woman's heart, he should abuse her.   *Last Chronicle of Barset*, xliv.

5365. It's dogged as does it.   Ibid., lxi.

TRUMBULL, JOHN, U.S. poet, 13 April, 1750—11 May, 1831

5366. For any man with half an eye
      What stands before him may espy ;
      But optics sharp it needs, I ween,
      To see what is not to be seen.   *McFingal*, i. 65.

5367. What has posterity done for us,
      That we, lest they their rights should lose,
      Should trust our necks to gripe of noose ?   Ibid., ii. 124.

TUER, ANDREW WHITE, publisher, 24 Dec. 1838—24 Feb. 1900
5368. English as she is spoke.
                              Title of reprint of Portuguese-English conversation guide.

TUPPER, MARTIN FARQUHAR, author, 17 July, 1810—29 Nov. 1889
5369. Well-timed silence hath more eloquence than speech.
                              Proverbial Philosophy, 1st series. *Of Discretion.*

5370. A good book is the best of friends, the same to-day and for ever.   Ibid., *Of Reading.*

5371. A babe in a house is a well-spring of pleasure.
                              Ibid., *Of Education.*

TURGENEV, IVAN SERGEIEVITCH, Russian novelist, 9 Nov. 1818—
      3 Sept. 1883

5372. I agree with no man's opinions. I have some of my own.
                              Fathers and Sons, xiii.

5373. Go and try to disprove death. Death will disprove you, and that's all !   Ibid., xxvii.

5374. Whatever a man prays for, he prays for a miracle. Every prayer reduces itself to this : ' Great God, grant that twice two be not four.'   *Prayer.*

TURNER, WILLIAM JAMES REDFERN, poet, 13 Oct. 1889—18 Nov.
      1946
5375.   When I was but thirteen or so
               I went into a golden land,
               Chimborazo, Cotopaxi
               Took me by the hand.   *Romance.*

TWAIN, MARK (SAMUEL LANGHORNE CLEMENS), U.S. author, 30 Nov.
      1835—21 April, 1910

5376. They spell it Vinci and pronounce it Vinchy ; foreigners always spell better than they pronounce. *The Innocents Abroad*, xix.

5377. This poor little one-horse town.
                              Sketches. The Undertaker's Chat.

5378. The statements was interesting, but tough.
The Adventures of Huckleberry Finn, xvii.

5379. Cauliflower is nothing but cabbage with a college education.
Pudd'nhead Wilson's Calendar.

5380. In Boston they ask, How much does he know ?   In New York, How much is he worth ?   In Philadelphia, Who were his parents ?
What Paul Bourget thinks of us.

5381. There ain't a-going to *be* no core.   Tom Sawyer Abroad, i.

5382. A classic is something that everybody wants to have read and nobody wants to read.
Speeches. The Disappearance of Literature.

5383. The reports of my death are greatly exaggerated.
Cable from Europe to the Associated Press.

UDALL, NICHOLAS, schoolmaster, born 1505, buried 23 Dec. 1556

5384. As long liveth the merry man (they say)
    As doth the sorry man, and longer by a day.
Ralph Roister Doister, I. i.

UMBERTO I, King of Italy, 14 March, 1844—29 July, 1900

5385. È un incidente del mestiere.—It is one of the incidents of the profession.   After escaping assassination.

UNTERMEYER, LOUIS, U.S. author, 1 Oct. 1885—

5386.   God, though this life is but a wraith,
        Although we know not what we use,
        Although we grope with little faith,
        Give me the heart to fight—and lose.   Prayer.

VANBRUGH *or* VANBURGH, SIR JOHN, dramatist and architect, baptised 24 Jan. 1664, died 26 March. 1726

5387.   Much of a Muchness.   The Provoked Husband, I. i.

VANDIVER, WILLARD DUNCAN, U.S. Congressman, 30 March, 1854—30 May, 1932

5388.   I come from a state that raises corn and cotton and cockleburs and Democrats, and frothy eloquence neither convinces nor satisfies me.   I am from Missouri.   You have got to show me.
Speech at a naval banquet in Philadelphia, 1899.

VAUGHAN, HENRY, Welsh poet, 17 April, 1622—23 April, 1695

5389.   'Tis now clear day : I see a rose
        Bud in the bright east, and disclose
        The pilgrim sun.   The Search.

5390.   Happy those early days ! when I
        Shin'd in my angel-infancy.
        Before I understood this place
        Appointed for my second race,
        Or taught my soul to fancy aught
        But a white celestial thought.   The Retreat.

5391. And in those weaker glories spy
Some shadows of eternity.   *Ibid.*

5392. But felt through all this fleshy dress
Bright shoots of everlastingness.   *Ibid.*

5393. My soul, there is a country
    Far beyond the stars.   *Peace.*

5394. I saw Eternity the other night,
Like a great ring of pure and endless light,
    All calm, as it was bright ;
And round beneath it, Time in hours, days, years,
    Driv'n by the spheres
Like a vast shadow mov'd ; in which the world
    And all her train were hurl'd.   *The World.*

5395. They are all gone into the world of light,
    And I alone sit lingering here.   *They are all gone.*

5396. I see them walking in an air of glory,
    Whose light doth trample on my days ;
My days, which are at best but dull and hoary,
    Mere glimmering and decays.   *Ibid.*

5397. I cannot reach it ; and my striving eye
Dazzles at it, as at eternity.   *Childhood.*

VAUX OF HARROWDEN, THOMAS VAUX, 2nd Baron, 1510—October,
    1556

5398. For Age with stealing steps,
    Hath clawed me with his clutch.
                    The Aged Lover renounceth Love.

VERE, EDWARD DE, *see* Oxford

VICTORIA, QUEEN, 24 May, 1819—22 Jan. 1901

  5399. We are not amused.
            When an equerry told a questionable story at Windsor.

VILLIERS, GEORGE, *see* Buckingham, 2nd Duke of

VILLON, FRANÇOIS, French poet, 1431—1485 ?

5400. Mais où sont les neiges d'antan ?
        —But where are the snows of yester-year ?
            Ballade des dames du temps jadis—Ballade of Old-time Ladies.

VINCENT OF LERINS, Saint, died A.D. 450 ?

  5401. Quod semper, quod ubique, quod ab omnibus creditum est.
— What always, what everywhere, what by everyone has been believed.
            [Definition of catholicity.]   *Commonitorium,* ii.

VIRGIL *or* VERGIL (PUBLIUS VERGILIUS MARO), Roman poet, 15 Oct. 70—21 Sept. 19 B.C.

5402. Tityre, tu patulae recubans sub tegmine fagi
Silvestrem tenui musam meditaris avena.
—You, Tityrus, reclining under cover of a spreading beech tree, practise the woodland muse on a slender reed.
Eclogues (Bucolics), i. 1.

5403. Et penitus toto divisos orbe Britannos.
—And the Britons wholly sundered from all the world.
Ibid., 66.

5404. Arcades ambo.
—Arcadians both. Ibid., vii. 4.

5405. Non omnia possumus omnes.
—We cannot all do all things. Ibid., viii. 63.

5406. Ultima Thule.
—Farthest Thule. *Georgics*, I. 30.

5407. Felix, qui potuit rerum cognoscere causas.
—Happy he who has been able to learn the causes of things.
Ibid., II. 490.

5408. Sed fugit interea, fugit irreparabile tempus.
—But meanwhile it is flying, time is flying that cannot be recalled. Ibid., III. 284.

5409. Arma virumque cano.
—Arms and the man I sing. *Aeneid*, I. 1.

5410. Forsan et haec olim meminisse juvabit.
—Perhaps even these things it will some day give pleasure to recall. Ibid., 203.

5411. Mens sibi conscia recti.
—A mind conscious of its rectitude. Ibid., 604.

5412. Non ignara mali miseris succurrere disco.
—Not ignorant of ill do I learn to aid the wretched. Ibid., 630.

5413. Timeo Danaos et dona ferentes.
—I fear the Greeks even when they bring gifts. Ibid., II. 49.

5414. In utrumque paratus.
—Prepared for either event. Ibid., 61.

5415. Crimine ab uno
Disce omnes.
—From one piece of villainy judge them all. Ibid., 65.

5416. Horresco referens.
—I shudder to recall it. Ibid., 204.

5417. Tacitae per amica silentia lunae.
—Amid the friendly silence of the still moon. Ibid., 255.

5418. Quantum mutatus ab illo.
—How changed from him whom we knew Ibid., 274.

5419. Dis aliter visum.
—The will of the gods was otherwise. Ibid., 428.

5420. Auri sacra fames.
—Accursed hunger for gold. Ibid., III. 57.

5421. Monstrum horrendum, informe, ingens, cui lumen ademptum.
—A monster frightful, shapeless, huge, bereft of sight.

Ibid., 658.

5422.   Varium et mutabile semper
Femina.
—A fickle and changeable thing is woman ever. Ibid., IV. 569.

5423. Possunt, quia posse videntur.
—They are able because they seem to be able.   Ibid., V. 231.

5424.   Facilis descensus Averno :
Noctes atque dies patet atri janua Ditis ;
Sed revocare gradum, superasque evadere ad auras,
Hoc opus, hic labor est.
—Easy is the descent to Avernus ; night and day stands open
the gate of gloomy Pluto ; but to recall the step, and pass
out to the upper air—this is the toil, this the labour.

Ibid., VI. 126.

5425. Parcere subjectis et debellare superbos.
—To spare the humbled and subdue the proud.   Ibid., 853.

5426. O mihi praeteritos referat si Juppiter annos.
—O, if Jupiter would restore to me the years that are past !

Ibid., VIII. 560.

5427. Macte nova virtute, puer, sic itur ad astra.
—Good luck to your youthful valour, boy.   Such is the way
to the stars.   Ibid., IX. 641.

5428. Sic vos non vobis mellificatis apes.
—So do you bees make honey, not for yourselves.   *Attributed.*

5429. Mantua me genuit, Calabri rapuere, tenet nunc
Parthenope.   Cecini pascua, rura, duces.
—Mantua bore me, the Calabrians carried me off, Naples
holds me now.   I sang of pastures, farms, leaders.

His own epitaph.

VOLTAIRE, FRANÇOIS MARIE AROUET DE, French author and
philosopher, 21 Nov. 1694—30 May, 1778

5430. Si Dieu n'existait pas, il faudrait l'inventer.—If God did
not exist, it would be necessary to invent Him.
Épîtres, xcvi.   *A l'auteur du livre des trois imposteurs.—Letters,*
xcvi.   *To the Author of the Book of the Three Impostors.*

5431. Tout est pour le mieux dans le meilleur des mondes possibles.
—All is for the best in the best of possible worlds.   [Dr. Pangloss.]
Candide, i.

5432. Dans ce pays-ci, il est bon de tuer de temps en temps un
amiral pour encourager les autres.—In this country [England] it is
good to kill an admiral from time to time, to encourage the others.
[In allusion to the shooting of Admiral Byng.]   Ibid., xxiii.

5433. Cela est bien dit, répondit Candide, mais il faut cultiver
notre jardin.—' That is well said,' replied Candide, ' but we must
cultivate our garden.'   [i.e. we must attend to our own affairs.]

Ibid., xxx.

5434. Ils ne se servent de la pensée que pour autoriser leurs injustices, et n'emploient les paroles que pour déguiser leurs pensées.— They use thought only to warrant their injustice, and employ words only to conceal their thoughts.

> *Dialogue* xiv. *Le Chapon et la poularde.—The Capon and the Pullet.*

WADE, JOSEPH AUGUSTINE, Irish composer, 1796 ?—15 July, 1845

5435. Meet me by moonlight alone. *Meet me by Moonlight.*

WALLACE, WILLIAM ROSS, U.S. poet, 1819—5 May, 1881

5436.　　　　But a mightier power and stronger
　　　　　Man from his throne has hurled,
　　　　　And the hand that rocks the cradle
　　　　　Is the hand that rules the world.
> *The Hand that rules the World.*

WALLAS, GRAHAM, sociologist, 31 May, 1858—10 Aug. 1932

5437. Just as it is impossible to sing, or to speak a foreign language, well, with one's mouth and throat in a ' gentlemanly ' position, so it may prove to be the case that one cannot think effectively if one's main purpose in life is to be a gentleman. *The Great Society*, x.

WALLER, EDMUND, poet, 3 March, 1606—21 Oct. 1687

5438. The yielding marble of her snowy breast.
> *On a Lady passing through a Crowd of People.*

5439. So was the huntsman by the bear oppress'd
　　　　Whose hide he sold—before he caught the beast !
> *Battle of the Summer Islands*, ii. 38.

5440.　　　　That which her slender waist confin'd
　　　　　Shall now my joyful temples bind ;
　　　　　No monarch but would give his crown
　　　　　His arms might do what this has done. *On a Girdle.*

5441.　　　　A narrow compass ! and yet there
　　　　　Dwelt all that's good, and all that's fair :
　　　　　Give me but what this riband bound,
　　　　　Take all the rest the sun goes round. **Ibid.**

5442.　　　　Others may use the ocean as their road,
　　　　　Only the English make it their abode.
> *Of a War with Spain*, 25.

5443.　　　　For all we know
　　　　　Of what the blessed do above
　　　　　Is, that they sing, and that they love.
> *While I listen to thy Voice.*

5444.　　　　Go, lovely rose !
　　　　Tell her, that wastes her time and me,
　　　　　That now she knows,
　　　　When I resemble her to thee,
　　　　How sweet and fair she seems to be. *Go, Lovely Rose.*

5445.   The soul's dark cottage, batter'd and decay'd,
     Lets in new light through chinks that time has made ;
     Stronger by weakness, wiser men become,
     As they draw near to their eternal home.
     Leaving the old, both worlds at once they view
     That stand upon the threshold of the new.
                              On the foregoing Divine Poems.

WALPOLE, HORACE *or* HORATIO, 4th EARL OF ORFORD, author,
     24 Sept. 1717—2 March, 1797

5446.   It is charming to totter into vogue.
                Letters.   To George Augustus Selwyn, 2 Dec. 1765.

5447.   This world is a comedy to those that think, a tragedy to those
that feel.   *Ibid., To Sir Horace Mann,* 31 Dec. 1769.

WALPOLE, SIR ROBERT, 1st EARL OF ORFORD, Prime Minister, 26 Aug.
     1676—18 March, 1745

5448.   All those men have their price.   [Referring to ' pretended
patriots.'   Usually misquoted as ' All men have their price.']
                         W. Coxe, *Memoirs Of Walpole,* IV. 369.

5449.   They now ring the bells, but they will soon wring their hands.
                    On the declaration of war with Spain, 1739.

5450.   The balance of power.
                    Speech in House of Commons, 13 Feb. 1741.

WALSH, WILLIAM, poet, 1663—18 March, 1708

5451.   And sadly reflecting
          That a lover forsaken
             A new love may get,
          But a neck when once broken
             Can never be set.   *The Despairing Lover,* 17.

5452.   I can endure my own despair,
          But not another's hope.   *Of all the Torments.*

WALTON, IZAAK, writer on angling, 9 Aug. 1593—15 Dec. 1683

5453.   Some innocent, harmless mirth, of which, if thou be a severe,
sour-complexioned man, then I here disallow thee to be a competent
judge.   *The Compleat Angler.   Epistle to the Reader.*

5454.   I am, Sir, a Brother of the Angle.   Ibid., I. i.

5455.   Thus use your frog. . . .   Put your hook, I mean the arming-
wire, through his mouth, and out at his gills ; and then with a fine
needle and silk sew the upper part of his leg, with only one stitch, to
the arming-wire of your hook ; or tie the frog's leg, above the upper
joint, to the armed-wire ; and, in so doing, use him as though you
loved him, that is, harm him as little as you may possibly, that he may
live the longer.   Ibid., viii.

5456.   This dish of meat is too good for any but anglers, or very
honest men.   Ibid.

5457. And [blessing] upon all that are lovers of virtue ; and dare trust in His providence ; and be quiet ; and go a-Angling.   Ibid., xxi.

WARBURTON, WILLIAM, Bishop of Gloucester, 24 Dec. 1698—7 June, 1779

5458. Orthodoxy is my doxy ; heterodoxy is another man's doxy.
Remark to Lord Sandwich.   Priestly, *Memoirs*, i. 372.

WARD, ARTEMUS (CHARLES FARRAR BROWNE), U.S. humorist, 26 April, 1834—6 March, 1867

5459. I now bid you a welcome adoo.
Artemus Ward his Book.   The Shakers.

5460. My pollertics, like my religion, bein of a exceedin accommodatin character.   Ibid., *The Crisis.*

5461. N.B.—This is rote Sarcasticul.
Ibid., *A Visit to Brigham Young.*

5462. I girdid up my Lions and fled the Seen.   Ibid.

5463. Did you ever hav the measels, and if so how many ?
Ibid., *The Census.*

5464. Do me eyes deceive me earsight ?   Is it some dreams ?
Ibid., *Moses the Sassy.*

5465. I'm not a politician and my other habits air good.
Ibid., *Fourth of July Oration.*

5466. Why is this thus ?   What is the reason of this thusness ?
Artemus Ward's Lecture.

WARE, EUGENE FITCH, U.S. lawyer, 29 May, 1841—1911

5467. Oh, dewy was the morning, upon the first of May,
And Dewey was the admiral, down in Manila Bay ;
And dewy were the Regent's eyes, them royal orbs of blue,
And do we feel discouraged ?   We do not think we do !
Manila.

WARMAN, CY, U.S. journalist, 22 June, 1855—7 April, 1914

5468. Every daisy in the dell knows my secret, knows it well,
But yet I dare not tell, sweet Marie.   *Sweet Marie.*

WARREN, SAMUEL, lawyer and novelist, 23 May, 1807—29 July, 1877

5469. There is probably no man living, though ever so great a fool, that cannot do *something* or other well.   *Ten Thousand a Year*, xxviii.

WASHBURN, HENRY STEVENSON, U.S. author, 10 June, 1813—1903

5470.   We shall meet, but we shall miss him,
              There will be one vacant chair.   *The Vacant Chair.*

WASHINGTON, GEORGE, U.S. President, 22 Feb. 1732—14 Dec. 1799

5471. Father, I cannot tell a lie, I did it with my little hatchet.
Attributed.

*N

5472. We must consult Brother Jonathan [Jonathan Trumbull, Governor of Connecticut]. *Frequent remark during War of Independence.*
[Hence the use of ' Brother Jonathan ' for typical American.]

5473. It is our true policy to steer clear of permanent alliances with any portion of the foreign world.
Farewell Address, 17 Sept. 1796.

WATKYNS, ROWLAND, author, *fl.* 1662

5474. I love him not ; but shew no reason can
Wherefore, but this, *I do not love the man.*
Flamma sine Fumo : or Poems without Fictions. Antipathy.

WATSON, SIR WILLIAM, poet, 2 Aug. 1858—11 Aug. 1935

5475. Man looks at his own bliss, considers it,
Weighs it with curious fingers ; and 'tis gone.
The Fatal Scrutiny.

5476. Too avid of earth's bliss, he was of those
Whom Delight flies because they give her chase.
Byron the Voluptuary.

5477. O be less beautiful, or be less brief.   *Autumn.*

5478.   The staid, conservative
Came-over-with-the-Conqueror type of mind.
A Study in Contrasts, i. 42.

5479.   April, April,
Laugh thy girlish laughter ;
Then, the moment after,
Weep thy girlish tears !   *April.*

WATTS, ISAAC, hymn-writer, 17 July, 1674—25 Nov. 1748

5480.   Let dogs delight to bark and bite.
Divine Songs for Children, xvi. *Against Quarrelling.*

5481.   But, children, you should never let
Such angry passions rise ;
Your little hands were never made
To tear each other's eyes.   Ibid.

5482.   Birds in their little nests agree.
Ibid., xvii. *Love between Brothers and Sisters.*

5483.   How doth the little busy bee
Improve each shining hour,
And gather honey all the day
From every opening flower.
Ibid., xx. *Against Idleness and Mischief.*

5484.   For Satan finds some mischief still
For idle hands to do.   Ibid.

5485. 'Tis the voice of the sluggard ; I hear him complain,
' You have wak'd me too soon, I must slumber again.'
As the door on its hinges, so he on his bed,
Turns his sides and his shoulders and his heavy head.
Moral Songs, i. *The Sluggard.*

5486.　　　　　Our God, our help in ages past,
　　　　　　　Our hope for years to come,
　　　　　　　Our shelter from the stormy blast,
　　　　　　　And our eternal home.　　　　　　*Psalm xc.*
　　[The substitution of ' O ' for ' Our ' was made by John Wesley.]

5487.　　　　　A thousand ages in thy sight
　　　　　　　Are like an evening gone,
　　　　　　　Short as the watch that ends the night
　　　　　　　Before the rising sun.　　　　　　　　Ibid.

5488.　　　　　Time, like an ever-rolling stream,
　　　　　　　Bears all its sons away.　　　　　　　Ibid.

5489.　Hark ! from the tombs a doleful sound.　　*A Funeral Thought.*

WEATHERLY, FREDERIC EDWARD, song writer, 4 Oct. 1848—7 Sept.
　　1929

5490.　Where are the boys of the old Brigade ?　　*The Old Brigade.*

5491.　　　　　Then steadily, shoulder to shoulder,
　　　　　　　Steadily, blade by blade !
　　　　　　　Ready and strong, marching along,
　　　　　　　Like the boys of the old Brigade.　　　Ibid.

5492.　　　　　Roses are flow'ring in Picardy,
　　　　　　　But there's never a rose like you !

　　　　　　　　　　　　　　　　　　　Roses of Picardy.

WEAVER, *see* Wever

WEBBER, BYRON, author, 1838—1913

5493.　　　　　Hands across the sea !
　　　　　　　Feet on British ground !
　　　The old blood is bold blood, the wide world round.
　　　　　　　　　　　　　　　　　　Hands across the Sea.

WEBSTER, DANIEL, U.S. statesman, 18 Jan. 1782—24 Oct. 1852

5494.　Liberty and Union, now and for ever, one and inseparable.
　　　　　　　　　　　　　　Speech in Senate, 26 Jan. 1830.

5495.　He touched the dead corpse of public credit, and it sprang
upon its feet.　　　*Eulogy on Alexander Hamilton,* 10 March, 1831.

5496.　On this question of principle, while actual suffering was yet
afar off, they [the Colonies] raised their flag against a power to which,
for purposes of foreign conquest and subjugation, Rome in the height
of her glory is not to be compared,—a power which has dotted over
the surface of the whole globe with her possessions and military posts,
whose morning drum-beat, following the sun, and keeping company
with the hours, circles the earth with one continuous and unbroken
strain of the martial airs of England.　　*Speech in Senate,* 7 May, 1834.

5497.　I was born an American ; I will live an American ; I shall
die an American.　　　　　　　　　　Ibid., 17 July, 1850.

WEBSTER, JOHN, dramatist, 1580 ?—1625 ?

5498. Is not old wine wholesomest, old pippins toothsomest, old wood burn brightest, old linen wash whitest ? Old soldiers, sweetheart, are surest, and old lovers are soundest. *Westward Hoe*, II. ii.

5499.   Call for the robin redbreast and the wren,
            Since o'er shady groves they hover,
            And with leaves and flowers do cover
            The friendless bodies of unburied men.
                                        The White Devil, v. iv.

5500. Cover her face ; mine eyes dazzle : she died young.
                                        The Duchess of Malfi, IV. ii.

WELLINGTON, ARTHUR WELLESLEY, 1st DUKE OF, Field Marshal and Prime Minister, 29 April *or* 1 May, 1769—14 Sept. 1852

5501. Nothing except a battle lost can be half so melancholy as a battle won.   *Despatch*, 1815.

5502. There is no mistake ; there has been no mistake ; and there shall be no mistake.   *Letter to Mr. Huskisson*.

5503. Up, Guards, and at them !
                    Attributed order at Waterloo, 18 June, 1815.
            [His own account was that he said ' Stand up, Guards ! '
            and then gave the order to attack.]

5504. I never saw so many shocking bad hats in my life.
                                On seeing the first Reformed Parliament.

5505. The whole art of war consists in getting at what is on the other side of the hill.   *Attributed*.

5506. I care not one twopenny damn what becomes of the ashes of Napoleon Buonaparte.   Ibid.

5507. The battle of Waterloo was won on the playing fields of Eton.
                                                                    Ibid.

WELLS, HERBERT GEORGE, author, 21 Sept. 1866—13 Aug. 1946

5508. I was thinking jest what a Rum Go everything is.
                                                        Kipps, III. iii. 8.

5509. Sesquippledan verboojuice.   *Mr. Polly*, i. 5.

5510. The world may discover that all its common interests are being managed by one concern, while it still fails to realise that a world government exists.   *A Short History of the World*, lix.

5511. The shape of things to come.   *Title of book*.

WESLEY, CHARLES, Methodist preacher, 18 Dec. 1707—29 March, 1788

5512.   Jesus, lover of my soul,
                Let me to Thy bosom fly,
            While the nearer waters roll,
                While the tempest still is high.
                                        Jesus, Lover of my Soul.

5513.   Cover my defenceless head
                          With the shadow of Thy wing.   Ibid.

5514.   Gentle Jesus, meek and mild,
                      Look upon a little child,
                      Pity my simplicity,
                      Suffer me to come to Thee.
                                  Gentle Jesus, Meek and Mild.

WESLEY, JOHN, founder of Methodism, 17 June, 1703—2 March,
    1791

  5515. Certainly this [neatness of apparel] is a duty, not a sin.
' Cleanliness is, indeed, next to godliness.'
                                  Sermons, xciii.   *On Dress.*

  5516. I look upon all the world as my parish.
                                  Journal, 11 June, 1739.

5517.   Do all the good you can,
                      By all the means you can,
                      In all the ways you can,
                      In all the places you can,
                      At all the times you can,
                      To all the people you can,
                      As long as ever you can.   *Rule of Conduct.*

WESSEL, HORST, Nazi storm trooper, 9 Oct. 1907—23 Feb. 1930

5518. Die Fahnen hoch !—die Reihen dicht geschlossen !
      —Up with the Colours !—Close fast the ranks !
                                  Horst Wessel Song.

WESTBURY, RICHARD BETHELL, 1st BARON, Lord Chancellor, 30 June,
    1800—20 July, 1873

  5519. Then, sir, you will turn it over once more in what you are
pleased to call your mind.   [Retort to a solicitor.]
                      T. A. Nash, *Life of Lord Westbury*, II. 292.

  5520. A silly old man who does not understand even his silly old
trade. [Of a witness from the Herald's College.]   *Attributed.*

WESTCOTT, EDWARD NOYES, U.S. author, 27 Sept. 1846—31 March,
    1898

  5521. Do unto the other feller the way he'd like to do unto you
an' do it fust.   *David Harum*, xx.

WEVER *or* WEAVER, RICHARD, dramatist, *fl.* 1565 ?

5522.   In a herber green, asleep where as I lay,
                  The birds sang sweet in the middes of the day ;
                  I dreamed fast of mirth and play ;
                      In youth is pleasure, in youth is pleasure.
                                  Lusty Juventus.

WHATELY, RICHARD, Archbishop of Dublin, 1 Feb. 1787—1 Oct,
1863

5523. Happiness is no laughing matter. *Apophthegms*, page 218.

WHEWELL, WILLIAM, Master of Trinity College, Cambridge, 24 May,
1794—6 March, 1866

5524. Hence no force however great can stretch a cord however
fine, into an horizontal line which is accurately straight.
Elementary Treatise on Mechanics, 1st edition, page 44.
[Instance of unconscious versification.]

WHISTLER, JAMES ABBOTT MCNEILL, U.S. painter, 10 July, 1834—
17 July, 1903

5525. No, I ask it for the knowledge of a lifetime. [When asked
in a legal action, ' For two days' labour, you ask two hundred
guineas ? '] *The Gentle Art of making Enemies*, 5.

5526. I am not arguing with you—I am telling you. Ibid., 51.

5527. Why drag in Velasquez ? [To an enthusiast who said she
knew of only two painters in the world, himself and Velasquez.]
D. C. Seitz, *Whistler Stories*, 27.

5528. I'm lonesome. They are all dying. I have hardly a warm
personal enemy left. Ibid., 47.

WHITE, JOSEPH BLANCO, Irish author, 11 July, 1775—20 May, 1841
5529. Mysterious Night ! when our first parent knew
Thee from report divine, and heard thy name,
Did he not tremble for this lovely frame,
This glorious canopy of light and blue ? *To Night*.

5530. If Light can thus deceive, wherefore not Life ? Ibid.

WHITEFIELD, GEORGE, Methodist preacher, 16 Dec. 1714—30 Sept.
1770

5531. Hark ! the herald-angels sing
Glory to the new-born King.
Altered opening lines of Charles Wesley's
Christmas Hymn.

WHITEHEAD, WILLIAM, Poet Laureate, baptised 12 Feb. 1715, died
14 April, 1785

5532. Yes, I'm in love, I feel it now,
And Celia has undone me !
And yet I'll swear I can't tell how
The pleasing plague stole on me. *The Je ne sais quoi*.

5533. Her voice, her touch, might give th' alarm—
'Twas both, perhaps, or neither !
In short, 'twas that provoking charm
Of Celia all together. Ibid.

5534. Say, can you listen to the artless woes
Of an old tale, which every schoolboy knows ?
The Roman Father, prologue, 9

WHITING, WILLIAM, hymn-writer, 1 Nov. 1825—1878

5535. O hear us when we cry to Thee
      For those in peril on the sea.   *Eternal Father Strong to save.*

WHITMAN, WALT (WALTER), U.S. poet, 31 May, 1819—26 March, 1892

5536. I loafe and invite my soul.   *Song of Myself, i*

5537. I think I could turn and live with animals, they are so placid
      and self-contain'd ;
      I stand and look at them long and long.
      They do not sweat and whine about their condition ;
      They do not lie awake in the dark and weep for their sins ;
      They do not make me sick discussing their duty to God ;
      Not one is dissatisfied—not one is demented with the mania
      of owning things ;
      Not one kneels to another, nor to his kind that lived thousands
      of years ago ;
      Not one is respectable or industrious over the whole earth.
                                    Ibid., xxxii.

5538. I sound my barbaric yawp over the roofs of the world.
                                     Ibid., lii.

5539. Out of the cradle endlessly rocking,
      Out of the mocking-bird's throat, the musical shuttle.
               Out of the Cradle of endlessly rocking.

5540. O Captain ! my Captain ! our fearful trip is done,
      The ship has weather'd every rack, the prize we sought is won,
      The port is near, the bells I hear, the people all exulting,
      While follow eyes the steady keel, the vessel grim and daring ;
        But O heart ! heart ! heart !
         O the bleeding drops of red,
           Where on the deck my Captain lies,
             Fallen cold and dead.   *O Captain ! My Captain !*

WHITTIER, JOHN GREENLEAF, U.S. poet, 17 Dec. 1807—7 Sept. 1892

5541. For of all sad words of tongue or pen,
      The saddest are these : ' It might have been ! '   *Maud Muller.*

5542. Blessings on thee, little man,
      Barefoot boy, with cheek of tan !   *The Barefoot Boy.*

5543. Old Floyd Ireson, for his hard heart,
      Tarred and feathered and carried in a cart
      By the women of Marblehead.   *Skipper Ireson's Ride.*

5544. Dinna ye hear it ?—dinna ye hear it ?
      The pipes o' Havelock sound !   *The Pipes at Lucknow.*

5545. ' Shoot, if you must, this old grey head,
      But spare your country's flag,' she said.   *Barbara Frietchie.*

5546. ' Who touches a hair of yon grey head
      Dies like a dog ! March on ! ' he said.   *Ibid.*

WHUR, CORNELIUS, Methodist minister, 1782—12 March, 1853

5547.
Will not a beauteous landscape bright—
    Or music's soothing sound,
Console the heart—afford delight,
    And throw sweet peace around ?
They may, but never comfort lend
Like an accomplished female friend !
Village Musings. The Female Friend.

WHYTE-MELVILLE, GEORGE JOHN, Scottish author, 19 June, 1821
    —5 Dec. 1878

5548. We always believe our first love is our last, and our last
love our first. *Katerfelto*, xiv.

5549. The swallows are making them ready to fly,
    Wheeling out on a windy sky :
Good-bye, Summer, good-bye, good-bye. *Good-bye, Summer.*

5550. Wrap me up in my tarpaulin jacket,
    And say a poor buffer lies low. *The Tarpaulin Jacket.*

WILBERFORCE, SAMUEL, Bishop of Winchester, 7 Sept. 1805—19 July,
    1873

5551.
If I were a cassowary
    On the plains of Timbuctoo,
I would eat a missionary,
    Coat and bands and hymn-book too. *Attributed.*

WILCOX, ELLA WHEELER, U.S. poetess, 5 Nov. 1850—30 Oct. 1919

5552.
Laugh, and the world laughs with you ;
    Weep, and you weep alone ;
For the sad old earth must borrow its mirth,
    But has trouble enough of its own. *Solitude.*

5553.
So many gods, so many creeds,
    So many paths that wind and wind,
When just the art of being kind
Is all the sad world needs. *The World's Need.*

5554.
No question is ever settled
    Until it is settled right. *Settle the Question Right.*

WILDE, OSCAR FINGAL O'FLAHERTIE WILLS, Irish author, 16 Oct.
    1854—30 Nov. 1900

5555. There is no such thing as a moral or an immoral book. Books
are well written, or badly written. That is all.
The Picture of Dorian Gray, preface.

5556. All art is quite useless. Ibid.

5557. The only way to get rid of a temptation is to yield to it.
Ibid., ii.

5558. He knew the precise psychological moment when to say
nothing. Ibid.

5559. Meredith is a prose Browning, and so is Browning.
The Critic as Artist, I.

5560. As long as war is regarded as wicked, it will always have its fascination. When it is looked upon as vulgar, it will cease to be popular. Ibid., II.

5561. There is no sin except stupidity. Ibid.

5562. I can resist everything except temptation.
Lady Windermere's Fan, I.

5563. A man who knows the price of everything, and the value of nothing. [Definition of a cynic.] Ibid., III.

5564. Experience is the name everyone gives to his mistakes.
Ibid.

5565. One should never trust a woman who tells one her real age. A woman who would tell one that, would tell one anything.
A Woman of No Importance, I.

5566. I have nothing to declare except my genius.
At New York Custom House.

5567. I suppose that I shall have to die beyond my means.
When confronted with a large fee for an operation.

5568.   Tread lightly, she is near
      Under the snow,
    Speak gently, she can hear
      The daisies grow. *Requiescat.*

5569.   Yet each man kills the thing he loves,
      By each let this be heard,
    Some do it with a bitter look,
      Some with a flattering word.
    The coward does it with a kiss,
      The brave man with a sword.
The Ballad of Reading Gaol, i. 7.

5570.   The vilest deeds like poison-weeds
      Bloom well in prison-air :
    It is only what is good in Man
      That wastes and withers there :
    Pale Anguish keeps the heavy gate
      And the Warder is Despair. Ibid., v. 5.

5571.   Down the long and silent street,
    The dawn, with silver-sandaled feet,
    Crept like a frightened girl. *The Harlot's House.*

WILLARD, EMMA HART, U.S. educationist, 23 Feb. 1787—15 April, 1870

5572. Calm and peaceful shall we sleep,
Rocked in the cradle of the deep. *The Cradle of the Deep.*

WILLIAM III. (of Orange), King, 4 Nov. 1650—8 March, 1702

5573. There is one certain means by which I can be sure never to see my country's ruin : I will die in the last ditch.
D. Hume, *History of England*, lxv.

5574. Every bullet has its billet.
John Wesley's *Journal*, 6 June, 1765.

WILLS, WILLIAM GORMAN, Irish dramatist, 28 Jan. 1828—13 Dec. 1891

5575.   I'll sing thee songs of Araby,
                          And tales of fair Cashmere,
                      Wild tales to cheat thee of a sigh,
                          Or charm thee to a tear.
                                              I'll sing thee Songs of Araby.

WILSON, JOHN, bookseller, died 1889

5576.   O for a Booke and a shadie nooke,
                          Eyther in-a-doore or out ;
                      With the grene leaves whisp'ring overhede,
                          Or the Streete cryes all about.
                      Where I maie Reade all at my ease,
                          Both of the Newe and Olde ;
                      For a jollie goode Booke whereon to looke
                          Is better to me than Golde.
                                              For a catalogue of second-hand books.

WILSON, THOMAS, Bishop of Sodor and Man, 20 Dec. 1663—7 March, 1755

5577. It costs more to revenge [injuries] than to bear them.
                                              Maxims of Piety and Morality, 303.

WILSON, THOMAS WOODROW, U.S. President, 28 Dec. 1856—3 Feb. 1924

5578. There is such a thing as a man being too proud to fight.
                                              Address to foreign-born citizens, 10 May, 1915.

5579. The world must be made safe for democracy.
                                              Address to Congress asking for declaration of war,
                                              2 April, 1917.

WIMPERIS, ARTHUR HAROLD, dramatist, 3 Dec. 1874—14 Oct. 1953

5580.   I've gotter motter—
                          Always merry and bright !
                      Look around and you will find
                      Every cloud is silver-lined ;
                          The sun will shine
                          Although the sky's a grey one.
                      I've often said to meself, I've said,
                      ' Cheer up, cully, you'll soon be dead !
                          A short life and a gay one ! '
                                              The Arcadians, III.   *My Motter.*

WITHER, GEORGE, poet, 11 June, 1588—2 May, 1667

5581.   Shall I, wasting in despair,
                      Die, because a woman's fair ?
                      Or make pale my cheeks with care
                      'Cause another's rosy are ?
                          Be she fairer than the day
                          Or the flowery meads in May,
                          If she think not well of me,
                          What care I how fair she be ?
                                              The Author's Resolution in a Sonnet.

5582.   If she slight me when I woo,
            I can scorn and let her go.   Ibid.

WOLCOT, John ('PETER PINDAR'), poet, baptised 9 May, 1738, died
     14 Jan. 1819

5583.   What rage for fame attends both great and small!
        Better be d——d than mentioned not at all!
                        More Lyric Odes to the Royal Academicians, **viii.**

5584.   Care to our coffin adds a nail, no doubt;
                      And ev'ry grin so merry, draws one out.
                                          Expostulatory Odes, **xv.**

WOLFE, CHARLES, Irish poet, 14 Dec. 1791—21 Feb. 1823

5585.   Not a drum was heard, not a funeral note,
                      As his corse to the rampart we hurried.
                                          The Burial of Sir John Moore.

5586.   But he lay like a warrior taking his rest
                      With his martial cloak around him.   Ibid.

5587.   We carved not a line, and we raised not a stone,
                      But we left him alone with his glory.   Ibid.

WOLFE, JAMES, General, 2 Jan. 1727—13 Sept. 1759

    5588.   I would rather have written those lines [Gray's *Elegy*] than
take Quebec.   *The night before he was killed on the Plains of Abraham.*

WOLSEY, THOMAS, Cardinal and Lord Chancellor, 1475?—29 Nov.
     1530

    5589.   Had I served my God as diligently as I have served the king,
He would not have given me over in my grey hairs.
                        To Sir William Kingston, on the day of his death.

WOODWORTH, SAMUEL, U.S. poet, 13 Jan. 1784—9 Dec. 1842

5590.   The old oaken bucket, the iron-bound bucket,
        The moss-covered bucket, which hung in the well.
                                          The Old Oaken Bucket.

WOOLF, ADELINE VIRGINIA, authoress, 25 Jan. 1882—28 March,
     1941

    5591.   Those comfortably padded lunatic asylums which are known,
euphemistically, as the stately homes of England.
                        The Common Reader.   Lady Dorothy Nevill.

5592.   A room of one's own.   *Title of book.*

WORDSWORTH, DAME ELIZABETH, Principal of Lady Margaret Hall,
     Oxford, 22 June, 1840—30 Nov. 1932

5593.   If all the good people were clever,
                      And all clever people were good,
                      The world would be nicer than ever
                      We thought that it possibly could.   *Good and Clever.*

5594.
> But somehow, 'tis seldom or never
> The two hit it off as they should,
> The good are so harsh to the clever,
> The clever, so rude to the good !   Ibid.

WORDSWORTH, WILLIAM, Poet Laureate, 7 April, 1770—23 April, 1850

5595.
> In that sweet mood when pleasant thoughts
> Bring sad thoughts to the mind.
> > *Lines Written in Early Spring.*

5596.
> And 'tis my faith that every flower
> Enjoys the air it breathes.   Ibid.

5597.
> Nor less I deem that there are Powers
> Which of themselves our minds impress ;
> That we can feed this mind of ours
> In a wise passiveness.   *Expostulation and Reply.*

5598.
> Up ! up ! my friend, and quit your books ;
> Or surely you'll grow double.   *The Tables Turned.*

5599.
> Come forth into the light of things,
> Let Nature be your teacher.   Ibid.

5600.
> One impulse from a vernal wood
> > May teach you more of man,
> Of moral evil and of good,
> > Than all the sages can.   Ibid.

5601.
> > Sensations sweet
> Felt in the blood, and felt along the heart.
> *Lines Composed a Few Miles above Tintern Abbey*, 27.

5602.
> That best portion of a good man's life,
> His little, nameless, unremembered acts,
> Of kindness and of love.   Ibid., 33.

5603.
> > The sounding cataract
> Haunted me like a passion.   Ibid., 76.

5604.
> > I have learned
> To look on nature, not as in the hour
> Of thoughtless youth ; but hearing oftentimes
> The still, sad music of humanity,
> Nor harsh nor grating, though of ample power
> To chasten and subdue.   And I have felt
> A presence that disturbs me with the joy
> Of elevated thoughts : a sense sublime
> Of something far more deeply interfused,
> Whose dwelling is the light of setting suns,
> And the round ocean and the living air,
> And the blue sky, and in the mind of man.   Ibid., 88.

5605.
> Knowing that Nature never did betray
> The heart that loved her.   Ibid., 122.

5606.
> A primrose by a river's brim
> A yellow primrose was to him,
> And it was nothing more.   *Peter Bell*, I. 249.

5607.
> All silent and all damned !   Ibid., II. 516.

5608. What fond and wayward thoughts will slide
          Into a lover's head !—
    ' O mercy ! ' to myself I cried,
          ' If Lucy should be dead ! '

> *Strange Fits of Passion have I known.*

5609. She dwelt among the untrodden ways
          Beside the springs of Dove,
    A maid whom there were none to praise
          And very few to love :

5610. A violet by a mossy stone
          Half hidden from the eye !
    Fair as a star, when only one
          Is shining in the sky.

> *She dwelt among the Untrodden Ways.*

5611. But she is in her grave, and, oh,
          The difference to me !

> *Ibid.*

5612. No motion has she now, no force ;
          She neither hears nor sees,
    Rolled round in earth's diurnal course,
          With rocks, and stones, and trees.

> *A Slumber did my Spirit seal.*

5613. The stars of midnight shall be dear
    To her ; and she shall lean her ear
    In many a secret place
    Where rivulets dance their wayward round,
    And beauty born of murmuring sound
    Shall pass into her face.

> *Three Years she grew.*

5614. One that would peep and botanize
    Upon his mother's grave.

> *A Poet's Epitaph.*

5615. And you must love him, ere to you
    He will seem worthy of your love.

> *Ibid.*

5616. The sweetest thing that ever grew
    Beside a human door.

> *Lucy Gray.*

5617. Drink, pretty creature, drink !

> *The Pet Lamb.*

5618. She gave me eyes, she gave me ears;
    And humble cares, and delicate fears;
    A heart, the fountain of sweet tears;
          And love, and thought, and joy.

> *The Sparrow's Nest.*

5619. My heart leaps up when I behold
          A rainbow in the sky

> *My Heart leaps up.*

5620. The child is father of the man.

> *Ibid.*

5621.   The cattle are grazing,
          Their heads never raising ;
    There are forty feeding like one.

> *Written in March.*

5622. Sweet childish days, that were as long
    As twenty days are now.

> *To a Butterfly.*

5623. As high as we have mounted in delight
    In our dejection do we sink as low.

> *The Leech-Gatherer ; or, Resolution and Independence, 4.*

5624. I thought of Chatterton, the marvellous boy,
The sleepless soul that perished in his pride ;
Of him who walked in glory and in joy
Followed his plough, along the mountain-side :
By our own spirits are we deified ;
We poets in our youth begin in gladness ;
But thereof comes in the end despondency and madness.

Ibid., 7.

5625. Earth has not anything to show more fair.
            Sonnet, composed upon Westminster Bridge.

5626. This City now doth like a garment wear
The beauty of the morning.   Ibid.

5627. Dear God ! the very houses seem asleep ;
And all that mighty heart is lying still !   Ibid.

5628. Once did she hold the gorgeous East in fee.
            Sonnet, on the Extinction of the Venetian Republic.

5629. Men are we, and must grieve when even the shade
Of that which once was great, is passed away.   Ibid.

5630. Plain living and high thinking are no more :
The homely beauty of the good old cause
Is gone ; our peace, our fearful innocence,
And pure religion breathing household laws.
            Sonnet.   O Friend ! I know not which Way I must look.

5631. Milton ! thou should'st be living at this hour :
England hath need of thee : she is a fen
Of stagnant waters.   *Sonnet.   London, 1802.*

5632. Thy soul was like a star, and dwelt apart :
Thou hadst a voice whose sound was like the sea :
Pure as the naked heavens, majestic, free,
So didst thou travel on life's common way,
In cheerful godliness ; and yet thy heart
The lowliest duties on herself did lay.   Ibid.

5633. We must be free or die, who speak the tongue
That Shakespeare spake ; the faith and morals hold
Which Milton held.   *Sonnet.   It is not to be thought of.*

5634. And stepping westward seemed to be
A kind of heavenly destiny.   *Stepping Westward.*

5635. A voice so thrilling ne'er was heard
In springtime from the cuckoo-bird,
Breaking the silence of the seas
Among the farthest Hebrides.   *The Solitary Reaper.*

5636. For old, unhappy, far-off things,
And battles long ago.   Ibid.

5637. The music in my heart I bore,
Long after it was heard no more.   Ibid.

5638.   The good old rule
Sufficeth them, the simple plan,
That they should take, who have the power,
And they should keep who can.   *Rob Roy's Grave.*

5639. The swan on still St. Mary's Lake
Float double, swan and shadow. *Yarrow Unvisited.*

5640. O Cuckoo ! shall I call thee bird,
Or but a wandering voice ? *To the Cuckoo.*

5641. She was a phantom of delight
When first she gleamed upon my sight.
She was a Phantom of Delight.

5642. A dancing shape, an image gay,
To haunt, to startle, and waylay. Ibid.

5643. A creature not too bright or good
For human nature's daily food ;
For transient sorrows, simple wiles,
Praise, blame, love, kisses, tears, and smiles. Ibid.

5644. A perfect woman, nobly planned,
To warn, to comfort, and command. Ibid.

5645. I wandered lonely as a cloud
That floats on high o'er vales and hills,
When all at once I saw a crowd,
A host of golden daffodils ;
Beside the lake, beneath the trees.
Fluttering and dancing in the breeze.
I wandered Lonely as a Cloud.

5646. For oft, when on my couch I lie
In vacant or in pensive mood,
They flash upon that inward eye
Which is the bliss of solitude ;
And then my heart with pleasure fills,
And dances with the daffodils. Ibid.

5647. Spade ! with which Wilkinson hath tilled his lands.
To the Spade of a Friend.

5648. Stern daughter of the voice of God ! *Ode to Duty.*

5649. Thou dost preserve the stars from wrong ;
And the most ancient heavens, through Thee, are fresh and
strong. Ibid.

5650. The light that never was, on sea or land ;
The consecration, and the poet's dream.
*Elegiac Stanzas suggested by a Picture of Peele Castle in a
Storm.*

5651. But an old age serene and bright,
And lovely as a Lapland night,
Shall lead thee to thy grave. *To a Young Lady.*

5652. Where the statue stood
Of Newton, with his prism and silent face,
The marble index of a mind forever
Voyaging through strange seas of thought alone.
The Prelude, III. 61.

5653. Bliss was it in that dawn to be alive,
But to be young was very heaven ! Ibid., XI. 108.

5654. Who is the happy Warrior ? Who is he
That every man in arms should wish to be ?
Character of the Happy Warrior.

5655. Who, doomed to go in company with Pain,
And Fear, and Bloodshed, miserable train !
Turns his necessity to glorious gain.   Ibid.

5656. But who, if he be called upon to face
Some awful moment to which Heaven has joined
Great issues, good or bad for human kind,
Is happy as a lover.   Ibid.

5657. Nuns fret not at their convent's narrow room,
And hermits are contented with their cells.
            Sonnet. Nuns fret not.

5658. The world is too much with us ; late and soon,
Getting and spending, we lay waste our powers :
Little we see in Nature that is ours.
         Sonnet. The World is too much with us.

5659.   Great God ! I'd rather be
A Pagan suckled in a creed outworn ;
So might I, standing on this pleasant lea,
Have glimpses that would make me less forlorn ;
Have sight of Proteus rising from the sea ;
Or hear old Triton blow his wreathèd horn.   Ibid.

5660. The rainbow comes and goes,
And lovely is the rose.   *Ode on Intimations of Immortality.*

5661.   The sunshine is a glorious birth ;
      But yet I know, where'er I go,
That there hath passed away a glory from the earth.   Ibid.

5662. The cataracts blow their trumpets from the steep.   Ibid.

5663. The winds come to me from the fields of sleep.   Ibid.

5664. Whither is fled the visionary gleam ?
Where is it now, the glory and the dream ?   **Ibid.**

5665 Our birth is but a sleep and a forgetting :
The soul that rises with us, our life's star,
    Hath had elsewhere its setting,
      And cometh from afar :
    Not in entire forgetfulness,
    And not in utter nakedness,
But trailing clouds of glory do we come
    From God, who is our home :
Heaven lies about us in our infancy !
Shades of the prison-house begin to close
    Upon the growing boy,
But he beholds the light, and whence it flows
    He sees it in his joy ;
The youth, who daily farther from the east
    Must travel, still is Nature's priest,
     And by the vision splendid
     Is on his way attended ;
At length the man perceives it die away,
And fade into the light of common day.   **I**bid.

5666. As if his whole vocation
Were endless imitation.   Ibid.

5667. And custom lie upon thee with a weight,
    Heavy as frost, and deep almost as life !   *Ibid.*

5668.   Those obstinate questionings
    Of sense and outward things,
    Fallings from us, vanishings;
    Blank misgivings of a creature
Moving about in worlds not realised,
High instincts before which our mortal nature
Did tremble like a guilty thing surprised.   *Ibid.*

5669.   Truths that wake
To perish never.   *Ibid.*

5670.   Hence, in a season of calm weather,
        Though inland far we be,
        Our souls have sight of that immortal sea
    Which brought us hither.   *Ibid.*

5671. In years that bring the philosophic mind.   *Ibid.*

5672. To me the meanest flower that blows can give
Thoughts that do often lie too deep for tears.   *Ibid.*

5673. Two voices are there ; one is of the sea,
One of the mountains ; each a mighty voice :
In both from age to age thou didst rejoice,
They were thy chosen music, Liberty !
        *Sonnet.   Thought of a Briton on the Subjugation of
        Switzerland.*

5674.   The good die first,
And they whose hearts are dry as summer dust
Burn to the socket.   *The Excursion,* I. 500.

5675. A man he seems of cheerful yesterdays
And confident to-morrows.   *Ibid.,* VII. 557.

5676.   The Gods approve
The depth, and not the tumult, of the soul.   *Laodamia,* 74.

5677. An ampler ether, a diviner air.   *Ibid.,* 105.

5678. Ethereal minstrel ! Pilgrim of the sky !   *To a Skylark.*

5679. Type of the wise who soar, but never roam,
True to the kindred points of heaven and home.   *Ibid.*

5680. Scorn not the Sonnet.   Critic, you have frowned,
Mindless of its just honours ; with this key
Shakespeare unlocked his heart.
        Sonnet.   Scorn not the Sonnet.

5681. Nature's old felicities.   *The Trossachs.*

5682. And Lamb, the frolic and the gentle,
Has vanished from his lonely hearth.
        Extempore Effusion upon the Death of James Hogg.

5683. How fast has brother followed brother,
From sunshine to the sunless land !   *Ibid.*

5684. And thou art long, and lank, and brown,
As is the ribbed sea sand.
        Lines added to Coleridge's *Ancient Mariner.*

5685. And listens like a three years' child.   *Ibid.*

5686. Poetry is the spontaneous overflow of powerful feelings : it takes its origin from emotion recollected in tranquillity.

Lyrical Ballads, preface.

WORK, HENRY CLAY, U.S. song-writer, 1 Oct. 1832—8 June, 1884

5687. Bring the good old bugle, boys, we'll sing another song ;
Sing it with a spirit that will start the world along,
Sing it as we used to sing it—fifty thousand strong,
As we were marching through Georgia.

Marching through Georgia

5688. Father, dear father, come home with me now,
The clock in the steeple strikes one. *Come Home, Father.*

WOTTON, SIR HENRY, diplomat and poet, 1568—Dec. 1639

5689. How happy is he born and taught
That serveth not another's will ;
Whose armour is his honest thought,
And simple truth his utmost skill.

The Character of a Happy Life.

5690. And entertains the harmless day
With a religious book, or friend. Ibid.

5691. Lord of himself, though not of lands,
And, having nothing, yet hath all. Ibid.

5692. You meaner beauties of the night,
That poorly satisfy our eyes
More by your number than your light
You common people of the skies ;
What are you, when the moon shall rise ?

On his Mistress, the Queen of Bohemia.

5693. He first deceased ; she for a little tried
To live without him, liked it not, and died.

Upon the Death of Sir Albertus Morton's Wife.

5694. An ambassador is an honest man sent to lie abroad for the good of his country. *Written in a friend's album.*

WYATT, SIR THOMAS, poet, born 1503 ? buried 11 Oct. 1542

5695. And wilt thou leave me thus ?
Say nay, say nay, for shame !

Poems from the Devonshire MS. part I. xii.

5696. Forget not yet the tried intent
Of such a truth as I have meant ;
My great travail so gladly spent
Forget not yet ! *Ibid.,* xxvii.

XENOPHON, Greek historian, 430 ?—355 ? B.C.

5697. Θάλαττα θάλαττα.—The sea ! the sea !

Anabasis, IV. vii.

[Transliterated Thalatta, thalatta. Shout of Greek soldiers when they sighted the Euxine on their homeward march.]

XERXES, King of Persia, 519 ?—465 B.C.

5698. My men have become women, and my women men.
> *When Queen Artemisia's ship sank another at Salamis,*
> 480 B.C.

YEATS, WILLIAM BUTLER, Irish poet, 13 June, 1865—28 Jan. 1939

5699.   The land of faery,
Where nobody gets old and godly and grave,
Where nobody gets old and crafty and wise,
Where nobody gets old and bitter of tongue.
> *The Land of Heart's Desire.*

5700. Had I the heavens' embroidered cloths,
Enwrought with golden and silver light.
> *He wishes for the Cloths of Heaven.*

5701. I have spread my dreams under your feet ;
Tread softly, because you tread on my dreams.   Ibid.

5702. When you are old and grey and full of sleep,
And nodding by the fire, take down this book.
> *When you are Old.*

5703. She bid me take life easy, as the grass grows on the weirs ;
But I was young and foolish, and now am full of tears.
> *Down by the Salley Gardens.*

5704. I will arise and go now, and go to Innisfree,
And a small cabin build there, of clay and wattles made ;
Nine bean-rows will I have there, a hive for the honey-bee,
    And live alone in the bee-loud glade.
> *The Lake Isle of Innisfree.*

5705. When I play on my fiddle in Dooney,
Folk dance like a wave of the sea.   *The Fiddler of Dooney.*

YOUNG, ANDREW, Scottish schoolmaster, 23 April, 1807—30 Nov.
     1889

5706.   There is a happy land,
               Far, far away,
           Where saints in glory stand,
            Bright, bright as day.   *There is a Happy Land.*

YOUNG, EDWARD, poet, baptised 3 July, 1683, died 5 April, 1765

5707. Tired Nature's sweet restorer, balmy sleep !
He, like the world, his ready visit pays
Where fortune smiles ; the wretched he forsakes.
> *Night Thoughts*, Night i. 1.

5708. Night, sable goddess ! from her ebon throne
In rayless majesty, now stretches forth
Her leaden sceptre o'er a slumb'ring world.   Ibid., 18.

5709. Procrastination is the thief of time.   Ibid., 393.

5710. At thirty, man suspects himself a fool ;
Knows it at forty, and reforms his plan :
At fifty chides his infamous delay,
Pushes his prudent purpose to resolve ;
In all the magnanimity of thought
Resolves ; and re-resolves ; then, dies the same.   Ibid., 417.

5711. All men think all men mortal but themselves.   Ibid., 424.

5712. Who does the best his circumstance allows,
Does well, acts nobly ; angels could no more.
                                        Ibid., Night ii. 90.

5713. Some for renown, on scraps of learning dote,
And think they grow immortal as they quote.
                                Love of Fame, Satire i. 89.

5714.   Be wise with speed ;
A fool at forty is a fool indeed.   Ibid., Satire ii. 282.

5715. For her own breakfast she'll project a scheme,
Nor take her tea without a stratagem.   Ibid., Satire vi. 187.

5716. How commentators each dark passage shun,
And hold their farthing candle to the sun.   Ibid., Satire vii. 97.

5717. Their feet through faithless leather met the dirt,
And oftener chang'd their principles than shirt.
                                To Mr. Pope, Epistle i. 277.

5718. Accept a miracle instead of wit,—
See two dull lines with Stanhope's pencil writ.
                Lines written with Lord Chesterfield's diamond pencil.

ZAMOYSKI, JAN, Chancellor of Poland, 1541—3 June, 1605
    5719. The king reigns, but does not govern.
                                Speech in Polish Parliament, 1605.

ZANGWILL, ISRAEL, Jewish novelist, 14 Feb. 1864—1 Aug. 1926
    5720. Scratch the Christian and you find the pagan—spoiled.
                                The Children of the Ghetto, II. vi.

ZOLA, ÉMILE ÉDOUARD CHARLES ANTOINE, French novelist, 2 April,
    1840—29 Sept. 1902

    5721. J'accuse.—I accuse.
                Title of open letter to President of France in connection with
                the Dreyfus case, 13 Jan. 1898.

THE BIBLE

[The text used in the following quotations is that of the Authorised Version, except in a few instances which are indicated by notes. For convenience of reference, there is given below an alphabetical index of the books of the Old Testament and New Testament from which quotations have been taken.]

THE OLD TESTAMENT

5722. And God said, Let there be light : and there was light.   *Genesis*, i. 3.

5723. It is not good that the man should be alone.   Ibid., ii. 18.

5724. Bone of my bones, and flesh of my flesh.   Ibid., 23.

5725. Ye shall be as gods, knowing good and evil.   Ibid., iii. 5.

5726. In the sweat of thy face shalt thou eat bread.   Ibid., 19.

5727. For dust thou art, and unto dust shalt thou return.   Ibid.

5728. The mother of all living.   Ibid., 20.

5729. Am I my brother's keeper ?   Ibid., iv. 9.

5730. My punishment is greater than I can bear.   Ibid., 13.

5731. There were giants in the earth in those days.   Ibid., vi. 4.

5732. But the dove found no rest for the sole of her foot.   Ibid., viii. 9.

5733. Whoso sheddeth man's blood, by man shall his blood be shed.

    Ibid., ix. 6.

5734. Even as Nimrod the mighty hunter before the Lord.   Ibid., x. 9.

5735. In a good old age.   Ibid., xv. 15.

5736. His hand will be against every man, and every man's hand against
him.   Ibid., xvi. 12.

5737. Shall not the Judge of all the earth do right ?   Ibid., xviii. 25.

5738. Esau selleth his birthright for a mess of pottage.
[In the Genevan Bible.]   Ibid., xxv. chapter heading.

5739. The voice is Jacob's voice, but the hands are the hands of Esau.

    Ibid., xxvii. 22.

5740. This is none other but the house of God, and this is the gate of heaven.

    Ibid., xxviii. 17

5741. I will not let thee go, except thou bless me. Ibid., xxxii. 26.
5742. Behold, this dreamer cometh. Ibid., xxxvii. 19.
5743. Jacob saw that there was corn in Egypt. Ibid., xlii. 1.
5744. Bring down my grey hairs with sorrow to the grave. Ibid., 38.
5745. Ye shall eat of the fat of the land. Ibid., xlv. 18.
5746. Few and evil have the days of the years of my life been. Ibid., xlvii. 9.
5747. Unstable as water, thou shalt not excel. Ibid., xlix. 4.
5748. Now there arose up a new king over Egypt, which knew not Joseph.
Exodus, i. 8.
5749. Who made thee a prince and a judge over us ? Ibid., ii. 14.
5750. I have been a stranger in a strange land. Ibid., 22.
5751. A land flowing with milk and honey. Ibid., iii. 8.
5752. Darkness which may be felt. Ibid., x. 21.
5753. And they spoiled the Egyptians. Ibid., xii. 36.
5754. Thou shalt give life for life, eye for eye, tooth for tooth, hand for hand,
foot for foot. Ibid. xxi. 23.
5755. Thou shalt not seethe a kid in his mother's milk. Ibid., xxiii. 19.
5756. Thou shalt love thy neighbour as thyself. Leviticus, xix. 18.
5757. The Lord bless thee, and keep thee : The Lord make his face shine
upon thee, and be gracious unto thee : The Lord lift up his
countenance upon thee, and give thee peace. Numbers, vi. 24.
5758. Let me die the death of the righteous, and let my last end be like his !
Ibid., 10.
5759. Be sure your sin will find you out. Ibid., xxxii. 23.
5760. Thou shalt love the Lord thy God with all thine heart, and with all thy
soul, and with all thy might. Deuteronomy, vi. 5
5761. Thou shalt not muzzle the ox when he treadeth out the corn.
Ibid., xxv. 4.
5762. In the morning thou shalt say, Would God it were even ! and at even
thou shalt say, Would God it were morning ! Ibid., xxviii. 67.
5763. Jeshurun waxed fat, and kicked. Ibid., xxxii. 15.
5764. As thy days, so shall thy strength be. Ibid., xxxiii. 25.
5765. The eternal God is my refuge, and underneath are the everlasting
arms. Ibid., 27.
5766. Hewers of wood and drawers of water. Joshua, ix. 21.
5767. I am going the way of all the earth. Ibid., xxiii. 14.
5768. I arose a mother in Israel. Judges, v. 7.
5769. The stars in their courses fought against Sisera. Ibid., 20.
5770. She brought forth butter in a lordly dish. Ibid., 25.
5771. Why tarry the wheels of his chariots ? Ibid., 28.
5772. Have they not divided the prey ; to every man a damsel or two ?
Ibid., 30.
5773. Faint, yet pursuing them. Ibid., viii. 4.
5774. He smote them hip and thigh. Ibid., xv. 8.
5775. The Philistines be upon thee, Samson. Ibid., xvi. 9.
5776. Whither thou goest, I will go ; and where thou lodgest, I will lodge :
thy people shall be my people, and thy God my God : Where thou
diest, will I die, and there will I be buried : the Lord do so to me,
and more also, if ought but death part thee and me. Ruth, i. 16.
5777. Speak, Lord ; for thy servant heareth. 1 Samuel, iii. 9.

5778. Quit yourselves like men.   Ibid., iv. 9.
5779. Is Saul also among the prophets ?   Ibid., x. 11.
5780. A man after his own heart.   Ibid., xiii. 14.
5781. Agag came unto him delicately.   And Agag said, Surely the bitterness
     of death is past.   Ibid., xv. 32.
5782. Saul hath slain his thousands, and David his ten thousands.
                                                       Ibid., xviii. 7.
5783. Tell it not in Gath, publish it not in the streets of Askelon.
                                                       2 *Samuel*, i. 20.
5784. Saul and Jonathan were lovely and pleasant in their lives, and in
     their death they were not divided.   Ibid., 23.
5785. How are the mighty fallen in the midst of the battle !   Ibid., 25.
5786. Thy love to me was wonderful, passing the love of women.   Ibid., 26.
5787. Smote him under the fifth rib.   Ibid., ii. 23.
5788. Tarry at Jericho until your beards be grown.   Ibid., x. 5.
5789. The poor man had nothing, save one little ewe lamb.   Ibid., xii. 3.
5790. Thou art the man.   Ibid., 7.
5791. Would God I had died for thee, O Absalom, my son, my son !
                                                       Ibid., xviii. 33.
5792. A proverb and a byword among all people.   1 *Kings*, ix. 7.
5793. Behold, the half was not told me.   Ibid., x. 7.
5794. My father hath chastised you with whips, but I will chastise you
     with scorpions.   Ibid., xii. 11.
5795. He slept with his fathers.   Ibid., xiv. 20.
5796. How long halt ye between two opinions ?   Ibid., xviii. 21.
5797. He is talking, or he is pursuing, or he is in a journey, or peradventure
     he sleepeth, and must be awaked.   Ibid., 27.
5798. There ariseth a little cloud out of the sea, like a man's hand.   Ibid., 44.
5799. A still small voice.   Ibid., xix. 12.
5800. Hast thou found me, O mine enemy ?   Ibid., xxi. 20.
5801. And a certain man drew a bow at a venture, and smote the king of
     Israel between the joints of his harness.   Ibid., xxii. 34.
5802. Is it well with the child ?   And she answered, It is well.
                                                       2 *Kings*. iv. 26.
5803. There is death in the pot.   Ibid., 40.
5804. Are not Abana and Pharpar, rivers of Damascus, better than all the
     waters of Israel ?   Ibid., v. 12.
5805. Is thy servant a dog, that he should do this great thing ?
                                                       Ibid., viii. 13.
5806. The driving is like the driving of Jehu, the son of Nimshi ; for he
     driveth furiously.   Ibid., ix. 20.
5807. The man whom the king delighteth to honour.   *Esther*, vi. 9.
5808. From going to and fro in the earth, and from walking up and down
     in it.   *Job*, i. 7.
5809. Naked came I out of my mother's womb, and naked shall I return
      thither : the Lord gave, and the Lord hath taken away ;   blessed
     be the name of the Lord.   Ibid., 21.
5810. Skin for skin, yea, all that a man hath, will he give for his life.
                                                       Ibid., ii. 4

5811. There the wicked cease from troubling, and there the weary be at rest. Ibid., iii. 17.

5812. Man is born unto trouble, as the sparks fly upward. Ibid., v. 7.

5813. My days are swifter than a weaver's shuttle, and are spent without hope. Ibid., vii. 6.

5814. No doubt but ye are the people, and wisdom shall die with you. Ibid., xii. 2.

5815. Man that is born of a woman is of few days, and full of trouble. Ibid., xiv. 1.

5816. Miserable comforters are ye all. Ibid., xvi. 2.

5817. The king of terrors. Ibid., xviii. 14.

5818. I am escaped with the skin of my teeth. Ibid., xix. 20.

5819. I know that my redeemer liveth. Ibid., 25.

5820. Seeing the root of the matter is found in me. Ibid., 28.

5821. My desire is . . . that mine adversary had written a book. Ibid., xxxi. 35.

5822. Who is this that darkeneth counsel by words without knowledge ? Ibid., xxxviii. 2.

5823. When the morning stars sang together, and all the sons of God shouted for joy. Ibid., 7.

5824. Canst thou bind the sweet influences of Pleiades, or loose the bands of Orion ? Ibid., 31.

5825. He saith among the trumpets, Ha, ha ; and he smelleth the battle afar off, the thunder of the captains, and the shouting. Ibid., xxxix. 25.

5826. Canst thou draw out leviathan with an hook ? Ibid., xli. 1.

5827. As hard as a piece of the nether millstone. Ibid., 24.

5828. He maketh the deep to boil like a pot. Ibid., 31.

5829. Why do the heathen rage, and the people imagine a vain thing ? *Psalms*, ii. 1.

5830. Out of the mouth of babes and sucklings. Ibid., viii. 2.

5831. Thou hast made him a little lower than the angels. Ibid., 5.

5832. The fool hath said in his heart, There is no God. Ibid., xiv. 1. and liii. 1.

5833. He that sweareth to his own hurt, and changeth not. Ibid., xv. 4.

5834. The lines are fallen unto me in pleasant places ; yea, I have a goodly heritage. Ibid., xvi. 6.

5835. Keep me as the apple of the eye, hide me under the shadow of thy wings. Ibid., xvii. 8.

5836. Yea, he did fly upon the wings of the wind. Ibid., xviii. 10.

5837. The heavens declare the glory of God ; and the firmament showeth his handiwork. Ibid., xix. 1.

5838. Day unto day uttereth speech, and night unto night showeth knowledge. Ibid., 2.

5839. More to be desired are they than gold, yea, than much fine gold : sweeter also than honey and the honeycomb. Ibid., 10.

5840. He maketh me to lie down in green pastures : he leadeth me beside the still waters. Ibid., xxiii. 2.

5841. Though I walk through the valley of the shadow of death. Ibid., 4.

5842. Thy rod and thy staff they comfort me. Ibid.

5843. Weeping may endure for a night, but joy cometh in the morning.
Ibid., xxx. 5.

5844. My times are in thy hand. Ibid., xxxi. 15.

5845. Eschew evil, and do good : seek peace, and ensue it.
[Book of Common Prayer rendering.] Ibid., xxxiv. 14.

5846. I have been young, and now am old ; yet have I not seen the righteous
forsaken, nor his seed begging bread. Ibid., xxxvii. 25.

5847. Flourishing like a green bay tree. Ibid., 36.
[Book of Common Prayer rendering.]

5848. He heapeth up riches, and knoweth not who shall gather them.
Ibid., xxxix. 6.

5849. Blessed is he that considereth the poor. Ibid., xli. 1.

5850. As the hart panteth after the water brooks. Ibid., xlii. 1.

5851. Deep calleth unto deep. Ibid., 7.

5852. My tongue is the pen of a ready writer. Ibid., xlv. 1.

5853. God is our refuge and strength, a very present help in trouble.
Ibid., xlvi. 1.

5854. Man being in honour abideth not : he is like the beasts that perish.
Ibid., xlix. 12.

5855. The cattle upon a thousand hills. Ibid., l. 10.

5856. A broken and a contrite heart, O God, thou wilt not despise.
Ibid., li. 17.

5857. Oh that I had wings like a dove ! Ibid., lv. 6.

5858. But it was even thou, my companion, my guide, and mine own familiar
friend. [Book of Common Prayer rendering.] Ibid., 14.

5859. We took sweet counsel together. Ibid., 14.

5860. Vain is the help of man. Ibid., lx. 11 and cviii. 12.

5861. His enemies shall lick the dust. Ibid., lxii. 9.

5862. He putteth down one, and setteth up another. Ibid., lxxv. 7.

5863. They go from strength to strength. Ibid., lxxxiv. 7.

5864. For a day in thy courts is better than a thousand. I had rather be a
doorkeeper in the house of my God, than to dwell in the tents of
wickedness. Ibid., 10.

5865. Mercy and truth are met together ; righteousness and peace have
kissed each other. Ibid., lxxxv. 10.

5866. For a thousand years in thy sight are but as yesterday when it is past,
and as a watch in the night. Ibid., xc. 4.

5867. We spend our years as a tale that is told. Ibid., 9.

5868. The days of our years are threescore years and ten ; and if by reason
of strength they be fourscore years, yet is their strength labour and
sorrow ; for it is soon cut off, and we fly away. Ibid., 10.

5869. So teach us to number our days, that we may apply our hearts unto
wisdom. Ibid., 12.

5870. I will say of the Lord, He is my refuge and my fortress : my God ;
in him will I trust. Ibid., xci. 2.

5871. Nor for the pestilence that walketh in darkness ; nor for the destruction
that wasteth at noonday. Ibid., 6.

5872. As for man, his days are as grass : as a flower of the field, so he
flourisheth. Ibid., ciii. 15.

O

5873. For the wind passeth over it, and it is gone ; and the place thereof shall know it no more. *Ibid.*, 16.

5874. Wine that maketh glad the heart of man. *Ibid.*, civ. 15.

5875. They that go down to the sea in ships, that do business in great waters. *Ibid.*, cvii. 23.

5876. They reel to and fro, and stagger like a drunken man, and are at their wit's end. *Ibid.*, 27.

5877. I said in my haste, All men are liars. *Ibid.*, cxvi. 11.

5878. Precious in the sight of the Lord is the death of his saints. *Ibid.*, 15.

5879. This is the day which the Lord hath made ; we will rejoice and be glad in it. *Ibid.*, cxviii. 24.

5880. Thy word is a lamp unto my feet, and a light unto my path. *Ibid.*, cxix. 105.

5881. The sun shall not smite thee by day, nor the moon by night. *Ibid.*, cxxi. 6.

5882. Except the Lord build the house, they labour in vain that build it. *Ibid.*, cxxvii. 1.

5883. He giveth his beloved sleep. *Ibid.*, 2.

5884. Happy is the man that hath his quiver full of them. *Ibid.*, 5.

5885. Thy children like the olive branches round about thy table. [Book of Common Prayer rendering.] *Ibid.*, cxxviii. 3.

5886. Behold, how good and how pleasant it is for brethren to dwell together in unity ! *Ibid.*, cxxxiii. 1.

5887. We hanged our harps upon the willows. *Ibid.*, cxxxvii. 2.

5888. How shall we sing the Lord's song in a strange land ? *Ibid.*, 4.

5889. If I forget thee, O Jerusalem, let my right hand forget her cunning. *Ibid.*, 5.

5890. If I take the wings of the morning, and dwell in the uttermost parts of the sea. *Ibid.*, cxxxix. 9.

5891. I am fearfully and wonderfully made. *Ibid.*, 14.

5892. Put not your trust in princes. *Ibid.*, cxlvi. 3.

5893. Surely in vain the net is spread in the sight of any bird. *Proverbs*, i. 17.

5894. Wisdom crieth without ; she uttereth her voice in the streets. *Ibid.*, 20.

5895. Her ways are ways of pleasantness, and all her paths are peace. *Ibid.*, iii. 17.

5896. The path of the just is as the shining light, that shineth more and more unto the perfect day. *Ibid.*, iv. 18.

5897. Go to the ant, thou sluggard ; consider her ways, and be wise. *Ibid.*, vi. 6.

5898. Yet a little sleep, a little slumber, a little folding of the hands to sleep. *Ibid.*, 10.

5899. As an ox goeth to the slaughter. *Ibid.*, vii. 22.

5900. Wisdom is better than rubies. *Ibid.*, viii. 11.

5901. Stolen waters are sweet, and bread eaten in secret is pleasant. *Ibid.*, ix. 17.

5902. A wise son maketh a glad father : but a foolish son is the heaviness of his mother. *Ibid.*, x. 1.

5903. In the multitude of counsellors there is safety.

Ibid., xi. 14 and xxiv. 6.

5904. As a jewel of gold in a swine's snout, so is a fair woman which is without discretion. Ibid., 22.

5905. A righteous man regardeth the life of his beast ; but the tender mercies of the wicked are cruel. Ibid., xii. 10.

5906. Hope deferred maketh the heart sick. Ibid., xiii. 12.

5907. The way of transgressors is hard. Ibid., 15.

5908. He that spareth the rod hateth his son. Ibid., 24.

5909. The heart knoweth his own bitterness ; and a stranger doth not intermeddle with his joy. Ibid., xiv. 10.

5910. A soft answer turneth away wrath. Ibid., xv. 1.

5911. A merry heart maketh a cheerful countenance. Ibid., 13.

5912. Better is a dinner of herbs where love is, than a stalled ox and hatred therewith. Ibid., 17.

5913. A word spoken in due season, how good it is ! Ibid., 23.

5914. Pride goeth before destruction, and an haughty spirit before a fall.

Ibid., xvi. 18.

5915. The hoary head is a crown of glory, if it be found in the way of righteousness. Ibid., 31.

5916. He that repeateth a matter separateth very friends. Ibid., xvii. 9.

5917. A merry heart doeth good like a medicine. Ibid., 22.

5918. He that hath knowledge spareth his words. Ibid., 27.

5919. Even a fool, when he holdeth his peace, is counted wise. Ibid., 28.

5920. Whoso findeth a wife findeth a good thing. Ibid., xviii. 22.

5921. There is a friend that sticketh closer than a brother. Ibid., 24.

5922. He that hath pity upon the poor lendeth unto the Lord. Ibid., xix. 17.

5923. Wine is a mocker, strong drink is raging. Ibid., xx. 1.

5924. Every fool will be meddling. Ibid., 3.

5925. It is naught, it is naught, saith the buyer : but when he is gone his way, then he boasteth. Ibid., 14.

5926. It is better to dwell in a corner of the housetop, than with a brawling woman in a wide house. Ibid., xxi. 9.

5927. A good name is rather to be chosen than great riches. Ibid., xxii. 1.

5928. Train up a child in the way he should go : and when he is old, he will not depart from it. Ibid., 6.

5929. Riches certainly make themselves wings. Ibid., xxiii. 5.

5930. Look not thou upon the wine when it is red. Ibid., 31.

5931. At the last it biteth like a serpent, and stingeth like an adder.

Ibid., 32.

5932. As cold waters to a thirsty soul, so is good news from a far country.

Ibid., xxv. 25.

5933. Answer not a fool according to his folly, lest thou also be like unto him. Ibid., xxvi. 4.

5934. Answer a fool according to his folly, lest he be wise in his own conceit.

Ibid. 5.

5935. The sluggard is wiser in his own conceit than seven men that can render a reason. Ibid., 16.

5936. Whoso diggeth a pit shall fall therein. Ibid., 27.

5937. Boast not thyself of to-morrow; for thou knowest not what a day may bring forth. *Ibid.*, xxvii. 1.

5938. Faithful are the wounds of a friend. *Ibid.*, 6.

5939. A continual dropping in a very rainy day and a contentious woman are alike. *Ibid.*, 15.

5940. Iron sharpeneth iron; so a man sharpeneth the countenance of his friend. *Ibid.*, 17.

5941. Though thou shouldest bray a fool in a mortar among wheat with a pestle, yet will not his foolishness depart from him. *Ibid.*, 22.

5942. The wicked flee when no man pursueth: but the righteous are bold as a lion. *Ibid.*, xxviii. 1.

5943. He that maketh haste to be rich shall not be innocent. *Ibid.*, 20.

5944. Where there is no vision, the people perish. *Ibid.*, xxix. 18.

5945. The horseleach hath two daughters, crying, Give, give.
Ibid., xxx. 15.

5946. The way of an eagle in the air; the way of a serpent upon a rock; the way of a ship in the midst of the sea; and the way of a man with a maid. *Ibid.*, 19.

5947. The spider taketh hold with her hands, and is in king's palaces.
Ibid., 28.

5948. Who can find a virtuous woman? for her price is far above rubies.
Ibid., xxxi. 10.

5949. Her children arise up, and call her blessed. *Ibid.*, 28.

5950. Vanity of vanities; all is vanity. *Ecclesiastes*, i. 2.

5951. What profit hath a man of all his labour which he taketh under the sun? *Ibid.*, 3.

5952. One generation passeth away, and another generation cometh: but the earth abideth for ever. *Ibid.*, 4.

5953. All the rivers run into the sea; yet the sea is not full. *Ibid.*, 7.

5954. There is no new thing under the sun. *Ibid.*, 9.

5955. All is vanity and vexation of spirit. *Ibid.*, 14.

5956. He that increaseth knowledge increaseth sorrow. *Ibid.*, 18.

5957. One event happeneth to them all. *Ibid.*, ii. 14.

5958. To everything there is a season, and a time to every purpose under the heaven. *Ibid.*, iii. 1.

5959. A threefold cord is not quickly broken. *Ibid.*, iv. 12.

5960. God is in heaven, and thou upon earth: therefore let thy words be few. *Ibid.*, v. 2.

5961. Better is it that thou shouldest not vow, than that thou shouldest vow and not pay. *Ibid.*, 5.

5962. A good name is better than precious ointment; and the day of death than the day of one's birth. *Ibid.*, vii. 1.

5963. It is better to go to the house of mourning than to go to the house of feasting. *Ibid.*, 2.

5964. As the crackling of thorns under a pot, so is the laughter of the fool.
Ibid., 6.

5965. Say not thou, What is the cause that the former days were better than these? for thou dost not enquire wisely concerning this.
Ibid., 10.

5966. Be not righteous overmuch. Ibid., 16.

5967. God hath made man upright; but they have sought out many inventions. Ibid., 29.

5968. A living dog is better than a dead lion. Ibid., ix. 4.

5969. Whatsoever thy hand findeth to do, do it with thy might.
Ibid., 10.

5970. The race is not to the swift, nor the battle to the strong, neither yet bread to the wise, nor yet riches to men of understanding, nor yet favour to men of skill; but time and chance happeneth to them all.
Ibid., 11.

5971. Dead flies cause the ointment of the apothecary to send forth a stinking savour. Ibid., x. 1.

5972. For a bird of the air shall carry the voice, and that which hath wings shall tell the matter. Ibid., 20.

5973. Cast thy bread upon the waters: for thou shalt find it after many days. Ibid., xi. 1.

5974. In the place where the tree falleth, there it shall be. Ibid., 3.

5975. Truly the light is sweet, and a pleasant thing it is for the eyes to behold the sun. Ibid., 7.

5976. Rejoice, O young man, in thy youth. Ibid., 9.

5977. Remember now thy Creator in the days of thy youth, while the evil days come not, nor the years draw nigh, when thou shalt say, I have no pleasure in them. Ibid., xii. 1.

5978. And the grasshopper shall be a burden, and desire shall fail: because man goeth to his long home, and the mourners go about the streets.
Ibid., 5.

5979. Or ever the silver cord be loosed, or the golden bowl be broken, or the pitcher be broken at the fountain, or the wheel broken at the cistern.
Ibid., 6.

5980. Then shall the dust return to the earth as it was: and the spirit shall return unto God who gave it. Ibid., 7.

5981. Of making many books there is no end; and much study is a weariness of the flesh. Ibid., 12.

5982. Let us hear the conclusion of the whole matter: Fear God, and keep his commandments: for this is the whole duty of man. Ibid., 13.

5983. Let him kiss me with the kisses of his mouth: for thy love is better than wine. *The Song of Solomon*, i. 2.

5984. Stay me with flagons, comfort me with apples: for I am sick of love.
Ibid., ii. 5.

5985. For, lo, the winter is past, the rain is over and gone; The flowers appear on the earth; the time of the singing of birds is come, and the voice of the turtle is heard in our land. Ibid., 11.

5986. Take us the foxes, the little foxes, that spoil the vines. Ibid., 15.

5987. Until the day break, and the shadows flee away. Ibid., 17.

5988. Who is she that looketh forth as the morning, fair as the moon, clear as the sun, and terrible as an army with banners? Ibid., vi. 10.

5989. Set me as a seal upon thine heart, as a seal upon thine arm: for love is strong as death; jealousy is cruel as the grave. Ibid., viii. 6.

5990. Many waters cannot quench love. Ibid., 7.

5991. The ox knoweth his owner, and the ass his master's crib.

Isaiah, i. 3.

5992. Though your sins be as scarlet, they shall be as white as snow.

Ibid., 18.

5993. They shall beat their swords into plowshares, and their spears into pruninghooks ; nation shall not lift up sword against nation, neither shall they learn war any more. Ibid., ii. 4 and *Micah*, iv. 3.

5994. Grind the faces of the poor. Ibid., iii. 15.

5995. Woe unto them that call evil good, and good evil. Ibid., v. 20.

5996. Wizards that peep, and that mutter. Ibid., viii. 19.

5997. The wolf also shall dwell with the lamb, and the leopard shall lie down with the kid. Ibid., xi. 6.

5998. How art thou fallen from heaven, O Lucifer, son of the morning !

Ibid., xiv. 12.

5999. Watchman, what of the night ? Ibid., xxi. 11.

6000. Let us eat and drink ; for to-morrow we shall die. Ibid., xxii. 13.

6001. Whose merchants are princes. Ibid., xxiii. 8.

6002. For precept must be upon precept, precept upon precept ; line upon line, line upon line ; here a little, and there a little.

Ibid., xxviii. 10.

6003. The desert shall rejoice, and blossom as the rose. Ibid., xxxv. 1.

6004. Set thine house in order. Ibid., xxxviii. 1.

6005. All flesh is grass. Ibid., xl. 6.

6006. A bruised reed shall he not break, and the smoking flax shall he not quench. Ibid., xlii. 3.

6007. There is no peace, saith the Lord, unto the wicked. Ibid., xlviii. 22.

6008. How beautiful upon the mountains are the feet of him that bringeth good tidings, that publisheth peace. Ibid., lii. 7.

6009. A man of sorrows, and acquainted with grief. Ibid., liii. 3.

6010. All we like sheep have gone astray. Ibid., 6.

6011. He is brought as a lamb to the slaughter. Ibid., 7.

6012. Seek ye the Lord while he may be found, call ye upon him while he is near. Ibid., lv. 6.

6013. For my thoughts are not your thoughts, neither are your ways my ways, saith the Lord. Ibid., 8.

6014. All our righteousnesses are as filthy rags ; and we all do fade as a leaf. Ibid., lxiv. 6.

6015. Saying, Peace, peace ; when there is no peace.

Jeremiah, v. 14 and viii. 11.

6016. Is there no balm in Gilead ? Ibid., viii. 22.

6017. Can the Ethiopian change his skin, or the leopard his spots ?

Ibid., xiii. 23.

6018. Is it nothing to you, all ye that pass by ? behold, and see if there be any sorrow like unto my sorrow. *Lamentations*, i. 12.

6019. As if a wheel had been in the midst of a wheel. *Ezekiel*, x. 10.

6020. The fathers have eaten sour grapes, and the children's teeth are set on edge. Ibid., xviii. 2.

6021. Can these bones live ? Ibid., xxxvii. 3.

6022. Cast into the midst of a burning fiery furnace. *Daniel*, iii. 6.

6023. Thou are weighed in the balances, and art found wanting.

Ibid., v. 27.

6024. According to the law of the Medes and Persians, which altereth not.

Ibid., vi. 12.

6025. The Ancient of days.   *Ibid., vii. 13.*

6026. Many shall run to and fro, and knowledge shall be increased.

Ibid., xii. 4.

6027. They have sown the wind, and they shall reap the whirlwind.

Hosea, viii. 7.

6028. I have multiplied visions, and used similitudes.   *Ibid., xii. 10.*

6029. Your old men shall dream dreams, your young men shall see visions.

Joel, ii. 28.

6030. They shall sit every man under his vine and under his fig tree.

Micah, iv. 4.

6031. Write the vision, and make it plain upon tables, that he may run
that readeth it.   *Habakkuk, ii. 2.*

6032. Who hath despised the day of small things ?   *Zechariah, iv. 10.*

6033. I was wounded in the house of my friends.   *Ibid., xiii. 6.*

6034. But unto you that fear my name shall the Sun of righteousness arise
with healing in his wings.   *Malachi, iv. 2.*

The New Testament

6035. The voice of one crying in the wilderness, Prepare ye the way of the
Lord, make his paths straight.   *Matthew, iii. 3.*

6036 O generation of vipers, who hath warned you to flee from the wrath
to come ?   *Ibid., 7.*

6037. And now also the axe is laid unto the root of the trees.

Ibid., 10 and Luke, iii. 9.

6038. Man shall not live by bread alone, but by every word that proceedeth
out of the mouth of God.   *Ibid., iv. 4.*

6039. Blessed are the meek : for they shall inherit the earth.   *Ibid., v. 5.*

6040. Blessed are the pure in heart : for they shall see God.   *Ibid., 8.*

6041. Blessed are the peacemakers : for they shall be called the children
of God.   *Ibid., 9.*

6042. Ye are the salt of the earth : but if the salt have lost his savour, where-
with shall it be salted ?   *Ibid., 13*

6043. Ye are the light of the world. A city that is set on an hill cannot be
hid.   *Ibid., 14.*

6044. Let your light so shine before men, that they may see your good works,
and glorify your Father which is in heaven.   *Ibid., 16.*

6045. Whosoever shall say, Thou fool, shall be in danger of hell fire.

Ibid., 22.

6046. Till thou hast paid the uttermost farthing.   *Ibid., 26.*

6047. An eye for an eye, and a tooth for a tooth.   *Ibid., 38.*

6048. Whosoever shall smite thee on thy right cheek, turn to him the other
also.   *Ibid., 39.*

6049. Love your enemies.   *Ibid., 44.*

6050. He maketh his sun to rise on the evil and on the good, and sendeth
rain on the just and on the unjust.   *Ibid., 45.*

6051. When thou doest alms, let not thy left hand know what thy right hand doeth. Ibid., vi. 3.

6052. Our Father which art in heaven, Hallowed be thy name. Thy kingdom come. Thy will be done in earth, as it is in heaven. Give us this day our daily bread. And forgive us our debts, as we forgive our debtors. And lead us not into temptation, but deliver us from evil : For thine is the kingdom, and the power, and the glory, for ever. Amen. Ibid., 9.

6053. Where moth and rust doth corrupt, and where thieves break through and steal. Ibid., 19.

6054. Where your treasure is, there will your heart be also. Ibid., 21.

6055. No man can serve two masters. Ibid., 24.

6056. Ye cannot serve God and mammon. Ibid.

6057. Which of you by taking thought can add one cubit unto his stature ? Ibid., 27.

6058. Consider the lilies of the field, how they grow ; they toil not, neither do they spin. Ibid., 28.

6059. Seek ye first the kingdom of God, and his righteousness ; and all these things shall be added unto you. Ibid., 33.

6060. Take therefore no thought for the morrow ; for the morrow shall take thought for the things of itself. Sufficient unto the day is the evil thereof. Ibid., 34.

6061. Judge not, that ye be not judged. Ibid., vii. 1.

6062. Why beholdest thou the mote that is in thy brother's eye, but considerest not the beam that is in thine own eye ? Ibid., 3.

6063. Neither cast ye your pearls before swine. Ibid., 6.

6064. Ask, and it shall be given you ; seek, and ye shall find ; knock, and it shall be opened unto you. Ibid., 7.

6065. What man is there of you, whom if his son ask bread, will he give him a stone ? Ibid., 9.

6066. Therefore all things whatsoever ye would that men should do to you, do ye even so to them : for this is the law and the prophets. Ibid., 12.

6067. Wide is the gate, and broad is the way, that leadeth to destruction, and many there be which go in thereat. Ibid., 13.

6068. Strait is the gate, and narrow is the way, which leadeth unto life, anf few there be that find it. Ibid., 14.

6069. Beware of false prophets, which come to you in sheep's clothing, but inwardly they are ravening wolves. Ibid., 15.

6070. By their fruits ye shall know them. Ibid., 20.

6071. For he taught them as one having authority, and not as the scribes. Ibid., 29.

6072. There shall be weeping and gnashing of teeth. Ibid., viii. 12.

6073. The foxes have holes, and the birds of the air have nests ; but the Son of man hath not where to lay his head. Ibid., 20.

6074. Let the dead bury their dead. Ibid., 22.

6075. The harvest truly is plenteous, but the labourers are few. Ibid., ix. 37.

6076. Freely ye have received, freely give. Ibid., x. 8.

6077. Be ye therefore wise as serpents, and harmless as doves. Ibid., 16.

6078. The very hairs of your head are all numbered. Ibid., 30.

6079. He that findeth his life shall lose it : and he that loseth his life for my sake shall find it. Ibid., 39.

6080. What went ye out into the wilderness to see ? A reed shaken with the wind ? Ibid., xi. 7.

6081. Wisdom is justified of her children. Ibid., 19.

6082. Come unto me, all ye that labour and are heavy laden, and I will give you rest. Ibid., 28.

6083. He that is not with me is against me. Ibid., xii. 30 and *Luke*, xi. 23.

6084. Empty, swept, and garnished. Ibid., 44.

6085. The last state of that man is worse than the first. Ibid., 45.

6086. Some seeds fell by the way side. Ibid., xiii. 4.

6087. An enemy hath done this. Ibid., 28.

6088. When he had found one pearl of great price. Ibid., 46.

6089. A prophet is not without honour, save in his own country, and in his own house. Ibid., 57.

6090. Be of good cheer ; it is I ; be not afraid. Ibid., xiv. 27.

6091. If the blind lead the blind, both shall fall into the ditch.
Ibid., xv. 14.

6092. The dogs eat of the crumbs which fall from their masters' table.
Ibid., 27.

6093. Thou art Peter, and upon this rock I will build my church ; and the gates of hell shall not prevail against it. Ibid., xvi. 18.

6094. Get thee behind me, Satan. Ibid., 23.

6095. It is good for us to be here. Ibid., xvii. 4.

6096. Except ye be converted, and become as little children, ye shall not enter into the kingdom of heaven. Ibid., xviii. 3.

6097. But whoso shall offend one of these little ones which believe in me, it were better for him that a millstone were hanged about his neck and that he were drowned in the depth of the sea. Ibid., 6.

6098. If thine eye offend thee, pluck it out, and cast it from thee : it is better for thee to enter into life with one eye, rather than having two eyes to be cast into hell fire. Ibid., 9.

6099. Where two or three are gathered together in my name, there am I in the midst of them. Ibid., 20.

6100. Until seventy times seven. Ibid., 22.

6101. What therefore God hath joined together, let not man put asunder.
Ibid., xix. 6.

6102. Thou shalt love thy neighbour as thyself. Ibid., 19.

6103. It is easier for a camel to go through the eye of a needle, than for a rich man to enter into the kingdom of God. Ibid., 24.

6104. With men this is impossible ; but with God all things are possible.
Ibid., 26.

6105. But many that are first shall be last ; and the last shall be first.
Ibid., 30.

6106. Borne the burden and heat of the day. Ibid., xx. 12.

6107. The stone which the builders rejected, the same is become the head of the corner. Ibid., xxi. 42.

*o

6108. For many are called, but few are chosen. Ibid., xxii. 14.
6109. Render therefore unto Caesar the things which are Caesar's; and unto God the things that are God's. Ibid., 21.
6110. Ye pay tithe of mint and anise and cummin. Ibid., xxiii. 23.
6111. Blind guides, which strain at a gnat, and swallow a camel. Ibid., 24.
6112. Whited sepulchres, which indeed appear beautiful outward, but are within full of dead men's bones. Ibid., 27.
6113. Wars and rumour of wars. Ibid., xxiv. 6.
6114. For nation shall rise against nation, and kingdom against kingdom. Ibid., 7.
6115. The abomination of desolation. Ibid., 15.
6116. Wheresoever the carcase is, there will the eagles be gathered together. Ibid., 28.
6117. Eating and drinking, marrying and giving in marriage. Ibid., 38.
6118. Well done, thou good and faithful servant. Ibid., xxv. 21.
6119. Unto every one that hath shall be given, and he shall have abundance : but from him that hath not shall be taken away even that which he hath. Ibid., 29.
6120. I was a stranger, and ye took me in. Ibid., 35.
6121. Thirty pieces of silver. Ibid., xxvi. 15.
6122. Watch and pray, that ye enter not into temptation : the spirit indeed is willing, but the flesh is weak. Ibid., 41.
6123. All they that take the sword shall perish with the sword. Ibid., 52.
6124. Thy speech bewrayeth thee. Ibid., 73.
6125. He saved others ; himself he cannot save. Ibid., xxvii. 42.
6126. Eli, Eli, lama sabachthani ? that is to say, My God, my God, why hast thou forsaken me ? Ibid., 46.
6127. The sabbath was made for man, and not man for the sabbath. *Mark*, ii. 27.
6128. If a house be divided against itself, that house cannot stand. Ibid., iii. 25.
6129. He that hath ears to hear, let him hear. Ibid., iv. 9.
6130. My name is Legion. Ibid., v. 9.
6131. Clothed, and in his right mind. Ibid., 15.
6132. I see men as trees, walking. Ibid., viii. 24.
6133. What shall it profit a man, if he shall gain the whole world, and lose his own soul ? Ibid., 36.
6134. Where their worm dieth not, and the fire is not quenched. Ibid., ix. 44.
6135. Suffer the little children to come unto me, and forbid them not : for of such is the kingdom of God. Ibid., x. 14.
6136. Which devour widows' houses, and for a pretence make long prayers. Ibid., xii. 40.
6137. Go ye into all the world, and preach the gospel to every creature. Ibid., xvi. 15.
6138. Glory to God in the highest, and on earth peace, good will toward men. *Luke*, ii. 14.
6139. Physician, heal thyself. Ibid., iv. 23.
6140. The only son of his mother, and she was a widow. Ibid., vii. 12.

6141. No man, having put his hand to the plough and looking back, is fit for the kingdom of God. *Ibid.*, ix. 62.

6142. The labourer is worthy of his hire. *Ibid.*, x. 7.

6143. He passed by on the other side. *Ibid.*, 31.

6144. Go, and do thou likewise. *Ibid.*, 37.

6145. But one thing is needful : and Mary hath chosen that good part, which shall not be taken away from her. *Ibid.*, 42.

6146. Thou fool, this night thy soul shall be required of thee. *Ibid.*, xii. 20.

6147. Let your loins be girded about, and your lights burning. *Ibid.*, 35.

6148. Friend, go up higher. *Ibid.*, xiv. 10.

6149. For whosoever exalteth himself shall be abased ; and he that humbleth himself shall be exalted. *Ibid.*, 11.

6150. I have married a wife, and therefore I cannot come. *Ibid.*, 20.

6151. The poor, and the maimed, and the halt, and the blind. *Ibid.*, 21.

6152. Go out into the highways and hedges, and compel them to come in. *Ibid.*, 23.

6153. Rejoice with me ; for I have found my sheep which was lost. *Ibid.*, xv. 6.

6154. Joy shall be in heaven over one sinner that repenteth, more than over ninety and nine just persons, which need no repentance. *Ibid.*, 7.

6155. Wasted his substance with riotous living. *Ibid.*, 13.

6156. And he would fain have filled his belly with the husks that the swine did eat. *Ibid.*, 16.

6157. I cannot dig ; to beg I am ashamed. *Ibid.*, xvi. 3.

6158. The children of this world are in their generation wiser than the children of light. *Ibid.*, 8.

6159. Make to yourselves friends of the mammon of unrighteousness. *Ibid.*, 9.

6160. There was a certain rich man, which was clothed in purple and fine linen, and fared sumptuously every day. *Ibid.*, 19.

6161. Between us and you there is a great gulf fixed. *Ibid.*, 26.

6162. We are unprofitable servants : we have done that which was our duty to do. *Ibid.*, xvii. 10.

6163. The kingdom of God is within you. *Ibid.*, 21.

6164. Remember Lot's wife. *Ibid.*, 32.

6165. God, I thank thee, that I am not as other men are, extortioners, unjust, adulterers, or even as this publican. *Ibid.*, xviii. 11.

6166. God be merciful to me a sinner. *Ibid.*, 13.

6167. Out of thine own mouth will I judge thee. *Ibid.*, xix. 22.

6168. For if they do these things in a green tree, what shall be done in the dry ? *Ibid.*, xxiii. 31.

6169. Father, forgive them ; for they know not what they do. *Ibid.*, 34.

6170. Whose shoe's latchet I am not worthy to unloose. *John*, i. 27.

6171. Can there any good thing come out of Nazareth ? *Ibid.*, 46.

6172. The wind bloweth where it listeth, and thou hearest the sound thereof, but canst not tell whence it cometh, and whither it goeth. *Ibid.*, iii. 8.

6173. God so loved the world, that he gave his only begotten Son, that whosoever believeth in him should not perish, but have everlasting life. *Ibid.*, 16.

6174. Men loved darkness rather than light, because their deeds were evil.
           Ibid., 19.
6175. He was a burning and a shining light.   Ibid., v. 35.
6176. Judge not according to the appearance.   Ibid., vii. 24.
6177. He that is without sin among you, let him first cast a stone at her.
           Ibid., viii. 7.
6178. The truth shall make you free.   Ibid., 32.
6179. The night cometh, when no man can work.   Ibid., ix. 4.
6180. The hireling fleeth, because he is an hireling, and careth not for the
     sheep.   Ibid., x. 13.
6181. I am the resurrection, and the life.   Ibid., xi. 25.
6182. For the poor always ye have with you.   Ibid., xii. 8.
6183. A new commandment I give unto you, That ye love one another.
           Ibid., xiii. 34.
6184. Let not your heart be troubled : ye believe in God, believe also in me.
           Ibid., xiv. 1.
6185. In my Father's house are many mansions.   Ibid., 2.
6186. Greater love hath no man than this, that a man lay down his life for
     his friends.   Ibid., xv. 13.
6187. What I have written I have written.   Ibid., xix. 22.
6188. Silver and gold have I none; but such as I have give I thee. *Acts*, iii. 6.
6189. Thy money perish with thee.   Ibid., viii. 20.
6190. Breathing out threatenings and slaughter.   Ibid., ix. 1.
6191. It is hard for thee to kick against the pricks.   Ibid., 5.
6192. God is no respecter of persons.   Ibid., x. 34.
6193. Come over into Macedonia, and help us.   Ibid., xvi. 9.
6194. Certain lewd fellows of the baser sort.   Ibid., xvii. 5.
6195. For in him we live, and move, and have our being.   Ibid., 28.
6196. Gallio cared for none of those things.   Ibid., xviii. 17.
6197. Great is Diana of the Ephesians.   Ibid., xix. 34.
6198. It is more blessed to give than to receive.   Ibid., xx. 35.
6199. A citizen of no mean city.   Ibid., xxi. 39.
6200. Brought up in this city at the feet of Gamaliel.   Ibid., xxii. 3.
6201. With a great sum obtained I this freedom.   Ibid., 28.
6202. Hast thou appealed unto Caesar ?   Unto Caesar shalt thou go.
           Ibid., xxv. 12.
6203. Paul, thou art beside thyself ; much learning doth make thee mad.
           Ibid., xxvi. 24.
6204. Words of truth and soberness.   Ibid., 25.
6205. For this thing was not done in a corner.   Ibid., 26.
6206. Almost thou persuadest me to be a Christian.   Ibid., 28.
6207. They cast four anchors out of the stern, and wished for the day.
           Ibid., xxvii. 29.
6208. A law unto themselves.   *Romans*, ii. 14.
6209. (As some affirm that we say) Let us do evil, that good may come.
           Ibid., iii. 8.
6210. The wages of sin is death.   Ibid., vi. 23.
6211. And we know that all things work together for good to them that
     love God.   Ibid., viii. 28.

6212. If God be for us, who can be against us ? Ibid., 31.

6213. For I am persuaded that neither death, nor life, nor angels, nor principalities, nor powers, nor things present, nor things to come, Nor height, nor depth, nor any other creature, shall be able to separate us from the love of God, which is in Christ Jesus our Lord. Ibid., 38.

6214. Be not wise in your own conceits. Ibid., xii. 16.

6215. Vengeance is mine ; I will repay, saith the Lord. Ibid., 19.

6216. Therefore if thine enemy hunger, feed him ; if he thirst, give him drink : for in so doing thou shalt heap coals of fire on his head. Ibid., 20.

6217. Be not overcome of evil, but overcome evil with good. Ibid., 21.

6218. The powers that be are ordained of God. Ibid., xiii. 1.

6219. The night is far spent, the day is at hand. Ibid., 12.

6220. None of us liveth to himself. Ibid., xiv. 7.

6221. Absent in body, but present in spirit. 1 *Corinthians*, v. 3.

6222. Know ye not that a little leaven leaveneth the whole lump ? Ibid., 6.

6223. It is better to marry than to burn. Ibid., vii. 9.

6224. I am made all things to all men. Ibid., ix. 22.

6225. But I keep under my body, and bring it into subjection. Ibid., 27.

6226. All things are lawful for me, but all things are not expedient. Ibid., x. 23.

6227. For the earth is the Lord's, and the fulness thereof. Ibid., 26.

6228. If a woman have long hair, it is a glory to her. Ibid., xi. 15.

6229. Though I speak with the tongues of men and of angels, and have not charity, I am become as sounding brass, or a tinkling cymbal. Ibid., xiii. 1.

6230. When I was a child, I spake as a child, I understood as a child, I thought as a child : but when I became a man, I put away childish things. Ibid., 11.

6231. For now we see through a glass, darkly ; but then face to face. Ibid., 12.

6232. And now abideth faith, hope, charity, these three ; but the greatest of these is charity. Ibid., 13.

6233. Let all things be done decently and in order. Ibid., xiv. 40.

6234. Let us eat and drink ; for to-morrow we die. Ibid., xv. 32.

6235. Behold, I show you a mystery ; We shall not all sleep, but we shall all be changed, In a moment, in the twinkling of an eye, at the last trump. Ibid., 51.

6236. O death, where is thy sting ? O grave, where is thy victory ? Ibid., 55.

6237. Quit you like men, be strong. Ibid., xvi. 13.

6238. Not of the letter, but of the spirit. 2 *Corinthians*, iii. 6.

6239. For we walk by faith, not by sight. Ibid., v. 7.

6240. God loveth a cheerful giver. Ibid., ix. 7.

6241. For ye suffer fools gladly, seeing ye yourselves are wise. Ibid., xi. 19.

6242. A thorn in the flesh. Ibid., xii. 7.

6243. And he said unto me, My grace is sufficient for thee : for my strength is made perfect in weakness. Ibid., 9.

6244. The right hands of fellowship. *Galatians*, ii. 9.

6245. God is not mocked : for whatsoever a man soweth, that shall he also
reap. *Ibid.*, vi. 7.

6246. Let us not be weary in well-doing. *Ibid.*, 9.

6247. Be ye angry, and sin not : let not the sun go down upon your wrath.
Ephesians, iv. 26.

6248. Put on the whole armour of God. *Ibid.*, vi. 11.

6249. For me to live is Christ, and to die is gain. *Philippians*, i. 21.

6250. Work out your own salvation with fear and trembling. *Ibid.*, ii. 12.

6251. Whose God is their belly, and whose glory is in their shame.
Ibid., iii. 19.

6252. The peace of God, which passeth all understanding. *Ibid.*, iv. 7.

6253. Whatsoever things are true, whatsoever things are honest, whatsoever
things are just, whatsoever things are pure, whatsoever things are
lovely, whatsoever things are of good report ; if there be any virtue,
and if there be any praise, think on these things. *Ibid.*, 8.

6254. Touch not, taste not, handle not. *Colossians*, ii. 21.

6255. Labour of love. 1 *Thessalonians*, i. 3.

6256. Study to be quiet. *Ibid.*, iv. 11.

6257. Pray without ceasing. *Ibid.*, v. 17.

6258. Prove all things ; hold fast that which is good. *Ibid.*, 21.

6259. Not greedy of filthy lucre. 1 *Timothy*, iii. 3.

6260. Drink no longer water, but use a little wine for thy stomach's sake
and thine often infirmities. *Ibid.*, v. 23.

6261. The love of money is the root of all evil. *Ibid.*, vi. 10.

6262. Fight the good fight. *Ibid.*, 12.

6263. Science falsely so called. *Ibid.*, 20.

6264. I have fought a good fight, I have finished my course, I have kept
the faith. 2 *Timothy*, iv. 7.

6265. Unto the pure all things are pure. *Titus*, i. 15.

6266. Faith is the substance of things hoped for, the evidence of things not
seen. *Hebrews*, xi. 1.

6267. Whom the Lord loveth he chasteneth. *Ibid.*, xii. 6.

6268. Let brotherly love continue. *Ibid.*, xiii. 1.

6269. Be not forgetful to entertain strangers : for thereby some have entertained angels unawares. *Ibid.*, 2.

6270. Jesus Christ the same yesterday, and to-day, and for ever. *Ibid.*, 8.

6271. The tongue can no man tame ; it is an unruly evil. *James*, iii. 8.
[Commonly misquoted, ' The tongue is an unruly member.']

6272. Resist the devil, and he will flee from you. *Ibid.*, iv. 7.

6273. Honour all men. Love the brotherhood. Fear God. Honour the
king. 1 *Peter*, ii. 17.

6274. Giving honour unto the wife, as unto the weaker vessel. *Ibid.*, iii. 7.

6275. Charity shall cover the multitude of sins. *Ibid.*, iv. 8.

6276. Be sober, be vigilant ; because your adversary the devil, as a roaring
lion, walketh about, seeking whom he may devour. *Ibid.*, v. 8.

6277. The dog is turned to his own vomit again ; and the sow that was
washed to her wallowing in the mire. 2 *Peter*, ii. 22.

6278. Bowels of compassion. 1 *John*, iii. 17.

6279. God is love. *Ibid.*, iv. 8.

6280. There is no fear in love ; but perfect love casteth out fear.   Ibid., 18.
6281. Be thou faithful unto death, and I will give thee a crown of
          life.   *Revelation*, ii. 10.
6282. He shall rule them with a rod of iron.   Ibid., 27.
6283. I know thy works, that thou art neither cold nor hot : I would thou
          wert cold or hot.   Ibid., iii. 15.
6284. He went forth conquering, and to conquer.   Ibid., vi. 2.
6285. And I looked, and behold a pale horse : and his name that sat on him
          was Death.   Ibid., 8.
6286. And I saw a new heaven and a new earth : for the first heaven and the
          first earth were passed away ; and there was no more sea.

                                                                  Ibid., xxi. 1.

6287. And God shall wipe away all tears from their eyes ; and there shall
          be no more death, neither sorrow, nor crying, neither shall there be
          any more pain : for the former things are passed away. And he that
          sat upon the throne said, Behold, I make all things new.

                                                                  Ibid., xxi. 4.

6288. I am Alpha and Omega, the beginning and the end, the first and the
          last.   Ibid., xxii. 13.

THE APOCRYPHA

6289. Great is truth, and mighty above all things.   1 *Esdras*, iv. 41
6290. Miss not the discourse of the elders.   *Ecclesiasticus*, viii. 9.
6291. He that toucheth pitch shall be defiled therewith.   Ibid., xiii. 1.
6292. As the clear light is upon the holy candlestick, so is the beauty of the
          face in ripe age.   Ibid., xxvi. 17.
6293. Whose talk is of bullocks.   Ibid., xxxviii. 25.
6294. Let us now praise famous men, and our fathers that begat us.

                                                                 Ibid., xliv. 1.

6295. It was an holy and good thought.   2 *Maccabees*, xii. 45.
6296. And Nicanor lay dead in his harness.   Ibid., xv. 28.

THE BOOK OF COMMON PRAYER

6297. We have left undone those things which we ought to have done ; And
          we have done those things which we ought not to have done.

                               Morning Prayer.   General Confession.

6298. The noble army of Martyrs.   Ibid., *Te Deum.*
6299. O all ye Works of the Lord, bless ye the Lord : praise him, and magnify
          him for ever.   Ibid., *Benedicite.*
6300. Give peace in our time, O Lord.   Ibid., *Versicles.*
6301. Whose service is perfect freedom.

                          Ibid., *Second Collect, for Peace.*

6302. Have mercy upon us miserable sinners.   *Litany.*
6303. From envy, hatred, and malice, and all uncharitableness.   Ibid.
6304. The world, the flesh, and the devil.   Ibid.
6305. From battle and murder, and from sudden death.   Ibid.
6306. All sorts and conditions of men.

                          Prayer for All Conditions of Men

6307. Read, mark, learn, and inwardly digest.

Collect for the Second Sunday in Advent.

6308. Jews, Turks, Infidels, and Heretics.

Third Collect for Good Friday.

6309. Renounce the devil and all his works.   *Baptism of Infants.*

6310. The pomps and vanity of this wicked world.   *Catechism.*

6311. To keep my hands from picking and stealing.   Ibid.

6312. To do my duty in that state of life, unto which it shall please God to call me.   Ibid.

6313. An outward and visible sign of an inward and spiritual grace.   Ibid.

6314. If any of you know cause or just impediment.

Solemnisation of Matrimony.

6315. Brute beasts that have no understanding.   Ibid.

6316. Let him now speak, or else hereafter for ever hold his peace.   Ibid.

6317. To have and to hold from this day forward, for better for worse, for richer for poorer, in sickness and in health, to love and to cherish, till death us do part.   Ibid.

6318. To love, cherish, and obey.   Ibid.

6319. With this ring I thee wed, with my body I thee worship, and with all my worldly goods I thee endow.   Ibid.

6320. Those whom God hath joined together let no man put asunder.   Ibid.

6321. Laid violent hands upon themselves.   *Burial of the Dead.*

6322. Man that is born of a woman hath but a short time to live, and is full of misery.   Ibid.

6323. In the midst of life we are in death.   Ibid.

6324. We therefore commit his body to the ground ; earth to earth, ashes to ashes, dust to dust ; in sure and certain hope of the Resurrection to eternal life.   Ibid.

6325. We therefore commit his body to the deep, to be turned into corruption, looking for the resurrection of the body (when the Sea shall give up her dead).

Form of Prayer to be used at the Burial of their Dead at Sea.

6326. Of Works of Supererogation.

Articles of Religion. Title of Article xiv.

6327. A fond thing vainly invented.   Ibid., xxii.   *Of Purgatory.*

6328. A man may not marry his Grandmother.

Table of Kindred and Affinity.

AUTHORSHIP UNKNOWN

EARLY ENGLISH

6329. Þæs ofereode, þisses swa mæg !
    —That was got over, so may this be !   *Deor's Lament.*

6330. Hige sceal þe heardra, heorte þe cenre,
    Mod sceal þe mare, þe ure mægen lytlað.
    —Spirit shall be the stouter, heart the bolder, courage
       shall be the greater, as our might lessens.
                The Battle of Maldon, 312.

6331. Sumer is icumen in,
    Lhude sing cuccu !   *Cuckoo Song.*

6332. Everyman, I will go with thee, and be thy guide,
    In thy most need to go by thy side. [Knowledge.]
                Everyman, 522.

BALLADS

6333. I saw the new moon late yestreen
    Wi' the auld moon in her arm.   *Sir Patrick Spens.*

6334. Yestreen the Queen had four Maries,
    The night she'll hae but three ;
    There was Marie Seaton, and Marie Beaton,
    And Marie Carmichael, and me.   *The Queen's Maries.*

6335. As I was walking all alane
    I heard twa corbies making a mane.
    The tane unto the tither did say,
    ' Whar sall we gang and dine the day ?   *The Twa Corbies.*

6336. This ae nighte, this ae nighte,
    Every nighte and alle,
    Fire and fleet and candle-lighte,
    And Christe receive thy saule.   *A Lyke-Wake Dirge.*

6337. I wish I were where Helen lies,
    Night and day on me she cries ;
    O that I were where Helen lies,
    On fair Kirkconnell lea !   *Helen of Kirkconnell.*

6338. I lighted down my sword to draw,
    I hackèd him in pieces sma',
    I hackèd him in pieces sma',
    For her sake that died for me.   Ibid.

6339. Fight on, my men, Sir Andrew says,
    A little I'm hurt, but yet not slain ;
    I'll but lie down and bleed awhile,
    And then I'll rise and fight again.
           Ballad of Sir Andrew Barton.

SONGS AND CAROLS

6340. God rest you merry, gentlemen,
    Let nothing you dismay.   *God rest you Merry.*

6341. Please her the best you may,
    She looks another way.
    Alas and well-a-day !
        Phillida flouts me.   *The Disdainful Shepherdess.*

6342. There is a lady sweet and kind,
　　　　Was never face so pleased my mind ;
　　　　I did but see her passing by,
　　　　And yet I love her till I die.
　　　　　　　　　　　　There is a Lady Sweet and Kind.

6343. My love in her attire doth show her wit,
　　　　　It doth so well become her ;
　　　　For every season she hath dressings fit,
　　　　　For Winter, Spring, and Summer.
　　　　　　No beauty she doth miss
　　　　　　　When all her robes are on :
　　　　　　But Beauty's self she is
　　　　　　　When all her robes are gone.   *Madrigal.*

6344. 　　　I saw my Lady weep,
　　　　And Sorrow proud to be advancèd so
　　　　In those fair eyes where all perfections keep.
　　　　　　　John Dowland's *Third Book of Songs or Airs*, iii.

6345. Weep you no more, sad fountains ;
　　　　　What need you flow so fast ?
　　　　Look how the snowy mountains
　　　　　Heaven's sun doth gently waste !   Ibid., viii.

6346. Love not me for comely grace,
　　　　For my pleasing eye or face,
　　　　Nor for any outward part,
　　　　No, nor for a constant heart.   *Love not me for Comely Grace.*

6347. Over the mountains
　　　　　And over the waves,
　　　　Under the fountains
　　　　　And under the graves ;
　　　　Under floods that are deepest,
　　　　　Which Neptune obey,
　　　　Over rocks that are steepest,
　　　　　Love will find out the way.   *Love will find out the Way.*

6348. Begone, dull Care ! I prithee begone from me !
　　　　Begone, dull Care ! thou and I shall never agree.
　　　　　　　　　　　　　　　　Begone Dull Care.

6349. Though little, I'll work as hard as a Turk,
　　　　　If you'll give me employ,
　　　　To plough and sow, and reap and mow,
　　　　　And be a farmer's boy.   *The Farmer's Boy.*

6350. And this is law, I will maintain,
　　　　　Unto my dying day, Sir,
　　　　That whatsoever king shall reign,
　　　　　I will be the Vicar of Bray, Sir.   *The Vicar of Bray.*

6351. God save our gracious king,
　　　　Long live our noble king,
　　　　　God save the king !
　　　　Send him victorious,
　　　　Happy and glorious,
　　　　Long to reign over us,
　　　　　God save the king !   *God save the King.*
　　　　　　[Authorship claimed for Henry Carey and for James
　　　　　　Oswald.]

6352. ' Where are you going, my pretty maid ? '
       ' I am going a-milking, sir,' she said.
                          Where are you going, my Pretty Maid?

6353. ' What is your fortune, my pretty maid ? '
       ' My face is my fortune, sir,' she said.
       ' Then I won't marry you, my pretty maid.'
       ' Nobody asked you, sir,' she said.   Ibid.

6354. The noble Duke of York,
       He had ten thousand men,
       He marched them up to the top of the hill,
       And he marched them down again.
       When they were up, they were up,
       And when they were down, they were down,
       And when they were only half-way up,
         They were neither up nor down.   *The Noble Duke of York.*

6355. It is good to be merry and wise,
       It is good to be honest and true,
       It is best to be off with the old love,
       Before you are on with the new.
                          Songs of England and Scotland, II. 73.

6356. From the lone sheiling of the misty island
           Mountains divide us, and the waste of seas—
       Yet still the blood is strong, the heart is Highland,
           And we in dreams behold the Hebrides.
                                        Canadian Boat Song.

6357. Oh, ye'll tak' the high road, and I'll tak' the low road,
       And I'll be in Scotland afore ye,
       But me and my true love will never meet again,
       On the bonny, bonny banks o' Loch Lomond.
                          The Bonny Banks o' Loch Lomond.

6358. Farewell and adieu to you, fair Spanish Ladies,
           Farewell and adieu to you, Ladies of Spain,
       For we've received orders to sail for old England,
           But we hope in a short time to see you again.
               We'll rant and we'll roar, all o'er the wild ocean,
               We'll rant and we'll roar, all o'er the wild seas,
       Until we strike soundings in the Channel of Old England,
       From Ushant to Scilly is thirty-five leagues.   *Spanish Ladies.*

6359. Casey Jones, he mounted to the cabin,
       Casey Jones, with his orders in his hand !
       Casey Jones, he mounted to the cabin,
       Took his farewell trip into the promised land.   *Casey Jones.*

6360. Frankie and Johnny were lovers, O Lordy, how they could love.
       Swore to be true to each other, true as the stars above ;
           He was her man, and he done her wrong.
                                        Frankie and Johnny.

EPIGRAMS

6361. Had you seen these roads before they were made,
           You would lift up your hands and bless General Wade.
                   On roads made in the Scottish highlands, 1726–1729.

6362. Great Chatham, with his sabre drawn,
      Stood waiting for Sir Richard Strachan ;
      Sir Richard, longing to be at 'em,
      Stood waiting for the Earl of Chatham.
                          On the Walcheren Expedition, 1809.

6363. On Waterloo's ensanguined plain,
      Full many a gallant man was slain,
      But none, by bullet or by shot,
      Fell half so flat as Walter Scott.
                          On Walter Scott's ' Field of Waterloo.'

6364. I come first. My name is Jowett.
      I am the Master of the College.
      Everything that is, I know it.
      If I don't, it isn't knowledge.   *The Balliol Masque.*

6365. My name is George Nathaniel Curzon.
      I am a most superior person.   *Ibid.*

LIMERICKS

6366. There was a young lady of Riga,
      Who went for ride on a tiger ;
            They returned from the ride
            With the lady inside,
      And a smile on the face of the tiger.

6367. There was a young man of Devizes,
      Whose ears were of different sizes ;
            The one that was small
            Was no use at all ;
      The other won hundreds of prizes.

6368. There was an old man of Khartoum,
      Who kept two black sheep in his room.
            ' They remind me,' he said,
            ' Of two friends who are dead.'
      But he never would tell us of whom.

6369. There was a young man of Boulogne,
      Who sang a most topical song.
            It wasn't the words
            That frightened the birds,
      But the horrible *double entendre.*

6370. There was a young curate of Salisbury,
      Whose manners were quite halisbury-scalisbury ;
            He ran about Hampshire
            Without any pampshire,
      Till the vicar compelled him to walisbury.
      [Salisbury = Sarum, Hampshire = Hants.]

6371. There was an old man of Nantucket
      Who kept all his cash in a bucket,
            But his daughter, named Nan,
            Ran away with a man,
      And as for the bucket, Nantucket.

6372. There was a young lady named Bright,
      Who could travel much faster than light.
            She started one day
            In the relative way,
      And came back on the previous night.

6373. There's a wonderful family called Stein,
    There's Gert and there's Epp and there's Ein ;
        Gert's poems are bunk,
        Epp's statues are junk,
    And no one can understand Ein.
      [Gertrude Stein, Jacob Epstein, Albert Einstein.]

EPITAPHS AND INSCRIPTIONS

6374. What we gave, we have ;
    What we spent, we had ;
    What we left, we lost.   *Epitaph on the Earl of Devon*, 1419.

6375. Here sleeps in peace a Hampshire grenadier,
    Who caught his death by drinking cold small beer;
    Soldiers, take heed from his untimely fall,
    And when you're hot, drink strong, or not at all.
          From a Winchester churchyard.

6376. Here lie I, Martin Elginbrodde ;
    Hae mercy o' my soul, Lord God ;
    As I wad do, were I Lord God,
    And ye were Martin Elginbrodde.
        Quoted by George MacDonald in ' David Elginbrod.'

6377. Here lies a poor woman who always was tired,
    She lived in a house where help wasn't hired.
    The last words she said were : ' Dear friends, I am going
    Where washing ain't wanted, nor sweeping, nor sewing ;
    And everything there is exact to my wishes,
    For where folk don't eat there's no washing of dishes.
    In heaven loud anthems for ever are ringing,
    But having no voice I'll keep clear of the singing.
    Don't mourn for me now, don't mourn for me never ;
    I'm going to do nothing for ever and ever.'
          The Tired Woman's Epitaph.

6378. This is the grave of Mike O'Day
    Who died maintaining his right of way.
    His right was clear, his will was strong,
    But he's just as dead as if he'd been wrong.   *Modern.*

6379. Give me a good digestion, Lord,
    And also something to digest ;
    Give me a healthy body, Lord,
      With sense to keep it at its best ;
    Give me a healthy mind, good Lord,
      To keep the good and pure in sight,
    Which seeing sin is not appalled
      But finds a way to set it right ;
    Give me a mind that is not bored,
      That does not whimper, whine, or sigh ;
    Don't let me worry overmuch
      About the fussy thing called I.
    Give me a sense of humour, Lord,
      Give me the grace to see a joke,
    To get some happiness from life
      And pass it on to other folk.
          Prayer found in Chester Cathedral.

PARODIES]

6380. Ye gods ! annihilate but space and time
And make two lovers happy.
Martinus Scriblerus on the Art of Sinking in Poetry, xi.

6381. And thou Dalhousie, the great God of War,
Lieutenant-Colonel to the Earl of Mar. Ibid.
[Both of these are often ascribed to Pope.]

6382. He killed the noble Mudjokivis.
Of the skin he made him mittens,
Made them with the fur side inside
Made them with the skin side outside.
He, to get the warm side inside,
Put the inside skin side outside.
He, to get the cold side outside,
Put the warm side fur side inside.
That's why he put the fur side inside,
Why he put the skin side outside,
Why he turned them inside outside. *The Modern Hiawatha.*

WEATHER AND CALENDAR RHYMES

6383. First it rained, and then it snew,
Then it friz, and then it thew
And then it friz again.

6384. Please to remember
The fifth of November,
Gunpowder treason and plot ;
I see no reason
Why gunpowder treason
Should ever be forgot. *On Guy Fawkes Day.*

6385. Christmas is coming, the geese are getting fat,
Please put a penny in an old man's hat.
If you haven't got a penny, a ha'penny will do,
If you haven't got a ha'penny, God bless you.

Beggar's rhyme.

6386. Thirty days hath September,
April, June, and November ;
All the rest have thirty-one,
Excepting February alone,
Which has but twenty-eight days clear,
And twenty-nine at each leap year. *Old rhyme.*
[Many different versions.]

6387. The Ram, the Bull, the Heavenly Twins,
And next the Crab, the Lion shines,
The Virgin, and the Scales,
The Scorpion, Archer, and He-Goat,
The Man that bears the Watering-Pot,
And Fish with glittering tails. *Signs of the Zodiac.*

PROVERBS

COLLECTIONS OF PROVERBS REFERRED TO

[Opposite each proverb is indicated either the earliest of the standard collections in which it appears, or the century of its earliest-noted appearance in literature. References in brackets are to older forms of what is in essentials the same proverb. In many cases, of course, the proverb is older than any reference given.]

A. H.	A. Henderson, *Scottish Proverbs*, 1832.
B.	H. G. Bohn, *A Handbook of Proverbs*, 1855.
C.	J. Clarke, *Paroemiologia Anglo-Latina*, 1639.
C. R.	W. Camden, *Remaines Concerning Britaine*, 1614.
D.	M. A. Denham, *A Collection of Proverbs and Popular Sayings relating to the Seasons, the Weather, and Agricultural Pursuits*, 1846.
D. F.	D. Fergusson, *Scottish Proverbs*, 1641.
F.	T. Fuller, *Gnomologia : Adagies and Proverbs.* 1732.
G. H.	G. Herbert, *Outlandish Proverbs*, 1640 ; 2nd edition entitled *Jacula Prudentum*, 1651.
H.	J. Heywood, *A Dialogue containing the number in effect of all the Proverbs in the English Tongue*, 1546.
I.	R. Inwards, *Weather Lore : A Collection of Proverbs, Sayings and Rules concerning the Weather*, 1869.
J. H.	J. Howell, *Proverbs*, 1659.
K.	J. Kelly, *Complete Collection of Scottish Proverbs*, 1721.
L.	V. S. Lean, *Collectanea*, 1902–4.
P. R. A.	B. Franklin, *Poor Richard's Almanack*, 1758.
R.	J Ray, *English Proverbs*, 1670 and later editions.
T. D.	T. Draxe, *Bibliotheca Scholastica Instructissima, or A Treasury of Ancient Adagies and Sententious Proverbs*, 1616.
W. H.	W. C. Hazlitt, *English Proverbs and Proverbial Phrases*, 1869.

PROVERBS

6388. A bad bush is better than the open field.	*R.*
6389. A bad excuse is better than none.	16th cent.
6390. A bad penny always comes back.	19th cent.
6391. A bad workman quarrels with his tools.	*G. H.*
6392. A baker's wife may bite of a bun,	
A brewer's wife may drink of a tun,	
A fishmonger's wife may feed of a conger,	
But a servingman's wife may starve for hunger.	16th cent.
6393. A bald head is soon shaven.	*R.*
6394. A barber learns to shave by shaving fools.	*R.*
6395. A bargain is a bargain.	16th cent.
6396. A barley-corn is better than a diamond to a cock.	16th cent.
6397. A beggar can never be bankrupt.	*C.*
6398. A beggar's purse is bottomless.	16th cent.
6399. A belly full of gluttony will never study willingly.	*R.*
6400. A bird in the hand is worth two in the bush.	*Latin*
6401. A bit in the morning is better than nothing all day.	*R.*
6402. A black hen lays a white egg.	*French*
6403. A black [=dark] man is a jewel [*or* pearl] in a fair woman's eye.	
	R. (16th cent.)
6404. A black plum is as sweet as a white.	*T.D.*
6405. A blate [=shy] cat makes a proud mouse.	*D. F.*
6406. A blind man cannot judge colours.	*Latin*
6407. A blind man will not thank you for a looking-glass.	*F.*
6408. A blustering night, a fair day.	*G.H.*
6409. A boaster and a liar are all one.	14th cent.
6410. A bonny bride is soon buskit [=dressed].	*D.F.*
6411. A book that is shut is but a block.	*F.*
6412. A borrowed loan should come laughing home.	*F.*
6413. A bow long bent grows weak.	*H.*
6414. A bribe will enter without knocking.	*T.D.*
6415. A broken friendship may be soldered, but will never be sound.	*F.*
6416. A broken sleeve holdeth the arm back.	15th cent.
6417. A bully is always a coward.	19th cent.
6418. A bushel of March dust is worth a king's ransom.	16th cent.
6419. A buxom widow must be either married, buried, or shut up in	
a convent.	*Spanish*
6420. A carrion kite will never be a good hawk.	16th cent.
6421. A cat has nine lives.	*H.*
6422. A cat in gloves catches no mice.	16th cent.
6423. A cat may look at a king.	*H.*
6424. A cat's walk : a little way and back.	*W. H.*
6425. A child may have too much of his mother's blessing.	*C.*
6426. A chip of the old block.	17th cent.
6427. A city that parleys is half gotten.	*G. H.*
6428. A civil denial is better than a rude grant.	*F.*
6429. A close mouth catches no flies.	*Italian*

6430. A cock is crouse on his ain midden [*or* bold on his own
dunghill]   *Latin*

6431. A cold hand and a warm heart.   L.

6432. A cold May and a windy
Makes a full barn and a findy [=solid].   R.

6433. A collier's cow and an alewife's sow are always well fed. R.

6434. A covetous man is good to none, but worst to himself.   *Latin*

6435. A crab of the wood is sauce very good
For a crab of the sea.
The wood of a crab is good for a drab
That will not her husband obey.   *J. H.*

6436. A cracked bell can never sound well.   *F.*

6437. A crafty knave needs no broker.   *H.*

6438. A creaking gate [*or* door] hangs long. [Used figuratively of
long-lived invalids.]   18th cent.

6439. A cup in the pate is a mile in the gate [=way].   17th cent.

6440. A curst cow has short horns.   *Latin*

6441. A danger foreseen is half avoided.   *F.*

6442. A dear ship stands long in the haven.   *D. F.*

6443. A diligent scholar, and the master's paid.   *G. H.*

6444. A dog will not howl if you beat him with a bone.   *K. (J. H.)*

6445. A dog's nose and a maid's knees are always cold.   *R. (J. H.)*

6446. A drowning man will catch at a straw.   17th cent.

6447. A dry May and a dripping June
Bring all things into tune.   *I.*

6448. A dwarf on a giant's shoulder sees further of the two. *Latin*
A fair bride is soon busked, *see* A bonny bride, etc.

6449. A fair day in winter is the mother of a storm.   *G. H.*

6450. A fair exchange is no robbery.   17th cent. (*H.*)

6451. A famine in England begins at the horse-manger. [=When
oats are dear.]   *R. (C. R.)*

6452. A fat housekeeper makes lean executors.   *G. H.*

6453. A fault confessed is half redressed.   16th cent.

6454. A fool and his money are soon parted.   16th cent.

6455. A fool knows more in his own house than a wise man in another's. *G. H.*

6456. A fool may ask more questions in an hour than a wise man can
answer in seven years.   *R.*

6457. A fool may give a wise man counsel.   *K.* (14th cent.)

6458. A fool will not give his bauble for the Tower of London. 16th cent.

6459. A fool's bolt is soon shot.   13th cent.

6460. A forced kindness deserves no thanks.   *F.*

6461. A foul morn may turn to a fair day.   *F.*

6462. A fox is not taken twice in the same snare.   *Greek*

6463. A friend in court is better than a penny in purse.   15th cent.

6464. A friend in need is a friend indeed.   *Latin*

6465. A friend is never known till needed.   14th cent.

6466. A friend to all is a friend to none.   *Greek*

6467. A friend's frown is better than a fool's smile.   *J. H.*

6468. A full belly neither fights nor flies well.   *G. H.*

6469. A ganging fit is aye getting. [=A going foot is always getting.] *K.*

6470. A gift long waited for is sold, not given. *F.*
6471. A good beginning makes a good ending. 14th cent.
6472. A good conscience is a continual feast. *T. D.*
6473. A good deed is never lost. *T. D.*
6474. A good example is the best sermon. *F.*
6475. A good face is a letter of recommendation. 17th cent.
6476. A good face needs no band, and a pretty wench no land. *R.*
6477. A good horse cannot be of a bad colour. 17th cent.
6478. A good Jack makes a good Jill. *C. R.*
6479. A good lather is half the shave. *F.*
6480. A good man can no more harm than a sheep. *C. R.*
6481. A good name keeps its lustre in the dark. *R.*
6482. A good neighbour, a good morrow. 15th cent.
6483. A good paymaster never wants workmen. *F.*
6484. A good shift may serve long, but it will not serve ever. *R.*
6485. A good surgeon must have an eagle's eye, a lion's heart, and
    a lady's hand. *R.*
6486. A good tale ill told is marred in the telling. *Latin*
6487. A good tale is none the worse for being twice told. *K.*
6488. A good thing is soon snatched up. *R.*
6489. A good wife and health is a man's best wealth. *F.*
6490. A good wife makes a good husband. *H.*
6491. A great city, a great solitude. *Greek*
6492. A great dowry is a bed full of brambles. *G. H.*
6493. A great fortune is a great slavery. *Latin*
6494. A great ship asks deep waters. *G. H.*
6495. A green winter [*or* Christmas] makes a fat churchyard. *R.*
6496. A green wound is soon healed. *R.*
6497. A growing youth has a wolf in his belly. 17th cent.
6498. A grunting horse and a groaning wife seldom fail their master. *H.*
6499. A guilty conscience needs no accuser. 18th cent. (16th cent.)
6500. A hair of the dog that bit you. [=A drink to cure the effect of
    a previous debauch.] *H.*
6501. A handful of good life is better than a bushel of learning. *G. H.*
6502. A head like a snake,
    A neck like a drake,
    A back like a beam,
    A belly like a bream,
    A foot like a cat.
    A tail like a rat. [Points of a good greyhound.] *R.*
6503. A heavy purse makes a light heart. 16th cent.
6504. A hedge between keeps friendship green. 18th cent.
6505. A high building, a low foundation. *C. R.*
6506. A honey tongue, a heart of gall. 16th cent.
6507. A hook's well lost to catch a salmon. *J. D.*
6508. A horse stumbles that has four legs. *G. H.*
6509. A hungry man is an angry man. *J. H.*
6510. A king without learning is but a crowned ass. 16th cent.
6511. A lame traveller should get out betimes. *F.*
6512. A lawyer never goes to law himself. *Italian*

6513. A lazy sheep thinks its wool heavy. *F.*
6514. A lazy youth, a lousy age. 18th cent.
6515. A leg of a lark is better than the body of a kite. *H.*
6516. A liar is not believed when he speaks the truth. *Latin*
6517. A lie begets a lie. *F.*
6518. A light purse makes a heavy heart. 16th cent.
6519. A light-heeled mother makes a heavy-heeled daughter. *R.*
6520. A lion may be beholden to a mouse. 17th cent.
6521. A lion's skin is never cheap. 17th cent.
6522. A lisping lass is good to kiss. *R.*
6523. A little body doth often harbour a great soul. *R.*
6524. A little good is soon spent. *C. R.*
6525. A little house well filled.
　　　A little land well tilled,
　　　And a little wife well willed. *R.*
6526. A little of everything is nothing in the main. *F.*
6527. A little pot is soon hot. *H.*
6528. A long tongue is a sign of a short hand. [=Lavish promise is
　　　followed by poor performance.] *G. H.*
6529. A low hedge is easily leaped over. *C. R.*
6530. A mackerel sky and mares' tails
　　　Make lofty ships carry low sails. *I.*
6531. A mackerel sky is never long dry. *I.*
6532. A maid oft seen, and a gown oft worn,
　　　Are disesteemed and held in scorn. *R.*
6533. A maid that laughs is half taken. *R.*
6534. A maiden with many wooers often chooses the worst. *K.*
6535. A man, a horse, and a dog are never weary of each other's
　　　company. 18th cent.
6536. A man among children will be long a child, a child among men
　　　will be soon a man. *F.*
6537. A man at sixteen will prove a child at sixty. *F.*
6538. A man can do no more than he can. *R.*
6539. A man cannot whistle and drink at the same time. 16th cent.
6540. A man is as old as he feels, and a woman as old as she
　　　looks. 19th cent.
6541. A man is known by the company he keeps. 17th cent.
6542. A man is weal or woe as he thinks himself so. *K.*
6543. A man knows his companion in a long journey and a little inn. *F.*
6544. A man may bear till his back break. *C.*
6545. A man may love his house well, though he ride not on the ridge.
　　　[=Does not proclaim it from the house-top.] *H.*
6546. A man may woo where he will, but he will wed where his hap is. *D. F.*
6547. A man of many trades begs his bread on Sundays. *F.*
6548. A man of straw is worth a woman of gold. 16th cent.
6549. A man of words and not of deeds is like a garden full of weeds. *J. H.*
6550. A man surprised is half beaten. *F.*
6551. A man without a smiling face must not open a shop. *Chinese*
6552. A man's best fortune, or his worst, is a wife. *J. H.*
　　　A man's house is his castle, *see* An Englishman's house, etc.

6553. A May flood never did good. *C.*

6554. A miss is as good as a mile. 19th cent.

6555. A moneyless man goes fast through the market. *F.*

6556. A mouse in time may bite in two a cable. *H.*

6557. A new broom sweeps clean.. *H.*

6558. A nice wife and a back door
Do often make a rich man poor. 15th cent.
[The wife spends and the servants steal.]

6559. A nod from a lord is a breakfast for a fool. *F.*

6560. A nod is as good as a wink to a blind horse. 19th cent.

A peck of March dust is worth a king's ransom. *see* A bushel, etc.

6561. A penny for your thoughts. *H.*

6562. A penny saved is a penny gained [*or* got]. 17th cent.

6563. A pennyweight of love is worth a pound of law. *K.*

6564. A pitiful look asks enough. *G. H.*

6565. A poor man's table is soon spread. *T. D.*

6566. A pound of care will not pay an ounce of debt. 16th cent.

6567. A pretty kettle of fish [=a muddle]. 18th cent.

6568. A proud man hath many crosses. *F.*

6569. A quiet conscience sleeps in thunder. *F.*

6570. A ragged colt may make a good horse. *H.*

6571. A rainbow in the morning is the shepherd's warning ;
A rainbow at night is the shepherd's delight. *I.*

6572. A right Englishman knows not when a thing is well. *R.*

6573. A rolling eye, a roving heart. 17th cent.

6574. A rolling stone gathers no moss. *H.*

6575. A runaway monk never praises his convent. *Italian*

6576. A saint abroad and a devil at home. 17th cent.

6577. A scald [=scabby] head is soon broken. 15th cent.

6578. A Scot, a rat, and a Newcastle grindstone travel all the world
over. 17th cent.

6579. A Scottish man is wise behind the hand. [=Afterwards.] *D. F.*

6580. A Scottish mist will wet an Englishman to the skin. *C.*

6581. A ship and a woman are ever repairing. *G. H.*

6582. A short horse is soon curried. 14th cent.

6583. A short life and a merry one. 17th cent.

6584. A small leak will sink a great ship. *F.*

6585. A small pack becomes a small pedlar. *French*

6586. A smiling boy seldom proves a good servant. *R.*

6587. A snow year, a rich year. *G. H.*

6588. A solitary man is either a brute or an angel [*or* either a God or a
beast.] *F.*

6589. A stern chase is a long chase. 19th cent.

6590. A stick is quickly found to beat a dog with. 16th cent.

6591. A stitch in time saves nine. *F.*

6592. A storm in a teacup. 19th cent.

6593. A straight stick is crooked in the water. 17th cent.

6594. A swarm of bees in May is worth a load of hay,
But a swarm in July is not worth a fly. *R.*

6595. A tale never loses in the telling. *K. (T. D.)*

6596. A tale twice told is cabbage twice sold. *F.*
6597. A thief knows a thief as a wolf knows a wolf. *T. D.*
6598. A tocherless [=dowerless] dame sits long at hame. *K.*
6599. A toom [= empty] purse makes a blate [=shy] merchant. *R.*
6600. A traveller may lie by authority. 14th cent.
6601. A true jest is no jest. 14th cent.
6602. A watched pot never boils. 19th cent.
6603. A whistling woman and a crowing hen
Are neither fit for God nor men. *K.*
6604. A white wall is a fool's paper. 16th cent.
6605. A wife brings but two good days, her wedding day and death
day. *Greek*
6606. A wight [=strong] man never wanted a weapon. *D. F.*
6607. A wild goose never laid a tame egg. *B.*
6608. A wilful man will have his way. 19th cent.
6609. A wise man changes his mind, a fool never will. 17th cent.
6610. A woman, a dog [*or* ass], and a walnut tree,
The more you beat them, the better they'll be. *R.* (16th cent.)
[Several versions with ' spaniel ' for ' dog.']
6611. A woman conceals what she knows not. *G. H.*
6612. A woman is an angel at ten, a saint at fifteen, a devil at forty, and
a witch at fourscore. 17th cent.
6613. A woman is to be from her house three times: when she is
christened, married, and buried. *G.*
6614. A woman's advice is a poor thing, but he is a fool who does not
take it. *Spanish*
6615. A woman's mind and winter wind change oft. *C.*
6616. A woman's strength is in her tongue. *J. H.*
6617. A woman's tongue is the last thing about her that dies. 17th cent.
6618. A woman's work is never done. *R.*
6619. A wonder lasts but nine days. *H.* (14th cent.)
6620. A word spoken is past recalling. 16th cent.
6621. A work ill done must be done twice. *J. H.*
6622. A young courtier, an old beggar. 16th cent.
6623. A young man should not marry yet, an old man not at all. *Greek*
6624. Accidents will happen in the best-regulated families. 19th cent.
6625. Actions speak louder than words. 20th cent.
6626. Adversity makes a man wise, not rich. *R.*
6627. Afraid of his own shadow. 16th cent.
6628. After a storm comes a calm. 16th cent.
6629. After death, the doctor. [Too late.] 16th cent.
6630. After dinner sit awhile; after supper walk a mile. 16th cent.
6631. After meat, mustard. [When it is of no use.] 16th cent.
6632. Age and wedlock tames man and beast. *C. R.*
6633. Agree, for the law is costly. *C. R.*
6634. Agues come on horseback, but go away on foot. 17th cent.
6635. Alike every day makes a clout [=rag] on Sunday. [=If you always
wear your best clothes they will soon wear out.] *K.*
6636. All are good lasses, but whence come the bad wives? *K.*
6637. All are not friends that speak us fair. *C.*

6638. All are not merry that dance lightly.   15th cent.
6639. All cats are grey in the dark.   *H.*
6640. All covet, all lose.   13th cent.
6641. All doors open to courtesy.   *F.*
6642. All fellows at football. [=On the playing-field, all are on equality.]
                                                       16th cent.
6643. All fish are not caught with flies.   16th cent.
6644. All flesh is not venison.   *G. H.*
6645. All his geese are swans.   16th cent.
6646. All is fair in love and war.   17th cent.
6647. All is fish that comes to net.   16th cent.
6648. All is lost that is put in a riven dish.   *C.*
6649. All is not gold that glitters.   *Latin*
6650. All is not lost that is in danger.   *R.*
6651. All is over but the shouting.   19th cent.
6652. All is well that ends well.   15th cent.
6653. All is well with him who is beloved of his neighbours.   *G. H.*
6654. All lay load on the willing horse.   *R. (H.)*
6655. All Lombard Street to a China orange.   [Lombard Street is a
      banking centre.]   19th cent. (18th cent.)
6656. All men can't be first.   *F.*
6657. All men can't be masters.   *H.*
6658. All my eye and Betty Martin. [=All humbug.]   18th cent.
6659. All promises are either broken or kept.   16th cent.
6660. All roads lead to Rome.   14th cent.
6661. All Stuarts are not sib [=related] to the king.   *K.*
6662. All tarred with the same brush.   19th cent.
6663. All the keys hang not at one man's girdle.   *H.*
6664. All the months in the year curse a fair Februeer.   *R.*
6665. All the world and his wife.   18th cent.
6666. All things are difficult before they are easy.   *F.*
6667. All things come to those who wait.   *French*
6668. All truths are not to be told.   14th cent.
6669. All weapons of war cannot arm fear.   16th cent.
6670. All work and no play makes Jack a dull boy.   *J. H.*
6671. Almost and Very [*or* Well] nigh saves many a lie.   *C.*
6672. Almost was never hanged.   *C.*
6673. Alms never make poor.   *G. H.*
6674. Always in the saddle, never on his way. [Of equestrian statues.]
                                                       16th cent.
6675. Always taking out of the meal-tub, and never putting in, soon
      comes to the bottom.   18th cent.
6676. An ague in the spring is physic for a king.   *J. H.*
6677. An ape's an ape, a varlet's a varlet.
      Though they be clad in silk or scarlet.   *F.* (16th cent.)
6678. An apple a day keeps the doctor away.   20th cent.
6679. An apple, an egg, and a nut, you may eat after a slut.   *R.*
6680. An artist lives everywhere.   16th cent.
6681. An ass is but an ass, though laden with gold.   17th cent.
6682. An ass loaded with gold climbs to the top of the castle.   *F.*

6683. An atheist is one point beyond the devil.   *F.*
6684. An egg will be in three bellies in twenty-four hours.   *R.*
6685. An empty sack cannot stand upright.   17th cent.
6686. An English summer, three hot days and a thunderstorm.   19th cent.
6687. An Englishman is never happy but when he is miserable, a Scotchman
      never at home but when he is abroad, and an Irishman never at
      peace but when he is fighting.   19th cent.
6688. An Englishman's house is his castle.   *R.*
6689. An honest man's word is as good as his bond.   *R.*
6690. An hour in the morning is worth two in the evening.   *B.*
6691. An idle youth, a needy age.   *G. H.*
6692. An ill stake standeth longest.   *J. H.*
6693. An ill wound is cured, not an ill name.   *G. H.*
6694. An inch in a miss is as good as an ell.   *C. R.*
6695. An iron hand in a velvet glove.   *French*
6696. An oak is not felled at one stroke.   15th cent.
6697. An old cat laps as much as a young kitten.   *C. R.*
6698. An old cat sports not with her prey.   *G. H.*
6699. An old dog bites sore.   *H.*
6700. An old fox needs no craft.   *C.*
6701. An old head on young shoulders.   *C.*
6702. An old knave is no babe.   *H.*
6703. An old man is a bed full of bones.   *R.*
6704. An old man never wants a tale to tell.   *F*
6705. An old physician and a young lawyer.   [Are best.]   *G. H.*
6706. An old poacher makes the best keeper.   19th cent. (14th cent.)
6707. An old soldier, an old fool.   *French*
6708. An open door may tempt a saint.   *J. H.*
6709. An ounce of discretion is worth a pound of learning.   *R.*
6710. An ounce of fortune is worth a pound of forecast.   17th cent.
6711. An ounce of mother-wit is worth a pound of clergy [=learning].
                                                                              17th cent.
6712. An ounce of wit that's bought is worth a pound that's taught.   *F.*
6713. An ox is taken by the horns, and a man by the tongue.   *G. H.*
6714. An unbidden guest knows not where to sit.   14th cent.
6715. Anger and haste hinder good counsel.   *B.*
6716. Another's bread costs dear.   *G. H.*
6717. Any port in a storm.   18th cent.
6718. Anything for a quiet life.   *R.*
6719. Ars est celare artem.—Art lies in concealing art.   *Latin*
6720. As a man is friended, so the law is ended.   16th cent.
6721. As bald as a coot.   15th cent.
6722. As calm as a clock.   19th cent.
6723. As clean as a whistle.   19th cent.
6724. As close as wax.   18th cent.
6725. As cold as charity.   17th cent.
6726. As cross as a bear with a sore head.   19th cent.
6727. As cross as nine highways.   *B.*
6728. As cross as two sticks.   19th cent.
6729. As dead as a door-nail.   14th cent.

6730. As dead as mutton. 18th cent.
6731. As drunk as a lord. 17th cent.
6732. As drunk as a mouse. 14th cent.
6733. As drunk as a wheelbarrow. R.
6734. As dry as a bone. 16th cent.
6735. As dull [or dead] as ditchwater. 18th cent.
6736. As fine as fivepence. 16th cent.
6737. As fit as a fiddle. R.
6738. As flat as a pancake. 18th cent. (16th cent.)
6739. As full as an egg is of meat. 16th cent.
As good be hanged for a sheep as a lamb, see As well be hanged, etc.
6740. As good be out of the world as out of the fashion. C.
6741. As good lost as found. H.
6742. As good play for nought as work for nought. H.
6743. As jolly as a sandboy. 19th cent.
6744. As large as life. 18th cent.
6745. As lazy as Ludlam's dog, that leaned his head against a wall to bark. R.
6746. As lean as a rake. 14th cent.
6747. As like as two peas. 16th cent.
6748. As mad as a hatter. 19th cent.
6749. As mad as a March hare. 14th cent.
6750. As melancholy as a cat. 16th cent.
6751. As melancholy as a sick monkey. 19th cent.
6752. As merry as a cricket. H.
6753. As merry as a grig. 18th cent.
6754. As merry as mice in malt. C.
6755. As mild as a lamb. 16th cent.
6756. As neat as a new pin. 18th cent.
6757. As nimble as a cow in a cage. H.
6758. As nimble as an eel in a sandbag. F.
6759. As old as Paul's [or Paul's steeple]. 17th cent.
6760. As old as the hills. 19th cent.
6761. As plain as a pikestaff. [Originally ' packstaff,' with which the pedlar carried his pack over his shoulder.] 16th cent.
6762. As plain as the nose on a man's face. C.
6763. As poor as a church mouse. J. H.
6764. As poor as Job. 14th cent.
6765. As proud as a peacock. 13th cent.
6766. As proud as Lucifer. 14th cent.
6767. As quick as thought. 13th cent.
6768. As quiet as a mouse. 17th cent.
6769. As red as a turkey-cock. 17th cent.
6770. As right as a trivet. 19th cent.
6771. As right as ninepence. 19th cent.
6772. As right as rain. 19th cent.
6773. As seasonable as snow in summer [or harvest]. 16th cent.
6774. As sick as a dog. 16th cent.
6775. As slender in the middle as a cow in the waist. R.
6776. As slippery as an eel. 15th cent.

P

6777. As soft as butter. 16th cent.
6778. As soft as silk. 14th cent.
6779. As soon as man is born he begins to die. *German*
6780. As soon goes the young sheep as the old to market [*or* pot]. 16th cent.
6781. As sore fight wrens as cranes. *D. F.*
6782. As sound as a bell. 16th cent.
6783. As sound as a trout [*or* roach]. 13th cent.
6784. As sure as a gun. 17th cent.
6785. As sure as death. 16th cent.
6786. As sure as eggs is eggs. 17th cent.
6787. As sure as God made little apples. 19th cent.
6788. As sure as God's in Gloucestershire. 17th cent.
6789. As sweet as a nut. 16th cent.
6790. As the day lengthens the cold strengthens. *R.*
6791. As the fool thinks, so the bell clinks. 17th cent.
6792. As the goodman saith, so say we ;
   But as the goodwife saith, so must it be. *R.*
6793. As the old cock crows, the young one learns. 14th cent.
6794. As the touchstone trieth gold, so gold trieth men. *F.* (16th cent.)
6795. As they brew, so let them drink [*or* bake]. 16th cent. (13th cent.)
6796. As true as a turtle to her mate. 15th cent.
6797. As true as God's in heaven. *R.*
6798. As true as Gospel. 16th cent.
6799. As true as steel. 14th cent.
6800. As true as the dial to the sun. 17th cent.
6801. As ugly as sin. 19th cent.
6802. As warm [*or* hot] as toast. 15th cent.
6803. As weak as water. 14th cent.
6804. As welcome as flowers in May. 17th cent.
6805. As welcome as water in one's shoes. *J. H.*
6806. As well as the beggar knows his dish [*or* bag]. *H.*
6807. As well be hanged for a sheep as a lamb. *R.*
6808. As wise as a man of Gotham. [Gotham was proverbial for folly.] *J.H.*
6809. As you make your bed, so you must lie on it. 16th cent.
6810. As your wedding-ring wears, your cares will wear away. *R.*
6811. Ask a kite for a feather, and she'll say, she has but just enough
   to fly with. *F.*
6812. Ask much to have a little. *G. H.*
6813. Ask my fellow if I be a thief. *H.*
6814. Ask no questions and you will be told no lies. 18th cent.
6815. Ask the mother if the child be like his father. *F.*
6816. At a great bargain, pause. *G. H.*
6817. At a round table there's no dispute of place. *R.*
6818. At court, everyone for himself. 14th cent.
6819. At Easter let your clothes be new,
   Or else be sure you will it rue. *L.*
6820. At every dog's bark seem not to awake. [=Do not fuss about
   trifles.] *H.*
6821. At latter Lammas. [=Never.] 16th cent.
6822. At length the fox is brought to the furrier. *G. H.*

6823. At open doors dogs come in. *D. F.*
6824. At the end of the game you'll see who's the winner. *F. (G. H.)*
6825. Athanasius contra mundum.—Athanasius against the world. *Latin*
6826. Audi alteram partem.—Hear the other side. *Latin*
6827. Autre tempts, autre mœurs.—Other times, other manners. *French*
6828. Away goes the devil when he finds the door shut against him. *Italian*
6829. Bacchus hath drowned more men than Neptune. *F.*
6830. Bachelor's fare : bread and cheese and kisses. 18th cent.
6831. Bachelors' wives and maids' children are always well taught. *H.*
6832. Back may trust but belly won't. [=You can wait for clothes, but
　　　not for food.] 19th cent.
6833. Bad is the best. 16th cent.
6834. Bare as the birch at Yule even. 19th cent.
6835. Bare walls make giddy housewives. *C. R.*
6836. Bare words make no bargain. *C.*
6837. Barking dogs seldom bite. 16th cent.
6838. Barnaby bright, Barnaby bright :
　　　The longest day and the shortest night. *J. H.*
　　　[St. Barnabas' day, 11 June, in Old Style reckoned longest.]
6839. Bashfulness is an enemy to poverty. *Latin*
6840. Be a friend to thyself, and others will befriend thee. *K.*
6841. Be as you would seem to be. *G. H.*
6842. Be it better, be it worse,
　　　Be ruled by him that bears the purse. 14th cent.
6843. Be just before you are generous. 18th cent.
6844. Be long sick, that you may be soon hale. *K.*
6845. Be not too bold with your betters. *J. H.*
6846. Be not too hasty to outbid another. *R.*
6847. Be still, and have thy will. 16th cent. (15th cent.)
6848. Be sure before you marry of a house wherein to tarry. *Italian*
6849. Bear and forbear. 16th cent.
6850. Bear wealth, poverty will bear itself. *D. F*
6851. Bear with evil, and expect good. *G. H*
6852. Beauty draws more than oxen. *G. H.*
6853. Beauty is but a blossom. *T. D.*
6854. Beauty is but skin-deep. 17th cent.
6855. Beauty is potent, but money is omnipotent. *R.*
6856. Beauty will buy no beef. *F.*
6857. Beauty without bounty avails nought. 16th cent.
6858. Bees that have honey in their mouths have stings in their tails.
　　　15th cent.
6859. Before one can say Jack Robinson. 18th cent.
6860. Before you make a friend eat a bushel of salt with him. *Latin*
6861. Beggars cannot be choosers. *H.*
6862. Being on sea, sail ; being on land, settle. *G. H.*
6863. Believe well and have well. *H.*
6864. Bells call others to church, but go not themselves. *G. H.* (16th cent.)
6865. Benefits please, like flowers, while they are fresh. *G. H.*
6866. Best is best cheap. [=The best bargain.] *H.*
6867 Best to bend while 'tis a twig. 16th cent.

6868. Better a clout [=patch] than a hole out. *C. R.*
6869. Better a finger off than always aching. 13th cent.
6870. Better a fortune in a wife than with a wife. *K.*
6871. Better a lean peace than a fat victory. 17th cent.
6872. Better a little fire to warm us, than a great one to burn us. 16th cent.
6973. Better a mischief than an inconvenience. *C.*
6874. Better a mouse in the pot than no flesh at all. *C. R.*
     Better a wee bush than nae bield [=no shelter], *see* A bad bush, etc.
6875. Better an egg to-day than a hen to-morrow. *Italian*
6876. Better an empty house than an ill tenant. *F.*
6877. Better an open enemy than a false friend. 17th cent.
6878. Better bairns greet [=children weep] than bearded men. *D. F.*
6879. Better be a fool than a knave. *G. H.*
6880. Better be alone than in bad company. *C.* (15th cent.)
6881. Better be an old man's darling than a young man's warling [=object of contempt]. *H.*
6882. Better be born lucky than rich. *C.*
6883. Better be envied than pitied. *Greek*
6884. Better be happy than wise. *H.*
6885. Better be stung by a nettle than pricked by a rose. [=Better be wronged by an enemy than by a friend.] *J. H.*
6886. Better be sure than sorry. 19th cent.
6887. Better be ill spoken of by one before all than by all before one. *J. H.*
6888. Better be poor than wicked. *B.*
6889. Better be the head of a dog than the tail of a lion. *R.*
6890. Better be the head of the yeomanry than the tail of the gentry. *C.*
6891. Better be unmannerly than troublesome. *J. H.*
6892. Better bow than break. 15th cent. (14th cent.)
6893. Better buy than borrow. *D. F.*
6894. Better come at the latter end of a feast than the beginning of a fray. *H.*
6895. Better cut the shoe than pinch the foot. *F.*
6896. Better die a beggar than live a beggar. *R.*
6897. Better early than late. 13th cent.
6898. Better give a shilling than lend a half a crown. *J. H.*
6899. Better go about than fall into a ditch. *J. H.*
6900. Better go away longing than loathing. *F.*
6901. Better go to bed supperless than rise in debt. *R.*
6902. Better go to heaven in rags than to hell in embroidery. *F.*
6903. Better good afar off than evil at hand. *G. H.*
6904. Better have an old man to humour than a young rake to break your heart. *W. H.*
6905. Better have one plough going than two cradles. 16th cent.
6906. Better hazard once than be always in fear. *F.*
6907. Better keep now than seek anon. *J. H.*
6908. Better kiss a knave than be troubled with him. *C. R.*
6909. Better late than never. *Greek.*
6910. Better leave than lack. *H.*
6911. Better lose a jest than a friend. 16th cent.
6912. Better luck next time. 19th cent.
6913. Better my hog dirty home than no hog at all. *R.*

6914. Better one house filled than two spilled [=spoiled]. [Said when two unpleasant people marry.] *R.*

6915. Better one's house too little one day than too big all the year after. *R.*

6916. Better pay the butcher than the doctor. 19th cent.

6917. Better ride on an ass that carries me than a horse that throws me. *G.H.*

6918. Better say Here it is than Here it was. *D. F.*

6919. Better sell than live poorly. *F.*

6920. Better sit idle than work for nothing. 17th cent.

6921. Better sit still than rise up and fall. 15th cent.

6922. Better small fish than an empty dish. *R.*

6923. Better some of a pudding than none of a pie. *R.*

6924. Better spare at brim than at bottom. [=Save early and avoid being in want later.] *H.*

6925. Better spare to have of thine own than ask of other men. *G. H.*

6926. Better speak to the master than the man. 17th cent.

6927. Better suffer ill than do ill. *C.*

6928. Better the devil you know than the devil you don't know. 19th cent.

6929. Better the foot slip than the tongue. 16th cent.

6930. Better the last smile than the first laughter. *H.*

6931. Better unborn than untaught. *H.* (13th cent.)

6932. Better untaught than ill taught. *R.*

6933. Better wear out shoes than sheets. [Sound men wear out shoes, sick men sheets.] *K.*

6934. Better wed over the mixen [=dung-heap] than over the the moor. [=Choose a partner from near at home.] *D. F.*

6935. Between Scylla and Charybdis. *Greek*

6936. Between the beetle [=mallet] and the block. 16th cent.

6937. Between the devil and the deep sea. 17th cent.

6938. Between the hammer and the anvil. *Latin*

6939. Between two stools one falls to the ground. *Latin*

6940. Between you and me and the post [*or* bedpost]. [=In confidence.] 19th cent.

6941. Beware beginnings. *C.*

6942. Beware of a silent dog and still water. *Latin*

6943. Beware of after-claps. 16th cent.

6944. Beware of breed. [=Ill breed.] *R.*

6945. Beware of Had I wist. 14th cent.

6946. Beware of the forepart of a woman, the hind part of a mule, and all sides of a priest. 16th cent.

6947. Beware of the man of one book. *Latin*

6948. Birchen twigs break no ribs. *C.*

6949. Birds of a feather flock together. 16th cent.

6950. Birth is much, but breeding is more. *C.*

6951. Bis dat qui cito dat.—He gives twice who gives quickly. *Latin.*

6952. Biting and scratching is Scots folk's wooing. *D. F.*

6953. Bitter pills may have wholesome effects. *F.*

6954. Black will take no other hue. *H.*

6955. Blessings are not valued till they are gone. *F.*

6956. Blind man's holiday. [=Twilight.] 16th cent.

6957. Blood is thicker than water. [=Relationship is a strong bond.]
19th cent.

6958. Blood will have blood. 16th cent.

6959. Blow first and sip afterwards. R.

6960. Blow the wind never so fast,
It will lower at the last. F.

6961. Blushing is virtue's colour. 17th cent.

6962. Born on Monday, fair in the face ;
Born on Tuesday, full of God's grace ;
Born on Wednesday, sour and sad ;
Born on Thursday, merry and glad ;
Born on Friday, worthily given ;
Born on Saturday, work hard for your living ;
Born on Sunday, you will never know want. 19th cent.
[See Monday's child, etc.]

6963. Born on the wrong side of the blanket. [=Illegitimate.] 18th cent.

6964. Borrowed garments never sit well. F.

6965. Both together do best of all. C.

6966. Bought wit is best, but may cost too much. R.

6967. Boys will be boys. 17th cent.

6968. Boys will be men. D. F.

6969. Brag is a good dog, but Holdfast is a better. R.

6970. Bread is the staff of life. 17th cent.

6971. Bridges were made for wise men to walk over and fools to ride over. R.

6972. Bring a cow to the hall and she'll run to the byre. D. F.

6973. Building and marrying of children are great wasters. G. H.

6974. Building is a sweet impoverishing. G.H.

6975. Business is business. 18th cent.

6976. Butter is gold in the morning, silver at noon, and lead at
night. 16th cent.

6977. Butter is mad twice a year. [When very hard or very soft.] 17th cent.

6978. Buy at a fair but sell at home. T. D.

6979. By hook or by crook [=By fair means or foul.] H. (14th cent.)

6980. By the street of By and by one arrives at the house of Never.
Spanish

6981. By Tre, Pol, and Pen,
You shall know the Cornish men. [Cornish prefixes.] R.

6982. Cadgers are aye cracking of crooksaddles. [=Carriers are always
talking of pack-saddles.—People tend to talk ' shop.'] D. F.

6983. Caesar's wife must be above suspicion. Latin

6984. Calf love, half love ; old love, cold love. 19th cent.

6985. Call me cousin, but cozen me not. R.

6986. Call no man happy till he dies. 17th cent.

6987. Calm weather in June sets corn in tune. 16th cent.

6988. Cards are the devil's books. 17th cent.

6989. Care is no cure. 16th cent.

6990. Care killed a cat. 16th cent.

6991. Cast ne'er a clout till May be out. F.

6992. Cast not out the foul water till you bring in the clean. D. F.

6993. Cat will after kind. H. (13th cent.)

6994. Cats eat what hussies [=housewives] spare. [=What is niggardly
saved is often squandered.] 16th cent.
6995. Cauld kail het again. [=Cold cabbage warmed up.] *Latin*
6996. Caveat emptor.—Let the buyer beware. [=The quality of the
article is his concern.] *Latin*
6997. Change of weather is the discourse of fools. *J. H.*
6998. Charity begins at home. 14th cent.
6999. Che sarà, sarà.—What will be, will be. *Italian*
7000. Cheat me in the price but not in the goods. *F.*
7001. Cheese it is a peevish elf,
It digests all things but itself. *Latin*
7002. Children and chicken must be always picking. 16th cent.
7003. Children and fools have merry lives. *C.*
7004. Children and fools speak the truth. *H.*
7005. Children are certain cares, but uncertain comforts. *C.*
7006. Children are poor men's riches. *R.*
7007. Children pick up words as pigeons pease,
And utter them again as God shall please. *R.*
7008. Children should be seen and not heard. 19th cent.
7009. Children suck the mother when they are young, and the father
when they are old. *R.*
7010. Children, when little, make parents fools ; when great, mad. *G. H.*
7011. Choose a horse made, and a wife to make. *G. H.*
7012. Choose a wife rather by your ear than your eye. *F.*
7013. Choose for yourself and use for yourself. *C.*
7014. Choose neither a woman nor linen by candle-light. 16th cent.
7015. Choose none for thy servant who have served thy betters. *G. H.*
7016. Christmas comes but once a year.
But when it comes it brings good cheer. 16th cent.
7017. Church work goes on slowly. 17th cent.
7018. Cider is treacherous because it smiles in the face and then cuts
the throat. 17th cent.
7019. Circumstances alter cases. 19th cent.
7020. Civility costs nothing. 19th cent.
7021. Claw me, and I'll claw thee. [Of mutual flattery.] 16th cent.
7022. Clergymen's sons always turn out badly. 19th cent.
7023. Cloudy mornings turn to clear evenings, *H.*
7024. Cold broth hot again, that loved I never ;
Old love renewed again, that loved I ever. *F.*
7025. Cold of complexion, good of condition. *R.*
7026. Cold pudding settles love. 17th cent.
7027. Cold weather and crafty knaves come out of the north. *J. H.*
7028. Come day, go day, God send Sunday. [The sluggard's wish.] *K.*
7029. Come not to counsel uncalled. 16th cent.
7030. Command your man and do it yourself. *R.*
7031. Common fame is a common liar. 17th cent.
7032. Common fame is seldom to blame. *R.*
7033. Comparisons are odious. 15th cent.
7034. Conceited [=ingenious] goods are quickly spent. *R.*
7035. Confess and be hanged. 16th cent.

7036. Confession is good for the soul. *K.*

7037. Constant dropping wears away the stone. *Greek*

7038. Content is the philosopher's stone, that turns all it touches into gold. *F.*

7039. Content lodges oftener in cottages than palaces. *F.*

7040. Cool words scald not the tongue. *F.*

7041. Corruptio optimi pessima.—Corruption of best is worst. *Latin*

7042. Counsel breaks not the head. *G. H.*

7043. Counsel is no command. *F.*

7044. Courtesy on one side only lasts not long. *G. H.*

7045. Courting and wooing bring dallying and doing. *C. R.*

7046. Covetousness brings nothing home. *C.*

7047. Covetousness bursts the sack. 19th cent. (16th cent.)

7048. Craft against craft makes no living. *G. H.*

7049. Craft must have clothes, but truth loves to go naked. *F.*

7050. Credit keeps the crown of the causeway. [=Is not ashamed to show itself.] *K.*

7051. Creditors have better memories than debtors. *J. H.*

7052. Critics are like brushers of noblemen's clothes. *G. H.*

7053. Crooked logs make straight fires. 17th cent.

7054. Cross the stream where it is ebbest [=shallowest]. 17th cent.

7055. Crosses are ladders to heaven. *T. D.*

7056. Crows are never the whiter for washing themselves. *K*

7057. Cucullus non facit monachum.—The cowl does not make the monk. *Latin.*

7058. Cunning [=skill] is no burden. 16th cent.

7059. Curiosity is ill manners in another's house. *F.*

7060. Curses, like chickens, come home to roost. 14th cent.

7061. Custom is second nature. 14th cent.

7062. Custom is the plague of wise men and the idol of fools. *B.*

7063. Custom makes all things easy. 16th cent.

7064. Custom without reason is but ancient error. 17th cent.

7065. Dally not with money or women. *G. H.*

7066. Danger and delight grow on one stock. 16th cent.

7067. Dangers are overcome by dangers. *G. H.*

7068. Daughters and dead fish are no keeping wares. *F.*

7069. Dawted [=petted] daughters make daidling [=silly] wives. 19th cent.

7070. De gustibus non est disputandum.—There is no disputing about tastes. *Latin*

7071. De minimis non curat lex.—The law does not concern itself about trifles. *Latin*

7072. De mortuis nil nisi bonum.—Concerning the dead [speak] nothing but good. *Latin*

7073. Dead men don't bite. *Latin*

7074. Dead men tell no tales. 17th cent.

7075. Dead mice feel no cold. *R.*

7076. Death and marriage make term day. *D. F.*

7077. Death defies the doctor. *K.*

7078. Death is the grand leveller. *F.*

7079. Death keeps no calendar. *G. H.*

7080. Death pays all debts.   16th cent.
7081. Death's day is doom's day.   16th cent.
7082. Deaths foreseen come not.   *G. H.*
7083. Debt is better than death.   *J. H.*
7084. Debt is the worst poverty.   *F.*
7085. Debtors are liars.   *G. H.*
7086. Deeds are fruits, words are but leaves.   *T. D.*
7087. Deeds are males and words are females.   16th cent.
7088. Deem the best till the truth be tried out.   15th cent.
7089. Delays are dangerous.   14th cent.
7090. Deliberating is not delaying.   *F.*
7091. Denying a fault doubles it.   17th cent.
7092. Dependence is a poor trade.   *F.*
7093. Desert and reward seldom keep company.   17th cent.
7094. Desires are nourished by delays.   *T. D.*
7095. Despair gives courage to a coward.   *F.*
7096. Desperate diseases must have desperate remedies [*or* cures].   *Latin*
7097. Diamond cut diamond.   [Of people matched in cunning.]   17th cent.
7098. Diet cures more than doctors.   19th cent.
7099. Diffidence is the right eye of prudence.   *F.*
7100. Diligence is the mother of good luck.   17th cent.
7101. Dinners cannot be long where dainties want.   *H.*
7102. Discreet women have neither eyes nor ears.   *G. H.*
7103. Discretion is the better part of valour.   16th cent.
7104. Diseases are the interests of pleasures.   *R.*
7105. Disgraces are like cherries, one draws another.   *G. H.*
7106. Dissembled sin is double wickedness.   *T. D.*
7107. Divide et impera.—Divide and rule.   *Latin*
7108. Do and undo, the day is long enough.   *C.*
7109. Do as I say, not as I do.   *H.*
7110. Do as most men do, and men will speak well of you.   *H.*
7111. Do as you would be done by.   16th cent.
7112. Do as you're bidden and you'll never bear blame.   *R.*
7113. Do evil and look for the like.   16th cent.
7114. Do it well that thou mayest not do it twice.   *F.*
7115. Do not all you can ; spend not all you have ; believe not all you
     hear ; and tell not all you know.   *B.*
7116. Do not halloo till you are out of the wood.   19th cent.
7117. Do not keep a dog and bark yourself.   16th cent.
7118. Do not meet troubles half-way.   16th cent.
7119. Do not put all your eggs in one basket.   18th cent.
7120. Do not spur a free horse.   *Latin.*
7121. Do on the hill as you would do in the hall.   *D. F.*
7122. Do the likeliest and hope the best.   *D. F.*
7123. Do well and have well.   14th cent.
7124. Do what thou oughtest and come what can come.   *J. H.*
7125. Do wrong once and you'll never hear the end of it.   17th cent
7126. Dog does not eat dog.   18th cent.
7127. Dogs bark as they are bred.   *K.*
7128. Dogs bark before they bite.   *H.*

*P

7129. Dogs that bark at a distance never bite. *C. R.*

7130. Dogs wag their tails not so much in love to you as to your bread.

17th cent.

7131. Draff is good enough for swine. 16th cent.

7132. Drawn wells are seldom dry. [=Things are improved by use.] *C.*

7133. Drawn wells have sweetest water. *C.*

7134. Dreams go by contraries. 15th cent.

7135. Dree out [=endure] the inch as you have done the span. *K.*

7136. Drift is as bad as unthrift. *J. H.*

7137. Drink only with the duck. [=Water only.] 14th cent.

7138. Drink wine, and have the gout ; drink none, and have the gout.

16th cent.

7139. Drive the nail that will go. 17th cent.

7140. Drunken folks seldom take harm. 18th cent.

7141. Dry bread at home is better than roast meat abroad. *G. H.*

7142. Dulce bellum inexpertis.—War is pleasant to those who have
not tried it. *Latin*

7143. Dumb folks get no lands. 14th cent.

7144. Dummy [=a dumb man] cannot lie. *D. F.*

7145. Each bird loves to hear himself sing. *H.*

7146. Each cross hath its inscription. *C.*

7147. Early master, soon knave [=servant]. [Early independence
causes extravagance, making employment necessary.] 14th cent.

7148. Early to bed and early to rise
Makes a man healthy, wealthy, and wise. *C.* (16th cent.)

7149. Ease and success are fellows. 14th cent.

7150. East, west, home's best. *B.*

7151. Easy come, easy go. [Of quickly acquired fortunes.] 19th cent.

7152. Eat at pleasure, drink by measure. *French*

7153. Eat to live, but do not live to eat. *Latin*

7154. Eaten bread is forgotten. *C. R.*

7155. Eating and scratching wants but a beginning. [Said to people
who have a poor appetite.] *K.*

7156. Education begins a gentleman, conversation completes him. *F.*

7157. Ἐγγύη· πάρα δ' ἄτη—[Act as] surety ; ruin is at hand. *Greek*

7158. Either a feast or a fast. *F.*

7159. Empty vessels make the most sound [or noise.] 16th cent.

7160. England is the paradise of women, the hell of horses, and the
purgatory of servants. *D. F.* (16th cent.)

7161. Enough is as good as a feast. 15th cent.

7162. Envy never enriched any man. *R. (T. D.)*

7163. Envy shoots at others and wounds herself. 16th cent.

7164. Even a fly hath its spleen. *Latin*

7165. Even a worm will turn. *H.*

7166. Even reckoning makes long friends. *H.*

7167. Evening red and morning grey
Help the traveller on his way ;
Evening grey and morning red
Bring down rain upon his head. *D.*

7168. Ever drunk, ever dry. 16th cent.

7169. Ever sick of the slothful guise,
Loth to bed and loth to rise. *C.*

7170. Every ass loves to hear himself bray. *F.*

7171. Every bean hath its black. *C.*

7172. Every bird likes its own nest best. *French*

7173. Every cloud has a silver lining. 19th cent.

7174. Every dog has his day. *H.*

7175. Every dog is a lion at home. *Italian*

7176. Every door may be shut but death's door. *Italian*

7177. Every herring must hang by its own gill. *C.*

7178. Every honest miller has a golden thumb. *R.* (16th cent.)

7179. Every horse thinks his own pack heaviest. *F.*

7180. Every Jack has his Jill. *R.*

7181. Every little helps. 18th cent.

7182. Every man at forty is a fool or a physician. *R.*

7183. Every man can rule [*or* tame] a shrew but he who has her. *H.*

7184. Every man for himself, and God for us all. *H.*

7185. Every man has his faults. *C.*

7186. Every man is a fool sometimes, and none at all times. *K.*

7187. Every man is best known to himself. *T. D.*

7188. Every man is the architect of his own fortune. *Latin*

7189. Every man must eat a peck of dirt before he dies. *C.*

7190. Every man to his trade. *Greek*

7191. Every miller draws water to his own mill. *R.* (16th cent.)

7192. Every one can keep house better than her mother till she trieth. *F.*

7193. Every one is kin to the rich man. *Italian*

7194. Every one to his taste, as the old woman said when she kissed
her cow. *H.*

7195. Every one's faults are not written in their foreheads. *R.*

7196. Every path hath a puddle. *G. H.*

7197. Every shoe fits not every foot. 17th cent.

7198. Every sin brings its punishment with it. *G. H.*

7199. Every tub must stand on its own bottom. 16th cent.

7200. Every white hath its black, and every sweet its sour. 18th cent.

7201. Everybody's business is nobody's business. 17th cent.

7202. Everything hath an end, and a pudding hath two. 16th cent.

7203. Everything is the worse for wearing. *C.*

7204. Everything must have a beginning. 16th cent.

7205. Evil to him that evil thinks. 16th cent.

7206. Ex Africa semper aliquid novi.—Out of Africa always something new. *Latin*

7207. Ex nihilo nihil fit.—Nothing comes of nothing. *Latin*

7208. Ex pede Herculem.—From his foot [you may know] Hercules.
[=A small piece shows the quality of the whole.] *Latin*

7209. Ex ungue leonem.—By his claw [you may know] the lion. *Latin*

7210. Example is better than precept. *Latin*

Exchange is no robbery, *see* A fair exchange, etc.

7211. Experience is the mistress of fools. 16th cent.

7212. Extreme right is extreme wrong. *Latin*

7213. Extremes meet. 18th cent.

7214. Face to face the truth comes out. *F.*

7215. Facts are stubborn things. 18th cent.

7216. Faint heart never won fair lady. 16th cent.

7217. Fair and foolish, little and loud,
Long and lazy, black and proud ;
Fat and merry, lean and sad,
Pale and peevish, red and bad. [Of women's colours.] 16th cent.

7218. Fair and softly goes far. 14th cent.

7219. Fair folk are aye fushionless [=pithless]. *K.*

7220. Fair in the cradle and foul in the saddle. *C.*

7221. Fair maidens wear no purses. [=A girl is not expected to pay her shot.] *K.*

7222. Fair play's a jewel. 19'h cent.

7223. Fair words break no bones. 15th cent.

7224. Fair words butter no parsnips. *C.*

7225. Fair words make fools fain [=pleased]. (*H.* 13th cent.)

7226. Fall not out with a friend for a trifle. *C.*

7227. Fame is but the breath of the people. *F.*

7228. Familiarity breeds contempt. *Latin*

7229. Far-fetched and dear bought is good for ladies. *H.*

7230. Far fowls have fair feathers. *K.*

7231. Far from eye, far from heart. 13th cent.

7232. Fast bind, fast find. *H.*

7233. Fat paunches make lean pates. *Greek*

7234. Fat sorrow is better than lean sorrow. [=Better be rich and miserable than poor and miserable.] *R.*

7235. Fate leads the willing but drives the stubborn. *Latin*

7236. Faults are thick where love is thin. *J. H.*

7237. Feather by feather the goose is plucked. *Italian*

7238. February fill dyke. 16th cent.

7239. February makes a bridge, and March breaks it. *G. H.*

7240. Feed a cold and starve a fever. 19th cent.

7241. Feed by measure and defy the physician. *H.*

7242. Festina lente.—Hasten slowly. *Latin*

7243. Few words are best. 16th cent.

7244. Few words to the wise suffice. *H.*

7245. Fiat experimentum in corpore vili.—Let the experiment be made on a worthless body. *Latin*

7246. Fiat justitia, ruat coelum.—Let justice be done, though heaven fall. *Latin*

7247. Fields have eyes, and woods have ears. 13th cent.

7248. Finding's keeping. 19th cent.

7249. Fine feathers make fine birds. *R.*
Fine words butter no parsnips, *see* Fair words, etc.

7250. Finis coronat opus.—The end crowns the work. *Latin*

7251. Fire is a good servant but a bad master. 17th cent.

7252. Fire that is closest kept burns most of all. *Latin*

7253. First catch your hare. [Misquotation from a cookery-book.] 18th cent.

7254. First come, first served. 16th cent.

7255. First creep and then go [=walk]. 15th cent.

7256. First deserve and then desire. *C. R.*

7257. First think and then speak. *C.*

7258. First thrive and then wive. *C.*

7259. Fish and company stink in three days. 16th cent.

7260. Fish is cast away that is cast in dry pools. *H.*

7261. Fish must swim thrice—once in the water, a second time in the sauce, and a third time in wine in the stomach. *French*

7262. Five hours sleepeth a traveller, seven a scholar, eight a merchant, and eleven every knave. 17th cent.

7263. Fling dirt enough, and some will stick. *Latin*

7264. Follow love and it will flee,
Flee love and it will follow thee. *R.* (16th cent.)

7265. Follow not truth too near the heels, lest it dash out thy teeth. *G. H.*

7266. Follow the river and you'll get to the sea. *F.*

7267. Fools and bairns should not see half-done work. *K.*

7268. Fools and madmen speak the truth. 17th cent.

7269. Fools are fain of flittin. [=Fond of moving.] *D. F.*

7270. Fools build houses, and wise men buy them. *R.*

7271. Fools cut their fingers, but wise men cut their thumbs. [=The folly of wise men is greater.] 18th cent.

7272. Fools make feasts and wise men eat them. *C.* (16th cent.)

7273. Fools tie knots and wise men loose them. *C.*

7274. For a flying enemy make a golden [*or* silver] bridge. *French*

7275. For a morning rain leave not your journey. 16th cent.

7276. For age and want, save while you may !
No morning sun lasts a whole day. *P. R. A.*

7277. For every evil under the sun
There is a remedy or there is none :
If there be one, try and find it ;
If there be none, never mind it. *W. H.*

7278. For want of a nail the shoe is lost ; for want of a shoe the horse is lost ; for want of a horse the rider is lost. *G. H.*

7279. For want of company, welcome trumpery. *R.*

7280. Forbearance is no acquittance. *H.*

7281. Forbid a thing, and that we will do. 14th cent.

7282. Forewarned, forearmed. *Latin*

7283. Forgive and forget. *H.*

7284. Forgive any sooner than thyself. *Spanish*

7285. Fortiter in re, suaviter in modo.—Strong in action, gentle in method. *Latin*

7286. Fortune can take from us nothing but what she gave us. *Latin*

7287. Fortune favours fools. *Latin*

7288. Fortune favours the brave. *Latin*

7289. Fortune knocks once at least at every man's gate. *W. H.*

7290. Foul in the cradle and fair in the saddle. *C. R.*

7291. Four eyes see more than two. *Latin*

7292. Friends are like fiddle-strings, they must not be screwed too tight. *B.*

7293. Friends are thieves of time. 17th cent.

7294. Friends may meet, but mountains never greet. *R.* (16th cent.)

7295. Friends tie their purses with a cobweb thread. *B.*

7296. Friendships multiply joys and divide griefs. *B.*

7297. From a choleric man withdraw a little ; from him that says nothing, for ever. *G. H.*

7298. From hell, Hull and Halifax, good Lord deliver us. [Beggars' saying, Hull and Halifax being of old very strict in enforcing the law against them.] 16th cent.

7299. From pillar to post [*or* post to pillar]. [=From whipping-post to pillory.] 15th cent.

7300. Frost and fraud both end in foul. *C. R.*

7301. Full of courtesy, full of craft. *C.* (16th cent.)

7302. Gadding gossips shall dine on the pot-lid. *F.*

7303. Game is cheaper in the market than in the fields and woods. *F.*

7304. Gaming, women, and wine, while they laugh, they make men pine. *G. H.*

7305. Gear [=property] is easier gained than guided. *R.*

7306. Gentility is but ancient riches. *G. H.*

7307. Gentility without ability is worse than plain beggary. *R.*

7308. Gentry sent to market will not buy one bushel of corn. 16th cent.

7309. Get a name to rise early, and you may lie all day. *K.*

7310. Giff gaff [=one gift for another] makes good friends. *R.*

7311. Give a bairn his will, and a whelp his fill, and none of these two will thrive. *K.*

7312. Give a dog a bad name and hang him. *K.*

7313. Give a lie twenty-four hours' start, and you can never overtake it. *L.*

7314. Give a loaf, and beg a shive [=slice]. *R.*

7315. Give a man luck, and throw him into the sea. *C.*

7316. Give a thief rope enough, and he'll hang himself. *R.*

7317. Give a thing and take again
And you shall ride in hell's wain. *R.*

7318. Give and spend, and God will send. *B.*

7319. Give him an inch, and he'll take an ell. 17th cent. (*H.*)
Give him rope enough and he'll hang himself, *see* Give a thief rope, etc.

7320. Give losers leave to speak [*or* talk]. *H.*

7321. Give me a child for the first seven years, and you may do what you like with him afterwards. [A Jesuit saying.] *L.*

7322. Give never the wolf the wether to keep. *D. F.*

7323. Give the devil his due. 16th cent.

7324. Giving much to the poor doth increase a man's store. *G. H.*

7325. Glasses and lasses are brittle ware. *K.*

7326. Gluttony kills more than the sword. 16th cent.

7327. Γνῶθι σεαυτόν—Know thyself. *Greek*

7328. Go down the ladder when thou marriest a wife ; go up when thou choosest a friend. *R.*

7329. Go farther and fare worse. *H.*

7330. Go not for every grief to the physician, for every quarrel to the lawyer, nor for every thirst to the pot. *G. H.*

7331. Go to bed with the lamb, and rise with the lark. 16th cent.

7332. God comes to see us without a bell. *Spanish*

7333. God comes with leaden feet, but strikes with iron hands.   16th cent.
7334. God defend me from my friends ; from my enemies I can defend
    myself.   17th cent. (15th cent.)
7335. God heals and the doctor takes the fee.   *G. H.*
7336. God help the poor, for the rich can help themselves.   *K.*
7337. God help the rich, the poor can beg.   *J. H.*
7338. God helps them that help themselves.   *G. H.* (16th cent.)
7339. God is better pleased with adverbs than with nouns.   [=With
    what is done well and lawfully.]   16th cent.
7340. God makes and apparel shapes, but it is money that finishes the man.   *R.*
7341. God never sends mouths but he sends meat.   *H.*
7342. God send you joy, for sorrow will come fast enough.   *T. D.*
7343. God send me a friend that may tell me of my faults ; if not, an
    enemy, and he will.   *R.*
7344. God sends cold after clothes.   [=He supplies men according to their
    needs.]   *H.*
7345. God sends fortune to fools.   *H.*
7346. God sends meat and the devil sends cooks.   16th cent.
7347. God tempers the wind to the shorn lamb.   *French*
7348. God's mill grinds slow but sure.   *Greek*
7349. Gold goes in at any gate except heaven's.   *R.*
7350. Good advice is beyond price.   *Latin*
7351. Good ale is meat, drink and cloth.   17th cent.
7352. Good ale will make a cat speak.   *R.*
7353. Good and quickly seldom meet.   *G. H.*
7354. Good clothes open all doors.   *F.*
7355. Good company on the road is the shortest cut.   *Italian*
7356. Good harvests make men prodigal, bad ones provident.   *R.*
7357. Good in the mouth and bad in the maw.   17th cent.
7358. Good is good, but better carries it.   *G. H.*
7359. Good masters make good servants.   19th cent.
7360. Good men [*or* people] are scarce.   17th cent.
7361. Good riding at two anchors, men have told,
    For if one break the other may hold.   *Greek*
7362. Good swimmers at length are drowned.   *G. H.*
7363. Good take-heed doth surely speed.   *C.*
7364. Good to fetch a sick man sorrow and a dead man woe.   [Said
    to those who loiter on errands.]   *R.*
7365. Good ware makes quick markets.   *Latin*
7366. Good weight and measure is heaven's treasure.   *F.*
7367. Good will should be taken for part payment.   *D. F.*
7368. Good wine needs no bush.   [The old sign of a tavern was a bunch
    of ivy.]   16th cent.
7369. Good words cost nought.   16th cent.
7370. Good words without deeds
    Are rushes and reeds.   *J. H.*
7371. Good workmen are seldom rich.   *G. H.*
7372. Goods are theirs who enjoy them.   16th cent.
7373. Gossiping and lying go together.   *F.*
7374. Grasp all, lose all.   18th cent.

7375. Great barkers are no biters. *C. R.*

7376. Great boast, small roast. *H.*

7377. Great bodies move slowly. *K.*

    Great cry and little wool, *see* Much cry, etc.

7378. Great men's sons seldom do well. *Latin*

7379. Great minds think alike.   20th cent. (17th cent.)

7380. Great spenders are bad lenders. *C.*

7381. Great strokes make not sweet music. *G. H.*

7382. Great talkers are great liars.   18th cent.

7383. Great trees are good for nothing but shade. *G. H.*

7384. Great trees keep down little ones. *F.*

7385. Great winds blow upon high hills.   16th cent.

7386. Greedy folk have long arms. *K.*

7387. Grey hairs are death's blossoms. *R.*

7388. Gutta cavat lapidem non vi sed saepe cadendo.—The drop hollows
    the stone not by force but by often falling. *Latin*

7389. Had I fish, is good without mustard. [A retort to those who talk
    of what they would do if they had so-and-so.] *C. R.*

7390. Hae ye gear, hae ye nane,
    Tine heart and a's gane.
    [=Have you goods, have you none, lose heart and all's
    gone.] *B.*

7391. Hail brings frost in the tail. *C.*

7392. Hair and hair makes the carle's [=fellow's] head bare.
    [=A large store may be brought to nothing by taking
    away a little at a time.] *C.*

7393. Half a loaf is better than no bread. *H.*

    Half the world knows not how the other half lives, *see* One half
    of the world, etc.

7394. Hall binks are sliddery. [=Hall benches are slippery. The
    favour of the great is uncertain.] *D. F.*

7395. Handsome is that handsome does.   *R.* (16th cent.)

7396. Hang him that hath no shift and him that hath one too many. *K.*

7397. Hanging and wiving go by destiny. *H.*

7398. Hap [=good luck] and a halfpenny are world's gear [=goods]
    enough. *C.*

7399. Happy is he that is happy in his children. *F.*

7400. Happy is he whose friends were born before him. [=He who
    has a position ready-made.] *R.*

7401. Happy is the bride the sun shines on, and the corpse the rain
    rains on.   17th cent.

7402. Happy is the child whose father goes to the devil. [And leaves
    a great estate got by extortion.]   16th cent.

7403. Happy is the country which has no history.   19th cent.

7404. Happy is the wooing that is not long a-doing.   16th cent.

7405. Happy man be his dole. [=May happiness be his lot.] *H.*

7406. Hard fare makes hungry bellies. *C.*

7407. Hard with hard never made good wall. [=Mortar is needed.
    Refractory spirits will not agree.] *Latin*

7408. Hard words break no bones.   16th cent

7409. Hares may pull dead lions by the beard. *Latin*
7410. Harm watch, harm catch. 15th cent.
7411. Harvest comes not every day, though it come every year. F.
7412. Haste and wisdom are things far odd. H.
7413. Haste comes not alone. [There is always some trouble with it.] G. H.
7414. Haste is from hell [*or* the devil.] 17th cent.
7415. Haste makes waste. H.
7416. Haste trips up its own heels. F.
7417. Hasty climbers have sudden falls. R. (16th cent.)
7418. Hasty gamesters oversee themselves. R.
7419. Hate not at the first harm. C.
7420. Hatred is blind, as well as love. F.
7421. Have a horse of thine own and thou mayest borrow another. J. H.
7422. Have an eye to the main chance. 16th cent.
7423. Have but few friends, though many acquaintances. J. H.
7424. Have God and have all. D. F.
7425. Have not thy cloak to make when it begins to rain. F. (C.)
7426. Hawks will not pick hawks' eyes out. 16th cent.
7427. He begins to die that quits his desires. G. H.
7428. He brings a staff to break his own head. 16th cent.
7429. He can give little to his servant who licks his own trencher. G. H.
7430. He can ill be master that never was scholar. C.
7431. He cannot say Bo to a goose. 16th cent.
7432. He cannot speak well that cannot hold his tongue. F. (17th cent.)
7433. He carries fire in one hand and water in the other. 15th cent.
7434. He carries well to whom it weighs not. G. H.
7435. He commands enough that obeys a wise man. G. H.
7436. He complains wrongfully on the sea that twice suffers shipwreck. G. H.
7437. He could eat me without salt. [=He hates me bitterly.] K.
7438. He dances well to whom fortune pipes. 16th cent.
7439. He deserves not the sweet that will not taste the sour. *Latin*
He dwells far from neighbours that is fain to praise himself,
see He hath ill neighbours, etc.
7440. He giveth twice that gives in a trice. *Latin*
7441. He goes a great voyage that goes to the bottom of the sea. F.
7442. He goes far that never turns. H.
7443. He goes long barefoot that waits for dead men's shoes. H.
7444. He goes not out of his way that goes to a good inn. G. H.
7445. He has a good estate, but that the right owner keeps it from him. R.
7446. He has a great fancy to marriage that goes to the devil for a wife. F.
7447. He has brought his pigs to a fine market. J. H. (16th cent.)
7448. He has but a short Lent that must pay money at Easter. F. (J. H.)
7449. He has a fault of a wife that marries mam's pet. K.
7450. He has much prayer but little devotion. H.
7451. He has not a penny to bless himself with. H.
7452. He has not lost all who has one cast left. F.
7453. He has wit at will that with an angry heart can hold him still D. F.
7454. He hath ill neighbours that is fain to praise himself. 16th cent.
7455. He has great need of a fool that plays the fool himself. G. H.

7456. He hath no leisure who useth it not. *G. H.*

7457. He hath not lived that lives not after death. *G. H.*

7458. He hath slept well that remembers not he hath slept ill. *F.*

7459. He is a fool that forgets himself. 14th cent.

7460. He is a fool that is not melancholy once a day. *R.*

7461. He is a fool that marries at Yule,
For when the corn's to shear the bairn's to bear. *K.*

7462. He is a fool who makes his doctor his heir. *Latin*

7463. He is a good friend that speaks well of us behind our backs. *R.*

7464. He is a good man whom fortune makes better. *F.*

7465. He is a good physician who cures himself. 15th cent.

7466. He is a great necromancer, for he asks counsel of the dead.
[=Of books.] *G. H.*

7467. He is an ill cook that cannot lick his own fingers. *H.*

7468. He is an ill guest that never drinks to his host. *R.*

7469. He is blind enough who sees not through the holes of a sieve. *R.*

7470. He is born in a good hour who gets a good name. 15th cent.

7471. He is either dead or teaching school. *Greek*

7472. He is happy that thinks himself so. *Latin*

7473. He is idle that might be better employed. *F.*

7474. He is lifeless that is faultless. *H.*

7475. He is no man's enemy but his own. *C.*

7476. He is not a wise man who cannot play the fool on occasion.
F. (16th cent.)

7477. He is not laughed at that laughs at himself first. *F.*

7478. He is not poor that hath little, but he that desireth much. *G. H.*

7479. He is not wise that is not wise for himself. *Latin*

7480. He is only bright that shines by himself. *G. H.*

7481. He is poor indeed that can promise nothing. *R.* (*C.*)

7482. He is rich enough that wants nothing. *Latin*

7483. He is unworthy to live who lives only for himself. *F.*

7484. He is wise enough that can keep himself warm. *H.*

7485. He is wise that is ware in time. 14th cent.

7486. He is wise that knows when he is well enough. *H.*

7487. He knows enough that can live and hold his peace. 16th cent.

7488. He laughs best that laughs last. 18th cent.

7489. He laughs ill that laughs himself to death. *C.*

7490. He lives long that lives well. 16th cent.

7491. He lives unsafely that looks too near on things. *G. H.*

7492. He loses his thanks who promises and delays. *T. D.*

7493. He loseth indeed that loseth at last. *F.*

7494. He loseth nothing that loseth not God. *G. H.*

7495. He loves me for little that hates me for naught. *D. F.*

7496. He makes a rod for his own back. *H.* (14th cent.)

7497. He may freely receive courtesies that knows how to requite
them. *R.*

7498. He may ill run that cannot go [=walk.] *H.*

7499. He may well be contented who needs neither borrow nor
flatter. *R.* (15th cent.)

7500. He must have iron nails that scratches a bear. *R.*

7501. He must have leave to speak who cannot hold his tongue. *D. F.*
7502. He must needs swim that is held up by the chin. *H.*
7503. He must rise betimes that will cozen with the devil. *J. H.*
7504. He must rise early that would please everybody. *R.*
7505. He must stoop that hath a low door. *R.*
7506. He never broke his hour that kept his day. *R.*
7507. He never lies but when the holly is green. [=He lies always.] *D. F.*
7508. He never tint [=lost] a cow that grat [=wept] for a needle. *D. F.*
7509. He preaches well that lives well. 17th cent.
7510. He preacheth patience that never knew pain. *B.*
7511. He quits his place well that leaves his friend there. *G. H.*
7512. He rides sure that never fell. 15th cent.
7513. He rises over early that is hanged ere noon. *D. F.*
7514. He should have a long spoon that sups with the devil. 14th cent.
7515. He sits full still that has riven breeks [=trousers.] *D. F.*
7516. He sits not sure that sits too high. 17th cent.
7517. He smells best that smells of nothing. *Latin*
7518. He stands not surely that never slips. *G. H.*
7519. He sups ill who eats up all at dinner. *French*
7520. He teacheth ill who teacheth all. *J. H.*
7521. He that asketh faintly beggeth a denial. *Latin*
7522. He that believes all, misseth ; he that believes nothing, hits not. *G. H.*
7523. He that bewails himself hath the cure in his hands. *G. H.*
7524. He that bites on every weed must needs light on poison. *C.*
7525. He that blames would buy. *G. H.*
7526. He that blows in the dust fills his eyes with it. *G. H.*
7527. He that borrows must pay again with shame or loss. *R.*
7528. He that brings up his son to nothing, breeds a thief. *F.*
7529. He that burns his house warms himself for once. *G. H.*
7530. He that burns most shines most. *G. H.*
7531. He that buys a house ready wrought hath many a pin and nail
for nought. *C. R.*
7532. He that buys land buys many stones ;
He that buys flesh buys many bones ;
He that buys eggs buys many shells ;
He that buys good ale buys nothing else. *R.*
7533. He that by the plough would thrive
Himself must either hold or drive. *R.*
7534. He that can make a fire well can end a quarrel. *G. H.*
7535. He that can stay obtains. *French*
7536. He that cannot abide a bad market deserves not a good one. *R.*
7537. He that cannot make sport should mar none. *K.*
7538. He that cannot pay, let him pray. *R.*
7539. He that chastiseth one amendeth many. *T. D.*
7540. He that comes first to the hill may sit where he will. *D. F.*
7541. He that cometh last to the pot is the soonest wroth. *H.*
7542. He that commits a fault thinks everyone speaks of it. *G. H.*
7543. He that could know what would be dear
Need be a merchant but one year. *H.*
7544. He that counts all costs will ne'er put plough in the earth. *D. F.*

7545. He that desires honour is not worthy of honour.   17th cent.

7546. He that does bidding deserves no dinging [=beating].   *D. F.*

7547. He that does not love a woman sucked a sow.   *F.*

7548. He that does you an ill turn will never forgive you.   *K.*

7549. He that doth lend doth lose his friend.   *W. H.* (17th cent.)

7550. He that doth nothing doth ever amiss.   17th cent.

7551. He that doth what he should not shall feel what he would not.   *G. H.* (16th cent.)

7552. He that doth what he will doth not what he ought.   *G. H.*

7553. He that eats till he is sick must fast till he is well.   *F.*

7554. He that falls to-day may rise to-morrow.   17th cent.

7555. He that feareth every bush must never go a-birding.   16th cent.

7556. He that fears death lives not.   *G. H.*

7557. He that fears you present will hate you absent.   *F.*

7558. He that fights and runs away may live to fight another day.   *Greek*

7559. He that gains well and spends well needs no account book.   *G.H.*

7560. He that gapeth till he be fed,
Well may he gape until he be dead.   *H.*

7561. He that gives me small gifts would have me live.   *French*

7562. He that goes barefoot must not plant thorns.   *G. H.*

7563. He that goes to bed thirsty riseth healthy.   *G. H.*

7564. He that goeth far hath many encounters.   *G. H.*

7565. He that goeth out with often loss
At last comes home by weeping cross.   *R.*

7566. He that gropes in the dark finds that he would not.   *J. H.*

7567. He that handles thorns shall prick his fingers.   *R.*

7568. He that has a wife has a master.   *K.*

7569. He that has no children knows not what is love.   17th cent.

7570. He that has no gear to tine [=goods to lose] has shins to pine [=to suffer pain]. [=Corporal punishment may be used when the offender cannot pay a fine.]   *D. F.*

7571. He that has two hoards will get a third.   *D. F.*

7572. He that hath a good harvest may be content with some thistles.   *C.*

7573. He that hath a head of wax must not walk in the sun.   *G. H.*

7574. He that hath an ill name is half hanged.   *H.*

7575. He that hath but one eye must be afraid to lose it.   *G. H.*

7576. He that hath it and will not keep it,
He that wants it and will not seek it,
He that drinks and is not dry,
Shall want money as well as I.   *J. H.*

7577. He that hath lost his credit is dead to the world.   *G. H.*

7578. He that hath no head needs no hat.   *R.*

7579. He that hath no ill fortune is troubled with good.   *G. H.*

7580. He that hath no money needeth no purse.   *T. D.*

7581. He that hath nothing is not contented.   *R.*

7582. He that hath one hog makes him fat ; and he that hath one son makes him a fool.   *G. H.*

7583. He that hath plenty of goods shall have more.   *H.*

7584. He that hath right, fears ; he that hath wrong, hopes.   *G. H.*

7585. He that hath shipped the devil must make the best of him.   *R.*

7586. He that hath some land must have some labour.   *C.*

7587. He that hath time, and looks for time, loseth time.   *C. R.* (16th cent.)

7588. He that hears much and speaks not at all, shall be welcome both in bower and hall.   *R.*

7589. He that hides can find.   15th cent.

7590. He that hopes not for good fears not evil.   *G, H.*

7591. He that is a master must serve.   *G. H.*

7592. He that is angry at a feast is rude.   *G, H.*

7593. He that is angry without a cause, must be pleased without amends. *H.*

7594. He that is born to be hanged shall never be drowned.   *G. R.*

7595. He that is busy is tempted by but one devil; he that is idle, by a legion.   *F.*

7596. He that is down, down with him.   *C.*

7597. He that is fallen cannot help him that is down.   *G. H.*

7598. He that is fed at another's hand may stay long ere he be full.   *G. H.*

7599. He that is foolish in the fault, let him be wise in the punishment. *G. H.*

7600. He that hath done ill once will do it again   *B.*

7601. He that is ill to himself will be good to nobody.   *K.*

7602. He that is in a town in May loseth his spring.   *G. H.*

7603. He that is master of himself will soon be master of others.   *B.*

7604. He that is not handsome at twenty, nor strong at thirty, nor rich at forty, nor wise at fifty, will never be handsome, strong, rich, or wise.   *G. H.*

7605. He that is once born, once must die.   *G. H.*

7606. He that is too secure [=over-confident] is not safe.   *F.*

7607. He that kisseth his wife in the market-place shall have many teachers.   *C. R.*

7608. He that knows little soon repeats it.   *R.*

7609. He that knows nothing doubts nothing.   *G. H.*

7610. He that labours and thrives spins gold.   *G. H.*

7611. He that lends gives.   *G. H.*

7612. He that lies on the ground can fall no lower.   *Latin*

7613. He that lives ill, fear follows him.   *G. H.*

7614. He that lives in hope danceth without music.   *G. H.*

7615. He that lives most dies most.   *G. H.*

7616. He that lives not well one year sorrows seven after.   *G. H.*

7617. He that lives well is learned enough.   *G. H.*

7618. He that loseth his due gets not thanks.   *G. D.*

7619. He that loseth his wife and sixpence hath lost a tester [=sixpenny piece].   *R.*

7620. He that loves glass without G,
Take away L and that is he.   *R.*

7621. He that loves the tree loves the branch.   *G. H.*

7622. He that makes a good war makes a good peace.   *G. H.*

7623. He that makes a thing too fine breaks it.   *G. H.*

7624. He that makes himself a sheep shall be eaten by the wolf.
    G. H. (16th cent.)

7625. He that marries a widow and three children marries four thieves.   *R.*

7626. He that marries a widow will often have a dead man's head thrown in his dish.   *H.*

7627. He that marries ere he be wise will die ere he thrive. *H.*

7628. He that marries for wealth sells his liberty. *G. H.*

7629. He that marries late marries ill. *G. H.* (16th cent.)

7630. He that may not do as he would must do as he may. *Latin*

7631. He that mischief hatcheth mischief catcheth. *C. R.*

7632. He that mocks a cripple ought to be whole. 16th cent.

7633. He that never climbed never fell. *H.*

7634. He that once deceives is ever suspected. *G. H.*

7635. He that once hits will ever be shooting. *G. H.*

7636. He that passeth a winter's day escapes an enemy. *French*

7637. He that pays last never pays twice. *R.*

7638. He that pities another remembers himself. *G. H.*

7639. He that praiseth himself spattereth himself. *G. H.*

7640. He that preacheth giveth alms. *G. H.*

7641. He that promises too much means nothing. *F.*

7642. He that pryeth into every cloud may be stricken with a thunderbolt. *R.*

7643. He that puts on a public gown must put off a private person. *F.*

He that reckons without his host must reckon twice, *see* To reckon without one's host.

7644. He that respects not is not respected. *G. H.*

7645. He that riseth first is first dressed. *G. H.*

7646. He that runs fast will not run long. *B.*

7647. He that runs in the dark may well stumble. *R.*

7648. He that saveth his dinner will have the more for his supper. [=The man who saves when young will have more to spend when he is old.] *French*

7649. He that seeks trouble never misses. *G. H.*

7650. He that sends a fool means to follow him. *G. H.*

7651. He that serves everybody is paid by nobody. 17th cent.

7652. He that serves well need not be afraid to ask his wages. *G. H.*

7653. He that shames shall be shent [=disgraced]. *D. F.*

7654. He that shoots oft shall at last hit the mark. *Latin*

7655. He that shows his purse longs to be rid of it. *C.*

7656. He that sings on Friday will weep on Sunday. *G. H.*

7657. He that spares the bad injures the good. *Latin*

7658. He that speaks me fair and loves me not, I'll speak him fair and trust him not. *T. D*

7659. He that speaks sows, and he that holds his peace gathers. *G. H.*

7660. He that stays in the valley shall never get over the hill. *R.*

7661. He that strikes with his tongue must ward with his head. *G. H.*

7662. He that studies his content wants it. *G. H.*

7663. He that stumbles and falls not mends his pace. *G. H.*

7664. He that takes not up a pin slights his wife. *G. H.*

7665. He that talks much of his happiness summons grief. *G. H.*

7666. He that talks to himself speaks to a fool. *K.*

7667. He that teaches himself has a fool for his master. 17th cent.

7668. He that tells a secret is another's servant. *G. H.*

7669. He that tells his wife news is but newly married. *G. H.*

7670. He that thinks too much of his virtues bids others think of his vices. *W. H,*

7671. He that travels far knows much. *R.*

7672. He that was born under a three-halfpenny [*or* threepenny] planet
shall never be worth two pence [*or* a groat]. *R*

7673. He that will eat the kernel must crack the nut. *Latin*

7674. He that will France [*or* England] win must with Scotland first
begin. 16th cent.

7675. He that will enter into Paradise must have a good key. *G. H.*

7676. He that will not be counselled cannot be helped. *C.*

7677. He that will not be ruled by his own dame shall be ruled by his
stepdame. [=Those who cannot be prevailed upon by
gentle means must have harsher treatment.] *H.*

7678. He that will not be saved needs no preacher. *R.*

7679. He that will not have peace, God gives him war. *G. H.*

7680. He that will not stoop for a pin shall never be worth a pound. *R.*

7681. He that will not when he may, when he will he shall have nay.
H. (10th cent.)

7682. He that will thrive must ask leave of his wife. *H.* (15th cent.)

7683. He that will thrive must rise at five,
He that hath thriven may lie till seven. 16th cent.

7684. He that will to Cupar maun [=must] to Cupar. [=Wilful people
must have their way. The Fife courts of Justice were
formerly at Cupar.] *K.*

7685. He that winketh with the one eye and looketh with the other, I
will not trust him though he were my brother. *H.*

7686. He that wipes the child's nose kisseth the mother's cheek. *G. H.*

7687. He that woos a maid must come seldom in her sight,
But he that woos a widow must woo her day and night. *C.*

7688. He that would be old long must be old betimes. 17th cent. (16th cent.)

7689. He that would be well needs not go from his own house. *G. H.*

7690. He that would hang his dog gives out first that he is mad.
R. (16th cent.)

7691. He that would have good luck in horses must kiss the parson's
wife. *R.*

7692. He that would have what he hath not should do what he doth not. *H.*

7693. He that would know what shall be must consider what hath been. *F.*

7694. He that would learn to pray, let him go to sea. *R.*

7695. He that would live for aye must eat sage in May. *R.*

7696. He that would live in peace and rest
Must hear and see and say the best. *R.*

7697. He that would no evils do must shun all things that long
[=belong] thereto. *C.*

7698. He that would the daughter win
Must with the mother first begin. *R.*

7699. He thinks not well that thinks not again. *G. H.*

7700. He to whom God gave no sons the devil gives nephews. *B.*

7701. He warms too near that burns. *G. H.*

7702. He was a bold man that first ate an oyster. 17th cent.

7703. He was hanged that left his drink behind him. [Only a man
running for his life would do so.] *R.*

7704. He was scant [=short] of news that told his father was hanged. *K.*

7705. He who commences many things finishes but few. *Italian*

7706. He who does not rise early never does a good day's work. *T. D.*

7707. He who lies down with dogs will rise with fleas. *Latin*

7708. He who never was sick dies the first fit. *F.*

7709. He who pays the piper may call the tune. 17th cent.

7710. He who rides on a tiger can never dismount. *Chinese*

7711. He who says what he likes shall hear what he does not like. *Latin*

7712. He who swells in prosperity will shrink in adversity. *B.*

7713. He wrongs not an old man that steals his supper from him. *G. H.*

7714. Heads I win, tails you lose. 17th cent.

7715. Health and money go far. *G. H.*

7716. Health and wealth create beauty. *B.*

7717. Health and sickness surely are men's double enemies. *G. H.*

7718. Health is better than wealth. 16th cent.

7719. Health is not valued till sickness comes. *F.*

7720. Hear all parties. *H.*

7721. Hear and see and be still. 15th cent.

7722. Hear twice before you speak once. *B.*

7723. Hearken to reason, or she will be heard. *G. H.*

7724. Hearts may agree though heads differ. *F.*

Heaven helps those that help themselves, *see* God helps them, etc.

7725. Hell and Chancery are always open. *F.*

7726. Hell is full of good meanings and wishes. *G. H.*

Hell is paved with good intentions. *see* The road to hell, etc.

7727. Hell is wherever heaven is not. 17th cent.

7728. Help, hands ! for I have no lands. 16th cent.

7729. Help me to salt, help me to sorrow. 19th cent.

7730. Here to-day and gone to-morrow. *P. R. A.*

7731. Hereafter comes not yet. *H.*

7732. Heresy may be easier kept out than shook off. *G. H.*

7733. Hew not too high lest the chips fall in thine eye. 14th cent.

7734. Hide nothing from thy minister, physician, and lawyer.
G. H. (16th cent.)

7735. High places have their precipices. *F.*

High words break no bones, *see* Hard words, etc.

7736. His bark is worse than his bite. *Latin*

7737. His bashful mind hinders his good intent. *R.*

7738. His bread is buttered on both sides. [=He is well-to-do.] *R.*

7739. His hair grows through his hood. [=He is in want.] 15th cent.

7740. His heart is in his boots [*formerly* hose]. 15th cent.

7741. His heart is in his mouth. 16th cent.

7742. His money burns a hole in his pocket. [=He feels a strong desire to spend it.] 16th cent.

7743. His wits are wool-gathering. [=He is absent-minded.] 16th cent.

7744. History repeats itself. 19th cent.

7745. Hold fast when you have it. *H.*

7746. Hold your hands off other folks' bairns, till you get some of your own. *B.*

7747. Home is home, be it never so homely. *H.*

7748. Homer sometimes nods. *Latin*

7749. Honest men marry soon, wise men not at all. *R.*
7750. Honesty is the best policy. 16th cent.
7751. Honesty may be dear bought, but can never be an ill pennyworth. *K.*
7752. Honey in the mouth saves the purse. *Italian*
7753. Honey is dear bought if licked off thorns. 12th cent.
7754. Honey is sweet, but the bee stings. *G. H.*
7755. Honi soit qui mal y pense.—Shame take him that shame thinketh. *French*
7756. Honour and ease are seldom bedfellows. *C.*
7757. Honour and profit lie not in one sack. *G. H.*
7758. Honour will buy no beef. 17th cent.
7759. Honour without profit is a ring on the finger. *Spanish*
7760. Honours change manners. *Latin*
7761. Hope for the best and prepare for the worst. 16th cent.
7762. Hope is a good breakfast but a bad supper. 17th cent.
7763. Hope is a lover's staff. *B.*
7764. Hope is as cheap as despair. *F.*
7765. Hope is the poor man's bread. *Italian*
7766. Hope well and have well. 16th cent.
7767. Hot love is soon cold. *H.*
7768. Humanum est errare.—To err is human. *Latin*
7769. Humble hearts have humble desires. *G. H.*
7770. Hunger breaks through stone walls. *H.*
7771. Hunger finds no fault with the cookery. *F.*
7772. Hunger is the best sauce. *Latin*
7773. Hunger makes dinners, pastime suppers. *G. H.*
7774. Hungry bellies have no ears. *Latin*
7775. Hungry dogs will eat dirty puddings. *H.*
7776. Hungry flies bite sore. *H.*
7777. Husbands are in heaven whose wives scold not. *H.*
7778. Hypocrisy is a homage that vice pays to virtue. *French*
7779. I am very wheamow [=nimble] said the old woman, when she stepped into the milk-bowl. *R.*
7780. I can see as far into a millstone as another. *H.*
7781. I cannot be your friend and your flatterer too. 17th cent.
7782. I gave the mouse a hole, and she is become my heir. *G. H.*
7783. I had rather have your room than your company. 16th cent.
7784. I have other fish to fry. [=Other business to attend to.] 17th cent.
7785. I know him not though I should meet him in my dish. 17th cent.
7786. I know no more than the man in the moon about it. 19th cent.
7787. I know no more than the Pope of Rome about it. *R.*
7788. I live, and lords do no more. 16th cent.
7789. I love my friends well, but myself better. *French.*
7790. I love thee like pudding, if thou wert pie I'd eat thee. *R.*
7791. I may see him need, but I'll not see him bleed. *C.*
7792. I pensieri stretti ed il viso sciolto.—The thoughts close and the countenance open. *Italian*
7793. I say little [*or* nothing] but I think the more. *H.* (15th cent.)
7794. I stout [=proud] and thou stout, who shall bear the ashes out? *H.*
7795. I taught you to swim, and now you'd drown me. *F.*

7796. I was not born yesterday. 19th cent.
7797. I wept when I was born, and every day shows why. *G. H.*
7798. I will either grind or find. *R.*
7799. I will keep no more cats than will catch mice. *R.*
7800. I will neither meddle nor make. 16th cent.
7801. I will not change a cottage in possession for a kingdom in
    reversion. *R.*
7802. I will not keep a dog and bark myself. 16th cent.
7803. I will not make a toil of a pleasure. 17th cent.
7804. I will not make my dish-clout my table-cloth. *R.*
7805. I will not pull the thorn out of your foot and put it into my own. *R.*
7806. I will trust him no further than I can fling him. *R.*
7807. I wot well how the world wags, he is most loved that hath most
    bags. *R.*
7808. I would not call the king my cousin. [=I would be so happy.] *K.*
7809. I would not touch him with a pair of tongs. *R.*
7810. Idle brains are the devil's workshop. *R.*
7811. Idle folks have the least leisure. 19th cent.
7812. Idle men are dead all their life long. *F.*
7813. Idle people take the most pains. *R.*
7814. Idleness is the key of beggary. *R.*
7815. Idleness is the parent of all vice [*or* the root of all evil]. 15th cent.
7816. Idleness makes the wit rust. *F.*
7817. Idleness must thank itself if it go barefoot. *R.*
7818. If a good man thrive, all thrive with him. *G. H.*
7819. If a man deceive me once, shame on him ; if he deceive me twice,
    shame on me. *K.*
7820. If a woman were little as she is good
    A peascod would make her a gown and a hood. *Italian*
7821. If all fools wore white caps we should seem a flock of geese. *G. H.*
7822. If all men say that thou art an ass, then bray. *T. D.*
7823. If an ass goes a-travelling, he'll not come home a horse. *F.*
7824. If anything stay, let work stay. *R.*
7825. If Candlemas day be fair and bright, [2 Feb.]
    Winter will have another flight ;
    If on Candlemas day it be shower and rain,
    Winter is gone and will come not again. *R.*
7826. If every man mend one, all shall be amended. *H.*
7827. If folly were grief, every house would weep. *G. H.*
7828. If fools went not to market, bad wares would not be sold. *Spanish*
7829. If great men would have care of little ones, both would last
    long. *G. H.*
7830. If hope were not, heart would break. 13th cent.
7831. If I had not lifted up the stone, you had not found the jewel. *R.*
7832. If Ifs and Ans were pots and pans
    There'd be no trade for tinkers. 19th cent.
7833. If it were not for the belly the back might wear gold. *F.*
7834. If Jack's in love, he's no judge of Jill's beauty. *F.*
7835. If Janiveer's calends be summerly gay,
    'Twill be winterly weather till the calends of May. *F.*

7836. If money be not thy servant, it will be thy master.   17th cent.
7837. If my shirt knew my design, I'd burn it.   *F.* (17th cent.)
7838. If on the eighth of June it rain,
    It foretells a wet harvest, men sain.   *F.*
7839. If one sheep leap o'er the dyke [=ditch], all the rest will follow.   *K.*
7840. If one will not another will ; so are all maidens married.   *H.*
7841. If physic do not work, prepare for the kirk.   *R.*
7842. If St. Paul's be fine and clear   [25 Jan.]
    It doth betide a happy year.   16th cent. (14th cent.)
7843. If St. Vitus's day be rainy weather   [15 June]
    It will rain for thirty days together.   *D.*
7844. If the adder could hear and the blindworm could see,
    Neither man nor beast would ever go free.   19th cent.
7845. If the beard were all, the goat might preach.   17th cent.
7846. If the bed could tell all it knows, it would put many to the
    blush.   *J. H.*
7847. If the brain sows not corn, it plants thistles.   *G. H.*
7848. If the cap fits, wear it.   18th cent.
7849. If the cock goes crowing to bed.
    He's sure to rise with a watery head.   [=It will rain.]   *D.*
7850. If the counsel be good, no matter who gave it.   *F.*
7851. If the devil find a man idle, he'll set him to work.   *K.*
7852. If the doctor cures, the sun sees it ; but if he kills, the earth hides it. *K.*
7853. If the dog bark, go in ; if the bitch bark, go out.   *R.*
7854. If the first of July it be rainy weather,
    'Twill rain, more or less, for four weeks together.   *F.*
7855. If the grass grow in Janiveer,
    It grows the worse for't all the year.   *R.*
7856. If the ice will bear a man before Christmas, it will not bear a
    goose after.   *I.*
7857. If the laird slight the lady, so will all the kitchen boys.   *K.*
7858. If the lion's skin cannot, the fox's shall.   [=If force will not
    answer, craft will.]   *French*
7859. If the mountain will not come to Mahomet, Mahomet must go to
    the mountain.   *R.*
7860. If the oak's before the ash,
    Then you'll only get a splash ;
    If the ash precedes the oak,
    Then you may expect a soak.   *W. H.*
7861. If the old dog barks, he gives counsel.   *G. H.*
7862. If the pills were pleasant, they would not want gilding.   *F.* (*T. D.*)
7863. If the sky falls we shall catch [*or* have] larks.   *H.*
7864. If the staff be crooked, the shadow cannot be straight.   *G. H.*
7865. If the sun in red should set.
    The next day surely will be wet ;
    If the sun should set in grey,
    The next will be a rainy day.   *I.*
7866. If the twenty-fourth of August be fair and clear,
    Then hope for a prosperous autumn that year.   *F.*
7867. If the wise erred not, it would go hard with fools.   *G. H.*

7868. If there be a rainbow in the eve,
It will rain and leave ;
But if there be a rainbow in the morrow,
It will neither lend nor borrow. *R.*

7869. If there were no knaves and fools, all the world would be alike. *F.*

7870. If things were to be done twice, all would be wise. *G. H.*

7871. If thou dealest with a fox, think of his tricks. *F.*

7872. If thou hast not a capon, feed on an onion. *R.*

7873. If we are bound to forgive an enemy, we are not bound to trust him. *F.*

7874. If wind blows on you through a hole,
Make your will and take care of your soul. *P. R. A.*

7875. If wise men play the fool, they do it with a vengeance. *B.*

7876. If wishes were horses, beggars would ride. *K.*

7877. If ye would know a knave, give him a staff. *G. H.*

7878. If you always say No, you'll never be married. *K.*

7879. If you are too fortunate, you will not know yourself ; if you are too
unfortunate, nobody will know you. *F.*

7880. If you beat spice it will smell the sweeter. *F.*

7881. If you can kiss the mistress, never kiss the maid. *R.*

7882. If you cannot bite, never show your teeth. *R.*

7883. If you don't like it, you may lump [=put up with] it. 19th cent.

7884. If you drink in your pottage, you'll cough in your grave. *R.*

7885. If you make a jest, you must take a jest. 18th cent.

7886. If you have done no ill the six days, you may play the seventh. *F.*

7887. If you have no enemies, it is a sign fortune has forgot you. *F.*

7888. If you kill one flea in March you kill a hundred. *L.*

7889. If you leap into a well, Providence is not bound to fetch you out. *F.*

7890. If you lie upon roses when young, you'll lie upon thorns when old. *F.*

7891. If you pay not a servant his wages, he will pay himself. *F.*

7892. If you put nothing into your purse, you can take nothing out. *F.*

7893. If you run after two hares, you will catch neither. *Latin*

7894. If you sing before breakfast, you'll cry before night. 16th cent.

7895. If you squeeze a cork, you will get but little juice. *F.*

7896. If you swear, you'll catch no fish. 17th cent.
If you touch pot you must touch penny, *see* Touch pot, etc.

7897. If you trust before you try,
You may repent before you die. *R.* (16th cent.)

7898. If you want a thing well done, do it yourself. *L.*

7899. If you want a thing done, go ; if not, send. *P. R. A.*

7900. If you wish good advice, consult an old man. *Portuguese*

7901. If you wish to live and thrive,
Let the spider run alive. 19th cent.

7902. If you would fruit have,
You must bring the leaf to the grave. *R.*
[=Transplant in autumn.]

7903. If you would know secrets, look for them in grief or pleasure. *G. H.*

7904. If you would know the value of money, try to borrow some. *G. H.*

7905. If you would live well for a week, kill a hog ; if you would live well
for a month, marry ; if you would live well all your life, turn
priest. 19th cent.

7906. If you would make an enemy, lend a man money, and ask it of him again. *Portuguese*

7907. If you would wish the dog to follow you, feed him. *B.*

7908. If your ear burns, someone is talking about you. *H.*

7909. If your hand be bad, mend it with good play. [At cards.] *F.*

7910. If youth knew what age would crave, it would both get and save. *R.*

7911. Ignorance is the mother of devotion. 16th cent.

7912. Ignorance is the mother of impudence. *B.*

7913. Ignotum per ignotius.—[Explaining] what is unknown by what is still more unknown. *Latin*

7914. Il faut reculer pour mieux sauter.—One must draw back in order to leap better. *French*

7915. Ill beef ne'er made good broo [=broth]. *K.*

7916. Ill comes in ells and goes out by inches. *G. H.*

7917. Ill comes upon waur's [=worse's] back. *K.*

7918. Ill doers are ill deemers. *K.*

7919. Ill-gotten gains [or goods] seldom prosper. 16th cent.

7920. Ill-gotten goods thrive not to the third heir. *Latin*

7921. Ill gotten, ill spent. *Latin*

7922. Ill luck is good for something. *C. R.*

7923. Ill natures never want a tutor. *F.*

7924. Ill news travels fast [or comes apace]. 16th cent.

7925. Ill ware is never cheap. *G. H.*

7926. Ill weeds grow apace. *French*

7927. Ill will never said well. 15th cent.

7928. In a calm sea every man is a pilot. *R.*

7929. In a good house all is quickly ready. *G. H.*

7930. In a retreat the lame are foremost. *G. H.*

7931. In a thousand pounds of law there is not an ounce of love. *R.*

7932. In all games it is good to leave off a winner. *F.*

7933. In an ermine spots are soon discovered. *F.*

7934. In April, come he will;   [The cuckoo.]
In May, he sings all day ;
In June he alters his tune ;
In July he prepares to fly ;
In August, go he must ;
If he stay till September,
'Tis as much as the oldest man can ever remember. *I.*

7935. In at one ear and out at the other. 14th cent.

7936. In choosing a wife and buying a sword we ought not to trust another. *G. H.*

7937. In dock, out nettle.   [Signifying inconstancy.] 14th cent.

7938. In doing we learn. *G. H.*

7939. In every art it is good to have a master. *G. H.*

7940. In every country the sun rises in the morning. *G. H.*

7941. In fair weather prepare for foul. *F.*

7942. In for a penny, in for a pound. 17th cent.

7943. In giving and taking it is easy mistaking. *B.*

7944. In love is no lack. 15th cent.

7945. In love's wars, he who flieth is conqueror. *F.*

7946. In March, the birds begin to search ;
In April, the corn begins to fill ;
In May, the birds begin to lay. *W. H.*

7947. In my own city my name, in a strange city my clothes procure me
respect. *R.*

7948. In settling an island, the first building erected by a Spaniard will
be a church ; by a Frenchman, a fort ; by a Dutchman, a
warehouse ; and by an Englishman, an alehouse. 18th cent.

7949. In space comes grace. *H.*

7950. In sports and journeys men are known. *G. H.*

7951. In the coldest flint there is hot fire. 16th cent.

7952. In the country of the blind the one-eyed man is king. 16th cent.

7953. In the deepest water is the best fishing. *R.*

7954. In the end things will mend. *J. H.*

7955. In the grave, dust and bones jostle not for the wall. *F.*

7956. In the house of the fiddler all fiddle. *G. H.*

7957. In the husband wisdom, in the wife gentleness. *G. H.*

7958. In the old of the moon, a cloudy morning bodes a fair afternoon. *R.*

7959. In the world, who knows not to swim goes to the bottom. *G. H.*

7960. In time of prosperity friends will be plenty ;
In time of adversity not one among twenty. *J. H.*

7961. In trust is treason. 15th cent.

7962. In vain he craves advice that will not follow it. *R.*

7963. In vino veritas.—In wine there is truth. *Latin.*

7964. Industry is fortune's right hand, and frugality her left. *R.*

7965. Inglese italianato è un diavolo incarnato.—An Englishman
Italianate is a devil incarnate. *Italian.*

7966. Injuries don't use to be written on ice. *F.*

7967. Innocence itself sometimes hath need of a mask. *F.*

7968. Innocent actions carry their warrant with them. *F.*

7969. Interest will not lie. 17th cent.

7970. Into the mouth of a bad dog often falls a good bone. *C.*

7971. It chances in an hour, that happens not in seven years. 16th cent.

7972. It cost more to do ill than to do well. *G. H.*

7973. It early pricks that will be a thorn. 14th cent.

7974. It is a bad cause that none dare speak in. *C.*

7975. It is a bad cloth that will take no colour. *H.*

7976. It is a bad sack that will abide no clouting. *H.*

7977. It is a bold [*or* wily] mouse that breeds [*or* nestles] in the cat's
ear. 15th cent.

7978. It is a dear collop that is cut out of thine own flesh. *H.*

7979. It is a foolish sheep that makes the wolf his confessor. *R.*

7980. It is a good horse that never stumbles,
And a good wife that never grumbles. *R.*

7981. It is a good tongue that says no ill, and a better heart that thinks
none. *K.*

7982. It is a hard-fought field where none escapes. *H.*

7983. It is a hard winter when one wolf eats another. 16th cent.

7984. It is a long lane that has no turning. *R.*

7985. It is a pain both to pay and pray. *D. F.*

7986. It is a poor dog that is not worth the whistling.   *H.*
7987. It is a poor heart that never rejoices.   19th cent.
7988. It is a poor stake that cannot stand one year in the ground. *H.*
7989. It is a proud horse that will not bear his own provender. *H.*
7990. It is a rank courtesy when a man is forced to give thanks for his own. *R.*
7991. It is a sad burden to carry a dead man's child. 17th cent.
7992. It is a sad house where the hen crows louder than the cock. 16th cent.
7993. It is a sair dung [=sore beaten] bairn that dare not greet
  [=weep].   *D. F.*
7994. It is a silly bargain where nobody gets. *F.* (16th cent.)
7995. It is a silly fish that is caught twice with the same bait. *F.*
7996. It is a silly goose that comes to the fox's sermon. 16th cent.
7997. It is a sin to belie the devil. 16th cent.
7998. It is a sin to steal a pin. 19th cent.
7999. It is a wise child that knows its own father. 18th cent. (16th cent.)
8000. It is always term time in the court of conscience. *F.*
8001. It is an ill battle [*or* army] where the devil carries the colours. *R.* (*C.*)
8002. It is an ill bird that fouls its own nest. 13th cent.
8003. It is an ill counsel that hath no escape. *G. H.*
8004. It is an ill procession where the devil bears the cross [*or* holds the
  candle].   *T. D.*
8005. It is an ill wind that blows nobody good. *H.*
8006. It is as hard to please a knave as a knight. *R.*
8007. It is better to marry a shrew than a sheep. 16th cent.
8008. It is better to hear the lark sing than the mouse squeak [*or* cheep]. *B.*
8009. It is comparison that makes men miserable. *F.*
8010. It is day still while the sun shines. *R.*
8011. It is easier to build two chimneys than to maintain one. *G. H.*
8012. It is easier to fall than rise. *C. R.*
8013. It is easier to pull down than to build up. 16th cent.
8014. It is easier to raise the devil than to lay him. 18th cent.
8015. It is easy to be wise after the event. 17th cent.
8016. It is easy to bowl down hill *C.*
8017. It is easy to rob an orchard when none keeps it. *C.*
8018. It is good beating proud folks, for they will not complain. *C.*
8019. It is good fishing in troubled waters. 16th cent.
8020. It is good sheltering under an old hedge. *R.*
8021. It is good sleeping in a whole skin. *H.*
8022. It is good to be merry and wise. [Said when merriment becomes
  foolish.]   *H.*
8023. It is good to be near of kin to an estate. *R.*
8024. It is good to beware by other men's harms. *Latin*
8025. It is good to fear the worst, the best will be the welcomer [*or* save
  itself].   *T. D.*
8026. It is good to have a hatch before the door. [=To keep silence.] *H.*
8027. It is good to have some friends both in heaven and in hell. *G. H.*
8028. It is Greek to me. [=Unintelligible.] 16th cent.
8029. It is hard to halt before a cripple. [He will soon see if you are
  shamming.]   14th cent.
8030. It is hard to be wretched, but worse to be known so. *G. H.*

8031. It is hard to laugh and cry both with a breath.   *C.*
8032. It is hard to please all.   15th cent.
8033. It is hard to sit in Rome and strive against the Pope.   *D. F.*
8034. It is hard to wive and thrive both in a year.   15th cent.
8035. It is ill fishing before the net. [=Anticipating gains.]   *H.*
8036. It is ill healing of an old sore.   *H.*
8037. It is ill jesting with edged tools.   16th cent.
8038. It is ill putting a naked sword in a madman's hand.   *H.*
8039. It is ill speaking between a full man and a fasting.   *D. F.*
8040. It is ill striving against the stream.   13th cent.
8041. It is ill taking the breeks off a Hielandman.   19th cent.
8042. It is ill to drive black hogs in the dark.   *R.*
8043. It is ill waiting for dead men's shoes.   16th cent.
8044. It is lawful to learn even from an enemy.   *Latin*
8045. It is love that makes the world go round.   *French*
8046. It is merry in hall when beards wag all.   14th cent.
8047. It is merry when gossips meet.   *C.*
8048. It is merry when knaves meet.   *H.*
8049. It is more easy to praise poverty than to bear it.   *H.*
8050. It is more pain to do nothing than something.   *G. H.*
8051. It is never too late to mend.   17th cent.
8052. It is no more pity to see a woman weep than to see a goose go barefoot.   16th cent.
8053. It is no play where one greets [=weeps] and another laughs.   *D. F.*
8054. It is no sin to sell dear, but a sin to give ill measure.   *K.*
8055. It is no time to stoop when the head is off.   *D. F.*
8056. It is no use crying over spilt milk.   *J. H.*
8057. It is not all butter that the cow yields.   *H.*
8058. It is not as thy mother says, but as thy neighbours say.   *F.*
8059. It is not good to want and to have.   *D. F.*
8060. It is not how long, but how well we live.   *R.*
8061. It is not lost that a friend gets.   *D. F.*
8062. It is not lost that comes at last.   17th cent.
8063. It is not the suffering, but the cause, that makes a martyr.   17th cent.
8064. It is not What is she, but What has she.   17th cent.
8065. It is safe taking a shive [=slice] of a cut loaf.   *R.* (16th cent.)
8066. It is the men who make a city.   *Greek*
8067. It is the nature of the beast.   *R.*
8068. It is the pace that kills.   19th cent.
8069. It is the unforeseen [*or* unexpected] that always happens.   19th cent.
8070. It is too late to grieve when the chance is past.   *C. R.*
8071. It is too late to spare when the bottom is bare [*or* when all is spent].   *Latin*
8072. It is very hard to shave an egg.   *C.*
8073. It is wit to pick a lock and steal a horse, but wisdom to let them alone.   *J. H.*
8074. It matters not what religion an ill man is of.   *F.*
8075. It must be true that all men say.   *H.*
8076. It never rains but it pours.   19th cent. (18th cent.)
8077. It never troubles a wolf how many the sheep be.   17th cent.

8078. It signifies nothing to play well if you lose. *F.*

8079. It takes all sorts to make a world. 17th cent.

8080. It takes two to make a quarrel. 19th cent.

8081. It will be all the same a hundred years hence. *B.*

8082. Jack is as good as his master. 19th cent.

8083. Jack of all trades and master of none. 18th cent.

8084. Jack Sprat could eat no fat,
His wife could eat no lean ;
And so, betwixt them both, you see,
They licked the platter clean. *C.*

8085. Jack would be a gentleman if he could speak French. *H.*

8086. Janiveer [=January] freeze the pot by the fire. *R.*

8087. Joan is as good as my lady in the dark. 17th cent.

8088. Jouk and let the jaw gae by. [=Dodge and let the splash go past.] *K.*

8089. Jove laughs at lovers' perjuries. *Latin*

8090. Judex damnatur ubi nocens absolvitur.—The judge is condemned
when the guilty is acquitted. *Latin*

8091. Justice pleaseth few in their own house. *G. H.*

8092. Kame sindle, kame sair. [=Comb seldom, comb sore.] *D. F.*

8093. Keek in my kail pot, glower in my ambry. [=Peer in my cabbage
pot, stare in my cupboard. Said to those who pry officiously.] *K.*

8094. Keep a calm sough. [=Keep a quiet tongue.] 19th cent·

8095. Keep a thing seven years and you will find a use for it. 17th cent.

8096. Keep counsel thyself first. *C.*

8097. Keep good men company and you shall be of the number. *G. H.*

8098. Keep some till more come. *R.*

8099. Keep something for a sore foot. [=Save for age or distress.] *K.*

8100. Keep the common road, and thou'rt safe. *F.*

8101. Keep your ain fish-guts for your ain sea-maws [=gulls]. [=Keep
your leavings for your own friends.] *K.*

Keep your breath to cool your porridge, *see* Save your breath, etc.

8102. Keep your eyes wide open before marriage and half shut afterwards. *P. R. A.*

8103. Keep your mouth shut and your eyes open. 18th cent.

8104. Keep your shop and your shop will keep you. 17th cent.

8105. Kick an attorney downstairs and he'll stick to you for life. *L.*

8106. Kindle not a fire that you cannot extinguish. *B.* (16th cent.)

8107. Kindness cannot be bought for gear [=goods]. *D. F.*

8108. Kindness is lost that is bestowed on children and old folks. *C.*

8109. Kindnesses, like grain, increase by sowing. *B.*

8110. Kings and bears oft worry their keepers. *D. F.*

8111. King's chaff is worth other men's corn. *D. F.*

8112. Kings have long arms. *Greek*

8113. Kings have many ears and many eyes. *Greek*

8114. Kiss and be friends. 14th cent.

8115. Kissing goes by favour. *C. R.*

8116. Kitchen physic is the best physic. 16th cent.

8117. Kitty Swerrock where she sat,
Come reach me this, come reach me that.
[Said to lazy girls who ask for things to be reached to them.] *K.*

Q

8118. Knavery may serve a turn, but honesty never fails.   *R.*

8119. Knaves and fools divide the world.   *R.*

8120. Knaves imagine nothing can be done without knavery.   *F.*

8121. Knowledge is folly, except grace guide it.   *G. H.*

8122. Knowledge is no burden.   *G. H.*

8123. Knowledge is power.   19th cent. (17th cent.)

8124. Knowledge makes one laugh, but wealth makes one dance.   *G. H.*

8125. Knowledge without practice makes but half an artist.   *F.*

8126. Κοινὰ τὰ τῶν φίλων.—The things of friends are in common.   *Greek*

8127. Laborare est orare.—To work is to pray.   *Latin*

8128. Labour as long-lived, pray as ever dying.   *G. H.*

8129. Lad's love [=southernwood] is lassies' delight, and if lads won't love, lassies will flite [=scold].   19th cent.

8130. Lad's love's a busk of broom, hot awhile and soon done.   *R.*

8131. Land was never lost for want of an heir.   *R.*

8132. Lasses are lads' leavings.   *R.*

8133. Last but not least.   16th cent.

8134. Last make fast. [When going through a gate.]   *J. H.*

8135. Late repentance is seldom true.   *Latin*

8136. Laugh and grow fat.   16th cent.

8137. Law, logic, and Switzers may be hired to fight for anybody.   16th cent.

8138. Law makers should not be law breakers.   17th cent. (14th cent.)

8139. Law catches flies, but lets hornets go free.   15th cent.

8140. Lawsuits consume time, and money, and rest, and friends.   *G. H.*

8141. Lawyers' houses are built on the heads of fools.   *G. H.*

8142. Lazy folk take the most pains.   18th cent.

8143. Leal heart lied never.   18th cent.

8144. Lean liberty is better than fat slavery.   *F.*

8145. Learn weeping and thou shalt gain laughing.   *G. H.*

8146. Learn wisdom by the follies of others.   *B.*

8147. Learning makes a good man better and an ill man worse.   *F.*

8148. Least said soonest mended.   15th cent.

8149. Least talk most work.   17th cent.

8150. Leave a jest when it pleases you best.   *G. H.*

8151. Leave is light. [=It is an easy matter to ask leave.]   *H.*

8152. Leave off while the play is good.   14th cent.

8153. Leave off with an appetite.   16th cent.

8154. Lend and lose ; so play fools.   *R.*

8155. Lend not horse, nor wife, nor sword.   16th cent.

8156. Lend your money and lose your friend.   *R.*

8157. Less of your courtesy and more of your purse.   *C.*

8158. Let all live as they would die.   *G. H.*

8159. Let alone makes many a loon. [=Neglect makes many a rascal.]   *D. F.*

8160. Let another's shipwreck be your sea-mark.   17th cent.

8161. Let bygones be bygones.   17th cent. (*H.*)

Let every herring hang by its own tail, *see* Every herring, etc.

8162 Let every pedlar carry his own pack [*or* burden].   *J. H.*

8163. Let him that is cold blow at the coal.   *H.*

8164. Let him that would be happy for a day, go to the barber ; for a week, marry a wife ; for a month, buy him a new horse ; for a year, build him a new house ; for all his lifetime, be an honest man. *Italian*

8165. Let his own wand ding [=rod beat] him. [=Let him bear the results of his own folly.] *K.*

8166. Let not a child sleep upon bones. [=On the nurse's lap.] *R.*

8167. Let not your tongue cut your throat. *B.*

8168. Let patience [=a kind of dock] grow in your garden alway. *H.*

8169. Let sleeping dogs lie. 14th cent.

8170. Let that flee [=fly] stick to the wall. 18th cent.

8171. Let that which is lost be for God. *Spanish*

8172. Let the cobbler stick to his last. *Latin*

8173. Let the world slide [*or* wag.]. 16th cent.

8174. Let them laugh that win. *H.*

8175. Let well alone. 14th cent.

8176. Let your letter stay for the post, not the post for the letter. *R.*

8177. Let your purse be your master. *C.*

8178. Liars begin by imposing upon others, but end by deceiving themselves. *B.*

8179. Liars should have good memories. *Latin*

8180. Life is half spent before we know what it is. *G. H.*

8181. Life is made up of little things. *L.*

8182. Life is sweet. 14th cent.

8183. Life lies not in living but in liking. *R.*

8184. Life without a friend is death without a witness. *G. H.*

8185. Life would be too smooth if it had no rubs in it. *F.*

8186. Light burdens, long borne, grow heavy. *H.*

8187. Light cares speak, great ones are dumb. *Latin*

8188. Light gains make heavy purses. [Because light gains come often, great only occasionally.] *H.*

8189. Lightly come, lightly go. 15th cent.

8190. Like a bull in a china shop. 19th cent.

8191. Like a dying duck in a thunderstorm. 18th cent.

8192. Like a house on fire. [=Rapidly.] 19th cent.

8193. Like a fish out of water. *Latin*

8194. Like a hen on a hot griddle. [=Fidgety.] 19th cent.

8195. Like a red rag to a bull. 16th cent.

8196. Like a toad under a harrow. 19th cent. (13th cent.)

8197. Like author, like book. *R.*

8198. Like blood, like good, and like age, make the happiest marriage. *C.*

8199. Like cures like. *Latin*

8200. Like father, like son. 14th cent.

8201. Like herrings in a barrel. [=Packed close.] 19th cent.

8202. Like lips, like lettuce. [Of an ass eating thistles.] *Latin*

8203. Like master, like man. *Latin*

8204. Like mother, like daughter. 16th cent.

8205. Like punishment and equal pain both key and keyhole do sustain. *C.*

8206. Like the curate's egg, good in parts. 19th cent.

8207. Like water off a duck's back. 19th cent.

8208. Like will to like. *Latin*
8209. Likely lies in the mire when Unlikely gets over. *D. F.*
8210. Likeness causeth liking. *C.*
8211. Lilies are whitest in a blackamoor's hand. *F.*
8212. Listeners hear no good of themselves. *R.*
8213. Littera scripta manet.—The written letter remains. *Latin*
8214. Little and often fills the purse. 17th cent.
8215. Little birds that can sing and won't sing must be made to sing. *R.*
8216. Little by little as the cat ate the flickle [=flitch]. *H.*
8217. Little goods, little care. *T. D.*
8218. Little intermeddling makes good friends. *D. F.*
8219. Little journeys and good cost bring safe home. *G. H.*
8220. Little kens the wife that sits by the fire
How the wind blows cold in Hurle-burle-swyre. *D. F.*
[=Those in shelter know little of others' troubles. Hurle-
burle-swyre is a Scottish mountain pass.]
8221. Little knoweth the fat sow what the lean doth mean. *H.*
8222. Little pitchers have long [*or* wide] ears. *G. H. (H.)*
8223. Little sticks kindle the fire, great ones put it out. *G. H.*
8224. Little strokes fell great oaks. 16th cent.
8225. Little thieves are hanged, but great ones escape. *C.*
8226. Little things are pretty. *R.*
8227. Little things please little minds. *Latin*
8228. Live and learn. *C.*
8229. Live and let live. *Dutch*
8230. Living well is the best revenge. *G. H.*
8231. London Bridge was made for wise men to go over and fools to go
under. [The old bridge was dangerous for light wherries to shoot.]
C.
8232. Long a widow weds with shame. *J. H.*
8233. Long absent, soon forgotten. *T. D.*
8234. Long beards heartless,
Painted hoods witless,
Gay coats graceless
Makes England thriftless. 16th cent.
[A taunting rhyme made up by the Scots.]
8235. Long foretold, long last ;
Short notice, soon past. [Of the barometer.] 19th cent.
8236. Long looked for comes at last. 15th cent.
8237. Long-tongued wives go long with bairn. [=They tell everyone
as soon as it is in prospect.] *R.*
8238. Look at your corn in May,
And you'll come weeping away ;
Look at the same in June,
And you'll come home in another tune. *C.*
8239. Look before you leap. 14th cent.
8240. Look high and fall low. *P.*
Look not a gift horse in the mouth, *see* Never look, etc.
8241. Look on the bright side. 19th cent
Look to the main chance, *see* Have an eye, etc.

8242. Lookers-on see most of the game. *16th cent.*
8243. Lose an hour in the morning and you'll be all day hunting for it. *19th cent.*
8244. Lose nothing for want of asking. *16th cent.*
8245. Losers are always in the wrong. *B.*
8246. Loth to bed and loth out of it. *D. F.*
8247. Loth to drink and loth to leave it off. *D. F.*
8248. Love and a cough cannot be hid. *Latin*
8249. Love and business teach eloquence. *G. H.*
8250. Love and lordship like no fellowship. *Latin*
8251. Love and pride stock Bedlam. *F.*
8252. Love asks faith, and faith asks firmness. *G. H.*
8253. Love begets love. *Latin*
8254. Love comes in at the window and goes out at the door. *C. R.*
8255. Love does much but money does all. *French*
8256. Love is blind. *14th cent.*
8257. Love is full of trouble [*or* fear]. *16th cent. (14th cent.)*
8258. Love is lawless. *Latin*
8259. Love is never without jealousy. *17th cent.*
8260. Love is not found in the market. *G. H.*
8261. Love is sweet in the beginning but sour in the ending. *T. D.*
8262. Love is the loadstone of love. *F.*
8263. Love is the true price of love. *G. H.*
8264. Love laughs at locksmiths. *19th cent.*
8265. Love lives in cottages as well as in courts. *R. (16th cent.)*
8266. Love locks no cupboards. *C.*
8267. Love makes all hearts gentle. *G. H.*
8268. Love makes one fit for any work. *G. H.*
8269. Love me little, love me long. *H.*
8270. Love me, love my dog. *Latin*
8271. Love of lads and fire of chats [=chips] is soon in and soon out. *15th cent.*
8272. Love rules his kingdom without a sword. *G. H.*
8273. Love will creep where it cannot go [=walk]. [Originally ' Kind [=Nature] will creep,' kind being later mistaken for kindness or love.] *17th cent.*
8274. Love will find a way. *16th cent.*
8275. Love your neighbour, yet pull not down your hedge. *G. H.*
8276. Lovers live by love as larks live by leeks. *H.*
8277. Loving comes by looking. *C.*
8278. Lucky men need no counsel. *B.*
8279. Lucy light, Lucy light,
The shortest day and the longest night. *R.*
[St. Lucy's Day, 21 Dec. in Old Style, was reckoned shortest.]
8280. Maidens must be mild and meek, swift to hear and slow to speak. *K.*
8281. Maidens should be mim till they're married, and then they may burn kirks. *K.*
8282. Maids say nay and take. *R. (16th cent.)*
8283. Maids want nothing but husbands, and when they have them they want everything. *R.*

8284. Make a virtue of necessity. *Latin*
8285. Make hay while the sun shines. *H.*
8286. Make not balks of good ground. [Do not waste opportunities.] *C.R.*
8287. Make not mickle [=much] of little. *D. F.*
8288. Make not thy tail broader than thy wings. [=Do not have too many attendants.] *J. H.*
8289. Make not two sorrows of one. *H.*
8290. Make the best of a bad bargain. *R.*
8291. Make yourself all honey and the flies will devour you. *Italian*
8292. Malice is mindful. *C.*
8293. Malt is above meal [*or* wheat] with him. [=He is drunk.] *H.*
8294. Man doth what he can, and God what He will. *T. D.*
8295. Man is a bubble. *Greek*
8296. Man is the measure of all things. *Greek*
8297. Man proposes, God disposes. *Latin*
8298. Man, woman, and devil, are the three degrees of comparison. *F.*
8299. Manchester bred : long in the arms, and short in the head. *W. H.*
8300. Manners maketh man [*or* Manners make the man]. 14th cent.
8301. Man's extremity is God's opportunity. 17th cent.
8302. Many a good cow hath a bad calf. *H.*
8303. Many a little makes a mickle [=great]. *Greek*
8304. Many a man speirs the gate [=asks the way] he knows full well. *D. F.*
8305. Many a one for land takes a fool by the hand. [=Marries her or him.] *R. (C.)*
8306. Many a true word is spoken in jest. 14th cent.
8307. Many blame the wife for their own thriftless life. *B.*
8308. Many estates are spent in the getting,
Since women, for tea, forsook spinning and knitting,
And men, for punch, forsook hewing and splitting. *P. R. A.*
8309. Many go out for wool and come home shorn. *Spanish*
8310. Many hands make light work. *Latin*
8311. Many have been ruined by buying good pennyworths. *F.*
8312. Many hips and haws, many frosts and snaws. *D.*
8313. Many kinsfolk and few friends. *H.*
8314. Many kiss the child for the nurse's sake. *H.* (13th cent.)
8315. Many kiss the hand they wish cut off. *G. H.*
8316. Many sands will sink a ship. *C.*
Many strokes fell great oaks, *see* Little strokes, etc.
8317. Many talk of Robin Hood that never shot in his bow,
And many talk of Little John that never did him know. *R.*
8318. Many things grow in the garden that were never sown there. *Spanish*
8319. Many would be cowards if they had courage enough. *F.*
8320. March borrows of April
Three days, and they be ill. *F.*
8321. March comes in like a lion and goes out like a lamb. *R.*
8322. March in Janiveer, Janiveer in March I fear. *R.*
8323. March many weathers. *R.*
8324. March wind and May sun
Makes clothes white and maids dun. *R.*

8325. March winds and April showers
Bring forth May flowers. *D.*

8326. Marriage is a lottery. 17th cent.

8327. Marriage is honourable, but housekeeping is a shrew. *R.*

8328. Marriages are made in heaven. 16th cent.

8329. Marriage, with peace, is this world's paradise ; with strife, this
life's purgatory. 17th cent.

8330. Marry first and love will follow. 17th cent.

8331. Marry in haste, and repent at leisure. 16th cent.

8332. Marry in Lent, live to repent. 19th cent.

8333. Marry in May, you'll rue it for aye. *Latin*

8334. Marry with your match. *Latin*

8335. Marry your son when you will, your daughter when you can. *G. H.*

8336. May bees don't fly this month. [A retort to people who say
'Maybe.'] *K.*

8337. Measure is a merry mean. 14th cent.

8338. Measure thrice before you cut once. *Italian*

8339. Meat and matins [*or* mass] hinder no man's journey. *C.*

8340. Meat is much, but manners is more. *C.*

8341. Μηδὲν ἄγαν—Nothing too much. *Greek*

8342. Men are blind in their own cause. *D. F.*

8343. Men are not to be measured by inches. *F.*

8344. Men cut large thongs of other men's leather. *Latin*

8345. Men have faults, women only two :
There's nothing good they say, and nothing good they do.

17th cent.

8346. Men leap over where the hedge is lowest. *H.*

8347. Men may meet, but mountains never. 16th cent.

8348. Men muse as they use. *R.*

8349. Mend your clothes and you may hold out this year. *G. H.*

8350. Merry is the feast-making till we come to the reckoning. *R.*

8351. Merry meet, merry part. *R.*

8352. Mettle is dangerous in a blind horse. *R.*

8353. Mickle [=big] head, little wit. *D. F.*

8354. Might is right. 14th cent.

8355. Milk says to wine, Welcome friend. *G. H.*

8356. Mills and wives are ever wanting. *Italian.*

8357. Mint [=give warning] ere you strike. *D. F.*

8358. Mischief comes by the pound and goes away by the ounce.

F. (16th cent.)

8359. Misfortunes come on wings and depart on foot. *B.*

8360. Misfortunes never come singly. 14th cent.

8361. Misreckoning is no payment. *H.*

8362. Mocking is catching. *R.*

8363. Monday for wealth,
Tuesday for health,
Wednesday the best day of all :
Thursday for crosses,
Friday for losses,
Saturday no luck at all. [Days for marrying.] 19th cent.

8364. Monday's child is fair of face,
Tuesday's child is full of grace,
Wednesday's child is full of woe,
Thursday's child has far to go,
Friday's child is loving and giving,
Saturday's child works hard for its living ;
But the child who is born on the Sabbath day
Is lucky and happy and good and gay. *19th cent.*
8365. Money begets money. *Italian*
8366. Money is often lost for want of money. *T. D.*
8367. Money is round and rolls away. *Italian*
8368. Money is the sinews of war. *Latin*
8369. Money makes the man. *Greek*
8370. Money makes the mare to go. *16th cent.*
8371. Money talks. *17th cent.*
8372. More belongs to marriage than four bare legs in a bed. *H.*
8373. More hair than wit. [Long hair was supposed to denote lack of
brains.] *16th cent.*
8374. More haste less speed. *H.*
8375. More have repented speech than silence. *G. H.*
8376. More know Tom Fool than Tom Fool knows. *18th cent.*
8377. More than enough is too much. *17th cent.*
8378. More than we use is more than we want. *F.*
8379. Morning dreams are true. *Latin*
8380. Much bruit, little fruit. *French*
8381. Much coin, much care. *Latin*
8382. Much cry and little wool. *15th cent.*
8383. Much water goes by the mill the miller knows not of. *H.*
8384. Much would have more. *14th cent.*
8385. Muck and money go together. *R.*
8386. Murder will out. *14th cent. (13th cent.)*
8387. Music helps not the toothache. *G. H.*
8388. Must is a king's word. *17th cent.*
8389. My belly thinks my throat cut. [=I am hungry.] *16th cent.*
8390. My son's my son till he gets him a wife,
My daughter's my daughter all her life. *R.*
8391. Name not a rope in his house that hanged himself. *G. H.*
8392. Names and natures do often agree. *C.*
8393. Nature abhors a vacuum. *17th cent.*
8394. Nature does nothing in vain. *17th cent.*
8395. Nature draws more than ten oxen. *R.*
8396. Nature has given us two ears, two eyes, and but one tongue ; to
the end we should hear and see more than we speak. *Greek*
8397. Nature passes nurture. *16th cent.*
8398. Nature requires five,
Custom taketh seven,
Idleness takes nine,
And Wickedness eleven. [Hours of sleep.] *D.*
8399. Naughty boys sometimes make good men. *17th cent.*
8400. Ne sutor ultra crepidam.—Let not the cobbler go beyond his last. *Latin*

8401. Near is my coat, but nearer is my shirt [*or* Near is my kirtle [*or* petticoat] but nearer is my smock.] *Latin*

8402. Near is my shirt, but nearer is my skin. 16th cent.

8403. Nearest the heart, nearest the mouth. [When one person is named instead of another by mistake.] *D. F.*

8404. Nearest the King, nearest the widdie [=gallows]. *D. F.*

8405. Necessity is the mother of invention. 16th cent.

8406. Necessity knows no law. *Latin*

8407. Neck or nothing. *R.*

8408. Need makes the old wife trot. 15th cent.

8409. Needles and pins, needles and pins,
When a man's married his trouble begins. 19th cent.

8410. Needs must when the devil drives.. 15th cent.

8411. Neither fish nor flesh nor good red herring. *H.*

8412. Neither great poverty not great riches will hear reason. *B.*

8413. Neither praise nor dispraise thyself ; thy actions serve the turn. *G. H.*

8414. Never a barrel the better herring. [=Nothing to choose between them.] *H.*

8415. Never ask pardon before you are accused. *B.*

8416. Never be ashamed to eat your meat. *Latin*

8417. Never cast dirt into that fountain of which thou hast sometime drunk. *R.*

8418. Never catch at a falling knife or a falling friend. 19th cent.

8419. Never cross a bridge till you come to it. 19th cent.

8420. Never draw your dirk when a dunt [=blow] will do. *A. H.*

8421. Never is a long day. 14th cent.

8422. Never judge from appearances. 16th cent.

8423. Never look a gift horse in the mouth. *Latin*

8424. Never put off till to-morrow what may be done to-day. 14th cent.

8425. Never refuse a good offer. *R.*

8426. Never say die. 19th cent.

8427. Never sigh, but send. *R.*

8428. Never too old [*or* late] to learn. *R.*

8429. Never trouble trouble till trouble troubles you. 19th cent.

8430. Never venture out of your depth till you can swim. *B.*

8431. Never was cat or dog drowned, that could but see the shore. *Italian*

New brooms sweep clean, *see* A new broom, etc

8432. New lords, new laws. 16th cent.

8433. Night is the mother of counsel. *Greek*

8434. Nine tailors make a man. 17th cent.

8435. No better than she should be. [=Immoral.] 17th cent.

8436. No butter will stick to his bread. [=Everything goes wrong with him.] *H.*

8437. No case : abuse the plaintiff's attorney. 17th cent.

8438. No churchyard is so handsome that a man would desire straight to be buried there. *G. H.*

8439. No day passeth without some grief. *R.*

8440. No fence against a flail. *R.*

8441. No folly to being in love. *R.*

*Q

8442. No fool like an old fool. *H.*

8443. No friend like the penny. *Spanish*

8444. No gains without pains. 16th cent.

8445. No garden without its weeds. *F.*

8446. No joy without annoy [*or* alloy]. *C.*

8447. No living man all things can. *Latin*

8448. No lock will hold against the power of gold. *G. H.*

8449. No longer pipe, no longer dance. [Of people who are kind only while getting benefits.] *C. R.*

8450. No man can both sup and blow at once. *D. F.*

8451. No man can play the fool so well as the wise man. *D. F.*

8452. No man cries stinking fish. *F.*

8453. No man hath a worse friend than he brings from home. *R.*

8454. No man is a match for a woman till he is married. 19th cent.

8455. No man is born wise. 17th cent.

8456. No man is his craft's master the first day. *C.*

8457. No man is wise at all times. *Latin*

8458. No man loveth his fetters, be they made of gold. *H.*

8459. No man will another in the oven seek, except that himself have been there before. [Often said of mother and daughter.] *H.*

8460. No mill, no meal. *Greek*

8461. No mischief but a woman or a priest is at the bottom of it. *Latin*

8462. No money, no Swiss. [Swiss mercenaries will not fight unless they are paid.] *French*

8463. No names, no pack drill. 20th cent.

8464. No news is good news. *Italian*

No pains, no gains, *see* No gains without pains.

8465. No penny, no paternoster. [=Priests will not serve without payment.] 16th cent.

8466. No profit to honour, no honour to religion. *G. H.*

8467. No receiver, no thief. *H.*

8468. No remedy but patience. *T. D.*

8469. No rose without a thorn. 15th cent.

8470. No safe wading in an unknown water. *C.*

8471. No sunshine but hath some shadow. *R.*

8472. No sweet without sweat. *C.*

8473. No taxation without representation. 18th cent.

8474. No time like the present. 17th cent.

8475. No weather is ill if the wind be still. *C.*

8476. No wisdom like silence. *Greek*

8477. Nodum in scirpo quaerere.—To seek for a knot in a bulrush. [=To find difficulties where there are none.] *Latin*

8478. None is offended but by himself. *Latin*

8479. None knows the weight of another's burden. *G. H.*

8480. None so blind as those who won't see. 16th cent.

8481. None so deaf as those who won't hear. 16th cent.

8482. None so old that he hopes not for a year of life. *Latin*

8483. Northampton stands on other men's legs. [Because it is the centre of the boot trade.] 17th cent.

8484. Not God above gets all men's love. *Greek*

8485. Not to advance is to go back. *Latin*
8486. Not to be fit to hold a candle to him. [=Not to be compared with
   him. From the custom of holding candles before shrines. 18th cent.
8487. Not to be sneezed at. [=Not to be despised.] 19th cent.
8488. Nothing dries sooner than a tear. *Latin*
8489. Nothing for nothing. 18th cent.
8490. Nothing hath no savour. *H.*
8491. Nothing have, nothing crave. *J. H.*
8492. Nothing is certain but death and the taxes. *L.*
8493. Nothing is certain but uncertainty. *Latin*
8494. Nothing is impossible to a willing heart. *H.*
8495. Nothing like leather. [In the cobbler's opinion. =Each believes
   in his own trade.] 17th cent.
8496. Nothing must be done hastily but killing of fleas. *R.*
8497. Nothing so bad but it might have been worse. 19th cent.
8498. Nothing so crouse [=pert] as a new washen louse. [Of ragged
   people who get new clothes.] *D. F.*
8499. Nothing succeeds like success. 19th cent.
8500. Nothing venture, nothing have [*or* win]. 17th cent. (14th cent.)
8501. Nothing worse than a familiar enemy. [=One belonging to one's
   household.] 14th cent.
8502. Nulla dies sine linea.—No day without a line. [From a tradition
   regarding the industry of the painter Apelles.] *Latin*
8503. Nurture is above nature. *French*
8504. Oaks may fall when reeds stand the storm. *F.*
8505. Obedience is much more seen in little things than in great. *F.*
9506. Obscurum per obscurius.—The obscure [explained] by the more
   obscure.] *Latin*
8507. Of a pig's tail you can never make a good shaft. *G. H.*
8508. Of all tame beasts I hate sluts. *R.*
8509. Of enough men leave. [=If there are no leavings, there can hardly
   have been enough.] *D. F.*
8510. Of evil grain no good seed can come. *R.* (*T. D.*)
8511. Of him that speaks ill, consider the life more than the word. *G. H.*
8512. Of idleness comes no goodness. *R.*
8513. Of little meddling cometh great rest [*or* ease.] *H.* (14th cent.)
8514. Of saving cometh having. *T. D.*
8515. Of soup and love, the first is the best. *F.*
8516. Of sufferance cometh ease [*or* rest]. 14th cent.
8517. Of thy sorrow be not too sad, of thy joy be not too glad. 15th cent.
8518. Of two evils choose the least. 14th cent.
8519. Of wine the middle, of oil the top, of honey the bottom, is the
   best. *Latin*
8520. Often and little eating makes a man fat. *R.*
8521. Often to the water, often to the tatter. [Of linen.] *R.*
8522. Old age is honourable. *B.*
8523. Old age, though despised, is coveted by all. *B.*
8524. Old and tough, young and tender. *R.*
8525. Old bees yield no honey. *R.*
8526. Old friends and old wine are best. *T. D.*

8527. Old maids lead apes in hell. 16th cent.
8528. Old men and travellers may lie by authority. *C. R.*
8529. Old men are twice children. *Greek*
8530. Old men go to death ; death comes to young men. *G. H.*
8531. Old men, when they scorn young, make much of death. *G. H.*
8532. Old men will die and children soon forget. 16th cent.
8533. Old muck-hills will bloom. *R.*
8534. Old porridge is sooner heated than new made. [=Old lovers are sooner reconciled than new loves begun.] *R.*
8535. Old praise dies unless you feed it. *G. H.*
8536. Old sin makes new shame. 14th cent.
Omelets are not made without breaking of eggs, *see* You cannot make an omelet, etc.
8537. On Candlemas Day throw candle and candlestick away. *R.*
8538. On painting and fighting look aloof. [One is dangerous, the other loses effect close at hand.] *G. H.*
8539. On St. Valentine all the birds of the air in couples do join. [St. Valentine's day, 14 Feb.] 14th cent.
8540. On the first of April
Hunt the gowk another mile. *D.*
    [Gowk=cuckoo, here=April fool.]
8541. On Valentine's day will a good goose lay. [14 Feb.] *R.*
8542. Once a knave and ever a knave. *J. H.*
8543. Once a parson, always a parson. 19th cent.
8544. Once bitten, twice shy. 19th cent.
8545. Once in ten years one man hath need of another. 16th cent.
8546. Once wood and aye the waur. [=Once mad and always the worse. Recovery from madness is seldom complete.] *D. F.*
8547. One and none is all one. [=One is negligible.] *Spanish*
8548. One beats the bush, and another catches the birds. 14th cent.
8549. One beggar is enough at a door. *C.*
8550. One beggar is woe that another by the door should go. 14th cent.
8551. One, but that one a lion. *Greek*
8552. One cannot be in two places at once. 17th cent.
8553. One day of pleasure is worth two of sorrow. *F.*
8554. One enemy is too many, and a hundred friends too few. *German*
8555. One eye of the master sees more than ten of the servants'. *G. H.*
8556. One eye-witness is better than ten ear-witnesses. *Latin*
8557. One father is more than a hundred schoolmasters. *G. H.*
8558. One flower makes no garland. *G. H.*
8559. One fool makes many. *G. H.*
8560. One foot is better than two crutches. *G. H.*
8561. One for sorrow,
Two for mirth,
Three for a wedding,
Four for a birth. [Omens from magpies.] *D.*
8562. One God, no more, but friends good store. *C.*
8563. One good turn deserves [*or* asks *or* requires] another. 15th cent.
8564. One hair of a woman draws more than a team of oxen. 16th cent.
8565. One half of the world does not know how the other half lives. *G. H.*

8566. One hand washeth the other, and both the face. *Latin*
8567. One hour to-day is worth two to-morrow. *F.*
8568. One hour's sleep before midnight is worth two after. *G. H.*
8569. One ill weed mars a whole pot of pottage. *H.*
8570. One ill word asketh another. *H.*
8571. One law for the rich and another for the poor. 19th cent.
8572. One lie makes many. *Latin*
8573. One mad action is not enough to prove a man mad. *F.*
8574. One man may steal a horse while another may not look over a hedge. 19th cent. (*H.*)
8575. One man's meat is another man's poison. *Latin*
8576. One may know by your nose what pottage you love. [=Strong drink.] 16th cent.
8577. One may see day at a little hole. *H.*
8578. One mule scrubs another. *Latin*
8579. One must draw the line somewhere. 19th cent.
8580. One nail drives out another. 13th cent.
8581. One of these days is none of these days. *B.*
8582. One pair of legs is worth two pairs of hands. 16th cent.
8583. One scabbed sheep infects a whole flock. *Latin*
8584. One slumber invites another. *G. H.*
8585. One swallow does not make a summer. *Greek*
8586. One sword keeps another in the sheath. *G.H.*
8587. One tale is good till another is told. *F.* (16th cent.)
8588. One to-day is worth two to-morrows. 17th cent.
8589. One tongue is enough for a woman. *R.*
8590. One volunteer is worth two pressed men. 18th cent.
8591. One year a nurse, and seven years the worse. *R.*
8592. One year of joy, another of comfort, and all the rest of content [A marriage wish.] *R.*
8593. Opinion rules the world. 17th cent.
8594. Opportunity makes the thief. 13th cent.
8595. Οὐδὲ Ἡρακλῆς πρὸς δύο.—Not even Hercules could contend against two. *Greek*
8596. Our last garment is made without pockets. *Italian*
8597. Our sins and our debts are often more than we think. *J. H.*
8598. Out of debt, out of danger. *C.*
8599. Out of sight, out of mind. 13th cent.
8600. Out of the frying-pan into the fire. *H.*
8601. Oxford for learning, London for wit, Hull for women, and York for a tit [=horse]. *W. H.*
8602. Pain past is pleasure. 16th cent.
8603. Painted pictures are dead speakers. *R.*
8604. Painters and poets have leave to lie. 16th cent.
8605. Pale moon doth rain, red moon doth blow, White moon doth neither rain nor snow. *C.*
8606. Pardon all but thyself. *G. H.*
8607. Past cure, past care. 16th cent.
8608. Paternoster built churches, and Our Father pulls them down. 17th cent.

8609. Patience is a flower that grows not in every garden.   *H.*

8610. Patience is a plaster for all sores.   *C.* (14th cent.)

8611. Patience, money, and time bring all things to pass.   *G. H.*

8612. Pay beforehand was never well served.   16th cent.

8613. Pay what you owe, and what you're worth you'll know.   *F.*

8614. Peace makes plenty.   15th cent.

8615. Peebles for pleasure.   19th cent.

8616. Penny and penny laid up will be many.   *C.*

8617. Penny wise, pound foolish.   *C. R.*

8618. Pens may blot, but they cannot blush.   16th cent.

8619. Pension never enriched a young man.   *G. H.*

8620. People who live in glass houses should never throw stones.   *G. H.*

8621. Pigs love that lie together.   *R.*

8622. Pigs might fly, but they are very unlikely birds.   19th cent.

8623. Plain dealing is a jewel, though they that use it commonly die beggars.   16th cent.

8624. Plain dealing is praised more than practised.   *C.*

8625. Play with your peers. [Said to young folk who are cheeky to their elders.]   *D. F.*

8626. Play, women and wine undo men laughing.   *J. H.*

8627. Pleasant hours fly fast.   *F.*

8628. Please the eye and plague the heart.   17th cent.

8629. Pleasing ware is half sold.   *G. H.*

8630. Pleasure has a sting in its tail.   17th cent.

8631. Plenty makes dainty.   *R.*

8632. Plough deep while others sleep
And you shall have corn to sell and to keep.   *D.* (*J. H.*)

8633. Poeta nascitur, non fit.—A poet is born, not made.   *Latin*

8634. Poets are born, but orators are made.   *Latin*

8635. Poor and liberal, rich and covetous.   *G. H.*

8636. Poor folk are fain [=glad] of little.   *D. F.*

8637. Poor folks' friends soon misken [=fail to know them].   *K.*

8638. Poor men seek meat for their stomach ; rich men stomach for their meat.   16th cent.

8639. Poor men's tables are soon spread.   *R.*

8640. Possession is nine [*or* eleven] points of the law.   17th cent.

8641. Post hoc ; ergo propter hoc.—After this ; therefore on account of this.   *Latin*

8642. Pour not water on a drowned mouse   *C.*

8643. Poverty breeds strife.   *R.*

8644. Poverty is in want of much, avarice of everything.   *Latin*

8645. Poverty is no sin.   *G. H.*

8646. Poverty is no vice but an inconvenience.   16th cent.

8647. Poverty is not a shame, but the being ashamed of it is.   *F.*

8648. Poverty is the mother of all arts and trades.   17th cent.

8649. Poverty is the mother of health.   14th cent.

8650. Poverty parteth fellowship [*or* friends].   14th cent.

8651. Practice makes perfect.   *Latin*

8652. Practise what you preach.   17th cent.

8653. Praise day at night, and life at the end.   *G. H.*

8654. Praise makes good men better and bad men worse.   *F.* (17th cent.)

8655. Praise to the face is open disgrace.   *L.*

8656. Prayers and provender hinder no man's journey.   *G. H.*

8657. Prettiness makes no pottage.   *R.*

8658. Prevention is better than cure.   *Latin*

8659. Pride and grace dwell never in one place.   *F.*

8660. Pride breakfasted with Plenty, dined with Poverty, and supped
with Infamy.   *P. R. A.*

8661. Pride feels no cold.   *R.*

8662. Pride goes before, and shame follows after.   14th cent.

8663. Pride is as loud a beggar as want, and a great deal more saucy.   *F.*

8664. Pride will have a fall.   16th cent.

8665. Proffered service stinks.   *Latin*

8666. Promise is debt.   14th cent.

8667. Promises and pie-crusts are made to be broken.   18th cent.

8668. Prospect is often better than possession.   *F.*

8669. Prove thy friend ere thou have need.   15th cent.

8670. Proverbs are the daughters of daily experience.   *Dutch*

8671. Provide for the worst, the best will save itself.   *H.*

8672. Providence is better than rent.   *G. H.*

8673. Public money is like holy water, everyone helps himself to it.   *Italian*

8674. Public reproof hardens shame.   *F.*

8675. Puff not against the wind.   *C. R.*

8676. Punctuality is the politeness of princes.   *French*

8677. Punctuality is the soul of business.   *B.*

8678. Put a coward to his mettle, and he'll fight the devil.   *K.*

8679. Put not thy hand between the bark and the tree. [=Do not
meddle in family matters.]   *H.*

8680. Put that in your pipe and smoke it. [=Put up with it.]   19th cent.

8681. Put your shoulder to the wheel.   17th cent.

8682. Quality without quantity is little thought of.   *K.*

8683. Quarrelling dogs come halting home.   *K.*

8684. Quartan agues kill old men and cure young.   *Italian*

8685. Queen Anne is dead. [=The news is stale.]   18th cent.

8686. Qui facit per alium facit per se.—He who does a thing through
another does it himself.   *Latin*

8687. Quick at meat, quick at work.   *C.*

8688. Quickly come, quickly go.   17th cent.

8689. Quietness is best.   *A. H.*

8690. Quos Deus vult perdere, prius dementat.—Whom God wishes to
destroy He first makes mad.   *Latin*

8691. Quot homines, tot sententiae.—So many men, so many opinions.
   Latin

8692. Rain before seven : fine before eleven.   19th cent.

8693. Rain, rain, go to Spain,
Fair weather come again.   *J. H.*

8694. Raise no more spirits than you can conjure down.   *C.*

8695. Rather sell than be poor.   *R.*

8696. Rats desert a sinking ship [*or* a falling house].   17th cent.

8697. Raw dads [=chunks] make fat lads.   *K.*

8698. Ready money is a ready medicine.   16th cent.
8699. Ready money will away.   *R.*
8700. Reason lies between the spur and the bridle.   *G. H.*
8701. Reason rules all things.   *T. D.*
8702. Reckless youth makes rueful age.   16th cent.
8703. Red sky at night, shepherd's delight :
    Red sky in the morning, shepherd's warning.   16th cent.
8704. Religion is the best armour, but the worst cloak.   *F.*
8705. Remove an old tree and it will die.   16th cent.
8706. Repentance comes too late.   15th cent.
8707. Reserve the master-blow.   [=Do not teach all your skill, lest your
    pupil overreach you.]   *J. H.*
8708. Respect a man, he will do the more.   *J. H.*
8709. Respice finem.—Look to the end.   *Latin*
8710. Revenge is sweet.   16th cent.
8711. Rice for good luck, and bauchles [=old shoes] for bonny bairns.
    [Referring to the wedding custom.]   19th cent.
8712. Rich folk have many friends.   *K.*
8713. Rich men have no faults.   *F.*
8714. Riches are but the baggage of fortune.   *J. H.*
8715. Riches are gotten with pain, kept with care, and lost with
    grief.   16th cent.
8716. Riches are like muck, which stink in a heap, but spread abroad
    make the earth fruitful.   16th cent.
8717. Riches bring oft harm, and ever fear.   *H.*
8718. Riches serve a wise man but command a fool.   *French*
8719. Ride softly that you may get home the sooner.   *R.*
8720. Right wrongs no man.   *A. H.*
8721. Rome was not built in a day.   *Latin*
8722. Rue and thyme grow both in one garden.   *K.*
8723. Rule youth well, for age will rule itself.   *D. F.*
8724. Sadness and gladness succeed each other.   *C.*
    Safe bind, safe find, *see* Fast bind, etc.
8725. St. Bartholomew brings the cold dew.   [24 Aug.]
8726. St. Benedick, sow thy pease, or keep them in thy rick.
    [21 March.]   *R.*
8727. St. Matthie sends sap into the tree.   [St. Matthias's day =
    24 Feb.]   *R.*
8728. St. Swithin's day, if thou dost rain,   [15 July.]
    For forty days it will remain ;
    St. Swithin's day, if thou be fair,
    For forty days 'twill rain na mair.   16th cent.
8729. St. Thomas grey, St. Thomas grey,   [21 Dec.]
    The longest night and the shortest day.   19th cent.
8730. Salmon and sermon have their season in Lent.   *J. H.*
8731. Salt seasons all things.   *J. H.*
8732. Salus populi suprema est lex.—The safety of the people is the
    highest law.   *Latin*
8733. Samson was a strong man, but he could not pay money before he
    had it.   *J. H.*

8734.	Satan reproves [*or* rebukes] sin.	17th cent.
8735.	Save a thief from the gallows and he will cut your throat.	*C. R.*
8736.	Save something for the man that rides on the white horse. [=For white-haired old age.]	*C.*
8737.	Save your breath to cool your porridge.	16th cent.
8738.	Say as men say, but think to yourself.	*C.*
8739.	Say no ill of the year till it be past.	*G. H.*
8740.	Say to pleasure, Gentle Eve, I will none of your apple.	*G. H.*
8741.	Say well is good but Do well is better.	*C.*
8742.	Say well or be still.	15th cent.
8743.	Saying is one thing and doing another.	*H.*
8744.	Scald not your lips in another man's pottage.	*R.* (16th cent.)
8745.	Scatter with one hand, gather with two.	*J. H.*
8746.	Schoolboys are the reasonablest people in the world ; they care not how little they have for their money.	*R.*
8747.	Score twice before you cut once. [=Plan carefully before taking an irrevocable step.]	17th cent.
8748.	Scorn at first makes after-love the more.	*B.*
8749.	Scorning is catching.	*R.*
8750.	Scotsmen aye reckon frae an ill hour.	*K.*
8751.	Scratch a Russian and you'll find a Tartar.	19th cent.
	Scratch me and I'll scratch you, *see* You scratch my back, etc.	
8752.	Se non è vero, è molto ben trovato.—If it is not true, it is very well invented.	*Italian.*
8753.	Search not too curiously lest you find trouble.	*J. H.*
8754.	Second thoughts are best.	*Latin*
8755.	See a pin and let it lie, You'll want a pin before you die. See a pin and pick it up, All the day you'll have good luck.	19th cent.
8756.	See Naples and then die.	*Italian*
8757.	Seeing is believing.	*C.*
8758.	Seek till you find, and you'll not lose your labour.	*R.*
8759.	Seek your salve where you get your sore.	*D. F.*
8760.	Seldom comes a better. [When a bad one goes.]	13th cent.
8761.	Seldom seen, soon forgotten.	14th cent.
8762.	Self do, self have.	*H.*
8763.	Self-love is a mote in every man's eye.	*R.*
8764.	Self-praise is no recommendation.	17th cent.
8765.	Self-preservation is the first law of nature.	17th cent.
8766.	Send a fool to the market, and a fool he'll return.	16th cent.
8767.	Send a wise man on an errand, and say nothing to him.	14th cent.
8768.	Servants should put on patience when they put on a livery.	*F.*
8769.	Servants should see all and say nothing.	18th cent.
8770.	Service is no inheritance.	15th cent.
8771.	Service without reward is punishment.	*G. H.*
8772.	Set a beggar on horseback and he'll ride to the devil [*or* to the gallows *or* ride a gallop.]	16th cent.
8773.	Set a stout heart to a stey brae [=steep hill].	*K.*
8774.	Set a thief to catch a thief.	*R.*

8775. Set good against evil.   *G. H.*

8776. Set the saddle on the right horse.   *T. D.*

8777. Set trees poor and they will grow rich, set them rich and they will grow poor.   *R.*

8778. Seven hours' sleep will make a clown forget his design.   *F.*

8779. Seven may be company but nine are confusion.   *F.* (17th cent.)

8780. Shame in a kindred cannot be avoided.   *C. R.*

8781. Shameless [*or* shameful] craving must have shameful nay.   *H.*

8782. Share and share alike.   17th cent.

8783. She that is born a beauty is half married.   *F.*

8784. Shear your sheep in May and shear them all away.   *R.*

8785. Ships fear fire more than water.   *G. H.*

8786. Short acquaintance brings repentance.   *R.*

8787. Short and sweet.   16th cent.

8788. Short pleasure, long lament.   15th cent.

8789. Short reckonings are soon cleared.   *F·*

8790. Short reckonings make long friends.   16th cent.

8791. Short rede [=counsel], good rede.   13th cent.

8792. Short shooting loseth the game.   *H.*

8793. Show me a liar and I will show you a thief.   17th cent.

8794. Show me not the meat, but show me the man.   *C.*

8795. Show me the man, and I'll show you the law.   *D. F.*

8796. Si vis pacem, para bellum.—If you want peace, prepare for war.   *Latin*

8797. Sickness is felt, but health not at all.   *F.*

8798. Sickness tells us what we are.   *F.*

8799. Silence gives consent.   14th cent.

8800. Silence is golden.   19th cent. (*G. H.*)

8801. Silence is the best ornament of a woman.   *R.* (16th cent.)

8802. Silence was never written down.   *Italian.*

8803. Silence seldom doth harm.   *R.*

8804. Silks and satins put out the kitchen fire.   *G. H.*

8805. Sins are not known till they be acted.   *G. H.*

8806. Sit in your place, and none can make you rise.   *G. H.*

8807. Six hours for a man, seven for a woman, and eight for a fool. [Of sleep.]   18th cent.

8808. Six of one and half a dozen of the other.   19th cent.

8809. Slander leaves a scar behind it.   *T. D.*

8810. Sleep without supping and wake without owing.   *G. H.*

8811. Sloth is the key to poverty.   17th cent.

8812. Slow and [*or* but] sure.   *C.* (*T. D.*)

8813. Slow at meat, slow at work.   *K.*

8814. Sluts are good enough to make slovens' pottage.   *C.*

8815. Small birds must have meat.   [=Children must be fed.]   *C.*

8816. Small invitation will serve a beggar.   *B.*

Small pitchers have wide ears, *see* Little pitchers, etc.

8817. Small profits and quick returns.   19th cent.

8818. Small rain lays great dust.   *R.*

8819. Small sorrows speak ; great ones are silent.   *Latin*

8820. Smoke follows the fairest.   *Greek*

8821. Sneeze on a Monday, you sneeze for danger;
Sneeze on a Tuesday, you kiss a stranger;
Sneeze on a Wednesday, you sneeze for a letter;
Sneeze on a Thursday, for something better;
Sneeze on a Friday, you sneeze for sorrow;
Sneeze on a Saturday, see your sweetheart to-morrow;
Sneeze on a Sunday, your safety seek,
The Devil will have you the whole of the week. *W. H.*

8822. So got, so gone. *R.*

8823. So many countries, so many customs. *R.* (11th cent.)

8824. So many servants, so many enemies. *Latin*

8825. So we have the chink, we will bear with the stink. *Latin*

8826. Soft fire makes sweet malt. 16th cent.

8827. Soft words and hard arguments. *R.*

8828. Some are wise and some are otherwise. *J. H.*

8829. Some evils are cured by contempt. *G. H.*

8830. Some have hap [=luck], some stick in the gap. *C.*

8831. Sometimes the best gain is to lose. *G. H.*

8832. Somewhat is better than nothing. *H.*

8833. Soon crooketh the tree that good gambrel would be. [Gambrel =
butcher's bent hanger for carcases.] 15th cent.

8834. Soon enough if well enough. *Latin*

8835. Soon got, soon spent. *H.*

8836. Soon hot, soon cold. 15th cent.

8837. Soon learnt, soon forgotten. 14th cent.

8838. Soon ripe, soon rotten. *Latin*

8839. Sorrow and an evil life maketh soon an old wife. *C.*

8840. Sorrow comes unsent for. *Latin*

8841. Sorrow is dry. *French*

8842. Sorrow is good for nothing but sin. *J. H.*

8843. Sorrow will pay no debt. *R.*

8844. Sow with the hand, and not with the whole sack. *Greek*

8845. Spare the rod and spoil the child. *C.* (*Bible.*)

8846. Spare to speak and spare to speed. 14th cent.

8847. Spare well and spend well. 16th cent.

8848. Spare when you're young, and spend when you're old. *R.*

8849. Sparing is the first gaining. 16th cent.

8850. Speak fair and think what you will *C. R.*

8851. Speak fitly or be silent wisely. *G. H.* (*C.*)

8852. Speak not of my debts unless you mean to pay them. *G. H.*

8853. Speak well of the dead. *Latin*

8854. Speak well of your friend, of your enemy say nothing. *B.*

8855. Speak when your spoken to; come when you're called. *R.*

8856. Spectacles are death's arquebuse. *G. H.*

8857. Speech is the picture of the mind. *R.*

8858. Speed the plough! 17th cent. (15th cent.)

8859. Spend and be free, but make no waste. *C.*

8860. Spend and God will send. 14th cent.

8861. Spend not where you may save; spare not where you must spend. *R.*

8862. Spies are the ears and eyes of princes. *G. H.*

8863. Spit in your hands and take better hold. *H.*
8864. Sport is sweetest when there be no spectators. *C.*
8865. Spread the table, and contention will cease. *R.*
8866. Standing pools gather filth. *C.*
8867. Stay a little, and news will find you. *G. H.*
8868. Stay a while, that we may end the sooner. *G. H.*
8869. Step after step the ladder is ascended. *G. H.*
8870. Sticks and stones may break my bones, but words will never hurt me. 19th cent.
8871. Still waters run deep. 19th cent. (14th cent.)
8872. Stolen pleasures are sweetest. 17th cent.
8873. Stone-dead hath no fellow. 17th cent.
8874. Straws show which way the wind blows. 17th cent.
8875. Stretch your arm no further than your sleeve will reach. 16th cent.
8876. Stretch your legs according to your coverlet. *G. H.* (13th cent.)
8877. Strike while the iron is hot. 14th cent.
8878. Success is never blamed. *F.*
8879. Such beginning, such end. *H.*
8880. Such welcome, such farewell. *H.*
8881. Sue a beggar and get a louse. *C.*
8882. Suffer and expect. *G. H.*
8883. Sunday's child is full of grace,
Monday's child is full in the face,
Tuesday's child is solemn and sad,
Wednesday's child is merry and glad,
Thursday's child is inclined to thieving,
Friday's child is free in giving,
Saturday's child works hard for its living. 19th cent.
[Days of birth. *See* Monday's child, etc.]
8884. Sus Minervam.—A pig [teaching] Minerva. [=Teach your grand-mother.] *Latin*
8885. Sweep before your own door. 17th cent.
8886. Sweet discourse makes short days and nights. *R.*
8887. Sweet meat will have sour sauce. *H.* (15th cent.)
8888. Sweetest wine makes sharpest vinegar. 16th cent.
8889. Sweetheart and Honeybird keeps no house. *R.*
8890. Swine, women and bees cannot be turned. *R.*
8891. Tailors and writers must mind the fashion. *F.*
8892. Tak awa' Aberdeen and twal' mile round aboot, an' far [=where] are ye ? [On Aberdeen's importance.] 19th cent.
8893. Tak your ain will, an' then ye'll no die o' the pet [=ill humour]. *K.*
8894. Take a farthing from a thousand pounds, it will be a thousand pounds no longer. 18th cent.
8895. Take away fuel, take away flame. *C.*
8896. Take away my good name and take away my life. *R.*
8897. Take care of the pence and the pounds will take care of them-selves. 18th cent.
8898. Take heed is a good rede [=counsel]. 16th cent.
8899. Take heed of a person marked, and a widow thrice married. [Marked=with some natural defect.] *G. H.*

8900. Take heed of a stepmother : the very name of her sufficeth. **G. H.**
8901. Take heed of an ox before, an ass behind, and a monk on all
  sides. *Spanish*
8902. Take heed of enemies reconciled and of meat twice boiled. *R.*
8903. Take heed of the vinegar of sweet wine. *G. H.*
8904. Take heed you find not that you do not seek. *R.*
8905. Take not a musket to kill a butterfly. *W. H.*
8906. Take the bit and the buffet with it. [=Put up with some ill
  usage where you get advantage.] *K.*
8907. Take things as they come. 17th cent.
8908. Take things as you find them. *L.*
8909. Take time by the forelock. 16th cent.
8910. Take time while time is, for time will away. *R.* (16th cent.)
8911. Take your wife's first advice and not her second. 17th cent.
8912. Take your will of it, as the cat did of the haggis. *K.*
8913. Talk is but talk ; but 'tis money buys lands. *R.*
8914. Talk of an angel and you'll hear his wings. *L.*
8915. Talk of the devil, and he'll appear. 17th cent.
8916. Talking pays no toll. *G. H.*
8917. Tarry-long brings little home. *F.*
8918. Teach your grandmother to suck eggs. 18th cent. (16th cent.)
8919. Teaching others teacheth yourself. *F.*
8920. Tell a lie and find the truth. *Spanish*
8921. Tell me with whom thou goest and I'll tell thee what thou
  doest. 16th cent.
8922. Tell [=count] money after your own father. *C. (T. D.)*
8923. Tell not all you know, nor do all you can. *Italian*
8924. Tell that to the Marines. [Expressing incredulity.] 19th cent.
8925. Tell the truth and shame the devil. 16th cent.
8926. Tempora mutantur, nos et mutamur in illis.—Times change and
  we change with them. *Latin*
8927. Tempus fugit.—Time flies. *Latin*
8928. Thank you for nothing. 16th cent.
8929. That cock won't fight. [=That story won't be accepted.] 19th cent.
8930. That fish will soon be caught that nibbles at every bait. *F.*
8931. That is a game that two can play at. 19th cent.
8932. That is but an empty purse that is full of other men's money. *R.*
8933. That is well spoken that is well taken. 16th cent.
8934. That suit is best that best suits me. *C.*
8935. That which doth blossom in the spring will bring forth fruit in the
  autumn. *T. D.*
8936. That which is easily done is soon believed. *R.*
8937. That which is evil is soon learned. *C.*
8938. That which proves too much proves nothing. *F.*
8939. That which two will takes effect. *Latin*
8940. That which was bitter to endure may be sweet to remember. *F.*
8941. The absent are always in the wrong. *G. H.*
8942. The ass that brays most eats least. *R.*
8943. The axe goes to the wood where it borrowed its helve. *F.*
8944. The bait hides the hook. *F.*

8945. The beggar may sing before the thief. *Latin*
8946. The belly hates a long sermon. *F.*
8947. The belly is not filled with fair words. *C.*
8948. The belly teaches all arts. *Latin*
8949. The best bred have the best portion. *G. H.*
8950. The best fish swim near the bottom. *C.*
8951. The best horse needs breaking, and the aptest child needs teaching. *C.*
8952. The best is behind. 16th cent.
8953. The best mirror is an old friend. *R.*
8954. The best of friends must part. 17th cent.
8955. The best of the sport is to do the deed and say nothing. *G. H.*
8956. The best patch is off the same cloth. *F.*
8957. The best physicians are Dr. Diet, Dr. Quiet, and Dr. Merryman. *Latin*
8958. The best remedy against an ill man is much ground between. *G. H.*
8959. The best smell is bread, the best savour salt, the best love that of children. *G. H.*
8960. The best thing for the inside of a man is the outside of a horse. [=Riding exercise.] 19th cent.
8961. The best things are worst to come by. *C.*
8962. The best throw of the dice is to throw them away. 16th cent.
8963. The better the day the better the deed. 17th cent.
8964. The better workman, the worse husband. *T. D.*
8965. The black ox has trod on his foot. [=Care has come on him.] *H.*
8966. The blind eat many a fly. 15th cent.
8967. The body is sooner dressed than the soul. *G. H.*
8968. The boot is on the other leg. [=Things are the other way about.] 19th cent.
8969. The boughs that bear most hang lowest. 17th cent.
8970. The brother had rather see the sister rich than make her so. *R.*
8971. The burnt child dreads the fire. 14th cent.
8972. The busiest men have the most leisure. 19th cent.
8973. The buyer needs a hundred eyes, the seller not one. *Italian*
8974. The calf, the goose, the bee :
    The world is ruled by these three. 17th cent.
    [=Parchment, pen, and wax.]
8975. The calmest husbands make the stormiest wives. 17th cent.
8976. The camel going to seek horns lost his ears. *Latin*
8977. The cat and dog may kiss, yet are none the better friends. 13th cent.
8978. The cat is hungry when a crust contents her. *R.*
8979. The cat knows whose lips she licks. *Latin*
8980. The cat would eat fish but would not wet her feet. 13th cent.
8981. The chamber of sickness is the chapel of devotion. *T. D.*
8982. The charitable gives out at the door and God puts in at the window. *R.*
8983. The chickens are the country's, but the city eats them. *G. H.*
8984. The child says nothing but what it heard by the fire. *G. H.*
8985. The children in Holland take pleasure in making
    What the children in England take pleasure in breaking. 19th cent.

8986. The clartier [=dirtier] the cosier. 19th cent.
8987. The coaches won't run over him. [=He is in jail.] *R.*
8988. The comforter's head never aches. *G. H.*
8989. The common horse is worst shod. *H.*
8990. The company makes the feast. 17th cent.
8991. The covetous spends more than the liberal. *G. H.*
8992. The cow knows not what her tail is worth till she hath lost it. *G. H.*
8993. The crow thinks her own bird fairest. 16th cent.
8994. The cuckold is the last that knows of it. *C. R.*
8995. The cuckoo comes in April,
  Sings a song in May ;
  Then in June another tune,
  And then she flies away. *W. H.*
8996. The cunning wife makes her husband her apron. *R.*
  The cure is worse than the disease, *see* The remedy, etc.
8997. The danger past and God forgotten. *G. H.*
8998. The darkest hour is before the dawn. 17th cent.
8999. The day has eyes and the night has ears. *D. F.*
9000. The day is short and the work is long. 15th cent.
9001. The dead have few friends. 14th cent.
9002. The death of wolves is the safety of the sheep. 16th cent.
9003. The devil always leaves a stink behind him. 16th cent.
9004. The devil dances in an empty pocket. 15th cent.
9005. The devil divides the world between atheism and superstition. *G. H.*
9006. The devil gets up to the belfry by the vicar's skirts. *J. H.*
9007. The devil is a busy bishop in his own diocese. 16th cent.
9008. The devil is kind to his own. 17th cent.
9009. The devil is good when he is pleased. *C.* (16th cent.)
9010. The devil is in the dice. *R.*
9011. The devil is not so black as he is painted. 16th cent.
9012. The devil lies brooding in the miser's chest. *F.*
9013. The devil lurks behind the cross. *Spanish*
9014. The devil take the hindmost. 17th cent.
9015. The devil tempts all, but the idle man tempts the devil. *Turkish*
9016. The devil was sick, the devil a monk would be ;
  The devil was well, the devil a monk was he. *Latin*
9017. The devil wipes his tail with the poor man's pride. *J. H.*
9018. The devil's children have the devil's luck. *R.*
9019. The devil's meal is all bran. [=Ill-gotten gains are disappointing.]
  Italian
9020. The diligent spinner has a large shift. [=Industry gives comfort.]
  Spanish
9021. The dog that licks ashes trust not with meal. *G. H.*
9022. The eagle does not catch flies. *Latin*
9023. The early bird catches the worm. *C. R.*
9024. The earthen pot must keep clear of the brass vessel. *F.*
9025. The ebb will fetch off what the tide brings in. *R.*
9026. The effect speaks, the tongue needs not. *G. H.*
9027. The end crowns all. *Latin*
9028. The end justifies the means. 17th cent.

9029. The end of fishing is not angling but catching. *F.*

9030. The English never know when they are beaten. 19th cent.

9031. The Englishman weeps, the Irishman sleeps, but the Scotchman gangs while [=goes till] he gets it. *K.*

9032. The envious man shall never want woe. *C. R.*

9033. The escaped mouse ever feels the taste of the bait. *G. H.*

9034. The evening crowns the day. 17th cent.

9035. The evils we bring on ourselves are the hardest to bear. *L.*

9036. The exception proves [=tests] the rule. 17th cent.

9037. The eye is bigger than the belly. 16th cent.

9038. The eye is the pearl of the face. 16th cent.

9039. The eye of the master will do more work than both his hands. *P. R. A.*

9040. The eye that sees all things else sees not itself. 16th cent.

9041. The eyes have one language everywhere. *G. H.*

9042. The face is the index of the heart [*or* mind]. *Latin*

9043. The fairer the hostess the fouler the reckoning. *J. H.*

9044. The fairer the paper the fouler the blot. *F.*

9045. The fairest rose at last is withered. 16th cent.

9046. The fairest silk is soonest stained. 16th cent.

The farthest away about is the nearest way home, *see* The longest way round, etc.

9047. The fat is in the fire. 16th cent.

9048. The father to the bough, the son to the plough. [=If the father is hanged, the son inherits the land.] 16th cent.

9049. The feet of the deities are shod with wool. [As they bring judgment.] *Latin*

9050. The fewer his years, the fewer his tears. *F.*

9051. The fire which lights us at a distance will burn us when near. *B.*

9052. The first and last frosts are the worst. *G. H.*

9053. The first blow is half the battle. 18th cent.

9054. The first blow makes the wrong, but the second makes the fray. 17th cent.

9055. The first breath is the beginning of death. *F.*

9056. The first dish pleaseth all. *G. H.*

9057. The first faults are theirs that commit them, the second theirs that permit them. *F.*

9058. The first glass for thirst, the second for nourishment, the third for pleasure, and the fourth for madness. 16th cent.

9059. The first service a child doth his father is to make him foolish. *G. H.*

9060. The first wife is matrimony, the second company, the third heresy. *Italian*

9061. The first year let your house to your enemy ; the second to your friend ; the third, live in it yourself. *W. H.*

9062. The fly sat upon the axletree of the chariot-wheel and said What a dust do I raise ! *Greek*

9063. The folly of one man is the fortune of another. 17th cent.

9064. The fool asks much, but he is more fool that grants it. *T. D.*

9065. The fool is busy in everyone's business but his own. *F.*

9066. The fool saith, Who would have thought it ? *T. D.*

9067. The fool wanders, the wise man travels. *F.*

9068. The foot on the cradle and hand on the distaff is the sign of a good
    housewife. *Spanish*

9069. The fox fares best when he is cursed. 17th cent.

9070. The fox knows much, but more he that catcheth him. *G. H.*

9071. The fox may grow grey, but never good. 17th cent.

9072. The fox preys farthest from his hole. *J. H.*

9073. The fox's wiles will never enter the lion's head. 16th cent.

9074. The friar preached against stealing, and had a goose [*or* pudding]
    in his sleeve. *G. H.*

9075. The frog cannot out of her bog. *R.*

9076. The frog said to the harrow, Cursed be so many lords. 13th cent.

9077. The full moon brings fair weather. B.

9078. The further you go, the further behind. 15th cent.

9079. The gallows will have its own at last. *B.*

9080. The game is not worth the candle. *G. H.*

9081. The German's wit is in his fingers. *G. H.*

9082. The goat must browse where she is tied. *G. H.*

9083. The golden age never was the present age. *F.*

9084. The good mother says not, Will you ? but gives. *G. H.*

9085. The good or ill hap of a good or ill life
    Is the good or ill choice of a good or ill wife. *F.*

9086. The goodman is the last who knows what's amiss at home. *R.*

9087. The gown is his that wears it, and the world his that enjoys it. *G. H.*

9088. The grace of God is gear [=goods] enough. *D. F.*

9089. The grapes are sour. *Greek.*

9090. The great and the little have need of one another. *F.*

9091. The great would have none great, and the little all little. *G. H.*

9092. The greater the truth, the greater the libel. 18th cent.

9093. The greatest burdens are not the gainfullest. *R.*

9094. The greatest clerks [=scholars] are not the wisest men. *Latin*

9095. The greatest respect is due to children. *Latin*

9096. The greatest step is that out of doors. *G. H.*

9097. The greatest talkers are always the least doers. *C. R.* (16th cent.)

9098. The greatest wealth is contentment with a little. *J. H.*

9099. The groat is ill saved that shames the master. *C. R.*

9100. The groundsel [=door-sill] speaks not, save what it heard of the
    hinges. *G. H.*

9101. The gull comes against the rain. *R.* (*T. D.*)

9102. The hand that gives gathers. *J. H.*

9103. The handsomest flower is not the sweetest. *B.*

9104. The hare starts when a man least expects it. 14th cent.

9105. The hasty man never wants woe. 14th cent.

9106. The head and feet keep warm,
    The rest will take no harm. *French*

9107. The healthful man can give counsel to the sick. *G. H.*

9108. The heart's letter is read in the eyes. *G. H.*

9109. The higher the ape goes, the more he shows his tail. *G. H.* (16th cent.)

9110. The higher the plum tree, the riper the plum ;
    The richer the cobbler, the blacker his thumb. *R.*

9111. The higher up, the greater fall. 16th cent.

9112. The highest branch is not the safest roost. *B.*
9113. The highest flood has the lowest ebb. 16th cent.
9114. The highway is never about. *C.*
9115. The hindmost dog may catch the hare. 16th cent.
9116. The hog never looks up to him that threshes down the acorns. *F.*
9117. The hole calls the thief. *G. H.*
9118. The horse that draws his halter is not quite escaped. *C.*
9119. The horse thinks one thing, and he that saddles him another.

17th cent.
9120. The house goes mad when women gad. 19th cent.
9121. The house is a fine house when good folks are within. *G. H.*
9122. The house shows the owner. *G. H.*
9123. The ignorant hath an eagle's wings and an owl's eyes. *G. H.*
9124. The iron entered into his soul. [From a mistranslation in the
Vulgate of Psalm cv. 18, ' He was laid in iron.'] *Latin*
9125. The Italians are wise before the deed, the Germans in the deed,
the French after the deed. *G. H.*
9126. The Jews spend at Easter, the Moors at marriages, the Christians
in suits. *G. H.*
9127. The king can do no wrong. 17th cent.
9128. The king can make a knight, but not a gentleman. 17th cent
9129. The king never dies. [Legal maxim.] *Latin*
9130. The king's cheese goes half away in parings. [Among his
attendants.] *J. H.*
9131. The king's word is more than another man's oath. 16th cent.
9132. The lame goes as far as the staggerer. *G. H.*
9133. The lame post brings the truest news. *F.*
9134. The lame tongue gets nothing. *C. R.*
9135. The lapwing cries farthest from her nest. 16th cent.
9136. The larks fall there ready roasted. [A sluggard's dream.] *French*
9137. The last drop makes the cup run over. 17th cent.
9138. The last straw breaks the camel's back. 19th cent. (17th cent.)
9139. The last suitor wins the maid. *R.*
9140. The least foolish is wise. *G. H.*
9141. The less wit a man has, the less he knows that he wants it. *F.*
9142. The life of man is a winter's day and a winter's way. *R.*
9143. The lion is not so fierce as he is painted. *G. H. (T. D.)*
9144. The little cannot be great unless he devour many. *G. H.*
9145. The lone sheep is in danger of the wolf. *C.*
9146. The longest day must have an end. 17th cent.
9147. The longest way round is the nearest way home. 17th cent.
9148. The love of money and the love of learning rarely meet. *G. H.*
9149. The love of the wicked is more dangerous than their hatred. *F.*
9150. The lower millstone grinds as well as the upper. *R.*
9151. The mad dog bites his master. *F.*
9152. The magician mutters, and knows not what he mutters. *R.*
9153. The man shall have his mare again. 16th cent.
9154. The market is the best garden. *G. H.*
9155. The master absent and the house dead. *G. H.*
9156. The master's eye makes the horse fat. *Greek*

9157. The master's footsteps fatten the soil. *J. H.* (16th cent.)
9158. The mill cannot grind with the water that is past. *G. H.*
9159. The mind is the man. *Latin*
9160. The miserable man maketh a penny of a farthing, and the liberal of a farthing sixpence. *G. H.*
9161. The mob has many heads, but no brains. *F.*
9162. The money you refuse will never do you good. *B.*
9163. The moon does not heed the barking of dogs. *Latin*
9164. The moon is a moon still, whether it shine or not. *F.*
9165. The more cost the more honour. *D. F.* (16th cent.)
9166. The more danger, the more honour. *R.* (16th cent.)
9167. The more knave, the better luck, 16th cent,
9168. The more laws, the more offenders. *Latin*
9169. The more light a torch gives, the shorter it lasts. *F.*
9170. The more mischief the better sport. *K.*
9171. The more noble the more humble. *T. D.*
9172. The more the merrier ; the fewer the better cheer [*or* fare]. *H.*
9173. The more thy years, the nearer thy grave. *C. R.*
9174. The more wit the less courage. *F.*
9175. The more women look in their glass, the less they look to their house. *G. H.*
9176. The more you stir, the worse it will stink. *H.*
9177. The morning hour has gold in its mouth. *German*
9178. The mother of mischief is no bigger than a midge's wing. *D. F.*
9179. The mother-in-law remembers not that she was a daughter-in-law. *J. H.*
9180. The mouse that has but one hole is quickly taken. 14th cent.
9181. The nearer the bone, the sweeter the flesh. 16th cent.
9182. The nearer the church, the farther from God. 14th cent.
9183. The nightingale and cuckoo sing both in one month. *C.*
9184. The noblest vengeance is to forgive. 16th cent.
9185. The nurse is valued till the child has done sucking. *F.*
9186. The nurse's tongue is privileged to talk. *R.*
9187. The offender never pardons. *G. H.*
9188. The offspring of those that are very young or very old lasts not. *G. H.*
9189. The parings of a pippin are better than the whole crab. *F.*
9190. The parson always christens his own child first. *R.*
9191. The peacock hath fair feathers but foul feet. *T. D.*
9192. The penny is well spent that saves a groat. *C. R.*
9193. The persuasion of the fortunate sways the doubtful. *G. H.*
9194. The pine wishes herself a shrub when the axe is at her root. *F.*
9195. The pitcher goes so often to the well that it is broken at last. 14th cent.
9196. The plough goes not well if the ploughman hold it not. *G.*
9197. The poor man pays for all. *C.*
9198. The poor man's shilling is but a penny. [Because he buys at the dearest rate.] *K.*
9199. The postern door makes thief and whore. *C. R.*
9200. The pot calls the kettle black. 17th cent.

9201. The pride of the rich makes the labours of the poor. *C.*
9202. The priest forgets that he was clerk. 16th cent.
9203. The prodigal robs his heir, the miser himself. *F.*
9204. The proof of the pudding is in the eating. *C. R.*
9205. The properer man, the worse luck. *R.*
9206. The reasons of the poor weigh not. *G. H. (T. D.)*
9207. The receiver is as bad as the thief. 17th cent.
9208. The remedy for injuries is not to remember them. *Italian*
9209. The remedy for love is—land between. *Spanish*
9210. The remedy is worse than the disease. 17th cent.
9211. The resolved mind hath no cares. *G. H.*
9212. The rich knows not who is his friend. *G. H.*
9213. The rich never want for kindred. *B.*
The river past and God forgotten, *see* The danger past, etc.
9214. The road to hell is paved with good intentions. 19th cent. (16th cent.)
9215. The robin and the wren are God's cock and hen,
The martin and the swallow are God's bow and arrow. 19th cent.
9216. The rotten apple injures its neighbours. *Latin*
9217. The rough net is not the best catcher of birds. *H.*
9218. The same heat that melts the wax will harden the clay. 16th cent.
9219. The same knife cuts bread and fingers. *T. D.*
9220. The sandal tree perfumes the axe that fells it. *Indian*
9221. The scholar may waur [=worst] the master. *K.*
9222. The Scot will not fight till he sees his own blood. 19th cent.
9223. The sea and the gallows refuse none. 18th cent.
9224. The sea complains it wants water. *C.*
9225. The sea hath fish for every man. 16th cent.
9226. The sea refuses no river. *F.*
9227. The shoe will hold with the sole. *H.*
9228. The shortest answer is doing. *G. H.*
9229. The sickness of the body may prove the health of the soul. *B.*
9230. The sight of you is good for sore eyes. 18th cent.
9231. The sign invites you in, but your money must get you out. *F.*
9232. The singing man keeps his shop in his throat. *G. H.*
9233. The slothful man is the beggar's brother. *K.*
9234. The sluggard makes his night till noon. *F.*
9235. The sluggard's convenient season never comes. *F.*
9236. The smith and his penny are both black. *G. H.*
9237. The smith hath always a spark in his throat. [=Is always thirsty.] *R.*
9238. The smoke of a man's own house is better than the fire of another. *Latin*
9239. The snail slides up the tower at last, though the swallow mounteth it not. *F.*
9240. The soul is not where it lives, but where it loves. 16th cent.
9241. The soul needs few things, the body many. *G. H.*
9242. The still sow eats up all the draff. 15th cent.
9243. The sting is in the tail. 17th cent.
9244. The sting of a reproach is the truth of it. *F.*
9245. The stone that lieth not in your way need not offend you. *F.*

9246. The stream cannot rise above its source. *F.*
9247. The subject's love is the king's life-guard. *Latin*
9248. The submitting to one wrong brings on another. *Latin*
9249. The sun can be seen by nothing but its own light. *F.*
9250. The sun is never the worse for shining on a dunghill. 14th cent.
9251. The sun shines upon all alike. 16th cent.
9252. The swan sings before death. *Latin*
9253. The table robs more than the thief. *G. H.*
9254. The tailor makes the man. 17th cent.
9255. The tale runs as it pleases the teller. *F.*
9256. The taste of the kitchen is better than the smell. *W. H.*
9257. The thief is sorry he is to be hanged, but not that he is a thief. *F.*
9258. The thin end of the wedge is to be feared. 19th cent.
9259. The third time pays for all. 16th cent.
9260. The thread breaks where it is weakest. *G. H.*
9261. The thunderbolt hath but his clap. *T. D.*
9262. The tide never goes out so far but it always comes in again.

    19th cent.
9263. The tired ox treads surest. *Latin*
9264. The tongue breaks bone, though itself has none. 13th cent.
9265. The tongue is ever turning to the aching tooth. *Italian*
9266. The tongue is not steel yet it cuts. *H.*
9267. The tongue of idle persons is never idle. *F.*
9268. The tongue talks at the head's cost. *G. H.*
9269. The treason is loved but the traitor is hated. 17th cent.
9270. The tree falls not at the first stroke. 16th cent.
9271. The truest jests sound worst in guilty ears. *R.*
9272. The unexpected always happens. *Latin*
9273. The vale discovereth the hill. 16th cent.
9274. The virtue of a coward is suspicion. *G. H.*
9275. The war is not done so long as my enemy lives. *G. H.*
9276. The way to an Englishman's heart is through his stomach. 19th cent.
9277. The way to be safe is never to feel secure. *F.*
9278. The way to bliss lies not on beds of down. *C.*
9279. The weakest goes to the wall. 15th cent.
9280. The Welshman keeps nothing till he has lost it. 17th cent.
9281. The wholesomest meat is at another man's cost. *J. H.*
9282. The wife is the key of the house. *T. D.*
9283. The wind keeps not always in one quarter. *C.*
9284. The wine in the bottle does not quench thirst. *G. H.*
9285. The wine will taste of the cask. 16th cent.
9286. The wise hand doth not all that the foolish mouth speaks. *G. H.*
9287. The wish is father to the thought. *Latin*
9288. The wolf eats oft of the sheep that have been warned. *G. H.*
9289. The world is a ladder for some to go up and some down. *J. H.*
9290. The world is his who enjoys it. 18th cent.
9291. The worse for the rider, the better for the bider. [=Where roads
    are muddy, the soil is good.] *C.*
9292. The worse luck now, the better another time. *K.*
9293. The worse the passage, the more welcome the port. *F.*

9294. The worst of law is that one suit breeds twenty. *G. H.*
9295. The worst wheel of a cart creaks most. 15th cent.
9296. The worth of a thing is best known by the want of it. *R.*
9297. The worth of a thing is what it will bring. 17th cent.
9298. The young pig grunts like the old sow. *R.*
9299. There are as good fish in the sea as ever came out of it. 19th cent.
9300. There are black sheep in every flock [*or* fold]. 19th cent.
9301. There are many ways to fame. *G. H.*
9302. There are more maids than Malkin, and more men than Michael. *R.*
9303. There are more men threatened than struck. *G. H.*
9304. There are more ways to kill a dog than hanging. *R.*
9305. There are more ways to the wood than one. *H.*
9306. There are no birds in last year's nest. *Spanish*
9307. There are no fans in hell. *Arabic*
9308. There are spots even on the sun. 19th cent.
9309. There are two sides to every question. 19th cent.
9310. There are wheels within wheels. [=Complex influences are at work.] 17th cent.
9311. There came nothing out of the sack but what was in it. *G. H.*
9312. There is a devil in every berry of the grape. 17th cent.
9313. There is a good time coming. 19th cent.
9314. There is a measure in all things. 14th cent
9315. There is a remedy for everything but death. 16th cent.
9316. There is a salve for every sore. 16th cent.
9317. There is a time for all things. 14th cent.
9318. There is a witness everywhere. *F.*
9319. There is always a something. 19th cent.
9320. There is but an hour in a day between a good housewife and a bad. *R*
9321. There is but one good wife in the world, and every man thinks
       he has her. 17th cent.
9322. There is a difference between staring and stark blind [*or* mad]. *H*
9323. There is falsehood in fellowship *H.*
9324. There is great force hidden in a sweet command. *G. H.*
9325. There is honour among thieves. 18th cent.
9326. There is little for the rake after the besom [=broom]. *D. F.*
9327. There is luck in odd numbers. 16th cent.
9328. There is many a fair thing found false. *D. F*
9329. There is no fire without some smoke. *H*
9330. There is no general rule without some exception. 17th cent.
9331. There is no going to heaven in a sedan. *F*
9332. There is no jollity but hath a smack of folly in it. *G. H.*
9333. There is no love lost between them. [=They hate each other,
       but formerly=They love mutually.] 17th cent.
9334. There is no medicine against death. *Latin*
9335. There is no medicine for fear. *D. F.*
9336. There is no pack of cards without a knave. 16th cent.
9337. There is no redemption from hell. 14th cent
9338. There is no such flatterer as a man's self. *F.*
9339. There is no tree but bears some fruit. *C*
9340. There is no venom to that of the tongue. *J. H.*

9341. There is no wool so white but a dyer can make it black.   16th cent.
9342. There is nobody will go to hell for company.   *G. H.*
9343. There is reason in roasting of eggs.   *J. H.*
9344. There is who despises pride with a greater pride.   *Greek*
9345. There may be blue and better blue.   *K.*
9346. There needs a long time to know the world's pulse.   *G. H.*
9347. There was never a slut but had a slit, there was never a daw
    [=drab] but had twa. [Said to girls whose clothes have tears
    in them.]   *K.*
9348. There were no ill language if it were not ill taken.   *G. H.*
9349. There will be sleeping enough in the grave.   *P. R. A.*
9350. There would be no great ones if there were no little ones.   *G. H.*
9351. There's many a slip 'twixt the cup and the lip.   *Greek*
9352. There's no mischief in the world done,
    But a woman is always one.
       [=A woman is at the bottom of it.]   *R.*
9353. They agree like bells ; they want nothing but hanging.   *R.*
9354. They are far behind that may not follow. [Said to encourage
    those who are outstripped.]   *K.*
9355. They buy good cheap [=a bargain] that bring nothing home.   *D. F.*
9356. They cleave [*or* hang *or* hold] together like burrs.   *H.*
9357. They die well that live well.   *C.*
    They laugh best that laugh last, *see* He laughs best, etc.
9358. They love dancing well that dance among thorns.   *C. R.*
9359. They love me for little that hate me for naught.   *R.*
9360. They love too much that die for love.   *R.*
9361. They must hunger in frost that will not work in heat.   *H.*
9362. They need much whom nothing will content.   *C.*
9363. They say so, is half a lie.   *Italian*
9364. They take a long day that never pay.   *R.*
9365. They talk of Christmas so long that it comes.   *G. H.*
9366. They that are bound must obey.   13th cent.
9367. They that be in hell ween there is none other heaven.   *H.*
9368. They that bourd wi' cats maun counts on scarts. [=They that
    jest with cats must count on scratches.]   *A. H.*
9369. They that have got good store of butter may lay it thick on their
    bread.   *C.*
9370. They that have no other meat
    Bread and butter are glad to eat.   *C.*
9371. They that live longest must die at last.   *R.*
9372. They that think none ill are soonest beguiled.   *H.*
9373. They that walk much in the sun will be tanned at last.   *R.* (16th cent.)
9374. They think a calf a muckle [=large] beast that never saw a
    cow.   *A. H.*
9375. They who live longest will see most.   *Spanish*
9376. They who love most are least set by.   *J. H.*
9377. They who would be young when they are old must be old when
    they are young.   *R.*
9378. Things are as they be taken.   *C.*
9379. Things at the worst will mend.   17th cent.

9380. Things done cannot be undone. *H.*
9381. Things hardly attained are longer retained. *C.*
9382. Things past cannot be recalled. *H.*
9383. Things present are judged by things past. 16th cent.
9384. Things well fitted abide. *G. H.*
9385. Think much, speak little, and write less. *Italian*
9386. Think of ease, but work on. *G. H.*
9387. Think to-day and speak to-morrow. *B.*
9388. Think well of all men. *J. H.*
9389. Think with the wise, but talk with the vulgar [=ordinary people]. *Greek*
9390. Thinking is very far from knowing. *B.*
9391. This rule in gardening never forget,
   To sow dry and to set wet. *R.*
9392. This world is nothing except it tend to another. *G. H.*
9393. Though a lie be well dressed it is ever overcome. *G. H.*
9394. Though I say it that should not. 16th cent.
9395. Though love is blind, yet 'tis not for want of eyes. *F.*
9396. Though modesty be a virtue, yet bashfulness is a vice. *F.*
9397. Though old and wise, yet still advise [=take counsel]. *G. H.*
9398. Though the sore be healed, yet a scar may remain. *F.*
9399. Though the sun shines, leave not your cloak at home. *Spanish*
9400. Thought is free. 14th cent.
9401. Threatened men [*or* folks] live long. 16th cent.
9402. Threats without power are like powder without ball. 18th cent.
9403. Three are too many to keep a secret, and too few to be merry. *F.*
9404. Three failures and a fire make a Scotsman's fortune. 19th cent.
9405. Three great evils come out of the North, a cold wind, a cunning knave, and a shrinking cloth. 17th cent.
9406. Three helping one another bear the burden of six. *G. H.*
9407. Three may keep counsel if two be away. *H.*
9408. Three removes are as bad as a fire. *P. R. A.*
9409. Three things drive a man out of his house—smoke, rain, and a scolding wife. *Bible*
9410. Three women and a goose make a market. *Italian*
9411. Thrift is good revenue. *Latin*
9412. Thrift is the philosopher's stone. *F.*
9413. Thursday come, and the week is gone. *G. H.*
9414. Time and chance reveal all secrets. 18th cent.
9415. Time and thinking tame the strongest grief. *K.*
9416. Time and tide wait for no man. 16th cent.
9417. Time fleeth away without delay. *C.*
9418. Time is a file that wears and makes no noise. *Italian*
9419. Time is money. 18th cent.
9420. Time is the rider that breaks youth. *G. H*
9421. Time lost cannot be won again [*or* Time past cannot be recalled]. 14th cent.
9422. Time tries all things. 16th cent.
9423. Time trieth truth. *H.*
9424. To a child all weather is cold. *G. H*

9425. To a crazy ship all winds are contrary. *G. H.*

9426. To be a good spender God is the treasurer. *G. H.*

9427. To a red man read thy rede, [=Give your counsel.]
With a brown man break thy bread,
At a pale man draw thy knife,
From a black man keep thy wife.
  The red is wise, the brown trusty,
  The pale envious, and the black lusty. *D. F.*
  [Refers to the different complexions.]

9428. To add insult to injury. *Latin*

9429. To be beloved is above all bargains. *G. H.*

9430. To be born with a silver spoon in one's mouth. *C.*

9431. To be in a person's bad [*or* good] books. [=In [*or* out of] favour.] 19th cent.

9432. To be in the wrong box. [=In an awkward position.] 16th cent.

9433. To be on one's last legs. [=Near death.] 16th cent.

9434. To be too busy gets contempt. *G. H.*

9435. To be under a cloud. [=In disgrace.] 17th cent.

9436. To bear away the bell. [=To be first.] 14th cent.

9437. To bear two faces in one hood. [=To be double-faced.] 15th cent.

9438. To beat about the bush. [=To approach a subject indirectly.] 16th cent.

9439. To bend the bow of Ulysses. [=To emulate a great man's achievements.] *Greek*

9440. To blow one's own trumpet. [=To praise oneself.] 16th cent.

9441. To break my head and then give me a plaster. 15th cent.

9442. To break Priscian's head. [=To be guilty of bad grammar. Priscian was a Latin grammarian.] 16th cent.

9443. To bring a noble to ninepence. [=To waste money. The noble was worth 6s. 8d.] *H.*

9444. To bring haddock to paddock. [=To lose everything.] *H.*

9445. To build castles in Spain. [=Daydreams.] 15th cent.

9446. To build castles in the air. [=Daydreams.] 16th cent.

9447. To burn one's boats. [=To commit oneself irrevocably.] 19th cent.

9448. To burn the candle at both ends. *R.*

9449. To bury the hatchet. [=To make peace.] 18th cent.

9450. To buy a pig in a poke. *H.*

9451. To buy and sell and live by the loss. *T. D.*

9452. To call a spade a spade. [=To speak plainly.] *Latin*

9453. To carry coals to Newcastle. [Newcastle being a main source of coal.] 16th cent.

9454. To carry [*or* draw] water in a sieve. *Latin*

9455. To cast water into the sea [*or* Thames]. 14th cent.

9456. To catch a Tartar. [=To make a capture that is beyond control.] 17th cent.

9457. To catch a weasel asleep. 19th cent.

9458. To comb one's head with a stool. [=To thrash him.] 16th cent.

9459. To come from little good to stark nought. *R.*

9460. To come up to the scratch. [=To come forward for an encounter.] 19th cent.

R

9461. To count one's chickens before they are hatched.   16th cent.
9462. To cry out before one is hurt.   16th cent.
9463. To cry with one eye and laugh with the other.   14th cent.
9464. To cut off one's nose to spite one's face.   *French*
9465. To cut the coat according to the cloth. [=To keep within one's
    means.]   *H.*
9466. To cut the grass [*or* ground] from under a person's feet. [=To
    thwart him.]   16th cent.
9467. To deceive oneself is very easy.   *G. H.*
9468. To deserve [*or* lie for] the whetstone. [=To be a great liar, a
    whetstone round the neck being the former penalty for this.]
    15th cent.
9469. To dig one's grave with one's teeth. [By overeating.]   *French*
9470. To draw the long bow. [=To exaggerate.]   *R.*
9471. To fiddle while Rome is burning. [=To trifle during a crisis.]
    17th cent.
9472. To find a mare's nest. [=A discovery that amounts to nothing.]
    16th cent.
9473. To fish for a herring and catch a sprat.   C.
9474. To flog a dead horse. [=To argue on an outworn theme.]   19th cent.
9475. To fry in one's own grease.   14th cent.
9476. To gain teacheth how to spend.   *G. H.*
9477. To give a thing and take a thing
Is to wear the devil's gold ring.   17th cent.
9478. To haul over the coals. [=To call to account.]   16th cent.
9479. To have a bee in one's bonnet. [=To be crazy on some one point.]
    17th cent.
9480. To have a bone in one's leg. [A joking excuse.]   *R.*
9481. To have a crow to pluck [*or* pull] with one. [=To have a
    complaint to make.]   15th cent.
9482. To have a finger in the pie [=To be concerned in the affair.]
    16th cent.
9483. To have a rod in pickle for someone. [=To have punishment in
    store for him.]   16th cent.
9484. To have [*or* hold] a wolf by the ears. [So that you can neither
    hold on nor let go.]   *Greek*
9485. To have bats in the belfry. [=To be crazy.]   20th cent.
9486. To have many [*or* other] irons in the fire.   16th cent.
9487. To have one's labour for one's pains.   16th cent.
9488. To have one foot in the grave.   16th cent.
9489. To have the wrong sow by the ear.   *H.*
9490. To have two strings to one's bow.   15th cent.
9491. To heap Ossa upon Pelion. [Alluding to the attempt of the
    Giants to scale heaven.]   *Greek*
9492. To help a lame dog over a stile.   *H.*
9493. To hit the nail on the head. [=To speak to the point.]   16th cent.
9494. To hold a candle to the devil. [=To assist in evil.]   15th cent.
9495. To keep [*or* hold] one's nose to the grindstone. [=To work without
    stopping.]   *H.*
9496. To keep one's tongue between one's teeth.   17th cent.

9497. To keep the wolf from the door. [=To avert want.] *H.*
9498. To kill the goose that lays the golden eggs. *Greek*
9499. To kill two birds with one stone. 17th cent.
9500. To kiss the rod. [To submit meekly to correction.] 16th cent.
9501. To know how many beans make five. 18th cent.
9502. To know on which side one's bread is buttered. *H.*
9503. To know where the shoe pinches. 14th cent.
9504. To know which way the wind blows. *H.*
9505. To laugh on the wrong side of one's mouth [*or* face]. 17th cent.
9506. To lay it on with a trowel. [=To flatter grossly.] 16th cent.
9507. To lay up for a rainy day. [=To provide for a time of want.]
16th cent.
9508. To lead one by the nose. [=To dominate him.] *Latin*
9509. To leave no stone unturned. [=To try all methods.] *Greek*
9510. To let the cat out of the bag. [=To disclose a secret.] 18th cent.
9511. To lick into shape. [=To train or mould.] 17th cent.
9512. To look as if butter would not melt in one's mouth. [=To look
very innocent.] 16th cent.
9513. To look at both sides of a penny. [=To be very saving.] 19th cent.
9514. To look for a needle in a haystack. *Latin*
To lose the ship for a halfpennyworth of tar, *see* To spoil the ship, etc.
9515. To make a mountain out of a molehill. 16th cent.
9516. To make a person turn in his grave. 19th cent.
9517. To make bricks without straw. *Bible*
9518. To make ducks and drakes of. [=To squander.] 16th cent.
9519. To make ends meet. [=To live within one's means.] *C.*
9520. To make fish of one and flesh [*or* fowl] of another. [=To
discriminate unfairly.] *C.*
9521. To make two bites of a cherry. [=To do a small task in two
stages.] *French*
9522. To pay a person in his own coin. [=To retaliate in the same way
as he has injured you.] 16th cent.
To pile Ossa upon Pelion, *see* To heap Ossa, etc.
9523. To play first [*or* second] fiddle. [=To take the leading [*or*
subordinate] part.] 19th cent.
9524. To pour oil upon the waters. [=To compose a quarrel.] 19th cent.
9525. To promise and give nothing is comfort to a fool. *T. D.*
9526. To put a spoke in one's wheel. [=To put an obstacle in the way.
Reference is to the pin used to lock wheels.] 17th cent. (16th cent.)
9527. To put one's best foot foremost. [=To make a strong effort.]
17th cent.
9528. To put one's nose out of joint. [=To supplant him.] 16th cent.
9529. To put salt on a bird's tail. [Jokingly said to be a way of catching
it.] 16th cent.
9530. To put the cart before the horse. *Latin*
9531. To reckon without one's host. 16th cent. (15th cent.)
9532. To rob Peter to pay Paul. 14th cent.
9533. To run with the hare and hunt with the hounds.
19th cent. (15th cent.)
9534. To scare a bird is not the way to catch it. *C.*

9535. To see which way the cat jumps. [=How events will turn
    out.]   19th cent.

9536. To send away with a flea in his ear. [=Peremptorily.]   *H.*

9537. To set the Thames on fire. [=To create a sensation.]   18th cent.

9538. To shut the stable door when the steed is stolen.   *French*

9539. To smell of the lamp. [=To show studied effort.]   *Greek*

9540. To sow one's wild oats. [=To indulge in youthful excesses.]
                      16th cent.

9541. To split hairs. [=To make fine distinctions.]   *R.*

9542. To spoil the ship [*originally* sheep] for a halfpennyworth of tar.   *C. R.*

9543. To stand in one's own light. [=To spoil one's own chances.]   *H.*

    To stew in one's own iuice, *see* To fry in one's own grease.

9544. To take a leaf out of one's book. [=To follow his example.]
                      19th cent.

9545. To take counsel of one's pillow. [=To allow a night's interval
    before making a decision.]   16th cent.

9546. To take one down a peg or two. [=To humble his pride.]   16th cent.

9547. To take one up before he is down.   16th cent.

9548. To take the bull by the horns. [=To face a difficulty.]   19th cent.

9549. To take the chestnuts out of the fire with the cat's paw.   16th cent.

9550. To take the gilt off the gingerbread. [=To make a thing less
    attractive.]   19th cent.

9551. To take the law into one's own hands. [=To act without
    authority.]   17th cent.

9552. To take the rough with the smooth.   15th cent.

9553. To take the will for the deed.   15th cent.

9554. To take the wind out of one's sails. [=To put him at a dis-
    advantage.]   19th cent.

9555. To tell tales out of school.   *H.*

9556. To throw a sprat to catch a whale. [=To do a small favour in
    the hope of a great return.]   19th cent.

9557. To throw dust in one's eyes. [To mislead.]   *T. D.*

9558. To throw good money after bad.   19th cent.

9559. To throw the helve after the hatchet. [=To throw away what
    remains, because your losses have been so great.]   *H.*

9560. To turn an honest penny. [=To make money.]   *H.*

9561. To turn cat in pan. [=To change sides.]   17th cent.

9562. To turn over a new leaf. [=To amend one's ways.]   *H.*

9563. To wash a blackamoor white. [=To waste effort.]   *Greek*

9564. To wash dirty linen in public. [=To publish family scandals.]
                      19th cent.

9565. To wear one's heart upon one's sleeve. [=To make one's feelings
    apparent to everyone.]   17th cent.

9566. To wear the breeches. [Of a wife who dominates her husband.]
                    16th cent. (15th cent.)

9567. To wear the willow. [=To mourn the loss of a sweetheart.]
                    16th cent.

9568. To wet one's whistle. [=To have a drink.]   14th cent.

9569. Toasted cheese hath no master.   *R.*

9570. To-day a man, to-morrow a mouse.   *R.*

9571. To-day is Yesterday's pupil. *Latin*
9572. To-day me, to-morrow thee. 13th cent.
9573. To-morrow come never. *R.*
9574. To-morrow is a new day. 16th cent.
9575. Too many cooks spoil the broth. 16th cent.
9576. Too much breaks the bag. *Spanish*
9577. Too much consulting confounds. *F.*
9578. Too much of one thing is good for nothing. 14th cent.
9579. Too much praise is a burden. 17th cent.
9580. Too much taking heed is loss. *G. H.*
9581. Too too will in two. [Friends that are too intimate will
    quarrel.] *R.*
9582. Touch a galled horse, and he'll wince [*or* kick]. 18th cent. (14th cent.)
9583. Touch pot, touch penny. [=No credit given.] 17th cent.
9584. Touch wood, it's sure to come good. [Touching wood is a charm
    to avert ill-luck after boasting.] 20th cent.
9585. Tout passe, tout casse, tout lasse.—All passes, all breaks, all
    wearies. *French*
9586. Translators, traitors. *Italian*
9587. Trash and trumpery is the highway to beggary. *R.*
9588. Travel makes a wise man better, but a fool worse. *F.*
    Tread on a worm and it will turn, *see* Even a worm, etc.
9589. True blue will never stain. *J. H.*
9590. True lovers are shy when people are by. 18th cent.
9591. Trust me, but look to thyself. *F.*
9592. Trust not a horse's heel, nor a dog's tooth. *R.*
9593. Trust not a new friend nor an old enemy. *K.*
9594. Truth and oil are ever above. *G. H.*
9595. Truth fears no colours. *R.*
9596. Truth finds foes where it makes none. *R.*
9597. Truth hath a good face, but bad clothes. *J. H.*
9598. Truth is God's daughter. *F.*
9599. Truth is stranger than fiction. 19th cent.
9600. Truth is truth to the end of the reckoning. 16th cent.
9601. Truth lies at the bottom of a well. *Greek*
9602. Truth may be blamed but cannot be shamed. 16th cent.
9603. Truth needs not many words. 16th cent.
9604. Truth never grows old. *F.*
9605. Truth and roses have thorns about them. *B.*
9606. Truth seeks no corners. 16th cent.
9607. Try before you trust. 15th cent.
9608. Try your friend before you have need of him. 15th cent.
9609. Try your skill in gilt first, and then in gold. *C.*
9610. Turkey, carps, hops, pickerel, and beer
    Came into England all in one year. 17th cent.
    [Pickerel=young pike. The year is supposed to be 1520.]
9611. Turn your money when you hear the cuckoo, and you'll never be
    without it during the year. *W. H.*
9612. Two anons and a by and by is an hour and a half. *C. R.*
9613. Two attorneys can live in a town when one cannot. *L.*

9614. Two blacks do not make a white. [=Another's fault does not excuse your own.] *K.*

Two can play at that game, *see* That is a game, etc.

9615. Two cats and a mouse,
Two wives in one house,
Two dogs and a bone,
Never agree in one. *R.*

9616. Two daughters and a back door are three arrant thieves. [The daughters spend, and the servants filch.] *D. F.*

9617. Two dogs fight for a bone, and a third runs away with it. 16th cent.

9618. Two dry sticks will kindle a green one. *R.*

9619. Two ears to one tongue, therefore hear twice as much as you speak. *Greek*

9620. Two eyes can see more than one. *C.R.* (16th cent.)

9621. Two fools in one house [*or* bed] are too many. 16th cent.

9622. Two heads are better than one. *H.*

9623. Two hungry meals make the third a glutton. *H.*

9624. Two in distress make trouble less. *B.*

9625. Two is company, three is none. 19th cent.

Two may keep counsel if one be away, *see* Three may keep, etc.

9626. Two negatives make an affirmative. 16th cent.

9627. Two of a trade can never agree. *R.*

9628. Two Sir Positives can scarce meet without a skirmish. *F.*

9629. Two sparrows on one ear of corn make an ill agreement. *G. H.*

9630 .Two things a man should never be angry at ; what he can help, and what he cannot help *K.*

9631. Two things doth prolong thy life : A quiet heart and a loving wife. 17th cent.

9632. Two to one in all things against the angry man. *F.*

9633. Two wrongs don't make a right. 19th cent.

9634. Under the blanket the black one is as good as the white *F.*

9635. Under the furze is hunger and cold,
Under the broom is silver and gold. *R.*

9636. Under water, famine ; under snow, bread. *G. H.*

9637. Unkissed, unkind. 16th cent.

9638. Unknown [*or* uncouth], unkissed. 14th cent.

9639. Unlucky in love, lucky at play. 18th cent.

9640. Unminded, unmoaned. *H.*

9641. Unsound minds, like unsound bodies, if you feed, you poison. *G. H.*

9642. Up hill spare me ;
Down hill forbear me ;
Plain way, spare me not,
Let me not drink when I am hot. [How to use a horse.] *F.*

9643. Use legs and have legs. *R.*

Use makes perfectness, *see* Practice makes perfect.

9644. Use the means, and God will give the blessing. *T. D.*

9645. Vainglory blossoms but never bears. *F.*

9646. Valour that parleys is near yielding. *G. H.*

9647. Valour would fight, but discretion would run away. *R.*

9648. Vanity is the sixth sense. 19th cent.

9649. Variety is pleasing.	*Greek*
9650. Varnishing hides a crack.	*F.*
9651. Venture not all in one bottom.	*Latin*
9652. Verbum sat sapienti.—A word is enough to the wise.	*Latin*
9653. Vice makes virtue shine.	*F.*
9654. Vice ruleth where gold reigneth.	17th cent.
9655. Virtue and a trade are the best portion for children.	*G. H.*
9656. Virtue and happiness are mother and daughter.	*B.*
9657. Virtue is its own reward.	*Latin*
9658. Virtue never grows old.	*G. H.*
9659. Virtue which parleys is near a surrender.	18th cent.
9660. Virtues all agree, but vices fight one another.	*F.*
9661. Vows made in storms are forgotten in calms.	*F.*
9662. Vox et praeterea nihil.—A voice and nothing besides.	*Latin*
9663. Vox populi vox Dei.—The voice of the people is the voice of God.	*Latin*
9664. Wage will get a page. [=You will get servants if you have the money to hire them.]	*K.*
9665. Wake not a sleeping lion.	16th cent.
9666. Walls have ears.	17th cent.
9667. Want is the mother of industry.	*B.*
9668. Want makes strife 'twixt man and wife.	*B.*
9669. Want of wit is worse than want of wealth.	*K.*
9670. Want will be your master.	18th cent.
9671. Wanton kittens may make sober cats.	*F.*
9672. War, hunting, and law [*or* love] are as full of trouble as pleasure.	*G. H.*
9673. War is death's feast.	*G. H.*
9674. War makes thieves, and peace hangs them.	*G. H.*
9675. Wars bring scars.	*R.*
9676. Wash your hands often, your feet seldom, and your head never.	*R.*
Waste makes want, *see* Wilful waste, etc.	
9677. Waste not, want not.	18th cent.
9678. Water, fire, and soldiers quickly make room.	*G. H.*
9679. We are born crying, live complaining, and die disappointed.	*F.*
9680. We are bound to be honest, but not to be rich.	*W. H.*
9681. We bachelors grin, but you married men laugh till your hearts ache.	*R.*
9682. We can drink of the burn when we cannot bite of the brae [=hill]. [=People who lack bread can always get water.]	*D. F.*
9683. We can live without our friends, but not without our neighbours.	*K.*
9684. We can shape coat and sark [=shirt] for them, but we cannot shape their weird [=fate].	*K.*
9685. We cannot come to honour under coverlet.	*G. H.*
9686. We leave more to do when we die, than we have done.	*G. H.*
9687. We may give advice, but we cannot give conduct.	*P. R. A.*
9688. We must live by the quick, not by the dead.	16th cent.
9689. We must not lie down and cry, God help us.	17th cent.
9690. We never find that a fox dies in the dirt of his own ditch. [=Men are rarely hurt by the things they are accustomed to.]	*R.*
9691. We never miss the water till the well runs dry.	*K.*

9692. We see not what sits on our shoulder. *C.*
9693. We shall lie all alike in our graves. *C.*
9694. We shall see what we shall see. 19th cent.
9695. We soon believe what we desire. *Latin*
9696. Weak food best fits weak stomachs. 15th cent.
9697. Weak men had need be witty. *C.*
9698. Weal and woman never pan [=close together]. 19th cent. (*C.*)
9699. Wealth is best known by want. *F.*
9700. Wealth is like rheum, it falls on the weakest parts. *G. H.*
9701. Wealth makes wit waver. *D. F.*
9702. Wealth makes worship. *C.*
9703. Wedlock is a padlock. *R.*
9704. Weeds want no sowing. *F.*
9705. Weening is not measure. *G. H.*
9706. Weigh right, and sell dear. 16th cent.
9707. Weight and measure take away strife. *G. H.*
9708. Welcome death, quoth the rat, when the trap fell. *J. H.*
9709. Welcome evil, if thou comest alone. *G. H.*
9710. Welcome is the best cheer. [=In hospitality the spirit is the thing.] *Greek*
9711. Well begun is half done. *Latin*
9712. Well may he smell fire whose gown burns. *G. H.*
9713. Well to work and make a fire,
It doth care and skill require. *R.*
9714. Were there no hearers, there would be no backbiters. *G. H.*
9715. What can you expect from a hog but a grunt. *P. R. A.* (*R.*)
9716. What can't be cured must be endured. 14th cent.
9717. What costs little is little esteemed. 17th cent.
9718. What God will no frost can kill. *R.*
9719. What greater crime than loss of time ? *F.*
9720. What is bolder than a miller's neckcloth, which takes a thief by the throat every morning ? *German*
9721. What is bought is cheaper than a gift. *R.*
9722. What is bred in the bone will not out of the flesh. *H.* (13th cent.)
9723. What is done by night appears by day. 14th cent.
9724. What is got over the devil's back is spent under his belly.
[=What is got by oppression is spent in luxury.] 17th cent.
9725. What is lost in the hundred [=district] will be found in the shire. 17th cent. (*H.*)
9726. What is new is not true, what is true is not new. 19th cent.
9727. What is sauce for the goose is sauce for the gander. *R.*
9728. What is the good of a sun-dial in the shade ? *F.*
9729. What is worth doing is worth doing well. 19th cent.
9730. What man has done, man can do. 19th cent.
9731. What may be done at any time will be done at no time. *K.*
9732. What one day gives another takes away from us. *G. H.*
9733. What one knows, it is sometimes useful to forget. *Latin*
9734. What soberness conceals, drunkenness reveals. *Latin*
9735. What the eye doesn't see the heart doesn't grieve over.
19th cent. (*H.*)

9736. What the fool does in the end, the wise man does at the beginning.
19th cent.

9737. What the heart thinks the tongue speaks. 15th cent.

9738. What's yours is mine, and what's mine's my own. 18th cent.

9739. When a couple are newly married, the first month is honeymoon,
or smick smack : the second is, hither and thither : the third is
thwick thwack: the fourth, the devil take them that brought
thee and I together. R.

9740. When a dog is drowning, everyone offers him drink. G. H.

9741. When a friend asks, there is no to-morrow. G. H.

9742. When age is jocund, it makes sport for death. G. H.

9743. When ale [or drink or wine] is in, wit is out. H. (14th cent.)

9744. When all men have what belongs to them it cannot be much. G. H.

9745. When all men speak, no man hears. K.

9746. When all sins grow old, covetousness is young. G. H. (16th cent.)

9747. When April blows his horn, [=When it thunders.]
It's good both for hay and corn. R.

9748. When at Rome do as the Romans do. Latin

9749. When Candlemas day is come and gone, [2 Feb.]
The snow lies on a hot stone. R.

9750. When caught by the tempest, whatever it be,
If it lightens and thunders beware of a tree. D.

9751. When children stand quiet they have done some ill. G. H.
When drink is in, wit is out, see When ale is in, etc.

9752. When Fortune knocks, open the door. 17th cent.

9753. When Greek meets Greek, then comes the tug of war. [Common
misquotation of No. 2409 supra.] 17th cent.

9754. When house and land are gone and spent,
Then learning is most excellent. 18th cent.

9755. When I did well, I heard it never ;
When I did ill, I heard it ever. K.

9756. When I lent I was a friend,
When I asked I was unkind. 16th cent.

9757. When in doubt, leave out. [A newspaper maxim.] 20th cent.

9758. When it rains and the sun shines at the same time, the devil is
beating his wife. French

9759. When it thunders the thief becomes honest. Italian

9760. When love puts in, friendship is gone. 17th cent.

9761. When many strike on an anvil, they must strike by measure. R.

9762. When need is highest, help is nighest. 13th cent.

9763. When one door shuts another opens. Spanish

9764. When Oxford draws knife. England's soon at strife. 17th cent.

9765. When poverty comes in at the door, love flies out at the window.
17th cent.

9766. When round the moon there is a brugh, [=halo.]
The weather will be cold and rough. D.

9767. When sorrow is asleep wake it not. J. H.

9768. When the belly is full, the bones would be at rest. H

9769. When the cat is away the mice will play. 16th cent.

9770. When the cat winketh, little wots the mouse what the cat thinketh. R.

*R

9771. When the clouds are upon the hills,
  They'll come down by the mills.   *R.*

9772. When the corn is in the shock,
  The fish are on the rock.   *W. H.*

9773. When the cuckoo comes she eats up all the dirt. [=The mire
  dries up.]   17th cent.

9774. When the cuckoo comes to the bare thorn,
  Sell your cow and buy your corn :
  But when she comes to the full bit,
  Sell your corn and buy your sheep.   *R.*

9775. When the cup is full, carry it even.   14th cent.

9776. When the devil is blind. [=Never.]   *J. H.*

9777. When the fern is as high as a ladle,
  You may sleep as long as you are able.   *R.*

9778. When the fox preaches, beware the geese.   *H.*

9779. When the goodman is from home, the goodwife's table is soon
  spread.   *R.*

9780. When the gorse [*or* furze] is out of bloom, kissing is out of fashion.
  [Gorse is always in bloom.]   *P. R. A.*

9781. When the head aches, all the body is the worse.   *Latin*

9782. When the husband drinks to the wife, all would be well ; when
  the wife drinks to the husband, all is well.   *R.*

9783. When the mist comes from the hill,
  Then good weather it doth spill ;
  When the mist comes from the sea,
  Then good weather it will be.   *D.*

9784. When the moon's in the full, then wit's in the wane.   *D.*

9785. When the sand doth feed the clay. [In a wet summer.]
  England woe and welladay !
  When the clay doth feed the sand,   [In a dry summer.]
  Then it is well with England.   *R.*

9786. When the sun is highest he casts the least shadow.   *F.*

9787. When the sun sets bright and clear,
  An easterly wind you need not fear.   *D.*

9788. When the sun sets in a bank,
  A westerly wind we shall not want.   *D.*

9789. When the tree is fallen, all go with their hatchet.   *Greek*

9790. When the wind is in the east
  It's good for neither man nor beast.   *J. H.*

9791. When the wind is in the north
  The skilful fisher goes not forth.   *D.*

9792. When the wind is in the south
  It blows the bait in the fish's mouth.   17th cent.

9793. When the wind is in the west
  The weather is at the best.   17th cent.

9794. When thieves fall out, honest men come by their own.   *H.*

9795. When things are at the worst they will mend.   16th cent.

9796. When thou dost hear a toll or knell
  Then think upon thy passing bell.   *J. H.*

9797. When thy neighbour's house doth burn, then look to your own. *Latin*

9798. When war begins hell opens. *G. H.*

9799. When we have gold we are in fear, when we have none we are in danger. *R.*

When wine is in, wit is out, *see* When ale is in, etc.

9800. When wine sinks, words swim. *K.*

9801. When you are an anvil, hold you still ;
When you are a hammer, strike your fill. 16th cent.

When you are at Rome, do as Rome does, *see* When in Rome, etc.

9802. When you are well hold yourself so. *K.*

9803. When you bow, bow low. *Chinese*

9804. When you can tread on nine daisies at once, spring has come. 19th cent.

9805. When you christen the bairn, you should know what to call it. *K.*

9806. When you go to dance, take heed whom you take by the hand. *C.*

9807. When you have told [=counted] your cards, you'll find you have gained but little. *H.*

9808. Where bees are, there is honey. *R.*

9809. Where coin is not common, commons [=provisions] must be scant. *H.*

9810. Where God hath his church, the devil will have his chapel.
R. (16th cent.)

9811. Where God helps, nought harms. 14th cent.

9812. Where honour ceases, knowledge decreases. *C.*

9813. Where it is well with me, there is my country. *Latin*

9814. Where no fault is, there needs no pardon. *C.*

9815. Where nothing is, a little doth ease. *H.*

9816. Where nothing is, the king must lose his right. *H.*

9817. Where shall the ox go but he must labour ? *G. H.*

9818. Where the bee sucks honey, the spider sucks poison. 16th cent.

9819. Where the dam leaps over, the kid follows. *F.*

9820. Where the devil cannot come, he will send. *German*

9821. Where the heart is past hope, the face is past shame. 16th cent.

9822. Where the horse lies down, there some hairs will be found. 16th cent.

9823. Where the water is shallow no vessel will ride. *C.*

9824. Where there are three physicians, there are two atheists. *Latin*

9825. Where there is peace, God is. *G. H.*

9826. Where there is whispering, there is lying. *R.*

9827. Where there's a will there's a way. *G. H.*

9828. Where vice is, vengeance follows. *C.*

9829. Where your will is ready, your feet are light. *G. H.*

9830. Whether the pitcher strikes the stone, or the stone the pitcher, it is bad for the pitcher. 17th cent.

9831. While the discreet advise, the fool doth his business. *G. H.*

9832. While the dog [*or* hound] gnaws the bone, companions would he none. *Latin*

9833. While the dust is on your feet, sell what you have bought. *R.*

9834. While the grass grows the horse starves. *Latin*

9835. While the leg warmeth the boot harmeth. *H.*

9836. While the tall maid is stooping, the little one hath swept the house. *Italian*

9837. While there is life there is hope. *Latin*

9838. White hands cannot hurt. *Spanish*
9839. White silver draws black lines. 16th cent.
9840. Who can sing so merry a note
As he that cannot change a groat ? *H.*
9841. Who chatters to you will chatter of you. 19th cent.
9842. Who draweth his sword against his prince must throw away the
scabbard. *J. H.*
9843. Who gives away his goods before he is dead,
Take a beetle and knock him on the head. *R.*
9844. Who gives to all, denies all. *G. H.*
9845. Who goes a-borrowing goes a-sorrowing. 16th cent.
9846. Who goes a-mothering finds violets in the lane. [Parents visited
on Mothering Sunday, Mid-Lent.] 20th cent.
9847. Who goes to bed supperless, all night tumbles and tosses. *Italian*
9848. Who goes to Westminster for a wife, to Paul's for a man, and to
Smithfield for a horse, may meet with a whore, a knave, and a
jade. *J. H.*
9849. Who hastens a glutton, chokes him. *G. H.*
9850. Who hath none to still him, may weep out his eyes. *G. H.*
9851. Who is worse shod than the shoemaker's wife ? *H.*
9852. Who keeps company with the wolf will learn to howl. 16th cent.
9853. Who knows most says least. *Italian*
9854. Who lives by hope will die by hunger. *Italian*
9855. Who marries does well, who marries not does better. 17th cent.
9856. Who marrieth for love without money, hath merry nights and
sorry days. *R.*
9857. Who may hold that will away ? *H.*
9858. Who meddleth in all things may shoe the gosling. [=May waste
his time.] *H.*
9859. Who more busy than he that hath least to do ? *T. D.*
9860. Who more ready to call her neighbour scold, than the arrantest
scold in the parish ? *C.*
9861. Who more than he is worth doth spend,
He makes a rope his life to end. *R.*
9862. Who preacheth war is the devil's chaplain. *R.*
9863. Who spends more than he should, shall not have to spend when
he would. *R.*
9864. Who spits against heaven, it falls in his face. *G. H.*
9865. Who swims in sin shall sink in sorrow. 16th cent.
9866. Who will not be ruled by the rudder must be ruled by the rock. *Italian*
9867. Who will not keep a penny never shall have many. *C.*
9868. Whom we love best, to them we can say least. *R.*
9869. Whoredom and grace dwelt ne'er in one place. *K.*
9870. Whoso hath but a mouth shall ne'er in England suffer drouth.
[The rain will fill it.] *R.*
9871. Wide will wear but tight will tear. *R.*
9872. Widows are always rich. *R.*
9873. Widows' children turn out well. 19th cent.
9874. Wife and children are bills of charges. *J. H.*
9875. Wiles help weak folk. *D. F.*

9876. Wilful waste makes woeful want.	*K.*
9877. Will is the cause of woe.	*C.*
9878. Will will have will, though will woe win.	*H.*
9879. Willows are weak, yet they bind other wood.	*G. H.*
9880. Win at first and lose at last.	*R.*
9881. Win gold and wear gold.	16th cent.
9882. Wine and wenches empty men's purses.	16th cent.
9883. Wine is a turncoat, first a friend, then an enemy.	*G. H.*
9884. Wine is old men's milk.	16th cent.
9885. Wine makes all sorts of creatures at table.	*G. H.*
9886. Wink and choose.	*C.*
9887. Wink at small faults.	*C.*

Winter and wedlock tames man and beast, *see* Age and wedlock, etc.

9888. Winter eateth what summer getteth.	15th cent.
9889. Winter finds out what summer lays up.	*R.*
9890. Winter never rots in the sky.	17th cent.
9891. Winter's thunder and summer's flood	
Never boded Englishman good.	*R.*
9892. Winter's thunder makes summer's wonder.	*C. R*
9893. Winter weather and women's thoughts change oft.	15th cent.
9894. Wisdom sometimes walks in clouted shoes.	*F.*
9895. Wise men are caught with wiles.	*C.*
9896. Wise men care not for what they cannot have.	*R.*
9897. Wise men have their mouths in their hearts, fools their hearts in	
their mouths.	15th cent.
9898. Wise men learn by other men's mistakes ; fools, by their own.	*Latin*
9899. Wise men make proverbs and fools repeat them.	18th cent.
9900. Wise men propose, and fools determine.	17th cent.
9901. Wishers and wolders [=woulders] be small householders.	16th cent.
9902. Wishes can never fill a sack.	*Italian*
9903. Wit once bought is worth twice taught.	*R.*
9904. With empty hands men may no hawks allure.	14th cent.
9905. With Latin, a horse, and money, thou wilt pass through the	
world.	*Italian*
9906. Without business, debauchery.	*G. H.*
9907. Without danger we cannot get beyond danger.	*G. H.*
9908. Wives must be had, be they good or bad.	*C.*
9909. Woe to the house where there is no chiding.	*G. H.*
9910. Woman is the woe of man.	*Latin*
9911. Women and dogs set men together by the ears.	16th cent.
9912. Women and hens by too much gadding are lost.	17th cent.
9913. Women and music should never be dated.	18th cent.
9914. Women and their wills are dangerous ills.	17th cent.
9915. Women and wine, game and deceit,	
Make the wealth small and the wants great.	*K.*
9916. Women are always in extremes.	*C.*
9917. Women are born in Wiltshire, brought up in Cumberland, lead	
their lives in Bedfordshire, brings their husbands to Bucking-	
ham, and die in Shrewsbury.	17th cent.

9918. Women are necessary evils. 16th cent.
9919. Women are saints in church, angels in the street, devils in the
    kitchen, and apes in bed. 16th cent.
9920. Women in state affairs are like monkeys in glass-shops. *J. H.*
9921. Women laugh when they can and weep when they will. *G. H.*
9922. Women must have the last word. 16th cent.
9923. Women must have their wills when they live, because they make
    none when they die. *R.*
9924. Women, priests, and poultry never have enough. *J. H.*
9925. Women's jars breed men's wars. 17th cent.
9926. Wonder is the daughter of ignorance. 17th cent. (16th cent.)
9927. Wood half-burnt is easily kindled. *G. H.*
9928. Wood in a wilderness, moss in a mountain, and wit in a poor
    man's breast, are little thought of. *D. F.*
9929. Words are but sands, it's money buys lands. *J. H.*
9930. Words are but wind, but blows unkind. *J. H.*
9931. Words are wind. 13th cent.
9932. Words cut more than swords. 13th cent.
9933. Worse things happen at sea. 19th cent.
9934. Wranglers never want words. *R.*
9935. Write down the advice of him who loves you, though you like it
    not at present. 17th cent.
9936. Wrong never comes right. 19th cent.
9937. Years know more than books. *G. H.*
9938. Yelping curs will raise mastiffs. *K.*
9939. Yesterday will not be called again. 16th cent.
9940. You are a fool to steal if you can't conceal. *B.*
9941. You are a man among the geese when the gander is away. *R.*
9942. You are come of a blood and so is a pudding. *D. F*
9943. You are good to fetch the devil a priest. [Said to those who
    loiter.] *K.*
9944. You are of so many minds, you'll never be married. *K.*
9945. You cackle often, but never lay an egg. *F.*
9946. You can call a man no worse than unthankful. *C.*
9947. You can have no more of a cat than the skin. 16th cent.
9948. You cannot catch old birds with chaff. *R.* (15th cent.)
9949. You cannot drive a windmill with a pair of bellows. *G. H.*
9950. You cannot eat your cake and have it. *H.*
9951. You cannot get blood [*or* water] out of a stone. *Latin*
9952. You cannot know wine by the barrel. *G. H.*
9953. You cannot lose what you never had. 17th cent.
9954. You cannot make a silk purse out of a sow's ear. *J. H.*
9955. You cannot make an omelet without breaking eggs. *French*
9956. You cannot make people honest [*or* sober] by Act of Parliament.
    20th cent.
9957. You cannot see the city for the houses. 16th cent.
9958. You cannot see the wood for the trees. *H.*
9959. You cannot teach an old dog new tricks. *C. R.*
9960. You have a head and so has a pin. 18th cent.
9961. You know good manners, but you use but few. *R.*

9962. You may be a wise man though you can't make a watch. *R.*
9963. You may ding the deil [=beat the devil] into a wife, but you'll never ding him out of her. *K.*
9964. You may go and shake your ears. [Expressing contempt.] 16th cent.
9965. You may know by a handful the whole sack. *F.*
9966. You may know by a penny how a shilling spends. *R.*
9967. You may poke a man's fire after you have known him seven years, but not before. *L.*
9968. You may take a horse to the water, but you can't make him drink. *H.*
9969. You may trust him with untold gold. *C.*
9970. You might have knocked me down with a feather. [=I was greatly surprised.] 19th cent.
9971. You must ask your neighbour if you shall live in peace. *C.*
9972. You must go into the country to hear what news at London. *R.*
9973. You must look where it is not, as well as where it is. *F.*
9974. You must lose a fly to catch a trout. *G. H.*
9975. You must not let your mouse-trap smell of blood. *F.*
9976. You must not pledge your own health. *R.*
9977. You must take the fat with the lean. *R.*
9978. You never know what you can do till you try. 19th cent.
9979. You never speak but your mouth opens. *R.*
9980. You pay more for your schooling than your learning is worth. *C.*
9981. You pays your money and you takes your choice. *L.*
9982. You scratch my back and I'll scratch yours. 17th cent.
9983. You see what we must all come to, if we live. *R.*
9984. You should never rub your eyes but with your elbow. [=Not at all.]
9985. You think all is lost that goes beside your own mouth. 17th cent.
9986. You were born when wit was scant. *R.*
9987. You were bred in Brazen-Nose College. [=You have plenty of assurance.] *F.*
9988. You will never be mad, you are of so many minds. *R.*
9989. You will scratch a beggar one day before you die. [=You will be a beggar.] *C.*
9990. You would be over the stile ere you come at it. *H.*
9991. You would do little for God if the devil were dead. *D. F.*
9992. You would spy faults if your eyes were out. *R.*
9993. Young cocks love no coops. *C. R.*
9994. Young men may die, old men must. 16th cent.
9995. Young men think old men fools, and old men know young men to be so. 16th cent.
9996. Young men's knocks old men feel. [=We pay in age for what happened in youth.] *R.*
9997. Young prodigal in a coach will be old beggar barefoot. *F.*
9998. Young saint, old devil. 15th cent.
9999. Your lips hang in your light. [=You talk foolishly.] *H.*
10000. Your mind is chasing mice. [=Wool-gathering.] *K.*
10001. Your trumpeter is dead. [Reproaching a braggart.] *K.*
10002. Youth and age will never agree. *D. F.*

10003. Youth and white paper take any impression. *R.*

10004. Youth will be served. 19th cent.

10005. Youth will have its course [*or* swing]. 16th cent.

10006. Yule is come, and Yule is gone,
    And we have feasted well ;
So Jack must to his flail again,
    And Jenny to her wheel. *D.*

10007. Zeal without knowledge is fire without light. *F.*

10008. Zeal without prudence is frenzy. *F.*

INDEX

INDEX

INDEX

529

Action, how like an angel, in, 4239
   lies in his true nature, 4287
   lose the name of, 4253
   nor utterance, 4041
   not knowledge but, 2049
   strong in, 7285
   to the word, suit, 4265
   used their dearest, 4417
Actions are what they are, 558
   innocent, 7968
   serve the turn, 8413
   speak louder, 6625
Active men, honest minds and, 1562
Actor leaves, well-graced, 3702
Actors in the world, best, 4240
   were all spirits, 4750
Acts, little, nameless, 5602
   our angels are, our, 1535
   the best, 124
   the four first, 214
A-cursing, like a very drab, 4250
Adam and Eve were dispossessed, 267
   and of Eve, son of, 3335
   dolve and Eve span, 130
   the goodliest man, 2834
   whipp'd the offending, 3964
Added unto you, all these things shall
   be, 6059
Adder could hear, if, 7844
   stingeth like, 5931
Adding one to one, goes on, 389
Addison, to the volumes of, 2110
Adieu, bid your servant, 4793
   for evermore, 542
   my native shore, 605
   she cries, 1584
Administered is best, whate'er is best,
   3247
Admirable, how express and, 4239
Admiral, good to kill an, 5432
Admiralty, blood be the price of, 2281
Admire an' for to see, for to, 2317
   fools, 3181
   where none, 2498
Ado there was, much, 276
A-doing, not long, 7404
Adonais, the soul of, 4868
Adonis in loveliness, 2046
Adoo, bid you a welcome, 5459
Adoration, duty, and observance, all, 4120
Adores thee, he who, 2952
Adorn, that he did not, 2113
Adsum, and fell back, said, 5300
Adullam, political Cave of, 289
Ἀδύνατα εἰκότα, προαιρεῖσθαι, 49
Advance, not to, 8485
Advantage, mutual and general, 911
Adventure, awfully big, 165
   meet the great, 148
   most beautiful, 1564
Adventures are to the adventurous, 1271
Adventuring both, by, 3760
Adverbs, God is better pleased with,
   7339

Adversary had written a book, that
   mine, 5821
   never sallies out and sees her, 2915
Adversitate fortunae, in omni, 252
Adversity, bruised with, 3579
   cross'd with, 3600
   in time of, 7960
   makes a man wise, 6626
   sweet are the uses of, 4067
   will shrink in, 7712
Adversity's sweet milk, 3665
Advice, if you wish, 7900
   in vain he craves, 7962
   is beyond price, good, 7350
   is seldom welcome, 874
   of him who loves you, 9935
   that will not follow, 7962
   valuable or even earnest, 5337
   we may give, 9687
   woman seldom asks, 18
   woman's, 6614
   your wife's first, 8911
Advices, lengthen'd, sage, 522
Advise, yet still, 9397
A-dying, unconscionable time, 833
Aequora vectus, multa per, 814
Aere perennius, 1994
Aesthetic line, the high, 1629
Afeard, a soldier and, 4626
Affair, no half-and-half, 1661
Affairs, ordering your, 4720
Affection beaming in one eye, 1219
   cannot hold the bent, 4146
Affections dark as Erebus, 3811
   mild, of, 3308
Affirmative or a negative, 3351
   two negatives make, 9626
Afflict me, how dost thou, 3574
   the best, 1751
Affright, the bad, 1751
Affront me, well-bred man will not, 1059
Afghanistan's plains, on, 2309
Afraid, be not, 6090
   of God, many are, 2434
   of his own shadow, 6627
Afric shore, sent from, 2784
Africa aliquid semper novi, ex, 7206
   always something new, out of, 7206
   and her prodigies, 314
   I speak of, 3919
After this ; therefore on account of this,
   8641
After-claps, beware of, 6943
After-love the more, makes, 8748
Afternoon, bodes a fair, 7958
   multitude call, 3620
   seemed always, 5154
Agag came unto him delicately, 5781
Again and again, I do it, 764
Against me, he that is not with me is,
   6083
   us, who can be, 6212
Agamemnon, brave men lived before,
   1995

American, If I were an, 839
  not a Virginian but, 1882
Americans, when they die, good, **43**
Amfalula-Tree, in the, 1480
Amiable but degraded race, 1316
  weakness, 1488
Amicably if they can, 3352
Amicitia est, firma, 3450
A-milking, I am going, 6352
Amiral, bon de tuer un, 5432
Amiss at home, knows what's, 9086
  doth ever, 7550
  nothing shall come, 436
Ammunition, pass the, 1542
Amnis, dum defluat, 1999
Amo, amas, I love a lass, 3067
  odi et, 813
  te, Sabidi, non, 2581
Amor che move il sole, 1141
Amoris integratio, 5286
Amos Cottle ! what a name, 601
A-mothering, who goes, 9846
Amphibrachys hastes, 994
Amphimacer strikes his thundering
  hoofs, 994
Amurath an Amurath succeeds, 3918
Amused, we are not, 5399
Anaesthesia, perpetual, 2618
Analytic, skill'd in, 562
Anapaests throng, swift, 994
Anarch, thy hand, great, 3229
Ancestor, I am my own, 2183
Ancestry back, trace my, 1647
  without pride of, 1291
Ancêtre, moi je suis mon, 2183
Anchors, riding at two, 7361
  they cast four, 6207
Ancient of Days, the, 1742, 6025
  people, that marry, 1570
Ancientry, wronging the, 4713
Anderson my jo, John, 514
Ἀνήριθμον γέλασμα, 26
Angel and half bird, half, 412
  appear to each lover, 3100
  beautiful and ineffectual, 73
  brightest fell, 4618
  domesticate the Recording, 5023
  dropp'd down from the clouds, as if
    an, 3870
  faces smile, those, 3048
  from his side, curse his better, 4471
  girt with golden wings, 2721
  is a man, better, 4818
  is man an ape or, 1265
  ministering, 3483, 4328
  of Death, 286
  say, hear thy guardian, 1431
  talk of, 8914
  the Recording, 5017, 5023
  unpursu'd, dreadless, 2855
  woman think him an, 5298
Angel's wings, clip an, 2205
Angeli, non Angli, sed, 1789
Angel-infancy, shin'd in, 5390

Angels, a little lower than, 5831
  alone, that soar above, 2472
  and ministers of grace, 4207
  and of gods, fault of, 3208
  are bright still, 4618
  are, our acts or, 1535
  are painted fair, 3078
  could do no more, 5712
  fear to tread, where, 3185
  glittering and sparkling, 5356
  in the street, 9919
  not Angles but, 1789
  now walk the, 2561
  of Jesus, 1468
  of light, 1468
  on the side of the, 1265
  prostrate fall, let, 3135
  round my head, four, 23
  sing thee to thy rest, 4346
  sung this strain, guardian, 5332
  to my bed, four, 23
  tremble while they gaze, 1775
  trumpet-tongued, 4556
  unawares, entertained, 6269
  visits like those of, 229
  weep, as make the, 4394
  weep, tears such as, 2787
  white, like two, 285
Angels' visits, short and bright, 3054
Angel-visits, few and far between, like,
  700
Anger and haste hinder, 6715
  is a short madness, 2001
  more in sorrow than, 4192
  'twas surely in an, 505
Angle, Brother of the, 5454
Anglers, too good for any but, 5456
Angles, but angels, not, 1789
Angli, sed angeli, non, 1789
Angling but catching, not, 9029
Angry, and sin not, be ye, 6247
  at a feast, 7592
  at, two things a man should never be,
    9630
  man, against, 9632
  man, hungry man is, 6509
  without a cause, 7593
  word, speak no, 33
Anguish keeps the heavy gate, 5570
  lessen'd by another's, 3631
  of all sizes, 1889
Angusta domi, res, 2186
Animal, man is a noble, 319
  man is a tool-using, 740
Animals are such agreeable friends,
  1412
  paragon of, 4239
  turn and live with, 5537
  we are vertebrate, 2611
Anna, here thou, great, 3191
Annabel Lee, I and my, 3157
Annals, short and simple, 1758
  true, writ your, 4685
Anni labuntur, fugaces, 147, 1990

Bear it, no man alive could, 4826
  no mortal can, 1595
  till his back break, 6544
Bear's ethereal grace, 759
Bear-baiting, Puritan hated, 2516
Beard of formal cut, 4090
  Old Man with a, 2398
  were all, if, 7845
Bearded like the pard, 4090
Beards be grown, until your, 5788
  heartless, long, 8234
  wag all, when, 8046
Beast, before he caught, 5439
  cocoa is a vulgar, 890
  it is the nature of, 8067
  life of his, 5905
  man and bird and, 976
  marks of the, 1812
  that wants discourse of reason, 4186
  with two backs, 4413
  working out the, 5236
Beastie, cowrin, tim'rous, 483
Beastly, rooms at college was, 2274
Beasts, brute, 6315
  fled to brutish, 4033
  of all tame, 8508
  that perish, like, 5854
Beat them, the more you, 6610
Beata mea Domina, 2991
Beaten, known when they are, 9030
  may be said, that is, 577
  surprised is half, 6550
Beatitude, ninth, 3316
Beaumont lie a little further, bid, 2171
  lie a little nearer Spenser, 171
Beauteous things, all, 1038
Beauties flee, whither I follow her, 352
  of the night, meaner, 5692
Beautiful as woman's blush, 2367
  lovers of the, 3133
  many men, so, 966
  my beautiful, 3055
  my blue-eyed, my, 688
  O be less, 5477
  one was, 642
  outward, appear, 6112
  things, see the, 1478
  they stand, how, 1863
  to last, too, 430
  upon the mountains, 6008
Beauty, a thing of, 2203
  and her chivalry, her, 609
  as could die, as much, 2168
  born of murmuring sound, 5613
  cannot tame, breast, 132
  coming in solemn, 2601
  crieth in an attic, 589
  draws more than oxen, 6852
  draws us, 3190
  faded, 3141
  health and wealth create, 7716
  in a brow of Egypt, 3730
  in his life, daily, 4465
  in their summer, 3568

Beauty is but a blossom, 6853
  is but skin-deep, 6854
  is potent, 6855
  is to me, thy, 3161
  is truth, 2221
  itself doth of itself persuade, 4777
  keen unpassioned, 299
  lies, perhaps some, 2689
  like a dial-hand, 4808
  lives with kindness, 3602
  loveliest things of, 2602
  no judge of Jill's, 7834
  nor good talk, 'tisn't, 2348
  of a thousand stars, 2564
  of an aged face, 697
  provoketh thieves, 4065
  she doth miss, no, 6343
  she that is born, 8783
  she walks in, 634
  spring nor summer's, 1289
  stands in the admiration only of weak minds, 2887
  still, such seems your, 4807
  they grew in, 1866
  to the moon, unmask her, 4198
  too rich for use, 3638
  took from those who loved them, 1167
  truly blent, 4135
  veiling an Indian, 3792
  what once had, 3209
  will buy no beef, 6856
  with my nails, come near your, 3540
  without bounty, 6857
Beauty's charming, look not thou on, 3509
  ensign yet, 3670
  rose might never die, 4780
  self she is, 6343
  worthiness, combined in, 2560
Beaux, where none are, 2498
Beaver on, with his, 3870
Beckons me away, 5349
Bed, and so to, 3126
  as you make your, 6809
  be blest that I lie on, 23
  by day, have to go to, 5040
  by night, 1708
  could tell all it knows, if, 7846
  each within our narrow, 806
  early to, 7148
  four angels to my, 23
  four bare legs in, 8372
  from his brimstone, 989, 4966
  full of bones, 6703
  full of brambles, 6492
  loth to, 7169, 8246
  of down, thrice-driven, 4427
  of honour lain, in the, 577
  so he on his, 5485
  supperless, go to, 6901
  supperless, goes to, 9847
  to the brown, blue, 1721
  two fools in one, 9621
  welcome to your gory, 527

Betime, to business that we love we rise, 4659
Betimes, he must rise, 7503
  should get out, 6511
  to be up, 4138
Betray us in deepest consequence, 4542
Betsey and I are out, 736
Better and better, getting, 1044
  be, doth make men, 2176
  be it, 6842
  bettered expectation, 3922
  book, can write a, 1447
  carries it, 7358
  for being a little bad, 4408
  for worse, for, 6317
  man than I am, 2308
  or wiser behind, not left a, 1718
  seldom comes, 8760
  spared a better man, 3879
  striving to, 4482
  than she should be, no, 8435
  than he knew, builded, 1448
  the world with ablow, 2603
  thing, far, far, 1251
  things and approve them, I see, 3083
  without, I'd been, 3095
Betters, bold with your, 6845
  who have served, 7015
Betty Martin, my eye and, 6658
Bewails himself, he that, 7523
Beware by other men's harms, 8024
  I bid you, 2332
  when the great God lets loose a thinker, 1440
Bewitch me, do more, 1898
Bewitched with the rogue's company, 3831
Bewrayeth thee, speech, 6124
Bible, but litel on the, 859
Bibles laid open, 1889
Biblia a-biblia, 2357
Βιβλίον, μέγα, μέγα κακόν, 683
Bidden, do as you're, 7112
Bidding, he that does, 7546
Bider, better for, 9291
Bier ye cannot fashion, better, 103
Bigamy, sir, is a crime, 2925
Bigger they come, 1521
Bilin' down his repoort, 1665
Billboard lovely as a tree, 3020
Billee, youngest he was little, 5306
Billows, takes the ruffian, 3903
Bills of charges, children are, 9874
Billy and me, way for, 1927
  heart to poke poor, 1736
Bind, fast find, fast, 7232
  them, heart and brow, 3074
Biography is about chaps, 208
  no history, only, 1435
Βίος βραχύς, ὁ, 1915
Birch at Yule even, bare as, 6834
Birchen twigs break no ribs, 6948
Bird, a rare, 2187
  clung to, spray the, 370

Bird each fond endearment tries, 1702
  early, 9023
  immortal, 2217
  in the hand, a, 6400
  in the sight of any, 5893
  is on the Wing, 1491
  it is an ill, 8002
  like a singing, 3416
  likes its own nest, 7172
  loves to hear himself, 7145
  might haply inhabit, 4164
  of dawning, 4175
  of March, sea-blue, 5231
  of night, amorous, 2865
  of the air, 5972
  of the wilderness, 1925
  of Time has but a little way to fly, 1491
  on the wing, like a. 266
  that shunn'st the noise of folly, 2702
  thou never wert, 4854
  to scare, 9534
  trills, the Attic, 2893
Bird's throat, the sweet, 4077
Birdie say, does little, 5190
Birds, another catches, 8548
  begin to lay, 7946
  begin to search, 7946
  charm of earliest, 2837
  choirs of singing, 453
  do sing, pretty, 3024
  do sing, when, 4121
  fine feathers make fine, 7249
  frightened the, 6369
  how can ye chant, 527
  i' the cage, like, 4524
  in last year's nest, 9306
  in the high Hall-garden, 5241
  in their little nests agree, 5482
  kill two, 9499
  nest of singing, 2114
  of a feather, 6949
  of calm sit brooding, 2672
  of the air, all, 8539
  outside despair to get in, 2937
  sang, late the sweet, 4799
  sang sweet, 5522
  sing, and no, 2233
  sing madrigals, 2573
  sit courin, 5123
  so happy as we, no, 2401
  that sing and won't sing, 8215
  time of the singing of, 5985
  to sing, suffers little, 3584
  very unlikely, 8622
  with chaff, catch old, 9948
Bird-song at morning, 5053
Birkenhead drill, to the, 2314
Birnam wood to high Dunsinane hill, 4615
Birth, day of one's, 5962
  have smiled, on my, 5127
  he himself is subject to his, 4197
  is but a sleep, our, 5665
  is much, 6950

S

Blind man cannot judge colours, 6406
  man will not thank you, 6407
  man's holiday, 6956
  none so, 8480
  old man of Scio's rocky isle, 631
  staring and stark, 9322
  the halt and the, 2596, 6151
  to Him, olives they were not, 2383
  with dust and smoke, 3044
Blindly, never lov'd sae, 532
Blindworm could see, [if], 7844
Blink, tint the blythe, 1129
Bliss and woe, mingle human, 3506
  it excels all other, 1406
  looks at his own, 5475
  source of all my, 1712
  too avid of earth's, 5476
  was it, 5653
  way to, 9278
  where ignorance is, 1750
  winged hours of, 700
Blithesome and cumberless, 1925
Block, beetle and, 6936
  book that is shut is, 6411
  chip of the old, 471, 6426
  in the rough-hewn, 3109
  itself, the old, 471
  you insensible, 138
Blockhead, bookful, 3184
  no man but a, 2147
Blocks, you stones, you, 3998
Blood and iron, 224
  be shed, by man shall his, 5733
  be the price of admiralty, 2281
  clean from my hand, wash, 4578
  felt in the, 5601
  for his country, good enough to shed,
    3407
  fountain fill'd with, 1102
  freeze thy young, 4214
  hey-day in the, 4293
  I smell the, 4506
  in him, so much, 4627
  inhabits our frail, 4163
  is bold blood, old, 5493
  is fet from fathers of warproof, 3978
  is strong, still the, 6356
  is tame, it's humble, 4293
  is thicker than water, 6957
  is very snow-broth, 4385
  is warm within, whose, 3756
  more stirs, 3827
  must have its course, young, 2261
  out of a stone, get, 9951
  pure and eloquent, 1290
  reigns, red, 4714
  simple faith than Norman, 5152
  smell of, 9975
  stepp'd in so far, in, 4609
  streams in the firmament, 2566
  summon up the, 3977
  till he sees his own, 9222
  to stir men's, 4041
  toil, tears, and sweat, 907

Blood, weltering in his, 1373
  whoso sheddeth man's, 5733
  will have blood, 6958
  with cold, thicks man's, 961
  you are come of a, 9942
Blood's a rover, 2014
Bloody but unbowed, head, 1872
  likely, not, 4835
  man is that, what, 4534
Bloom, blight in its, 5122
  is shed, its, 525
  old muck-hills will, 8533
  on a woman, sort of, 166
  sae fresh and fair, 527
  sight of vernal, 2821
  sweet of earliest, 1014
Blooms each thing, 3024
Blossom, beauty is but, 6853
  bud bursting into, 684
  by blossom, 5106
  in purple and red, 5248
  in the spring, 8935
  under the, 4755
  with pleasure, 370
Blossoms, birds. and bowers, 1896
  but never bears, 9645
  down through the, 3062
  straying, mid, 996
Blot, art to, 3301
  creation's, 1606
  scratching a, 1655
  the fouler the, 9044
Blotted a thousand, would he had, 2179
  it out for ever, 5017
  out a line, never, 2179
Blow [puff] at once, sup, and, 8450
  first, 6959
  kindly here, 3386
  on whom I please, to, 4087
  wind ! come, wrack ! 4638
Blow [knock], but a word and a, 447
  first, 9053, 9054
  liberty's in every, 539
  might be the be-all, 4554
  remember thy swashing, 3627
Blowing, nor'-wester's, 3155
Blown with reckless violence, 4401
Blows [puffs] a man up, it, 3849
  nobody good, 8005
  the wind to-day, 5056
Blows [knocks] [are] unkind, 9930
Blue above and the blue below, 3339
  and better blue, 9345
  Beard's domestic chaplain, 1193
  darkly deeply beautifully, 4969
  grappling in the central, 5170
  Hobbs hints, 375
  Presbyterian true, 569
  ran the flash across, 419
  till all look, 1540
  were her eyes, 2445
  will never stain, true, 9589
Blue-eyed, beautiful, my, 688
Blunder free us, frae mony a, 495

Blunder, it is a, 1550
Blundered, some one had, 5211
Blunders, one of Nature's, 1051
Blush, beautiful as woman's, 2367
  put many to, 7846
  to find it fame, 3304
  unseen, born to, 1763
  would it bring a, 1253
Blushed, saw its God, and, 1121
Blushes, beat away those, 3950
Blushing is virtue's colour, 6961
Blut und Eisen, 224
Bo to a goose, say, 7431
Boast, small roast, great, 7376
Boaster and a liar, 6409
Boasteth, when he is gone 5925
Boastings as the Gentiles use, 2294
Boat and went to sea, took, 5305
  beautiful pea-green, 2399
  is on the shore, my, 645
  speed, bonny, 266
Boatman, do not tarry, 703
Boats, messing about in, 1740
  to burn one's, 9447
Bodice, aptly lac'd, 3330
Bodie forme doth take, 4991
Bodies by, bore dead, 3825
  hale souls out of, 3933
  move slowly, great, 7377
  of unburied men, 5499
  unsound, 9641
Bodkin, with a bare, 4253
Body and in soul, in, 3466
  and soul, overthrow of, 557
  Charlotte, having seen his, 5303
  demd, damp, moist, 1209
  fill'd and vacant mind, 3985
  give me a healthy, 6379
  he is through your, 263
  hit a body, gin a, 2612
  I keep under my, 6225
  I thee worship, with my, 6319
  is sooner dressed, 8967
  is the worse, all, 9781
  joint and motive of her, 4371
  little, 6523
  meet a body, gin a, 550, 2612
  [needs] many [things], 9241
  on a worthless, 7245
  pent, here in the, 2939
  perfect little, 281
  sound mind in a sound, 2194
  Thersites', 4703
  thought, her, 1290
  to be kicked, no, 5347
  to that pleasant country's earth, gave
    his, 3698
  to the deep, commit, 6325
  to the ground, commit, 6324
Body's vest aside, casting, 2591
Bog, cannot out of her, 9075
  or steep, o'er, 2816
  profound as that Serbonian, 2806
  to an admiring, 1257

Boil [an egg], the vulgar, 3303
  like a pot, maketh the deep to, 5828
Boils, watched pot never, 6602
Bois, n'irons plus aux, 134
Bokes, clad in blak or reed, 854
Bold and forth on, 4686
  bad man, a, 4983
  be not too, 4987, 6845
  every where Be, 4987
  man, he was, 7702
Boldest held his breath, 707
Boldness, again boldness, 1142
Bolt is soon shot, fool's, 6459
Bombast, serious swelling into, 1394
Bombastes, must meet, 3382
Bombazine would have shown, 1582
Bombs bursting in air, 2250
Bond, let him look to his, 3784
  'tis not in the, 3802
  word is as good as, 6689
Bondman, check'd like a, 4051
Bondman's key, in a, 3772
Bone, as curs mouth, a, 902
  beat him with, 6444
  dry as, 6734
  in one's leg, have, 9480
  of my bones, 5724
  often falls a good, 7970
  the nearer, 9181
  tongue breaks, 9264
Bone, what is bred in, 9722
Bones are coral made, 4736
  bed full of, 6703
  buys many, 7532
  curst be he that moves my, 4820
  fair words break no, 7223
  for his honour'd, 2678
  full of dead men's, 6112
  interred with their, 4030
  live, can these, 6021
  mock'd the dead, 3565
  over the stones, rattle his, 3053
  sit in my, 4943
  sleep upon, 8166
  stones may break, 8870
  that lay scatter'd by, 3565
  together fly, rattling, 1365
  tongs and the, 3726
  words break no, 7408
  would be at rest, 9768
Bonfire, everlasting, 4579
Bon-mots from their places, plucking,
  2975
  not enough, 2048
Bonnet, bee in one's, 9479
  in antique ruff and, 2096
Bonnets, all the Blue, 3511
Bonnie bay at morning, 1115
  blithe as she's, 5122
Bononcini, compar'd to, 592
Bonum, nil nisi, 7072
Booby for another, give her, 1586
Boojum, the Snark was a, 800
Book, a book's a, 597

Book about, not throw this, 194
  all the world knows me in my, 2938
  another damned, thick, square, 1672
  as good almost kill a man as kill a
    good, 2913
  beware of the man of one, 6947
  can write a better, 1447
  dainties that are bred in, 3614
  doth share the glory, 3633
  frowst with a, 2334
  genius I had when I wrote, 5087
  go, little, 5047
  great, great evil, 683
  he can read, give a man, 5334
  he who destroys a good, 2913
  I can read anything which I call,
    2357
  I directe to thee, 844
  I never read a, 4946
  I'll drown my, 4754
  in cloistre, upon a, 852
  is the best of friends, good 5370
  is the precious life-blood, good, 2914
  like author, like, 8197
  medley of my, 2184
  moral or an immoral, 5555
  Nature was his, 248
  no such thing as a moral, 5555
  of knowledge fair, 2821
  of Nature, the, 1962
  of secrecy, nature's, 4645
  of songs and sonnets, 4348
  of Verse, 1493
  of Verses, 1494
  quarrel by the, 4123
  take a leaf out of one's, 9544
  take down this, 5702
  that is not a year old, never read any,
    1446
  that is shut, 6411
  that mine adversary had written,
    5821
  to make one, 2142
  to read, wants a, 893
  wants to read a, 893
  what is the use of, 760
  where men may read strange matters,
    4550
  where's the, 905
  with a religious, 5690
  word for word without, 4129
Booke, a jollie goode, 5576
  and a shadie nooke, 5576
  go, little, 4
Bookful blockhead, 3184
Books, all saws of, 4222
  and pictures, muddled with, 2274
  are good enough, 5027
  are not seldom talismans and spells,
    1090
  are to be tasted, some, 116
  are well written, 5555
  at the British Museum, 588
  authority from others', 3608

Books cannot always please, 1111
  deep vers'd in, 2895
  devil's, 6988
  else appear so mean, all, 435
  for good manners, 4123
  [I love] old, 1723
  I'll burn my, 2567
  in a person's bad, 9431
  in the running brooks, 4067
  knowing I loved, 4731
  lard their lean, 553
  my only, 2968
  next o'er his, 3220
  of making many, 5981
  quit your, 5598
  reading valueless, 3439
  skim the cream of others', 2975
  spectacles of, 1393
  that you may carry to the fire, 2163
  [that you may] hold readily in your
    hand, 2163
  the arts, the academes, 3616
  through, do you read, 2139
  were read, his, 201
  which are no books, 2357
  years know more than, 9937
  you need, all the, 435
Books' clothing, things in, 2358
Boot harmeth, 9835
  is on the other leg, 8968
  saddle, to horse, 347
Boots—boots—boots—boots, 2319
  displace pair of, 3382
  heart is in his, 7740
  ran out at the heels of, 1539
Bo-peep, as if they started at, 1992
Border, bound for the, 3511
  off a sunny, 2628
  she gaed o'er the, 534
  through all the wide, 3476
Bore, every hero becomes a, 1443
Borealis race, like the, 525
Boreas, cease, rude, 5020
Bores and Bored, two mighty tribes, 668
  of the dreariest hue, 1796
Born, as soon as a man is, 6779
  better never been, 2996
  better to be lowly, 4757
  crying, we are, 9679
  for you alone was, 3394
  he that is once, 7605
  I wept when I was, 7797
  in a cellar, 1538
  in a good hour, 7470
  natural to die as to be, 109
  never was, 5059
  on the wrong side, 6963
  out of my due time, 2994
  under that I was, 3932
  when wit was scant, 9986
  with a silver spoon, 9430
  would thou hadst ne'er been, 4462
  yesterday, not, 7796
Borogoves, mimsy were the, 774

Bread-sauce, time-honoured, 2069
Break, better bow than, 6892
  break, break, 5184
Breakfast, for her own, 5715
  sing before, 7894
Breakfasts at five o'clock, 796
Breaking, take pleasure in, 8985
Breaks it, he that makes a thing too
  fine, 7623
Breast, boiling bloody, 3734
  forward, marched, 423
  in the human, 3234
  marble of her snowy, 5438
  on her white, 3188
  soothe a savage, 1022
  spirit in a loyal, 3673
  that beauty cannot tame, 132
  wail or knock the, 2906
  with sweetness fills, 807
  within his own clear, 2726
Breastplate, what stronger, 3542
Breath, allowing him a, 3695
  at all, thou no, 4530
  be rude, although thy, 4091
  call the fleeting, 1761
  can make them, 1695
  first, 9055
  flatter'd its rank, 618
  fly away, 4148
  having lost her, 4650
  I hate, whose, 4682
  in pain, draw thy, 4314
  lightly draws its, 1001
  out-sweeten'd not, 4702
  save your, 8737
  thou art, a, 4397
  weary of, 1970
  with bated, 3772
  with tempestuous, 2031
Breathes there the man, 3467
Breathing, closer is He than, 5219
  health and quiet, 2203
  out threatenings, 6190
Breathless, power breathe, 4650
  we flung us, 294
Bred, because they so were, 1359
  best, 8949
  en bawn in a briar-patch, 1830
  in the bone, what is, 9722
Breeches, so have your, 721
  wear the, 9566
  were blue, his, 990, 4967
Breed and brew along there, 1328
  beware of, 6944
  of men, this happy, 3684
  of noble bloods, 4006
Breeding is more, 6950
  to show your, 4900
Breeds without the Law, lesser, 2294
Breeks, men't my auld, 3395
  off a Hielandman, taking, 8041
  that has riven, 7515
Breeze, bird, and flower, 3512
  blew, the fair, 958

Breeze can bear, far as, 633
  cooling western, 3179
  fluttering and dancing in, 5645
  leaves are winnowed by, 928
  mid blossoms, 995
  rain and tossing, 67
  refreshes in the, 3241
Breezes, by the midnight, 4852
Breezy, Sneezy, Freezy, 1433
Breffny, little waves of, 1733
Breitmann gife a barty, Hans, 2415
Brer Fox, he lay low, 1828
Brethren, the great Twin, 2526
  to dwell together, 5886
Brevis esse laboro, 2005
Brevity is the soul of wit, 4229
Brew, as they, 6795
Brewer's wife, 6392
Bribe will enter, 6414
Bricht moonlicht nicht, 2389
Bricks are alive at this day, 3546
  without straw, make, 9517
Bridal lamp, light the, 2865
  of the earth and sky, 1891
Bride, happy is, 7401
  hath paced into the hall, 955
  into slumbers like, 1530
  is soon buskit, bonny, 6410
  makes a happy, 5145
  my bonny bonny, 1807
  still unravish'd, 2218
Bride-bed to have deck'd, 4330
Bridegroom, fresh as a, 3824
Brides of Enderby, play, 2059
Bridesmaid, happy, 5145
Bridge, make a golden, 7274
  never cross, 8419
Bridges were made for wise men to walk
  over, 6971
Bridle-reins a shake, gae, 542
Brief, I struggle to be, 2005
  or be less, 5477
Brier-patch, bred en bawn in, 1830
Briers, how full of, 4064
Brig, mate of the Nancy, 1612
Brigade, boys of the old, 5490, 5491
Bright and beautiful, things, 32
  and fierce and fickle, 5201
  both lovely and, 3504
  bright as day, 5706
  he is only, 7480
  things come to confusion, 3707
  young lady named, 6372
Brightest and best, 1857
Brightness, all her original, 2785
  falls from the air, 3025
Brignal banks are wild, 3500
Brillig, 'twas, 774
Brim, better spare at, 6924
  bubbles winking at, 2212
Brimming, and bright, and large, 61
Brimstone bed, from his, 989, 4966
Bring, what it will, 9297
Bristol City, sailors of, 5305

Britain a fit country, make 2432
first, at Heaven's command, 5332
is a world by itself, 4696
is going to make war, 215
Britain's crown, from, 1319
Britannia needs no bulwarks, 705
rule the waves, 5332
Britannos, divisos orbe, 5403
Brither, lo'ed him like a, 523
British and Armoric knights, 2784
ground, feet on, 5493
man, blood of a, 4506
manhood, piece of, 738
Britons never will be slaves, 5332
wholly sundered from all the world,
5403
Broached, he bravely, 3734
Broadcloth without, 1093
Broken and a contrite heart, 5856
at last, [pitcher] is, 9195
made to be, 8667
Broken-hearted, half, 594
ne'er been, 532
Broker, needs no, 6437
Broo, ne'er made good, 7915
Brooches, I will make you, 5053
Brook along, my forest, 973
and river meet, where, 2449
fast by a, 184
is deep, where the, 3541
like of a hidden, 970
that turns a mill, 3398
Brooks, after the water, 5850
I sing of, 1896
too broad for leaping, 2020
Broom, busk of, 8130
is silver and gold, under, 9635
sweeps clean, new, 6557
Broth hot again, cold, 7024
too many cooks spoil, 9575
Brother, closer than, 5921
followed brother, 5683
hail and farewell, 815
I grew so like my, 2412
man, gently scan, 493
near the throne, no, 3291
though he were my, 7685
turns, still to my, 1682
Brother's keeper, am I my, 5729
Brotherhood, crown thy good with, 172
love the, 6273
Brotherly love continue, 6268
Brothers and their murder'd man, two,
2206
be for a' that, 548
too, all the, 4150
we band of, 3991
Brow, grace was seated on this, 4292
in that victorious, 54
is beld, now your, 514
is wet, his, 2447
lifted slowly her white, 1561
on thine azure, 628
pure unclouded, 773
*S

Brow was brent, bonnie, 514
Brown [is] trusty, 9427
man break thy bread, with, 9427
Browning, a prose, 5559
Since Chaucer was alive, 2370
some " Pomegranate," from, 323
Brows, gathering her, 520
Bruce has aften led, 537
Brugh, round the moon, 9766
Bruise and bless, made to, 2628
for an inward, 3826
Bruit, little fruit, much, 8380
Brunck, learn'd professor, 3319
Brush, tarred with the same, 6662
work with so fine, 99
Brushers of noblemen's clothes, 7052
Brushes of comet's hair, 2285
Brute or an angel, 6588
Brute, et tu, 679
Brutes men, had made, 3110
without you, we had been, 3078
Brutus is an honourable man, 4031
once, there was a, 4007
Tarquin and Caesar each had his,
1881
the fault, dear, 4005
you too, 679
Bubble, man is, 8295
mostly froth and, 1731
Bubbles, earth has, 4540
winking, beaded, 2212
Buck in spring, like a, 2288
Bucket, as for the, 6371
old oaken, 5590
which hung in the well, 5590
Buckhurst choose, I would, 3391
Buckingham, bring their husbands to,
9917
high-reaching, 3567
so much for, 915
Buckram men grown out of two, eleven,
3844
suits, rogues in, 3843
Bud again, be a, 2209
and bloom forth brings, 5067
bursting, young, 684
nip him in the, 3389
Buds of May, darling, 4783
summer's velvet, 3967
Buffer lies low, poor, 5550
Buffet, take the bit and, 8906
Buffoon, statesman and, 1346
Buffs, private of the, 1319
Bug in a rug, snug as, 1559
Bugle, blow, 5196
bring the good old, 5687
Bugles, blow out, you, 300
sang truce, our, 710
Bugloss, the blue, 1109
Build me straight, 2459
not boast, lives to, 3455
the house, except the Lord, 5882
up, easier to pull down than, 8013
Builded better than he knew, 1448

Canakin clink, let me, 4436
Candid where we can, be, 3231
Candle and candlestick away, throw, 8537
  as a white, 697
  at both ends, burn, 9448
  burns at both ends, 2659
  devil holds, 8004
  fit to hold, 592, 8486
  game is not worth, 9080
  hold their farthing, 5716
  light such a, 2386
  out, out brief, 4636
  throws his beams, how far, 3812
  to my shames, hold, 3782
  to the devil, hold, 9494
  two old chairs and half a, 2402
Candle-ends, called him, 794
Candle-light, by yellow, 5040
  choose neither a woman nor linen by, 7014
  colours seen by, 329
  sleet and, 6336
Candlemas day be fair, if, 7825
  day is come, when, 9749
  day it be shower, if on, 7825
  Day, on, 8537
Candles are all out, their, 4565
Candlestick, upon the holy, 6292
Candlestick-maker much acquaints, 417
Cane, conduct of a clouded, 3198
Canker galls the infants, 4198
Cankers of a calm world, 3872
Cannibals that each other eat, 4422
Cannon in front of them, 5213
  to right of them, 5213
Cannon's mouth, even in, 4090
  opening roar, 611
Canopy of light and blue, 5529
  rich embroider'd, 3552
Cant, clear your mind of, 2159
Cantie wi' mair, 543
Cantons, write loyal, 4136
Cants which are canted, 5016
Canvas, splash at a ten-league, 2285
Cap by night, a, 1680
  fits, wear it, if, 7848
Capa que cubre todos, 821
Capacity can soar to, highest that human, 2917
Caparisons don't become a young woman, 4888
  no, 4888
Capax imperii nisi imperasset, 5114
Cape, round the, 357
  St. Vincent to the North-west, 366
  Turk, not yet doubled, 2641
Capers, lovers run into strange, 4076
Capitol betrayed the, 3079
Capon, if thou hast not, 7872
  lined, with good, 4090
Captain, becomes his captain's, 4654
  bold, cook and a, 1612
  can, more than his, 4654

Captain lies, on the deck, 5540
  my Captain, O, 5540
  of the Gate, 2519
  or Colonel, 2755
Captains and the Kings depart, 2293
  by the hundred, 1610
  thunder of the, 5825
Car, drive the rapid, 1145
Caravan, put up your, 1920
  starts for the Dawn of Nothing, 1506
  the innumerable, 429
Caravanserai, batter'd, 1497
Carcase is, wheresoever, 6116
Carcasses of unburied men, 4682
Card, speak by the, 4321
Cardinal's chair, sat on, 140
Cards are the devil's books, 6988
  shuffle the, 820
  when you have told, 9807
  without a knave, no, 9336
Care, a fig for, 1908
  and skill require, 9713
  at the horseman's back, 685
  begone, dull, 6348
  beyond to-day, no, 1749
  bringers of worry and, 1796
  for nobody, I, 216
  golden, 3914
  Hippoclides does not, 1914
  is no cure, 6989
  is over, then the, 5139
  keeps his watch, 3654
  killed a cat, 6990
  little goods, little, 8217
  much coin, much, 8381
  neither cauld nor, 3007
  not for what they cannot have, 9896
  now with me past, 3690
  past cure, past, 8607
  pound of, 6566
  punch with, 302
  ravell'd sleave of, 4576
  so wan with, 3814
  to our coffin adds a nail, 5584
  weary fu' o', 528
  with judicious, 487
  woman's tender, 1103
Care's an enemy to life, 4128
Cared for none of those things, 6196
Career, awe a man from the, 3936
  open to talents, 3017
  which might damage, 168
Cares, against eating, 2695
  and strife, void of, 3142
  are dumb, great, 8187
  deprest with, 1592
  humble, 5618
  resolved mind hath no, 9211
  speak, light, 8187
  that infest the day, 2453
  will wear away, 6810
  with crosses and with, 4989
  worn with life's, 1114
Caressing, kind its, 945

Chief Justice was rich, 2512
  the brilliant, 2501
Chieftain o' the pudding-race, 502
  to the Highlands bound, 703
Chiel's amang you takin notes, 517
Child a home, who gives a, 2604
  a little, 1001
  a most wholesome food, 5082
  a treat, who gives, 2604
  again, make me a, 29
  all weather is cold, to, 9424
  among men, 6536
  and she was a child. I was, 3157
  any christom, 3973
  as yet a, 3288
  at sixty, prove a, 6537
  be like his father, if, 6815
  behold the, 3246
  carry a dead man's, 7991
  doth his father, service, 9059
  first, his own, 9190
  getting wenches with, 4713
  give me, 7321
  half devil and half, 2291
  happy English, 5127
  happy is, 7402
  has done sucking, till, 9185
  has its fairy godmother, 5318
  I spake as a, 6230
  I stand, a little, 1906
  I thought as a, 6229
  I understood as a, 6230
  is father of the man, 5620
  imposes on the man, 1359
  is it well with, 5802
  it is a wise, 7999
  like a froward, 5139
  like a three years', 5685
  like a tired, 4842
  look upon a little, 5514
  love to gaze upon a, 684
  many kiss, 8314
  may have too much, 6425
  Monday's, 8364
  my absent, 3744
  needs teaching, aptest, 8951
  nurse for a poetic, 3468
  of misery, 2381
  of the pure unclouded brow, 773
  on a cloud I saw a, 232
  Rowland to the dark tower came, 4506
  says nothing, 8984
  she bare, toward the, 1103
  should always say what's true, 5041
  show'st thee in a, 4480
  sleep upon bones, let not, 8166
  sometimes say Poor, 3114
  spoil, 8845
  sprightly and forward, 875
  Sunday's, 8883
  sweet, my, 5205
  that knows his own, 3777
  the Heav'n-born, 2670
  to have a thankless, 4487

Child, train up, 5928
  upon her knee, set his, 5205
  well nursed, young healthy, 5082
  what it is to be a, 5318
  whose father goes to the devil, 7402
  will be long a, 6536
  you idiotic, 1666
Child's nose, wipes, 7686
  sob in the silence, 325
Childhood, in my days of, 2363
  shows the man, 2891
Childhood's hour, from, 2971
Childish things, put away, 6230
Childishness, second, 4090
Children and chicken, 7002
  and fools, 7003, 7004
  and old folks, bestowed on, 8108
  are certain cares, 7005
  are heard, voices of, 234
  are poor man's riches, 7006
  arise up, her, 5949
  become as little, 6096
  dear, was it yesterday, 56
  follow through the wet, 755
  follow'd, even, 1704
  Friend for little, 2655
  happy in his, 7399
  he that has no, 7569
  in Holland, 8985
  justified of her, 6081
  like the olive branches, 5885
  maids', 6831
  make parents fools, 7010
  marrying of, 6973
  men are but, 1390
  of the Lord, 33
  old men are twice, 8529
  pick up words, 7007
  respect is due to, 9095
  scream, heard his, 1735
  should be seen and not heard, 7008
  should be seen, not heard, 1735
  shout, little, 5307
  soon forget, 8532
  stand quiet, when, 9751
  suck the mother, 7009
  suffer the little, 6135
  to come unto me, 6135
  turn out well, widows', 9873
  uncertain comforts, 7005
  weeping, hear the, 324
Children's Hour, known as, 2452
Chill it was, bitter, 2207
Chimaeras dire, Hydras and, 2808
Chimborazo, Cotopaxi, 5375
Chime, higher than the sphery, 2737
  to guide their, 2585
Chimes at midnight, heard, 3908
  jingles, little, 732
Chimley-piece, bottle on, 1221
Chimney corner, old men from, 4909
  he made a, 3546
  maintain one, 8011
Chimneys, easier to build two, 8011

Credula postero, quam minimum, 1987
Credulity, season of, 836
  who listen with, 2106
Creed, a Calvinistic, 838
  outworn, suckled in, 5659
  sapping a solemn, 617
Creeds, keys of all, 5225
  so many, 5553
  than in half the, 5232
Creeks and inlets, through, 938
Creep and then go, 7255
  make your flesh, 1190
  shall sweetly, 3952
  where it cannot go, 8273
Creetur, a lone lorn, 1233
Crest, joy brightens his, 2873
Crew complete, with all her, 1069
  darling of our, 1181
  no gale dismayed, 803
Crib, ass his master's, 5991
Cricket, merry as, 6752
  on the hearth, 2705
Cried in vain, John he, 1072
Cries, night and day on me she, 6337
Crime, featureless and commonplace, 1307
  madden to, 630
  Napoleon of, 1314
  of being a young man, 835
  plus qu'un, 1550
  punishment fit the, 1649
  reach the scene of, 1426
  this coyness were no, 2586
  what greater, 9719
  worse than a, 1550
Crimes, follies, and misfortunes, register of, 1601
Crimine ab uno disce omnes, 5415
Cripple, halt before, 8029
  he that mocks, 7632
Crispian, feast of, 3989
Critic, in logic a great, 562
  the good, 1552
  you have frowned, 5680
Critic's eye, view me with, 1467
Critical, sternly, 1870
Criticism, cant of, 5016
  definition of, 71
Criticisms, they pass no, 1412
Critics!—appall'd I venture, 529
  are like brushers, 7052
  before you trust in, 599
  much confide in, 5073
Critique, le bon, 1552
Cromwell, Charles the First [had his], 1881
  damned, see, 3254
  guiltless, some, 1764
Crony, trusty, drouthy, 523
Crooked in the water, 6593
  if the staff be, 7864
  straight, set the, 2994
Crooksaddles, cracking of, 6982

Crop, a-watering last year's, 1413
Cross as a bear, 6726
  as nine highways, 6727
  as two sticks, 6728
  devil bears, 8004
  e'en though it be a, 6
  hath its inscription, 7146
  last at His, 158
  lurks behind, 9013
  no crown, no, 3125
  of Jesus, with the, 149
  on the bitter, 3815
  she wore, sparkling, 3188
Crosse he bore, a bloodie, 4981
Crosses are ladders, 7055
  between the, 2529
  proud man hath, 6568
Crossways, things at home are, 736
Crotchets in thy head, 4352
Crouch, still bidding, 349
Crouse, nothing so, 8498
Crow makes wing to the rooky wood, 4596
  thinks her own bird fairest, 8993
  to pluck, to have, 9481
Crowd, muse in a, 330
  'twas in a, 176
Crowd's ignoble strife, far from the madding, 1766
Crowds, if you can talk with, 2330
Crown, all the forces of, 840
  better than his, 3799
  conquer a, 3077
  head that wears a, 3905
  is in my heart, 3553
  likeness of a kingly, 2809
  not the king's, 4391
  of glory, hoary head is, 5915
  of life, give thee, 6281
  put on my, 4671
  the tripled, 3348
  to gain, a kingly, 1859
  within the hollow, 3695
  would give his, 5440
Crowned, and again discrowned, 2030
Crowns all, the end, 9027
  and pounds, give, 2015
  resign, I'd, 2544
Crows and choughs, 4515
  are never the whiter, 7056
Crow-toe, tufted, 2752
Crucified, dear Lord was, 34
Cruel, not to trust, 4815
  only to be kind, 4300
Cruelty, farewell, fair, 4137
Cruise, all on our last, 5025
Crumb, craved no, 1657
Crumbs which fall, 6092
Crush of worlds, 15
Crust contents her, 8978
  with water and a, 2204
Crutch, shoulder'd his, 1700
Crutches, better than two, 8560
Cry and little wool, much, 8382

Dangerous, have in me something, 4331
such men are, 4008
thing, little learning is a, 3170
Dangers are overcome by dangers, 7067
who brave, its, 2461
Dansons sur un volcan, 3451
Dante never stays too long, 2509
Danube, rude hut by, 623
Dappled things, glory be to God for, 1978
Dare do all that may become a man, 4560
do, what men, 3949
never grudge the throe, 403
' not ' wait upon ' I would,' 4559
what man dare, I, 4604
you who, 2633
Darien, upon a peak in, 2201
Daring spirit pall, no danger can, 1156
Dares do more is none, who, 4560
Darest thou then, 3481
Dark, after that the, 5282
all cats are grey in, 6639
and bright, best of, 634
and doubtful, from the, 1110
and the daylight, between, 2452
and true and tender, 5201
at one strike comes, 963
children fear to go in, 108
dark, dark, 2900
drive black hogs in, 8042
ever-during, 2821
go home in the, 1880
good as my lady in, 8087
he that gropes in, 7566
he that runs in, 7647
hellish, 5070
illumine, what in me is, 2767
irrecoverably, 2900
wanderers of the, 4494
we are for the, 4667
with excess of bright, 2822
Darkies have to part, 1544
Darkness again and a silence, 2467
as a bride, encounter, 4400
born, in silent, 1135
buries all, universal, 3229
came down on the field, 5293
dawn on our, 1857
deepens, the, 2496
do devour it, jaws of, 3707
go out into the, 1839
instruments of, 4542
leaves the world to, 1754
peering, into that, 3159
prince of, 4503
rather than light, 6174
scatters the rear of, 2687
visible, 2769
walketh in, 5871
what of the, 2411
which may be felt, 5752
Darling, Charlie is my, 3011
of my heart, 733
old man's, 6881
somebody's, 2352

Darlings, wealthy curled, 4414
Dart, feather on the fatal, 602
shook a dreadful, 2809
Time shall throw a, 321
Darter's youngest darter, 3145
Dastard in war, 3479
Dat, bis dat cito, 6951
Date, all too short, 4783
Dated, women and music should never be.
9913
Daughter am I in my mother's house,
2282
Duke-and-a-Duchess's, 143
harping on my, 4233
heavy-heeled, 6519
let them all to, 5309
like mother, like, 8204
my daughter's my, 8390
O my ducats ! 3783
of the gods, 5157
of the voice of God, 5648
taken his little, 2444
when you can, [marry], 8335
win, he that would, 7698
Daughter-in-law, that she was, 9179
Daughters and a back door, two, 9616
and dead fish, 7068
dawted, 7069
none of Beauty's, 637
of my father's house, I am all the, 4150
Dauntless in war, so, 3477
David his ten thousands, 5782
Daw but had twa, never, 9347
Dawn and sunset, seen, 2601
before, 8998
comes up like thunder, 2310
crept like a frightened girl, 5571
doth rise, dappled, 2686
exhalations of, 1000
rosy-fingered, 1952
Dawn's early light, by the, 2250
Daws to peck at, for, 4411
Day, about the break of, 3058
across the, 5176
advent of each dangerous, 148
alternate Night and, 1497
and night, con the pages, 2008
another blue, 754
appears by, 9723
as one shall see in a summer's, 3714
at night, praise, 8653
at the close of, 185
back with Policeman, 2336
be never so longe, 1840
beware of the, 701
break, until, 5987
burden and heat of, 6106
come day, go, 7028
comes, w'en de great, 1833
dearly love but one, 734
ebbs out life's little, 2497
enjoy bright, 2726
entertains the harmless, 5690
every dog has, 7174

Death, ere thou hast slain, 321
  everything but, 9315
  for his ambition, 4029
  fortunate in the occasion of, 5113
  from sudden, 6305
  give me liberty or give me, 1883
  gone to her, 1970
  had left it almost fair, 4921
  has been abroad, Angel of, 286
  has brimmed his banks, river of, 3044
  has broach'd him to, 1181
  has stopped the ears, 2017
  hath a thousand doors, 2610
  had not hope of, 1137
  he taketh all away, 1041
  he that fears, 7556
  his court, keeps, 3695
  his dart shook, 2880
  his name that sat on him was, 6285
  how wonderful is, 4838
  I cry, for restful, 4797
  I here importune, 4663
  i' the other [eye], set, 4001
  improved by, 3448
  in life, 5199
  in love with easeful, 2216
  in that sleep of, 4253
  in the pot, there is, 5803
  in the ranks of, 2965
  into the world, brought, 2765
  is as a lover's pinch, 4672
  is certain to all, 3906
  is past, bitterness of, 5781
  is the grand leveller, 7078
  itself awakes, 3903
  itself, look on, 4582
  keeps no calendar, 7079
  lays his icy hand, 4902
  like sleep might steal on me, 4842
  lives not after, 7457
  love thee better after, 332
  make one in love with, 4879
  makes equal, 1908
  make much of, 8531
  makes sport for, 9742
  men fear, 108
  no medicine against, 9334
  nor life, neither, 6213
  now boast thee, 4674
  of each day's life, 4576
  of princes, heavens themselves blaze
    forth, 4018
  of the righteous, die, 5758
  old men go to, 8530
  one that had been studied in his, 4545
  or life shall thereby be the sweeter,
    4397
  over them triumphant, 2880
  pays all debts, 7080
  penalty, abolish the, 2197
  perchance of, 5335
  prepare for, 2087
  proud to take us, make, 4665
  Reaper whose name is, 2433

Death, reports of my, 5383
  ruling passion strong in, 3264
  sense of, 4399
  silence deep as, 707
  silent halls of, 429
  sleep is a, 320
  so noble, in a, 2906
  someone's, 397
  sure as, 6785
  swan sings before, 9252
  that stroke of, 2112
  the doctor, after, 6629
  there is no, 2530
  there shall be no more, 6287
  they were not divided, in, 5784
  this fell sergeant, 4342
  thou wast not born for, 2217
  to us, 'tis, 2418
  to what we fear of, 4402
  try to disprove, 5373
  ugly sights of, 3565
  under the ribs of, 2731
  untimely, 3216
  us do part, till, 6317
  valley of the shadow of, 5841
  vasty Hall of, 63
  wages of sin is, 6210
  way to dusty, 4636
  we are in, 6323
  welcome, 9708
  what should it know of, 1001
  where is thy sting, 6236
  why fear, 1564
  will disprove you, 5373
  without a witness, 8184
  years of fearing, 4022
Death's arquebuse, 8856
  blossoms, 7387
  counterfeit, sleep, 4582
  dateless night, 4788
  day is doom's day, 7081
  door, 7176
  feast, war is, 9673
  pale flag, 3670
  second self, 4799
Death-bed, gone to his, 841
Deaths foreseen come not, 7082
Debauchery, without business, 9906
Debellare superbos, 5425
Debt is better than death, 7083
  is the worst poverty, 7084
  out of, 8598
  pay an ounce of, 6566
  posterity most in, 2057
  rise in, 6901
  sorrow will pay no, 8843
  to pay, a double, 1708
Debtors are liars, 7085
  as we forgive, 6052
  better memories than, 7051
Debts, death pays all, 7080
  forgive us our, 6052
  he that dies pays, 4748
  speak not of my, 8852

Decay, by laws of time, 1038
hastes to swift, 2099
muddy vesture of, 3809
subject to, 1354
Deceased, he first, 5693
name of the late, 2327
Deceit, we hug the dear, 1043
Deceive, first we practise to, 3482
me once, if a man, 7819
me twice, if he, 7819
oneself, to, 9467
Deceived, desire to be, 558
Deceiver, I'm a gay, 1016
Deceivers ever, men were, 3934
Deceives, he that once, 7634
December, drear-nighted, 2232
seek roses in, 599
Decencies, content to dwell in, 3269
Decency, want of, 3410
Decent, to what is, 1973
Decently and in order, 6233
things be done, 6233
Decide, the moment to, 2477
who shall, 3275
Deck, stood on the burning, 1864
Declare, nothing to, 5566
Decliner of honours and titles, 1465
Dedans, ceux qui sont au, 2937
Dee, across the sands of, 2255
lived on the river, 216
Dee [die], I wad, 125
Deed and abide it, do the, 2996
and repent it, do the, 2996
by the doer's, 4378
in all my life, one good, 3585
in every eye, blow the horrid, 4556
is never lost, good, 6473
of dreadful note, 4594
so shines a good, 3812
take the will for, 9553
the better the, 8963
till thou applaud, 4595
wise before, 9125
without a name, 4613
Deed's achieved, matchless, 4915
Deeds are fruits, 7086
are males, 7087
emblems of, 630
ill done, makes, 3751
know, so little men their own, 5314
like poison-weeds, 5570
must not be thought, 4575
my lady please, doughty, 1737
not years, live in, 124
of men, looks quite through, 4009
relate, these unlucky, 4474
turn sourest by, 4805
were evil, because, 6174
which make up life, 341
years of noble, 5264
Deep a lower deep, in the lowest, 2826
almost as life, 5667
and crisp and even, 3030
and massy, close and high, 3473

Deep calleth unto deep, 5851
cradle of the, 5572
dive into the bottom of, 3828
for me, in terms too, 1631
from the great deep to the great deep, 5252
from the vasty, 3855
her home is on the, 705
home on the rolling, 3453
in the shady sadness, 2229
slimy bottom of the, 3565
still waters run, 8871
sweep through the, 704
tempest o'er the, 5345
there's danger on the, 179
to boil, he maketh, 5828
young man, singularly, 1631
Deeper than did ever plummet sound, 4754
Deer, a-chasing the wild, 518
go weep, stricken, 4277
I was a stricken, 1083
rats and such small, 4502
Defac'd deflower'd, and now to death devote, 2876
Defaming and defacing, 5255
Défauts de leur qualités, 131
Defect in her, some, 4745
of Henry King, chief, 202
perfection, make, 4650
Defects of their qualities, 131
Defence and ornament, 225
at one gate to make, 2902
or apology, make a, 831
Defend, he had promised to, 2514
me from my friends, 7334
Defender, I mean the Faith's, 591
Defer or neglect it, not, 1790
Deficiency, supply their, 3376
Defiled, shall be, 6291
Deform'd, unfinish'd, 3559
Dégagé, half so, 1053
Degeneration, fatty, 5021
Degree, in an extreme, 3351
suits with our, 327
Degrees, name you the, 4123
scorning the base, 4011
Deil's awa wi' the Exciseman, 533
Deils he'll mak them, clever, 503
Δεινά, πολλά τά, 4953
Deities, feet of, 9049
Dejection do we sink, in, 5623
Delay, chides his infamous, 5710
reprov'd each dull, 1702
sweet reluctant amorous, 2833
there lies no plenty, in, 4140
Delaying, deliberating is not, 7090
saved the State, by, 1456
Delays are dangerous, 7089
nourished by, 7094
promises and, 7492
Delenda est Carthago, 808
Deliberates, woman that, 13
Deliberating is not delaying, 7090

T

Dies pays all debts, he that, 4748
  the first fit, 7708
  the same, then, 5710
  when an old man, 3023
Dies irae, dies illa, 817
  sine linea, nulla, 8502
Diet cures more, 7098
  Dr. Quiet, Dr., 8957
  sober in your, 2931
Dieu n'existait pas, si, 5430
Difference, made all the, 1568
  to me, the, 5611
  wear your rue with, 4315
Difficult, all things are, 6666
  do you call it, 2165
Difficulty and labour, with, 2818
Diffidence is the right eye, 7099
Dig, I cannot, 6157
  till you gently perspire, 2334
Digest, inwardly, 6307
  something to, 6379
Digestion bred, from pure, 2845
  give me a good, 6379
  sour, prove in, 3680
  wait on appetite, 4600
Digests all things but itself, 7001
Dignified, man who is, 896
Dignity compos'd, for, 2796
  of history, 254
Diligence is the mother of good luck, 7100
Dimidium facti, 1998
Dine at Ware, I should, 1075
  if this should stay to, 801
  late, I shall, 2375
  on the pot-lid, 7302
  that jurymen may, 3193
Dined to-day, I have, 4947
Dines on the following day, 796
Ding, chiels that winna, 499
  the deil into a wife, 9963
Dinging, deserves no, 7546
Dingle, or bushy dell, 2723
Dining-room will be well lighted, 2375
Dinkey-Bird is singing, 1480
Dinner cool, no fear lest, 2852
  eats up all at, 7519
  he that saveth, 7648
  lubricates business, 3520
  sit awhile, after, 6630
Dinner-bell, tocsin of the soul, 663
Dinners cannot be long, 7101
  hunger makes, 7773
Diocese, in his own, 9007
Diplomacy is to do and say, 1677
Dirce in one boat, with, 2372
Directions, rode madly off in all, 2394
Directories, Pocket Books, 2357
Dirge is sung, 1009
Dirk, never draw your, 8420
Dirt, eat a peck of, 7189
  enough, fling, 7263
  feet met, 5717
  never cast, 8417

Dirt of his own ditch, dies in, 9690
  painted child of, 3294
Dirty work again, at his, 3287
Dis aliter visum, 5419
Dis's waggon, from, 4719
Disappointed, never be, 3316
Disappointment every day, by, 1096
Disaster, laugh at all, 2459
  meet with Triumph and, 2329
Disasters, had the fewest, 1154
  trace the day's, 1706
Disclosure, sky makes no, 373
Discobulus, standeth, the, 589
Discontent, hang the head as, 719
  in pensive, 4989
  winter of our, 3557
Discord, bray'd horrible,2856
  harmony not understood, 3242
Discords sting, their, 1931
Discouraged, de we feel, 5467
Discourse, bid me, 4773
  dialect and, 579
  of the elders, 6290
  subtle and sinewy to, 2917
  sweet, 8886
  with such large, 4305
Discovery, never made a, 4916
Discreet advise, while, 9831
Discretion is the better part, 7103
  ounce of, 6709
  woman without, 5904
  would run away, 9647
Discrowned, crowned and again, 2080
Disdain and scorn, 3937
  my Dear Lady, 3926
Disease is incurable, 3891
  meet the, 3137
  my life, long, 3289
  shapes of foul, 5234
  worse than, 9210
Diseases are the interests, 7104
  desperate, 7096
  desperate grown, 4302
  remedy to all, 556
Disgrace, open, 8656
  with fortune, in, 4786
Disgraces are like cherries, 7105
Disguises which we wear, 2838
Dish, empty, 6922
  fit for the gods, 4014
  in a lordly, 5770
  meet him in my, 7785
  nor wash, 4744
  pleaseth all, first, 9056
  put in a riven, 6648
Dish-clout my tablecloth, make, 7804
Dishes, no washing of, 6377
Dismay, let nothing you, 6340
Dismount, can never, 7710
Disobedience, Man's first, 2765
Disorder in the dress, 1897
  with most admired, 4606
Dispaires, comfortless, 4989
Dispoged, when I am so, 1221

Dog it was that died, 1690
  little toy, 1479
  living, 5968
  love me, love my, 8270
  man, a horse, and a, 6535
  mine enemy's, 4521
  more ways to kill, 9304
  new tricks, teach an old, 9959
  one of the two dogs meets, with a
    third, 1484
  over a stile, help. 9492
  shall bear him company, 3236
  sick as, 6774
  smarts, this, 1484
  something better than, 5168
  that bit you, hair of, 6500
  that licks ashes, 9021
  to beat, 6590
  to follow you, wish, 7907
  to tear, giving your heart to a, 2332
  to throw at a, 4063
  went mad, the, 1689
  will have his day, 4333
  will not howl, 6444
Dog Hollow, 3045
Dog's tooth, [trust not], 9592
  walking on his hinder legs, 2131
Dogerel, may wel be rym, 869
Dogged as does it, it's, 5365
Dogs, all by the name of, 4587
  and a bone, two, 9615
  and all, little, 4507
  are fighting, two, 1484
  bark as they are bred, 7127
  bark at me, 3559
  bark before they bite, 7128
  between two, 3538
  come in, at open doors, 6823
  delight to bark, let, 5480
  eat of the crumbs, 6092
  fight for a bone, two, 9617
  heed the barking of, 9163
  hungry, 7775
  lie, let sleeping, 8169
  of war, let slip, 4028
  over stiles, lame, 2265
  quarrelling, 8683
  seldom bite, barking, 6837
  that bark at a distance, 7129
  throw physic to, 4632
  wag their tails, 7130
  who lies down with, 7707
Doing [is] another [thing], 8743
  joy's soul lies in, 4363
  or suffering, 2771
  shortest answer is, 9228
  then be up and, 2442
  well, worth, 9729
  what he does, by, 895
Δοκεῖν ἄριστος, ἀλλ᾽ εἶναι, οὐ γάρ, 25
Dole, happy man be his, 7405
Doll, had a sweet little, 2263
  in the world, prettiest, 2263, 2264

Dollar, the almighty, 2062
Dollars, however plenty, 933
Dolore, nessun maggior, 1139
Dolores, splendid and sterile, 5100
Dolphin's back, mermaid on, 3715
Dolphin-chamber, in my, 3896
Dome, that rounded Peter's, 1448
Domestiques, admirez par leurs, 2935
Domina, beata mea, 2991
Domitian, from the death of, 1602
Don John of Austria, 881
Don, remote and ineffectual, 199
Dona ferentes, et, 5413
Done at all, surprised to find it, 2131
  at any time, may be, 9731
  been and gone and, 1614
  betters what is, 4720
  by, do as you would be, 7111
  cannot be undone, 9380
  determined, dared and, 4915
  for you, what have I, 1876
  if you want a thing, 7899
  is done, what's, 4589
  it is well, 4675
  may compute what's, 494
  quickly, well it were, 4554
  so little, 3381, 5230
  something, 2448
  we ought not to have, 6297
  well begun is half, 9711
  when 'tis done, if it were, 4554
  would 'twere, 3588
Done-to-death, called, 5357
Doom, regardless of their, 1749
  to the crack of, 4616
Doom's day, death's day is, 7081
Doomsday is near, 3871
Doon, banks and braes o', 527
Dooney, on my fiddle in, 5705
Door, before his cottage, 4961
  beside a human, 5616
  beside the golden, 2392
  came out by the same, 1502
  creaking, 6438
  daughters and a back, 9616
  forc'd me from the, 3000
  form from off my, 3160
  good John, shut the, 3282
  have a hatch before, 8026
  keep the wolf from, 9497
  knocking on the moonlit, 1170
  [love] goes out at, 8254
  may be shut, every, 7176
  may tempt, open, 6708
  nice wife and a back, 6558
  on its hinges, as, 5485
  open the, 9752
  sat at her ivied, 690
  should go, another by, 8550
  shut the stable, 9538
  shut, when he finds, 6828
  shuts, when one, 9763
  stood open at our feast, 952
  sweep before your, 8885

Dreams of thee, I arise from, 4847
old men shall dream, 6029
out of mind, put my, 5090
that are done, 5090
that wave before the half-shut eye, 5329
to sell, there were, 190
waken from his summer, 4845
you tread on my, 5701
Dreamt that I dwelt in marble hal's, 439
Dree out the inch, 7135
Dress and manners, 4823
be plain in, 2931
sweet disorder in, 1897
this fleshly, 5392
well, we don't, 4823
Dressed, first, 7645
in all his trim, 4806
when he's well, 1217
Dressings fit, for every season, 6343
Drest, still to be, 2178
Dries sooner, nothing, 8488
Drift is as bad, 7136
Drill, no names, no pack, 8463
Drink, a taste for, 1660
and the devil, 5036
before I go, I may, 513
behind him, left his, 7703
by measure, 7152
cannot whistle and, 6539
deep, or taste not, 3170
every creature, 1048
everyone offers him, 9740
is in, when, 9743
is raging, strong, 5923
loth to, 8247
nor any drop to, 960
of the burn, we can, 9682
only with the duck, 7137
or to sleep, not my design to, 1126
pretty creature, 5617
reasons we should, 30
so let them, 6795
strong, or not at all, 6375
think that I can, 5057
till all look blue, 1540
to me only, 2169
when I am hot, let me not, 9642
with me, fly, 3070
with me, sit and, 196
you can't make him, 9968
Drinking is the soldier's pleasure, 1371
largely sobers, 3170
poor and unhappy brains for, 4434
with constant, 1047
Drinks, and gapes for drink, 1047
and is not dry, 7576
long time between, 2979
to his host, never, 7468
Drivel, the ropy, 1609
Driveller and a show, a, 2091
Driveth furiously, he, 5806
Driving, in riding and, 1457

Driving of Jehu, like the, 5806
spend my life in, 2150
Droite recule, ma, 1537
Drone, lazy yawning, 3967
Dronken, whan that he wel, 862
Droop and drowse, begin to, 4596
Drop hollows the stone, 7388
it if I tried, can't, 2317
last, 9137
to drink, nor any, 960
Dropping, constant, 7037
continual, 5939
Droppings of warm tears, 328
Drops from off the eaves, 2710
of red, bleeding, 5540
Dross that is not Helena, 2563
Drouth, in England suffer, 9870
Drown me, now you'd, 7795
what pain it was to, 3565
Drowned, chance of being, 2123
good swimmers at length are, 7362
in the depths, 6097
never was cat, 8431
shall never be, 7594
the third, as he, 1735
Drowning man will catch, 6446
mark upon him, no, 4727
Drowsy man, dull ear of, 3745
Drowsyhed, land of, 5329
Drudge, a harmless, 2102
disobedient, for a, 1714
Drudgery, to that dry, 2364
Drum ecclesiastic, 560
rumble of a distant, 1495
spirit-stirring, 4452
them up the Channel, 3039
to England, take my, 3039
vith a hole in it, 1195
was heard, not a, 5585
Drums, bangin' er de, 1833
beat the, 2980
begin to roll, when, 2303
from the noise of our own, 4677
like muffled, 2439
thr' rolling, 5202
Drunk as a lord, 6731
as a mouse, 6732
as a wheelbarrow, 6733
ever dry, ever, 7168
hasten to be, 1379
I am, not so think as you, 5002
where I got, 3319
Drunkard, rolling English, 888
Drunkards, liars and adulterers, 4478
Drunken folks seldom take harm, 7140
man, stagger like, 5876
where I got more, 3319
Drunkenness reveals, 9734
Dry as a bone, 6734
as the remainder biscuit, 4086
drawn wells are seldom, 7132
ever drunk, ever, 7168
Oh ! I am so, 1470
till a' the seas gang, 541

Dry, what shall be done in, 6168
Dryden, prefaces of, 5073
  taught to join, 3300
  wanted or forgot, 3301
Ducats, O my Christian, 3783
Duchess, that's my last, 379
Duck, drink only with, 7137
  like a dying, 8191
  my dainty, 4724
Duck's back, water off, 8207
Ducks and drakes of, make, 9518
  on a pond, four, 41
Duddy, wow, but they were, 3395
Due, he that loseth his, 7618
Duke of York, noble, 6354
Duke's son—cook's son, 2318
Dukedom, prize above my, 4731
Dulce et decorum est, 1992
Dull and hoary, but, 5396
  as ditchwater, 6735
  at whiles, though it's, 2265
  boy, makes Jack a, 6670
  gentle, yet not, 1172
  so dead in look, so, 3883
  we ourselves are, 4376
Dulness ever loves a joke, 3221
Dumb, a beggar that is, 3358
  as a drum vith a hole, 1195
  folks get no lands, 7143
Dumblane, flower o', 5122
Dummheit, mit der, 3456
Dummy cannot lie, 7144
Dunce that has been kept at home, 1057
  that has been sent to roam, 1057
  with wits, a, 3225
Dundee, in bonny, 3507
Dungeon, himself is his own, 2726
  live upon the vapour of, 4448
  scourged to his, 429
Dunghill, on his own, 6430
  shining on, 9250
Dunt will do, when a, 8420
Δύο, οὐδὲ Ἡρακλῆς πρός, 8595
Dupe of to-morrow, 1096
Dusk lit by one large star, 2629
  ran between the streets, 24
Dust alone remains of thee, 3209
  and bones jostle not, 7955
  and heat, not without, 2915
  and silence of the upper shelf, 2504
  be equal made, in, 4902
  blossom in their, 4903
  bushel of March, 6418
  cinders, ashes, 2204
  come to, 4704, 4705, 4706
  come to worse than, 2019
  do I raise, what, 9062
  enclosed here, to dig, 4820
  excuse my, 3098
  from whence he sprung, 3467
  he that blows in, 7526
  in one's eyes, throw, 9557
  is on your feet, while, 9833
  knight's bones are, 995

    *T

Dust, less than the, 1975
  lick the, 5861
  nigh is grandeur to, 1452
  on an Empire's, 608
  our paper, make, 3694
  pays us but with, 3365
  provoke the silent, 1761
  quintessence of, 4239
  return to the earth, 5980
  shalt thou return, unto, 5727
  small rain lays, 8818
  that is a little gilt, 4369
  this quiet, 1259
  thou art, 2438, 5727
  to dust, 6324
  trace the noble, 4325
  would hear her and beat, 5248
  write it [good turn] in, 2976
  writes in, 123
  you are not worth, 4511
Dust's your wages, 2019
Dust-heap called ' history,' 222
Dusty, cobweb-covered, 589
Dutch [Holland], I said it in, 797
  the fault of the, 727
Dutch [wife], swop for my dear old, 899
Dutchman, a warehouse, 7948
Duties, brace ourselves to, 909
  if I had no, 2150
  on herself did lay, 5633
  property has its, 1330
Duty, a divided, 4424
  as the subjects owes, 3593
  below he did his, 1182
  daily stage of, 2246
  declares that it is, 4825
  done that which was our, 6162
  England expects that every man will
    do his, 3035
  is the king's, subject's, 3984
  not a sin, 5515
  not for meed, for, 4073
  of being happy, 5029
  of man, whole, 5982
  path of, 5209
  thank God, I have done my, 3036
  to do my, 6312
  to God, discussing, 5537
  we so much underrate, 5029
  which lies nearest, 742
  which thou knowest to be, 742
  whispers low, 1452
Dwarf on a giant's shoulder, 6448
Dwell together in unity, 5886
Dwelling-place, blest is, 1925
Dye one's whisker's green, 792
Dyer's hand, like the, 4812
Dying, Egypt, dying, I am, 4663
  groans of the, 3472
  man to dying men, 173
  men, upon the lips of, 60
  shall go down, 3467
  they are all, 5528

Eye, glad me with its soft black, 2971
  half hidden from the, 5610
  has danced, many an, 1929
  hath not seen it, 1868
  hath the merriest, 3538
  have an eagle's, 6485
  he that hath but one, 7575
  heav'n in her, 2863
  her cheek, her lip, language in her, 4371
  holds him with his glittering, 954
  however blue, where's, 2224
  I eyed, when first your, 4807
  I have a good, 3928
  in a fair woman's, 6403
  in my mind's, 4189
  in the twinkling of an, 6235
  in the wink of an, 5046
  is bigger than the belly, 9037
  is the pearl, 9038
  Lesbia hath a beaming, 2960
  lest the chips fall in, 7733
  lifting up a fearful, 4972
  loathsome to the, 2066
  locked up from mortal, 1118
  man with half an, 5366
  master's, 9156
  mote in every man's, 8763
  negotiate for itself, 3930
  never rub your, 9984
  of heaven to garnish, 3748
  of heaven visits, that, 3681
  of the master, 9039
  of the master sees, 8555
  offend thee, if thine, 6098
  or face, pleasing, 6346
  please, 8628
  rolling, 6573
  sees not itself, 9040
  sees with equal, 3233
  so inquiring, 2370
  still-soliciting, 4476
  sublime declar'd absolute rule, 2832
  that sees all things, 9040
  then can I drown an, 4788
  to the main chance, 7422
  tongue, sword, 4260
  was bright, saw her, 950
  will mark our coming, 651
  winketh with one, 7685
  with a threatening, 3746
  with his keener, 2593
  with how blank an, 993
  with lack-lustre, 4082
Eyeball, like a coal his, 4914
Eyebrow, to his mistress', 4090
Eyeless in Gaza, 2899
Eyelids down, weigh my, 3902
  heavy and red, 1965
  tinged the, 3106
Eyes again so royal, of, 4674
  and lemonade, black, 2950
  are cast, where'er these, 4959
  as the fairy-flax, blue, 2445
  bein' only, 1200

Eyes, buyer needs a hundred, 8973
  can see more, two, 9620
  could see, as long as, 2012
  dazzle, mine, 5500
  deceive me earsight, do, 5464
  did one inhabit, where, 3565
  drink to me only with thine, 2169
  dry one's, 372
  evermore peep through, 3754
  fields have, 7247
  from star-like, 730
  from women's, 3616
  gather to the, 5198
  glow, whose little, 1903
  good for sore, 9230
  have one language, 9041
  have seen the glory, mine, 2029
  her aspect and her, 634
  in April, men's, 1329
  in Huncamunca's, 1483
  in those fair, 6344
  is censured by our, 2571
  kindling her undazzled, 2919
  kiss that mortal's, 442
  lids of Juno's, 4719
  light that lies in woman's, 2967
  like stars, start from their spheres,
    make thy, 4214
  look your last, 3671
  look'd from thoughtful, 3113
  look'd love, soft, 609
  love in her sunny, 1049
  love-darting, 2735
  many ears and many, 8113
  may weep, wakeful, 2369
  may wink, runaways', 3663
  night has a thousand, 268
  nor ears, neither, 7102
  not for want of, 9395
  observing with judicious, 5358
  of gold and bramble-dew, 5055
  of men, as in a theatre, 3702
  of men, persuade, 4777
  of most unholy blue, 2961
  of wonder, dreaming, 773
  one whose subdued, 4474
  ope their golden, 4695
  open, [keep], 8103
  out, pick hawks', 7426
  owl's, 9123
  pair of sparkling, 1662
  pearls that were his, 4736
  play the woman with mine, 4624
  poorly satisfy our, 5692
  quaint enamell'd, 2752
  quiet, 5054
  rain influence, bright, 2693
  rapt soul sitting in, 2700
  read in, 9108
  ride sparkling in, 3937
  see more, four, 7291
  see with mortal, 50
  severe, with, 4090
  she gave me, 5618

Falsehood framed, heart for, 4892
    grapple, let her and, 2920
    hath, goodly outside, 3769
    in fellowship, 9323
Falstaff sweats to death, 3833
Faltered more or less, 5050
Fame, bandits in the paths of, 529
    common, 7031, 7032
    damned to everlasting, 3254
    elates thee, while, 2951
    great heir of, 2678
    I slight, nor, 3202
    inspires, fair, 3291
    is but the breath, 7227
    is no plant that grows on mortal soil, 2747
    is the spur, 2746
    many ways to, 9301
    nor yet a fool to, 3288
    rage for, 5583
    shall be damned to, 3223
    shall be outworn, thy, 2996
    soon spread around, 1073
    that wit could ever win, 442
    titles, wealth and, 3209
    unknown, to, 1769
    was but a dream, lust of, 291
Fames eternall beadroll, on, 4988
Familiar, but by no means vulgar, 4200
    but not coarse, 2110
    in his mouth as household words, 3990
    palpable and, 1000
Familiarity breeds contempt, 7228
Families, best-regulated, 6624
    resemble one another, happy, 5353
Family, every unhappy, 5353
    form one, 1910
Famine in England, 6451
    under water, 9636
Famous, found myself, 674
    men, let us now praise, 6294
Fan, brain him with his lady's, 3836
    use so large a, 792
Fancies are more giddy, our, 4145
Fancy, a young man's, 5167
    bred, where is, 3789
    bright-eyed, 1777
    feign'd, by hopeless, 5199
    not express'd in, 4201
    of most excellent, 4323
    painted her, all my, 759, 2613
    power of, 4107
    roam, ever let the, 2223
    sweet and bitter, 4116
    whispers of, 2106
Fanny's way, only pretty, 3102
Fans in hell, no, 9307
Fantastic toe, the light, 2684
    tripped the light, 230
Fantasy, all made of, 4120
    nothing but vain, 3636
Fantasy's hot fire, not, 3466
Far and few, far and few, 2400
    between, short and, 229

Far, far, away, 5706
    from eye, far from heart, 7231
    he that goeth, 7564
    that never turns, goes, 7442
    to go, has, 8364
Fare, hard, 7406
    surveyed the unaccustomed, 4922
    thee well, for ever, 641
    worse, go farther and, 7329
Fared sumptuously every day, 6160
Fares, how he, 3046
Farewell ! a long farewell, 4760
    and adieu to you, 6358
    content, 4452
    for a mute, 2058
    for ever, 4054
    goes out sighing, 4367
    hail and, 815
    need not bid, 2239
    no sadness of, 5282
    remorse, 2827
    such welcome, such, 8880
    to Lochaber, 3370
Farce est jouée, 3355
    is played, the, 3355
Fardels bear, who would, 4253
Far-fetched and dear bought, 7229
Farm, his little snug, 4966
    his snug little, 989
Farmers stood, embattled, 1451
Farrago libelli, nostri, 2184
Farther and fare worse, go, 7329
Farthing, at a single, 811
    from a thousand pounds, 8894
    maketh a penny of, 9160
    [maketh] sixpence, of, 9160
    uttermost, 6046
Farthings, Latin word for three, 3611
Fashion, after the high Roman, 4665
    faithful in my, 1301
    glass of, 4260
    must mind, 8891
    out of, 6740
    out of the, 918
Fashioned so slenderly, 1970
Fashnable fax, 5289
Fast [quick] they follow, so, 4317
    we live, too, 58
Fast [go hungry], feast or, 7158
    till he is well, must, 7553
Fasting, between a fou man and a, 3518
Fat and greasy citizens, 4070
    and grows old, one is, 3840
    and kicked, waxed, 5763
    and merry, 7217
    could eat no, 8084
    friend, who's your, 426
    is in the fire, 9047
    let me have men about me that are 4008
    laugh and grow, 8136
    makes a man, 8520
    of others' works, 553
    of the land, eat of, 5745

Fat oxen, who drives, 2160
  she help'd him to, 144
  should himself be, 2160
  sow, little knoweth, 8221
  with the lean, take, 9977
Fate, all influence, all, 1535
  cannot touch me, 4947
  conspire, with, 1517
  drives the stubborn, 7235
  equall'd with me in, 2820
  foreknowledge, will and, 2804
  hanging breathless on, 2460
  heart for every, 646
  hides the book of, 3232
  in the storms of, 3200
  leads the willing, 7235
  let this be my, 3317
  limits of a vulgar, 1778
  master of my, 1873
  no armour against, 4902
  summons, when, 1354
  take a bond of, 4614
  too much, fears his, 2942
  torrent of his, 2092
  why should they know their, 1750
  with a heart for any, 2442
Fates a jest, owe the, 2337
  masters of their, 4005
Father, after your own, 8922
  bred, without, 2697
  child that knows, 7999
  dear father, 5688
  dies, cry not when, 2097
  goes to the devil, 7402
  heard his children scream, 1735
  is more, one, 8557
  it is a wise, 3777
  like son, like, 8200
  maketh a glad, 5902
  my true-begotten, 3776
  urged me sair, my, 153
  was hanged, told his, 7704
  when they are old, [suck], 7009
  which art in heaven, 6052
  which is in heaven, glorify, 6044
Father William, you are hale, 4965
  you are old, 763, 4965
Fatherland, dear, 3457
Fathers, ashes of his, 2519
  God of our, 2292
  of war-proof, 3978
  slept with his, 5795
  that begat us, 6294
Fathom five, full, 4736
Fauld, sheep are in the, 152
Fault, all fault who hath no, 5258
  and his sorrows, his, 2952
  and not the actor, condemn, 4390
  confessed, 6453
  doubles it, denying, 7091
  excusing of a, 3749
  he that commits, 7542
  I see, hide the, 3306
  is, where no, 9814

Fault or stain, without, 281
  seeming monstrous, 4104
  the glorious, 3207
  the worse, make, 3749
  which needs it, 1887
Faultless, faultily, 5238
  lifeless that is, 7474
  piece to see, 3172
Faults a little blind, to, 3327
  are not written in their foreheads, 7195
  are thick, 7236
  best men are moulded out of, 4408
  every man has, 7185
  first, 9057
  has she no, 3310
  I love thee, with all, 1080
  lie gently on him, 4767
  men have, 8345
  not for thy, 621
  observed, all his, 4051
  of man, bear with, 719
  rich men have no, 8713
  teeth and forehead of, 4287
  tell of my, 7343
  to scan, their, 1701
  vile ill-favour'd, 4355
  wink at small, 9887
  with all her, 903
  you would spy, 9992
Faustus must be damned, 2566
Faute, c'est une, 1550
Favour, kissing goes by, 8115
  wi' wooin' was fashous, 3009
Favourite has no friend, 1753
Favours call, nor for her, 3202
  hangs on princes', 4761
  I've felt all its, 945
Fawne, to crowche, to, 4989
Fear and Bloodshed, 5655
  and danger, continual, 1918
  and trembling, with, 6250
  arming me from, 292
  be always in, 6906
  cannot arm, 6669
  cheefly from, 3146
  follows him, 7013
  imagining some, 3731
  in children, natural, 108
  increased with tales, 108
  is affront, 1912
  [lives] without, 2055
  love casteth out, 6280
  never negotiate out of, 2248
  no medicine for, 9335
  no more the heat, 4704
  the worst, good to, 8025
  thou not at all, 5108
  'tis time to, 4692
  with hope farewell, 2827
Feared, it is just as I, 2398
Fearful and dizzy 'tis, 4515
Fearfully and wonderfully made, 5891
Fears attack, when, 685
  delicate, 5618

Fears do make us traitors, 4617
  our hopes belied, 1963
  present, 4543
  than wars or women have, more, 4761
  that I may cease to be, 2231
  you present, that, 7557
Feast, as good as, 7161
  as you were going to, 2178
  at the latter end of, 6894
  company makes, 8990
  continual, 6472
  door stood open at, 952
  imagination of, 3682
  or a fast, 7158
Feasted well, we have, 10006
Feasting, to the house of, 5963
Feast-making, merry is, 8350
Feasts, fools make, 7272
  wise men eat, 7272
Feather, ask a kite for, 6811
  by feather, 7237
  knocked me down with, 9970
  never moults a, 1214
  view'd his own, 602
Feathers but foul feet, fair, 9191
  far fowls have fair, 7230
  green, by, 205
  make fine birds, fine, 7249
Feature, cheated of, 3559
Featured like him, 4787
February alone, excepting, 6386
  fill dyke, 7238
  makes a bridge, 7239
Februeer, curse a fair, 6664
Fed, always well, 6433
  at another's hand, 7598
  gapeth till he be, 7560
  look up and are not, 2750
  on, appetite had grown by what it,
    4184
Federation of the world, 5171
Feeble up, help the, 4687
Feed by measure, 7241
  him, if you would wish the dog to
    follow you, 7907
  it, dies unless you, 8535
  you poison, if you, 9641
Feeds and breeds by a composture, 4690
Feel them most, who shall, 3215
  what he would not, 7551
  what wretches feel, 4498
Feeling as to sight, sensible to 4568
  had fed the, 2560
  petrifies the, 497
Feelings, not in figures, 124
  overflow of powerful, 5686
Feels the noblest, 124
Fees, dream on, 3635
Feet are light, your, 9829
  beneath her petticoat, 5062
  clang of hurrying, 101
  comes with leaden, 7333
  dreams under your, 5701
  fail beneath my, 5240

Feet, fall at her flying, 716
  from under a person's, 9466
  had run, from to-day my, 24
  her pretty, 1902
  I sat against her, 5098
  in soda water, wash, 1423
  keep thou my, 3047
  low at her, 3442
  nearer than hands and 5219
  never fail, let my due, 2711
  of Gamaliel, at the, 6200
  of him that bringeth good tidings, 6008
  of the many-twinkling, 629
  repose unscanned, 3322
  standing with reluctant, 2449
  those blessed, 3815
  tremble under her, 5248
  with flying, 610
  with silver-sandaled, 5571
  would not wet, 8980
Felice, ricordarsi del tempo, 1139
Felicem fuisse, 252
Felicitas, curiosa, 3139
Felicite, what more, 4990
Felicities, Nature's old, 5681
Felicity, absent thee from, 4344
  studied, 3139
  their green, 2232
  we make, our own, 2098
Felix opportunitate mortis, 5113
  qui potuit, 5407
Fell, from morn to noon he, 2790
  half so flat, 6363
  help me when I, 5125
  like the stick, 3090
  never climbed, never, 7633
  rides sure that never, 7512
  the instant that he, 3486
Fella, also on the unjust, 269
Feller, sweetes' li'l', 5006
Fellow, he's a Good, 1514
  I shot his, 3760
  if I be a thief, ask my, 6813
  many a good tall, 3826
  of no mark, 3864
  want of it the, 3250
  with the best king, 3996
Fellow-feeling makes one, 1578
Fellow-rover, a laughing, 2598
Fellows as I do, what should such, 4257
  at football, all, 6642
  Nature hath framed strange, 3754
Fellowship, falsehood in, 9324
  like no, 8250
  right hands of, 6244
Felt as a man, 186
Female of sex it seems, 2903
  of the species, 2300
Femina, varium et mutabile, 5422
Feminine gender, she's of, 3067
Femme, cherchez la, 1399
Fen of stagnant waters, 5631
  wild-fire dances on, 126
Fence against a flail, no, 8440

Fish are not caught, all, 6643
  are on the rock, 9772
  best, 8950
  better small, 6922
  cries stinking, 8452
  daughters and dead, 7068
  for every man, 9225
  had I, 7389
  he has gone to, 2403
  I was a, 4929
  in the sea, as good, 9299
  is cast away, 7260
  it is a silly, 7995
  kettle of, 6567
  must swim thrice, 7261
  no more land, say, 298
  nor flesh, neither, 8411
  of one, make, 9520
  out of water, like, 8193
  that hath fed of that worm, eat of, 4304
  to fry, I have other, 7784
  will soon be caught, 8930
  with glittering tails, 6387
  you'll catch no, 7896
Fish-ball, bread with one, 2376
Fisher goes not forth, 9791
Fishermen three, rocked, 1478
Fishers went sailing, three, 2256
Fishes gnaw'd upon, men that, 3565
  live, I marvel how, 4693
  talk, if you were to make little, 1728
Fish-guts, keep your ain, 8101
Fishified, how art thou, 3655
Fishing before the net, 8035
  best, 7953
  end of, 9029
  in troubled waters, 8019
Fishmonger's wife, 6392
Fist instead of a stick, 560
Fit [well, suitable] as a fiddle, 6737
  audience find, though few, 2859
  for God nor man, neither, 6603
Fit [foot], ganging, 6469
Fithele, or gay sautrye, 854
Fitted abide, things well, 9384
Fittest, survival of the, 1144, 4976
Five, how many beans make, 9501
  in five score, not, 3320
  must rise at, 7683
  nature requires, 8398
  thousand a year, if I had, 5294
Fivepence, fine as, 6736
Flag [standard] flying, keep the Red, 1027
  has braved, whose, 704
  has flown, English, 2284
  her holy, 1930
  of England, meteor, 706
  of our Union for ever, 2988
  spare your country's 5545
  was still there, our, 2250
Flag [lose vigour] or fail, we shall not, 908
Flagons, stay me with, 5984
Flail, no fence against, 8440
Flame, Chloe, is my real, 3326

Flame, feed his sacred, 992
  hard, gemlike, 3108
  nor private, dares to shine, nor public,
    3229
  so full of subtile, 187
  take away, 8895
Flames, through their paly, 3982
  must waste away, his, 730
  went by her like thin, 3424
Flanders fields, in, 2529
Flat as a pancake, 6738
  insipid, many times, 1394
Flatter, neither borrow nor, 7499
Flattered, being then most, 4015
Flatterer as a man's self, no such, 9338
  friend and, 7781
Flatterers besieged, by, 3291
  tell him he hates, 4015
Flattering with delicacy, 92
Flattery, is paid with, 2104
  sincerest of, 1018
Flavour, gives it all its, 1082
Flax shall he not quench, 6006
Flea has smaller fleas, 5075
  in his ear, with, 9536
  in March, kill one, 7888
Fleas have little fleas, great, 1171
  killing of, 8496
  rise with, 7707
  to go on, greater, 1171
Fled, all but he had, 1864
  far away, now 'tis, 945
  Him, I, 5313
Flee [run away] fro the prees, 843
  from you, [devil] will, 6272
Flee [fly] stick to the wall, let, 8170
Fleece was white as snow, 1802
Fleet thou canst not see, Spanish, 4897
  was moor'd, 1583
Fleets of iron framed, 1320
  sweep over thee, ten thousand, 626
Flesh and blood so cheap, 1967
  at all, no, 6874
  bring me, 3031
  could not all this, 3879
  creep, make your, 1190
  cut out of thine own, 7978
  fair and unpolluted, 4327
  he that buys, 7532
  how art thou fishified, 3655
  is bruckle, the, 1404
  is grass, all, 6005
  is heir to, that, 4253
  is not venison, all, 6644
  is weak, 6122
  of another, [make], 9520
  of my flesh, 5724
  take off my, 4943
  the sweeter the, 9181
  thorn in, 6242
  what a change of, 188
  which walls about our life, 3695
  will not out of, 9722
  would melt, too solid, 4182

Fleshed, bravely hast thou, 3880
Fleshly School of Poetry, 433
Flies [*insects*] bite sore, hungry, 7776
  catches no, 6429
  dead, 5971
  eagle does not catch, 9022
  not caught with, 6643
  to wanton boys, as, 4510
  will devour you, 8291
  with large blue, 4923
Flies [*moves in air*] an eagle flight, 4686
  wades or creeps or, 2816
Flight, above the vulgar, 3005
  attained by sudden, 2464
  never-ending, 2800
  of the self-same, 3760
  which soonest take, 3054
Fling him, further than I can, 7806
Flint, everlasting, 3659
  in the coldest, 7951
  snore upon, 4701
Flit ere you can point, 525
Flittin, fools are fain of, 7269
Flock, black sheep in, 9300
  infects a whole, 8583
  together, 6949
Flocks are thoughts, her, 2649
  my father feeds, 1940
  of light, in fleecy, 282
Flog a dead horse, to, 9474
Flood, highest, 9113
  into this angry, 4003
  never did good, May, 6553
  plung'd beneath that, 1102
  taken at the, 4052
Floods that are deepest, 6347
Floor, curled up on the, 1836
  I stand on, truly as, 741
  I swept the, 1622
  my fleece-like, 4852
  nicely sanded, 1708
Florence, rode past fair, 2206
Floures in the mede, alle, 845
  love I most these, 845
  white and rede, 845
Flourisheth, so he, 5872
Flourishing like a green bay tree, 5847
Flow, dark as winter was, 708
  how well soe'er, 3292
  like thee, could I, 1172
  so fast, what need you, 6345
Flower, a little western, 3716
  but a little faded 2028
  canst not stir a, 5315
  enjoys the air, every, 5596
  from every opening, 5483
  handsomest, 9103
  Heaven in a wild, 238
  in the crannied wall, 5220
  is born to blush unseen, 1763
  look like the innocent, 4551
  makes no garland, one, 8558
  modest crimson-tippèd, 496
  not pick one, 2661

Flower o' Dumblane, sweet, 5122
  of a blameless life, white, 5250
  of the field, as, 5872
  paints the wayside, 696
  that blows, meanest, 5672
  that never sets, constellated, 4860
  that once has blown, 1501
  that sad embroidery wears, 2752
  that smiles to-day, 1899
  that's like thy face, 4702
  this midsummer, 4913
  tree, fruit and, 2837
  you seize the, 525
Flower-bell, fancy from a, 397
Flower-de-luce being one, 4719
Flower-pots, your damned, 353
Flowers, anew, returning seasons bring, 3141
  appear on the earth, 5985
  are at my feet, see what, 2215
  bring forth May, 8325
  ensnared with, 2589
  for you, here's, 4718
  in May, welcome, as, 6804
  in the garden, 5047
  June, and July, 1896
  of all hue, 2831
  of middle summer, 4718
  of the Forest, 1430
  on chaliced, 4695
  only treads on, 4978
  play with, 3973
  reared that bunch, 344
  shall rise, blushing, 3167
  she comes again, with the, 2410
  strew thy green with, 4694
  that bloom in the spring, 1653
  that grow between, 2443
  that thou let'st fall, 4719
  touch a hundred, 2661
  with fairest, 4702
Flowret of the vale, meanest, 1773
Fluffy, just fluffy, 1884
Flung himself from the room, 2393
Flunked, he never. 1846
Flute, blows out his brains upon, 417
Flutes and soft recorders, 2783
  to the tune of, 4649
Fly [*insect*], blind eat many, 8966
  curious, thirsty, 3070
  hath its spleen, 7164
  I do not want to be a, 1667
  man is not a, 3237
  not worth a, 6594
  said a spider to a, 2032
  sat upon the axletree, 9062
  small gilded. 4517
  that sips treacle, 1593
  you must lose, 9974
Fly [*flee*] him when he comes back, 4753
  to others that we know not of, 4253
  which way shall I, 2826
  with, just enough to, 6811
Flyin'-fishes play, where, 2310

Fool will not give his bauble, 6458
Fool's bolt is soon shot, 6459
Foolish in the fault, 7599
   is wise, least, 9140
   thing, never said, 3390
   to make him, 9059
Foolishness depart from him, will not, 5941
Fools and bairns, 7267
   and madmen, 7268
   are fain of flittin, 7269
   are my theme, 596
   at the wicket, flannelled, 2289
   built on the heads of, 8141
   by shaving, 6394
   contest, let, 3247
   determine, 9901
   discourse of, 6997
   dreading e'en, 3291
   fain, fair words make, 7225
   fortune favours, 7287
   gladly, ye suffer, 6241
   [have] their hearts in their mouths, 9897
   idol of, 7062
   in one house, two, 9621
   it would go hard with, 7867
   [learn] by their own [mistakes], 9898
   mistress of, 7211
   never-failing vice of, 3169
   'od rot 'em, 4924
   repeat [proverbs], 9899
   rush in, 3185
   see these poor, 3130
   shame the, 3285
   should be so deep-contemplative, 4084
   so play, 8154
   the money of, 1916
   the Paradise of, 2824
   these mortals be, what, 3723
   think old men, 9995
   to go under, for, 8231
   to suckle, 4432
   twenty-seven millions, mostly, 750
   went not to market, if, 7828
   who came to scoff, 1703
   wore white caps, if, 7821
   would keep, none but, 4397
   yesterdays have lighted, 4636
Foot, and the Forty-Second, 1957
   depart on, 8359
   feeble of, 270
   for foot, 5754
   for the sole of her, 5732
   foremost, put one's best, 9527
   in the grave, one, 9488
   is better, one, 8560
   keep something for a sore, 8099
   less prompt, 68
   lie at the proud, 3752
   like a cat, 6502
   make crouch beneath, 414
   more light, a, 3491
   ox has trod on, 8965

Foot, pinch, 6895
   shall pass, with shining, 1518
   shoe fits not every, 7197
   slip, better, 6929
   so light a, 3659
   speaks, her, 4371
   was never tied, on fleeter, 3495
Football, all fellows at, 6642
Footfall and the next, between one, 2647
Footing seen, no, 4773
Foot-in-the-grave young man, 1637
Footman, was, 4927
Foot-path way, jog on, 4716
   poor, narrow, 501
Footprints on the sands of time, 2441
Footstep falls, where soft, 192
Footsteps, master's, 9157
Foppery of the world, excellent, 4478
For ever, and for ever, 3196
Forbear and to persevere, 5035
   bear and, 6849
   for Jesus' sake, 4820
   me, down hill, 9642
Forbearance ceases to be a virtue, 459
   is no acquittance, 7280
Forbid a thing, 7281
   it, Almighty God, 1883
   live a man, 4535
Force hidden, great, 9324
   however great, no, 5524
   no argument but, 322
   who overcomes by, 2788
Ford there was none, where, 3478
Forearmed, forewarned, 7282
Forecast, worth a pound of, 6710
Forefathers, the rude, 1756
   think of your, 5
Forehead, middle of her, 2468
   of ivory, 2991
Foreheads villainous low, 4752
   written in, 7195
Foreign hands, by, 3208
   troop was landed, 839
   world, with any portion of, 5473
Foreigners always spell better, 5376
Foremost fighting fell, 612
   none who would be, 2521
Forest dim, fade away into, 2212
   on forest hung about his head, 2229
   primeval, this is, 2457
Forests are rended, when, 3505
   of the night, in, 235
   shook, from the, 4807
Foretell, expiring do, 3683
Foretold, long, 8235
Forever, man has, 388
Forewarned, forearmed, 7282
Forget and smile, better, 3413
   best sometimes, 4438
   best to, 418
   forgive and, 7283
   if thou wilt, 3419
   lest we, 2293
   not yet, 5696

Forget, sometimes useful to, 9733
  thee, if I, 5889
  them all, you'll, 3189
  women and elephants never, 3097
Forgetful be, she may, 1103
Forgetfulness a prey, to dumb, 1767
  not in entire, 5665
  steep my senses in, 3902
  sweets of, 185
Forget-me-nots of the angels, 2458
Forgets, heart that has truly lov'd never, 2957
  himself, he is a fool that, 7459
Forgetting, the world, 3213
Forgive and forget, 7283
  any sooner than thyself, 7284
  divine to, 3183
  good to, 418
  them as a Christian, 94
  them, Father, 6169
  us our debts, 6052
  vengeance is to, 9184
  you, will never, 7548
Forgiveness, ask of thee, 4524
  give—and take, 1513
  to the injured, 1387
Forgot, all the rest, 4785
Forgotten man, the, 3402
  nothing, 5119
  seldom seen, soon, 8761
  soon, 8233
  soon learnt, soon, 8837
Forks and hope, with, 798
Forlorn, make me less, 5659
Form and feature, in, 2412
  and moving how express and admirable, in, 4239
  divine, what [avails], 2368
  lifts its awful, 1705
  mould of, 4260
Former days were better, 5965
  or the latter, 3351
Forms unseen, by, 1009
  vents in mangled, 4086
Forsaken me, why hast thou, 6126
  when he's, 1958
Forspent, clean, 2383
  with love and shame, 2383
Forsworn, so sweetly were, 4405
Fort, hold the, 247
Fortes ante Agamemnona, vixere, 1995
Fortiter in re, 7285
  pecca, 2492
Fortress built by Nature, 3684
Fortunatam natam me consule, 927
Fortunate, I rejoice at it, 4029
  if you are too, 7879
Fortune, adversity of, 252
  and men's eyes, 4786
  and to fame unknown, to, 1769
  architect of his own, 7188
  baggage of, 8714
  beguiling, of, 945
  can take from us, 7286

Fortune favours fools, 7287
  favours the brave, 7288
  gift of, 3941
  good night, 4485
  great, 6493
  has forgot you, 7887
  he that hath no ill, 7579
  in a wife, better a, 6870
  knocks once, 7289
  knocks, when, 9752
  leads on to, 4052
  make a Scotsman's, 9404
  makes better, 7464
  man's best, 6552
  means to men most good, when, 3746
  method of making, 1784
  of another, 9063
  of outrageous, 4253
  ounce of, 6710
  pipes to whom, 7438
  rail'd on Lady, 4080
  sick in, 4478
  smiles, where, 5707
  till heaven hath sent me, 4081
  to fools, God sends, 7345
  troubled with good, 7579
  what is your, 6353
Fortune's buffets and rewards, 4268
  cap we are not the very button, on, 4236
  golden smile, 498
  ice prefers, 1341
  right hand, 7964
Fortunes, pride fell with, 4062
Fortune-teller, juggler and, 3580
Forty, a fool at, 5714
  days it will remain, 8728
  devil at, 6612
  every man at, 7182
  every man over, 4833
  feeding like one, 5621
  knows it at, 5710
  rich at, 7604
  to fifty, from, 3149
  Year, till you come to, 5304
  years on, 270
Forty-nine, nineteen [takes] to, 2267
Forty-three, pass for, 1615
Forward and not back, look, 1801
  those behind cried, 2521
Fou for weeks thegither, 523
  I was na, 480
  o' love divine, 482
Fought, from morn till even, 3978
  so long, he had, 3698
  with us upon St. Crispin's day, 3992
Foul, frost and fraud both end in, 7300
  is fair, 4533
  strange, and unnatural, 4215
  thank the gods I am, 4106
Found, all they ever, 3387
  Him in the shining of the stars, 5266
  it, I have, 44
  less often sought than, 673

Found me, hast thou, 5800
  out by accident, 2362
  while he may be, 6012
Foundation, low, 6505
Foundations quiver, hell's, 150
Fount, meander level with, 2941
Fountain, cast dirt into, 8417
  fill'd with blood, 1102
  heads, 1534
  like the bubble on, 3496
  troubled, like a, 3592
Fountain's murmuring wave, 184
  silvery column, 988
Fountains, Afric's sunny, 1860
  sad, 6345
  under the, 6347
Founts falling, white, 880
  level with their, 2507
Four eyes see more, 7291
  for a birth, 8561
  grant that twice two be not, 5374
Four-footed things, of all, 892
Fourscore, witch at, 6612
Fourth estate of the realm, 2506
  [glass] for madness, 9058
Fowl and mushrooms, 1186
  concerning wild, 4164
Fowles maken melodys, smale, 847
Fowls have fair feathers, far, 7230
Fox fares best when he is cursed, 9069
  if thou dealest with, 7871
  is brought to the furrier, 6822
  is not taken twice, 6462
  knows much, 9070
  may grow grey, 9071
  needs no craft, old, 6700
  preaches, when, 9778
  preys farthest, 9072
  than that of the, 250
Fox's sermon, comes to, 7996
  [skin] shall, 7858
  wiles, 9073
Foxes have holes, 6073
  take us the, 5986
  that spoil the vines, 5986
Frailties, draw his, 1771
Frailty, thy name is woman, 4185
Frame began, universal, 1368
  stirs this mortal, 992
  tremble for this lovely, 5529
France, I saw the Queen of, 464
  order this matter better in, 5018
  sun rises bright in, 1129
  vasty fields of, 3963
  win, he that will, 7674
Francesca di Rimini, 1636
Frank, haughty, rash, 2501
Frankie and Johnny were lovers, 6360
Frater, ave atque vale, 815
Fraud, frost and, 7300
Fray, beginning of, 6894
  second [blow] makes, 9054
Fredome is a nobill thing, 136
Free as Nature first made man, 1386

Free, from God he could not, 1448
  in my soul am, 2472
  know our will is, 2134
  man is born, 3429
  neither man or beast would ever go,
    7844
  or die, we must be, 5633
  should himself be, 2160
  that moment they are, 1079
  the fresh, the ever, 3339
  they for to be, 3458
  thou art, 53
  till all are free, no one can be perfectly,
    4974
  truth shall make you, 6178
  yearning to breathe, 2392
Freed, thousands He hath, 826
Freedom and truth, fight for, 2051
  and whiskey gang thegither, 492
  flame of, 5109
  infringement of, 3150
  new birth of, 2421
  obtained I this, 6201
  ring, let, 4933
  service is perfect, 6301
  shall awhile repair, 1009
  shrieked—as Kosciusko fell, 699
  slowly broadens down, 5158
  to the free, assure, 2420
  to the slave, in giving, 2420
  yet thy banner, 622
Freedom's cause, bled in, 1981
Freely ye have received, 6076
Freeman casting . . . vote, 1935
Freemen, who rules o'er, 2160
Freeze the pot, Janiveer, 8086
French, if he could speak, 8085
  or Turk, or Proosian, 1626
  [wise] after the deed, 9125
Frenchman, a fort, 7948
  I praise the, 1063
Frenchmen, did march three, 3981
  sent below, ten thousand, 3115
Frensh of Paris was to hir unknowe, 851
  she spak ful faire, 851
Frenzy, demoniac, 2879
  rolling, in a fine, 3730
  zeal without prudence is, 10008
Fresh and strong, through Thee, 5649
  benefits please while, 6865
Freshness, dewy, 4957
Fret, living, we, 418
Friar, Apollo turned fasting, 2640
  many a, 140
Friars, white, black and grey, 2823
Fricassee or a ragout, in, 5082
Friday, born on, 6962
  for losses, 8363
  he that sings on, 7656
  sneeze on, 8821
Friday's child, 8364
Friend, a fav'rite has no, 1753
  a suspicious, 3291
  accomplished female, 5547

U

Generation passeth away, one, 5952

Generations, takes three, 3119

  tread thee down, 2217

Generous, be just before you are, 6843

Génie n'est autre chose, 438

Genius and the mortal instruments, 4012

  does what it must, 2503

  found respectable, 333

  I had, what a, 5087

  is one per cent, inspiration, 1409

  kindles, true, 3291

  nothing to declare except, 5566

  was such, whose, 1713

Genteel, no dancing bear was so, 1053

Gentes, multas per, 814

Gentil knight, parfit, 849

Gentiles use, boastings as, 2294

Gentility, a cottage of, 991, 4968

  is but ancient riches, 7306

  without ability, 7307

Gentle as falcon, 4913

Gentleman and scholar, 491

  education begins, 7156

  at least, is a, 890

  grand old name of, 5235

  Jack would be, 8085

  knight but not, 9128

  main purpose in life is to be, 5437

  man who is always talking about being, 5072

  nomination of, 4337

  prince of darkness is, 4503

  the first true, 1162

  to make a, 3119

  who was then the, 130

Gentlemanly position, mouth and throat in, 5437

Gentlemen and Ladies, was, 1259

  go by, while the, 2339

  God Almighty's, 1351

  great-hearted, 346

  of England, ye, 3099

  were not seamen, 2517

Gently, use all, 4262

Gentry sent to market, 7308

  tail of, 6890

Genus irritabile vatum, 2004

  omne, hoc, 1983

Geography is about maps, 208

Γεωμετρίαν, βασιλικὴν ἀτραπὸν ἐπί, 1459

Geometry, no royal road to, 1459

George the First was always reckoned vile, 2374

[George] the Fourth descended, when from earth, 2374

George the Second, but viler, 2374

George the Third, 210, 1881

  any good of, 2374

Georges ended, the, 2374

Georgia, marching through, 5687

Γηράσκω δ' αἰεὶ πολλὰ διδασκόμενος, 4951

German [Teuton] Hermann's a, 3320

  lairdie, wee wee, 1132

German [germane] to the matter, more, 4339

German's wit, 9081

Germans in Greek are sadly to seek, 3320

  [wise] in the deed, 9125

Germany over all, 1922

Germens spill at once, all, 4490

Gert and there's Epp and there's Ein, 6373

Gert's poems are bunk, 6373

Gesetz werden, Maxime solle ein allgemeines Gesetz, 2195

Gesture dignity and love, in every, 2863

Get what you want, 4930

Getting and spending, 5658

  up late, habit of, 796

Gets, bargain where nobody, 7994

Ghost of him, make a, 4212

  of the mourning, 1278

  some old lover's, 1288

  stubborn unlaid, 2728

  there needs no, 4224

  to each frustrate, 392

  vex not his, 4531

  what beckoning, 3206

  will walk, your, 361

Ghosts from an enchanter fleeing, 4844

  they have deposed, haunted by, 3695

Giant dies, as when a, 4399

  dies, the, 1786

  tyrannous to use it like, 4393

Giant's shoulder, on, 6448

  strength, excellent to have, 4393

Giants in the earth, there were, 5731

Gibes, great master of, 1268

  now, where be your, 4324

Giddy, I am, 4365

Giff gaff makes good friends, 7310

Gift, cheaper than, 9721

  long waited for, 6470

  which God has given, 3466

Giftie gie us, wad some Power, 495

Gifts, gives me small, 7561

Gods themselves cannot recall, 5166

  when they bring, 5413

  will not be distributed as, 933

Gig, crew of the captain's, 1612

Gilding pale streams, 4790

  would not want, 7862

Gilead, balm in, 6016

Gill, hang by its own, 7177

Gilpin, away went, 1073

  was a citizen, John, 1070

Gilt first, try your skill in, 9609

  off the gingerbread, take, 9550

Ginger shall be hot i' the mouth, 4142

Gingerbread, gilt off, 9550

Giraffe, neck of the, 759

Girdle, at one man's, 6663

Girl, an unlesson'd, 3793

  cleanly young, 3317

  goes walking, not a, 1329

  in the corps de bally, 1633

  in the kiss of one, 422

Good thing is soon snatched up, 6488
thing that I can do, 1790
time coming. 2536, 9313
to do, know what were, 3762
to me, he wos wery, 1245
to me is lost, all, 2827
to me, never done no, 2317
to nobody, 7601
to stark naught, from little, 9459
to us, portend no, 4477
tourne, whose doth us, 2976
trust that somehow, 5227
we oft might win, lose, 4386
will be the final goal, 5227
will toward men, 6138
will, won my right, 2544
work together for, 6211
you can, do all the, 5517
you'll do, little, 1413
Good-bye, and so, 1402
Goodliest man, Adam the, 2834
Goodman is from home, when, 9779
is the last who knows, 9086
saith, so say we, as, 6792
Goodness and the grace, thank, 5127
does disdain comparison, 2606
from fear and also from, 3146
in things evil, 3983
is, how awful, 2842
never fearful, 4403
Goods, all my worldly, 2402
are theirs who enjoy them, 7372
conceited, 7034
ill-gotten, 7919, 7920
not [cheat] in, 7000
who gives away his, 9843
with all my worldly, 6319
Goodwife saith, so must it be, as 6792
Goose go barefoot, see, 8052
is plucked, 7237
it is a silly, 7996
it will not bear, 7856
lay, will a good, 8541
royal game of, 1709
sauce for, 9727
say Bo to, 7431
that lays the golden eggs, 9498
three women and, 9410
to kill, 9498
wild, 6607
Gordian knot of it, 3965
Gore, avenge the patriotic, 3371
Gored several persons, 262
Gorgonised me from head to foot, 5213
Gorgons and Hydras, 2808
Gormed, I'm, 1241
Gorse is out of bloom, 9780
Gosling, shoe, 9858
Gospel, preach, 6137
true as, 6798
Gossip pines, pines are, 1523
Gossiping and lying, 7373
Gossips, gadding, 7302
meet, merry when, 8047

Got over, that was, 6329
so gone, so, 8822
Gotham, wise as a man of, 6808
Gotham's three Wise Men, 3117
Gotte helfe mir, 2491
Gotter vergebens kämpfen, 3456
Gott-trunkener Mensch, 3056
Γούνασι κεῖται, θεῶν ἐν, 1950
Gout, combined with, 1660
drink none, and have, 7133
drink wine and have, 7138
or stone, without, 3317
Gouvernement qu'elle mérite, 2547
Govern others, that would, 2607
reigns but does not, 5719
wrong, right to, 3226
Governed, the world is, 3087
Government at Washington still lives,
1575
can be long secure, no, 1272
essence of free, 681
exists, world, 5510
for forms of, 3247
highest form of, 4977
is impossible, 1266
it deserves, has, 2547
land of settled, 5158
of the people, 2421
Gowans fine, pu'd the, 511
Gowd for a' that, man's the, 546
Gower, O moral, 844
Gowk another mile, hunt, 8540
Gown and a hood, peascod would make,
7820
burns, whose, 9712
by the gateway haunts, 3348
is his that wears it, 9087
like a satin, 3094
of glory, 3361
oft worn, 6532
pluck'd his, 1704
puts on a public, 7643
Gowns, one that hath two, 3957
Gr-r-r—you swine, 355
Grace and strength, give us, 5035
bear's ethereal, 759
does it with a better, 4141
for comely, 6346
for sweet attractive, 2832
full of, 8364, 8883
full of God's, 6962
guide it, except, 8121
in space comes, 7949
inward and spiritual, 6313
is given of God, 935
is sufficient, my, 6243
of a day, tender, 5186
of God, but for, 271
of God is gear enough, 9088
quarrel with the noblest, 4745
their God—His, 504
to have thy Princes, 4989
to use it so, if I have, 2681
was in all her steps, 2863

Graceful and humane, in act, 2796
Graces, inherit heaven's, 4804
Gracious unto thee, be, 5757
Gradum, revocare, 5424
Grain at a breath, reaps, 2443
  of evil, 8510
  will grow, say which, 4538
Grammar, heedless of, 142
Gramophone, puts a record on, 1424
Grampian hills, on the, 1940
Granary floor, careless on, 2228
Grand and comfortable, baith, 162
Grandchild, his little, 4961
Grandmother, may not marry, 6328
  teach your, 8918
Grandsire, sit like his, 3756
Grange, at the moated, 4404
Grant, rude, 6428
Grants it, more fool that, 9064
Grape, devil in every berry of, 9312
  that can . . . Sects confute, 1507
Grapes are sour, 9089
  blood of lusty, 1531
  fathers have eaten sour, 6020
  of wrath are stored, 2029
Grapeshot, a whiff of, 745
Grapple them to thy soul, 4200
Grasp all, lose all, 7374
  it like a man, 1913
  reach should exceed, 394
Grass above me, green, 3419
  destroy a blade of, 264
  from under, cut, 9466
  grow in Janiveer, if, 7855
  grows on the weirs, as, 5703
  grows, while, 9834
  I fall on, 2589
  in the sunny, 2044
  is green, that, 5011
  kissed the lovely, 294
  star-scatter'd on, 1518
  to grow, two blades of, 5079
  turned out to, 4922
  was cut out of the, 891
Grasshopper shall be a burden, 5978
Grasshoppers, wings of, 3635
Grave [*tomb*], a little little, 3696
  a tear, drop on his, 2352
  adorn'd, thy humble, 3208
  as a carpet hang upon, 4694
  as now my bed, on my, 320
  between the cradle and the, 1408
  but she is in her, 5611
  dark and silent, 3365
  dig the, 5048
  Duncan is in his, 4591
  earliest at His, 158
  funeral marches to, 2439
  ghost come from, 4224
  is lying, her heart in his, 2962
  is not its goal, 2438
  kind of healthy, 4937
  lead but to the, 1759
  methought I saw, 3362

Grave, now in his colde, 867
  of Mike O'Day, 6378
  one foot in, 9488
  one small, 756
  pompous in the, 319
  secrets of the, 3106
  seek out a soldier's, 673
  shall lead theee to thy, 5651
  shine sweetly on my, 184
  sleeping enough in, 9349
  straight and dusty to, 5022
  strew'd thy, 4330
  sweeten thy sad, 4702
  that I may dread, 2247
  the nearer thy, 9173
  there lies a lonely, 35
  turn in his, 9516
  upon his mother's, 5614
  where is thy victory, 6236
  with one's teeth, dig, 9469
  with sorrow to the, 5744
  without a, 627
  you'll cough in, 7884
Grave [*serious*] and reverend signiors, 4415
  to gay, steer from, 3256
  to light, from, 1380
Grave's a fine and private place, 2588
Graves are sever'd, their, 1866
  find ourselves dishonourable, 4005
  let's talk of, 3694
  lie all alike in, 9693
  of the martyrs, about, 5056
  stood tenantless, 4171
  under the, 6347
Gravity, [only test] of humour, 3535
Grease, fry in one's own, 9475
Great and small, attends, 5583
  and small, creatures, 32
  and small, things both, 977
  and the little, 9090
  bodies move slowly, 7377
  far above the, 1778
  is to be misunderstood, to be, 1437
  know well I am not, 5259
  man helped the poor, 2520
  men are . . . bad men, 2
  men go, streets where, 1524
  men have not commonly been scholars, 1939
  men, lives of, 2441
  men reached, heights by, 2464
  men would have care of little ones, if, 7829
  men's sons, 7378
  ones eat up the little, 4693
  ones, there would be no, 9350
  produce anything, 3377
  rightly to be, 4307
  rule of men entirely, 2499
  some are born, 4151
  that he is grown so, 4006
  that which once was, 5629
  thing to pursue, 389

Great was ever achieved, nothing, 1441
  when some occasion is presented,
    always, 1394
  would have none great, 9091
Greater still, and so on, 1171
  than they are, makes mine, 4050
Greatest event, how much, 1551
  happiness for the greatest numbers,
    2047
  men, world knows nothing of, 5129
Greatness, farewell to all my, 4760
  far-off touch of, 5259
  in me there dwells no, 5259
  is a-ripening, 4760
  some achieve, 4151
  thrust upon 'em, some have, 4151
Greece, Athens. the eye of, 2892
  bulwark of, 3148
  fulmin'd over, 2894
  glory that was, 3162
  Italy, and England, 1367
  might still be free, 660
  the direful spring, to, 3203
  the isles of, 659
Greedy folk have long arms, 7386
  of filthy lucre, 6259
Greek, he could speak, 561
  manuscripts, brown, 395
  meets Greek, when, 9753
  said it in German and, 797
  Sir, is like lace, 2157
  small Latin and less, 2173
  to me, it is, 8028
Greeks, I fear the, 5413
  joined Greeks, when, 2409
Green, heard on the, 234
  knaves in Kendal, 3845
  night, lamps in a, 2584
  peculiar tint of yellow, 993
  sported on the, 4961
  thought in a green shade, 2590
  tree, do these things in, 6169
  trip upon the, 4773
  winter, 6495
Greenhouse too, loves a, 1084
Greenland's icy mountains, 1860
Green-sward, single on, 2625
Greet [salute] thee, how should I, 595
Greet [weep], bairn that dare not, 7993
  better bairns, 6878
  it gars me, 522
Greets, no play where one, 8053
Grenadier, Hampshire, 6375
  Who comes here ? A, 1254
Grenadiers of Austria, 1318
Greta woods are green, 3500
Grew, as fixed as if it, 993
  together, so we, 3724
Grey, but not with years, 640
  my gallant, 3488
Greyhound, this fawning, 3829
Greyhounds in the slips, 3979
Griddle, hen on a hot, 8194
Grief, acquainted with, 6009

    *U

Grief and laughter little while with, 2575
  and pain, after long, 5249
  canker and the, 672
  enough for thee, 1788
  every one can master a, 3939
  fills the room up, 3744
  is past, 431
  or pleasure, look for them in, 7903
  perk'd up in a glistering, 4757
  plague of sighing and, 3849
  should be past, 4711
  silent manliness of, 1711
  smiling at, 4149
  summons, 7665
  tame the strongest, 9415
  that does not speak, 4621
  with proverbs, patch, 3958
  without some, 8439
Griefs, [friendships] divide, 7296
  still am I king of, 3700
  that bow, 54
  that harass, all, 2085
Grieve, it is too late to, 8070
Grieving, Margaret are you, 1979
Grig, merry as, 6753
Grimes is dead, old, 1787
Grin, he own'd with a, 4968
  so merry, every, 5584
  vanquish Berkeley by, 308
  wears one universal, 1482
Grind, one demd horrid, 1211
  or find. either, 7798
  slowly, mills of God, 2456
Grinder, who serenely grindest, 686
Grinds He all, with exactness, 2456
  lower millstone, 9150
Grindstone, keep one's nose to, 9495
  Newcastle, 6578
Groan, condemn'd alike to, 1750
  with bubbling, 627
Groat, cannot change, 9840
  is ill saved, 9099
  saves, 9192
  shall never want, 7672
Grooves, down the ringing, 5174
  in determinate, 1825
Gropes in the dark, he that, 7566
Gross to sink, not, 4773
Grossness, losing all its, 466
Ground between, much, 8958
  choose thy, 673
  fathom-line could never touch, 3828
  from under, cut, 9466
  he that lies on, 7612
  I see thee stare, up-on, 868
  make not balks of good, 8286
  not fail, solid, 5240
  on the holy, 3029
  plat of rising, 2704
  purple all the, 2752
  rise from the, 3870
  to a more removed, 4210
  to shades of under, 718
Groundlings, split the ears of, 4263

Hands, I warm'd both, 2371
  large and sinewy, 2446
  lift up your, 6361
  little folding of, 5898
  many, 8310
  more work than both, 9039
  of fellowship, right, 6244
  off other folks' bairns, hold your, 7746
  often, wash, 9676
  oozing out at the palms of, 4890
  organs, dimensions, 3785
  spit in your, 8863
  strikes with iron, 7333
  take the law into one's own, 9551
  that the rod of empire might have
    sway'd, 1762
  to do, for idle, 5484
  upon themselves, laid violent, 6321
  wave their, 2058
  were never made, little, 5481
  will soon wring their, 5449
  with crooked, 5181
  with empty, 9904
  without falling into, 218
  worth two pairs of, 8582
Handsome about him, every thing, 3957
  at twenty, 7604
  in three hundred pounds a-year, looks,
    4355
  is that handsome does, 7395
  well-shaped man, 81
  will never be, 7604
Handsomer far, others are, 1463
Handy-dandy, change places, 4519
Hang him, give a dog a bad name and,
  7312
  himself, he'll, 7316
  lowest, that bear most, 8969
  myself to-day, will not, 886
  on him, she would, 4184
  themselves in hope, 1570
  together, we must all, 1556
  wretches, 3193
  wrong fler than no fler, better, 1247
  you, we will, 1643
  yourself, you would, 2137
Hanged, Almost was never, 6672
  as well be, 6807
  born to be, 7594
  confess and be, 7035
  ere noon, that is, 7513
  half, 7574
  himself, in his house that, 8391
  knows he is to be, 2151
  sorry he is to be, 9257
  that left his drink, 7703
  told his father was, 7704
Hanging and wiving, 7397
  of his cat, 274
  prevents a bad marriage, good, 4133
  want nothing but, 9353
Hangs my dear, rope that, 1591
Hanner, lost our little, 22
Hap and a halfpenny, 7398

Hap, good or ill, 9085
  some have, 8830
Happens not in seven years, 7971
Happier than I know, feel that I am, 2862
  things, remembering, 5169
Happiest women have no history, 1416
Happiness for the greatest numbers,
  greatest, 2047
  emblem of, 1925
  from life, get some, 6379
  great task of, 5050
  is no laughing matter, 5523
  is produced, so much, 2146
  lifetime of, 4826
  our being's end, 3248
  pursuit of, 2071
  right to consume, 4821
  talks much of, 7665
  through another man's eyes, 4119
  too swiftly flies, 1750
  without producing it, consume, 4821
  wreck of, 638
Happy and glorious, 6351
  angry and poor and, 884
  as a lover, 5656
  as kings, all be as, 5045
  but when he is miserable, never, 6687
  could I be with either, 1594
  duty of being, 5029
  fields, farewell, 2773
  for a day, would be, 8164
  for you, it is, 92
  he who crowns, 1697
  human race was most, 1602
  I were but little, 3931
  in his children, 7399
  in nothing else so, 3688
  is he, 7399, 7400
  is he born and taught, 5689
  man be his dole, 7405
  swains, Muses sing of, 1107
  than wise, better be, 6884
  that thinks himself so, 7472
  the man, 1381, 3142, 3165
  those that were good shall be, 2285
  till all are, 4974
  till he dies, call no man, 6986
  time when we were, 1139
  to have been, 252
  which of us is, 5295
  who has once been, 249
Harass'd, to attain, too, 58
Harbinger, perfume her, 2903
Hard as a piece of the nether millstone,
  5827
  nothing's so, 1905
  times, come again, 1547
  with hard, 7407
Hardens a' within, it, 497
Harder thing, hast borne, 1954
Hardest to bear, 9035
Hardy became a sort of village atheist,
  898
Hare, as thou woldest finde, 868

Heart to glow, made my, 4972
  to heart, and mind to mind, 3466
  to move, your, 3394
  to poke poor Billy, 1736
  to resolve, 1604
  to soften another man's, 5364
  untainted, 3542
  untravell'd fondly turns, 1682
  upon my sleeve, wear, 4411
  upon one's sleeve, 9565
  was as that of a little child, 5300
  was in the sea, my, 153
  was like to break, my, 153
  way to an Englishman's, 9276
  weighs upon the, 4631
  which others bleed for, 1024
  whispers the o'erfraught, 4621
  winning each, 1180
  with an angry. 7453
  with pleasure fills, 5646
  with words, unpack my, 4250
  within, a warm, 1093
  within, and God o'erhead, 2440
  within blood-tinctured, 323
  would break, 7830
  would fain deny, 4630
  would hear her and beat, 5248
Heart's core, rest at, 3415
  core, wear him in, 4269
  Desire, nearer to, 1517
  in the Highlands, 518
  letter, 9108
  undoing, my, 2967
Heart-ache, end the, 4253
Hearth, a clean, 2354
  and stool and all, 1020
  from his lonely, 5682
Hearths, sweep their, 1035
Hearts are dry as summer dust, 5674
  are light, somewhere, 5307
  are more than coronets, kind, 5152
  are yearning, while, 1541
  beat happily, thousand, 609
  endure, that human, 2098
  ensanguined, 1087
  gentle, makes all, 8267
  humble, 7769
  in love use their own tongues, 3930
  in their mouths, 9897
  may agree, 7724
  men with Splendid, 297
  now broken, cheerful, 2969
  of his countrymen, first in, 2407
  other lips and other, 441
  quell the stubborn, 5144
  sweetness that inspired, 2560
  that beat as one, two, 2473
  that hate thee, cherish, 4764
  that yearn, finite, 369
  though stout and brave, 2439
  unto wisdom, apply, 5869
  we leave behind, live in, 713
  who have stout, 221
Heart-strings prove it, 1039

Heart-throbs, count time by, 124
Heat, fantastic summer's, 3682
  me these irons hot, 3747
  that melts the wax, 9218
Heated than new made, sooner, 8534
Heath, a wind on the, 259
  on my native, 3516
Heathen in his blindness, 1862
  rage, why do the, 5829
  to break the, 5263
Heather looks, know I how, 1258
Heave and the halt and the hurl, 2270
Heaven a perfect round, in, 401
  airs from, 4207
  all [hours] to, 2167
  all that we believe of, 3078
  and a new earth, new, 6286
  and Charing Cross, betwixt, 5317
  and earth, differ as, 5256
  and earth, more things in, 4226
  and earth shall pass away, 3469
  and earth, unfolds both, 3707
  and home, kindred points of, 5679
  and in hell, friends both in, 8027
  and the first earth were passed away,
    first, 6286
  approving, 5323
  are cast, to pitying, 3197
  as the great eye of, 4984
  betwixt, breadth of, 330
  blessed part to, 4766
  breaks the serene of, 4957
  candidate of, 1364
  climbing, 4861
  doth with us as we with torches, 4383
  drowsy, make, 3615
  ever-moving spheres of, 2565
  fairer person lost not, 2796
  fall, though, 7246
  first-born, offspring of, 2819
  for climate, 160
  for, what's a, 394
  from all creatures hides the book of
    Fate, 3232
  gained from, 1770
  garden hard by, 267
  God's in his, 342
  gold bar of, 3421
  house as nigh, 2977
  how he fell from, 2790
  husbandry in, 4565
  I'm farther off from, 1960
  in a rage, puts, 239
  in a sedan, going to, 9331
  in a wild flower, 238
  in rags, go to, 6902
  in the nurseries of, 5312
  infinite meadows of, 2458
  into the kingdom of, 6096
  is above all yet, 4759
  is easily made, Persian's, 2950
  is he in, 3073
  is not, wherever, 7727
  is thick inlaid, 3809

Heaven itself that points out, 14
itself would stoop to her, 2737
ladders to, 7055
leave her to, 4220
lies about us, 5665
little souls to, 1469
on earth, 2830
on the walls of, 2561
of all their wish, 298
of hell, make a, 2774
open face of, 2199
or to hell, summons thee to, 4570
quit the port o', 3039
sends ane to, 479
smiles, 4875
than serve in, 2775
that leads men to this hell, 4816
there may be, 381
these the gems of, 2837
this is the gate of, 5740
thorny way to, 4199
those who win, 371
to earth, glance from, 3730
too, souls in, 2225
tries the earth, 2478
turns in the wards of, 5314
was falling, when, 2026
we are all going to, 1573
ween there is none other, 9367
which we ascribe to, 4376
who spits against, 9864
Heaven's, any gate except, 7349
gates, at, 2495
glories shine, see, 292
height, blue, 2648
jewelled crown, in, 2530
last best gift, 2846
light forever shines, 4866
street, in, 2604
wide champain, through, 2855
wide pathless way, 2703
Heavens above that plain, starry, 5333
clothed with the, 5355
declare the glory of God, 5837
does dwell, who in, 479
fill with shouting, 5170
from the blue, 1674
look bright, the, 2964
most ancient, 5649
pure as the naked, 5632
spangled, 8
were to break, if, 1993
with black, hung be, 3536
Heavy as frost, 5667
loads on thee, many, 1464
on him, Earth, lie, 1464
Hebrides, among the farthest, 5635
in dreams behold, 6356
Hecuba to him, what's, 4248
Hedge, alang the flow'ry, 5123
between, a, 6504
for to hide it in, 498
is lowest, where, 8346
low, 6529

Hedge, may not look over, 8574
pull not down your, 8275
under an old, 8020
Hedgehogs dressed in lace, 1931
Hedgerows, with the wild, 200
Hedges, unkempt about those, 295
Heed is a good rede, take, 8898
too much taking, 9580
Heel, trust not a horse's, 9592
Heels, trips up his own, 7416
Height, city of dreadful, 257
grandeur cloth'd, 3473
my soul can reach, 332
nor depth, nor, 6213
Heights by great men reached, 2464
Heir, for want of, 8131
makes the doctor, 7462
she is become my, 7782
thrive not to the third, 7920
Helen, and the rest, 718
lies, I wish I were where, 6337
like another, 1375
make me immortal, 2563
of Troy, mother of, 3106
thy beauty is to me, 3161
Helen's beauty, sees, 3730
eye, dust hath closed, 3025
Hell and Chancery, 7725
and ten to, 479
begin raising, 2406
better to reign in, 2775
blasts from, 4207
broke loose, all, 2843   [1514
daub his Visage with the Smoke of,
down, down to, 3556
fire, be cast into, 6098
fire, in danger of, 6045
for company, 160
for company, go to, 9342
gape not, ugly, 2567
grew darker at their frown, 2813
[has] a fury like a woman scorn'd, nor,
1023
Hull, and Halifax, 7298
I suffer seems a heav'n, 2826
if I owned Texas and, 4882
in embroidery, [go to], 6902
is a city, 4849
is full of good meanings, 7726
is paved, road to, 9214
is wherever heaven is not, 7727
it is, what, 4989
itself breathes out contagion, 4283
leads men to this, 4816
leads up to light, out of, 2803
make a heav'n of, 2774
myself am, 2826
never mentions, 3280
no fans in, 9307
no redemption from, 9337
on earth, it would be, 4826
opens, when war begins, 9798   [4619
pour the sweet milk of concord into,
shall not prevail against it, 6093

Highest, we needs must love, 5265
Highgate Hill, down the, 170
Highland scab and hunger, 505
Highlands bound, to the, 703
  in the, 5054
  my heart's in, 518
Highly, what thou wouldst, 4548
Highway is never about, 9114
Highwayman came riding, 3061
Highways and hedges, go out into, 6152
Hill, city that is set on, 6043
  comes first to, 7540
  do on the, 7121
  down the Highgate, 170
  laughing is heard on, 234
  mine be a cot beside, 3398
  mine be the breezy, 184
  of yon high eastward, 4176
  on a heaven-kissing, 4292
  on the windy, 294
  other side of, 5505
  retir'd, sat on a, 2804
  shall never get over, 7660
  spare me, up, 9642
  there is a green, 34
  to sit upon a, 3551
  to the top of the, 6354
  torrent is heard on, 185
  vale discovereth, 9273
  with green hath clad, 5067
Hills, amid the, 2010
  and far away, o'er, 5176
  and valleys, 2572
  blow upon high, 7385
  hillmen desire their, 2271
  look over on the South, 5310
  of the South Country, 195
  old as, 6760
  on moors and windy, 2601
  on the Grampian, 1940
  peep o'er hills, 3171
  the great black, 115
  these high wild, 3687
  to the reverberate, 4136
  upon a thousand, 5855
  we shall fight in the, 908
  whose heads touch heaven, 4421
Hill-side's dew-pearled, 342
Himmel weht, vom blauen, 1674
Hind that would be mated by the lion, 4375
Hindmost, devil take, 9014
Hinds shall bring, village, 1014
  soil'd by rude, 1113
Hinge nor loop, no, 4454
Hinges grate, on their, 2814
  what it heard of, 9100
Hint a fault, just, 3291
  a matter's inwardness, 2326
Hip and thigh, smote them, 5774
  catch him once upon, 3766
  I have thee on the, 3904
Hippoclides does not care, 1914
Hippocrene, the blushful, 2212

Hippopotamus, it was a, 801
Hips and haws, many, 8312
Hire, worthy of his, 6142
Hired the money, they, 1034
  to fight, may be, 8137
Hireling fleeth becuse he is an hireling, 6180
  to a state, 2105
Histories make men wise, 118
History, country which has no, 7403
  dignity of, 254
  dust-heap called, 222
  is but the biography of great men, 747
  is philosophy, 1261
  repeats itself, 7744
  strange eventful, 4090
  there is properly no, 1435
  what's her, 4149
  which is . . . register of the crimes, 1601
Hit, a very palpable, 4341
  from far, [love] can, 1894
  it off, the two, 5594
Hitch your wagon to a star, 1445
Hither, as their coming, 4523
Hits, he that once, 7635
Hive for the honey-bee, 5704
Hoarding went to hell, for, 3550
Hoards, he that has two, 7571
Hoarse or mute, unchang'd to, 2858
Hobbes clearly proves, 5074
Hobbs hints blue, 375
Hoe, leans upon his, 2555
  take a large, 2334
  with outstretch'd, 1067
Hog, ah could eat, 2643
  at all, no, 6913
  dirty home, better my, 6913
  he that hath one, 7582
  kill, 7905
  never looks up, 9116
  the fattest, 2605
  what can you expect from, 9715
Hogs in the dark, drive black, 8042
Hoist with his own petar, 4301
' Hold, enough,' first cries, 4643
  fast that which is good, 6258
  fast when you have it, 7745
  if one break, the other may, 7361
  or drive, himself must, 7533
  out this year, 8349
  take better, 8863
  that will away, 9857
  the fort, 247
  yourself so, 9802
Holdfast is a better [dog], 6969
  is the only dog, 3975
Holds thee, guess now who, 331
Hole, at a little, 8577
  calls the thief, 9117
  farthest from his, 9072
  has but one, 9180
  if wind blows on you through, 7874
  in a' your coats, 517

Honour and ease, 7756
  and profit, 7757
  and the sea, 211
  ceases, where, 9812
  comes, a pilgrim, 1009
  doth forget, new-made, 3738
  for his valour, 4029
  from me, take, 3673
  greater share of, 3987
  hath no skill in surgery, 3876
  he that desires, 7545
  if it be a sin to covet, 3988
  in one eye, set, 4001
  is a mere scutcheon, 3876
  is my life, mine, 3673
  is the subject of my story, 4002
  jealous in, 4090
  king delighteth to, 5807
  lain, in the bed of, 577
  love, obedience, 4630
  more cost, more, 9166
  more danger, more, 9166
  more, loved I not, 2471
  nation of men of, 464
  no profit to, 8466
  not without, 6089
  not worthy of, 7545
  peace I hope with, 1269
  peereth, so, 3591
  pluck up drowned, 3828
  pricks me on, 3876
  razed, from the book of, 4785
  rooted in dishonour, 5260
  set a leg, can, 3876
  that chastity of, 465
  to pluck bright, 3828
  we cannot come to, 9685
  while you strike him down, 3041
  will buy no beef, 7758
  without profit, 7759
Honour's at the stake, when, 4307
  truckle-bed, lie in, 577
  voice provoke, can, 1761
Honourable man, Brutus is, 4031
  men, so are they all, 4031
Honours, bears his blushing, 4760
  change manners, 7760
  mindless of its just, 5680
  perish, piled-up, 356
  thick upon him, 4760
  to the world, gave his, 4766
Hood, hair grows through, 7739
  him that wears a, 5057
Hoods witless, painted, 8234
Hook, bait hides, 8944
  draw out leviathan with, 5826
  for subscribers baits, 905
  or by crook, by, 6979
  through his mouth, put, 5455
Hook's well lost, 6507
Hoop, times of hood and, 5160
Hooping, out of all, 4098
Hoot, come from Rome al, 863
Hop forty paces, saw her, 4650

Hope abandon, all, 1136
  again, never to, 4761
  and fear set free, from, 5101
  and Glory, land of, 206
  bade the world farewell, 699
  break it to our, 4641
  but not another's, 5452
  clung feeding, 996
  [days] spent without, 5813
  deferred, 5906
  dream untroubled of, 3040
  elevates his crest, 2873
  fool'd with, 1388
  for the best, 7761
  for years to come, 5486
  he that lives in, 7614
  he who would not be frustrate of, 2910
  in sure and certain, 6324
  is a good breakfast, 7762
  is a lover's staff, 7763
  is as cheap as despair, 7764
  is better, my, 4160
  is but the dream, 3332
  is coldest, hits where, 4377
  is swift, true, 3572
  is the poor man's bread, 7765
  less quick to spring, 68
  like the gleaming taper's light, 1720
  men set their hearts upon, 1496
  more rich in, 4787
  never comes that comes to all, 2769
  no other medicine but, 4396
  nursing unconquerable, 65
  phantoms of, 2106
  pursued it with forks and, 798
  repose, in trembling, 1771
  springs eternal, 3234
  thou not much, 5108
  to feed on, 4989
  well and have well, 7766
  were not, if, 7830
  what is, 755
  whence this pleasing, 14
  while there is life there is, 9837
  white-handed, 2721
  who lives by, 9854
Hope's true gage, 3361
Hoped for, substance of things, 6266
Hopes and fears, for fifty, 397
  belied out fears, 1963
  decay, seen my fondest, 2971
  not for good, 7590
  of future years, all, 2460
  tender leaves of, 4760
  that have vanished, 1827
  vanity of human, 2100
  will cling, to weakest, 440
Hoppy, Croppy, Droppy, 1433
Hops and women, 1187
Horace, felicity of, 3139
  says is, what, 147
  whom I hated so, 621
Horatii curiosa felicitas, 3139
Horatius kept the bridge, 2524

Ignara mali, non, 5412
Ignorance, a childish, 1960
　daughter of, 9926
　is bliss, where, 1750
　is the mother, 7911, 7912
　Madam, pure, 2121
　of the law, 3529
　sedate, in, 2092
Ignorant has an eagle's wings, 9123
　of ill, not, 5412
　of what he's most assured, 4394
Ignotum per ignotius, 7913
　pro magnifico est, 5111
Ilium, topless towers of, 2563
Ill a-brewing towards my rest, 3778
　better suffer, 6927
　comes in by ells, 7916
　comes upon waur's back, 7917
　cure for this, 2334
　deeds, means to do, 3751
　doers are ill deemers, 7918
　final goal of, 5227
　gotten, ill spent, 7921
　he that hath done, 7600
　he thinks no, 4794
　if you have done no, 7886
　it costs more to do, 7972
　make strong themselves by, 4597
　man is, what religion, 8074
　man worse, [makes], 8147
　spoken of, better be, 6887
　they have done some, 9751
　to himself, he that is, 7601
　will never said well, 7927
Ill-doing, doctrine of, 4708
Ill-favoured thing, but mine own, 4122
Ill-gotten gains, 7919
Illiterate him, I say, 4883
Ills a prey, to hast'ning, 1695
　away, washes all man's, 1462
　dangerous, 9914
　to come, no sense of, 1749
　we have, bear those, 4253
Image gay, 5642
　of myself, best, 2847
Imaginary, all our wants are, 255
Imagination all compact, of, 3729
　amend them, if, 3735
　bodies forth, 3730
　into his study of, 3952
　of a boy, 2235
　of a man, mature, 2235
　to sweeten my, 4518
Imaginations are as foul, 4270
Imaginings, horrible, 4543
Imitation, endless, 5666
　is the sincerest, 1018
Immodest words admit of no defence, 3410
Immoral man, a most, 2266
Immortal as itself, being, 4211
　part of myself, lost, 4440
　think they grow, 5713
Immortality, longing after, 14

Immortality, nurslings of, 4873
Immortals, President of the, 1815
Impact has its measure, 2612
Imparadis'd in one another's arms, 2835
Impatience would be so much fretted, 2137
Impavidum ferient ruinae, 1993
Impeachment, own the soft, 4891
Impediment, cause or just, 6314
Impediments, admit, 4813
　to great enterprises, 111
Impera, divide et, 7107
Imperfections by, pass my, 1467
Imperially, learn to think. 823
Imperii, capax, 5114
Implications, with horrid, 1739
Importunate, rashly, 1970
Importunity, ever-haunting, 2364
Impossibile est, quia, 5288
Impossibilities, plausible, 49
Impossibility, nearly an, 943
Impossible, because it is, 5288
　I wish it were, 2165
　nothing is, 8494
　with men this is, 6104
Imposters, treat those two, 2329
Impoverishing, sweet, 6974
Impression, take any, 10003
Impudence, Cockney, 3441
　mother of, 7912
Impulse from a vernal wood, 5600
　of the moment, 92
　this or that poor, 356
In at one ear, 7935
　I went, out by the same Door as, 1502
　who's out, who's, 4524
Inactivity, wise and masterly, 2538
Inanimate things, depravity of, 1806
Incense, gods themselves throw, 4525
　hangs, what soft, 2215
Inch a king, every, 4516
　dree out, 7135
　give him, 7319
　to gain, no painful, 938
Inchcape Rock, it is the, 4963
Inches, goes out by, 7916
Incident of the dog, 1312
Incidente, è un, 5385
Incidents, one of the, 5385
Incivility and procrastination, 1176
Inclination leads, read just as, 2129
inclined to, sins they are, 572
Include me out, 1729
Income twenty pounds, 1238
　will supply, moderate, 255
Inconvenience, no vice but, 8646
　poverty is, 8646
Inconvenient, confoundedly, 4938
Incorruptible, the seagreen, 746
Increase, we desire, 4781
Increment, unearned, 2658
Ind, wealth of Ormus and of, 2792
Independence, Declaration of, 900
Independent, of being, 498

Janiveer in March I fear, 8322
Janiveer's calends be summerly gay, if, 7835
Janua Ditis, patet atri, 5424
Japanese action with prudence, reconcile, 913
Jardin, il faut cultiver, 5433
Javan or Gadire, isles of, 2903
Jaw gae by, let, 8088
Jaws, ponderous and marble, 4208
Jealous confirmations, to, 4449
  eyes, scornful yet, 3291
  one not easily, 4474
Jealousy, beware, my lord, of, 4446
  full of artless, 4308
  injustice, 1912
  is cruel as the grave, 5989
  never without, 8259
Jeers, gibes and flouts and, 1268
Jehu, like the driving of, 5806
Jellies soother than the creamy curd, 2210
Jenny kissed me, 2045
  to her wheel, 10006
Jenny's case, vengeance of, 4360
Jericho, tarry at, 5788
Jerusalem, if I forget thee, 5889
  the golden, 3026
  till we have built, 242
Jessamine, pale, 2752
Jest, a scornful, 2085
  and youthful jollity, 2683
  be laughable, swear, 3754
  better lose, 6911
  except ye owe the Fates, 2337
  fellow of infinite, 4323
  for ever, good, 3832
  he had his, 1348
  if you make, 7885
  is no jest, true, 6601
  leave, 8150
  life is a, 1585
  put his whole wit in, 187
  true word is spoken in, 8306
  with them, be slow to, 2337
  you must take, 7885
Jest's prosperity lies in the ear of him that hears it, 3622
Jested, quaffed, and swore, 1319
Jester, become a fool and, 3921
Jesters, with shallow, 3865
Jesting with edged tools, 8037
Jests sound worst, truest, 9271
  to his memory for, 4901
Jesu, by a nobler deed, 826
Jesus Christ her Lord, is, 5058
  Christ the same, 6270
  gentle, 5514
  lover of my soul, 5512
  stand up for, 1398
  the blood of, 217
  the very thought of Thee, 807
  with the Cross of, 149
  ye belong to, 33

Jesus' name, power of, 3135
Jeunesse savait, si, 1458
Jew, an Ebrew, 3842
  else, I am a, 3842
  eyes, hath not a, 3785
Jewel, black man is, 6403
  caught my heav'nly, 4905
  fair play's a, 7222
  in a ten-times-barr'd-up chest, 3673
  in an Ethiope's ear, 3638
  in its head, precious, 4067
  of gold in a swine's snout, 5904
  of their souls, immediate, 4445
  you had not found, 7831
Jewels five words long, 5194
  for a set of beads, 3696
  moving, 5356
Jews might kiss, 3188
  spend at Easter, 9126
  Turks, Infidels, 6308
Jhesus, that gentilman, 154
Jigging veins of rhyming mother wits, 2557
Jill, every Jack has, 7180
Jingo if we do, by, 2038
Job, poor as, 6764
Job, we will finish the, 912
  you have a responsible, 3022
Jobiska's, for his Aunt, 2403
Joe, poor old, 1548
Jog on, the foot-path way, 4716
John Anderson my jo, 514
John Bull, greatest of all, 669
John Naps of Greece, old, 3586
John of Gaunt, old, 3672
John Richard William Alexander Dwyer, 4927
Johnny Groat's, Maidenkirk to, 517
Johnson, imitation of, 472
  is dead, 1808
  no arguing with, 1727
  put you in mind of, 1808
  the Great Cham, 4950
Johnson's sayings, 3124
Joined, whom God hath, 6320
Joint, nose out of, 9528
Joints, his square-turn'd, 3470
Joke, Dulness ever loves a, 3221
  grace to see a, 6379
  had he, for many a, 1706
  relations with a good, 893
Jollies, 'er Majesty's, 2314
  they done it, the, 2314
Jollity and game, turn'd to, 2884
  but hath a smack of folly, no, 9332
Jolly as a sandboy, 6743
  credit in being, 1218
Jonathan, consult Brother, 5472
Jonson's learned sock, 2694
Jordan's wave, on this side, 35
Jorkins, I have a partner, 1240
Joseph, knew not, 5748
Josephus, Histories of, 2357
Jostle not, dust and bones, 7955

Justice, even-handed, 4555
  in the course of, 3799
  kind of wild, 110
  pleaseth few, 8091
  sad-eyed, 3967
  thou shalt have, 3803
  was done, 1815
  was for doing, 1487
  which is the, 4519
  with her lifted scale, 3217
  with mercy, temper, 2878
Justinian Stubbs, Esquire, 4927
Justitia, fiat, 7246

Kail het again, cauld, 6995
Κακά, πάντα τἀνθρώπων, 1462
Kalendas Graecas, ad, 87
Kame sindle, kame sair, 8092
Kann nicht anders, ich, 2491
Kansas had better stop raising corn, 2406
Kaspar's work was done, 4961
Keats, what porridge had, 375
  who kill'd John, 670
Keek in my kail pot, 8093
Keel, follow eyes the, 5540
  ploughs air, her, 828
Keep a thing seven years, 8095
  and pass, and turn, 1453
  it by me, I love to, 2076
  it, hath it and will not, 7576
  now, better, 6907
  some till more come, 8098
  something for a sore foot, 8099
  to the right, if you, 1457
  who can, they should, 5638
  you, shop will, 8104
Keeper, am I my brother's, 5729
  poacher makes the best, 6706
Keepers, oft worry their, 8110
Keeping, finding's, 7248
  men off, by, 1590
Keerless man in his talk, 1846
Κείμεθα, τῇδε, 4911
Keith of Ravelston, 1278
Ken, as far as angels', 2768
Kens the wife, little, 8220
Kensal Green, by way of, 889
Kent, apples, cherries, 1187
Kentucky home, my old, 1544
Kerke the narre, to, 4979
Kernel, he that will eat, 7673
Kettle black, pot calls, 9200
  of fish, 6567
Kew, come down to, 3060
  his Highness' dog at, 3313
Key and keyhole do sustain, 8205
  must have a good, 7675
  to which I found no, 1505
  under thy own life's, 4373
  with this, 5680
  with this same, 416
Keys hang not, all, 6663
  he bore, two massy, 2748
Khartoum, old man of, 6368

Khayyám, come with old, 1501
Kibe, galls his, 4322
Kick, a penalty, 3349
  against the pricks, 6191
  an attorney downstairs, 8105
  land him one solid, 2395
  me downstairs, why, 2244
Kicked until they can feel, 580
  waxed fat and, 5763
Kirkshaws, little tiny, 3917
Kid follows, 9819
  lie down with, 5997
  thou shalt not seethe, 5755
Kidlings blithe, than, 1588
Kidney, man of my, 4359
Kill a wife with kindness, 3590
  and die, must men, 4876
  thou shalt not, 941
  you if you quote it, 455
Killed, some sleeping, 3695
  with report that old man eloquent, 2757
Kills me some six or seven dozen of Scots, 3838
  the thing he loves, 5569
Kilmeny gaed up the glen, 1923
Kin, a little more than, 4178
  good to be near of, 8023
  makes the whole world, 4368
  to the rich man, every one is, 7193
Kind, art of being, 5553
  as she is fair, 3602
  cat will after, 6993
  cruel, only to be, 4300
  enjoy her while she's, 1383
  had it been early, 2120
  lady sweet and, 6342
  less than, 4178
  makes one wondrous, 1578
  of a people, what, 913
  praise the Lord, for he is, 2669
  so courteous, so, 4913
  to Him, leaves were, 2383
Kindle when we will, cannot, 59
Kindled, wood half-burnt is easily, 9927
Kindly, never lov'd sae, 532
Kindness and of love, of, 5602
  beauty lives with, 3602
  cannot be bought, 8107
  forced, 6460
  in another's trouble, 1731
  is lost, 8108
  kill a wife with, 3590
  little deeds of, 758
  milk of human, 4547
  save in the way of, 5351
  tak a cup o', 510
  that I can show, 1790
Kindnesses increase by sowing, 8109
Kindred, grave Jonas, 112
  never want for, 9213
  shame in, 8780
Kine, keeps the shadowy, 1278
King, and farewell, 3695

King, arose up a new, 5748
  as easily as a, 4007
  as I have served the, 5589
  authority forgets a dying, 5268
  can do no wrong, 227, 9127
  can mak a belted knight, 547
  can make a knight, 9128
  cat may look at, 6423
  delighteth to honour, whom, 5807
  divinity doth hedge, 4312
  do, what must the, 3696
  does, for his, 1888
  every inch a, 4516
  fellow with the best, 3996
  from an anointed, 3692
  glory to the new-born, 5531
  God bless the, 591
  God save the, 6351
  great and mighty, 3390
  hae we got for a, 1132
  heart and stomach of, 1427
  himself has follow'd, 1678
  honour the, 6273
  in Babylon, I was a, 1875
  is a thing men have made, 3531
  is it not brave to be, 2559
  lad that's born to be, 266
  long live our noble, 6351
  lose the name of, 3696
  must lose his right, 9816
  my cousin, not call, 7808
  nearest, 8404
  never dies, 9129
  no bishop, no, 2067
  nor prince shall tempt me, 104
  not sib to, 6661
  observing with judicious eyes, 5358
  of England cannot enter, 840
  of good fellows, best, 3996
  of kings, 4840
  of shreds and patches, 4295
  of terrors, 5817
  reigns, but does not govern, 5719
  ruthless, 1779
  sees thee, think the, 1888
  served my, 4765
  shall be contented, 3696
  shall reign, whatsoever, 6350
  so excellent a, 4183
  sovereign lord the, 3390
  they have a, 3967
  to reverence the, 5263
  under which, 3920
  without learning, 6510
  year's pleasant, 3024
King, defect of Henry, 202
  Pandion, he is dead, 156
  Wenceslas looked out, 3030
King's chaff, 8111
  cheese goes half way, 9130
  life-guard, 9247
  name is a tower of strength, 3573
  word is more, 9131
  word, must is, 8388

Kingdom against kingdom, 6114
  come, palaces in, 2604
  come, thy, 6052
  for a little grave, 3696
  for thine is the, 6052
  in reversion, for, 7801
  is, my mind to me, 1406
  like to a little, 4012
  of God, fit for, 6141
  of God is within you, 6163
  of God, of such is, 6135
  of God, seek ye, 6059
  to a peopled, 3867
Kingdoms, scourging, 2557
Kings, all be as happy as, 5045
  and bears oft worry, 8110
  and Senates, cashiering, 739
  are arming, when, 3509
  but the breath of, 488
  city of two, 2525
  come bow to it, bid, 3742
  commit, whatever madness, 1997
  crept out again, 326
  depart, captains and, 2293
  descended of so many, 4675
  dread and fear of, 3799
  have long arms, 8112
  have many ears, 8113
  in the hearts of, 3799
  it makes gods, 3572
  ken, he gart, 82
  like sleepin', 1115
  may be blest, 524
  pride of, 3230
  right divine of, 3226
  royal throne of, 3684
  ruin'd sides of, 189
  saddest of all, 2080
  sport of, 4952
  stories of the death of, 3695
  that fear their subjects' treachery
    3552
  their titles take, conquering, 826
  walk with, 2330
  will be tyrants, 467
Kinquering congs, 4996
Kinsfolk, many, 8313
Kipling, Rudyards cease from, 5012
Kirk, prepare for, 7841
Kirkconnel lea, on fair, 6337
Kirks, they may burn, 8281
Kirkwall, from Valencia to, 2326
Kirtle, near is my, 8401
Kiss a body, gin a body, 550
  a stranger, you, 8821
  ae fond, 530
  again with tears, 5193
  and be friends, 8114
  and part, let us, 1326
  but in the cup, leave, 2169
  cat and dog may, 8977
  coward does it with, 5569
  good to, 6522
  haunts me night and day, 5138

X

Labyrinthine buds the rose, 338
Lace for your cape, 4724
  Greek is like, 2157
Lacedaemon, in lordly, 2525
Lacedaemonians, tell the, 4911
Laces, tying up her, 2627
Lack, eat into itself, for, 573
  of many a thing, sigh, 4788
Lacrimae, hinc illae, 5284
Lad that's born to be king, 266
  when I was a, 1622
Lad's love's a busk of broom, 8130
  love is lassies' delight, 8129
Ladder, climbed the dusty, 5344
  go down, 7328
  is ascended, 8869
  traffic of Jacob's, 5317
  world is, 9289
Laden, labour and are heavy, 6082
Ladies, ate in hall among, 2548
  be but young and fair, 4086
  dead, in praise of, 4809
  good for, 7229
  intellectual, lords of, 649
  of St. James's, 1280
  of Spain, 6358
  over-offended, 5010
  spend their time in making nets, 5083
  with store of, 2693
Ladies' favours, rhyme themselves into,
  3995
  lips, o'er, 3635
Lads and Girls, 1259
  and girls, golden, 4704
  are far away, though, 1541
  love of, 8271
  raw dads make fat, 8697
  that thought there was no more be-
    hind, 4707
  that will die in their glory, 2018
  won't love, if, 8129
Lads' leavings, lasses are, 8132
Lady, a love for any, 3120
  a most beautiful, 1165
  here comes the, 3659
  in the land, ain't a, 899
  Joan is as good as my, 8087
  never won fair, 7216
  of my delight, the, 2649
  of Shallott, 5147
  seems of ivory, my, 2991
  sweet and kind, 6342
  sweet, arise, my, 4695
  through, pulls a, 2576
  thy mother a, 3504
  with a Lamp, 2466
Lady's in the case, when a, 1587
Lady-smocks all silver-white, 3623
Lafayette, we are here, 5004
Laggard in love, 3479
Laid me down with a will, 5048
Laird o' Cockpen, 3007
  slight the lady, if, 7857
Lairdie, wee, wee German, 1132

Lake of blue, starless, 993
  or moorish fen, by, 2728
  on still St. Mary's, 5639
Λακεδαιμονίοις, ἀγγειλον, 4911
Lakes, light shakes across, 5196
Lamb, dwell with, 5997
  go to bed with, 7331
  goes out like, 8321
  Mary had a little, 1802
  mild as, 6755
  save one little ewe, 5789
  shorn, 7347
  skin of an innocent, 3545
  to the shorn, 5019
  to the slaughter, as, 6011
  was sure to go, 1802
Lamb, the frolic and the gentle, 5682
Lambs could not forgive, 1226
  we were as twinn'd, 4708
Lame and impotent conclusion, 4433
  are foremost, 7930
  goes as far, 9132
  post brings the truest news, 9133
  tongue gets nothing, 9134
Lamely and unfashionable, 3559
Lament, long, 8788
Lammas, at latter, 6821
Lamp, I lift my, 2392
  in the evening, light, 195
  is shattered, when, 4872
  Lady with a, 2466
  smell of, 9539
  unto my feet, 5880
Lamps, a thousand silver, 193
  are going out all over Europe, 1792
  like golden, 2584
  shone, bright the, 609
Lancaster, time-honour'd, 3672
Lance in rest, looked like, 2288
Lancelot brave, not even, 5255
  or Pelleas, or Pellenore, 2888
Land alone, on this, 1910
  being on, settle, 6862
  between, remedy for love is, 9209
  charter of the, 5332
  England's the one, 297
  flowing with milk and honey, 5751
  from the holy, 3359
  green and pleasant, 242
  he that buys, 7532
  he that hath some, 7586
  ill fares the, 1695
  in a strange, 5888
  in this favoured, 5307
  in which it seemed always afternoon
    5154
  into a golden, 5375
  into the promised, 6359
  into the silent, 3417
  is bright, look, the, 939
  kennst du das, 1674
  know ye the, 630
  knowest thou the, 1674
  marched into their, 105

*X

Loved not at first sight, who ever loved, that, 2571, 4109
  not wisely, one that, 4474
  one all together, and, 421
  out upon it, I have, 5066
  sae kindly, never, 532
  so long, that he, 3397
  the Human Race, wish I, 3368
  the man, I, 2180
  thee since my day began, 5278
  them, from those who, 1167
  therefore must be, 3582
  thou hast not, 4075
  you Wednesday, if I, 2662
Love-in-idleness, maidens call it, 3716
Loveliness I never knew, her, 950
  increases, its, 2203
  needs not the foreign aid of ornament, 5326
  portion of the, 4865
  to believe in, 5318
Lovely and a fearful thing, 656
  and more temperate, more, 4783
  and pleasant in their lives, 5784
  on all things, 1166
  once he made more, 4865
  things, not dream thine, do, 2259
Lover, all as frantic, 3730
  all mankind love a, 1438
  and his lass, it was, 4121
  and sensualist, 1870
  forsaken, 5451
  give repentance to, 1691
  I sighed as a, 1605
  of trees, you, 361
  pale and wan, fond, 5064
  sighing like furnace, 4090
  to the heart of her, 3062
  without indiscretion, 1811
  woman loves her, 657
Lover's ear will hear the lowest sound, 3615
  eyes will gaze an eagle blind, 3615
  head, slide into a, 5608
  staff, hope is, 7763
Love-rhymes, regent of, 3613
Lovers are round her, sighing, 2962
  are shy, true, 9590
  are soundest, old, 5498
  happy, make two, 6380
  live by love, 8276
  love the spring, 4121
  love the western star, 3464
  meeting, journeys end in, 4139
  must consign to thee, 4706
  pair of star-cross'd, 3625
  quarrels of, 5286
  we that are true, 4076
  whisp'ring, 1693
Lovers' brains, through, 3635
  eyes, hiding love from, 1127
  perjuries, at, 3645, 8089
  tongues by night, 3651
Loves a rosy cheek, he that, 730

Loves another best, who, 4722
  his fellow men, who, 2042
  I have, two, 4818
  I prize as the dead carcasses, 4682
  is love, all she, 657
  kills the thing he, 5569
  me for little, 7495
  no one who . . . unhappy, 163
  not where it lives but where it, 9240
  on to the close, truly, 2957
  remain, if our, 361
  woman whom nobody, 1036
Lovesome thing, a garden is, 311
Lovest me, an thou, 3848
Loveth best all things, 977
  well both man and bird, 976
  well, of him that, 5068
Loving and giving, 8364
  comes by looking, 8277
  longest . . . when hope is gone, 96
  mere folly, most, 4092
  never call it, 330
  so faithful, so, 1116
Low, he that is, 451
  man seeks a little thing, 389
  raise and support, what is, 2767
  soft, gentle and, 4528
  water, tide turns at, 1434
Lowells talk only to Cabots, 261
Lower at the last, it will, 6960
  can fall no, 7612
  than the angels, 5831
Lowlands shall meet thee, 701
Lowliness is young ambition's ladder, 4011
Loyal and neutral, 4584
Loyalties, impossible, 70
Loyalty, learned body wanted, 5358
Lucifer, come not, 2567
  falls like, 4761
  proud as, 6766
  son of the morning, 5998
Luck, all the day you'll have good, 8755
  another time, better, 9292
  devil's, 9018
  give a man, 7315
  in horses, have good, 7691
  in odd numbers, 9327
  is good for something, ill, 7922
  light in ragged, 1870
  more knave, better, 9167
  mother of good, 7100
  next time, better, 6912
  now, worse, 9292
  the worse, 9205
  would have it, as good, 4357
Lucky and happy, 8364
  at play, 9639
  better be born, 6882
  men need no counsel, 8278
Lucre, filthy, 6259
Lucy light, 8279
  should be dead, if, 5608

Maid, last suitor wins, 9139
  my pretty, 6352, 6353
  never kiss, 7881
  of Astolat, lily, 5257
  of Athens, ere we part, 603
  oft seen, 6532
  sad brow and true, 4099
  slain by a fair cruel, 4148
  sphere-descended, 1013
  that laughs, 6533
Maiden, and mistress, 5104
  gentle, 4858
  meditation, fancy-free, 3716
  never bold, 4419
  of bashful fifteen, 4894
  smiled, archly the, 2463
  that orbed, 4852
  the maddest, 2620
  with many wooers, 6534
Maidenkirk to Johnny Groat's, 517
Maidenly, so joyously, so, 4912
Maidens be, as many, 950
  like moths, 604
  married, so are all, 7840
  must be mild and meek, 8280
  should be mim, 8281
  watching, all her, 5204
  wear no purses, 7221
  young fair, 5054
Maids and village hinds, 1014
  dance in a ring, 3024
  dun, [makes], 8324
  lead apes, old, 8527
  May when they are, 4114
  say nay and take, 8282
  strange seraphic pieces, 5356
  surpass, all other, 2544
  than Malkin, more, 9301
  that weave their thread with bones, 4147
  want nothing but husbands, 8283
  with seven mops, seven, 779
Maimed and set at naught, 589
Main, from out the azure, 5332
  silent, flooding in, 938
  skims along the, 3180
Maisie is in the wood, 3508
Maîtresses, j'aurai des, 1598
Majestic though in ruin, 2801
Majestical, being so, 4172
Majesty, attribute to awe and, 3799
  busied in his, 3967
  in rayless, 5708
  this earth of, 3684
Majorities, decision by, 1668
Majority, one on God's side is, 3144
Make anything, does not, 3140
  neither meddle nor, 7800
Maker, serve therewith my, 2761
Makes me or fordoes me, 4466
  so many, reason He, 2425
Making, take pleasure in, 8985
Maladies and miseries, cure of, 751

Malady most incident to maids, 4719
Malcontents, loiterers and, 3613
Male, more deadly than, 2300
Malice domestic, 4591
  is mindful, 8292
  never was his aim, 5076
  set down aught in, 4474
  towards none, with, 2424
Malkin, more maids than, 9302
Mallecho, miching, 4272
Mallow waves her silky leaf, 1109
Malt does more than Milton, 2021
  is above meal, 8293
  makes sweet, 8826
Mam's pet, marries, 7449
Mamble, I never went to, 1328
Mammon of unrighteousness, 6159
  serve God and, 6056
Mammy heerd him holler, 3387
Man, a horse, and a dog, 6535
  after his own heart, 5780
  alive, means for every, 4381
  all that may become, 4560
  all the faults of, 719
  all things can, no, 8447
  all this scene of, 3230
  among children, 6536
  assurance of a, 4292
  at sixteen, 6537
  being in honour abideth not, 5854
  by courtesy a, 100
  call up my, 3507
  can do no more than he can, 6538
  child is father of, 5620
  closing full in, 1368
  comes and tills the field, 5165
  could ease a heart, where's the, 3094
  delights not me, 4239
  dispute it like a, 4623
  do all things like a, 1888
  doth what he can, 8294
  even such a, 3883
  for the sabbath, not, 6127
  from his throne has hurled, 5436
  get a new, 4744
  has done, what, 9730
  he was her, 6360
  heaven had made her such, 4423
  his prey was, 3201
  in the case, get to, 2316
  in the moon, no more than, 7786
  is a bubble, 8295
  is . . . a civic animal, 48
  is a noble animal, 319
  is a pliable animal, 1295
  is a tool-using animal, 740
  is as old as he feels, 6540
  is born unto trouble, 5812
  is his own star, 1535
  is Nature's sole mistake, 1644
  is so in the way, a, 1581
  [is taken] by the tongue, 6713
  is the hunter, 5203

Matrimony, safest in, 4884
Matty, meddlesome, 5126
Maud, Maud, Maud, Maud, 5241
Maurice died, since, 284
Maw, bad in, 7357
Mawkishness, proceeds, 2235
Maxim be my virtue's guide, 2929
  should become a universal law, my,
    2195
Maxime solle ein allgemeines Gesetz
    werden, 2195
May be out, till, 6991
  bees don't fly, 8336
  chills the lap of, 1684
  cold, and windy, 6432
  crowned with milk-white, 282
  dry, 6447
  flood never did good, 6553
  flowers, bring forth, 8325
  he sings all day, in, 7934
  in a town in, 7602
  look at your corn in, 8238
  marry in, 833
  merry month of, 155
  shear your sheep in, 8784
  sings a song in, 8995
  sun, March wind and, 8324
  swarm of bees in, 6594
  the birds begin to lay, in, 7946
  there's an end of, 2022
  till the kalends of, 7835
  will be fine next year, 2023
May's new-fangled mirth, 3609
May-cloud, the swinging, 2628
Mayde, meke as is a, 848
Maying, that we two were, 2260
May-morn, till that, 419
Maypoles, I sing of, 1896
Maze, a mighty, 3230
Mazes lost, in wand'ring, 2804
Mægen lytlað, þe ure, 6330
Me for him, got taking, 2412
Meadow or plain, in, 5105
Meadows, feet have touch'd, 5242
  green, kissing, 4790
  in the dreaming, 3062
  of heaven, infinite, 2458
  paint the, 3623
  trim with daisies pied, 2689
Meads in May, flowery, 5581
Meal is all bran, devil's, 9019
  malt is above, 8293
  no mill, no, 8460
  trust not with, 9021
Meal-tub, taking out of, 6675
Meals, two hungry, 9623
Mean [base] even for man, too, 5290
  nothing common did, or, 2593
  stupid, dastardly, 1850
Mean [signify], I know not what they,
    5198
  not careful what they, 3584
Mean [middle] measure is a merry, 8337
Meandering, five miles, 985

Meanest of mankind, 3254
Meaning doesn't matter, 1630
  teems with hidden, 1656
  to some faint, 1355
Meannesses which are too mean, 5290
Means [agency] at all, by any, 1996
  die beyond my, 5567
  end justifies, 9028
  end must justify, 3328
  produce no effect, small, 2656
  straitened, 2186
  to boot, appliances and, 3905
  to do ill, sight of, 3751
  use the, 9644
  you can, by all the, 5517
Means [signifies] nothing, 7641
Meant than meets the ear, more is, 2709
  well, lies one who, 5034
Measels, did you ever hav, 5463
Measles, love is like, 2077
  love's like the, 2078
Measure in all things, 9314
  is a merry mean, 8337
  me, lads they, 2612
  must strike by, 9761
  of all things, 8296
  serves to grace, 3326
  shrunk to this little, 4024
  sin to give ill, 8054
  thrice, 8338
  weening is not, 9705
  wielder of the stateliest, 5278
Measured, men are not to be, 8343
Measures, not men, but, 461
Meat abroad, roast, 7141
  and canna eat, some hae, 551
  and drink to me, it is, 4117
  and matins, 8339
  and on us all, on our, 1906
  and we can eat, we hae, 551
  ashamed to eat, 8416
  cannot eat but little, 5057
  doth this our Caesar feed, upon what,
    4006
  drink, and cloth, 7351
  for their stomach, seek, 8638
  God sends, 7341, 7346
  in the hall, 5047
  is much, 8340
  it feeds on, mock, 4446
  one man is appointed to buy, 3531
  one man's, 8575
  show me not, 8794
  small birds must have, 8815
  sweet, 8887
  that have no other, 9370
  this dish of, 5456
  twice boiled, 8902
  wholesomest, 9281
Meats, funeral baked, 4188
Meddle nor make, neither, 7800
Meddlesome Matty, 5126
Meddleth in all things, 9858
Meddling, of little, 8513

Μηδὲν ἄγαν, 8341
Medes and the Persians, law of, 6024
Medicine against death, no, 9334
  for fear, no, 9335
  merry heart like, 5917
  ready, 8698
Medicines to make me love, 3331
Medio tutissimus ibis, 3082
Meditation, in maiden, 3716
Mediterranean, the blue, 4845
Meek and mild, 5514
  blessed are, 6039
  borne his faculties so, 4556
  than fierce, safer being, 411
Meekest man and the gentlest, 2548
Meet a body, gin a body, 550
  again, if we do, 4054
  again, shall we three, 4532
  again, till we, 3372
  again, will never, 6357
  and mingle, all things, 4848
  him in my dish, though I should, 7785
  make ends, 9519
  me by moonlight, 5435
  men may, 8347
  merry part, merry, 8351
  never the twain shall, 2287
  thee, if I should, 595
  wheel-barrows tremble when, 501
Meeter, deemed it, 3118
Meeting, broke the good, 4606
Meke as is a mayde, 848
Melancholy as a cat, 6750
  as a sick monkey, 6751
  green and yellow, 4149
  hence, loathed, 2682
  mark'd him for her own, 1769
  moping, 2879
  most musical, most, 2702
  nought so sweet, 552
  O sweetest, 1533
  of mine own, 4110
  once a day, 7460
  out of a song, suck, 4078
  sate retir'd, 1012
  villainous, 4479
  what charm can soothe, 1691
Meliora, proboque, video, 3083
Melodies are sweet, heard, 2219
Melody, blund'ring kind of, 1353
  luve's like the, 540
Melodye, smale fowles maken, 847
Melons, stumbling on, 2589
Melrose aright, view fair, 3461
Member, joint, or limb, in, 2809
  unruly, 6271
Même chose, plus c'est la, 2196
Meminisse juvabit, haec, 5410
Memorial, completed a, 1994
Memories, a night of, 2369
  flocks of the, 2650
  have good, 8179
Memory brings the light, 2969
  dear son of, 2678

Memory dear, to, 2430
  do honour his, 2180
  from the table of, 4222
  holds a seat, while, 4222
  how sweet their, 1101
  made such a sinner of, 4729
  of all he stole, 3220
  of man runneth not, 226
  pluck from the, 4631
  strengthens as you lay burdens upon
    it, 1177
  the warder of the brain, 4563
  vibrates in the, 4869
Men and women merely players, 4090
  are but children, 1390
  are created equal, 2071
  are men, but, 4438
  are not to be measured, 8343
  are we and must grieve, 5629
  as he, can be such, 69
  as trees, walking, see, 6132
  at most differ as Heaven and earth,
    5256
  betray, finds too late that, 1691
  biography of great, 747
  busy hum of, 2692
  but measures, not, 461
  cheerful ways of, 2821
  dare trust themselves with men, I
    wonder, 4688
  decay, 1695
  divine, [had made], 3110
  do a-land, as, 4693
  do, whatever, 2184
  enlarge the views of, 1817
  for fear of little, 40
  for Pieces, with, 1508
  have become women, my, 5698
  have faults, 8345
  he had ten thousand, 6354
  I've studied, 2619
  in His ways with, 5266
  in the catalogue ye go for, 4587
  loved darkness, 6174
  may come and men may go, 5189
  must work, 2257
  not thrones and crowns but, 1432
  off, by keeping, 1590
  quit you like, 6237
  quit yourselves like, 5778
  should brothers be, 1910
  so beautiful, the many, 966
  sorts and conditions of, 6306
  that were boys when I was, 196
  the best of, 1162
  think all men mortal, all, 5711
  we've got the, 2038
  who march away, 1819
  whose cities he saw, 1951
  will sometimes jealous be, 719
  women, and Herveys, 2933
Men's men, 1417
Mend, at the worst will, 9379
  in the end things will, 7954

Murders, twenty mortal, 4603
Murex up, who fished the, 375
Murmurs creep, with pleasing, 3179
  hear our mutual, 661
Murther, foul and midnight, 1782
Mus, nascetur ridiculus, 2006
Musam meditamur avena, 4935
  silvestrem, 5402
Muscles of his brawny arms, 2446
Muse [goddess], let's sing of rats, 1741
  meditate the thankless, 2744
  of fire, O for a, 3962
  of the many-twinkling feet. 629
  practise the woodland, 5402
  rise, honest, 3278
  transports of a British, 5124
  worst-natured, 3391
Muse [ponder] as they use, men, 8348
Muses, all the charm of, 5277
  sing of happy swains, 1107
Museum, books at the British, 588
Mushrooms, broiled fowl and, 1186
Music arose with its voluptuous swell, 609
  be the food of love, if, 4127
  creep in our ears, 3809
  discourse most eloquent, 4279
  fading in, 3788
  hath charms, 1022
  hear the sea-maid's, 3715
  helps not, 8387
  in himself, man that hath no, 3811
  in its roar, 625
  in my heart I bore, 5637
  is, how sour sweet, 3703
  make not sweet, 7381
  makes as healthful, 4297
  makes sweet, 3598
  mute, will make, 5254
  night shall be filled with, 2453
  of men's lives, with, 3703
  on the waters, like, 637
  one chord of, 3337
  shed, soul of, 2953
  sphere-descended, 1013
  that gentlier on the spirit lies, 5155
  the colour, the, 2596
  the condition of, 3107
  there, [for] the, 3177
  they were thy chosen, 5673
  though I'm full of, 453
  to attending ears, 3651
  when I hear sweet, 3810
  when soft voices die, 4869
Music's soothing sound, 5547
Musical as is Apollo's lute, 2729
Musicians that shall play to you, 3862
Music-makers, we are the, 3076
Musing there an hour, 660
Musket moulds in his hands, 1479
  take not, 8905
Musk-roses, with sweet, 3719
Must, Duty whispers low, Thou, 1452
  is a king's word, 8388
Mustard, after meat, 6631

Mustard and cress, now for, 1619
  good without, 7389
Mutamur in illis, 8926
Mutant, caelum, non animum, 2003
Mutato nomine, 1982
Mutatus ab illo, quantum, 5418
Mute, is she not pure, 3442
Mutiny, to rise and, 4042
Mutter, wizards that, 5996
Mutters, knows not what he, 9152
Mutton, dead as, 6730
  joint of, 3917
Muzzle the ox, thou shalt not, 5761
Myriad-minded Shakespeare, 1003
Myrte still, 1674
Myrtle, cypress and, 630
  is still, the, 1674
Myrtles brown, ye, 2738
Mystery, comprehend its, 2161
  I show you a, 6235
  lose myself in a, 313
  of things, take upon's, 4524
  pluck out the heart of, 4280
Mystic, wonderful, 5251

Nactus es, Spartam, 925
Nag, gait of a shuffling, 3858
Naiad airs, thy, 3162
  the guardian, 3489
Nail drives out another, 8580
  for want of, 7278
  it down, 2534
  made to the, 1985
  on the head, hit, 9493
  that will go, drive, 7139
  to our coffin adds a, 5584
Nailed for our advantage, 3815
Nails, he must have iron, 7500
Naked came I out of my mother's womb,
  5809
  every day he clad, 1688
  though lock'd up in steel, 3542
Nakedness, not in utter, 5665
Namby-pamby madrigals, 1608
Namby Pamby's little rhymes, 732
Name Achilles assumed, what, 317
  age without a, 2974
  Amos Cottle, what a, 601
  answered to his, 5300
  as lazy as the, 1328
  at which the world grew pale, 2090
  blushes at the, 2061
  by any other, 3644
  by her golden, 3062
  change the, 1982
  deed without a, 4613
  filches from me my good, 4445
  gathered together in my, 6099
  gets a good, 7470
  give a dog a bad, 7312
  halloo your, 4136
  hallowed be thy, 6052
  has left but the, 2952
  he that hath an ill, 7574

Y

Ocean gain, seen the hungry, 4796
  make the mighty, 757
  of truth, great, 3049
  sweeps the laboured mole away, 2099
  unfathom'd caves of, 1763
  upon a painted, 959
  wave, life on the, 3453
Ocean's bosom unespied, in, 2583
Ocean-fowl, wheeling, 5187
Oceans, portable and compendious, 1120
O'clock, it is ten, 4082
Odd numbers, luck in, 9327
  think it exceedingly, 2350
  your astonishment's, 2350
Odds, facing fearful, 2519
  is gone, the, 4664
Ode and elegy and sonnet, 2096
  I intended an, 1281
Oderint dum metuant, 1
Odi et amo, 813
  profanum vulgus, 1991
Odious ! in woollen ! 3262
  comparisons are, 7033
Odour, stealing and giving, 4127
Odours from the spicy shore, 2828
  led my steps astray, 4859
  when sweet violets sicken, 4869
Odyssey, surge and thunder of, 2379
Oedipus, Davus sum, non, 5285
  I'm Davus, not, 5285
Ofereode, þæs, 6329
Off ag'in, on ag'in, 1665
Offence, be pardon'd and retain, 4286
  is rank, my, 4285
  what dire, 3186
  yet detest th', 3212
Offended but by himself, none is, 8478
Offender, love th', 3212
  most notorious, 4949
  never pardons, 9187
Offenders, the more, 9168
Offending, head and front of my, 4416
Offer, never refuse a good, 8425
Offering be, poor the, 2243
Office boy to an Attorney's firm, 1622
  clear in his great, 4556
  hath but a losing, 3884
  I sit in an, 3022
  insolence of, 4253
Offices as public trusts, 681
Officer of mine, never more be, 4439
Officers of sorts, king and, 3967
Offside—No Ball, 3349
Offspring, its new-fledg'd, 1702
  of those that are very young, 9188
  source of human, 2839
O'Flynn, Father, 1745
Often and little eating, 8520
Oil in it, with boiling, 1651
  incomparable, 648
  the top, of, 8519
  upon the waters, pour, 9524
Οἴνοπα πόντον, ἐπί, 1946
Ointment, better than precious, 5962

Ointment of the apothecary, 5971
Old Age a regret, 1273
  age has brought to me, 5013
  age, in a good, 5735
  age is coveted by all, 8523
  age is honourable, 8522
  age of cards, an, 3271
  age serene and bright, 5651
  age, should accompany, 4630
  age, up to extreme, 52
  age, virtuous in, 3316
  along with me, grow, 402
  and bitter of tongue, 5699
  and crafty and wise, 5699
  and godly and grave, 5699
  and grey, when you are, 5702
  and never be, 2018
  and new at once, 397
  and tough, 8524
  and wise, though, 9397
  as he feels, man is, 6540
  as St. Paul's, 6759
  as she looks, woman, 6540
  as the hills, 6760
  aside, last to lay, 3176
  betimes, must be, 7688
  books, old wines, 1723
  but mellow, a man not, 3143
  dog new tricks, teach, 9959
  Father William, you are, 763, 4965
  folks, bestowed on, 8108
  friend, in an, 2574
  friends are best, 3527
  I grow, 4951
  if I live to be, 3317
  lie upon thorns when, 7890
  long, he that would be, 7688
  love everything that's, 1723
  lovers are soundest, 5498
  man, a hearty, 4965
  man, consult, 7900
  man do but die, what can, 1958
  man is a bed full of bones, 6703
  man never wants a tale, 6704
  man not [marry] at all, 6623
  man of St. Bees, 1664
  man to have had so much blood, 4627
  man to humour, 6904
  man, very foolish fond, 4522
  man, weak and despised, 4492
  man with a beard, 2398
  man, wrongs not, 7713
  man young, sight to make, 5159
  man's darling, 6881
  man's eye, in every, 3654
  man's talk, 3145
  men are, how subject, 3910
  men are twice children, 8529
  men feel young men's knocks, 9996
  men know when an old man dies, 3023
  men know young men to be [fools], 9995
  men make much of death, 8531
  men may lie, 8528
  men must [die], 9994

Old men shall dream dreams, 6029
  men, value the talk of, 811
  men will die, 8532
  men's dream, 1344
  men's milk, wine is, 9884
  min agreeable, is the, 1213
  none so, 8482
  now am, 5846
  plain men have rosy faces, 5054
  redress the balance of, 729
  she is not yet so, 3793
  some day before I'm, 2335
  spend when you're, 8848
  they shall not grow, 220
  times, old manners, 1723
  to learn, never too, 8428
  'un thinking of the, 1234
  unhappy, far-off things, 5636
  very young or very, 9188
  when they are young, 9377
  where nobody gets, 5699
  wine, in, 2574
  wine wholesomest, 5498
  you never can be, 4807
'Ole, knows of a better, 127
Oliver Twist has asked, 1205
Omelet, you cannot make, 9955
Ὁμιλίαι κακαί, 2616
Omnia possumus omnes, non, 5405
Ὀμωμοχ᾿, ἡ γλῶσσ᾿, 1460
On, Stanley, on, 3484
Once, through this world but, 1790
One and inseparable, 5494
  and none is all one, 8547
  before all, by, 6887
  but that one a lion, 8551
  for sorrow, 8561
  grew before, only, 5079
  of these days, 8581
  remains, the, 4866
  thing, too much of, 9578
  to come, and one to go, 788
  to one, goes on adding, 389
  too many, that hath, 7396
One-and-twenty, when I was, 2015
One-eyed man is king, 7952
One-horse town, little, 5377
Onion, feed on, 7872
Onward lend thy guiding hand, a little, 2898
Ope his mouth, could not, 563
Open door may tempt, 6708
  fly, on a sudden, 2814
Opened unto you, shall be, 6064
Opens, another [door], 9763
Operation, requires a surgical, 4939
Ophiuchus, fires the length of, 2811
Opinion, error of, 2072
  gross and scope of, 4168
  public, 2054
  rules the world, 8593
  still, of his own, 584
Opinions, between two, 5796
  bought golden, 4558

Opinions, I agree with no man's, 5372
  of my own, some, 5372
  so many men, so many, 5287, 8691
  stiff in, 1346
Opium des Voikes, Religion ist, 2594
  of the people, 2594
Opossum, agile as a young, 684
Opportunity makes the thief, 8594
  maximum of, 4830
Opposed may beware of thee, bear't
  that the, 4201
Opposition, without a formidable, 1272
Oppression bitter, to make, 4249
  rumour of, 1078
Optics sharp it needs, 5366
Optimi pessima, corruptio, 7041
Opus, finis coronat, 7250
  hic labor est, hoc, 5424
Oracle, I am Sir, 3758
Oracles are dumb, the, 2674
Oracular tongue, use of my, 4886
Orange bright, the, 2584
  to a China, 6655
Oranges gleam, golden, 1674
Orare, laborare est, 8127
Orations, make no long, 2985
Orator, I am no, 4040
  without an, 4777
Orators are made, 8634
  to the famous, 2894
  when they are out, 4112
Orb, changes in her circled, 3647
  lighted on this, 464
  quail and shake the, 4666
  which thou behold'st, smallest, 3809
Orbis erat, quod prius, 3445
  si fractus illabatur, 1993
  terrarum, judicat, 85
Orbs of blue, them royal, 5467
Orchard closes, pleasant, 327
  easy to rob, 8017
  little peach in, 1477
Order, best words in the best, 1004
  changeth, old, 5270
  in the land, keeps, 3322
  is heaven's first law, 3249
  of your going, upon, 4607
  raised a point of, 1836
  teach the act of, 3967
  this matter better, 5018
Orders in his hand, with, 6359
  obedient to their, 4911
Ordinances, by external, 2111
Ordinary young man, 2618
Ore, with new-spangled, 2753
Organ blow, the pealing, 2711
  of her life, every, 3952
  seated one day at, 3336
Organ-voice of England, 5221
Orient laugheth, al the, 864
Oriflamme, be your, 2527
Original, their great, 8
  thought is often, 1937
Orion, loose the bands of, 5824

Pope [*bishop*], strive against, 8033
Pope [*poet*], better to err with, 600
  Mr., very pretty poem, 213
Popery, inclines a man to, 1569
Popish liturgy, a, 838
Poplar's gentle and tall, 3038
Poplars are fell'd, 1094
Poppies, a-flutter with, 361
  blow, the, 2529
  nodding, 1109
  pleasures are like, 525
Poppy, blindly scattereth her, 318
  flushed print in a, 5311
  nor mandragora, 4450
Populi, salus, 921, 8732
Populus Romanus, utinam, 682
Porcelain, dainty rogue in, 2638
Pores, pass through the, 4853
Porpentine, quills upon the fretful, 4214
Porridge, cool your, 8737
  had John Keats, what, 375
  is sooner heated, old, 8534
Port [*harbour*] after stormie seas, 4985
  in a storm, any, 6717
  is near, the, 5540
  the more welcome, 9293
Port [*wine*] for men, 2155
  go fetch a pint of, 5179
Port [*mien*] as meke, of his, 848
Portal, from its ivory, 3323
Porters, poor mechanic, 3967
Portion for children, best, 9655
  have the best, 8949
  he wales a, 487
  in us, have no, 1299
Portray men as they ought to be portrayed, I, 4955
Ports and happy havens, 3681
Positives, two Sir, 9628
Possession, better than, 8668
  for ever, a, 5346
  is nine points, 8640
  lies, in thy, 4674
  would not show, virtue, 3951
Possessions, all my, 1428
Possest, cuts off what we, 1388
Possibilities, unconvincing, 49
Possible, O that 'twere, 5249
  with God all things are, 6104
Possunt, quia posse videntur, 5423
Post [*mail*], lame, 9133
  o'er land and ocean, 2761
  [*stay*] for the letter, 8176
Post between you and me and, 6940
  from pillar to, 7299
Post hoc; ergo propter, 8641
Postchaise, driving briskly in, 2150
Posteriors of this day, 3620
Posterity done, what has, 3388, 5367
  hope of, 1291
  mankind and, 2057
  shall sway, thy, 1055
  think of your, 5
Postern door makes thief, 9199

Postern, latched its, 1822
Postume, anni labuntur, 147
Postumus, Postumus, alas, 1990
Postures were, same our, 1287
Posy, with her maiden, 5242
Pot by the fire, freeze, 8086
  calls the kettle black, 9200
  cometh last to, 7541
  death in the, 5803
  is soon hot, little, 6527
  must keep clear, earthen, 9024
  never boils, watched, 6602
  shall have ten hoops, 3544
  young sheep to, 6780
Potations, banish strong, 2985
Potato, bashful young, 1632
Potomac, quiet along the, 191
Pottage, if you drink in, 7884
  in another's man's, 8744
  mess of, 5738
  prettiness makes no, 8657
  whole pot of, 8569
  you love, what, 8576
Pouch on side, 4090
Poultice, silence like a, 1932
Pouncet-box, held a, 3824
Pound, comes by, 8358
  foolish, penny wise, 8617
  give thee a silver, 703
  in for, 7942
  shall never be worth, 7680
  'tis for a thousand, 1073
  to be fined forty, 799
Pounds a year, rich with forty, 1699
  a year, three hundred, 4355
  a year, two hundred, 583
  draw for a thousand, 19
  take a farthing from a thousand, 8894
  will take care of themselves, 8897
Pours, never rains but it, 8076
[Poverty], being ashamed of, 8647
  breeds strife, 8643
  but not my will, 3669
  comes in at the door, 9765
  debt is the worst, 7084
  depress'd, worth by, 2086
  dined with, 8660
  enemy to, 6839
  great, 8412
  is in want of much, 8644
  is no disgrace, 4938
  is no sin, 8645
  is no vice, 8646
  is not a shame, 8647
  is the mother of all arts, 8648
  is the mother of health, 8649
  key to, 8811
  more easy to praise, 8049
  parteth fellowship, 8650
  parteth friends, 8650
  will bear itself, 6850
Pow, blessings on your frosty, 514
Powder without ball, 9402
Powder's runnin' low, when, 3039

Power and stronger, mightier, 5436
  and the glory, 6052
  balance of, 5450
  doth then show likest God's, earthly,
    3799
  force of temporal, 3799
  knowledge is, 8123
  lead life to sovereign, 5150
  of speech, strange, 974
  pomp of, 1759
  proud Edward's, 538
  relentless, 1751
  self-dependent, 2099
  shall fall short in, 341
  tends to corrupt, 2
  than use, rather in, 4373
  that pities me, 1686
  to chasten, of ample, 5604
  to hurt, that have, 4804
Powers, deem that there are, 5597
  princedoms, virtues, 2853
  that be, 6218
  we lay waste our, 5658
Poy, I haf von funny leedle, 3
Practice makes perfect, 8651
  what you preach, 8652
Prague, beautiful city of, 3342
Praise, all his pleasure, 3101
  as they turn from, 332
  at the shout of, 150
  blame, love, 5643
  damn with faint, 3291
  dies, old, 8535
  foolish face of, 3291
  girded with, 1742
  him and magnify him, 6299
  himself, is fain to, 7454
  if there be any, 6253
  it, or blame it too much, scarcely can,
    1713
  makes good men better, 8654
  named thee but to, 1804
  nor dispraise thyself, neither, 8413
  oblique, 2154
  of whom to be disprais'd were no small,
    2889
  record, no panegyric need, 1157
  swells the note of, 1760
  there were none to, 5609
  things thou wouldst, 1167
  to the face, 8655
  to their right, 3813
  too much, 9579
  world conspires to, 3310
Praised more than practised, 8624
Praiser of times past, 2007
Praiseth himself, he that, 7639
Praising what is lost, 4382
Prattle to be tedious, thinking his, 3702
Praxed's ear to pray, Saint, 395
Pray as ever dying, 8128
  he that would learn to, 7694
  let him, 7538
  one to watch and one to, 23

Pray, pain both to pay and, 7985
  remain'd to, 1703
  Saint Praxed's ear to, 395
  so, so give alms, 4720
  to whom the Romans, 2522
  to work is to, 8127
  without ceasing, 6257
Prayer all his business, 3101
  but little devotion, much, 7450
  doth teach us all, 3799
  erects a house of, 1155
  four [hours] spend in, 948
  lift one thought in, 998
  more things are wrought by, 5271
  pray but one, 2989
  reduces itself to this, 5374
Prayers and provender hinder no man's
    journey, 8656
  fall to thy, 3921
  feed on, 3123
  for a pretence make long, 6136
  which are age his alms, 3123
  wouldn't say his, 3387
Prayeth best who loveth best, 977
  well, he, 976
Prays for, whatever a man, 5374
Preach again, never sure to, 173
  goat might, 7845
  practise what you, 8652
Preached against stealing, 9074
  as never sure, 173
Preacher cries, sacred, 1282
  here lies the, 2074
  needs no, 7678
Preaches well that lives well, 7509
Preacheth, he that, 7640
Preaching, a woman's, 2131
Precedent to precedent, from, 5158
Precept, better than, 7210
  ending with some, 3324
  upon precept, 6002
Precepts in thy memory, 4200
Precincts, left the warm, 1767
Precious, one half so, 1515
  to me, were most, 4623
Precipices, high places have, 7735
Precise in every part, too, 1898
Precisian, devil turned, 2608
Predestination in the stride, 2273
  round enmesh me, with, 1512
Predominance, by spherical, 4478
Prefaces, read all the, 5073
Preferment out, to seek, 3596
Prejudices a man so, it, 4946
Premier pas, il n'y a que le, 1153
Prentice han' she tried on man, 475
Preparation, dreadful note of, 3982
  no formal, 263
Prepared for either event, 5414
Presbyter is but old Priest, new, 2763
Presbyterian true blue, 569
Presence, lord of thy, 3737
  made better by their, 1418
  scanter of your maiden, 4204

Presence that disturbs me, 5604
Present [*now*], act in the living, 2440
  are judged, things, 9383
  day, deficiencies of, 2106
  day, pleasures of, 1282
  day, seize the, 1987
  has latched its postern, 1822
  in spirit, 6221
  no time like, 8474
  nor things to come, things, 6213
  [seem] worst, things, 3893
Present [*gift*], for an un-birthday, 786
Presentment, counterfeit, 4292
Presents endear Absents, 2356
President, rather be right than be, 931
Press, liberty of the, 2182
Pressed men, worth two, 8590
Pretender, God bless, 591
Prettiness makes no pottage, 8657
Pretty is, every thing that, 4695
  little things are, 8226
Prevention is better than cure, 8658
Previous study, result of, 92
Prey, destined, 4827
  fastened on her, 3356
  have they not divided, 5772
  sports not with, 6698
Preys do rouse, to their, 4596
Priam's curtain, drew, 3883
Price, all those men have, 5448
  cheat me in, 7000
  of everything, knows, 5563
  of love, true, 8263
  pearl of great, 6088
  raise the volume's, 5073
  set her own, 3110
Prick and sting her, to, 4220
Pricking, knight was, 4980
Pricks, kick against, 6191
Pride and grace, 8659
  breakfasted with Plenty, 8660
  crueltie, and ambition, 3366
  dined with Poverty, 8660
  feels no cold, 8661
  fell with my fortunes, 4062
  goes before, 8662
  goeth before destruction, 5914
  is as loud a beggar, 8663
  naething here but Highland, 505
  never-failing vice, 3169
  not exempt from, 2373
  perished in his, 5624
  pomp, and circumstance, 4452
  poor man's, 9017
  that apes humility, 991, 4968
  that licks the dust, 3296
  vain was the sage's, 3305
  will have a fall, 8664
  with a greater pride, despises, 9344
Priest, all sides of, 6946
  continues what the nurse began, 1359
  fetch the devil a, 9943
  forgets that he was clerk, 9202
  pale-eyed, 2675

Priest, still is Nature's, 5665
  turn, 7905
  woman or, 8461
  writ large, old, 2763
Priests, tapers, temples, 3214
Prime, lovely April of her, 4781
Primrose by a river's brim, 5606
  first-born child of Ver, 1536
  pale, 4702
  path of dalliance, 4199
  sweet as the, 1710
  that forsaken dies, rathe, 2752
  was to him, a, 5606
  way, go the, 4579
Primroses that die unmarried, 4719
Prince, draweth his sword against, 9842
  on this afflicted, 1530
  who made thee a, 5749
Princerple, I *don't* believe in, 2481
Princes and lords may flourish, 1695
  ears and eyes of, 8862
  put not your trust in, 5892
  sweet aspect of, 4761
Princess, fitting for a, 4675
Principalities, nor powers, 6213
Principle, necessary and fundamental, 227
  rebels from, 467
Principles, chang'd their, 5717
  religious and moral, 78
Print it, 'sdeath! I'll, 3285
  it, some said, 450
  left the flushed, 5311
  see one's name in, 597
  seeing our names in, 884
Printing, invented the art of, 739
  to be used, caused, 3547
Prior, what once was Matthew, 3335
Priscian a little scratched, 3618
Priscian's head, to break, 9442
Prison, let's away to, 4524
  make, walls do not, 2472
Prison-air, bloom well in, 5570
Prisoner's life, passing on, 4387
Prison-house, secrets of my, 4214
Private, drunken, 1319
  person, put off, 7643
Privilege, for the glorious, 498
Prize, bound for the, 4800
  we sought is won, 5540
Prizes, to offer glittering, 221
  won hundreds of, 6367
Probationer, a young, 1364
Proceedings, subsequent, 1836
Procession, it is an ill, 8004
Proconsul, the great, 2513
Procrastination is the thief of time, 5709
Procul hinc, qui, 3042
Prodigal in a coach, young, 9997
  make men, 7356
  robs his heir, 9203
Prodigies, Africa and her, 314
  surprise, what, 2091
Pro-di-gi-ous! 3514

Repose, gives way to in, 4566
 in statue-like, 31
 manners had not, 5151
 seek not yet, 1431
Reprehend anything, if I, 4886
Representation, no taxation without, 8473
Reproach, sting of, 9244
Reprobation, fall to, 4471
Reproof on her lip, 2475
 public, 8674
 Valiant, fourth, 4123
Republic her station, gave, 2988
Republican form of government, 4977
Republicans, we are, 452
Reputation dies, at every word a, 3192
 I have lost my, 4440
 seeking the bubble, 4090
 written out of, 212
Requited, both are alike, 3085
Res angusta domi, 2186
Researches, with no deep, 1110
Resemble her to thee, 5444
Resent, no individual could, 5076
Reside in thrilling region, 4401
Residence, a forted, 4407
Resistance, wrong that needs, 133
Resisted, know not what's, 494
Resolution, native hue of, 4253
Resolve, a heart to, 1604
Resolves ; and re-resolves, 5710
Respect a man, 8708
 greatest, 9095
Respectable, genius found, 333
 not one is, 5537
 seldom even ordinarily, 2617
 to what is, 1973
Respected, is not, 7644
Respecter of persons, no, 6192
Respects not, he that, 7644
Rest [repose], absence of occupation is
 not, 1062
 angels sing thee to, 4346
 brave who sink to, 1008
 cometh great, 8513
 dove found no, 5732
 far, far better, 1251
 gets him to, 3985
 I will give you, 6082
 now cometh, 2665
 now she's at, and so am I, 1366
 of sufferance cometh, 8516
 perturbed spirit, 4227
 rest, for evermore, 3415
 seals up all in, 4799
 so may he, 4767
 without, 1675
Rest [remainder], name led all the, 2043
 nowhere, Eclipse first, 3068
 the sun goes round, take all, 5441
Reste, j'y suis, j'y, 2543
Resting-place, laid it in, 4921
Result happiness, 1238
Resurrection, hope of the, 6324

Resurrection, I am the, 6181
 looking for, 6325
Retained, longer, 9381
Retirement, must be no, 1800
 rural quiet, 5323
 urges sweet return, short, 2871
Retort Courteous, first, 4123
Retreat, a friend in my, 1063
 I will not, 1579
 in, 7930
Return, never must, 2742
Returning were as tedious as go o'er, 4609
Returns, quick, 8817
 whence they say none, 810
Reveal himself to his servants, 2918
Revelry by night, sound of, 609
Revels by a forest side, midnight, 2791
 now are ended, 4750
Revenge, best, 8230
 capable and wide, 4458
 had stomach, my, 4469
 if not victory is yet, 2795
 is sweet, 8710
 kind of wild justice, 110
 spur my dull, 4305
 study of, 2770
 sweet as my, 4683
 sweet is, 652
Revenges, times brings in, 4165
Revenons à nos moutons, 246
Revenue, thrift is good, 9411
Reverence, claims to, 5140
 none so poor to do him, 4034
Reviewers, chorus of indolent, 5222
Reviewing, read a book before, 4946
Révolution, c'est une, 2385
Revolutions are not made with rose-
 water, 2502
 that makes, 1600
Reward, desert and, 7093
 service without, 8771
 virtue is its own, 9657
Rewards and fairies, 1035
 are distant, 2111
Reynolds is laid, here, 1718
Rhein, die Wacht am, 3457
Rhetoric, he could not ope, for, 563
Rhetorician, sophistical, 1270
Rheumatic of shoulder, 270
Rhine, watch on the, 3457
 wide and winding, 615
Rhinoceros, the arm'd, 4604
Rhone, rushing of the arrowy, 616
Rhyme being no necessary adjunct, 2921
 build the lofty, 2739
 making beautiful old, 4809
 nor reason, received nor, 4995
 outlive this powerful, 4792
 the rudder is of verses, 574
 themselves into ladies' favours, 3995
 those that write in, 578
Rhymes, Namby Pamby's little, 732
Rhyming mother wits, 2557
 planet, born under, 3960

Rib, under the fifth, 5787
Riband bound, what this, 5441
  in the cap of youth, 4316
  just for a, 348
Ribs, birchen twigs break no, 6948
Rice, beside the ungather'd, 2451
  for good luck, 8711
  same old, 2366
Rich and covetous, 8635
  and rare were the gems, 2954
  and strange, something, 4736
  at forty, 7604
  better be born lucky than, 6882
  beyond the dreams of avarice, 2944
  can help themselves, 7336
  enough, he is, 7482
  ever by chance grow, 5309
  folk have many friends, 8712
  gifts wax poor, 4255
  God help, 7337
  good workmen are seldom, 7371
  he that makes haste to be, 5943
  knows not who is his friend, 9212
  man, a certain, 6160
  man, kin to, 7193
  man to enter into the kingdom of God,
    6103
  men have no faults, 8713
  never want for kindred, 9213
  not [bound] to be, 9680
  one law for, 8571
  pride of, 9201
  quiet, and infamous, 2512
  see the sister, 8970
  [trees] will grow, 8777
  with forty pounds, passing, 1699
  woman, as easy to marry, 5296
Richard's himself again, 916
Richardson for the story, read, 2137
Richer for poorer, for, 6317
Riches, ancient, 7306
  are but the baggage, 8714
  are gotten with pain, 8715
  [are] kept with care, 8715
  are like muck, 8716
  [are] lost with grief, 8715
  [bring] ever fear, 8717
  bring oft harm, 8717
  command a fool, 8718
  embarrassment of, 39
  great, 8412
  grow in hell, 2789
  he heapeth up, 5848
  his best, 1696
  I hold in light esteem, 291
  infinite, 2569
  make themselves wings, 5929
  poor men's, 7006
  rather than great, 5927
  serve a wise man, 8718
Richesses, l'embarras de, 39
Richest, that man is, 5343
Richmond Hill, lass of, 2544
Richmonds in the field, six, 3577

Richness, here's, 1208
Rick, keep them in thy, 8726
Rid of it, idea of getting, 2076
  of it, longs to be, 7655
Ride a gallop, he'll, 8772
  for me, I, 384
  forth at evening, 1526
  in triumph through Persepolis, 2559
  not on the ridge, 6545
  over, for fools to, 6971
  softly, 8719
Rideau, tirez le, 3355
Rider and his horse, between, 5071
  and horse, friend, foe, 614
  is lost, 7278
  on so proud a back, proud, 4774
  steed that knows his, 607
  worse for, 9291
Rides sure that never fell, 7512
Ridicule, du sublime au, 3016
Ridiculous, no spectacle so, 2508
  one step above, 3091
  sublime to the, 3016
Ridiculous mus, nascetur, 2006
Riding's a joy, sing, 384
Ridley, be of good comfort, Master, 2386
Rifle, jest roll to your, 2309
Rift within the lute, 5254
Riga, young lady of, 6366
Right as a trivet, 6770
  as men strive for, 332
  as ninepence, 6771
  as rain, 6772
  born to set it, 4228
  divine of kings, 3226
  do well and, 1895
  every single one of them is, 2297
  extreme, 7212
  fears, he that hath, 7584
  finds a way to set it, 6379
  generalities of natural, 900
  if you keep to, 1457
  in ev'ry cranny but, 1097
  is withdrawing, my, 1537
  Judge of all the earth do, 5737
  little, tight little, 1184
  of way, died maintaining, 6378
  or wrang, makes us, 478
  or wrong, our country, 1152
  than be President, rather be, 931
  there is none to dispute, 1064
  thirsting for the, 5209
  too fond of the, 1714
  was clear, his, 6378
  were worsted, though, 423
  Whatever is, is, 3242
  whose life is in the, 3247
  with firmness in, 2424
  wrong never comes, 9936
  wrongs no man, 8720
Righteous are bold as a lion, 5942
  cause, armour of, 427
  die the death of, 5758
  forsaken, not seen, 5846

Righteous man regardeth the life of his beast, 5905
overmuch, be not, 5966
Righteousness and peace have kissed, 5865
arise, Sun of, 6034
in the way of, 5915
Righteousnesses are as filthy rags, 6014
Rights, certain unalienable, 2071
duties as well as, 1330
should lose, lest they, 5367
of an Englishman, 2182
Rim, over the mountain's, 357
utmost purple, 5176
Ring I thee wed, with this, 6319
like a great, 5394
on her wand, gold, 2954
on the finger, 7759
out the old, 5233
so worn, 1114
the bells, they now, 5449
time, only pretty, 4121
wear the devil's gold, 9477
Ring-a-rosie, tots sang, 230
Rings for buddin' Sally, 689
Rio, I'd like to roll to, 2335
Riot, rash fierce blaze of, 3683
Riotous living, with, 6155
Ripe, from hour to hour we, 4083
soon rotten, soon, 8838
Ripeness is all, 4523
Riper stage, amuse his, 3246
Rise again, now they, 4603
and fight again, I'll, 6339
and trip away, then, 2373
at five, must, 7683
betimes, he must, 7503
early, get a name to, 7309
early, he must, 7504
early, who does not, 7706
easier to fall than, 8012
loth to, 7169
none can make you, 8806
on stepping-stones, 5223
sun to thee may never, 1026
to-morrow, may, 7554
up and fall, 6921
Rises, gives light as soon as he, 1558
over early, he, 7513
Riseth first, he that, 7645
River, Alph the sacred, 983
and o'er the lea, up, 1927
by the door, living, 5047
Dee, lived on the, 216
even the weariest, 5101
floated on, majestic, 61
follow, 7266
he swam the Eske, 3478
in the reeds by, 334
join the brimming, 5189
like the foam on, 3496
save the rush of, 191
sea refuseth no, 9226
snow falls in the, 525

River sweeping, proud, 5137
to flow away, waits for, 1999
we'll gather at the, 2486
Rivers, by shallow, 2573
cannot quench, 3554
of Damascus, 5804
run into the sea, all, 5953
wide, brooks and, 2689
Rivulets dance their wayward round, 5613
myriads of, 5208
Roach, sound as, 6783
Road all runners come, 2016
beset the, 1512
keep the common, 8100
lies long and straight, 5022
made the rolling English, 888
my mistress still the open, 5052
no royal, 1459
one that on a lonesome, 972
rule of the, 1457
takes no private, 3255
that leads him to England, 2128
they are upon the, 1074
to hell is paved, 9214
to Samarkand, Golden, 1526
was a ribbon of moonlight, 3061
wind up-hill, does the, 3420
ye'll tak' the high, 6357
Roads diverged, two, 1568
had you seen these, 6361
lead to Rome, all, 6660
walk'd along our, 2370
Roam, absent from Him I, 2939
if here at night you, 2087
sadly I, 1546
though we may, 3116
where'er I, 1682
where'er we, 1683
Roamin' in the gloamin', 2388
Roaming, where are you, 4139
Roar, cannon's opening, 611
like a torrent, 3180
with sullen, 2704
you as gently, 3713
Roareth thus, this that, 1673
Roast an egg, the learned, 3303
great boast, small, 7376
Roasted, larks fall, 9136
Rob an orchard, easy to, 8017
Peter to pay Paul, 9532
Robbed at all, he's not, 4451
that smiles, the, 4426
Robbery, exchange is no, 6450
to highway, 5301
Robbing, think little of, 1176
Robe, give me my, 4671
Robes about him, singing, 2808
and furr'd gowns hide all, 4520
are gone, when all, 6343
are on, when all her, 6343
riche, or fithele, 854
these my sky, 2715
your tyrants wear, 4843

Saints, pair of carved, 3696
  soul is with the, 995
  the ransomed, 38
  thy slaughter'd, 2760
  with my lost, 332
Sair, kame sindle, kame, 8092
Sairey, little do we know, 1224
Sake, for old sake's, 2264
Saki, you shall pass, 1519
Salad days, my, 4648
Salesman should select, 2396
Salisbury, young curate of, 6370
Sally, none like pretty, 733
Salmon and sermon, 8730
  it was the, 1189
  to catch a, 6507
Salt, eat me without, 7437
  have lost his savour, 6042
  help me to, 7729
  of the earth, ye are, 6042
  on a bird's tail, 9529
  seasons all things, 8731
  with him, eat a bushel of, 6860
Salt-petre, villainous, 3826
Salus populi, 921, 8732
Salutary neglect, wise and, 462
Salute thee, Mantovano, I, 5278
Salvation, no relish of, 4288
  none of us should see, 3799
  work out your own, 6250
Salve for every sore, 9316
  seek your, 8759
Samarcand, from silken, 2210
Samarkand, Golden Road to, 1526
Same, it will be all the, 8081
  old slippers, 2366
  thing, the more it is, 2196
  to desire the, 3450
  to-day and for ever, 5370
  yesterday and to-day, 6270
Samite, clothed in white, 5251
Samphire, one that gathers, 4515
Sampler, serve to ply the, 2735
Samson, exclaimed Dominie, 3514
Samson, Philistines be upon thee, 5775
  was a strong man, 8733
Sana in corpore sano, mens, 2194
Sand against the wind, throw, 237
  as is the ribbed sea, 5685
  doth feed the clay, 9785
  little grains of, 757
  palace built upon, 2660
  roll down their golden, 1860
  shadows pass gigantic on, 1526
  through beds of, 61
  world in a grain of, 238
Sandal tree perfumes, 9220
Sandboy, jolly as, 6743
Sands and shelves, tawny, 2718
  are all dry, when the, 769
  begin to hem, 61
  dance on the, 4773
  ignoble things, 189
  many, 8316

Sands of Dee, across the, 2255
  unto these yellow, 4735
  with printless foot, on, 4753
Sandstone, chunk of old red, 1836
Sane than mad, fitter being, 411
Sang, ane end of ane old, 3066
Sapienti, verbum sat, 9652
Sappho loved and sung, 659
Sarcasticul, this is rote, 5461
Sashes, one of his nice new, 1736
Sat side by side, where we, 4880
Satan, bowing low, 2886
  exalted sat, 2792
  finds some mischief still, 5484
  Nick, or Clootie, 489
  reproves sin, 8734
  stood unterrifi'd, 2811
  when ye tak him, 503
Satanic School, the, 4970
Satire be my song, let, 596
  for pointed, 3391
  or sense, 3293
  should wound with a touch that's
    scarcely felt, 2932
Saturday, born on, 6962
  no luck at all, 8363
  sneeze on, 8821
Saturday's child, 8364
Saturn, sat grey-haired, 2229
Satyr, Hyperion to a, 4183
Satyrs grazing on the lawns, 2570
Sauce for the goose, 9727
  hunger is the best, 7772
  second time in, 7261
  sour, 8887
Saucy, great deal more, 8663
Saul and Jonathan, 5784
  also among the prophets, 5779
  hath slain his thousands, 5782
Sauter, pour mieux, 7914
Savage, extreme, rude, 4815
  in woods the noble, 1386
Save, both get and, 7910
  Europe by her example, 3151
  himself he cannot, 6125
  one's own, matter enough, 382
  something for the man, 8736
  while you may, 7276
Saved, groat is ill, 9099
  he that will not be, 7678
  others, he, 6125
  penny, 6562
Saving cometh having, of, 8514
Saviour of the world. 593
  stung, with trait'rous kiss, 158
Saviour's birth is celebrated, 4175
Savour, keep seeming and, 4717
  nothing hath no, 8490
  salt, best, 8959
Saw of might, I find thy, 4109
Sawe, bene an old-sayd, 4979
Saws, full of wise, 4090
Say as men say, 8738
  do as I, 7109

Sea, to a most dangerous, 3792
  to shining sea, from, 172
  to Skye, over the, 266
  uttermost parts of, 5890
  was mountains rolling, 3155
  washes all man's ills, 1462
  waters of the dark blue, 633
  we have fed the, 2280
  when I put out to, 5281
  which brought us hither, 5670
  who hath desired the, 2270
  winds somewhere safe to, 5101
  within a walk of the, 196
  worse things happen at, 9933
  you'll get to, 7266
Sea-breakers, by lone, 3076
Sea-breeze hand in hand, with, 5310
Sea-change, doth suffer a, 4736
Sea-daisies feast on the sun, 5091
Seagreen Incorruptible, 746
Sea-king's daughter, 5214
Seal upon thine heart, as, 5989
Seals of love, but seal'd in vain, 4405
Sea-mark of my utmost sail, 4473
  shipwreck be, 8160
Sea-maws, for your ain, 8101
Seamen three, 3117
  were not gentlemen, 2517
Sea-monster, more hideous than, 4480
Search not too curiously, 8753
  not worth the, 3759
  will find it out, 1905
Seas again, down to the, 2597
  all o'er the wild, 6358
  breaking the silence of, 5635
  dangers of the, 3099
  gang dry, till a' the, 541
  guard our native, 704
  I come, over many, 814
  incarnadine, multitudinous, 4573
  isle in far-off, 343
  of perilous, 2217
  tossed upon cloudy, 3061
  waste of, 6356
  we shall fight on the, 908
Sea-shore, playing on the, 3049
Season comes, 'gainst that, 4175
  convenient, 9235
  of mists, 2227
  season'd are, by, 3813
  the soote, 5067
  to everything there is, 5958
  word spoken in due, 5913
Seasonable as snow in summer, 6773
Seasons and their change, all, 2837
  bring, returning, 3141
  come, few more, 256
  defend you from, 4497
  return, with the year, 2821
Seat, regain the blissful, 2765
Seats beneath the shade, 1693
Second [glass] for nourishment, 9058
  stroke intend, no, 2812
  thoughts are best, 8754

Second [wife is] company, 9060
Secret and a mystery, a, 2647
  bread eaten in, 5901
  he that tells, 7668
  knows it well, my, 5468
  none can utter, her, 3348
  so close, no, 5071
  too many to keep, 9403
Secrets, if you would know, 7903
  reveal all, 9414
Sect, slave to no, 3255
Sects, two-and-seventy jarring, 1507
Secure, he that is too, 7606
  never to feel, 9277
Securus judicat orbis, 85
Sedan, going to heaven in, 9331
Sedately in, monotonously out, 2926
Sedge has wither'd, 2233
Seduces, 'tis woman that, 1589
See all and say nothing, 8769
  as far into a millstone, 7780
  clearly is poetry, to, 3434
  day, one may, 8577
  fleet thou canst not, 4897
  her is to love her, to, 534
  her was to love her, 531
  more, never shall, 1787
  most, will, 9375
  not feel, how beautiful, 993
  not what sits on our shoulder, 9692
  not worth going to, 2156
  or seem, all that we, 3156
  oursels as ithers see us, 495
  something to, 360
  than be one, I'd rather, 454
  those who won't, 8480
  through all things, 3195
  what is not to be seen, 5366
  what we shall see, 9694
  what went ye out to, 6080
Seed can come, no good, 8510
  on the land, scatter, 695
Seeds fell by the wayside, 6086
  of April's sowing, 344
Seeing is believing, 8757
  worth, 2156
Seek all day, you shall, 3759
  and ye shall find, 6064
  anon, better keep now than, 6907
  another in the oven, 8459
  him here, we, 3073
  him, those Frenchies, 3073
  it, wants it and will not, 7576
  that you do not, 8904
  till you find, 8758
  ye first the kingdom of God, 6059
  ye the Lord, 6012
Seem, are things what they, 1837
  seldom what they, 1624
  things are not what they, 2437
  to be, be as you would, 6841
Seems, it is ; I know not, 4180
Seen and not heard, 7008
  because thou art not, 4091

Souls mounting up to God, 3424
  negotiate there, our, 1287
  out of men's bodies, hale, 3933
  times that try men's, 3089
  to heaven, little, 1469
  to play with, 382
  to warn th'immortal, 2561
  vanish like lightning, 5131
  were forfeit once, all, 4392
  with but a single thought, two, 2473
  ye contented your, 2289
  you may grind their, 3074
Soul-sides, boasts two, 399
Sound [*noise*] and fury, full of, 4636
  beauty born of, 5613
  burst of thunder, 1865
  doleful, 5489
  however rude the, 1607
  I heard, all the, 2011
  is forc'd, 231
  length and thund'ring, 1707
  like the sweet, 4127
  make the most, 7159
  must seem an echo, 3180
  save the rush, no, 191
  the whispering, 1094
  therof, thou hearest, 6172
  timid and tremulous, 769
  to heal the blows of, 1932
  well, can never, 6436
  with impetuous recoil and jarring 2814
Sound [*healthy*] as a bell, 6782
  as a roach, 6783
  as a trout, 6783
Soundings, until we strike, 6358
Sounds and sweet airs, 4749
  blowing martial, 2782
  concord of sweet, 3811
  will take care of themselves, 767
Soup and love, of, 8515
  I waved the turtle, 1611
  of the evening, 770
Sour and sad, 6962
  in the ending, 8261
  will not taste, 7439
Source, rise above its, 9246
  to mount, pants its, 2941
South Country, hills of, 195
  fierce and fickle is, 5201
  full of the warm, 2212
  rosy is the, 5244
Sovereign, civilities with, 2133
Sovereignest thing on earth, 3826
Sow [*pig*], alewife's, 6433
  by the ear, wrong, 9489
  eats up all, still, 9242
  like the old, 9298
  little knoweth the fat, 8221
  sucked, 7547
  that was washed, 6277
Sow [*seed*] dry and set wet, 9301
  one's wild oats, 9540
  with the hand, 8844
Sow's ear, silk purse out of, 9954

Soweth, whatsoever a man, 6245
Sowing, increase by, 8109
  weeds want no, 9704
Sown there, were never, 8318
Sows, and he shall not reap, 5107
Space and time, annihilate, 6380
Spade a spade, to call, 9452
  with which Wilkinson, 5647
Spades, the emblem of untimely graves,
    1087
Spain, castles in, 9445
  into the hands of, 5276
Span, inch as you have done, 7135
  less than a, 122
  thread the length of, 2603
Spangled heavens, 8
Spaniard will be a church, first building
    erected by, 7948
Spaniards too, thrash the, 1321
Spaniel, brach, or lym, 4508
Spanish soldier brag, 4928
  to tell her in, 352
Spare all I have, 1474
  at brim, better, 6924
  how much he can, 2154
  it is too late to, 8071
  me not, plain way, 9642
  me, up hill, 9642
  not where you must spend, 8861
  the humbled, 5425
  to have of thine own, 6925
  well and spend well, 8847
  when you're young, 8848
Spares the bad, he that, 7657
Sparing is the first gaining, 8849
Spark, illustrious, 1054
  in his throat, hath, 9237
  is left, nor human, 3229
Sparkle for ever, 5194
Sparks fly, upward, as the, 5812
Sparrow fall, hero perish or a, 3233
  in the fall of a, 4340
  is dead, my girl's, 809
  my girl's pet, 809
Sparrows build upon the trees, 928
  on one ear of corn, two, 9629
Sparta is yours, 925
Spartam nactus es, 925
Spartan kind, out of the, 3728
Spattereth himself, 7639
Speak fair, 8850
  fitly, 8851
  for yourself, why don't you, 2463
  gently, she can hear, 5568
  give losers leave to, 7320
  hear and see more than we, 8396
  him fair and trust him not, 7658
  in cause that none dare, 7974
  let him now, 6316
  little, think much, 9385
  Lord, 5777
  low, if you speak love, 3929
  must have leave to, 7501
  of me as I am, 4474

Strings do scarcely move, 231
Stripes and bright stars, 2250
Stripling Thames, crossing, 64
Strive, need'st not, 941
  to seek, to find, 5164
Stroke, at the first, 9270
  intend, no second, 2812
  not felled at one, 6696
Strokes, amorous of their, 4649
  fell great oaks, little, 8224
  great, 7381
Strong at thirty, 7604
  battle to the, 5970
  man after sleep, like a, 2919
  without rage, 1172
Stronger by weakness, 5445
Strove, a little while she, 650
  with none, I, 2371
Struck, more men threatened than, 9303
Struggle, in a contemptible, 460
  naught availeth, 937
Struggles of another, watch, 2489
Struts and frets his hour, 4636
  his dames before, 2687
Stuarts are not sib, all, 6661
Stubble-land, show'd like, 3824
Studie was but litel on the bible, 859
  what sholde he, 852
Studies serve for delight, 115
Studio, sine ira et, 5115
Studious let me sit, 5327
Study is a weariness, much, 5981
  is like the heaven's glorious sun, 3608
  labour and intent, 2909
  of mankind is man, 3243
  to be quiet, 6256
  what you most affect, 3587
  willingly, will never, 6399
Stuff, made of sterner, 4032
  perilous, 4631
  we are such, 4750
Stumble, may well, 7647
Stumbles and falls, he that, 7663
  horse that never, 7980
Stumps, fought upon his, 4837
Stupidity, no sin except, 5561
  struggle with, 3456
Sturdy and staunch he stands, 1479
Stygian set, ye, 2372
Style, attain an English, 2110
  definition of a, 5085
  est l'homme même, 437
  in so strange a, 3175
  is the man himself, 437
  refines, how the, 3182
Suaviter in modo, 7285
Subdue the proud, 5425
Subdued, both parties nobly are, 3912
  to what it works in, 4812
Subject owes the prince, as, 3593
Subject's duty is the king's, 3984
  love, 9247
Subjection, bring it into, 6225
Subjects are rebels, 467

Sublime au ridicule, du, 3016
  he that rode, 1775
  it was chust, 3003
  my object all, 1649
  one step above, 3091
  to the ridiculous, 3016
  true pathos and, 519
Submission, yielded with coy, 2833
Subscribers baits his hook, for, 905
  not printing any list of, 2158
Subside again, one by one, 2926
Substance might be call'd, 2809
  wasted his, 6155
Subtlest beast, serpent, 2870
Succeed, if at first you don't, 1911
Success, ease and, 7149
  ill-got had ever bad, 3550
  is never blamed, 8878
  is to labour, true, 5031
  not in mortals to command, 11
  nothing succeeds like, 8499
  with his surcease, 4554
Such a man there be, if, 3291
Suck, I have given, 4561
Sue a beggar, 8881
  we were not born to, 3674
Sueño, el que inventó el, 821
Suez, somewhere east of, 2312
Suffer and expect, 8882
  fools gladly, ye, 6241
  for it, the Greeks, 1997
  ill, better, 6927
  in the mind to, 4253
  me to come to Thee, 5514
Suffer'n, lounjun 'roun' en, 1831
Sufferance cometh ease, of, 8516
  in corporal, 4399
  is the badge, 3770
Suffering but the cause, not, 8063
  ended with the day, 31
  learn in, 4841
Sufferings, to each his, 1750
Sufficed, it greatly hath, 3006
Sufficiency, elegant, 5323
Sufficient unto the day, 6060
Suggestion, they'll take, 4740
  yield to that, 4543
Suing long to bide, in, 4989
Suit breeds twenty, one, 9294
  is best, that, 8934
  of plain, severe design, 2396
Suitor, think that you are Ann's, 4827
  wins, last, 9139
Suits me, best, 8934
  of solemn black, 4180
Sum, give no inconsiderable, 638
  of more, giving thy, 4069
  with a great, 6201
Sumer is icumen in, 6331
Summer, after many a, 5165
  All-hallown, 3822
  days do last, while, 4694
  does not make, 8585
  English, 6686

Summer getteth, that, 9883
  good-bye, 5549
  half be done, ere, 4775
  has set in, 1006
  if it takes all, 1744
  last rose of, 2963
  lasts, while, 4702
  lays up, 9889
  made glorious, 3557
  merrily, after, 4755
  set lip, 5311
  shall not fade, thy, 4784
Summer's day, compare thee to, 4783
  flood, 9891
  lease hath all too short a date, 4783
  rose, 2821
  wonder, makes, 9892
Summers' pride, shook three, 4807
Summits old in story, 5196
Summons comes, when thy, 429
  upon a fearful, 4173
Sun and breath, fail, 3442
  and moon were in the flat sea sunk,
    2725
  and the other stars, 1141
  and the rain are flying, 5056
  as the dial to, 258
  at the going down of, 220
  before the rising, 5487
  begins his state, 2688
  benighted walks under the midday,
    2726
  bosom-friend of the maturing, 2227
  can be seen by nothing but its own
    light, 9249
  candle to the, 5716
  clear as, 5988
  climbs slow, in front, 939
  dead no more do see, 1332
  disclose the pilgrim, 5389
  doth gently waste, 6345
  doth move, doubt that, 4232
  drum-beat, following the, 5496
  follow thy fair, 715
  for the eyes to behold, 5975
  glimmering tapers to, 1110
  go down upon your wrath, 6247
  goes to bed wi' the, 4718
  grows cold, till the, 5128
  had long since in the lap, 581
  heat o' the, 4704
  himself grow dim, 15
  in all his state, 31
  in bed, the, 2676
  in dim eclipse, 2786
  in his glory, smile like, 3323
  in red should set, if, 7865
  in the courts of the, 880
  is highest, when, 9786
  is laid to sleep, 2177
  is never the worse, 9250
  lasts, no morning, 7276
  laughed in the, 294
  looked over the mountain's rim, 357

Sun, loves to live i' the, 4079
  many an evening, 184
  must not walk in, 7573
  myself in Huncamunca's eyes, 1483
  never sets in the Spanish dominions,
    4928
  of righteousness, 6034
  of the burnish'd, 3775
  peer'd forth, worshipp'd, 3628
  reflecting upon the mud, 5133
  rises bright in France, 1129
  rises in the morning, 7940
  sees it, 7852
  sets bright and clear, 9787
  sets in a bank, 9788
  shall not smite thee by day, 5881
  shines always there, 4881
  shines, day still while, 8010
  shines, make hay while, 8285
  shines on, bride, 7401
  shines, though, 9399
  shines upon all, 9251
  should set in grey, 7865
  sinks low, as the, 3059
  sitting in the, 4961
  somewhere beneath the, 1039
  spots even on, 9308
  take warmth, from the, 1791
  that warms you here shall shine on me,
    3678
  the early-rising, 1901
  the selfsame, 4725
  to feel the, 326
  to meet the, 1768
  to rise, maketh his, 6050
  to the garish, 3664
  under the, 5951, 5954
  uprist, the glorious, 957
  views, descending, 251
  walk much in, 9373
  warm summer, 3386
  warms in the, 3241
  went down and the stars came out,
    5274
  white as the, 1030
  will be dimmed, glory of, 128
  will shine, the, 5580
  with the dying, 268
  you never loved the, 885
Sun's a thief, 4690
  bravado, met the, 170
  rim dips, 963
Sunbeam, impossible to be soiled as, 2911
  in a winter's day, 1408
Sunbeams flatter, which the, 691
  motes that people, 2698
  out of cucumbers, 5080
Sunday, born on, 6962
  from the week, does not divide, 4169
  God send, 7028
  killing of a mouse on, 274
  makes a clout on, 6635
  sneeze on, 8821
  will weep on, 7656

Sunday's child, 8883
Sundays, begs his bread on, 6547
   pulpits and, 1889
Sun-dial in the shade, 9728
   what is the good of, 9728
Sun-flower turns to her god, 2957
Sung, ever honour'd, ever, 1531
   from noon to noon, 2990
Sunium's marbled steep, 661
Sunless land, from sunshine to, 5683
Sunlight, somewhere in the, 2410
Sunrise, lives in Eternity's, 240
   pass, seen their, 891
Suns and universes ceased, 293
   can set and return, 811
   light of setting, 5604
Sunset and evening star, 5281
   fadeth, after, 4799
   ran . . . reeking, 366
Sunset-touch, there's a, 397
Sunshine after rain, like, 4775
   but hath some shadow, no, 8471
   is a glorious birth, 5661
   made a, 4984
   settles on its head, 1705
Sun-treader, 335
Sup and blow at once, 8450
   from home, before you, 2037
   sipped no, 1657
Supererogation, Works of, 6326
Superlative degree, 5363
Superstition, atheism and, 9005
Superstitions, end as, 2050
Supper from him, steals, 7713
   good breakfast but a bad, 7762
   if ever I ate a good, 42
   walk a mile, after, 6630
   will have more for, 7648
Supperless, go to bed, 6901
   goes to bed, 9847
Suppers, pastime [makes], 7773
Supping, sleep without, 8810
Supplied, can never be, 1695
Support him after, to, 4687
Sups ill, he, 7519
Sure as a gun, 6784
   as death, 6785
   as eggs is eggs, 6786
   as God made little apples, 6787
   as God's in Gloucestershire, 6788
   slow and, 8812
   than sorry, better be, 6886
Surety, [act as], 7157
Surface flow, upon the, 1389
Surfeit reigns, no crude, 2729
Surge and thunder of the Odyssey, 2379
   rude imperious, 3903
   the murmuring, 4515
Surgeon, good, 6485
Surmise, with a wild, 2201
Surname, out of his, 2505
Surpass her, nothing earthly could, 648
Surplusage, removal of, 3109
Surprise, to no little, 141

Surprise, what a, 944
Surprised is half beaten, man, 6550
Surprises, millions of, 1889
Surrender, dies but does not, 692
   unconditional and immediate, 1743
   virtue is near, 9659
   we shall never, 908
Surrey in a wilderness, meet, 3697
Survival of the fittest, 1144
Sus Minervam, 8884
Susceptible Chancellor, 1639
Suspect, hath reason to, 1486
   the thoughts of others, 3773
Suspected, ever, 7634
Suspicion always haunts the guilty mind,
   3555
   must be above, 6983
   virtue of a coward is, 9274
Sutor ultra crepidam, ne, 8400
Swaggering here, have we, 3721
Swain, a frugal, 1940
   no better than a homely, 3551
Swains commend her, all, 3601
Swallow dares, before the, 4719
   does not make a summer one, 8585
   flying south, 5200
   mounteth it not, 9239
   thou that knowest each, 5201
Swallow's wings, flies with, 3572
Swallows are making them ready to fly,
   5549
Swan and shadow, double, 5639
   dies the, 5165
   float double, 5639
   of Avon, sweet, 2175
   sings before death, 9252
Swanee Ribber, upon de, 1545
Swans, all his geese are, 6645
   asleep, sail like, 1525
   sing before they die, 999
Swap horses when crossing, 2423
Swashing and a martial outside, 4066
Swat, the Akond of, 2405
Sway, above this sceptred, 3799
   requir'd with gentle, 2833
   with an absolute, 3317
Sways, by submitting, 3272
Swear, if you, 7896
   me, Kate, like a lady, 3863
   to me, thou didst, 3896
Sweareth to his own hurt, 5833
Sweat and whine, do not, 5537
   no sweet without, 8472
   of thy face, in the, 5726
   to grunt and, 4253
   toil, tears and, 907
   wet with honest, 2447
Sweats to death, Falstaff, 3833
Sweep before your own door, 8885
Sweeping, nor sewing, nor, 6377
Sweet and fair she seems, how, 5444
   and glorious thing, 1992
   and low, 5195
   as a nut, 6789

Thought can win, shadowy, 2222
  for the morrow, no, 6060
  for want of, 1378
  hit on the same, 4898
  holy and good, 6295
  I shun the, 2648
  I thought he thought I slept, he, 3111
  is free, 9400
  is often original, 1937
  is speech, when, 3471
  it, who would have, 9066
  loftiness of, 1367
  magnanimity of, 5710
  of, little, 9928
  of Thee, the very, 807
  one grace, one, 2560
  perish the, 917
  pleasing-dreadful, 14
  quick as, 6767
  rear the tender, 5322
  she pined in, 4149
  sicklied o'er with the pale cast of, 4253
  so, go near to be, 3953
  so once, I, 1585
  steadfast of, 4913
  strikes me, sudden, 728
  sweet silent, 4788
  tell of saddest, 4857
  thing they call a, 3179
  think but one, 2989
  to a green, 2590
  to have common, 3268
  unproportion'd, 4200
  what oft was, 3173
  white celestial, 5390
  wish is father to, 9287
  wish was father to, 3915
  with but a single, 2473
  would destroy their paradise, 1750
Thoughts are best, second, 8754
  are not your thoughts, my, 6013
  as boundless, our, 633
  begin to have bloody, 4751
  change oft, women's, 9893
  close, 7792
  covers all a man's, 821
  dark soul and foul, 2726
  feeling of their masters', 2560
  fond and wayward, 5608
  his only friends, good, 717
  his own highest, 2237
  intent, on hospitable, 2851
  joy of elevated, 5604
  long, long, 2465
  more elevate, in, 2804
  my bloody, 4458
  my slaughterous, 4635
  no tongue, give, 4200
  not breaths, 124
  penny for your, 6561
  pleasant thoughts bring sad, 5595
  remain below, 4289
  restrain in me the cursed, 4566
  sensations rather than, 2236

    2 A

Thoughts that arise in me, 5184
  that breathe, 1777
  that do often lie too deep for tears,
    5672
  that nature gives way to, 4566
  that wander through eternity, 2797
  to conceal their, 5434
  will perish, 128
  with your fresh, 1979
  yet, with any such, 3974
Thousand, better than a, 5864
  pounds, draw for a, 19
  pounds no longer, 8894
  slimy things, 966
  such a day, spins, 3297
  ten thousand times ten, 38
  then another, 812
  years in thy sight, 5866
  years, thrice a, 24
Thousands at His bidding speed, 2761
  equally were meant, 5076
  had sunk, 710
  slain his, 5782
Thousandth Man will stand by your side,
    2324
Thread, any silk, any, 4724
  breaks, 9260
  feels at each, 3239
  with a cobweb, 7295
Threatened men live long, 9401
  more men, 9303
Threatenings and slaughter, 6190
Threats, no terror in your, 4049
  without power, 9402
Three are too many, 9403
  for a wedding, 8561
  gentlemen at once, 4889
  he stoppeth one of, 953
  helping one another, 9406
  may keep counsel, 9407
  per cents, 3521
  removes are as bad, 9408
  she'll hae but, 6334
  though he was only, 2668
  whole days together, 5066
  women and a goose, 9410
Threescore years and ten, 5868
Threshold, dares nor cross, 840
  of the new, upon, 5445
  set you at your, 2016
Thrice he assay'd, 2787
Thrift is good revenue, 9411
  is the philosopher's stone, 9412
  thrift, Horatio, 4188
Thrive and then wive, 7258
  he that will, 7682, 7683
  none of these two will, 7311
  with him, all, 7818
Thriven, he that hath, 7683
Throat, [cider] cuts, 7018
  cut a, 659
  cut, belly thinks, 8389
  cut your, 8735
  shop in his, 9232

Tooth for a tooth, 6047
　for tooth, 5754
　is not so keen, thy, 4091
　sharper than a serpent's, 4481
　to the aching, 9265
Toothache, could endure, 3959
　music helps not, 8387
Top, looking at the men at, 949
Topics, other fashionable, 1722
　you were but two, 2147
Top-peak, here's the, 391
Tops, think their slender, 1960
Torch, a bright, 2222
　gives, more light, 9169
　is at thy temple door, 3371
Torches, as we with, 4383
　to burn bright, teach, 3638
Tories own no argument, 322
Torrent is heard on the hill, 185
Torture one poor word, 1356
Tortures tried, heaven by, 3307
Torturing hour calls us, 2794
Tossed and gored several, 262
Tots sang " Ring-a-rosie,' 230
Totter into vogue, to, 5446
Touch, dares not put it to, 2942
　him further, nothing can, 4591
　him not and torture not, 4864
　him with a pair of tongs, not, 7809
　not, taste not, 6254
　pot, touch penny, 9583
　she hardly seemed to, 464
　that's scarcely felt, 2932
　wood, 9584
Touched nothing, he, 2113
Touchstone trieth gold, as, 6794
Tough and devilish sly, 1230
　interesting but, 5379
Tout est perdu, 1553
　passe, tout casse, 9585
Toves, the slithy, 774
Tower came, to the dark, 4506
　of London, for the, 6458
　yonder ivy-mantled, 4
Towers along the steep, no, 705
　and battlements, 2689
　burnt the topless, 2563
　cloud-capp'd, 4750
　of Julius, 1782
　ye antique, 1747
Town, all around the, 230
　damn'd distracting, 3311
　in May, in, 7602
　it is, a haunted, 2377
　little one-horse, 5377
　man made the, 1077
　mine own romantic, 3473
　of Bethlehem, little, 303
　or city, centre of each, 1938
　seaward from the, 2039
　surpasses, ne'er a, 521
　townsman of a stiller, 2016
Town-dweller, modern, 2055
Towns contend, seven, 3532

Toy dog is covered with dust, 1479
　foolish thing was but, 4166
Toys for your delight, 5053
　not to meddle with, 5042
Track, around the ancient, 2634
　come flying on our, 5333
　with a golden, 2428
Tract behind, leaving no, 4686
Trade abroad, venture, 3967
　every man to his, 7190
　gathers samphire, dreadful, 4515
　his silly old, 5520
　poor, 7092
　two of a, 9627
Trade's proud empire, 2099
Trades, jack of all, 8083
　man of many, 6547
　mother of all, 8648
Tradesmen, becomes none but, 4726
Trafficked for strange webs, 3106
Tragedy, comedy, history, 4240
　gorgeous, 2706
　to those that feel, 5447
　you *may* abuse a, 2126
Tragical-comical-historical-pastoral, 4241
Trail again, pull out on, 2277
　a-winding, long, long, 2254
　pull out on the Long, 2278
　that is always new, 2278
Train, as we rush in the, 5333
　attendant, for a, 498
　her starry, 2837
　up a child, 5928
　who follows in His, 1859
Train-band captain eke, 1070
Traitor is hated, 9269
Traitors, fears do make us, 4617
　jeer, 1027
Traitors' arms, more strong than, 4038
Tram, not a bus but a, 1825
Trance, no nightly, 2675
Tranquillity, recollected in, 5686
Transcendental kind, of a, 1630
Transgressors, way of, 5907
Transit gloria mundi, sic, 2245
Translated, thou art, 3722
Translators, traitors, 9586
Translunary things, brave, 1322
Transmitter, no tenth, 3455
Transportation for life, 799
Transports, permit the, 5124
Trap fell, when, 9708
Trash and trumpery, 9587
Travail, my labour for my, 4363
　so gladly spent, 5696
Travel all the world over, 6578
　forth, make me, 4791
　hopefully, to, 5031
　[makes] a fool worse, 9588
　makes a wise man better, 9588
Travell'd, much have I, 2200
Traveller, five hours sleepeth, 7262
　lame, 6511
　may lie, 6600

Truth and roses have thorns, 9605
and shame the devil, tell, 3856
and soberness, 6204
as I have meant, such, 5696
be tried out, till, 7088
brightness, purity and, 3078
cannot be shamed, 9602
children and fools speak, 7004
comes out, 7214
fears no colours, 9595
find, 8920
finds foes, 9596
fools and madmen speak, 7268
friend to, 3281
from his lips prevail'd, 1703
great is, 6289
has such a face, 1358
hath a good face, 9597
hath a quiet breast, 3677
[hath] bad clothes, 9597
his utmost skill, 5689
I hold it, 5223
in every shepherd's tongue, 3357
in wine there is, 7963
is as impossible to be soiled, 2911
[is] beauty, 2221
is clear, one, 3242
is God's daughter, 9598
is marching on, His, 2029
is stranger than fiction, 9599
is truth to the end, 9600
lay all undiscovered, 3049
lie which is half a, 5215
lies at the bottom of a well, 9601
loves to go naked, 7049
may be blamed, 9602
miscall'd simplicity, 4798
needs not many words, 9603
never grows old, 9604
put to the worse, who ever knew, 2920
quench'd the open, 3492
seeks no corners, 9606
shall be thy warrant, 3363
shall make you free, 6178
sits upon the lips, 60
sole judge of, 3244
sting of a reproach is, 9244
tell, 8925
that's brighter than gem, 422
the greater, 9092
the poets sings, 5169
this mournful, 2086
time trieth, 9423
to be a liar, doubt, 4232
tongues can poison, 981
too near, follow not, 7265
well known to most, 1097
what is, 107
when he speaks, 6516
which cunning times put on, 3792
will paint it, as, 1108
with Falsehood, strife of, 2477
with gold she weighs, 3217
Truth's sacred fort, 308

Truths are not to be told, all, 6668
fate of new, 2050
instruments of darkness tell us, 4542
that wake to perish never, 5669
to be self-evident, 2071
Try before you trust, 9607
till you, 9978
try again, 1911
Tub must stand on its own bottom, 7199
Tubal Cain was a man of might, 2535
Tuesday, born on, 6962
for health, 8363
sneeze on, 8821
Tuesday's child, 8364
Tug of war, then comes, 9753
of war, then was the, 2409
Tugs in a different way, 669
Tully, said I, no, 396
Tumble down, must, 4902
Tumbles and tosses, all night, 9847
Tumult and the shouting dies, 2293
Tun, drink of a, 6392
Tune and harsh, out of, 4261
bring all things into, 6447
call, 7709
singeth a quiet, 970
sweetly play'd in, 541
Tunes of Spain, slow old, 2601
Turf, a green grassy, 184
above thee, green be, 1804
that wraps their clay, 1009
Turk, bear, like the, 3291
malignant and a turban'd, 4474
out-paramoured the, 4499
the unspeakable, 753
work as hard as a, 6349
Turkey, carps, hops, 9610
Turkey, they always say in, 1194
Turkey-cock, red as, 6769
Turn again, pass and, 1453
cat in pan, 9561
deserves another, good, 8563
he that does you an ill, 7548
in his grave, 9516
it over once more, 5519
to him the other [cheek], 6048
Turned, bees cannot be, 8890
him right and round, 542
round, having once, 972
up, in case anything, 1236
Turning, lane that has no, 7984
Turnip than his father, have, 2097
Turnips cries, man who, 2097
Turns, goes far that never, 7442
Turpissimus, repente fuit, 2185
Turret, the Sultan's, 1490
Turtle [*dove*] is heard, voice of, 5985
love of the, 630
to her mate, true as, 6796
Turtle [*sea-tortoise*] eats, straight he, 375
soup, I waved the, 1611
Tuscany, even the ranks of, 2523
Tutor, ill natures never want, 7923
Twang, most melodious, 80

Weather, what dreadful hot, 97
  will be cold and rough, 9766
  winter, 9893
Weatherby George Dupree, 2668
Weave the warp and weave the woof,
    1780
  with toil and care, 4843
Web we weave, tangled, 3482
Wed, December when they, 4114
  it, think to, 4374
  over the mixen, 6934
  over the moor, 6934
  the fair Ellen, was to, 3479
  where his hap is, will, 6546
Wedding clothes, bought her, 13
  day and death day, 6605
  day, barefoot on her, 3589
  day, it is my, 1075
  day, that earliest, 2242
  in the church, saw, 3130
Wedding-ring wears, as, 6810
Wedge, thin end of, 9258
Wedlock hath oft compared been, 1147
  is a padlock, 9703
  tames man, age and, 6632
Wednesday, born on, 6962
  sneeze on, 8821
  the best day of all, 8363
Wednesday's child, 8364
Weds with shame, 8232
Wee, modest crimson-tippèd, 496
  sleekit, cowrin', 483
Weed [plant], bites on every, 7524
  mars, one ill, 8569
  pernicious, 1060
  who art so lovely fair, 4462
Weed [robe], rob Tellus of her, 4694
Weeds [plants]. garden full of, 6549
  grow apace, ill, 7926
  long live the, 1980
  no garden without, 8445
  reign o'er the land, 1109
  smell far worse than, 4805
  want no sowing, 9704
Weeds [robes] outworn, her winter, 4875
Week, days that's in the, 734
  [happy], for, 8164
  is gone, 9413
  live well for, 7905
  see what can be accomplished in, 5030
Weening is not measure, 9705
Weep, and you weep alone, 5552
  but never see, may, 2369
  every house would, 7827
  for her, that he should, 4248
  for you, the Walrus said, I, 783
  I saw my Lady, 6344
  no more, nor sigh, 1532
  not, my wanton, 1788
  or she will die, must, 5204
  out his eyes, may, 9850
  'tis that I may not, 662
  who would not, 3291
  you no more, 6345

Weeping and the laughter, 1299
  away, you'll come, 8238
  cross, comes home by, 7565
  may endure for a night, 5843
  there shall be, 6072
Weigh right, 9706
Weighed in the balances, 6023
Weighs not, to whom it, 7434
Weight and measure, 9707
  and measure, good, 7366
  he carries, 1073
  of another's burden, 8479
Weird sisters, the, 4536
  we cannot shape, 9684
Welcome as flowers in May, 6804
  as water in one's shoes, 6805
  bay deep-mouth'd, 651
  both in bower and hall, 7583
  death, 9708
  ever smiles, 4367
  evil, 9709
  friend, 8355
  is the best cheer, 9710
  singing to, 1468
  such farewell, such, 8880
  to your gory bed, 537
Welcomest when they are gone, 3537
Well [rightly], acts nobly, does, 5712
  all is well that ends, 6652
  all would be, 9782
  alone, let, 8175
  and fair, nothing but, 2906
  as the beggar knows his dish, 6806
  bed-time and all, 3875
  can't move her, looking, 5064
  done, 6118
  done, want a thing, 7898
  enough, knows when he is, 7486
  enough, soon enough if, 8834
  fast till he is, 7553
  he that would be, 7689
  it is not done, 2131
  laugh and be, 1786
  not how long but how, 8060
  oft we mar what's, 4482
  to make it, 5125
  'twill all be, 1514
  when I did, 9755
  when you are, 9802
  with him, all is, 6653
  with me, where it is, 9813
  with the child, is it, 5802
Well [hole], at the bottom of, 9601
  goes so often to, 9195
  if you leap into, 7889
  not so deep as a, 3662
  runs dry, till, 9691
Well-bred, sensible and, 1059
  very strange and, 1025
Well-content, sweet, 1149
Well-doing, weary in, 6246
Well-favoured man, to be, 3941
Wells are seldom dry, drawn, 7132
  have sweetest water, drawn, 7133

Will across the sky, wrote, 2391
  and you won't, you, 1298
  be done in earth, thy, 6052
  boy's will is the wind's, 2465
  complies against his, 584
  fix'd fate, free, 2804
  for the deed, take, 9553
  good, 7367
  have thy, 6847
  in us is over-ruled by fate, 2571
  is free, know our, 2134
  is not his own, his, 4197
  is ready, where your, 9829
  is the cause of woe, 9877
  live by one man's, 1972
  make your, 7874
  never said well, ill, 7927
  not another will, if one, 7840
  not when he may, 7681
  of it, take your, 8912
  puzzles the, 4253
  sign your, 2087
  take the place of reason, let, 2188
  take your ain, 8893
  th' unconquerable, 2770
  to do, the soul to dare, 3492
  was strong, his, 6378
  where there's a, 9827
  will have will, 9878
  woe win, though, 9878
William replied, Father, 764
Willie died, since little, 21
  there awa, wandering, 535
Willie Michie's banes, 503
Willie Winkie rins through the town, 2664
Willin', Barkis is, 1235
Willing horse, on the, 6654
Willow tree, all under the, 841
  wear the, 9567
Willows are weak, 9879
  harps upon, 5887
Wills, talk of, 3694
  when they live, have, 9923
Willy-nilly blowing, 1504
Wiltshire, born in, 9917
Wimpled, whining, purblind, wayward
  boy, 3613
Win at first, 9880
  gold and wear gold, 9882
  heads I, 7714
  let them laugh that, 8174
  nothing, 8500
  yet wouldst wrongly, 4548
Wince, galled horse, 9582
  let the galled jade, 4275
Wind along the Waste, 1504
  and the rain, hey, ho, 4166
  as large a charter as, 4087
  away, to keep the, 4326
  bay'd the whisp'ring, 1698
  be still, if, 8475
  beat of the off-shore, 2277
  blow, thou winter, 4091
  bloweth where it listeth, 6172

Wind blows, a soft, 1674
  blows cold, how, 8220
  blows, dust which the, 4511
  blows it back again, 237
  blows on you through a hole, if, 7875
  blows, which way, 8874, 9504
  by the winnowing, 2228
  can blaw, a' the airts, 507
  cold, 9405
  constancy in, 599
  does move, the gentle, 236
  ein sanfter, 1674
  fair stood the, 1324
  fill'd with a lusty, 828
  God tempers, 5019, 7347
  hear a voice in every, 1748
  hears Him in the, 3235
  hollow murmuring, 1530
  I go, like, 1503
  in that corner, sits, 3935
  is in the east, when, 9790
  is in the north, when, 9791
  is in the south, when, 9792
  is in the west, when, 9793
  it is an ill, 8005
  keeps not always in one quarter, 9283
  never so fast, blow, 6960
  of the western sea, 5195
  on the heath, 259
  on the moors, blows, 5056
  out of one's sails, take, 9554
  pass by me as the idle, 4049
  passeth over it, 5873
  puff not against, 8675
  shorter in, 270
  streaming to the, 2781
  streams . . . *against*, 623
  swoln with, 2750
  that follows fast, 1130
  that grand old harper, 4920
  they have sown, 6027
  'twas but the, 610
  upon the wings of, 5836
  warm western, 3386
  was a torrent of darkness, 3061
  was cold, 3460
  we shall not want, westerly, 9788
  wild West, 4844
  you need not fear, easterly, 9787
Wind's soft song, in the, 2410
Wind-flowers, pied, 4860
Windmill, you cannot drive, 9949
Window, love comes in at, 8254
  of the east, golden, 3628
  tirling at the, 2664
  where the sun came, 1959
Window-blind, walloping, 803
Window-panes, upon the, 1420
Windows, close, downy, 4674
  flare, crimson-blank, 2322
  I cleaned the, 1622
  not by eastern, 939
  richly dight, storied, 2711
  that exclude the light, 1772

Winds, and crack your cheeks, blow, 4490
  are breathing low, 4847
  are contrary, all, 9425
  blow, great, 7385
  come, come as the, 3505
  come to me, 5663
  courted by all the, 2903
  do blow, stormy, 704
  do shake, rough, 4783
  fed it, young, 4851
  imprison'd in the viewless, 4401
  of heaven, beteem, 4183
  of March with beauty, take, 4719
  of the World, give answer, 2283
  rides on the posting, 4699
  shoreward blow, 55
  speed with the light-foot, 1791
  Thy clarions, great, 901
  visitation of the, 3903
  were love-sick with them, 4649
Wine, and have the gout, drink, 7138
  and wenches, 9882
  ballast is old, 3117
  bin of, 5047
  bring me, 3031
  by the barrel, know, 9952
  doesn't get into the, 887
  fetch to me a pint o', 513
  Flask of, 1493
  gaming, women, and, 7304
  I'll not look for, 2169
  in old, 2574
  in the bottle, 9285
  in the stomach, in, 7261
  is a good familiar creature, 4442
  is a mocker, 5923
  is a turncoat, 9883
  [is] best, old, 8526
  is in, when, 9743
  is old men's milk, 9884
  it wasn't the, 1189
  Jug of, 1494
  look not thou upon, 5930
  makes all sorts of creatures, 9885
  mellow, like good, 3143
  needs no bush, good, 4126, 7368
  of life is drawn, 4583
  sinks, when, 9800
  spill'd the, 3110
  sweetest, 8888
  that maketh glad, 5874
  the middle, of, 8519
  there is truth, in, 7963
  use a little, 6260
  vinegar of sweet, 8903
  when it is red, 5930
  wholesomest, old, 5498
  will taste of the cask, 9285
Wine-cup glistens, taste not when, 3509
Wing, flits by on leathern, 1011
  shadow of Thy, 5513
Winged words, 1945
Wings, eagle's, 9123

Wings, girt with golden, 2721
  hear the beating of, 286
  in vain, beating, 73
  misfortunes come on, 8359
  O that I had, 5857
  on wide-waving, 1145
  shakes his dewy, 1146
  she claps her, 2495
  spreads his light, 3211
  tail broader than, 8288
  that which hath, 5972
  under the shadow of thy, 5835
  you'll hear his, 8914
Wink and choose, 9886
  and hold out mine iron, 3970
  at small faults, 9887
  I have not slept one, 4700
  nod is as good as, 6560
Winketh with one eye, 7685
Winner, good to leave off, 7932
  you'll see who's, 6824
Winning, O the glory of, 2626
  worth the wear of, 198
Winter and rough weather, 4077
  comes, if, 4846
  eateth, 9888
  ending in July, 667
  finds out, 9889
  frosty, but kindly, 4072
  green, 6495
  heel of limping, 3630
  in thy year, no, 425
  in't, there was no, 4666
  is dreary, 1958
  is gone, 7825
  is past, lo, the, 5985
  it is a hard, 7983
  ling'ring chills, 1684
  never rots in the sky, 9890
  of our discontent, 3557
  ruler of th'inverted year, 1086
  sad tale's best for, 4709
  Spring, and Summer, 6343
  suddenly was changed to Spring, 4859
  weather, 9893
  when the dismal rain, 4920
  wild, it was the, 2670
  will have another flight, 7825
Winter's day and a winter's way, 9142
  day, passeth, 7636
  pale, in, 4714
  rages, furious, 4704
  thunder, 9891, 9892
  traces, on, 5105
Winters cold, three, 4807
Wisdom, all men's, 3444
  all, vain, 2805
  and goodness to the vile seem vile, 4512
  and Wit are little seen, 275
  apply our hearts unto, 5869
  at one entrance quite shut out, 2821
  crieth without, 5894
  haste and, 7412
  is better than rubies, 5900